DOCUMENTS
of
American Constitutional & Legal History

VOLUME ONE

From Settlement through Reconstruction

EDITED BY

MELVIN I. UROFSKY

Virginia Commonwealth University

TEMPLE UNIVERSITY PRESS
Philadelphia

For Philip Eric Urofsky
with love and pride

First Edition
987654321
Copyright © 1989 by Alfred A. Knopf, Inc.

Published by Temple University Press.
All rights reserved under International and Pan-American Copyright Conventions.

Library of Congress Cataloging-in-Publication Data

Documents of American constitutional and legal history.

Includes bibliographies and indexes.
Contents: v. 1. From settlement through Reconstruction—v. 2. The Age of Industrialization to the present.
1. United States—Constitutional history—Sources. 2. United States—Constitutional law—Cases. I. Urofsky, Melvin I.
KF4502.D635   1989   342.73′029   88-13585
ISBN 0-87722-623-7 (v. 1)
ISBN 0-87722-624-5 (v. 2)

Manufactured in the United States of America

Text design: Sandra Josephson

Preface

The students and teachers using this collection of documents may be interested in knowing how it came to be, and the underlying ideas governing the selection of documents and their order.

In the constitutional history courses I took in college and graduate schools, my teachers did at times refer to the greater social, economic, and political events occurring outside the courtroom walls. But for the most part, the readings, the lectures, and the examinations emphasized the doctrines espoused by particular justices of the Supreme Court and their manifestation in certain cases. We rarely spoke about cases in the lower federal courts, and never even mentioned state tribunals, changes in legal training and the profession, or any of the many non–Supreme Court venues in which constitutional developments take place. When I attended law school many years later, history, like economics, psychology, and sociology, had made some minor inroads into the curriculum, but constitutional law remained an analysis of the "great cases" of the Supreme Court. And because law schools are training practitioners, most of these cases were of very recent vintage. One took a quick look at *Marbury, McCulloch,* and a few others for their contemporary doctrinal significance. One learned far more history in courses on contract and tort law than in courses on the Constitution.

When I first began teaching constitutional history, I did as my teachers had done, and the available texts and source books reinforced the notion that constitutional history and United States Supreme Court cases were one and the same. Then came the so-called "new" legal history, which, while still paying attention to the "great cases," began to look at developments in private law, in the state courts and constitutions, in the law schools and bar associations, and, in short, at anything that affected legal change in the country. Great constitutional scholars such as E. S. Corwin and J. Willard Hurst had, of course, been doing exactly that for years, but they were the exceptions. Now we realized that instead of being idiosyncratic their work was prophetic, pointing to what we now regard as the proper means of studying legal history—not in a vacuum populated solely by "great cases," but in the overall environment in which many factors affect legal development.

In this collection of documents, as in *A March of Liberty,* I have included the great cases, because they were and still are important. But I have also included decisions from state and lower federal courts, and a number of noncase items that affected American constitutional development. Out of the 125 selections in this volume, only a fourth of the documents are Supreme Court cases. This is because there was no Supreme Court for two-thirds of the period covered in this volume, settlement to Reconstruction, and because during the early nineteenth century some of the most exciting legal changes occured in the private law decisions of the state courts.

Organizing these documents presented some difficulties. While a straightforward chronological organization had the benefit of simplicity, it masked some of the connections between documents that needed to be emphasized. On the other hand, a topical arrangement would have excluded certain documents that did not fit into broader groupings. The final result is a topical and chronological arrangement that I hope has the merits of both approaches and overcomes the drawbacks. Each document has a brief introduction pointing out its significance and providing signposts so that the student may understand how it relates to larger developments. Cross-references to appropriate documents are included, as is a brief list of additional reading for those seeking further information.

Several people have been most generous in reading through this collection and their suggestions have strengthened it immeasurably. My editor and friend, Christopher J. Rogers, encouraged this project from the beginning, and his assistant, Niels Abboe, proved very helpful. Carolyn Viola-John saw the collection through the production process with a grace that made the whole business look easy. My thanks also to the designer, Sandra Josephson, and to the production supervisor, Jennifer Brett. Kermit L. Hall of the University of Florida read through the first version, and made a number of very useful suggestions for improving the selections and organization in order to make them useful to students. Helpful suggestions also came from Harold M. Hyman of Rice University and Rebecca S. Shoemaker of Indiana State University. Philip Urofsky took time out from his own studies to hunt down a number of documents. In the end, of course, the value of the selection will depend on its use to teachers and students alike, but I have tried to keep the choice broad enough to meet a variety of teaching interests.

Melvin I. Urofsky

Contents

Part VII   Slavery and the Dissolving Union   361

Part VIII   *Civil War and Reconstruction*   *447*

Part I

The Colonial Era

The settlers who came from England to the New World in the seventeenth and eighteenth centuries brought with them specific ideas of law and governance, ideas derived from their own history. Most important was the idea of government under law, the idea that no one, not even the king, could ignore the settled practices of the land. This idea dated back to Magna Carta (Document 1), and by the time of settlement had become the bedrock notion of English constitutionalism. Some of the ideas expressed in Magna Carta will be seen reflected in many of these documents down to the present day. In the early seventeenth century the influence of the Great Charter lay primarily in the fact that the settlers, the colonizing companies, and the Crown all assumed that the English law and rights derived from the Charter and enjoyed at home would also govern in the colonies (Document 2), for one could hardly expect people to brave the hardships of the wilderness if they would be penalized by a loss of liberty.

English settlers tried to recreate conditions similar to those they had left at home, but the North American frontier demanded changes. Land had been the most precious of all commodities in the Old World, and English common law reflected that scarcity. In the New World, however, land seemed to be virtually free and for the taking, but the settlers soon discovered that native Americans had far different views on what constituted ownership than did the English (Document 9). Assumptions about governmental powers over daily life also had to be reconsidered. The Virginia colony, after nearly being wiped out in its first decade, tried to establish some social stability through an extensive code of conduct (Document 3). The Separatists who arrived in Plymouth in 1620 imposed a basic frame of government on the settlement in order to avoid some of the problems faced at Jamestown (Document 4).

The idea of a basic outline of government was not new to Englishmen; although Great Britain has never had a formal constitution, the idea of "constitutionalism" ran deep in British political thought. What they meant was a body of commonly accepted rights and rules that over the centuries had

1

become a foundation upon which social order rested. The settlers built on this idea in their efforts to create viable colonial governments (Documents 5, 8). But they also went further and developed new ideas reflecting the more democratic society being created in the New World. Some of this may perhaps be attributed to the influence of the frontier, which fostered a more democratic and open society. Even if one does not fully accept the Turner frontier thesis, it does seem that frontier life at the least accelerated trends in English law that would not mature in the Mother Country until the nineteenth century. Roger Williams, for example, went against centuries of tradition in his call for religious freedom (Document 6), while American juries repudiated the harsh English libel laws to permit truth as a defense (Document 9).

Still, in the mid-eighteenth century, after 150 years of colonization, colonists along the eastern seaboard claimed to be Englishmen living under English law and under English forms of government. The changes that had taken place did not appear, at least at the time, as more than minor adjustments to local conditions. But as the documents in Part II show, these changes reflected significant alterations in the way people viewed the relationship between government and subjects, and the role of the law.

1

Magna Carta (1215)

The promises secured from King John by his barons amounted to little more than a restatement of the coronation pledges he and previous monarchs had made not to abuse their powers. But John Lackland had abused his authority, and in forcing him to repeat and put his signature to those promises, the barons not only reasserted their own powers, but established cardinal principles of English law: that a natural law—a fundamental, immutable law—exists, and that no one, not even a king, is above that law. This theme will become very important in American developments during the late colonial period. As the documents in Part II show, the colonists complained, not that the government of King George III had violated the laws of Parliament, but that King and Parliament had gone beyond the bounds permitted by natural law.

See J. C. Holt, *Magna Carta* (1965); W. F. Swindler, *Magna Carta: Legend and Legacy* (1965); and A. E. D. Howard, *The Road from Runnymede: Magna Carta and Constitutionalism in America* (1968).

---

14 For obtaining the common counsel of the kingdom concerning the assessment of aids (other than in the three cases aforesaid) or of scutage, We will cause to be summoned, severally by Our letters, the archbishops, bishops, abbots, earls, and great barons; We will also cause to be summoned, generally, by Our sheriffs and bailiffs, all those who hold lands directly of Us, to meet on a fixed day, but with at least forty days' notice, and at a fixed place. In all letters of such summons We will explain the cause thereof. The summons being thus made, the business shall proceed on the day appointed, according to the advice of those who shall be present, even though not all the persons summoned have come.

17 Common Pleas shall not follow Our Court, but shall be held in some certain place.

18 Recognizances of novel disseisin, mort d'ancestor, and darrein presentment shall be taken only in their proper counties, and in this manner: We or, if We be absent from the realm, Our Chief Justiciary shall send two justiciaries through each county four times a year, and they, together with

---

Source: Howard, *Magna Carta: Text and Commentary* (1964).

four knights elected out of each county by the people thereof, shall hold the said assizes in the county court, on the day and in the place where that court meets.

20   A free man shall be amerced for a small fault only according to the measure thereof, and for a great crime according to its magnitude, saving his position; and in like manner a merchant saving his trade, and a villein saving his tillage, if they should fall under Our mercy. None of these amercements shall be imposed except by the oath of honest men of the neighborhood.

28   No constable or other of Our bailiffs shall take corn or other chattels of any man without immediate payment, unless the seller voluntarily consents to postponement of payment.

38   In the future no bailiff shall upon his own unsupported accusation put any man to trial without producing credible witnesses to the truth of the accusation.

39   No free man shall be taken, imprisoned, disseised, outlawed, banished, or in any way destroyed, nor will We proceed against or prosecute him, except by the lawful judgment of his peers and by the law of the land.

40   To no one will We sell, to none will We deny or delay, right or justice.

45   We will appoint as justiciaries, constables, sheriffs, or bailiffs only such men as know the law of the land and will keep it well.

63   Wherefore We will, and firmly charge, that the English Church shall be free, and that all men in Our kingdom shall have and hold all the aforesaid liberties, rights, and concessions, well and peaceably, freely, quietly, fully, and wholly, to them and their heirs, of Us and Our heirs, in all things and places forever, as is aforesaid. It is moreover sworn, as well on Our part as on the part of the barons, that all these matters aforesaid shall be kept in good faith and without deceit. Witness the above-named and many others. Given by Our hand in the meadow which is called Runnymede, between Windsor and Staines, on the fifteenth day of June in the seventeenth year of Our reign.

2

Letters Patent to Sir
Humfrey Gylberte (1578)

Elizabeth I issued a number of patents to men like Sir Humphrey
Gilbert and Sir Walter Raleigh authorizing them to establish colonies
in North America and setting out their rights as proprietors as well as
their obligations to the Crown. Two crucial clauses in these patents
declared that settlers would retain the rights and privileges of Englishmen, and that the settlements should be governed under laws compatible with those of England. At the time neither the monarch nor the
exploration companies paid much attention to this clause; what other
law, after all, could apply in Her Majesty's colonies than that of England? One could not expect people attempting to tame a wilderness
to stop and write a new legal code when a perfectly fine one already
existed. Later, however, colonists relied on these clauses in their claims
to enjoy the full protection of English liberties and law.

See D. B. Quinn, *England and the Discovery of America* (1974), and A. L. Rowse,
The Expansion of Elizabethan England (1955).

Elizabeth by the grace of God Queene of England, &c. To all people to
whom these presents shall come, greeting.

   Know ye that of our especiall grace, certaine science and meere motion,
we have given and granted, and by these presents for us, our heires and
successours, doe give and graunt to our trustie and welbeloved servaunt Sir
Humphrey Gilbert of Compton, in our castle of Devonshire Knight, and to
his heires and assignes for ever, free libertie and licence from time to time,
and at all times for ever hereafter, to discover, finde, search out, and view
such remote, heathen and barbarous lands, countreys and territories not
actually possessed of any Christian prince or people, as to him, his heirs &
assignes, and to every or any of them, shall seeme good: and the same to have,
hold, occupie and enjoy to him, his heires and assignes for ever, with all
commodities, jurisdictions, and royalties both by sea and land; . . . And wee
doe likewise by these presents, for us, our heires and successours, give full
authoritie and power to the saide Sir Humfrey, his heires and assignes, and

Source: Thorpe, ed. 1 *Federal and State Constitutions* 49 (1909).

every of them, that hee and they, and every of any of them, shall and may at all and every time and times hereafter, have, take and lead in the same voyages, to travell thitherward, and to inhabite there with him, and every or any of them, such and so many of our subjects as shall willingly accompany him and them, and every or any of them, with sufficient shipping and furniture for their transportations, so that none of the same persons, nor any of them be such as hereafter shall be specially restrained by us, our heires and successors. . . .

And for uniting in more perfect league and amitie of such countreys, landes and territories so to bee possessed and inhabited as aforesayde, with our Realmes of England and Ireland, and for the better encouragement of men to this enterprise: wee doe by these presents graunt, and declare, that all such countreys so hereafter to bee possessed and inhabited as aforesayd, from thencefoorth shall bee of the allegiance of us, our heires, and successours. And wee doe graunt to the sayd sir Humfrey, his heires and assignes, and to all and every of them, and to all and every other person and persons, being of our allegiance, whose names shall be noted or entred in some of our courts of Record, within this our Realme of England, and that with the assent of the said sir Humfrey, his heires or assignes, shall nowe in this journey for discoverie, or in the second journey for conquest hereafter, travel to such lands, countries and territories as aforesaid, and to their and every of their heires: that they and every or any of them being either borne with our sayd Realmes of England or Ireland, or within any other place within our allegiance, and which hereafter shall be inhabiting within any the lands, countreys and territories, with such license as aforesayd, shall and may have, and enjoy all the priveleges of free denizens and persons native of England, and within our allegiance: any law, custome, or usage to the contrary notwithstanding.

And forasmuch, as upon the finding out, discovering and inhabiting of such remote lands, countreys and territories, as aforesayd, it shall be necessarie for the safety of all men that shall adventure themselves in those journeys or voiages, to determine to live together in Christian peace and civil quietnesse each with other, whereby every one may with more pleasure and profit, enjoy that whereunto they shall attaine with great paine and perill: wee for us, our heires and successours are likewise pleased and contented, and by these presents doe give and graunt to the sayd sir Humfrey and his heires and assignes for ever, that he and they, and every or any of them, shall and may, from time to time, for ever hereafter within the sayd mentioned remote lands and countreys, and in the way by the Seas thither, and from thence, have full and meere power and authoritie to correct, punish, pardon, governe and rule by their, and every or any of their good discretions and policies, as well in causes capitall or criminall, as civill, both marine and other, all such our subjects and others, as shall from time to time hereafter adventure themselves in the sayd journeys or voyages habitative or possessive, or that shall at any time hereafter inhabite any such lands, countreys or territories as aforesayd, or that shall abide within two hundred leagues of any sayd place or places, where the sayd sir Humfrey or his heires, or assignes, or any of them, or any of his, or their associats or companies, shall inhabite within sixe yeers next ensuing the date hereof, according to such statutes, lawes and ordinances, as shall be by him the said sir Humfrey, his heires and assignes, or every, or any of them, devised or established for the better government of the said people as aforesayd: so always that the sayd statutes, lawes and ordinances may be as neere as conveniently may, agreeable to the forme of the lawes & pollicy of England: and also, that they be not against the true Christian faith or religion now professed in the Church of England, nor in any wise to withdraw any of the subjects or people of those lands or places from the allegiance of us, our heires or successours, as their immediate Soveraignes under God. . . .

3

Virginia Rules on Conduct and Religion (1619)

Seventeenth-century England, for all its liberties, still placed numerous restrictions on the conduct of individuals. The existence of an established church also led to many political regulations regarding church attendance and other matters that today we would see as entirely religious. Faced by a hostile wilderness, colonial leaders felt the need for similar rules to ensure social stability. Virginians, however, were far less concerned with religion than their peers in New England. The Rules were designed to enforce social control after near anarchy in the early years had almost led to the colony's extinction. Moreover, the managers of the Virginia Company hoped that the Rules would attract new settlers by making the colony appear more civilized and less a

Source: Botein, *Early American Law and Society* 83 (1983).

wilderness outpost. Note also that in the absence of ecclesiastical authorities, the Virginia General Assembly assumed it had the power to define the duties of clergy.

See G. M. Brydon, *Virginia's Mother Church . . . 1607–1727* (1947); W. F. Craven, *The Southern Colonies in the Seventeenth Century* (1949).

Against Idleness, gaming, drunkenness & excesse in apparel, the Assembly hath enacted as followeth:

First in detestation of idlers, be it enacted, that if any man be found to live as an Idler, though a freed man, it shall be lawful for the Incorporation or Plantation to which he belongeth to appoint him a Master to serve for wages till he shewe apparent signes of amendment.

Against gaming at Dice & cards be it ordained by this present Assembly that the winner or winners shall lose all his or their winnings & both winners and loosers shall forfeit ten shillings a man, one ten shillings whereof to goe to the discoverer, & the rest to charitable & pious uses in the Incorporation where the faults are committed.

Against drunkenes be it also decreed, that if any private person be found culpable thereof, for the first time he is to be reprooved privately by the Minister, and second time publiquely, the Third time to lye in boltes 12 houres in the House of the Provost Marshall & to paye his fees, and if he still continue in that vice, to undergo such severe punishment, as the Governor & Councell shall think fitt to be inflicted on him. But if any Officer offende in this crime, the first time he shall receive a reproof from the Governour, the second time he shall openly be reproved in the Churche by the minister, & the third time he shall first be committed & then degraded. Provided it be understood, that the Governour hath always power to restore him when he shall in his discretion thinke fitt.

Against excesse of apparell, that every man be assessed in the Churche for all publique contributions, if he be unmarried according to his apparell, if he be married, according to his owne & his wives or either of their apparell.

For Reformation of Swearing, every freeman and Master of a family after thrice admonition shall give 5 shillings to the use of the churche where he dwelleth: and every servant after the like admonition, except his Master discharge the fine, shall be subject to whipping. Provided that the payment of the fine notwithstanding, the said servant shall acknowledge his fault publiquely in the Church.

All persons whatever upon Sabaoth days shall frequente divine service & sermons both forenoon and afternoone; and all suche as beare armes shall bring their pieces, swordes, power, & shotte. And Every one that shall transgresse this Law, shall forfeit three shillings a time to the use of the

Church, all lawful & necessary impediments excepted. But if a servant in this case shall willfully neglecte his Masters commande he shall suffer bodily punishmente.

All Ministers in the Colony shall once a year, namely in the month of Marche, bring to the Secretary of State a true account of all Christenings, burials & marriages, upon paine, if they faile, to be censured for their negligence by the Governour & Councell. Likewise, where there be no ministers, that the commanders of the place doe supply the same duty.

No maide or woman servant, either now resident in the Colonie, or hereafter to come, shall contract herselfe in marriage without either the consente of her parents or her Master or Mistress, or of the magistrate & Minister of the place both together. And whatsoever Minister shall marry or contracte any such persons without some of the foresaid consentes shall be subjecte to the severe censure of the Governour & Counsell.

All ministers shall duely read divine service, and exercise their ministerial function according to the Ecclesiastical Lawes and orders of the church of Englande, and every Sunday in the afternoon shall Catechize suche as are not yet ripe to come to the Communion. And whosoever of them shall be found negligent or faulty in this kinde shall be subject to the censure of the Governour and Councell.

The Ministers and Churchwardens shall seeke to prevent all ungodly disorders, as suspicions of whoredoms, dishonest company keeping with weomen and such like; the committers whereofe if, upon goode admonitions and milde reproofe they will not forbeare the said skandalous offences, they are to be presented and punished accordingly.

If any person after two warnings doe not amende his or her life in point of evident suspicion of Incontinency or of the commission of any other enormous sinnes, that then he or shee shall be presented by the Churchwardens and suspended for a time from the Churche by the minister. In which interim if the same person do not amend and humbly submitt him or herselfe to the churche, he is then fully to be excommunicate, and soon after a writt or warrant is to be sente from the Governour for the apprehending of his person & seizing all his goods. Provided alwayes, that all ministers doe meet once a quarter, namely at the feast of St. Michael the Arkangell, of the nativity of our Saviour, of the Annuntiation of the blessed Virgin, and about midsomer, at James Citty or any other place where the Governour shall reside, to determine whom it is fitt to excommunicate, and that they first present their opinion to the Governour ere they proceed to the acte of excommunication.

4

Mayflower Compact (1620)

The Separatists were the extreme Puritans who believed that the Church of England was so corrupt that the pure at heart had to leave it totally. A group which left England and landed at Plymouth knew of the troubles that had plagued the Jamestown colony in its first years because of a lack of well-defined governmental authority. Their leaders, aware of the problems at Jamestown, wanted to ensure that the settlement would not suffer from weak government. So before the colonists left the ship, they had to agree to abide by the government that would be established. The Separatists also carried, as part of their theological baggage, a belief in the compact theory of government, that is, that people agreed to join together in society, and in doing so consented to be governed. This English idea, which later played so important a role in the movement toward independence, will be expressed many times in our history. That it should take a written form, however, marks a significant step away from the more informal constitutionalism of the Mother Country. The Mayflower Compact is not a true constitution, but is important as the first American statement that governments rule by the consent of the governed. Despite its brevity, the Compact served as the only formal governance document of the colony for its seventy-one years of independent existence.

See S. E. Morison, ed., Bradford, *Of Plymouth Plantation, 1620–1647* (1959), and G. Langdon, *Pilgrim Colony: A History of New Plymouth, 1620–1691* (1966).

We whose names are underwritten, the loyal subjects of our dread Sovereign Lord King James, by the Grace of God of Great Britain, France, and Ireland King, Defender of the Faith, etc.

Having undertaken, for the Glory of God and advancement of the Christian Faith and Honour of our King and Country, a Voyage to plant the First Colony in the Northern Parts of Virginia, do by these presents solemnly and mutually in the presence of God and one of another, Covenant and Combine ourselves together into a Civil Body Politic, for our better ordering and preservation and furtherance of the ends aforesaid; and by virtue hereof to

Source: Morison, ed., Bradford, *Of Plymouth Plantation* 75 (1959).

enact, constitute and frame such just and equal Laws, Ordinances, Acts, Constitutions and Offices, from time to time, as shall be thought most meet and convenient for the general good of the Colony, unto which we promise all due submission and obedience. In witness whereof we have hereunder subscribed our names at Cape Cod, the 11th of November, in the year of the reign of our Sovereign Lord King James, of England, France and Ireland the eighteenth, and of Scotland the fifty-fourth. Anno Domini 1620.

5.

Fundamental Orders of Connecticut (1639)

Several of the smaller New England colonies also adopted compacts as the source of their governmental authority. The most elaborate of these documents, the Fundamental Orders of Connecticut (which united several towns in the Connecticut valley), provided for particular officers and branches of government and defined their authority and powers. Although the Orders resemble a modern constitution in outlining a scheme of government, a true constitution is superior to the agencies it establishes, while this document could be amended by the Connecticut General Court in the same manner as it used to change any statute.

See M. J. A. Jones, *Congregational Commonwealth* (1968); H. J. Santos, "The Birth of a Liberal State . . . ," 1 *Conn. L.R.* 386 (1968); and A. C. Bates, "Were the Fundamental Orders a Constitution?" 10 *Conn. Bar J.* 43 (1936).

Forasmuch as it hath pleased the All-mighty God by the wise disposition of his divyne pruvidence so to Order and dispose of things that we the Inhabitants and Residents of Windsor, Harteford and Wethersfield are now cohab-

Source: Thorpe, ed. 1 *Federal and State Constitutions* 519 (1909).

iting and dwelling in and uppon the River of Conectecotte and the Lands thereunto adioyneing; And well knowing where a people are gathered together the word of God requires that to mayntayne the peace and union of such a people there should be an orderly and decent Government established according to God, to order and dispose of the affayres of the people at all seasons as occation shall require; doe therefore assotiate and conioyne our selves to be as one Publike State or Commonwelth; and doe, for our selves and our Successors and such as shall be adioyned to us att any tyme hereafter, enter into Combination and Confederation togather, to mayntayne and presearve the liberty and purity of the gospell of our Lord Jesus which we now professe, as also the disciplyne of the Churches, which according to the truth of the said gospell is now practised amongst us; As also in our Civell Affaires to be guided and governed according to such Lawes, Rules, Orders and decrees as shall be made, ordered & decreed, as followeth:—

1.   It is Ordered . . . that there shall be yerely two generall Assemblies or Courts, the one the second thursday in Aprill, the other the second thursday in September, following; the first shall be called the Courte of Election, wherein shall be yerely Chosen . . . soe many Magestrats and other publike Officers as shall be found requisitte: Whereof one to be chosen Governour for the yeare ensueing and untill another be chosen, and noe other Magestrate to be chosen for more than one yeare; provided allwayes there be sixe chosen besids the Governour; which being chosen and sworne according to an Oath recorded for that purpose shall have power to administer justice according to the Lawes here established, and for want thereof according to the rule of the word of God; which choise shall be made by all that are admitted freemen and have taken the Oath of Fidelity, and doe cohabitte within this Jurisdiction, (having beene admitted Inhabitants by the major part of the Towne wherein they live,) or the major parte of such as shall be then present. . . .

4.   It is Ordered . . . that noe person be chosen Governor above once in two yeares, and that the Governor be alwayes a member of some approved congregation, and formerly of the Magestracy within this Jurisdiction; and all the Magestrats Freemen of this Commonwelth: . . .

5.   It is Ordered . . . that to the aforesaid Courte of Election the severall Townes shall send their deputyes, and when the Elections are ended they may proceed in any publike searvice as at other Courts. Also the other Generall Courte in September shall be for makeing of lawes, and any other publike occasion, which conserns the good of the Commonwelth. . . .

8.   It is Ordered . . . that Wyndsor, Hartford and Wethersfield shall have power, ech Towne, to send fower of their freemen as their deputyes to every Generall Courte; and whatsoever other Townes shall be hereafter added to this Jurisdiction, they shall send so many deputyes as the Courte shall judge meete, a resonable proportion to the number of Freemen that are in the said

Townes being to be attended therein; which deputyes shall have the power of the whole Towne to give their voats and alowance to all such lawes and orders as may be for the publike good, and unto which the said Townes are to be bownd.

9. It is ordered and decreed, that the deputyes thus chosen shall have power and liberty to appoynt a tyme and a place of meeting togather before any Generall Courte to aduise and consult of all such things as may concerne the good of the publike, as also to examine their owne Elections, whether according to the order, and if they or the gretest prte of them find any election to be illegall they may seclud such for prsent from their meeting, and returne the same and their resons to the Courte: and if yt proue true, the Courte may fyne the prty or prtyes so intruding and the Towne, if they see cause, and giue out a warrant to goe to a newe election in a legall way, either *in whole or* in prte. Also the said deputyes shall haue power to fyne any that shall be disorderly at their meetings, or for not coming in due tyme or place according to appoyntment; and they may returne the said fynes into the Courte if yt be refused to be paid, and the tresurer to take notice of yt, and to estreete or levy the same as he doth other fynes.

10. It is Ordered, sentenced and decreed, that euery Generall Courte, except such as through neglecte of the Gournor and the greatest prte of Magestrats the Freemen themselves doe call, shall consist of the Gouernor, or some one chosen to moderate the Court, and 4 other Magestrats at lest, wth the mayor prte of the deputyes of the seuerall Townes legally chosen; and in case the Freemen or mayor prte of them through neglect or refusall of the Gouernor and mayor prte of the magestrats, shall call a Courte, that yt shall consist of the mayor prte of Freemen that are prsent or their deputyes, wth a Moderator chosen by them: *In wch said Generall Courts shall consist the supreme power of the Commonwelth,* and they only shall haue power to make laws or repeale them; to graunt leuyes, to admitt of Freemen, dispose of lands vndisposed of,, to seuerall Townes or prsons, and also shall haue power to call ether Courte or Magestrate or any other prson whatsoeuer into question for any misdemeanour, and may for just causes displace or deale otherwise according to the nature of the offence; and also may deale in any other matter that concerns the good of this comon welth, excepte election of Magestrats, wch shall be done by the whole boddy of Freemen: In wch Courte the Gouernour or Moderator shall haue power to order the Courte to giue liberty of spech, and silence vnceasonable and disorderly speakeings, to put all things to voate, and in case the vote be equall to haue the casting voice. But non of these Courts shall be adiorned or dissolued wthout the consent of the major prte of the Court.

11. It is ordered, sentenced and decreed, that when any Generall Courte vppon the occasions of the Commonwelth haue agreed vppon any summe or somes of mony to be leuyed vppon the seuerall Townes wthin this Jurisdic-

tion, that a Committee be chosen to sett out and appoynt wt shall be the prportion of euery Towne to pay of the said leuy, prvided the Committees be made vp of an equall number out of each Towne.

6

The Bloudy Tenent of Persecution (1644)

ROGER WILLIAMS

Roger Williams had been exiled from Massachusetts Bay for his heretical notions of proper church and state relations, and he founded a refuge at Providence in Rhode Island. In 1643–44 he was in London securing a charter for Providence, at the same time that the Puritans had come to power and called the Westminster Assembly of Divines to plan England's ecclesiastical future. Still rankling from his expulsion, Williams entered the debate with several pamphlets, of which the lengthy "bloudy tenent" was aimed directly at the views of his arch opponent in the New World, the Puritan divine John Cotton. The work consists primarily of a dense and complex debate between Truth and Peace over the proper relations between church and state, but the basic argument is summed up in the opening "document," which is the basis for the debate. Williams's arguments are the first in the New World calling for freedom of conscience and a separation between the ecclesiastical and secular authorities. While they had little impact at the time, these ideas slowly infiltrated American political thought and emerge seemingly full-blown after the Revolution (see Documents 24, 25, and 27).

See O. E. Winslow, *Master Roger Williams* (1957); P. Miller, *Errand into the Wilderness* (1956); and E. S. Morgan, *Roger Williams: The Church and the State* (1967).

Source: Caldwell, ed. 3 *Complete Writings of Roger Williams* 3 (1963).

First, That the blood of so many hundred thousand soules of Protestants and Papists, spilt in the Wars of present and former Ages, for their respective Consciences, is not required nor accepted by Jesus Christ the Prince of Peace.

Secondly, Pregnant Scripturs and Arguments are throughout the Worke proposed against the Doctrine of persecution for cause of Conscience.

Thirdly, Satisfactorie Answers are given to Scriptures, and objections produced by Mr. Calvin, Beza, Mr. Cotton, and the Ministers of the New English Churches and others former and later, tending to prove the Doctrine of persecution for cause of Conscience.

Fourthly, The Doctrine of persecution for cause of Conscience, is proved guilty of all the blood of the Soules crying for vengeance under the Altar.

Fifthly, All Civill States with their Officers of justice in their respective constitutions and administrations are proved essentially Civill, and therefore not Judges, Governours or Defendours of the Spirituall or Christian state and Worship.

Sixthly, It is the will and command of God, that (since the comming of his Sonne the Lord Jesus) a permission of the most Paganish, Jewish, Turkish, or Antichristian consciences and worships, bee granted to all men in all Nations and Countries: and they are onely to bee fought against with that Sword which is only (in Soule matters) able to conquer, to wit, the Sword of Gods Spirit, the Word of God.

Seventhly, The State of the Land of Israel, the Kings and people thereof in Peace & War, is proved figurative and ceremoniall, and no patterne nor president for any Kingdome or civill state in the world to follow.

Eightly, God requireth not an uniformity of Religion to be inacted and inforced in any civill state; which inforced uniformity (sooner or later) is the greatest occasion of civill Warre, ravishing of conscience, persecution of Christ Jesus in his servants, and of the hypocrisie and destruction of millions of souls.

Ninthly, In holding an inforced uniformity of Religion in a civill state, wee must necessarily disclaime our desires and hopes of the Jewes conversion to Christ.

Tenthly, An inforced uniformity of Religion throughout a Nation or civill state, confounds the Civill and Religious, denies the principles of Christianity and civility, and that Jesus Christ is come in the Flesh.

Eleventhly, The permission of other consciences and worships then a state professeth, only can (according to God) procure a firme and lasting peace, (good assurance being taken according to the wisdome of the civill state for uniformity of civill obedience from all sorts.)

Twelfthly, lastly, true civility and Christianity may both flourish in a state or Kingdome, notwithstanding the permission of divers and contrary consciences, either of Jew or Gentile.

7

Frame of Government (1682)

WILLIAM PENN

All the colonies had to attract new settlers to survive and grow, and whether royal, company, or proprietary, had to offer some inducement to settlers. Some gave land; some held out hope of religious toleration (at least of certain beliefs), and all implied that a better life could be secured in the New World. William Penn, to whom Charles II gave the enormous tract of land the proprietor called "Pennsylvania," thought long and hard about the type of society he wished to foster. A Quaker, he knew firsthand about religious persecution and about how minority groups could be excluded from the political process. The "Frame of Government" represented not only an expression of advanced English political thought, but also a blueprint for what Penn hoped his colony would become. He hoped, he said in his preface, to establish a government that would not abuse its powers. This idea of limiting government derived in part from Magna Carta and from the compact theories expressed in Documents 4 and 5. As in so many theoretical constructs, the Frame proved somewhat defective when put into practice, but Penn, despite the restrictive sentiments in Article XXIII, agreed to changes when he arrived in the colony.

See M. M. Dunn, *William Penn: Politics and Conscience* (1967); G. Dargo, *Roots of the Republic* (1974); and G. B. Nash, "Framing of Government in Pennsylvania . . . ," 23 *W. and M. Q.* 183 (1966).

WHEREAS KING CHARLES the Second, by his Letters Patents, under the GREAT SEAL of *England,* for the Considerations therein mentioned, hath been graciously pleased to Give and Grant unto Me WILLIAM PENN (by the Name of WILLIAM PENN ESQUIRE, Son and Heir of SIR WILLIAM PENN deceased) and to My HEIRS and ASSIGNS forever, *All that Tract of Land or Province, called* PENNSILVANIA, *in* America, *with divers great Powers, Preheminencies, Royalties, Jurisdictions and Authorities necessary for the Well-being and Government thereof.*

Source: Dunn and Dunn, eds., 2 *Papers of William Penn* 211 (1982).

NOW KNOW YE, That for the *Well-being* and *Government* of the said *Province,* and for the *Encouragement* of all the FREE-MEN and PLANTERS that may be therein concerned, in pursuance of the Powers aforementioned, I the said WILLIAM PENN have *Declared, Granted* and *Confirmed,* and by these Presents for ME, my HEIRS and ASSIGNS do *Declare, Grant* and *Confirm* unto all the FREE-MEN, PLANTERS and ADVENTURERS of, in and to the said Province These LIBERTIES, FRANCHISES and PROPERTIES to be held, enjoyed and kept by the FREE-MEN, PLANTERS and INHABITANTS of and in the said *Province* of PENNSILVANIA forever.

Imprimis, That the *Government* of this *Province* shall, according to the *Powers* of the *Patent,* consist of the GOVERNOUR and FREE-MEN of the said *Province,* in the Form of a PROVINCIAL COUNCIL and GENERAL ASSEMBLY, by whom all *Laws* shall be made, Officers chosen and publick Affairs Transacted, as is hereafter respectively declared; That is to say,

II.   That the FREE-MEN of the said *Province* shall on the *Twentieth* day of the Twelfth Moneth, which shall be in this present year *One Thousand Six Hundred Eighty and Two,* Meet and Assembly in some fit place, of which timely Notice shall be beforehand given by the GOVERNOUR or his *Deputy,* and then and there shall chuse out of themselves SEVENTY TWO Persons of most Note for their *Wisdom, Virtue* and *Ability,* who shall meet on the Tenth day of the First Moneth next ensuing, and always be called and act as the PROVINCIAL COUNCIL of the said *Province.*

III.   That at the first Choice of such PROVINCIAL COUNCIL, *One Third part* of the said PROVINCIAL COUNCIL shall be chosen to serve for Three Years then next ensuing, *One Third part* for Two Years then next ensuing, and *One Third part* for One Year then next following such Election, and no longer; and that the said *Third* part shall go out accordingly. And on the Twentieth Day of the Twelfth Moneth, as aforesaid, yearly, forever afterward, the FREE-MEN of the said *Province* shall in like manner Meet and Assemble together, and then chuse *Twenty Four* Persons, being *One Third* of the said Number, to serve in PROVINCIAL COUNCIL for Three Years, it being intended, that *One Third* of the whole PROVINCIAL COUNCIL (always consisting and to consist of Seventy Two Persons, as aforesaid) falling off Yearly, it shall be yearly supplied by such new yearly Elections as aforesaid. And that no one Person shall continue therein longer than Three Years: And in case any Member shall decease before the last Election, during his time, that then at the next Election ensuing his Decease, another shall be chosen to supply his place for the remaining time he was to have served, and no longer.

IV.   That after the first Seven Years, every one of the said *Third parts* that goeth yearly off, shall be uncapable of being Chosen again for one whole Year following: That so all may be fitted for Government, and have Experience of the Care and Burden of it. . . .

VI.   That in this PROVINCIAL COUNCIL the GOVERNOUR or his *Deputy* shall or may alwayes *preside* and have a *Treble Voice;* and the said PROVINCIAL COUNCIL shall alwayes continue and sit upon its own *Adjournments* and *Committees.*

VII.   That the GOVERNOUR and PROVINCIAL COUNCIL shall prepare and propose to the GENERAL ASSEMBLY, hereafter mentioned, all BILLS, which they shall at any time think fit to be past into Laws within the said *Province;* which BILLS shall be Publisht and Affixed to the most noted Places in the Inhabited Parts thereof THIRTY Dayes before the Meeting of the GENERAL ASSEMBLY, in order to the passing of them into Laws, or rejecting of them, as the GENERAL ASSEMBLY shall see meet.

VIII.   That the GOVERNOUR and PROVINCIAL COUNCIL shall take Care, that all *Laws, Statutes* and *Ordinances,* which shall at any time be made within the said *Province,* be duely and diligently Executed.

IX.   That the GOVERNOUR and PROVINCIAL COUNCIL shall at all times have the Care of the *Peace* and *Safety* of the *Province;* and that nothing be by any Person attempted to the Subversion of this Frame of Government. . . .

XI.   That the *Governour* and *Provincial Council* shall at all times have Power to inspect the Management of the publick *Treasury,* and punish those who shall Convert any part thereof to any other use, than what hath been agreed upon by the GOVERNOUR, PROVINCIAL COUNCIL and GENERAL ASSEMBLY.

XII.   That the GOVERNOUR and PROVINCIAL COUNCIL shall erect and order all *publick Schools,* and encourage and reward the Authors of *useful Sciences* and *laudable Inventions* in the said Province.

XIII.   That for the better Management of the Powers and Trust aforesaid, the PROVINCIAL COUNCIL shall from time to time divide it self into Four distinct and proper Committees, for the more easie Administration of the Affairs of the Province, which divides the *Seventy Two* into four Eighteens, every one of which Eighteens shall consist of Six out of each of the *Three Orders* or *Yearly Elections,* each of which shall have a distinct portion of Business, as followeth. First, A *Committee* of PLANTATIONS, to scituate and settle Cities, Ports, Market-Towns and High-wayes, and to hear and decide all Suits and Controversies relating to *Plantations.* Secondly, a *Committee* of JUSTICE and SAFETY to secure the Peace of the Province, and punish the Male-Administration of those who subvert Justice to the Prejudice of the publick or private Interest. Thirdly, a *Committee* of TRADE and TREASURY, who shall regulate all Trade and Commerce according to Law, encourage Manufacture and Country-growth, and defray the publick Charge of the *Province.* And Fourthly, A *Committee* of MANNERS, EDUCATION and ARTS, that all Wicked and Scandalous Living may be prevented, and that *Youth* may be successively trained up in *Virtue* and *useful Knowledge* and *Arts;* the *Quorum* of each of which Committees being Six, that is, Two out of each of the three

Orders or yearly Elections, as aforesaid, make a *constant* or *standing Council* of twenty four, which will have the Power of the PROVINCIAL COUNCIL, being the *Quorum* of it, in all Cases not excepted in the fifth Article; and in the said *Committees* and *standing Council* of the *Province,* the GOVERNOUR or his *Deputy* shall or may *Preside,* as aforesaid. And in the Absence of the GOVERNOUR or his *Deputy:* if no one is by either of them appointed, the said *Committees* or *Council* shall appoint a *President* for that time, and not otherwise; and what shall be *resolved* at such *Committees,* shall be reported to the said *Council* of the *Province,* and shall be by them *Resolved* and *Confirmed* before the same shall be put in Execution: And that these respective *Committees* shall not sit at one and the same time, except in cases of necessity.

XIV.   And to the end that all Laws prepared by the GOVERNOUR and PROVINCIAL COUNCIL aforesaid, may yet have the more full Concurrence of the FREE-MEN of the *Province,* It is Declared, Granted and Confirmed, that at the time and Place or Places, for the Choice of a PROVINCIAL COUNCIL, as aforesaid, the said FREE-MEN shall Yearly chuse *Members* to serve in a GENERAL ASSEMBLY, as their *Representatives,* not exceeding Two Hundred Persons, who shall Yearly meet on the Twentieth Day of the second Moneth, which shall be in the Year 1683. following, in the *Capital Town* or *City* of the said *Province,* where during Eight Dayes the several *Members* may freely Confer with one another; and if any of them see meet, with a *Committee* of the PROVINCIAL COUNCIL (consisting of *Three* out of each of the Four *Committees* aforesaid, being *Twelve* in all) which shall be at that time purposely Appointed to receive from any of them Proposals for the Alteration or Amendment of any of the said proposed and promulgated *Bills;* and on the Ninth Day from their so meeting, the said GENERAL ASSEMBLY, after the reading over of the proposed *Bills* by the Clark of the PROVINCIAL COUNCIL, and the Occasions and Motives for them being opened by the GOVERNOUR or his DEPUTY, shall give their AFFIRMATIVE or NEGATIVE, which to them seemeth best, in such manner as hereafter is exprest: But not less than *two Thirds* shall make a *Quorum* in the Passing of Laws and Choice of such Officers as are by them to be Chosen.

XV.   That the Laws so prepared and proposed as aforesaid, that are Assented to by the GENERAL ASSEMBLY, shall be Enrolled, as Laws of the *Province,* with this Stile, BY THE GOVERNOUR, WITH THE ASSENT AND APPROBATION OF THE FREE-MEN IN PROVINCIAL COUNCIL AND GENERAL ASSEMBLY.

XVI.   That for the better Establishment of the *Government* and *Laws* of this *Province,* and to the end there may be an Universal Satisfaction in the laying of the *Fundamentals* thereof, the GENERAL ASSEMBLY shall or may for the first Year consist of all the FREE-MEN of and in the said Province; and ever after it shall be yearly Chosen, as aforesaid: which Number of TWO HUNDRED shall be Enlarged as the Country shall Encrease in People, so as it do not Exceed FIVE HUNDRED at any time: The Appointment and Proportion-

ing of which, as also the *Laying* and *Methodizing* of the Choice of the PROVIN-
CIAL COUNCIL and GENERAL ASSEMBLY in future times most Equally to the
Division of the *Hundreds* and *Counties,* which the *Country* shall hereafter be
divided into, shall be in the Power of the PROVINCIAL COUNCIL to *Propose,*
and the GENERAL ASSEMBLY to *Resolve.*

XVII.   That the GOVERNOUR and the PROVINCIAL COUNCIL shall Erect
from time to time *standing Courts of Justice* in such Places and Number, as they
shall judge Convenient for the good Government of the said *Province.* And
that the PROVINCIAL COUNCIL shall on the *Thirteenth Day* of the First
Moneth Yearly Elect and Present to the GOVERNOUR or his *Deputy* a double
Number of Persons to serve for *Judges, Treasurers, Masters* of *Rolls* within the
said *Province* for the Year next ensuing. And the FREE-MEN of the said
Province in their *County-Courts,* when they shall be erected, and till then, in
the GENERAL ASSEMBLY shall on the *Three and Twentieth* Day of the Second
Moneth yearly Elect and Present to the GOVERNOUR or his *Deputy* a *Double
Number* of Persons to serve for *Sheriffs, Justices* of *Peace* and *Coroners* for the
Year next ensuing; Out of which Respective *Elections* and *Presentments* the
GOVERNOUR or his *Deputy* shall Nominate and Commissionate the proper
Number for each Office the *Third day* after the said respective Presentments,
or else the First named in such Presentment for each Office shall stand and
serve for that Office the Year ensuing.

XVIII.   BUT for as much as the present Condition of the *Province* requires
some *Immediate Settlement,* and admits not of so quick a Revolution of *Officers,*
and to the end the said *Province* may with all convenient Speed be well
ordered and settled, I WILLIAM PENN do therefore think fit to Nominate and
Appoint such Persons for *Judges, Treasurers, Masters of the Rolls, Sheriffs, Justices
of the Peace* and *Coroners,* as are most fitly qualified for those Employments;
to whom I shall make and grant *Commissions* for the said *Offices,* respectively
to hold to them to whom the same shall be granted, for so long time as every
such Person shall *Well behave himself* in the *Office* or Place to him respectively granted, and no longer. And upon the Decease or Displacing of any of
the said Officers, the succeeding Officer or Officers shall be chosen as aforesaid. . . .

XXI.   And that at all times, when and so often as it shall happen, that the
GOVERNOUR shall or may be an *Infant* under the Age of One and Twenty
years, and no *Guardians* or *Commissioners* are appointed in writing by the
Father of the said Infant, or that such *Guardians* or *Commissioners* shall be
deceased, that during such Minority the PROVINCIAL COUNCIL shall from
time to time, as they shall see meet, constitute and appoint *Guardians* or
Commissioners, not exceeding *Three,* one of which three shall *Preside* as *Deputy*
and *Chief Guardian,* during such *Minority,* and shall have and execute with
the Consent of the other *Two* all the Power of a GOVERNOUR in all the
publick Affairs and Concerns of the said *Province.*

XXII.   That as often as any day of the Moneth, mentioned in any Article of this Charter, shall fall upon the *First Day* of the Week, commonly called the *Lords Day,* the Business appointed for that day shall be deferred till the next day, unless in case of Emergency.

XXIII.   That no *Act, Law* or *Ordinance* whatsoever, shall at any time here-after be made or done by the GOVERNOUR of this *Province,* his HEIRS or ASSIGNS, or by the FREE-MEN in the PROVINCIAL COUNCIL or the GENERAL ASSEMBLY, to *Alter, Change* or *Diminish* the *Form* or *Effect* of this CHARTER, or any *Part* or *Clause* thereof, or contrary to the true Intent and Meaning thereof, *without the Consent of the* GOVERNOUR, *his* HEIRS *or* ASSIGNS, *and Six Parts of Seven of the said* FREE-MEN *in* PROVINCIAL COUNCIL and GENERAL ASSEMBLY.

XXIV.   And *Lastly,* That I, the said WILLIAM PENN, for MY SELF, my HEIRS and ASSIGNS have *Solemnly Declared, Granted* and *Confirmed,* and do hereby *Solemnly Declare, Grant* and *Confirm,* That neither I, My HEIRS nor ASSIGNS *shall procure or do any thing or things, whereby the* Liberties *in this* Charter *contained and expressed, shall be infringed or broken:* And if any thing be procured by any Person or Persons contrary to these Premises, it shall be held of *no Force or Effect.* IN WITNESS whereof I the said WILLIAM PENN have unto this present CHARTER of LIBERTIES set my Hand and Broad Seal this Five and Twentieth Day of the Second Moneth, vulgarly called *April,* in the Year of our Lord One Thousand Six Hundred Eighty and Two.

William Penn.

8

Zenger's Case (1735)

The early interpretation of the trial of John Peter Zenger for seditious libel, and his acquittal by the jury, saw Zenger and his associates as patriotic republicans, and the decision as a landmark in legal develop-

Source: Katz, ed. (1972), J. Alexander, *A Brief Narrative of the Case and Trial of John Peter Zenger* 58 (1736).

ment. More recent scholarship sees Zenger as a narrow political partisan, as he and his colleagues sought immediate gain and had little interest in governmental reform. But although some scholars have downplayed the result and claim that the times, even without Zenger, would have led to similar reforms, others question this judgment. The law of seditious libel, which penalized the publication of any statement detrimental to character, did not allow truth as a defense—the *detriment* and not the truth was the issue. Zenger's case made truth a defense in American law, and even the infamous Sedition Law of 1798 (see Document 38) accepted this proposition. The Zenger case was the last colonial trial for seditious libel under the royal judges with one exception; changes in English law did not take place until nearly a century later. The following excerpt includes the opening statement of the prosecuting attorney, the Attorney General of the colony, Richard Bradley, and the response by the renowned Philadelphia attorney Andrew Hamilton, brought out of retirement to argue on Zenger's behalf.

See Katz, introduction to *A Brief Narrative . . .* (1972 ed.); H. L. Nelson, "Seditious Libel in Colonial America," 3 *Am. J. Leg. His.* 160 (1959); and L. W. Levy, *Emergence of a Free Press* (1985).

~~~~~~

Mr. Attorney General opened the information, which was as follows:

Mr. Attorney. May it please Your Honors, and you, gentlemen of the jury; the information now before the Court, and to which the Defendant Zenger has pleaded *not guilty,* is an information for printing and publishing *a false, scandalous and seditious libel,* in which His Excellency the Governor of this Province, who is the King's immediate representative here, is greatly and unjustly scandalized as a person that has no regard to law nor justice; with much more, as will appear upon reading the information. This of libeling is what has always been discouraged as a thing that tends to create differences among men, ill blood among the people, and oftentimes great bloodshed between the party libeling and the party libeled. There can be no doubt but you gentlemen of the jury will have the same ill opinion of such practices as the judges have always shown upon such occasions: But I shall say no more at this time until you hear the information. . . . To this information the Defendant has pleaded *not guilty,* and we are ready to prove it. . . .

Then *Mr. Hamilton,* who at the request of some of my friends was so kind as to come from Philadelphia to assist me on the trial, spoke.

Mr. Hamilton. May it please Your Honor; I am concerned in this cause on the part of Mr. Zenger the Defendant. The information against my client was sent me a few days before I left home, with some instructions to let me know how far I might rely upon the truth of those parts of the papers set forth in the information and which are said to be libelous. And though I am perfectly of the opinion with the gentleman who has just now spoke on the same side with me as to the common course of proceedings, I mean in putting Mr. Attorney upon proving that my client printed and published those papers mentioned in the information; yet I cannot think it proper for me (without doing violence to my own principles) to deny the publication of a complaint which I think is the right of every free-born subject to make when the matters so published can be supported with truth; and therefore I'll save Mr. Attorney the trouble of examining his witnesses to that point; and I do (for my client) confess that he both printed and published the two newspapers set forth in the information, and I hope in so doing he has committed no crime.

Mr. Attorney. Then if Your Honor pleases, since Mr. Hamilton has confessed the fact, I think our witnesses may be discharged; we have no further occasion for them.

Mr. Hamilton. If you brought them here only to prove the printing and publishing of these newspapers, we have acknowledged that, and shall abide by it. . . .

Mr. Chief Justice. Well Mr. Attorney, will you proceed?

Mr. Attorney. Indeed sir, as Mr. Hamilton has confessed the printing and publishing these libels, I think the jury must find a verdict for the King; for supposing they were true, the law says that they are not the less libelous for that; nay indeed the law says their being true is an aggravation of the crime.

Mr. Hamilton. Not so neither, Mr. Attorney, there are two words to that bargain. I hope it is not our bare printing and publishing a paper that will make it a libel: You will have something more to do before you make my client a libeler; for the words themselves must be libelous, that is, *false, scandalous, and seditious* or else we are not guilty.

[As Mr. Attorney has not been pleased to favor us with his argument, which he read, or with the notes of it, we cannot take upon us to set down his words, but only to show the book cases he cited and the general scope of his argument which he drew from those authorities. He observed upon the excellency as well as the use of government, and the great regard and reverence which had been constantly paid to it, both under the law and the gospel. That by government we were protected in our lives, religion and properties; and that for these reasons great care had always been taken to prevent everything that might tend to scandalize magistrates and others concerned in the administration of the government, especially the supreme magistrate. And that there were many instances of very severe judgments, and of punishments inflicted upon such, as had attempted to bring the government into contempt; by publishing false and scurrilous libels against it, or by speaking evil and scandalous words of men in authority; to the great disturbance of the public peace. And to support this, he cited 5 Coke 121 (suppose it should be 125), Wood's Instit. 430, 2 Lilly 168, I Hawkins 73.11.6. From these books he insisted that a libel was a malicious defamation of any person, expressed either in printing or writing, signs or pictures, to asperse the reputation of one that is alive or the memory of one that is dead; if he is a private man, the libeler deserves a severe punishment, but if it is against a magistrate or other public person, it is a greater offense; for this concerns not only the breach of the peace, but the scandal of the government; for what greater scandal of government can there be than to have corrupt or wicked magistrates to be appointed by the King to govern his subjects under him? And a greater imputation to the state cannot be than to suffer such corrupt men to sit in the sacred seat of justice, or to have any meddling in or concerning the administration of justice; And from the same books Mr. Attorney insisted that whether the person defamed is a private man or a magistrate, whether living or dead, whether the libel is true or false, or if the party against whom it is made is of good or evil fame, it is nevertheless a libel: For in a settled state of government the party aggrieved ought to complain for every injury done him in the ordinary course of the law. And as to its publication, the law had taken so great care of men's reputations that if one maliciously repeats it, or sings it in the presence of another, or delivers the libel or a copy of it over to scandalize the party, he is to be punished as a publisher of a libel. He said it was likewise evident that libeling was an offense against the law of God. *Act. XXIII. 5. Then said Paul, I wist not brethren, that he was the High Priest: For it is written, thou shalt not speak evil of the ruler of the People. 2 Pet. X. II. Despite government, presumptuous are they, self-willed, they are not afraid to speak evil of dignitaries, etc.* He then insisted that it was clear, both by the law of God and man, that it was a very great offense to speak evil of or to revile those in authority over us; and that Mr. Zenger had offended in a most notorious and gross manner in scandalizing His Excellency our Governor, who is the King's immediate representative and the supreme magistrate of this Province: For can there be anything more scandalous said of a Governor than what is published in those papers? Nay, not only the Governor, but both the Council and Assembly are scandalized; for there it is plainly said that *as matters now stand, their liberties and properties are precarious, and that slavery is like to be entailed on them and their posterity.* And then again Mr. Zenger says *the Assembly ought to despise the smiles or frowns of a governor; that he thinks the law is at an end; that we see men's deeds destroyed, judges arbitrarily displaced, new courts erected without consent of the legislature;* and *that it seems trials by juries are taken away when a governor pleases; that none can call anything their own longer than those in the administration will condescend to let them do it.*—And Mr. Attorney added that he did not know what could be said in defense of a man that had so notoriously scandalized the Governor and principal magistrates and officers of the government by charging them with depriving the people of their rights and liberties, and taking away trials by juries, and in short, putting an end to the law itself.—If this was not a libel, he said, he did not know what was one. Such persons as will take those liberties with governors and magistrates he thought ought to suffer for stirring up sedition and discontent among the people. And concluded by saying that the government had been very much traduced and exposed by Mr. Zenger before he was taken notice of; that at last it was the opinion of the Governor and Council that he ought not to be suffered to go on to disturb the peace of the government by publishing such libels against the Governor and the chief persons in the government; and therefore they had directed this prosecution to put a stop to this scandalous and wicked practice of libeling and defaming His Majesty's government and disturbing His Majesty's peace.

Mr. Chambers then summed up to the jury, observing with great strength of reason on Mr. Attorney's defect of proof that the papers in the information were *false, malicious, or seditious,* which was incumbent on him to prove to the jury, and without which they could not on their oaths say *that they were so, as charged.*]

Mr. Hamilton. May it please Your Honor; I agree with Mr. Attorney, that government is a sacred thing, but I differ very widely from him when he would insinuate that the just complaints of a number of men who suffer under a bad administration is libeling that administration. Had I believed that to be law, I should not have given the Court the trouble of hearing anything that I should say in this cause. I own when I read the information I had not the art to find out (without the help of Mr. Attorney's *innuendoes*) that the Governor was the person meant in every period of that newspaper; and I was inclined to believe that they were wrote by some who from an extraordinary zeal for liberty had misconstrued the conduct of some persons in authority into crimes; and that Mr. Attorney out of his too great zeal for power had exhibited this information to correct the indiscretion of my client; and at the same time to show his superiors the great concern he had lest they should be treated with any undue freedom. But from what Mr. Attorney has just now said, *to wit,* that this prosecution was directed by the Governor and Council, and from the extraordinary appearance of people of all conditions which I observe in Court upon this occasion, I have reason to think that those in the administration have by this prosecution something more in view, and that the people believe they have a good deal more at stake, than I apprehended: And therefore as it is become my duty to be both plain and particular in this cause, I beg leave to bespeak the patience of the Court.

I was in hopes, as that terrible Court, where those dreadful judgments were given and that law established which Mr. Attorney has produced for authorities to support this cause, was long ago laid aside as the most dangerous court to the liberties of the people of England that ever was known in that kingdom; that Mr. Attorney knowing this would not have attempted to set up a Star Chamber here, nor to make their judgments a precedent to us: For it is well known that what would have been judged treason in those days for a man to speak, I think, has since not only been practiced as lawful, but the contrary doctrine has been held to be law. . . .

Is it not surprising to see a subject, upon his receiving a commission from the King to be a governor of a colony in America, immediately imagining himself to be vested with all the prerogatives belonging to the sacred person of his Prince? And which is yet more astonishing, to see that a people can be so wild as to allow of and acknowledge those prerogatives and exemptions, even to their own destruction? Is it so hard a matter to distinguish between the majesty of our Sovereign and the power of a governor of the plantations? Is not this making very free with our Prince, to apply that regard, obedience and allegiance to a subject which is due only to our Sovereign? And yet in all the cases which Mr. Attorney has cited to show the duty and obedience we owe to the supreme magistrate, it is the King that is there meant and understood, though Mr. Attorney is pleased to urge them as authorities to prove the heinousness of Mr. Zenger's offense against the Governor of New York. The several plantations are compared to so many large corporations, and perhaps not improperly; and can anyone give an instance that the mayor or head of a corporation ever put in a claim to the sacred rights of majesty? Let us not (while we are pretending to pay a great regard to our Prince and his peace) make bold to transfer that allegiance to a subject which we owe to our King only. What strange doctrine is it to press everything for law here which is so in England? I believe we should not think it a favor, at present at least, to establish this practice. In England so great a regard and reverence is had to the judges, that if any man strikes another in Westminster Hall while the judges are sitting, he shall lose his right hand and forfeit his land and goods for so doing. And though the judges here claim all the powers and authorities within this government that a Court of King's Bench has in England, yet I believe Mr. Attorney will scarcely say that such a punishment could be legally inflicted on a man for committing such an offense in the presence of the judges sitting in any court within the Province of New York. The reason is obvious; a quarrel or riot in New York cannot possibly be attended with those dangerous consequences that it might in Westminster Hall; nor (I hope) will it be alleged that any misbehavior to a governor in the plantations will, or ought to be, judged of or punished as a like undutifulness would be to our Sovereign. From all which, I hope Mr. Attorney will not think it proper to apply his law cases (to support the cause of his Governor) which have only been judged where the King's safety or honor was concerned. It will not be denied but that a freeholder in the Province of New York has as good a right to the sole and separate use of his lands as a freeholder in England, who has a right to bring an action of trespass against his neighbor for suffering his horse or cow to come and feed upon his land, or eat his corn, whether enclosed or not enclosed; and yet I believe it would be looked upon as a strange attempt for one man here to bring an action against another, whose cattle and horses feed upon his grounds not enclosed, or indeed for eating and treading down his corn, if that were not enclosed. Numberless are the instances of this kind that might be given, to show that what is good law at one time and in one place is not so at another time and in another place; so that I think the law seems to expect that in these parts of the world men should take care, by a good fence, to preserve their property from the injury of unruly beasts. And perhaps there may be as good reason why men should take the same care to make an honest and upright conduct a fence and security against the injury of unruly tongues.

Mr. Attorney. I don't know what the gentleman means, by comparing cases of freeholders in England with freeholders here. What has this case to do with actions of trespass, or men's fencing their ground? The case before the Court is whether Mr. Zenger is guilty of libeling His Excellency the Governor of New York, and indeed the whole administration of the government?

Mr. Hamilton has confessed the printing and publishing, and I think nothing is plainer than that the words in the information are *scandalous, and tend to sedition, and to disquiet the minds of the people of this Province.* And if such papers are not libels, I think it may be said there can be no such thing as a libel.

Mr. Hamilton. May it please Your Honor; I cannot agree with Mr. Attorney: For though I freely acknowledge that there are such things as libels, yet I must insist at the same time that what my client is charged with is not a libel; and I observed just now that Mr. Attorney in defining a libel made use of the words *scandalous, seditious, and tend to disquiet the people;* but (whether with design or not I will not say) he omitted the word *false.*

Mr. Attorney. I think I did not omit the word *false:* But it has been said already that it may be a libel notwithstanding it may be true.

Mr. Hamilton. In this I must still differ with Mr. Attorney; for I depend upon it, we are to be tried upon this information now before the Court and jury, and to which we have pleaded *not guilty,* and by it we are charged with printing and publishing *a certain false, malicious, seditious and scandalous libel.* This word *false* must have some meaning, or else how came it there? I hope Mr. Attorney will not say he put it there by chance, and I am of opinion his information would not be good without it. But to show that it is the principal thing which, in my opinion, makes a libel, I put the case, if the information had been for printing and publishing a certain *true* libel, would that be the same thing? Or could Mr. Attorney support such an information by any precedent in the English law? No, the falsehood makes the scandal, and both make the libel. And to show the Court that I am in good earnest and to save the Court's time and Mr. Attorney's trouble, I will agree that if he can prove the facts charged upon us to be *false,* I'll own them to be *scandalous, seditious* and *a libel.* So the work seems now to be pretty much shortened, and Mr. Attorney has now only to prove the words *false* in order to make us guilty.

Mr. Attorney. We have nothing to prove; you have confessed the printing and publishing; but if it was necessary (as I insist it is not) how can we prove a negative? But I hope some regard will be had to the authorities that have been produced, and that supposing all the words to be true, yet that will not help them, that Chief Justice Holt in his charge to the jury in the case of Tutchin made no distinction whether Tutchin's papers were *true* or *false;* and as Chief Justice Holt has made no distinction in that case, so none ought to be made here; nor can it be shown in all that case there was any question made about their being *false* or *true.*

Mr. Hamilton. I did expect to hear that a negative cannot be proved; but everybody knows there are many exceptions to that general rule: For if a man is charged with killing another, or stealing his neighbor's horse, if he is innocent in the one case, he may prove the man said to be killed to be really alive; and the horse said to be stolen, never to have been out of his master's stable, etc., and this I think is proving a negative. But we will save Mr.

Attorney the problem of proving a negative, and take the *onus probandi* upon ourselves, and prove those very papers that are called libels to be *true.*

Mr. Chief Justice. You cannot be admitted, Mr. Hamilton, to give the truth of a libel in evidence. A libel is not to be justified; for it is nevertheless a libel that it is *true.*

9

Indian and White Views on Property (1742)

Colonists naturally brought with them concepts of property dominant in the Mother Country, in which individuals owned—that is, exercised complete control over—property, and where, for an exchange of value, property ownership could be sold or acquired. Indians, on the other hand, saw land as held collectively by the tribe. While they exercised rights, such as hunting, fishing, and farming, Indians did not "buy," "sell," or "own" land. Indians could allow others to share in land rights, and would accept gifts in return. The colonists believed that giving the Indians trinkets and other merchandise bought permanent title to the land. These two conflicting views of land and attached rights led to continual misunderstanding between settlers and Indians. The problem can be seen in this exchange between the Iroquois chief Canassateego and Lieutenant Governor George Thomas of Pennsylvania. The disagreement is even more unfortunate in light of the good relations William Penn had earlier established between his settlers and the Indians.

See W. E. Washburn, *The Indian and the White Man* (1964); I. Sutton, ed., *Indian Land Tenure* (1975), especially the piece on "Aboriginal Occupancy and Territoriality"; and A. F. C. Wallace, "Political Organization and Land Tenure . . . ," 13 *Sw. J. Anthro.* 301 (1957).

Source: Washburn, ed. *The Indian and the White Man* 329 (1964).

Canassateego:

Brethren, the Governor and Council, and all present,

According to our Promise we now propose to return you an Answer to the several Things mentioned to us Yesterday, and shall beg Leave to speak to publick Affairs first, tho' they were what you spoke to last. On this Head you Yesterday put us in Mind, first, of William Penn's early and constant Care to cultivate Friendship with all the Indians; of the Treaty we held with one of his Sons, about ten Years ago; and of the Necessity there is at this Time of keeping the Roads between us clear and free from all Obstructions. We are all very sensible of the kind Regard that good Man William Penn had for all the Indians, and cannot but be pleased to find that his Children have the same. We well remember the Treaty you mention, held with his Son on his Arrival here, by which we confirmed our League of Friendship, that is to last as long as the Sun and Moon endure. In Consequence of this, we, on our Part, shall preserve the Road free from all Incumbrances; in Confirmation whereof we lay down this String of Wampum. . . .

Brethren, we received from the Proprietor Yesterday, some Goods in Consideration of our Release of the Lands on the West-side of the Susquehannah. It is true, we have the full Quantity according to Agreement; but if the Proprietor had been here himself, we think, in Regard of our Numbers and Poverty, he would have made an Addition to them. If the Goods were only to be divided amongst the Indians present, a single Person would have but a small Portion; but if you consider what Numbers are left behind, equally entitled with us to a Share, there will be extremely little. We therefore desire, if you have the Keys of the Proprietor's Chest, you will open it, and take out a little more for us.

We know our Lands are now become more valuable. The white People think we do not know their Value; but we are sensible that the Land is everlasting, and the few Goods we receive for it are soon worn out and gone. For the future, we will sell no Lands but when the Proprietor is in the Country; and we will know beforehand, the Quantity of the Goods we are to receive. Besides, we are not well used with respect to the Lands still unsold by us. Your People daily settle on these Lands, and spoil our Hunting. We must insist on your removing them, as you know they have no Right to settle to the Northward of Kittochtinny-Hills. In particular, we renew our Complaints against some People who are settled at the Juniata, a Branch of the Susquehannah, and all the Banks of that River, as far as Mahaniay; and we desire they may be forthwith made to go off the Land, for they do great Damage to our Cousins the Delawares.

We have further to observe, with respect to the Lands lying on the West-side of the Susquehannah, that though the Proprietor has paid us for what his People possess, yet some Parts of that Country have been taken up by

Persons, whose Place of Residence is to the South of this Province, from whom we have never received any Consideration. This Affair was recommended to you by our Chiefs at our last Treaty; and you then, at our earnest Desire, promised to write a Letter to that Person who has the Authority over those People, and to procure us his Answer. As we have never heard from you on this Head, we want to know what you have done in it. If you have not done any Thing, we now renew our Request, and desire you will inform the Person whose People are seated on our Lands, that that Country belongs to us, in Right of Conquest—we having bought it with our Blood, and taken it from our Enemies in fair War; and we expect, as Owners of that Land, to receive such a Consideration for it as the Land is worth. We desire you will press him to send a positive Answer. Let him say Yes or No. If he says Yes, we will treat with him; if No, we are able to do ourselves Justice; and we will do it, by going to take Payment ourselves.

It is customary with us to make a Present of Skins, whenever we renew our Treaties. We are ashamed to offer our Brethren so few, but your Horses and Cows have eat the Grass our Deer used to feed on. This has made them scarce, and will, we hope, plead in Excuse for our not bringing a larger Quantity. If we could have spared more, we would have given more, but we are really poor; and desire you'll not consider the Quantity, but few as they are, accept them in Testimony of our Regard.

Lieutenant Governor Thomas:
Brethren,
We thank you for the many Declarations of Respect you have given us, in this solemn Renewal of our Treaties. We receive, and shall keep your String and Belts of Wampum, as Pledges of your Sincerity, and desire those we gave you may be carefully preserved, as Testimonies of ours.

In answer to what you say about the Proprietaries: they are all absent, and have taken the Keys of their Chest with them; so that we cannot, on their Behalf, enlarge the Quantity of Goods. Were they here, they might perhaps be more generous; but we cannot be liberal for them. The Government will, however, take your Request into Consideration; and in Regard to your Poverty, may perhaps make you a Present. . . .

The Number of Guns, as well as every Thing else, answers exactly with the Particulars specified in your Deed of Conveyance, which is more than was agreed to be given you. It was your own Sentiments, that the Lands on the West-side of the Susquehannah, were not so valuable as those on the East; and an Abatement was to be made, proportionable to the Difference in Value. But the Proprietor overlooked this, and ordered the full Quantity to be delivered, which you will look on as a Favour.

It is very true, that Lands are of late becoming more valuable; but what raises their Value? Is it not entirely owing to the Industry and Labour used by the white People, in their Cultivation and Improvement? Had not they come amongst you, these Lands would have been of no Use to you, any further than to maintain you. And is there not, now you have sold so much, enough left for all the Purposes of Living? What you say of the Goods, that they are soon worn out, is applicable to every Thing; but you know very well, that they cost a great deal of Money; and the Value of Land is no more, than it is worth in Money.

Part II ～～～～～～～～

Securing Independence

I
n 1754, at the conclusion of the French and Indian Wars, Great Britain stood triumphant, the ruler of a worldwide empire. But the war had drained England financially, and one government after another attempted unsuccessfully to raise a sufficient revenue to meet the costs of maintaining the empire as well as paying off the war debts.

The Crown at no time asked the American colonies to pay either principal or interest on the debt, but it seemed obvious to everyone that the thriving and prosperous colonies could easily afford to shoulder the costs of their own administration. To secure that revenue, however, Great Britain had to do something it had not done for over a century—govern its colonies. Although Parliament had passed numerous laws affecting the colonies, many of them had been ignored and unenforced. The problems of effectively governing over such a long distance led to what Edmund Burke later called "benign neglect." Affection and common heritage had kept colonies and Mother Country together, but those ties rapidly broke in a relatively short time.

Many historians trace the growing friction from the Writs of Assistance, the generalized search warrants that authorities sought to use against smugglers. James Otis's argument (Document 10) caught the popular imagination not so much for the novelty of his ideas as for the vivid manner in which he summed up a number of ideas prevalent in English political thought, some of which went all the way back to Magna Carta. At the same time, Parliament's growing authority (Document 11) made it inevitable that colonial autonomy and imperial needs would collide.

The first major collision came in the Stamp Act controversy of 1765–66 (Documents 12–14), which exposed the weakness of British rule. For the next ten years Parliament grappled with the problem of its unruly overseas subjects, who in turn developed ever more sophisticated arguments against parliamentary authority (Documents 15 and 16). Gradually a "republican ideology" became accepted by a majority of the colonists, who believed that government in the Mother Country had grown so corrupt as to threaten the colonists' rights as Englishmen. The best-known document making this charge is the Declaration of Independence (Document 18).

Although considered a radical document at the time, the Declaration of Independence stated nothing very new in either British or American political thought. Ideas of government controlled by law, of fundamental rules, of government by consent of the governed, had been part of the English heritage brought over by the early settlers and expanded upon by their descendants. The great power of the Declaration, therefore, lay only partly in its substance; Thomas Jefferson's masterful rhetoric breathed fire into it.

By 1776, of course, colonial leaders had begun exploring the sort of government wanted should independence be declared, and the proposal by John Adams (Document 17) captured much of the prevalent political thought of the time. Another concern of the colonists was securing their liberties, and by 1776 many believed that some form of written document, constitutional in nature, needed to be promulgated. Many states passed these bills of rights; that of Pennsylvania (Document 19) was among the earliest. A later compilation in Virginia served as a model for the federal Bill of Rights (Document 27).

Against the Writs of Assistance (1761)

JAMES OTIS

During the French and Indian Wars, British authorities decided to crack down on smuggling in New England, and sought writs of assistance, which were in essence open-ended search warrants, allowing officers to search any premises they chose. Such writs had been in use for a number of decades, but with the death of George II in 1760, all writs in his name expired. The surveyor-general of Boston sought new writs, and Massachusetts merchants hired James Otis to oppose their issuance. In his argument, Otis articulated the idea that measures that went "against the fundamental principles of law" were invalid, a concept that some considered revolutionary in 1761, but that would gain near-universal acceptance within the decade. One could find precedents for most of his arguments in British legal history, especially in the writings of Lord Coke, but Otis expressed them in a new and seemingly radical manner. John Adams, whose notes of the speech are our only record, called Otis's argument "the first scene of the first act of opposition to the arbitrary claims of Great Britain. Then and there, the child Independence was born." Note how quickly these ideas gained acceptance; see Documents 12 and 13.

See L. H. Gipson, *The Coming of the Revolution* (1954); M. H. Smith, *The Writs of Assistance Case* (1978); J. P. Reid, *Constitutional History of the American Revolution: The Authority of Rights* (1986).

~~~~~~

I take this opportunity to declare, that whether under a fee or not, (for in such a cause as this I despise a fee) I will to my dying day oppose, with all the powers and faculties God has given me, all such instruments of slavery on the one hand, and villainy on the other, as this writ of assistance is. It appears to me (may it please your honours) the worst instrument of arbitrary power, the most destructive of English liberty, and the fundamental principles of the constitution, that ever was found in an English law-book. I must therefore beg your honours patience and attention to the whole range of an

Source: Presser and Zainaldin, *Law and American History* 68 (1980).

argument, that may perhaps appear uncommon in many things, as well as points of learning, that are more remote and unusual, that the whole tendency of my design may the more easily be perceived, the conclusions better [discerned] and the force of them better felt.

I shall not think much of my pains in this cause as I engaged in it from principle. I was sollicited to engage on the other side. I was sollicited to argue this cause as Advocate-General, and because I would not, I have been charged with a desertion of my office; to this charge I can give a very sufficient answer, I renounced that office, and I argue this cause from the same principle; and I argue it with the greater pleasure as it is in favour of British liberty, at a time, when we hear the greatest monarch upon earth declaring from his throne, that he glories in the name of Briton, and that the privileges of his people are dearer to him than the most valuable prerogatives of his crown. And as it is in opposition to a kind of power, the exercise of which in former periods of English history, cost one King of England his head and another his throne. I have taken more pains in this cause, then I ever will take again: Although my engaging in this . . . has raised much resentment; but I think I can sincerely declare, that I cheerfully submit myself to every odious name for conscience sake; and from my soul I despise all those whose guilt, malice or folly has made my foes. . . . The only principles of public conduct that are worthy a gentleman, or a man are, to sacrifice estate, ease, health and applause, and even life itself to the sacred calls of his country. . . . I will proceed to the subject of the writ. . . . I will admit, that writs of one kind, may be legal, that is, special writs, directed to special officers, and to search certain houses, &c. especially set forth in the writ, may be granted by the Court of Exchequer at home, upon oath made before the Lord Treasurer by the person, who asks, that he suspects such goods to be concealed in THOSE VERY PLACES HE DESIRES TO SEARCH. The Act of 14th Car. II. [1662] which Mr. Gridley mentions proves this. And in this light the writ appears like a warrant from a justice of peace to search for stolen goods. Your Honours will find in the old book, concerning the office of a justice of peace, precedents of general warrants to search suspected houses. But in more modern books you will find only special warrants to search such and such houses specially named, in which the complainant has before sworn he suspects his goods are concealed; and you will find it adjudged that special warrants only are legal. In the same manner I rely on it, that the writ prayed for in this petition being general is illegal. It is a power that places the liberty of every man in the hands of every petty officer. . . .

In the first place the writ [that is sought by the customs officials in this case] is UNIVERSAL, being directed "to all and singular justices, sheriffs, constables and all other officers and subjects, &c." So that in short it is directed to every subject in the king's dominions; every one with this writ may be a tyrant: If this commission is legal, a tyrant may, in a legal manner also, controul, imprison or murder any one within the realm.

In the next place, IT IS PERPETUAL; there's no return, a man is accountable to no person for his doings, every man may reign secure in his petty tyranny, and spread terror and desolation around him, until the trump of the arch angel shall excite different emotions in his soul.

In the third place, a person with this writ, IN THE DAY TIME may enter all houses, shops, &c. AT WILL, and command all to assist.

Fourth, by this not only deputies, &c. but even THEIR MENIAL SERV-ANTS ARE ALLOWED TO LORD IT OVER US—What is this but to have the curse of Canaan with a witness on us, to be the servant of servants, the most despicable of God's creation. Now one of the most essential branches of English liberty, is the freedom of one's house. A man's house is his castle; and while he is quiet, he is as well guarded as a prince in his castle. This writ, if it should be declared legal, would totally annihilate this privilege. . . . This wanton exercise of this power is no chimerical suggestion of a heated Brain—I will mention some facts. Mr. Pew had one of these writs, and when Mr. Ware succeeded him, he endorsed this writ over to Mr. Ware, so that THESE WRITS ARE NEGOTIABLE from one officer to another, and so your Hon-ours have no opportunity of judging the persons to whom this vast power is delegated. Another instance is this.—Mr. Justice Wally had called this same Mr. Ware before him by a constable, to answer for a breach of the Sabbath day acts, or that of profane swearing. As soon as he had done, Mr. Ware asked him if he had done, he replied, yes. Well then, says he, I will shew you a little of my power—I command you to permit me to search your house for unaccustomed goods; and went on to search his house from the garret to the cellar, and then served the constable in the same manner. But to shew another absurdity in this writ, if it should be established, I insist upon it EVERY PERSON by 14th of Car. II. HAS THIS POWER as well as Custom-house officers; the words are, "it shall be lawful for any person or persons authorized, &c." What a scene does this open! Every man prompted by revenge, ill humour or wantonness to inspect the inside of his neighbour's house, may get a writ of assistance; others will ask it from self defence; one arbitrary exertion will provoke another, until society will be involved in tumult and in blood. Again these writs ARE NOT RETURNED. Writs in their nature are temporary things; when the purposes for which they are issued are answered, they exist no more; but these monsters in the law live forever, no one can be called to account. Thus reason and the constitution are both against this writ. Let us see what authority there is for it. No more than one instance can be found of it in all our law books, and that was in the zenith of arbitrary power, viz. In the reign of [Charles II] when Star-chamber powers were pushed in extremity by some ignorant clerk of the Exchequer. But had this writ been in any book whatever it would have been illegal. ALL PRECEDENTS ARE UNDER THE CONTROUL OF THE PRINCIPLES OF THE LAW. Lord Talbot says, it is better to observe these than any precedents though in the House of Lords, the last resort of the subject. No Acts of Parliament can establish such a writ; Though it should be made in the very words of the petition it would be void, "AN ACT AGAINST THE CONSTITUTION IS VOID." . . . But these prove no more than what I before observed, that *special* writs may be granted *on oath* and *probable suspicion*. The Act of 7th and 8th of William III. that the officers of the plantations shall have the same powers, &c. is confined to this sense, that an officer should show probable grounds, should take his oath on it, should do this before a magistrate, and that such magistrate, if he thinks proper should issue a special warrant to a constable to search the places. . . .

It is the business of this court to demolish this monster of oppression, and to tear into rags this remnant of Star Chamber tyranny— . . .

11

Parliamentary Omnipotence (1765)

WILLIAM BLACKSTONE

In the 1750s, William Blackstone gave a series of lectures at Oxford University on the laws of England. These were not technical lectures, as one might have heard at the Inns of Court (the training grounds for English solicitors and barristers), but were designed to elucidate the law to the sons of the gentry, who would be expected to serve as justices of the peace in their local shires, and then to take their proper place in Parliament. The published lectures were an immediate success, especially in America, where Blackstone's four volumes could easily be packed into two saddlebags and taken along as lawyers rode the rural court circuits. At the time Blackstone wrote, the monarch still had some real powers, but there is no question that the balance of governmental authority was rapidly shifting to the Parliament. This appealed to the colonists for several reasons, not the least of which was that they began to see their own assemblies as the locus of authority in the colonies; just as Parliament was gaining ascendancy over the king, so their assemblies would become dominant over the royal governors.

See A. Harding, *Social History of English Law* (1966).

Source: 1 *Commentaries on the Laws of England* 160 (1809 ed.).

We are next to examine the laws and customs relating to parliament, thus united together and considered as one aggregate body.

The powers and jurisdiction of parliament, says Sir Edward Coke, is so transcendent and absolute, that it cannot be confined, either for causes or persons, within any bounds. . . . It hath sovereign and uncontrolable authority in the making, confirming, enlarging, restraining, abrogating, repealing, reviving, and expounding of laws, concerning matters of all possible denominations, ecclesiastical, or temporal, civil, military, maritime, or criminal; this being the place where the absolute despotic power, which must in all governments reside somewhere, is intrusted by the constitution of these kingdoms. All mischiefs and grievances, operations and remedies, that transcend the ordinary course of the laws, are within the reach of this extraordinary tribunal. It can regulate or new-model the succession to the crown; as was done in the reign of Henry VIII and William III. It can alter the established religion of the land; as was done in a variety of instances, in the reigns of king Henry VIII and his three children. It can change and create afresh even the constitution of the kingdom and of parliaments themselves; as was done by the act of union [between England and Scotland], and the several statutes for triennial and septennial elections. It can, in short, do every thing that is not naturally impossible; and therefore some have not scrupled to call its power, by a figure rather too bold, the omnipotence of parliament. True it is, that what the parliament doth, no authority upon earth can undo. So that it is a matter most essential to the liberties of this kingdom, that such members be delegated to this important trust, as are most eminent for their probity, their fortitude, and their knowledge; for it was a known apophthegm of the great lord treasurer Burleigh, "that England could never be ruined but by a parliament;" and, as Sir Matthew Hale observes, this being the highest and greatest court, over which none other can have jurisdiction in the kingdom, if by any means a misgovernment should any way fall upon it, the subjects of this kingdom are left without all manner of remedy. . . .

It must be owned that Mr. Locke, and other theoretical writers, have held, that "there remains still inherent in the people a supreme power to remove or alter the legislative, when they find the legislative act contrary to the trust reposed in them; for, when such trust is abused, it is thereby forfeited, and devolves to those who gave it." But however just this conclusion may be in theory, we cannot practically adopt it, nor take any *legal* steps for carrying it into execution, under any dispensation of government at present actually existing. For this devolution of power, to the people at large, includes in it a dissolution of the whole form of government established by that people; reduces all the members to their original state of equality; and, by annihilating the sovereign power, repeals all positive laws whatsoever before enacted.

No human laws will therefore suppose a case, which at once must destroy all law, and compel men to build afresh upon a new foundation; nor will they make provision for so desperate an event, as must render all legal provisions ineffectual. So long therefore as the English constitution lasts, we may venture to affirm, that the power of parliament is absolute and without controul.

12

Virginia Stamp Act Resolutions (1765)

In order to pay the enormous debt generated by the war with France, Prime Minister George Grenville proposed, among other measures, revenue stamps ranging from three pence to six pounds, whose use would be required on all legal documents and printed materials, even playing cards. Stamp taxes had been in effect in England for a number of years, and no one anticipated the storm of protest they would incite in the colonies. The opposition found expression in numerous resolutions approved by the colonial legislatures. In Virginia, a new member, Patrick Henry, introduced seven resolutions, and in the ensuing debate made his famous "Caesar had his Brutus" speech. Although the assembly adopted only four of the resolutions, all seven received widespread newspaper publication. The resolutions are particularly clear in their assertion of colonists' rights as Englishmen. What had been tentative and radical only a few years earlier in Otis's resistance to the writs of assistance (Document 10) had become acceptable to moderates as well by 1765.

See E. S. Morgan and H. Morgan, *Prologue to Revolution: The Stamp Act Crisis* (1953); P. D. G. Thomas, *British Politics and the Stamp Act Crisis* (1975); and R. R. Beeman, *Patrick Henry* (1974).

Source: *Journal of House of Burgesses* 360 (1761–65).

Resolved, That the first adventurers and settlers of this His Majesty's Colony and Dominion of Virginia brought with them, and transmitted to their posterity, and all other His Majesty's subjects since inhabiting in this His Majesty's said Colony, all the liberties, privileges, franchises, and immunities, that have at any time been held, enjoyed, and possessed, by the people of Great Britain.

Resolved, That by two royal charters, granted by King James the First, the colonists aforesaid are declared entitled to all liberties, privileges, and immunities of denizens and natural subjects, to all intents and purposes, as if they had been abiding and born within the realm of England.

Resolved, That the taxation of the people by themselves, or by persons chosen by themselves to represent them, who can only know what taxes the people are able to bear, or the easiest method of raising them, and must themselves be affected by every tax laid on the people, is the only security against a burthensome taxation, and the distinguishing characteristick of British freedom, without which the ancient constitution cannot exist.

Resolved, That His Majesty's liege people of this his most ancient and loyal Colony have without interruption enjoyed the inestimable right of being governed by such laws, respecting their internal polity and taxation, as are derived from their own consent, with the approbation of their sovereign, or his substitute; and that the same hath never been forfeited or yielded up, but hath been constantly recognized by the kings and people of Great Britain.

Resolved therefore, That the General Assembly of this Colony have the only and sole exclusive right and power to lay taxes and impositions upon the inhabitants of this Colony, and that every attempt to vest such power in any person or persons whatsoever other than the General Assembly aforesaid has a manifest tendency to destroy British as well as American freedom.

Resolved. That His Majesty's liege people, the inhabitants of this Colony, are not bound to yield obedience to any law or ordinance whatever, designed to impose any taxation whatsoever upon them, other than the laws or ordinances of the General Assembly aforesaid.

Resolved, That any person who shall, by speaking or writing, assert or maintain that any person or persons other than the General Assembly of this Colony, have any right or power to impose or lay any taxation on the people here, shall be deemed an enemy to His Majesty's Colony.

Resolutions of the Stamp Act Congress (1765)

The Massachusetts House of Representatives sent a circular letter to the other colonies in June 1765, urging that they all send delegates to a meeting in New York in October to "consult together on the present circumstances of the colonies," that is, how they might cooperate in opposing the Stamp Act. Twenty-eight men from nine colonies met; three other colonies probably would have sent delegations but the Massachusetts letter arrived after their assemblies had adjourned. The so-called Stamp Act Congress petitioned the King and the House of Commons; it also drew up the following resolutions, which boldly denied Great Britain the right to tax the colonies without their consent. The Congress also rebutted the possibility of the colonies' being represented in Parliament, which in essence meant that Parliament had no right to tax the colonists in any form.

The Resolution put both the British government and the colonists in a difficult position. Few colonists believed that Parliament had no powers over the colonies, yet the Stamp Act Congress had seemed to deny the Crown any power to tax, the most fundamental of all governing powers. (Within a few years, in fact, just this idea gained acceptance; see Document 15.) Great Britain, finding it increasingly difficult to rule through "benign neglect," could hardly cede the taxing power without in effect giving up all claims of government. The formal response (see Document 14) exposed the weakness of the British position.

See Morgan and Thomas works cited in previous document.

The members of this Congress, sincerely devoted with the warmest sentiments of affection and duty to His Majesty's person and Government, inviolably attached to the present happy establishment of the Protestant succession, and with minds deeply impressed by a sense of the present and impending misfortunes of the British colonies on this continent; having considered as maturely as time will permit the circumstances of the said colonies, esteem

---

Source: Morgan and Morgan, *Prologue to Revolution* 62 (1963).

it our indispensable duty to make the following declarations of our humble opinion respecting the most essential rights and liberties of the colonists, and of the grievances under which they labour, by reason of several late Acts of Parliament.

I.   That His Majesty's subjects in these colonies owe the same allegiance to the Crown of Great Britain that is owing from his subjects born within the realm, and all due subordination to that august body the Parliament of Great Britain.

II.   That His Majesty's liege subjects in these colonies are intitled to all the inherent rights and liberties of his natural born subjects within the kingdom of Great Britain.

III.   That it is inseparably essential to the freedom of a people, and the undoubted right of Englishmen, that no taxes be imposed on them but with their own consent, given personally or by their representatives.

IV.   That the people of these colonies are not, and from their local circumstances cannot be, represented in the House of Commons in Great Britain.

V.   That the only representatives of the people of these colonies are persons chosen therein by themselves, and that no taxes ever have been, or can be constitutionally imposed on them, but by their respective legislatures.

VI.   That all supplies to the Crown being free gifts of the people, it is unreasonable and inconsistent with the principles and spirit of the British Constitution, for the people of Great Britain to grant to His Majesty the property of the colonists.

VII.   That trial by jury is the inherent and invaluable right of every British subject in these colonies.

VIII.   That the late Act of Parliament, entitled *An Act for granting and applying certain stamp duties, and other duties, in the British colonies and plantations in America, etc.,* by imposing taxes on the inhabitants of these colonies; and the said Act, and several other Acts, by extending the jurisdiction of the courts of Admiralty beyond its ancient limits, have a manifest tendency to subvert the rights and liberties of the colonists.

IX.   That the duties imposed by several late Acts of Parliament, from the peculiar circumstances of these colonies, will be extremely burthensome and grievous; and from the scarcity of specie, the payment of them absolutely impracticable.

X.   That as the profits of the trade of these colonies ultimately center in Great Britain, to pay for the manufactures which they are obliged to take from thence, they eventually contribute very largely to all supplies granted there to the Crown.

XI.   That the restrictions imposed by several late Acts of Parliament on the trade of these colonies will render them unable to purchase the manufactures of Great Britain.

XII.   That the increase, prosperity, and happiness of these colonies depend on the full and free enjoyments of their rights and liberties, and an intercourse with Great Britain mutually affectionate and advantageous.

XIII.   That it is the right of the British subjects in these colonies to petition the King or either House of Parliament.

Lastly, That it is the indispensable duty of these colonies to the best of sovereigns, to the mother country, and to themselves, to endeavour by a loyal and dutiful address to His Majesty, and humble applications to both Houses of Parliament, to procure the repeal of the Act for granting and applying certain stamp duties, of all clauses of any other Acts of Parliament, whereby the jurisdiction of the Admiralty is extended as aforesaid, and of the other late Acts for the restriction of American commerce.

14

Declaratory Act (1766)

The combination of colonial opposition and the protests of London merchants hit hard by the anti-stamp boycott led Parliament to repeal the Stamp Act in early 1766. But the British government did not want it to appear that it had caved in to riots and protests, so the Rockingham ministry secured the passage of the Declaratory Act, modeled on the Irish Declaratory Act of 1719. The Declaratory Act reaffirmed Parliament's unlimited right to tax, and was widely ignored in the colonies. Some scholars see the Declaratory Act as a sign of the growing British inability to govern the North American colonies; unable to enforce a legitimate tax, the government could now do little more than claim that it had a theoretical right, even if it no longer had the practical ability to collect the tax.

See the works cited in Document 12.

Source: Pickering, ed., 27 *Statutes at Large* 19 (1767).

~~~~~~

An act for the better securing the dependency of his Majesty's dominions in America *upon the crown and parliament of* Great Britain.

Whereas several of the houses of representatives in his Majesty's colonies and plantations in America, *have of late, against law, claimed to themselves, or to the general assemblies of the same, the sole and exclusive right of imposing duties and taxes upon his Majesty's subjects in the said colonies and plantations; and have, in pursuance of such claim, passed certain votes, resolutions, and orders, derogatory to the legislative authority of parliament, and inconsistent with the dependency of the said colonies and plantations upon the crown of* Great Britain: . . . be it declared . . . , That the said colonies and plantations in *America* have been, are, and of right ought to be, subordinate unto, and dependent upon the imperial crown and parliament of *Great Britain;* and that the King's majesty, by and with the advice and consent of the lords spiritual and temporal, and commons of *Great Britain,* in parliament assembled, had, hath, and of right ought to have, full power and authority to make laws and statutes of sufficient force and validity to bind the colonies and people of *America,* subjects of the crown of *Great Britain,* in all cases whatsoever.

II.   And be it further declared . . . , That all resolutions, votes, orders, and proceedings, in any of the said colonies or plantations, whereby the power and authority of the parliament of *Great Britain,* to make laws and statutes as aforesaid, is denied, or drawn into question, are, and are hereby declared to be, utterly null and void to all intents and purposes whatsoever.

15

Letter from a Farmer in Pennsylvania, II (1767)

JOHN DICKINSON

The forceful opposition to the Stamp Act led to its repeal, but the Crown still faced serious revenue problems. The new Chancellor of the Exchequer, Charles Townshend, seized upon a distinction made by some colonists between "internal" or local taxes, which only the colonial assemblies could impose, and "external" taxes to regulate trade, which Parliament could promulgate. The so-called Townshend Duties of 1767 were taxes in the guise of trade regulations, and although Townshend died in October of 1767, the taxes proved quite effective, bringing in over thirty thousand pounds annually. The colonists again protested.

One gauge of the growing intensity of colonial thought is that the leading argument came from a moderate, John Dickinson of Pennsylvania, who denied that Parliament could levy internal or external taxes, and held that it could not use control of trade to secure revenue. In many ways, Dickinson made explicit what had been implicit in the Stamp Act Resolution (Document 13). One of the most important of all the revolutionary-era pamphlets, Dickinson's *Letters* illustrate the importance of constitutional ideas in the struggle against Great Britain.

See F. McDonald, ed., *Empire and Nation* (1962); B. Bailyn, *The Ideological Origins of the American Revolution* (1967); and J. P. Reid, *Constitutional History of the American Revolution: The Authority to Tax* (1987).

My dear Countrymen,

There is another late act of parliament, which appears to me to be unconstitutional, and as destructive to the liberty of these colonies, as that mentioned in my last letter; that is, the act for granting the duties on paper, glass, etc.

The parliament unquestionably possesses a legal authority to *regulate* the trade of *Great Britain,* and all her colonies. Such an authority is essential to the relation between a mother country and her colonies; and necessary for

---

Source: McDonald, ed., *Empire and Nation* 7 (1962).

the common good of all. He who considers these provinces as states distinct from the *British Empire,* has very slender notions of *justice,* or of their *interests.* We are but parts of a *whole;* and therefore there must exist a power somewhere, to preside, and preserve the connection in due order. This power is lodged in the parliament; and we are as much dependent on *Great Britain,* as a perfectly free people can be on another.

I have looked over *every statute* relating to these colonies, from their first settlement to this time; and I find every one of them founded on this principle, till the *Stamp Act* administration.

All before, are calculated to regulate trade, and preserve or promote a mutually beneficial intercourse between the several constituent parts of the empire; and though many of them imposed duties on trade, yet those duties were always imposed *with design* to restrain the commerce of one part, that was injurious to another, and thus to promote the general welfare. The raising of a revenue thereby was never intended. Thus the King, by his judges in his courts of justice, imposes fines, which all together amount to a very considerable sum, and contribute to the support of government: But this is merely a consequence arising from restrictions that only meant to keep peace and prevent confusion; and surely a man would argue very loosely, who should conclude from hence, that the King has a right to levy money in general upon his subjects. Never did the *British* parliament, till the period above mentioned, think of imposing duties in *America* FOR THE PURPOSE OF RAISING A REVENUE. Mr. *Greenville* first introduced this language, in the preamble to the 4th of GEO. III Chap. 15, which has these words—"And whereas it is just and necessary that A REVENUE BE RAISED IN YOUR MAJESTY'S SAID DOMINIONS IN AMERICA, *for defraying the expences of defending, protecting, and securing the same:* We your Majesty's most dutiful and loyal subjects, THE COMMONS OF GREAT BRITAIN, in parliament assembled, being desirous to make some provision in this present session of parliament, TOWARD RAISING THE SAID REVENUE IN AMERICA, have resolved to GIVE and GRANT unto your Majesty the several rates and duties herein after mentioned." etc.

A few months after came the *Stamp Act,* which reciting this, proceeds in the same strange mode of expression, thus—"And whereas it is just and necessary, that provision be made FOR RAISING A FURTHER REVENUE WITHIN YOUR MAJESTY'S DOMINIONS IN AMERICA, *towards defraying the said expences,* we your Majesty's most dutiful and loyal subjects, the COMMONS OF GREAT BRITAIN, etc. GIVE and GRANT," etc. as before.

The last act, granting duties upon paper, etc. carefully pursues these modern precedents. The preamble is, "Whereas it is expedient THAT A REVENUE SHOULD BE RAISED IN YOUR MAJESTY'S DOMINIONS IN AMERICA, *for making a more certain and adequate provision for defraying the charge of the administration of justice, and the support of civil government in such provinces, where it shall be found necessary; and towards further defraying the expences of defending, protecting and securing the said dominions, we your Majesty's most dutiful and loyal subjects, the* COMMONS OF GREAT BRITAIN, *etc.* GIVE and GRANT," etc. as before.

Here we may observe an authority *expressly* claimed and exerted to impose duties on these colonies; not for the regulation of trade; not for the preservation or promotion of a mutually beneficial intercourse between the several constituent parts of the empire, heretofore the *sole objects* of parliamentary institutions; *but for the single purpose of levying money upon us.*

This I call an innovation; and a most dangerous innovation. . . .

Our great advocate, Mr. *Pitt,* in his speeches on the debate concerning the repeal of the *Stamp Act,* acknowledged, that *Great Britain* could restrain our manufactures. His words are these—"This kingdom, as the supreme governing and legislative power, has ALWAYS bound the colonies by her regulations and RESTRICTIONS in trade, in navigation, in MANUFACTURES—in everything, *except that of taking their money out of their pockets* WITHOUT THEIR CONSENT." Again he says, "We may bind their trade, CONFINE THEIR MANUFACTURES, and exercise every power whatever, *except that of taking their money out of their pockets* WITHOUT THEIR CONSENT." . . .

From what has been said, I think this uncontrovertible conclusion may be deduced, that when a ruling state obliges a dependent state to take certain commodities from her alone, it is implied in the nature of that obligation; is essentially requisite to give it the least degree of justice; and is inseparably united with it, in order to preserve any share of freedom to the dependent state; *that those commodities should never be loaded with duties,* FOR THE SOLE PURPOSE OF LEVYING MONEY ON THE DEPENDENT STATE.

Upon the whole, the single question is, whether the parliament can legally impose duties to be paid *by the people of these colonies only,* FOR THE SOLE PURPOSE OF RAISING A REVENUE, *on commodities which she obliges us to take from her alone,* or, in other words, whether the parliament can legally take money out of our pockets, without our consent. If they can, our boasted liberty is but

Vox et praeterea nihil.

A sound and nothing else.

A Farmer

16

Common Sense (1776)

THOMAS PAINE

As Americans moved toward independence, it proved increasingly difficult to overthrow long-established beliefs. In the agitation over the Stamp Act (Document 13) the patriots had blamed Parliament for the violation of their liberties, and in the late 1760s and early 1770s most of the revolutionary pamphlets had distinguished between the King, to whom the colonists allegedly gave glad loyalty, and the Parliament and the King's advisors, who were responsible for the attacks on British liberties. Tom Paine's *Common Sense,* one of the most brilliantly written of the revolutionary pamphlets, cut through this argument by laying blame on the King and exhorting the colonists to rid themselves of the delusion that the King in particular, or Great Britain in general, had their interests at heart.

See B. Bailyn, *Ideological Origins of the American Revolution* (1967); and A. O. Aldridge, *Man of Reason: Thomas Paine* (1959).

Some writers have so confounded society with government, as to leave little or no distinction between them; whereas they are not only different, but have different origins. Society is produced by our wants, and government by our wickedness; the former promotes our happiness *positively* by uniting our affections, the latter *negatively* by restraining our vices. The one encourages intercourse, the other creates distinctions. The first is a patron, the last a punisher.

Society in every state is a blessing, but Government, even in its best state, is but a necessary evil; in its worst state an intolerable one: for when we suffer, or are exposed to the same miseries *by a Government,* which we might expect in a country *without Government,* our calamity is heightened by reflecting that we furnish the means by which we suffer. Government, like dress, is the badge of lost innocence; the palaces of kings are built upon the ruins of the bowers of paradise. For were the impulses of conscience clear, uniform and irresistibly obeyed, man would need no other lawgiver; but that not being the case, he finds it necessary to surrender up a part of his property to furnish

Source: Fast, ed., *Selected Work of Tom Paine* 6 (1945).

means for the protection of the rest; and this he is induced to do by the same prudence which in every other case advises him, out of two evils to choose the least. Wherefore, security being the true design and end of government, it unanswerably follows that whatever form thereof appears most likely to ensure it to us, with the least expense and greatest benefit, is preferable to all others. . . .

I draw my idea of the form of government from a principle in nature which no art can overturn, viz. that the more simple any thing is, the less liable it is to be disordered, and the easier repaired when disordered; and with this maxim in view I offer a few remarks on the so much boasted constitution of England. That it was noble for the dark and slavish times in which it was erected, is granted. When the world was overrun with tyranny the least remove therefrom was a glorious rescue. But that it is imperfect, subject to convulsions, and incapable of producing what it seems to promise, is easily demonstrated.

Absolute governments, (tho' the disgrace of human nature) have this advantage with them, they are simple; if the people suffer, they know the head from which their suffering springs; know likewise the remedy; and are not bewildered by a variety of causes and cures. But the constitution of England is so exceedingly complex, that the nation may suffer for years together without being able to discover in which part the fault lies; some will say in one and some in another, and every political physician will advise a different medicine.

I know it is difficult to get over local or long standing prejudices, yet if we will suffer ourselves to examine the component parts of the English constitution, we shall find them to be the base remains of two ancient tyrannies, compounded with some new Republican materials.

First.—The remains of Monarchical tyranny in the person of the King.

Secondly.—The remains of Aristocratical tyranny in the persons of the Peers.

Thirdly.—The new Republican materials, in the persons of the Commons, on whose virtue depends the freedom of England.

The two first, by being hereditary, are independent of the People; wherefore in a *constitutional sense* they contribute nothing towards the freedom of the State.

To say that the constitution of England is an *union* of three powers, reciprocally *checking* each other, is farcical; either the words have no meaning, or they are flat contradictions.

To say that the Commons is a check upon the King, presupposes two things.

First.—That the King is not to be trusted without being looked after; or in other words, that a thirst for absolute power is the natural disease of monarchy.

Secondly.—That the Commons, by being appointed for that purpose, are either wiser or more worthy of confidence than the Crown.

But as the same constitution which gives the Commons a power to check the King by withholding the supplies, gives afterwards the King a power to check the Commons, by empowering him to reject their other bills; it again supposes that the King is wiser than those whom it has already supposed to be wiser than him. A mere absurdity!

There is something exceedingly ridiculous in the composition of Monarchy; it first excludes a man from the means of information, yet empowers him to act in cases where the highest judgment is required. The state of a king shuts him from the World, yet the business of a king requires him to know it thoroughly; wherefore the different parts, by unnaturally opposing and destroying each other, prove the whole character to be absurd and useless.

Some writers have explained the English constitution thus: the King, say they, is one, the people another; the Peers are a house in behalf of the King, the commons in behalf of the people; but this hath all the distinctions of a house divided against itself; and though the expressions be pleasantly arranged, yet when examined they appear idle and ambiguous; and it will always happen, that the nicest construction that words are capable of, when applied to the description of something which either cannot exist, or is too incomprehensible to be within the compass of description, will be words of sound only, and though they may amuse the ear, they cannot inform the mind: for this explanation includes a previous question, viz. *how came the king by a power which the people are afraid to trust, and always obliged to check?* Such a power could not be the gift of a wise people, neither can any power, *which needs checking,* be from God; yet the provision which the constitution makes supposes such a power to exist.

But the provision is unequal to the task; the means either cannot or will not accomplish the end, and the whole affair is a *Felo de se:* for as the greater weight will always carry up the less, and as all the wheels of a machine are put in motion by one, it only remains to know which power in the constitution has the most weight, for that will govern: and tho' the others, or a part of them, may clog, or, as the phrase is, check the rapidity of its motion, yet so long as they cannot stop it, their endeavours will be ineffectual: The first moving power will at last have its way, and what it wants in speed is supplied by time.

That the crown is this overbearing part in the English constitution needs not be mentioned, and that it derives its whole consequence merely from being the giver of places and pensions is self-evident; wherefore, though we have been wise enough to shut and lock a door against absolute Monarchy, we at the same time have been foolish enough to put the Crown in possession of the key.

The prejudice of Englishmen, in favour of their own government, by King, Lords and Commons, arises as much or more from national pride than reason.

Individuals are undoubtedly safer in England than in some other countries: but the will of the king is as much the law of the land in Britain as in France, with this difference, that instead of proceeding directly from his mouth, it is handed to the people under the formidable shape of an act of parliament. For the fate of Charles the First hath only made kings more subtle—not more just.

Wherefore, laying aside all national pride and prejudice in favour of modes and forms, the plain truth is that *it is wholly owing to the constitution of the people, and not to the constitution of the government* that the crown is not as oppressive in England as in Turkey.

An inquiry into the *constitutional errors* in the English form of government, is at this time highly necessary; for as we are never in a proper condition of doing justice to others, while we continue under the influence of some leading partiality, so neither are we capable of doing it to ourselves while we remain fettered by any obstinate prejudice. And as a man who is attached to a prostitute is unfitted to choose or judge of a wife, so any prepossession in favour of a rotten constitution of government will disable us from discerning a good one. . . .

As much hath been said of the advantages of reconciliation, which, like an agreeable dream, hath passed away and left us as we were, it is but right that we should examine the contrary side of the argument, and enquire into some of the many material injuries which these Colonies sustain, and always will sustain, by being connected with and dependant on Great Britain. To examine that connection and dependance, on the principles of nature and common sense, to see what we have to trust to, if separated, and what we are to expect, if dependant.

I have heard it asserted by some, that as America has flourished under her former connection with Great Britain, the same connection is necessary towards her future happiness, and will always have the same effect. Nothing can be more fallacious than this kind of argument. We may as well assert that because a child has thrived upon milk, that it is never to have meat, or that the first twenty years of our lives is to become a precedent for the next twenty. But even this is admitting more than is true; for I answer roundly that America would have flourished as much, and probably much more, had no European power taken any notice of her. The commerce by which she hath enriched herself are the necessaries of life, and will always have a market while eating is the custom of Europe.

But she has protected us, say some. That she hath engrossed us is true, and defended the Continent at our expense as well as her own, is admitted; and she would have defended Turkey from the same motive, *viz.* for the sake of trade and dominion.

Alas! we have been long led away by ancient prejudices and made large sacrifices to superstition. We have boasted the protection of Great Britain, without considering, that her motive was *interest* not *attachment;* and that she did not protect us from *our enemies* on *our account;* but from *her enemies* on *her own account,* from those who had no quarrel with us on any *other account,* and who will always be our enemies on the *same account.* Let Britain waive her pretensions to the Continent, or the Continent throw off the dependance, and we should be at peace with France and Spain, were they at war with Britain. The miseries of Hanover last war ought to warn us against connections.

It hath lately been asserted in parliament, that the Colonies have no relation to each other but through the Parent Country, *i.e.* that Pennsylvania and the Jerseys and so on for the rest, are sister Colonies by the way of England; this is certainly a very roundabout way of proving relationship, but it is the nearest and only true way of proving enmity (or enemyship, if I may so call it.) France and Spain never were, nor perhaps ever will be, our enemies as *Americans,* but as our being the *subjects of Great Britain.*

But Britain is the parent country, say some. Then the more shame upon her conduct. Even brutes do not devour their young, nor savages make war upon their families. Wherefore, the assertion, if true, turns to her reproach; but it happens not to be true, or only partly so, and the phrase *parent or mother country* hath been jesuitically adopted by the King and his parasites, with a low papistical design of gaining an unfair bias on the credulous weakness of our minds. Europe, and not England, is the parent country of America. This new World hath been the asylum for the persecuted lovers of civil and religious liberty from *every part* of Europe. Hither have they fled, not from the tender embraces of the mother, but from the cruelty of the monster; and it is so far true of England, that the same tyranny which drove the first emigrants from home, pursues their descendants still. . . .

To conclude, however strange it may appear to some, or however unwilling they may be to think so, matters not, but many strong and striking reasons may be given to show that nothing can settle our affairs so expeditiously as an open and determined declaration for independence. Some of which are,

First—It is the custom of Nations, when any two are at war, for some other powers, not engaged in the quarrel, to step in as mediators, and bring about the preliminaries of a peace; But while America calls herself the subject of Great Britain, no power, however well disposed she may be, can offer her mediation. Wherefore, in our present state we may quarrel on for ever.

Secondly—It is unreasonable to suppose that France or Spain will give us any kind of assistance, if we mean only to make use of that assistance for the purpose of repairing the breach, and strengthening the connection between Britain and America; because, those powers would be sufferers by the consequences.

Thirdly—While we profess ourselves the subjects of Britain, we must, in the eyes of foreign nations, be considered as Rebels. The precedent is somewhat dangerous to their peace, for men to be in arms under the name of subjects; we, on the spot, can solve the paradox; but to unite resistance and subjection requires an idea much too refined for common understanding.

Fourthly—Were a manifesto to be published, and despatched to foreign Courts, setting forth the miseries we have endured, and the peaceful methods which we have ineffectually used for redress; declaring at the same time that not being able longer to live happily or safely under the cruel disposition of the British Court, we had been driven to the necessity of breaking off all connections with her; at the same time, assuring all such Courts of our peaceable disposition towards them, and of our desire of entering into trade with them; such a memorial would produce more good effects to this Continent than if a ship were freighted with petitions to Britain.

Under our present denomination of British subjects, we can neither be received nor heard abroad; the custom of all Courts is against us, and will be so, until by an independence we take rank with other nations.

These proceedings may at first seem strange and difficult, but like all other steps which we have already passed over, will in a little time become familiar and agreeable; and until an independence is declared, the Continent will feel itself like a man who continues putting off some unpleasant business from day to day, yet knows it must be done, hates to set about it, wishes it over, and is continually haunted with the thoughts of its necessity.

17

Thoughts on Government (1776)

JOHN ADAMS

A few months before independence, George Wythe and John Adams spoke about the problems of the colonies' agreeing on how they should be governed in the future. Adams casually mentioned some ideas he had, and at Wythe's insistence put them into a letter, which Wythe soon had printed as *Thoughts on Government, in a Letter from a Gentleman to his Friend.* The pamphlet received wide attention and greatly influenced several states when they drew up new constitutions at the time of independence. (In fact, it was Adams who proposed the resolution adopted by the Continental Congress on May 10, 1776, calling on

Source: Peek, ed., *Political Writings of John Adams* 83 (1954).

all states not yet provided with a permanent constitution to adopt one.) We know, for example, that John Jay carried a copy of *Thoughts* with him when he left the Congress to draft the New York constitution. The pamphlet is important not in that it proposed new ideas but in that it summed up what Adams and many of his contemporaries considered the key ingredients of representative government. In it ran many of the threads already apparent in the earlier colonial documents (Documents 1, 4, and 7) as well as the allegedly radical ideas of Otis, Henry, and Dickinson (Documents 10, 12, and 15).

See G. Wood, *The Creation of the American Republic, 1776–1787* (1969); and P. Shaw, *The Character of John Adams* (1976).

My dear Sir: If I was equal to the task of forming a plan for the government of a colony, I should be flattered with your request and very happy to comply with it because, as the divine science of politics is the science of social happiness, and the blessings of society depend entirely on the constitutions of government, which are generally institutions that last for many generations, there can be no employment more agreeable to a benevolent mind than a research after the best.

Pope flattered tyrants too much when he said,

> For forms of government let fools contest,
> That which is best administered is best.
> [Essay on Man]

Nothing can be more fallacious than this. But poets read history to collect flowers, not fruits; they attend to fanciful images, not the effects of social institutions. Nothing is more certain from the history of nations and nature of man than that some forms of government are better fitted for being well administered than others. . . .

The foundation of every government is some principle or passion in the minds of the people. The noblest principles and most generous affections in our nature, then, have the fairest chance to support the noblest and most generous models of government.

A man must be indifferent to the sneers of modern Englishmen to mention in their company the names of Sidney, Harrington, Locke, Milton, Nedham, Neville, Burnet, and Hoadly. No small fortitude is necessary to confess that one has read them. The wretched condition of this country, however, for ten or fifteen years past has frequently reminded me of their principles and reasonings. They will convince any candid mind that there is no good government but what is republican. That the only valuable part of the British constitution is so because the very definition of a republic is "an empire of laws, and not of men." That, as a republic is the best of governments, so that particular arrangement of the powers of society or, in other words, that form of government which is best contrived to secure an impartial and exact execution of the laws is the best of republics.

Of republics there is an inexhaustible variety because the possible combinations of the powers of society are capable of innumerable variations.

As good government is an empire of laws, how shall your laws be made? In a large society inhabiting an extensive country, it is impossible that the whole should assemble to make laws. The first necessary step, then, is to depute power from the many to a few of the most wise and good. But by what rules shall you choose your representatives? Agree upon the number and qualifications of persons who shall have the benefit of choosing or annex this privilege to the inhabitants of a certain extent of ground.

The principal difficulty lies, and the greatest care should be employed, in constituting this representative assembly. It should be in miniature an exact portrait of the people at large. It should think, feel, reason, and act like them. That it may be the interest of this assembly to do strict justice at all times, it should be an equal representation, or, in other words, equal interests among the people should have equal interests in it. Great care should be taken to effect this and to prevent unfair, partial, and corrupt elections. Such regulations, however, may be better made in times of greater tranquility than the present; and they will spring up themselves naturally when all the powers of government come to be in the hands of the people's friends. At present, it will be safest to proceed in all established modes to which the people have been familiarized by habit.

A representation of the people in one assembly being obtained, a question arises whether all the powers of government—legislative, executive, and judicial—shall be left in this body? I think a people cannot be long free, nor ever happy, whose government is in one assembly. My reasons for this opinion are as follow:

1.   A single assembly is liable to all the vices, follies, and frailties of an individual—subject to fits of humor, starts of passion, flights of enthusiasm, partialities, or prejudice—and consequently productive of hasty results and absurd judgments. And all these errors ought to be corrected and defects supplied by some controlling power.

2.   A single assembly is apt to be avaricious and in time will not scruple to exempt itself from burdens which it will lay without compunction on its constituents.

3.   A single assembly is apt to grow ambitious and after a time will not hesitate to vote itself perpetual. This was one fault of the Long Parliament, but more remarkably of Holland, whose assembly first voted themselves from annual to septennial, then for life, and after a course of years, that all

vacancies happening by death or otherwise should be filled by themselves without any application to constituents at all.

4.   A representative assembly, although extremely well qualified and absolutely necessary as a branch of the legislative, is unfit to exercise the executive power for want of two essential properties, secrecy and dispatch.

5.   A representative assembly is still less qualified for the judicial power because it is too numerous, too slow, and too little skilled in the laws.

6.   Because a single assembly, possessed of all the powers of government, would make arbitrary laws for their own interest, execute all laws arbitrary for their own interest, and adjudge all controversies in their own favor.

But shall the whole power of legislation rest in one assembly? Most of the foregoing reasons apply equally to prove that the legislative power ought to be more complex, to which we may add that if the legislative power is wholly in one assembly and the executive in another or in a single person, these two powers will oppose and encroach upon each other until the contest shall end in war, and the whole power, legislative and executive, be usurped by the strongest.

The judicial power, in such case, could not mediate or hold the balance between the two contending powers because the legislative would undermine it. And this shows the necessity, too, of giving the executive power a negative upon the legislative; otherwise this will be continually encroaching upon that.

To avoid these dangers, let a distinct assembly be constituted as a mediator between the two extreme branches of the legislature, that which represents the people and that which is vested with the executive power.

Let the representative assembly then elect by ballot, from among themselves or their constituents or both, a distinct assembly which, for the sake of perspicuity, we will call a council. It may consist of any number you please, say twenty or thirty, and should have a free and independent exercise of its judgment and consequently a negative voice in the legislature.

These two bodies, thus constituted and made integral parts of the legislature, let them unite and by joint ballot choose a governor, who, after being stripped of most of those badges of domination called prerogatives, should have a free and independent exercise of his judgment and be made also an integral part of the legislature. This, I know, is liable to objections; and, if you please, you may make him only president of the council, as in Connecticut. But as the governor is to be invested with the executive power with consent of council, I think he ought to have a negative upon the legislative. If he is annually elective, as he ought to be, he will always have so much reverence and affection for the people, their representatives and counsellors, that, although you give him an independent exercise of his judgment, he will seldom use it in opposition to the two houses, except in cases the public utility of which would be conspicuous; and some such cases would happen. . . .

This mode of constituting the great offices of state will answer very well for the present; but if by experiment it should be found inconvenient, the legislature may at its leisure devise other methods of creating them; by elections of the people at large, as in Connecticut; or it may enlarge the term for which they shall be chosen to seven years, or three years, or for life; or make any other alterations which the society shall find productive of its ease, its safety, its freedom, or, in one word, its happiness.

A rotation of all offices, as well as of representatives and counsellors, has many advocates and is contended for with many plausible arguments. It would be attended no doubt with many advantages; and if the society has a sufficient number of suitable characters to supply the great number of vacancies which would be made by such a rotation, I can see no objection to it. These persons may be allowed to serve for three years and then be excluded three years, or for any longer or shorter term.

Any seven or nine of the legislative council may be made a quorum for doing business as a privy council, to advise the governor in the exercise of the executive branch of power and in all acts of state.

The governor should have the command of the militia and of all your armies. The power of pardons should be with the governor and council.

Judges, justices, and all other officers, civil and military, should be nominated and appointed by the governor with the advice and consent of council, unless you choose to have a government more popular; if you do, all officers, civil and military, may be chosen by joint ballot of both houses; or, in order to preserve the independence and importance of each house, by ballot of one house, concurred in by the other. Sheriffs should be chosen by the freeholders of counties; so should registers of deeds and clerks of counties.

All officers should have commissions under the hand of the governor and seal of the colony.

The dignity and stability of government in all its branches, the morals of the people, and every blessing of society depend so much upon an upright and skillful administration of justice that the judicial power ought to be distinct from both the legislative and executive, and independent upon both, that so it may be a check upon both, as both should be checks upon that. The judges, therefore, should be always men of learning and experience in the laws, of exemplary morals, great patience, calmness, coolness, and attention. Their minds should not be distracted with jarring interests; they should not be dependent upon any man, or body of men. To these ends, they should hold estates for life in their offices; or, in other words, their commissions should be during good behavior and their salaries ascertained and established by law. For misbehavior the grand inquest of the colony, the house of representatives, should impeach them before the governor and council, where they should have time and opportunity to make their defense; but, if convicted, should be removed from their offices and subjected to such other punishment as shall be thought proper. . . .

A constitution founded on these principles introduces knowledge among the people and inspires them with a conscious dignity becoming freemen; a general emulation takes place which causes good humor, sociability, good manners, and good morals to be general. That elevation of sentiment inspired by such a government makes the common people brave and enterprising. That ambition which is inspired by it makes them sober, industrious, and frugal. You will find among them some elegance, perhaps, but more solidity; a little pleasure, but a great deal of business; some politeness, but more civility. If you compare such a country with the regions of domination, whether monarchical or aristocratical, you will fancy yourself in Arcadia or Elysium.

If the colonies should assume governments separately, they should be left entirely to their own choice of the forms; and if a continental constitution should be formed, it should be a congress containing a fair and adequate representation of the colonies, and its authority should sacredly be confined to these cases, namely: war, trade, disputes between colony and colony, the post office, and the unappropriated lands of the crown, as they used to be called.

These colonies, under such forms of government and in such a union, would be unconquerable by all the monarchies of Europe.

18

Declaration of Independence (1776)

In many ways, the Declaration of Independence is the greatest of the political pamphlets of the revolutionary era, designed to justify the colonists' radicalism as a necessary means of protecting their rights as Englishmen. For the most part, succeeding generations have focused on Thomas Jefferson's magnificent generalizations about human liberty. For contemporaries, however, the list of grievances proved most important, for it allowed them to rationalize their rebellion in terms familiar not only to them, but to Englishmen as well. Politically, the Declaration

Source: Thorpe, 1 *Federal and State Constitutions* 3 (1909).

provided Americans with a convincing apologia for what they were doing, and because they succeeded in their revolution, we have tended to take their complaints at face value. But if George III was not a good King, neither was he the tyrant portrayed here. Moreover, Jefferson dramatized the colonial grievances by ascribing them to the King, although most of the laws had been passed by Parliament. As for the political theory, many of these ideas dated back to the founding of the colonies and before. Literate Englishmen had no trouble recognizing that the colonists were claiming rights they believed belonged historically to all of His Majesty's subjects.

See the classic by C. Becker, *The Declaration of Independence* (1922); G. Wills, *Inventing America: Jefferson's Declaration of Independence* (1978); and J. P. Reid, *Constitutional History of the American Revolution: The Authority of Rights* (1986).

~~~~~~

When in the course of human events, it becomes necessary for one people to dissolve the political bands which have connected them with another, and to assume the Powers of the earth, the separate and equal station to which the Laws of Nature and of Nature's God entitle them, a decent respect to the opinions of mankind requires that they should declare the causes which impel them to the separation.

We hold these truths to be self-evident, that all men are created equal, that they are endowed by their Creator with certain unalienable rights, that among these are Life, Liberty, and the pursuit of Happiness. That to secure these rights, Governments are instituted among Men, deriving their just powers from the consent of the governed. That whenever any Form of Government becomes destructive of these ends, it is the Right of the People to alter or to abolish it, and to institute new Government, laying its foundation on such principles and organizing its powers in such form, as to them shall seem most likely to effect their Safety and Happiness. Prudence, indeed, will dictate that Governments long established should not be changed for light and transient causes; and accordingly all experience hath shown, that mankind are more disposed to suffer, while evils are sufferable, than to right themselves by abolishing the forms to which they are accustomed. But when a long train of abuses and usurpations, pursuing invariably the same Object evinces a design to reduce them under absolute Despotism, it is their right, it is their duty, to throw off such Government, and to provide new Guards for their future security.—Such has been the patient sufferance of these Colonies; and such is now the necessity which constrains them to alter their former Systems of Government. The history of the present King of Great Britain is a history of repeated injuries and usurpations, all having in direct object the establishment of an absolute Tyranny over these States. To prove this, let Facts be submitted to a candid world.

He has refused his Assent to Laws, the most wholesome and necessary for the public good.

He has forbidden his Governors to pass Laws of immediate and pressing importance, unless suspended in their operation till his Assent should be obtained; and when so suspended, he has utterly neglected to attend to them.

He has refused to pass other Laws for the accommodation of large districts of people, unless those people would relinquish the right of Representation in the Legislature, a right inestimable to them and formidable to tyrants only.

He has called together legislative bodies at places unusual, uncomfortable, and distant from the depository of their public Records, for the sole purpose of fatiguing them into compliance with his measures.

He has dissolved Representative Houses repeatedly, for opposing with manly firmness his invasions on the rights of the people.

He has refused for a long time, after such dissolutions, to cause others to be elected; whereby the Legislative powers, incapable of Annihilation, have returned to the People at large for their exercise; the State remaining in the mean time exposed to all dangers of invasion from without, and convulsions within.

He has endeavoured to prevent the population of these States; for that purpose obstructing the Laws of Naturalization of Foreigners; refusing to pass others to encourage their migrations hither, and raising the conditions of new Appropriations of Lands.

He has obstructed the Administration of Justice, by refusing his Assent to Laws for establishing Judiciary powers.

He has made Judges dependent on his Will alone, for the tenure of their offices, and the amount and payment of their salaries.

He has erected a multitude of New Offices, and sent hither swarms of Officers to harass our People, and eat out their substance.

He has kept among us, in times of peace, Standing Armies without the Consent of our legislature.

He has affected to render the Military independent of and superior to the Civil Power.

He has combined with others to subject us to a jurisdiction foreign to our constitution, and unacknowledged by our laws; giving his Assent to their Acts of pretended Legislation:

For quartering large bodies of armed troops among us:

For protecting them, by a mock Trial, from Punishment for any Murders which they should commit on the Inhabitants of these States:

For cutting off our Trade with all parts of the world:

For imposing taxes on us without our Consent:

For depriving us of many cases, of the benefits of Trial by jury:

For transporting us beyond Seas to be tried for pretended offences:

For abolishing the free System of English Laws in a neighbouring Province, establishing therein an Arbitrary government, and enlarging its Boundaries so as to render it at once an example and fit instrument for introducing the same absolute rule into these Colonies:

For taking away our Charters, abolishing our most valuable Laws, and altering fundamentally the Forms of our Governments:

For suspending our own Legislatures, and declaring themselves invested with Power to legislate for us in all cases whatsoever.

He has abdicated Government here, by declaring us out of his Protection and waging War against us.

He has plundered our seas, ravaged our Coasts, burnt our towns, and destroyed the lives of our people.

He is at this time transporting large armies of foreign mercenaries to compleat the works of death, desolation, and tyranny, already begun with circumstances of Cruelty & perfidy scarcely paralleled in the most barbarous ages, and totally unworthy the Head of a civilized nation.

He has constrained our fellow Citizens taken Captive on the high Seas to bear Arms against their Country, to become the executioners of their friends and Brethren, or to fall themselves by their Hands.

He has excited domestic insurrections amongst us, and has endeavoured to bring on the inhabitants of our frontiers, the merciless Indian savages, whose known rule of warfare, is an undistinguished destruction of all ages, sexes, and conditions.

In every stage of these Oppressions We have Petitioned for Redress in the most humble terms: Our repeated Petitions have been answered only by repeated injury. A Prince, whose character is thus marked by every act which may define a Tyrant, is unfit to be the ruler of a free people.

Nor have We been wanting in attention to our British brethren. We have warned them from time to time of attempts by their legislature to extend an unwarrantable jurisdiction over us. We have reminded them of the circumstances of our emigration and settlement here. We have appealed to their native justice and magnanimity, and we have conjured them by the ties of our common kindred to disavow these usurpations, which, would inevitably interrupt our connections and correspondence. They too must have been deaf to the voice of justice and of consanguinity. We must, therefore, acquiesce in the necessity, which denounces our Separation, and hold them, as we hold the rest of mankind, Enemies in War, in Peace Friends.

We, therefore, the Representatives of the United States of America, in General Congress, Assembled, appealing to the Supreme Judge of the world for the rectitude of our intentions, do, in the Name, and by Authority of the good People of these Colonies, solemnly publish and declare, That these United Colonies are, and of Right ought to be free and independent states; that they are Absolved from all Allegiance to the British Crown, and that all political connection between them and the State of Great Britain, is and ought to be totally dissolved; and that as Free and Independent States, they have full Power to levy War, conclude Peace, contract Alliances, establish Commerce, and to do all other Acts and Things which Independent States may of right do. And for the support of this Declaration, with a firm reliance on the Protection of Divine Providence, we mutually pledge to each other our Lives, our Fortunes, and our sacred Honor.

The foregoing Declaration was, by order of Congress, engrossed, and signed by the following members:

JOHN HANCOCK

New Hampshire

Josiah Bartlett
William Whipple
Matthew Thornton

Massachusetts Bay

Samuel Adams
John Adams
Robert Treat Paine
Elbridge Gerry

Rhode Island

Stephen Hopkins
William Ellery

Connecticut

Roger Sherman
Samuel Huntington
William Williams
Oliver Wolcott

New York

William Floyd
Philip Livingston
Francis Lewis
Lewis Morris

New Jersey

Richard Stockton
John Witherspoon
Francis Hopkinson
John Hart
Abraham Clark

Pennsylvania

Robert Morris
Benjamin Rush
Benjamin Franklin
John Morton
George Clymer
James Smith
George Taylor
James Wilson
George Ross

Delaware

Caesar Rodney
George Read
Thomas M'Kean

Maryland

Samuel Chase
William Paca
Thomas Stone
Charles Carrol, of
   Carrollton

Virginia

George Wythe
Richard Henry Lee
Thomas Jefferson
Benjamin Harrison
Thomas Nelson, Jr.
Francis Lightfoot Lee
Carter Braxton

North Carolina

William Hooper
Joseph Hewes
John Penn

South Carolina

Edward Rutledge
Thomas Heyward, Jr.
Thomas Lynch, Jr.
Arthur Middleton

Georgia

Button Gwinnett
Lyman Hall
George Walton

Resolved, That copies of the Declaration be sent to the several assemblies, conventions, and committees, or councils of safety, and to the several commanding officers of the continental troops; that it be proclaimed in each of the United States, at the head of the army.

19

The Pennsylvania Bill of Rights (1776)

As states drew up their constitutions, most included some form of bill of rights. State framers were familiar with the view that fundamental rights ought to be embodied in some form of written expression to which people could refer, and upon which they could base their opposition to tyrannical government (see Document 28). The Pennsylvania constitution, which some people have labeled the "purest application of revolutionary political theory to government," made the listing of rights the very first article. The framers of this document obviously distrusted government, and in other sections did their best to limit its powers. The 1776 constitution lasted only fourteen years, and its experience was not untypical of several other state schemes drawn up in the flush of revolutionary fervor. Nearly all the revisions gave greater powers to the government and shifted powers from legislative to executive branches.

See A. Nevins, *The American States During and After the Revolution, 1775–1789* (1924); J. T. Main, *The Sovereign States, 1775–1783* (1973); and J. P. Selsam, *The Pennsylvania Constitution of 1776: A Study in Revolutionary Democracy* (1971).

I. That all men are born equally free and independent, and have certain natural, inherent and unalienable rights, amongst which are the enjoying and defending life and liberty, acquiring, possessing and protecting property, and pursuing and obtaining happiness and safety.

II. That all men have a natural and unalienable right to worship Almighty God, according to the dictates of their own consciences and understanding, and that no man ought, or of right can be compelled to attend any religious worship, or erect or support any place of worship, or maintain any ministry, contrary to, or against his own free will and consent, nor can any man who acknowledges the being of a God, be justly deprived or abridged of any civil right as a citizen, on account of his religious sentiments, or peculiar mode of religious worship; and that no authority can, or ought to be vested in, or

Source: Thorpe, ed., 5 *Federal and State Constitutions* 3082 (1909).

assumed by any power whatever, that shall in any case interfere with, or in any manner controul the right of conscience in the free exercise of religious worship.

III.   That the people of this state have the sole, exclusive and inherent right of governing and regulating the internal police of the same.

IV.   That all power being originally inherent in, and consequently derived from the people; therefore all officers of government, whether legislative or executive, are their trustees and servants, and at all times accountable to them.

V.   That government is, or ought to be, instituted for the common benefit, protection, and security of the people, nation or community; and not for the particular emolument or advantage of any single man, family, or set of men, who are a part only of that community; and that the community hath an indubitable, unalienable and indefeasible right to reform, alter or abolish government, in such manner as shall be by that community judged most conducive to the public weal.

VI.   That those who are employed in the legislative and executive business of the state, may be restrained from oppression, the people have a right, at such periods as they may think proper, to reduce their public officers to a private station, and supply the vacancies by certain and regular elections.

VII.   That all elections ought to be free, and that all free men, having a sufficient evident common interest with and attachment to the community, have a right to elect officers, or to be elected into office.

VIII.   That every member of society hath a right to be protected in the enjoyment of life, liberty and property, and therefore is bound to contribute his proportion towards the expense of that protection, and yield his personal service when necessary, or an equivalent thereto; but no part of a man's property can be justly taken from him or applied to public uses, without his own consent or that of his legal representatives; nor can any man who is conscientiously scrupulous of bearing arms be justly compelled thereto if he will pay such equivalent; nor are the people bound by any laws but such as they have in like manner assented to, for their common good.

IX.   That in all prosecutions for criminal offences, a man hath a right to be heard by himself and his council; to demand the cause and nature of his accusation; to be confronted with the witnesses, to call for evidence in his favor, and a speedy public trial by an impartial jury of the country, without the unanimous consent of which jury he cannot be found guilty; nor can he be compelled to give evidence against himself; nor can any man be justly deprived of his liberty, except by the laws of the land or the judgment of his peers.

X.   That the people have a right to hold themselves, their houses, papers and possessions free from search and seizure; and therefore warrants, without oaths or affirmations first made, affording a sufficient foundation for them, and whereby any officer or messenger may be commanded or required to search suspected places, or to seize any person or persons, his or their property not particularly described, are contrary to that right, and ought not to be granted.

XI.   That in controversies respecting property, and in suits between man and man, the parties have a right to trial by jury, which ought to be held sacred.

XII.   That the people have a right to freedom of speech, and of writing and publishing their sentiments; therefore the freedom of the press ought not to be restrained.

XIII.   That the people have a right to bear arms for the defence of themselves, and the state; and as standing armies in the time of peace, are dangerous to liberty, they ought not to be kept up; and that the military should be kept under strict subordination to, and governed by the civil power.

XIV.   That a frequent recurrence to fundamental principles and a firm adherence to justice, moderation, temperance, industry and frugality, are absolutely necessary to preserve the blessings of liberty, and, keep a government free. The people ought therefore to pay particular attention to these points in the choice of officers and representatives, and have a right to exact a due and constant regard to them from their legislatures and magistrates, in the making and executing such laws as are necessary for the good government of the state.

XV.   That all men have a natural inherent right to emigrate from one state to another that will receive them, or to form a new state in vacant countries, or in such countries as they can purchase, whenever they think that thereby they may promote their own happiness.

XVI.   That the people have a right to assemble together to consult for their common good, to instruct their representatives, and to apply to the legislature for redress of grievances by address, petition or remonstrance.

Part III

Becoming a Nation

With independence secured, the revolutionary generation turned to the task of establishing one nation out of thirteen fiercely independent states. Everyone recognized that the former colonies would have to form some sort of union, and in fact, the Continental Congress discussed the idea of a formal union even before it passed the Declaration of Independence. Although it took five years to work out the details, nearly all the delegates to the Congress that declared independence assumed that the colonies had to unite, and do so through a constitution.

A constitution defines the nature of a union, and America's first constitution, the Articles of Confederation (Document 20), reflected the experience of the colonies under British rule. The abuses of strong central government detailed in the Declaration of Independence (Document 18) led the drafting committee to design a federal union with a relatively weak central authority and the balance of power in the states.

For a decade, the United States lived under the Articles, and the Congress had some positive achievements to show for it. Congress concluded the war and negotiated a peace treaty, put down Indian uprisings in the West, and most important, established a public land policy (Document 22) and a method for admitting new states to the Union (Document 25) that would have far-reaching effects. Within the states, people continued to live under relatively familiar laws (Document 21), although the general democratic tenor of the times led to some sentiment against lawyers (Document 23). Perhaps most significant was the continued effort to establish and protect individual rights. The Pennsylvania Bill of Rights (Document 19) was only the beginning, and in 1786 Virginia took a major step in promoting individual liberties in the Statute for Religious Freedom (Document 24), a direct antecedent of the religious freedom embodied in the First Amendment.

But the deliberate weaknesses built into the Articles manifested themselves in a series of problems in the mid-1780s. The lack of an independent taxing power made it impossible for Congress to pay off either the principal or interest on the huge war loans, and in some years Congress barely received enough money to pay its current bills. Efforts to amend the Articles to give Congress greater fiscal autonomy received the approval of twelve states, but the amending process required unanimity, and Rhode Island vigorously opposed any move to give the central government more authority. Then came Shays's Rebellion in 1786, a pitiful uprising in western Massachusetts that scared many conservatives but had little chance of success. The state asked Congress for military help, and Congress could not respond. By then proponents of change had built up the momentum that led to the Philadelphia convention in the summer of 1787.

Nearly all the delegates recognized the need to either amend the Articles or replace them with a new constitution giving a national government greater power. Three proposals represented a variety of views (Document 26), and the final result, the Constitution (Document 27), marked a significant departure from the anticentrist philosophy of the Articles. This change did not satisfy everyone (Document 28), but the arguments of Hamilton, Madison, and Jay in *The Federalist* (Document 29) carried the day. With the Constitution ratified in the summer of 1788, Americans could turn in earnest to the task of creating a new nation.

The Articles of Confederation (1781)

The Articles of Confederation served for a decade as America's first constitution. John Dickinson's initial draft gave the central government more power than the delegates or the states were willing to concede at the time, and in order to get agreement, proponents of a federal union had to agree to a less powerful central government. Imperfect in many ways, the Articles nonetheless did allow the government of the new nation to function, in some areas quite effectively, and some scholars believe that with minor changes, it could have served for a number of years. Its weaknesses are most apparent when compared to the Constitution of 1787 (Document 27) with its explicit commitment to strong national government. One should note the many ways in which the Articles embodied various political ideas that had become commonplace during the decade before the Revolution, and also how they responded to the complaints in the Declaration of Independence.

See A. C. McLaughlin, *The Confederation and the Constitution, 1781–1789* (1905); M. Jensen, *The Articles of Confederation* (1940) and *The New Nation* (1950); E. S. Morgan, *The Birth of the Republic, 1763–1789* (1956); and F. W. Marks, *Independence on Trial* (1973).

To all to whom these Presents shall come, we the undersigned Delegates of the States affixed to our names send greeting.

Whereas the Delegates of the United States of America in Congress assembled did on the fifteenth day of November in the Year of our Lord One Thousand Seven Hundred and Seventy-seven, and in the Second Year of the Independence of America agree to certain articles of Confederation and perpetual Union between the States of Newhampshire, Massachusetts-bay, Rhodeisland, and Providence Plantations, Connecticut, New York, New Jersey, Pennsylvania, Delaware, Maryland, Virginia, North-Carolina, South-Carolina and Georgia in the Words following, viz.

"Articles of Confederation and perpetual Union between the States of Newhampshire, Massachusetts-bay, Rhodeisland and Providence Planta-

---

Source: Thorpe, ed., 1 *Federal and State Constitutions* 9 (1909).

tions, Connecticut, New-York, New-Jersey, Pennsylvania, Delaware, Maryland, Virginia, North-Carolina, South-Carolina and Georgia.

Article I.   The stile of this confederacy shall be "The United States of America."

Article II.   Each State retains its sovereignty, freedom and independence, and every power, jurisdiction and right, which is not by this confederation expressly delegated to the United States, in Congress assembled.

Article III.   The said States hereby severally enter into a firm league of friendship with each other, for their common defense, the security of their liberties, and their mutual and general welfare, binding themselves to assist each other, against all force offered to, or attacks made upon them, or any of them, on account of religion, sovereignty, trade or any other pretence whatever.

Article IV.   The better to secure and perpetuate mutual friendship and intercourse among the people of the different States in this Union, the free inhabitants of each of these States, paupers, vagabonds and fugitives from justice excepted, shall be entitled to all privileges and immunities of free citizens in the several States; and the people of each State shall have free ingress and regress to and from any other State, and shall enjoy therein all the privileges of trade and commerce, subject to the same duties, impositions and restrictions as the inhabitants thereof respectively, provided that such restrictions shall not extend so far as to prevent the removal of property imported into any State, to any other State of which the owner is an inhabitant; provided also that no imposition, duties or restriction shall be laid by any State, on the property of the United States, or either of them.

If any person guilty of, or charged with treason, felony, or other high misdemeanor in any State, shall flee from justice, and be found in any of the United States, he shall upon demand of the Governor or Executive power, of the State from which he fled, be delivered up and removed to the State having jurisdiction of his offence.

Full faith and credit shall be given in each of these States to the records, acts and judicial proceedings of the courts and magistrates of every other State.

Article V.   For the more convenient management of the general interests of the United States, delegates shall be annually appointed in such manner as the legislature of each State shall direct, to meet in Congress on the first Monday in November, in every year, with a power reserved to each State, to recall its delegates, or any of them, at any time within the year, and to send others in their stead, for the remainder of the year.

No State shall be represented in Congress by less than two, nor by more than seven members; and no person shall be capable of being a delegate for more than three years in any term of six years; nor shall any person, being a delegate, be capable of holding any office under the United States, for which he, or another for his benefit receives any salary, fees or emolument of any kind.

Each state shall maintain its own delegates in a meeting of the States, and while they act as members of the committee of the States.

In determining questions in the United States, in Congress assembled, each State shall have one vote.

Freedom of speech and debate in Congress shall not be impeached or questioned in any court, or place out of Congress, and the members of Congress shall be protected in their persons from arrests and imprisonments, during the time of their going to and from, and attendance on Congress, except for treason, felony, or breach of the peace.

Article VI.   No State without the consent of the United States in Congress assembled, shall send any embassy to, or receive any embassy from, or enter into any conference, agreement, alliance or treaty with any king, prince or state; nor shall any person holding any office of profit or trust under the United States, or any of them, accept of any present, emolument, office or title of any kind whatever from any king, prince or foreign state; nor shall the United States in Congress assembled, or any of them, grant any title of nobility.

No two or more States shall enter into any treaty, confederation or alliance whatever between them, without the consent of the United States in Congress assembled, specifying accurately the purposes for which the same is to be entered into, and how long it shall continue.

No State shall lay any imposts or duties, which may interfere with any stipulations in treaties, entered into by the United States in Congress assembled, with any king, prince or state, in pursuance of any treaties already proposed by Congress, to the courts of France and Spain.

No vessels of war shall be kept up in time of peace by any State, except such number only, as shall be deemed necessary by the United States in Congress assembled, for the defense of such State, or its trade; nor shall any body of forces be kept up by any State, in time of peace, except such number only, as in the judgment of the United States, in Congress assembled, shall be deemed requisite to garrison the forts necessary for the defense of such State; but every State shall always keep up a well regulated and disciplined militia, sufficiently armed and accoutred, and shall provide and constantly have ready for use, in public stores, a due number of field pieces and tents, and a proper quantity of arms, ammunition and camp equipage.

No State shall engage in any war without the consent of the United States in Congress assembled, unless such State be actually invaded by enemies, or shall have received certain advice of a resolution being formed by some nation of Indians to invade such State, and the danger is so imminent as not to admit of a delay, till the United States in Congress assembled can be consulted: nor shall any State grant commissions to any ships or vessels of war, nor letters of marque or reprisal, except it be after a declaration of war by the United States in Congress assembled, and then only against the kingdom or state and the subjects thereof, against which war has been so declared, and under such regulations as shall be established by the United States in Congress assembled, unless such State be infested by pirates, in which case vessels of war may be fitted out for that occasion, and kept so long as the danger shall continue, or until the United States in Congress assembled shall determine otherwise.

Article VII.   When land-forces are raised by any State of the common defence, all officers of or under the rank of colonel, shall be appointed by the Legislature of each State respectively by whom such forces shall be raised, or in such manner as such State shall direct, and all vacancies shall be filled up by the State which first made the appointment.

Article VIII.   All charges of war, and all other expenses that shall be incurred for the common defense or general welfare, and allowed by the United States in Congress assembled, shall be defrayed out of a common treasury, which shall be supplied by the several States, in proportion to the value of all land within each State, granted to or surveyed for any person, as such land and the buildings and improvements thereon shall be estimated according to such mode as the United States in Congress assembled, shall from time to time direct and appoint.

The taxes for paying that proportion shall be laid and levied by the authority and direction of the Legislatures of the several States within the time agreed upon by the United States in Congress assembled.

Article IX.   The United States in Congress assembled, shall have the sole and exclusive right and power of determining on peace and war, except in the cases mentioned in the sixth article—of sending and receiving ambassadors—entering into treaties and alliances, provided that no treaty of commerce shall be made whereby the legislative power of the respective States shall be restrained from imposing such imposts and duties on foreigners, as their own people are subjected to, or from prohibiting the exportation or importation of and species of goods or commodities whatsoever—of establishing rules for deciding in all cases, what captures on land or water shall be legal, and in what manner prizes taken by land or naval forces in the service of the United States shall be divided or appropriated—of granting letters of marque and reprisal in times of peace—appointing courts for the trial of piracies and felonies committed on the high seas and establishing courts for receiving and determining finally appeals in all cases of captures, provided that no member of Congress shall be appointed a judge of any of the said courts.

The United States in Congress assembled shall also be the last resort on appeal in all disputes and differences now subsisting or that hereafter may arise between two or more States concerning boundary, jurisdiction or any other cause whatever; which authority shall always be exercised in the manner following. Whenever the legislative or executive authority or lawful agent of any State in controversy with another shall present a petition to Congress, stating the matter in question and praying for a hearing, notice thereof shall be given by order of Congress to the legislative or executive authority of the other State in controversy, and a day assigned for the appearance of the parties by their lawful agents, who shall then be directed to appoint by joint consent, commissioners or judges to constitute a court for hearing and determining the matter in question: but if they cannot agree, Congress shall name three persons out of each of the United States, and from the list of such persons each party shall alternately strike out one, the petitioners beginning, until the number shall be reduced to thirteen; and from that number not less than seven, nor more than nine names as Congress shall direct, shall in the presence of Congress be drawn out by lot, and the persons whose names shall be so drawn or any five of them, shall be commissioners or judges, to hear and finally determine the controversy, so always as a major part of the judges who shall hear the cause shall agree in the determination: and if either party shall neglect to attend at the day appointed, without reasons, which Congress shall judge sufficient, or being present shall refuse to strike, the Congress shall proceed to nominate three persons out of each State, and the Secretary of Congress shall strike in behalf of such party absent or refusing; and the judgment and sentence of the court to be appointed, in the manner before prescribed, shall be final and conclusive; and if any of the parties shall refuse to submit to the authority of such court, or to appear or defend their claim or cause, the court shall nevertheless proceed to pronounce sentence, or judgment, which shall in like manner be final and decisive, the judgment or sentence and other proceedings being in either case transmitted to Congress, and lodged among the acts of Congress for the security of the parties concerned: provided that every commissioner, before he sits in judgment, shall take an oath to be administered by one of the judges of the supreme or superior court of the State where the cause shall be tried, "well and truly to hear and determine the matter in question, according to the best of his judgment, without favour, affection or hope of reward": provided also that no State shall be deprived of territory for the benefit of the United States.

All controversies concerning the private right of soil claimed under different grants of two or more States, whose jurisdiction as they may respect such lands, and the states which passed such grants are adjusted, the said grants or either of them being at the same time claimed to have originated antecedent to such settlement of jurisdiction, shall on the petition of either party to the Congress of the United States, be finally determined as near as may be in the same manner as is before prescribed for deciding disputes respecting territorial jurisdictions between different States.

The United States in Congress assembled shall also have the sole and exclusive right and power of regulating the alloy and value of coin struck by their own authority, or by that of the respective States—fixing the standard of weights and measures throughout the United States—regulating the trade and managing all affairs with the Indians, not members of any of the States, provided that the legislative right of any State within its own limits be not infringed or violated—establishing and regulating post-offices from one State to another, throughout all of the United States, and exacting such postage on the papers passing thro' the same as may be requisite to defray the expenses of the said office—appointing all officers of the land forces, in the service of the United States, excepting regimental officers—appointing all the officers of the naval forces, and commissioning all officers whatever in the service of the United States—making rules for the government and regulation of the said land and naval forces, and directing their operations.

The United States in Congress assembled shall have authority to appoint a committee, to sit in the recess of Congress, to be denominated "a Committee of the States," and to consist of one delegate from each State; and to appoint such other committees and civil officers as may be necessary for managing the general affairs of the United States under their direction—to appoint one of their number to preside, provided that no person be allowed to serve in the office of president more than one year in any term of three years; to ascertain the necessary sums of money to be raised for the service of the United States, and to appropriate and apply the same for defraying the public expenses—to borrow money, or emit bills on the credit of the United States, transmitting every half year to the respective States an account of the sums of money so borrowed or emitted,—to build and equip a navy—to agree upon the number of land forces, and to make requisitions from each State for its quota, in proportion to the number of white inhabitants in such State; which requisition shall be binding, and thereupon the Legislature of each State shall appoint the regimental officers, raise the men and cloath, arm and equip them in a soldier like manner, at the expense of the United States; and the officers and men so cloathed, armed and equipped shall march to the place appointed, and within the time agreed on by the United States in Congress assembled; but if the United States in Congress assembled shall, on consideration of circumstances judge proper that any State should not raise men, or should raise a smaller number of men than the quota thereof, such extra number shall be raised, officered, cloathed, armed and equipped in the same manner as the quota of such State, unless the legislature of such State shall judge that such extra number cannot be safely spared out of the same, in which case they shall raise, officer, cloath, arm and equip as many of such extra number as they judge can be safely spared. And the officers and men so cloathed, armed and equipped, shall march to the place appointed, and within the period agreed on by the United States in Congress assembled.

The United States in Congress assembled shall never engage in a war, nor grant letters of marque and reprisal in time of peace, nor enter into any treaties or alliances, nor coin money, nor regulate the value thereof, nor ascertain the sums and expenses necessary for the defence and welfare of the United States, or any of them, nor emit bills, nor borrow money on the credit of the United States, nor appropriate money, nor agree upon the number of vessels to be built or purchased, or the number of land or sea forces to be raised, nor appoint a commander in chief of the army or navy, unless nine states assent to the same: nor shall a question on any other point, except for adjourning from day to day be determined, unless by the votes of a majority of the United States in Congress assembled.

The Congress of the United States shall have power to adjourn to any time within the year, and to any place within the United States, so that no period of adjournment be for a longer duration than the space of six months, and shall publish the journal of their proceedings monthly, except such parts thereof relating to treaties, alliances or military operations, as in their judgment require secresy; and the yeas and nays of the delegates of each State on any question shall be entered on the Journal, when it is desired by any delegate; and the delegates of a State, or any of them, at his or their request shall be furnished with a transcript of the said journal, except such parts as are above excepted, to lay before the Legislatures of the several States.

Article X.   The committee of the States, or any nine of them, shall be authorized to execute, in the recess of Congress, such of the powers of Congress as the United States in Congress assembled, by the consent of nine States, shall from time to time think expedient to vest them with; provided that no power be delegated to the said committee, for the exercise of which, by the articles of confederation, the voice of nine States in the Congress of the United States assembled is requisite.

Article XI.   Canada acceding to this confederation, and joining in the measures of the United States, shall be admitted into, and entitled to all the advantages of this Union: but no other colony shall be admitted into the same, unless such admission be agreed to by nine States.

Article XII.   All bills of credit emitted, monies borrowed and debts contracted by, or under the authority of Congress, before the assembling of the United States, in pursuance of the present confederation, shall be deemed and considered as a charge against the United States, for payment and satisfaction whereof the said United States, and the public faith are hereby solemnly pledged.

Article XIII.   Every State shall abide by the determinations of the United States in Congress assembled, on all questions which by this confederation are submitted to them. And the articles of this confederation shall be inviolably observed by every State, and the Union shall be perpetual; nor shall any alteration at any time hereafter be made in any of them; unless such alteration be agreed to in a Congress of the United States, and be afterwards confirmed by the Legislatures of every State.

And whereas it has pleased the Great Governor of the world to incline the hearts of the Legislatures we respectively represent in Congress, to approve of, and to authorize us to ratify the said articles of confederation and perpetual union. Know ye that we the undersigned delegates, by virtue of the power and authority to us given for that purpose, do by these presents, in the name and in behalf of our respective constituents, full and entirely ratify and confirm each and every of the said articles of confederation and perpetual union, and all and singular the matters and things therein contained: and we do further solemnly plight and engage the faith of our respective constituents, that they shall abide by the determinations of the United States in Congress assembled, on all questions, which by the said confederation are submitted to them. And that the articles thereof shall be inviolably observed by the States we respectively represent, and that the Union shall be perpetual.

In witness thereof we have hereunto set our hands in Congress. Done at Philadelphia in the State of Pennsylvania the ninth day of July in the year of our Lord one thousand seven hundred and seventy-eight, and in the third year of the independence of America.

21

Vermont Reception Statute (1782)

One question raised by the Revolution was what law the new nation and states would now be governed under. Some Americans wanted to do away with English law entirely; others could not conceive of any other legal system. Aside from political and theoretical questions, there were practical ones as well. In whose name would writs now run if the colonists no longer pledged fealty to the King? How would judges be appointed, and what rules would they use in deciding cases?

Source: Brown, *British Statutes in American Law, 1776–1836* 23 (1964).

Nearly every state enacted a so-called "reception statute," which would, at least for the moment, keep the common law in effect until some permanent solution could be found. Between 1776 and 1784 eleven states made provision to receive common law, although they differed as to what year would demarcate the extent of the law. The Vermont statute, which is fairly typical, uses 1760; a few states went back into the seventeenth century. Eventually all new states (except Louisiana, which kept the French civil code) found it necessary to declare English common law as part of their jurisprudence.

Elizabeth's patents (Document 2) had established English law in the New World, and now it would have been difficult to accept any other law. The colonists had their hands full during and after the Revolution, and had no time to draft a civil code. Moreover, most believed English law fair, and thanks to the popularity of Blackstone, believed the English system of judges tailoring common law to specific circumstances better than the rigidity of the continental statutory arrangements. See, however, the codification movement of the mid-nineteenth century (Document 76).

See E. G. Brown, *British Statutes in American Law, 1776–1836* (1964); and W. E. Nelson, *The Americanization of the Common Law* (1975).

Whereas, it is impossible, at once, to provide particular statutes adapted to all cases wherein law may be necessary for the happy government of the people.

And whereas the inhabitants of this State have been habituated to conform their manners to the English laws, and hold their real estate by English tenures.

Be it enacted, &c that so much of the common law of England, as is not repugnant to the constitution or to any act of the legislature of this State, be, and is hereby adopted, and shall be, and continue to be, law within this state.

And whereas, the statute law of England is so connected and interwoven with the common law, that our jurisprudence would be incompleat without it; therefore,

Be it further enacted, that such statute laws and parts of laws of the kingdom of England, as were passed before [October 1, 1760] for the alteration and explanation of the common law, and which are not repugnant to the constitution, or some act of legislature, and are applicable to the circumstances of the State, are hereby adopted and made, and shall be and continue to be, law within this State, and all courts are to take notice thereof, and govern themselves accordingly.

Land Ordinance (1785)

Control of the great western lands had been a problem for the British, and would be one of the most acute issues facing the young republic. Under their colonial charters, many of the states "owned" lands west of the Appalachian mountains, and the closing of these lands to settlement in 1763 had caused much resentment. With independence the United States won title to the Northwest Territory in the Treaty of Paris, and the question now arose who would have control over those lands—the national government or the states. As a demand for ratifying the Articles, the smaller states, especially Maryland, successfully insisted that the large states cede their western lands to the national government. Congress dealt with these lands in a series of ordinances that established the nation's western land policy until 1862. In 1780 Congress resolved that these lands "shall be . . . formed into distinct Republican states" equal to existing states. In the 1785 Ordinance Congress took a major step in resolving the western land issue by providing for its orderly development, and two years later arranged for its governance as well (Document 25).

Congress saw sale of western lands as a source of revenue, but the lack of credit excluded many small farmers. Land speculation companies did most of the business in the territories for the next fifty years. The companies did, however, subdivide sections and sell small parcels on credit, thus helping achieve one of the act's goals—bringing in settlers.

See J. P. Bloom, ed., *The American Territorial System* (1974); M. Jensen, *The New Nation* (1950); P. J. Treat, *The National Land System, 1785–1820* (1910); and H. Tatter, "State and Federal Land Policy During the Confederation Period," 9 *Agr. His.* 176 (1935).

Be it ordained by the United States in Congress assembled, that the territory ceded by individual States to the United States, which has been purchased of the Indian inhabitants, shall be disposed of in the following manner:

A surveyor from each state shall be appointed by Congress or a Committee of the States, who shall take an oath for the faithful discharge of his duty, before the Geographer of the United States. . . .

The Surveyors, as they are respectively qualified, shall proceed to divide

Source: Ford et al., eds., 28 *Journals of the Continental Congress* 375 (1904–37).

the said territory into townships of six miles square, by lines running due north and south, and others crossing these at right angles, as near as may be, unless where the boundaries of the late Indian purchases may render the same impracticable, . . .

The lines shall be measured with a chain; shall be plainly marked by chaps on the trees, and exactly described on a plat; whereon shall be noted by the surveyor, at their proper distances, all mines, salt-springs, salt-licks and mill-seats, that shall come to his knowledge, and all water-courses, mountains and other remarkable and permanent things, over and near which such lines shall pass, and also the quality of the lands.

The plats of the townships respectively, shall be marked by subdivisions into lots of one mile square, or 640 acres, in the same direction as the external lines, and numbered from 1 to 36; always beginning the succeeding range of the lots with the number next to that with which the preceding one concluded. . . .

. . . And the geographer shall make . . . returns, from time to time, of every seven ranges as they may be surveyed. The Secretary of War shall have recourse thereto, and shall take by lot therefrom, a number of townships . . . as will be equal to one seventh part of the whole of such seven ranges, . . . for the use of the late Continental army. . . .

The board of treasury shall transmit a copy of the original plats, previously noting thereon the townships and fractional parts of townships, which shall have fallen to the several states, by the distribution aforesaid, to the commissioners of the loan-office of the several states, who, after giving notice . . . shall proceed to sell the townships or fractional parts of townships, at public vendue, in the following manner, viz.: The township or fractional part of a township No. 1, in the first range, shall be sold entire; and No. 2, in the same range, by lots; and thus in alternate order through the whole of the first range . . . provided, that none of the lands, within the said territory, be sold under the price of one dollar the acre, to be paid in specie, or loan-office certificates, reduced to specie value, by the scale of depreciation, or certificates of liquidated debts of the United States, including interest, besides the expense of the survey and other charges thereon, which are hereby rated at thirty six dollars the township, . . . on failure of which payment, the said lands shall again be offered for sale.

There shall be reserved for the United States out of every township the four lots, being numbered 8,11,26,29, and out of every fractional part of a township, so many lots of the same numbers as shall be found thereon, for future sale. There shall be reserved the lot No. 16, of every township, for the maintenance of public schools within the said township; also one-third part of all gold, silver, lead and copper mines, to be sold, or otherwise disposed of as Congress shall hereafter direct. . . .

And Whereas Congress . . . stipulated grants of land to certain officers and soldiers of the late Continental army . . . for complying with such engagements, Be it ordained, That the secretary of war . . . determine who are the objects of the above resolutions and engagements . . . and cause the townships, or fractional parts of townships, hereinbefore reserved for the use of the late Continental army, to be drawn for in such manner as he shall deem expedient.

23

Observations on Lawyers (1786)

HONESTUS

Although almost half the signers of the Declaration of Independence and more than half the members of the Constitutional Convention were lawyers, popular perceptions of the profession were at an all-time low in the decades immediately following the Revolution. Part of this discontent can be attributed to the business depression, for criticism of lawyers and courts rose as creditors used the legal system to collect debts. The laments of "Honestus" (Benjamin Austin, Jr.) were not new; during most of the colonial period one could find complaints of high fees and shoddy practices, as well as a call to do away with lawyers altogether. Some states severely restricted legal practice, and in Pennsylvania for a while the colony managed quite well without lawyers. The return of prosperity and the development of a national market economy soon boosted lawyers in prestige and income; criticism of the profession, however, continued. At least part of the antagonism to lawyers can be traced to the desire of Americans to create a new, simpler, and more democratic legal system. To some people, though, lawyers symbolized the complicated, expensive, and antidemocratic ways of the monarchy against which the Revolution had been fought.

See C. Warren, *A History of the American Bar* (1912); M. Bloomfield, *American Lawyers in a Changing Society, 1776–1876* (1976).

Source: Presser and Zainaldin, *Law and American History* 264 (1980).

Among the multiplicity of evils which we at present suffer, there are none more justly complained of, than those we labor under by the many pernicious practices in the profession of the law. It has therefore, become a subject of serious inquiry, whether this body of men, in a young republic, ought not to be controuled in their pleas.

Laws are necessary for the safety and good order of society, and consequently the execution of them is of great importance to be attended to. When therefore, *finesse* and gross impositions are practised, and under sanction of the law, every principle of equity and justice is destroyed, the persons concerned in such pernicious measures ought to be brought forward, and their conduct arraigned before the impartial tribunal of the people.

The study and practice of the law are doubtless an honourable employment; and when a man acts becoming the dignity of the profession, he ought to be esteemed by every member in the community. But when any number of men under sanction of this character are endeavouring to perplex and embarrass every judicial proceeding; who are rendering intricate even the most simple principles of law; who are involving individuals, applying for advice, in the most distressing difficulties; who are practising the greatest art in order to delay every process; who are taking the advantage of every accidental circumstance which an unprincipled person might have, by the lenity and indulgence of an honest creditor; who stand ready to strike up a bargain, (after rendering the property in a precarious state) to throw an honest man out of three quarters of his property. When such men pretend to cloak themselves under the sacredness of law, it is full time the people should inquire, "by what authority they do these things." . . .

The distresses of the people are now great, but if we examine particularly, we shall find them owing, in a great measure, to the conduct of some practitioners of the law. Seven-eighths of the causes which are now in their hands might have been settled by impartial referees. Why cannot the disputes of the merchant, &c. be adjusted by reference, rather than by a long tedious Court process? Or why should we engage lawyers who are wholly unacquainted with all mercantile concerns? Is it to swell the cost and then by a rule of Court have them finally determined by referees, which is generally the case? . . . If we look through the different counties throughout the Commonwealth, we shall find that the troubles of the people arise principally from debts enormously swelled by tedious law-suits.

The many pernicious modes of judiciary process which have taken place within a few years, are too notorious to mention; scarcely a petty office but has become a little distinct tribunal. What flagrant impositions are daily practised under sanction of law! The distressed individual is often reduced to the humiliating state of submitting to the extortion of official fees without any remedy. Is it not a disgrace to a free republic that the citizens should dread appealing to the laws of their country? To what purpose have we laws? . . .

It has, therefore, become necessary for the welfare and security of the Commonwealth, that some mode be adopted in order to render the laws a blessing, instead of an evil. For this purpose, it is requested that some acts should be passed, declaring that in all cases left to reference in future, the decision of the referees should be binding on the parties. In all judiciary processes, the Jury, to receive the evidence from the parties, and the Judges to give their opinion on any controverted points of law. The Jury in this manner would be possessed of all that was necessary to determine on the cause, viz. Law and Evidence, without the false glosses and subterfuges too often practised by lawyers.

If such regulations were made in our Courts, the Judges could determine with more precision; the Jury by taking the evidence, and points of law from the Judges, could, with more clearness, determine the cause; as in many instances, a Jury becomes puzzled in their judgment by the variety of sentiments advanced by lawyers. By this method the laws would be more justly executed, as the judges are under no influence from either party, their salaries being independent. But by our present mode, the lawyers become parties by their fees, and are too apt to delay the business while there is any prospect of further profit.

I would ask, whether there are many cases, that absolutely require the assistance of this "order?" Or if they were not admitted, whether any great inconvenience could arise? The law and evidence are all the essentials required, and are not the Judges with the Jury competent for these purposes? Why then this intervening "order?" The important study of law, should be followed solely with a view of doing justice; and gentlemen of talents, who meant to serve their country as Judges, should make the public good their chief object. They would not take up the profession as a set of needy persons, who meant by chicanery and finesse, to get a living by their practice; but they would make it a point of duty, so to understand the laws, as to distribute equal justice to the rich and poor; each individual would receive the benefit of the laws, and by a speedy and impartial determination, every man would have his cause decided without the imposition of enormous Court charges, and lawyers' fees. There would be no great danger of the Judges converting their authority to any destructive purposes, "as the municipal institutions are so fixed and determined, in this Commonwealth, that it must be difficult for the Judicial Authority to trample upon them with impunity." The perplexity of our laws, therefore, are chiefly owing to the embarrassments thrown in the way by many in the profession.

24

Virginia Statute for
Religious Freedom (1786)

The move to disestablish the Church of England, which enjoyed official status in parts of New York and all the colonies from Maryland to Georgia, became part of the revolutionary agenda. But disestablishment did not automatically lead to religious freedom; several New England states continued their established churches, and others imposed religious tests. But a trend soon developed that led from disestablishment to tolerance to freedom. The Virginia Bill of Rights of 1776, for example, included an article that "all men are equally entitled to the free exercise of religion, according to the dictates of conscience; and that it is the mutual duty of all to practice Christian forbearance, love, and charity towards each other." This did not satisfy Thomas Jefferson, who drafted the following bill in 1777; the legislature did not adopt it, however, until 1786. Whether or not Jefferson read Roger Williams, there is a direct link between the ideals of the "bloudy tenent" (Document 6) and the ideals expressed in the Statute and in the First Amendment. Again one can see the pattern of once-radical notions becoming accepted, mainstream principles.

See W. Miller, *The First Freedom* (1985); R. Rutland, *Birth of the Bill of Rights* (1955); the early chapters of E. A. Smith, *Religious Liberty in the United States* (1972); and D. Malone, *Jefferson and the Rights of Man* (1951).

Whereas Almighty God hath created the mind free; that all attempts to influence it by temporal punishments or burthens, or by civil incapacitations, tend only to beget habits of hypocrisy and meanness, and are a departure from the plan of the Holy author of our religion, who being Lord both of body and mind, yet chose not to propagate it by coercions on either, as was in his Almighty power to do; that the impious presumption of legislators and rulers, civil as well as ecclesiastical, who being themselves but fallible and uninspired men, have assumed dominion over the faith of others, setting up their own opinions and modes of thinking as the only true and infallible, and as such endeavouring to impose them on others, hath established and maintained false religions over the greatest part of the world, and through all time;

Source: Henning, 22 *Stat. at Large* 84 (1823).

that to compel a man to furnish contributions of money for the propagation of opinions which he disbelieves, is sinful and tyrannical; that even the forcing him to support this or that teacher of his own religious persuasion, is depriving him of the comfortable liberty of giving his contributions to the particular pastor, whose morals he would make his pattern, and whose powers he feels most persuasive to righteousness, and is withdrawing from the ministry those temporary rewards, which proceeding from an approbation of their personal conduct, are an additional incitement to earnest and unremitting labours for the instruction of mankind; that our civil rights have no dependence on our religious opinions, any more than our opinions in physics or geometry; that therefore the proscribing any citizen as unworthy the public confidence by laying upon him an incapacity of being called to offices of trust and emolument, unless he profess or renounce this or that religious opinion, is depriving him injuriously of those privileges and advantages to which in common with his fellow-citizens he has a natural right; that it tends only to corrupt the principles of that religion it is meant to encourage, by bribing with a monopoly of worldly honours and emoluments, those who will externally profess and conform to it; that though indeed these are criminal who do not withstand such temptation, yet neither are those innocent who lay the bait in their way; that to suffer the civil magistrate to intrude his powers into the field of opinion, and to restrain the profession or propagation of principles on supposition of their ill tendency, is a dangerous fallacy, which at once destroys all religious liberty, because he being of course judge of that tendency will make his opinions the rule of judgment, and approve or condemn the sentiments of others only as they shall square with or differ from his own; that it is time enough for the rightful purposes of civil government, for its officers to interfere when principles break out into overt acts against peace and good order; and finally, that truth is great and will prevail if left to herself, that she is the proper and sufficient antagonist to error, and has nothing to fear from the conflict, unless by human interposition disarmed of her natural weapons, free argument and debate, errors ceasing to be dangerous when it is permitted freely to contradict them:

Be it enacted by the General Assembly, That no man shall be compelled to frequent or support any religious worship, place, or ministry whatsoever, nor shall be enforced, restrained, molested, or burthened in his body or goods, nor shall otherwise suffer on account of his religious opinions or belief; but that all men shall be free to profess, and by argument to maintain, their opinion in matters of religion, and that the same shall in no wise diminish, enlarge, or affect their civil capacities.

And though we well know that this assembly elected by the people for the ordinary purposes of legislation only, have no power to restrain the acts of succeeding assemblies, constituted with powers equal to our own, and that therefore to declare this act to be irrevocable would be of no effect in law; yet we are free to declare, and do declare, that the rights hereby asserted are of the natural rights of mankind, and that if any act shall be hereafter passed to repeal the present, or to narrow its operation, such act will be an infringement of natural right.

25

The Northwest Ordinance (1787)

As settlers poured into the Northwest Territory, Congress realized that it would have to establish some provisions for government, and sooner than it had expected. From the beginning it had been assumed that one or more states would be carved out of the area, and they would enter the Union on an equal footing with the older states. The problem was how to make the transition from a relatively unpopulated frontier to statehood. The scheme set forward in the 1787 statute provided the basic mechanism for establishing government in the territories and then bringing those areas into the Union. The Land Ordinance marked the high point of Confederation government, and, with minor alterations, remained federal policy until 1862. It established for all time the principle that new states would be equal in every way to the original members of the Union, and thus prevented any division between old and new states, with the latter consigned to an inferior status.

See the essays in J. P. Bloom, ed., *The American Territorial System* (1974); T. C. Pease, "The Ordinance of 1787," 25 *M.V.H.R.* 167 (1938); and J. E. Eblen, "Origins of the United States Colonial System: The Ordinance of 1787," 51 *Wis. Mag. His.* 294 (1968).

Be it ordained by the authority aforesaid, That there shall be appointed from time to time by Congress, a governor, whose commission shall continue in force for the term of three years, unless sooner revoked by Congress; he shall

Source: Thorpe, ed., 2 *Federal and State Constitutions* 957 (1909).

reside in the district, and have a freehold estate therein in 1,000 acres of land, while in the exercise of his office.

There shall be appointed from time to time by Congress, a secretary, whose commission shall continue in force for four years unless sooner revoked; he shall reside in the district, and have a freehold estate therein in 500 acres of land, while in the exercise of his office. It shall be his duty to keep and preserve the acts and laws passed by the legislature, and the public records of the district, and the proceedings of the governor in his executive department, and transmit authentic copies of such acts and proceedings, every six months, to the Secretary of Congress: There shall also be appointed a court to consist of three judges, any two of whom to form a court, who shall have a common law jurisdiction, and reside in the district, and have each therein a freehold estate in 500 acres of land while in the exercise of their offices; and their commissions shall continue in force during good behavior.

The governor and judges, or a majority of them, shall adopt and publish in the district such laws of the original States, criminal and civil, as may be necessary and best suited to the circumstances of the district, and report them to Congress from time to time: which laws shall be in force in the district until the organization of the General Assembly therein, unless disapproved of by Congress; but afterwards the Legislature shall have authority to alter them as they shall think fit.

The governor, for the time being, shall be commander-in-chief of the militia, appoint and commission all officers in the same below the rank of general officers; all general officers shall be appointed and commissioned by Congress.

Previous to the organization of the general assembly, the governor shall appoint such magistrates and other civil officers in each county or township, as he shall find necessary for the preservation of the peace and good order in the same: After the general assembly shall be organized, the powers and duties of the magistrates and other civil officers shall be regulated and defined by the said assembly; but all magistrates and other civil officers not herein otherwise directed, shall, during the continuance of this temporary government, be appointed by the governor.

For the prevention of crimes and injuries, the laws to be adopted or made shall have force in all parts of the district, and for the execution of process, criminal and civil, the governor shall make proper divisions thereof; and he shall proceed from time to time as circumstances may require, to lay out the parts of the district in which the Indian titles shall have been extinguished, into counties and townships, subject however to such alterations as may thereafter be made by the legislature.

So soon as there shall be five thousand free male inhabitants of full age in the district, upon giving proof thereof to the governor, they shall receive authority, with time and place, to elect representatives from their counties or townships to represent them in the general assembly: *Provided,* That, for every five hundred free male inhabitants, there shall be one representative, and so on progressively with the number of free male inhabitants shall the right of representation increase, until the number of representatives shall amount to twenty-five; after which, the number and proportion of representatives shall be regulated by the legislature: *Provided,* That no person be eligible or qualified to act as a representative unless he shall have been a citizen of one of the United States three years, and be a resident in the district, or unless he shall have resided in the district three years; and, in either case, shall likewise hold in his own right, in fee simple, two hundred acres of land within the same: *Provided, also,* That a freehold in fifty acres of land in the district, having been a citizen of one of the states, and being resident in the district, or the like freehold and two years residence in the district, shall be necessary to qualify a man as an elector of a representative.

The representatives thus elected, shall serve for the term of two years; and, in case of the death of a representative, or removal from office, the governor shall issue a writ to the county or township for which he was a member, to elect another in his stead, to serve for the residue of the term.

The general assembly or legislature shall consist of the governor, legislative council, and a house of representatives. The Legislative Council shall consist of five members, to continue in office five years, unless sooner removed by Congress; any three of whom to be a quorum: and the members of the Council shall be nominated and appointed in the following manner, to wit: As soon as representatives shall be elected, the Governor shall appoint a time and place for them to meet together; and, when met, they shall nominate ten persons, residents in the district, and each possessed of a freehold in five hundred acres of land, and return their names to Congress; five of whom Congress shall appoint and commission to serve as aforesaid; and, whenever a vacancy shall happen in the council, by death or removal from office, the house of representatives shall nominate two persons, qualified as aforesaid, for each vacancy, and return their names to Congress; one of whom Congress shall appoint and commission for the residue of the term. And every five years, four months at least before the expiration of the time of service of the members of council, the said house shall nominate ten persons, qualified as aforesaid, and return their names to Congress; five of whom Congress shall appoint and commission to serve as members of the council five years, unless sooner removed. And the governor, legislative council, and house of representatives, shall have authority to make laws in all cases, for the good government of the district, not repugnant to the principles and articles in this ordinance established and declared. And all bills, having passed by a majority in the house, and by a majority in the council, shall be referred to the governor for his assent; but no bill, or legislative act whatever, shall be of any force without his assent. The governor shall have power to convene, prorogue, and dissolve the general assembly, when, in his opinion, it shall be expedient.

The governor, judges, legislative council, secretary, and such other officers as Congress shall appoint in the district, shall take an oath or affirmation of fidelity and of office; the governor before the president of congress, and all other officers before the Governor. As soon as a legislature shall be formed in the district, the council and house assembled in one room, shall have authority, by joint ballot, to elect a delegate to Congress, who shall have a seat in Congress, with a right of debating but not of voting during this temporary government.

And, for extending the fundamental principles of civil and religious liberty, which form the basis whereon these republics, their laws and constitutions are erected; to fix and establish those principles as the basis of all laws, constitutions, and governments, which forever hereafter shall be formed in the said territory: to provide also for the establishment of States, and permanent government therein, and for their admission to a share in the federal councils on an equal footing with the original States, at as early periods as may be consistent with the general interest:

It is hereby ordained and declared by the authority aforesaid, That the following articles shall be considered as articles of compact between the original States and the people and States in the said territory and forever remain unalterable, unless by common consent, to wit:

ART. 1.   No person, demeaning himself in a peaceable and orderly manner, shall ever be molested on account of his mode of worship or religious sentiments, in the said territory.

ART. 2.   The inhabitants of the said territory shall always be entitled to the benefits of the writ of *habeas corpus,* and of the trial by jury; of a proportionate representation of the people in the legislature; and of judicial proceedings according to the course of the common law. All persons shall be bailable, unless for capital offences, where the proof shall be evident or the presumption great. All fines shall be moderate; and no cruel or unusual punishments shall be inflicted. No man shall be deprived of his liberty or property, but by the judgment of his peers or the law of the land; and, should the public exigencies make it necessary, for the common preservation, to take any person's property, or to demand his particular services, full compensation shall be made for the same. And, in the just preservation of rights and property, it is understood and declared, that no law ought ever to be made, or have force in the said territory, that shall, in any manner whatever, interfere with or affect private contracts or engagements, *bona fide,* and without fraud, previously formed.

ART. 3.   Religion, morality, and knowledge, being necessary to good government and the happiness of mankind, schools and the means of education shall forever be encouraged. The utmost good faith shall always be observed towards the Indians; their lands and property shall never be taken from them without their consent; and, in their property, rights, and liberty, they shall never be invaded or disturbed, unless in just and lawful wars authorized by Congress; but laws founded in justice and humanity, shall from time to time be made for preventing wrongs being done to them, and for preserving peace and friendship with them. . . .

ART. 5.   There shall be formed in the said territory, not less than three nor more than five States. . . . And, whenever any of the said States shall have sixty thousand free inhabitants therein, such State shall be admitted, by its delegates, into the Congress of the United States, on an equal footing with the original States in all respects whatever, and shall be at liberty to form a permanent constitution and State government: *Provided,* the constitution and government so to be formed, shall be republican, and in conformity to the principles contained in these articles; and, so far as it can be consistent with the general interest of the confederacy, such admission shall be allowed at an earlier period, and when there may be a less number of free inhabitants in the State than sixty thousand.

ART. 6.   There shall be neither slavery nor involuntary servitude in the said territory, otherwise than in the punishment of crimes whereof the party shall have been duly convicted: *Provided, always,* That any person escaping into the same, from whom labor or service is lawfully claimed in any one of the original States, such fugitive may be lawfully reclaimed and conveyed to the person claiming his or her labor or service as aforesaid.

26

Proposals for Government (1787)

By the mid-1780s a number of Americans believed the government created under the Articles too weak to meet the needs of the new nation. Despite some impressive achievements of the Confederation Congress (including the negotiation of the peace treaty and the establishment of western land policy), the fact remained that the government could barely pay its bill, much less begin to retire the war debt. When Daniel Shays led an uprising of debt-ridden farmers in western Massachusetts, the Congress proved unable to heed the state's call for assistance in putting down the rebellion. Even people who believed that the Articles struck a proper balance between state and federal powers recognized that some adjustments would have to be made to give the national government more authority. Increasingly, however, prestigious figures such as George Washington, Alexander Hamilton, and James Madison called for replacement of the Articles by a new scheme of government, and their efforts led to the calling of the Constitutional Convention of 1787.

Following are three proposals made to the convention. The Virginia Plan, devised by James Madison and presented by Edmund Randolph, reflected the interests of the larger states. It proposed separate executive, legislative, and judicial branches in a strong national government whose decisions would be binding upon the states. The bicameral legislature would reflect the population of the states, with direct election of the lower house, which in turn would elect the senate.

Because the Virginia Plan apportioned congressional strength on the basis of population, the smaller states feared they would be dominated by the larger states. The New Jersey Plan, drafted by William Paterson, kept the older structure of Congress, with each state having only one vote. It too, however, granted more authority to the Congress than it had under the Articles. Neither proposal satisfied Alexander Hamilton of New York, who wanted an even stronger central government; his proposal received no support from the other delegates, and Hamilton soon returned to New York. He did, however, become a strong supporter of the proposed Constitution, and one of the writers of the *Federalist* (Document 28).

See M. Farrand, ed., *Records of the Federal Convention of 1787* (4 vols., 1911–1937); C. Rossiter, *1787: The Grand Convention* (1966); and L. W. Levy and D. J. Mahoney, eds., *The Framing and Ratification of the Constitution* (1987).

26a

The Virginia Plan

1.   Resolved that the Articles of Confederation ought to be so corrected and enlarged as to accomplish the objects proposed by their institution; namely "common defence, security of liberty and general welfare."

Source: Jensen, ed., 1 *Documentary History of the Ratification of the Constitution* 243 (1976).

2. Resolved therefore that the rights of suffrage in the National Legislature ought to be proportioned to the Quotas of contribution, or to the number of free inhabitants, as the one or the other rule may seem best in different cases.

3. Resolved that the National Legislature ought to consist of two branches.

4. Resolved that the members of the first branch of the National Legislature ought to be elected by the people of the several States every   for the terms of   ; to be of the age of   years at least, to receive liberal stipends by which they may be compensated for the devotion of their time to public service, to be ineligible to any office established by a particular State, or under the authority of the United States, except those peculiarly belonging to the functions of the first branch, during the term of service, and for the space of   after its expiration; to be incapable of reelection for the space of   after the expiration of their term of service, and to be subject to recall.

5. Resolved that the members of the second branch of the National Legislature ought to be elected by those of the first, out of a proper number of persons nominated by the individual Legislatures, to be of the age of years at least; to hold their offices for a term sufficient to ensure their independency; to receive liberal stipends by which they may be compensated for the devotion of their time to public service; and to be ineligible to any office established by a particular State, or under the authority of the United States, except those peculiarly belonging to the functions of the second branch, during the term of service, and for the space of   after the expiration thereof.

6. Resolved that each branch ought to possess the right of originating Acts; that the National Legislature ought to be impowered to enjoy the Legislative Rights vested in Congress by the Confederation and moreover to legislate in all cases to which the separate States are incompetent, or in which the harmony of the United States may be interrupted by the exercise of individual Legislation; to negative all laws passed by the several States, contravening in the opinion of the National Legislature the articles of Union; and to call forth the force of the Union against any member of the Union failing in its duty under the articles thereof.

7. Resolved that a National Executive be instituted; to be chosen by the National Legislature for the term of   years; to receive punctually, at stated times, a fixed compensation for the services rendered, in which no increase or diminution shall be made so as to affect the Magistracy, existing at the time of the increase or diminution, and to be ineligible a second time; and that besides a general authority to execute the National laws, it ought to enjoy the Executive rights vested in Congress by the Confederation.

8.   Resolved that the Executive and a convenient number of the National Judiciary, ought to compose a Council or revision with authority to examine every act of the National Legislature before it shall operate, and every act of a particular Legislature before a Negative thereon shall be final; and that the dissent of the said Council shall amount to a rejection, unless the Act of the National Legislature be passed again, or that of a particular Legislature be again negatived by   of the members of each branch.

9.   Resolved that a National Judiciary be established to consist of one or more supreme tribunals, and of inferior tribunals to be chosen by the National Legislature, to hold their offices during good behaviour; and to receive punctually at stated times fixed compensation for their services, in which no increase or diminution shall be made so as to affect the persons actually in office at the time of such increase or diminution. That the jurisdiction of the inferior tribunals shall be to hear and determine in the first instance, and of the supreme tribunal to hear and determine in the dernier resort, all piracies and felonies on the high seas, captures from an enemy; cases in which foreigners or citizens of other States applying to such jurisdictions may be interested, or which respect the collection of the National revenue; impeachments of any National officers, and questions which may involve the national peace and harmony.

10.   Resolved that provision ought to be made for the admission of States lawfully arising within the limits of the United States, whether from a voluntary junction of Government and Territory or otherwise, with the consent of a number of voices in the National legislature less than the whole.

11.   Resolved that a Republican Government and the territory of each State, except in the instance of a voluntary junction of Government and territory, ought to be guaranteed by the United States to each State.

12.   Resolved that provision ought to be made for the continuance of Congress and their authorities and privileges, until a given day after the reform of the articles of Union shall be adopted, and for the completion of all their engagements.

13.   Resolved that provision ought to be made for the amendment of the Articles of Union whensoever it shall seem necessary, and that the assent of the National Legislature ought not to be required thereto.

14.   Resolved that the Legislative Executive and Judiciary powers within the several States ought to be bound by oath to support the articles of Union.

15.   Resolved that the amendments which shall be offered to the Confederation, by the Convention ought at a proper time, or times, after the approbation of Congress to be submitted to an assembly or assemblies of Representatives, recommended by the several Legislatures to be expressly chosen by the people, to consider and decide thereon.

The New Jersey Plan

1. Resolved that the Articles of Confederation ought to be so revised, corrected, and enlarged as to render the federal Constitution adequate to the exigencies of Government, and the preservation of the Union.

2. Resolved that in addition to the powers vested in the United States in Congress, by the present existing articles of Confederation, they be authorized to pass acts for raising a revenue, by levying a duty or duties on all goods or merchandizes of foreign growth or manufacture, imported into any part of the United States, by Stamps on paper, vellum or parchment, and by a postage on all letters or packages passing through the general post-office, to be applied to such federal purposes as they shall deem proper and expedient; to make rules and regulations for the collection thereof; and the same from time to time, to alter and amend in such manner as they shall think proper: to pass Acts for the regulation of trade and commerce as well with foreign nations as with each other; provided that all punishments, fines, forfeitures and penalties to be incurred for contravening such acts rules and regulations shall be adjudged by the Common law Judiciaries of the State in which any offence contrary to the true intent and meaning of such Acts rules and regulations shall have been committed or perpetrated, with liberty of commencing in the first instance all suits and prosecutions for that purpose, in the superior common law Judiciary in such state, subject nevertheless, for the correction of errors, both in law and fact in rendering Judgement, to an appeal to the Judiciary of the United States.

3. Resolved that whenever requisitions shall be necessary, instead of the rule for making requisitions mentioned in the articles of Confederation, the United States in Congress be authorized to make such requisitions in proportion to the whole number of white and other free citizens and inhabitants of every age sex and condition including those bound to servitude for a term of years and three fifths of all other persons not comprehended in the foregoing description, except Indians not paying taxes; that if such requisitions be not complied with, in the time specified therein, to direct the collection thereof in the non-complying States and for that purpose to devise and pass acts directing and authorizing the same; provided that none of the powers hereby vested in the United States in Congress shall be exercised without the consent of at least   States, and in that proportion if the number of Confederated States should hereafter be increased or diminished.

Source: Jensen, ed., 1 *Documentary History of the Ratification of the Constitution* 251 (1976).

4.   Resolved that the United States in Congress be authorized to elect a federal Executive to consist of   persons, to continue in office for the term of   years, to receive punctually at stated times a fixed compensation for their services, in which no increase or diminution shall be made so as to affect the persons composing the Executive at the time of such increase or diminution, to be paid out of the federal treasury; to be incapable of holding any other office or appointment during their time of service and for   years thereafter; to be ineligible a second time, and removeable by Congress on application by a majority of the Executives of the several States; that the Executives besides their general authority to execute the federal acts ought to appoint all federal officers not otherwise provided for, and to direct all military operations; provided that none of the persons composing the federal Executive shall on any occasion take command of any troops so as personally to conduct any enterprise as General or in other capacity.

5.   Resolved that a federal Judiciary be established to consist of a supreme tribunal the Judges of which to be appointed by the Executive, and to hold their offices during good behaviour, to receive punctually at stated times a fixed compensation for their services in which no increase or diminution shall be made so as to affect persons actually in office at the time of such increase or diminution; that the Judiciary so established shall have authority to hear and determine in the first instance on all impeachments of federal officers, and by way of appeal in the dernier resort in all cases touching the rights of Ambassadors, in all cases of captures from an enemy, in all cases of piracies and felonies on the high Seas, in all cases in which foreigners may be interested, in the construction of any treaty or treaties, or which may arise on any of the Acts for regulation of trade, or the collection of the federal Revenue: that none of the Judiciary shall during the time they remain in office be capable of receiving or holding any other office or appointment during the time of service, or for thereafter.

6.   Resolved that all Acts of the United States in Congress made by virtue and in pursuance of the powers hereby and by the articles of Confederation vested in them, and all Treaties made and ratified under the authority of the United States, shall be the supreme law of the respective States so far forth as those Acts or Treaties shall relate to the said States or their Citizens, and that the Judiciary of the several States shall be bound thereby in their decisions, any thing in the respective laws of the Individual States to the contrary notwithstanding; and that if any State, or any body of men in any State shall oppose or prevent carrying into execution such acts or treaties, the federal Executive shall be authorized to call forth the power of the Confederated States, or so much thereof as may be necessary to enforce and compel an obedience to such Acts or an observance of such Treaties.

7.   Resolved that provision be made for the admission of new States into the Union.

8.   Resolved the rule for naturalization ought to be the same in every State.

9.   Resolved that a Citizen of one State committing an offence in another State of the Union, shall be deemed guilty of the same offence as if it had been committed by a Citizen of the State in which the offence was committed.

26c

Hamilton's Plan

1.   The Supreme Legislative power of the United States of America to be vested in two distinct bodies of men; the one to be called the Assembly, the other the Senate who together shall form the Legislature of the United States with power to pass all laws whatsoever subject to the Negative hereafter mentioned.

2.   The Assembly to consist of persons elected by the people to serve for three years.

3.   The Senate to consist of persons elected to serve during good behaviour; their election to be made by electors chosen for that purpose by the people. In order to this, the States to be divided into election districts. On the death, removal or resignation of any Senator his place to be filled out of the district from which he came.

4.   The supreme Executive authority of the United States to be vested in a Governor, to be elected to serve during good behaviour—His election to be made by Electors chosen by electors chosen by the people in the Election Districts aforesaid; or by electors chosen for that purpose by the respective Legislatures—provided that if an election be not made within a limited time, the President of the Senate shall be the Governor. The Governor to have a negative upon all laws about to be passed—and the execution of all laws passed—to be the Commander-in-Chief of the land and naval forces and of the militia of the United States—to have the entire direction of war when authorized or begun—to have, with the advice and approbation of the Senate, the power of making all treaties—to have the appointment of the heads

Source: Syrett, ed., 4 *Papers of Alexander Hamilton* 207 (1962).

or chief officers of the departments of finance, war, and foreign affairs—to have the nomination of all other officers (ambassadors to foreign nations included) subject to the approbation or rejection of the Senate—to have the power of pardoning all offences but treason, which he shall not pardon without the approbation of the Senate.

5.   On the death, resignation, or removal of the Governor, his authorities to be exercised by the President of the Senate (until a successor be appointed).

6.   The Senate to have the sole power of declaring war—the power of advising and approving all treaties—the power of approving or rejecting all appointments of officers except the heads or chiefs of the departments of finance, war, and foreign affairs.

7.   The supreme judicial authority of the United States to be vested in twelve judges, to hold their offices during good behavior, with adequate and permanent salaries. This court to have original jurisdiction in all causes of capture, and an appellate jurisdiction (from the courts of the several States) in all causes in which the revenues of the General Government or the citizens of foreign nations are concerned.

8.   The Legislature of the United States to have power to institute courts in each State for the determination of all causes of capture and of all matters relating to their revenues, or in which the citizens of foreign nations are concerned.

9.   The Governor, Senators, and all officers of the United States to be liable to impeachment for mal and corrupt conduct, and upon conviction to be removed from office, and disqualified for holding any place of trust or profit. All impeachments to be tried by a court, to consist of the judges of the Supreme Court, chief or senior judge of the Superior Court of law of each State—provided that such judge hold his place during good behavior and have a permanent salary.

10.   All laws of the particular States contrary to the Constitution or laws of the United States to be utterly void. And the better to prevent such laws being passed the Governor or President of each State shall be appointed by the General Government, and shall have a negative upon the laws about to be passed in the State of which he is Governor or President.

11.   No State to have any forces, land or naval—and the militia of all the States to be under the sole and exclusive direction of the United States, the officers of which to be appointed and commissioned by them.

27

Constitution of the United States (1787)

The Constitution adopted in 1787 has proved remarkably adaptable to the changing needs of the nation. William Gladstone once described it as "the most wonderful work ever struck off at a given time by the brain and purpose of man." In it the Framers summed up not only their own recent experiences in self-government, but centuries of British political thought as well. There has been a debate over whether the Constitution represents a "conservative counter-revolution" to the democratic principles of the Declaration of Independence embodied in the Articles of Confederation. Both constitutions derived from the same corpus of English thought, although they emphasized different strands. One can compare sections, but one should also remember that a constitution, unlike a statute, is not designed to be static or inflexible. How and what the Constitution became is in many ways more important than what the so-called "original intent" of the Framers may have been, although in the 1980s there has been some spirited debate on this issue.

See M. Kammen, ed., *The Origins of the American Constitution: A Documentary History* (1986); F. McDonald, *Novus Ordo Seclorum: The Intellectual Origins of the Constitution* (1985); and C. Rossiter, *1787: The Grand Convention* (1966).

We the People of the United States, in Order to form a more perfect Union, establish Justice, insure domestic Tranquility, provide for the common defence, promote the general Welfare, and secure the Blessings of Liberty to ourselves and our Posterity, do ordain and establish this Constitution for the United States of America.

Article I

Section 1.   All legislative Powers herein granted shall be vested in a Congress of the United States, which shall consist of a Senate and House of Representatives.

Source: 1 *U.S.C.A.* 25 (1987).

Section 2.   The House of Representatives shall be composed of Members chosen every second Year by the People of the several States, and the Electors in each State shall have the Qualifications requisite for Electors of the most numerous Branch of the State Legislature.

No Person shall be a Representative who shall not have attained to the Age of twenty five Years, and been seven Years a Citizen of the United States, and who shall not, when elected, be an Inhabitant of that State in which he shall be chosen.

Representatives and direct Taxes shall be apportioned among the several States which may be included within this Union, according to their respective Numbers, which shall be determined by adding to the whole Number of free Persons, including those bound to Service for a Term of Years, and excluding Indians not taxed, three fifths of all other Persons. The actual Enumeration shall be made within three Years after the first Meeting of the Congress of the United States, and within every subsequent Term of ten Years, in such Manner as they shall by Law direct. The Number of Representatives shall not exceed one for every thirty Thousand, but each State shall have at Least one Representative; and until such enumeration shall be made, the State of New Hampshire shall be entitled to chuse three, Massachusetts eight, Rhode Island and Providence Plantations one, Connecticut five, New-York six, New Jersey four, Pennsylvania eight, Delaware one, Maryland six, Virginia ten, North Carolina five, South Carolina five, and Georgia three.

When vacancies happen in the Representation from any State, the Executive Authority thereof shall issue Writs of Election to fill such Vacancies.

The House of Representatives shall chuse their Speaker and other Officers; and shall have the sole Power of Impeachment.

Section 3.   The Senate of the United States shall be composed of two Senators from each State, chosen by the Legislature thereof, for six Years; and each Senator shall have one Vote.

Immediately after they shall be assembled in Consequence of the first Election, they shall be divided as equally as may be into three Classes. The Seats of the Senators of the first Class shall be vacated at the Expiration of the second Year, of the second Class at the Expiration of the fourth Year, and of the third Class at the Expiration of the sixth Year, so that one third may be chosen every second Year; and if Vacancies happen by Resignation, or otherwise, during the Recess of the Legislature of any State, the Executive thereof may make temporary Appointments until the next Meeting of the Legislature, which shall then fill such Vacancies.

No Person shall be a Senator who shall not have attained to the Age of thirty Years, and been nine Years a Citizen of the United States, and who shall not, when elected, be an Inhabitant of that State for which he shall be chosen.

The Vice President of the United States shall be President of the Senate, but shall have no Vote, unless they be equally divided.

The Senate shall chuse their other Officers, and also a President pro tempore, in the Absence of the Vice President, or when he shall exercise the Office of President of the United States.

The Senate shall have the sole Power to try all Impeachments. When sitting for that Purpose, they shall be on Oath or Affirmation. When the President of the United States is tried the Chief Justice shall preside: And no Person shall be convicted without the Concurrence of two thirds of the Members present.

Judgment in Cases of Impeachment shall not extend further than to removal from Office, and disqualification to hold and enjoy any Office of honor, Trust or Profit under the United States: but the Party convicted shall nevertheless be liable and subject to Indictment, Trial, Judgment and Punishment, according to Law.

Section 4.   The Times, Places and Manner of holding Elections for Senators and Representatives, shall be prescribed in each State by the Legislature thereof; but the Congress may at any time by Law make or alter such Regulations, except as to the Places of chusing Senators.

The Congress shall assemble at least once in every Year, and such Meeting shall be on the first Monday in December, unless they shall by Law appoint a different Day.

Section 5.   Each House shall be the Judge of the Elections, Returns and Qualifications of its own Members, and a Majority of each shall constitute a Quorum to do Business; but a smaller Number may adjourn from day to day, and may be authorized to compel the Attendance of absent Members, in such Manner, and under such Penalties as each House may provide.

Each House may determine the Rules of its Proceedings, punish its Members for disorderly Behaviour, and, with the Concurrence of two thirds, expel a Member.

Each House shall keep a Journal of its Proceedings, and from time to time publish the same, excepting such Parts as may in their Judgment require Secrecy; and the Yeas and Nays of the Members of either House on any question shall, at the Desire of one fifth of those Present, be entered on the Journal.

Neither House, during the Session of Congress, shall, without the Consent of the other, adjourn for more than three days, nor to any other Place than that in which the two Houses shall be sitting.

Section 6.   The Senators and Representatives shall receive a Compensation for their Services, to be ascertained by law, and paid out of the Treasury of the United States. They shall in all Cases, except Treason, Felony and Breach of the Peace, be privileged from Arrest during their Attendance at the Session of their respective Houses, and in going to and returning from the same; and for any Speech or Debate in either House, they shall not be questioned in any other Place.

No Senator or Representative shall, during the Time for which he was elected, be appointed to any civil Office under the Authority of the United States, which shall have been created, or the Emoluments whereof shall have been encreased during such time; and no Person holding any Office under the United States, shall be a Member of either House during his Continuance in Office.

Section 7. All Bills for raising Revenue shall originate in the House of Representatives; but the Senate may propose or concur with amendments as on other Bills.

Every Bill which shall have passed the House of Representatives and the Senate, shall, before it become a Law, be presented to the President of the United States; If he approve he shall sign it, but if not he shall return it with his Objections to that House in which it shall have originated, who shall enter the Objections at large on their Journal, and proceed to reconsider it. If after such Reconsiderations two thirds of that House shall agree to pass the Bill, it shall be sent, together with the Objections, to the other House, by which it shall likewise be reconsidered, and if approved by two thirds of that House, it shall become a Law. But in all such Cases the Votes of both Houses shall be determined by Yeas and Nays, and the Names of the Persons voting for and against the Bill shall be entered on the Journal of each House respectively. If any Bill shall not be returned by the President within ten Days (Sunday excepted) after it shall have been presented to him, the Same shall be a Law, in like Manner as if he had signed it, unless the Congress by their Adjournment prevent its Return, in which Case it shall not be a Law.

Every Order, Resolution, or Vote to which the Concurrence of the Senate and House of Representatives may be necessary (except on a question of Adjournment) shall be presented to the President of the United States; and before the Same shall take Effect, shall be approved by him, or being disapproved by him, shall be repassed by two thirds of the Senate and House of Representatives, according to the Rules and Limitations prescribed in the Case of a Bill.

Section 8.   The Congress shall have Power To lay and collect Taxes, Duties, Imposts and Excises, to pay the Debts and provide for the common Defence and general Welfare of the United States; but all Duties, Imposts and Excises shall be uniform throughout the United States;

To borrow Money on the credit of the United States;

To regulate Commerce with foreign Nations, and among the several States, and with the Indian Tribes;

To establish an uniform Rule of Naturalization, and uniform Laws on the subject of Bankruptcies throughout the United States;

To coin Money, regulate the Value thereof, and of foreign Coin, and fix the Standard of Weights and Measures;

To provide for the Punishment of counterfeiting the Securities and current Coin of the United States;

To establish Post Offices and post Roads;

To promote the Progress of Science and useful Arts, by securing for limited Times to Authors and Inventors the exclusive Right to their respective Writings and Discoveries;

To constitute Tribunals inferior to the supreme Court;

To define and punish Piracies and Felonies committed on the high Seas, and Offences against the Law of Nations;

To declare War, grant Letters of Marque and Reprisal, and make Rules concerning Captures on Land and Water;

To raise and support Armies, but no Appropriation of Money to that Use shall be for a longer Term than two Years;

To provide and maintain a Navy;

To make Rules for the Government and Regulation of the land and naval Forces;

To provide for calling forth the Militia to execute the Laws of the Union, suppress Insurrections and repel Invasions;

To provide for organizing, arming, and disciplining, the Militia, and for governing such Part of them as may be employed in the Service of the United States, reserving to the States respectively, the Appointment of the Officers, and the Authority of training the Militia according to the discipline prescribed by Congress;

To exercise exclusive Legislation in all Cases whatsoever, over such District (not exceeding ten Miles square) as may, by Cession of particular States, and the Acceptance of Congress, become the Seat of the Government of the United States, and to exercise like Authority over all Places purchased by the Consent of the Legislature of the State in which the Same shall be, for the Erection of Forts, Magazines, Arsenals, dock-Yards, and other needful Buildings;—And

To make all Laws which shall be necessary and proper for carrying into Execution the foregoing Powers, and all other Powers vested by this Constitution in the Government of the United States, or in any Department or Officer thereof.

Section 9.   The Migration or Importation of such Persons as any of the States now existing shall think proper to admit, shall not be prohibited by the Congress prior to the Year one thousand eight hundred and eight, but a Tax or duty may be imposed on such Importation, not exceeding ten dollars for each Person.

The Privilege of the Writ of Habeas Corpus shall not be suspended, unless when in Cases of Rebellion or Invasion the public Safety may require it.

No Bill of Attainder or ex post facto Law shall be passed.

No Capitation, or other direct, Tax shall be laid, unless in Proportion to the Census or Enumeration herein before directed to be taken.

No Tax or Duty shall be laid on Articles exported from any State.

No Preference shall be given by any Regulation of Commerce or Revenue to the Ports of one State over those of another; nor shall Vessels bound to, or from, one State, be obliged to enter, clear or pay Duties in another.

No Money shall be drawn from the Treasury, but in Consequence of Appropriations made by Law; and a regular Statement and Account of the Receipts and Expenditures of all public Money shall be published from time to time.

No Title of Nobility shall be granted by the United States: And no Person holding any Office of Profit or Trust under them, shall, without the Consent of the Congress, accept of any present, Emolument, Office, or Title, of any kind whatever, from any King, Prince or foreign State.

Section 10.   No State shall enter into any Treaty, Alliance, or Confederation; grant Letters of Marque and Reprisal, coin Money; emit Bills of Credit, make any Thing but gold and silver Coin a Tender in Payment of Debts; pass any Bill of Attainder, ex post facto Law, or Law impairing the Obligation of Contracts, or grant any Title of Nobility.

No State shall, without the Consent of the Congress, lay any Imposts or Duties on Imports or Exports, except what may be absolutely necessary for executing its inspection Laws: and the net Produce of all Duties and Imposts, laid by any State on Imports or Exports, shall be for the Use of the Treasury of the United States; and all such Laws shall be subject to the Revision and Controul of the Congress.

No State shall, without the Consent of Congress, lay any Duty of Tonnage, keep Troops, or Ships of War in time of Peace, enter into any Agreement or Compact with another State, or with a foreign Power, or engage in War, unless actually invaded, or in such imminent Danger as will not admit of delay.

Article II

Section 1.   The executive Power shall be vested in a President of the United States of America. He shall hold his Office during the Term of four Years, and, together with the Vice President, chosen for the same Term, be elected, as follows

Each State shall appoint, In such Manner as the Legislature thereof may direct, a Number of Electors, equal to the whole Number of Senators and Representatives to which the State may be entitled in the Congress: but no Senator or Representative, or Person holding an Office of Trust or Profit under the United States, shall be appointed an Elector.

The Electors shall meet in their respective States, and vote by Ballot for two Persons, of whom one at least shall not be an Inhabitant of the same State with themselves. And they shall make a List of all the Persons voted for, and of the number of Votes for each; which List they shall sign and certify, and transmit sealed to the Seat of the Government of the United States, directed to the President of the Senate. The President of the Senate shall, in the Presence of the Senate and House of Representatives, open all the Certificates, and the Votes shall then be counted. The Person having the greatest number of Votes shall be the President, if such Number be a Majority of the whole Number of Electors appointed; and if there be more than one who have such Majority, and have an equal Number of Votes, then the House of Representatives shall immediately chuse by Ballot one of them for President; and if no Person have a Majority, then from the five highest on the List the said House shall in like Manner chuse the President. But in chusing the President, the Votes shall be taken by States, the Representation from each State having one Vote; a quorum for this Purpose shall consist of a Member or Members from two thirds of the States, and a Majority of all the States shall be necessary to a Choice. In every Case, after the Choice of the President, the Person having the greatest Number of Votes of the Electors shall be the Vice President. But if there should remain two or more who have equal Votes, the Senate shall chuse from them by Ballot the Vice President.

The Congress may determine the Time of chusing the Electors, and the Day on which they shall give their Votes; which Day shall be the same throughout the United States.

No Person except a natural born Citizen, or a Citizen of the United States, at the time of the Adoption of this Constitution, shall be eligible to the Office of President; neither shall any Person be eligible to that Office who shall not have attained to the Age of thirty five Years, and been fourteen Years a Resident within the United States.

In Case of the Removal of the President from Office, or of his Death, Resignation, or Inability to discharge the Powers and Duties of the said Office, the Same shall devolve on the Vice President, and the Congress may by Law provide for the Case of Removal, Death, Resignation or Inability, both of the President and Vice President, declaring what Officer shall then act as President, and such Officer shall act accordingly, until the Disability be removed, or a President shall be elected.

The President shall, at stated Times, receive for his Services, a Compensation, which shall neither be encreased nor diminished during the Period for which he shall have been elected, and he shall not receive within that Period any other emolument from the United States, or any of them.

Before he enter on the Execution of his Office, he shall take the following Oath or Affirmation:—"I do solemnly swear (or affirm) that I will faithfully execute the Office of President of the United States, and will to the best of my Ability, preserve, protect and defend the Constitution of the United States."

Section 2.   The President shall be Commander in Chief of the Army and Navy of the United States, and of the Militia of the several States, when called into the actual Service of the United States; he may require the Opinion, in writing, of the principal Officer in each of the executive Departments, upon any Subject relating to the Duties of their respective Offices, and he shall have Power to grant Reprieves and Pardons for Offences against the United States, except in Cases of Impeachment.

He shall have Power, by and with the Advice and Consent of the Senate, to make Treaties, provided two thirds of the Senators present concur; and he shall nominate, and by and with the Advice and Consent of the Senate, shall appoint Ambassadors, other public Ministers and Consuls, Judges of the supreme Court, and all other Officers of the United States, whose Appointments are not herein otherwise provided for, and which shall be established by Law: but the Congress may by Law vest the Appointment of such inferior Officers, as they think proper, in the President alone, in the Courts of Law, or in the Heads of Departments.

The President shall have Power to fill up all Vacancies that may happen during the Recess of the Senate, by granting Commissions which shall expire at the End of their next Session.

Section 3.   He shall from time to time give to the Congress Information of the State of the Union, and recommend to their Consideration such Measures as he shall judge necessary and expedient; he may, on extraordinary Occasions, convene both Houses, or either of them, and in Case of Disagreements between them, with Respect to the Time of Adjournment, he may adjourn them to such Time as he shall think proper; he shall receive Ambassadors and other public Ministers; he shall take Care that the Laws be faithfully executed, and shall Commission all the Officers of the United States.

Section 4.   The President, Vice President and all Civil Officers of the United States, shall be removed from Office on Impeachment for, and Conviction of, Treason, Bribery, or other high Crimes and Misdemeanors.

Article III

Section 1.   The judicial Power of the United States, shall be vested in one supreme Court, and in such inferior Courts as the Congress may from time to time ordain and establish. The Judges, both of the supreme and inferior Courts, shall hold their Offices during good Behaviour, and shall, at stated Times, receive for their Services, a Compensation, which shall not be diminished during their Continuance in Office.

Section 2.   The judicial Power shall extend to all Cases, in Law and Equity, arising under this Constitution, the Laws of the United States, and Treaties made, or which shall be made, under their Authority;—to all Cases affecting Ambassadors, other public Ministers and Consuls;—to all Cases of admiralty and maritime Jurisdiction;—to Controversies to which the United States shall be a Party;—to Controversies between two or more States;—between a State and Citizens of another State;—between Citizens of different States;—between Citizens of the same State claiming Lands under Grants of different States, and between a State, or the Citizens thereof, and foreign States, Citizens or Subjects.

In all Cases affecting Ambassadors, other public Ministers and Consuls, and those in which a State shall be Party, the Supreme Court shall have original Jurisdiction. In all the other Cases before mentioned, the supreme Court shall have appelate Jurisdiction, both as to Law and Fact, with such Exceptions, and under such Regulations as the Congress shall make.

The Trial of all Crimes, except in Cases of Impeachment, shall be by Jury; and such Trial shall be held in the State where the said Crimes shall have been committed; but when not committed within any State, the Trial shall be at such Place or Places as the Congress may by Law have directed.

Section 3.   Treason against the United States, shall consist only in levying War against them, or in adhering to their Enemies, giving them Aid and Comfort. No Person shall be convicted of Treason unless on the Testimony of two Witnesses to the same overt Act, or on Confession in open Court.

The Congress shall have Power to declare the Punishment of Treason, but no Attainder of Treason shall work Corruption of Blood, or Forfeiture except during the Life of the Person attainted.

Article IV

Section 1.   Full Faith and Credit shall be given in each State to the public Acts, Records, and judicial Proceedings of every other State. And the Congress may by general Laws prescribe the Manner in which such Acts, Records and Proceedings shall be proved, and the Effect thereof.

Section 2.   The Citizens of each State shall be entitled to all Privileges and Immunities of Citizens in the several States.

A Person charged in any State with Treason, Felony, or other Crime, who shall flee from Justice, and be found in another State, shall on Demand of the executive Authority of the State from which he fled, be delivered up, to be removed to the State having Jurisdiction of the Crime.

No Person held to Service or Labour in one State, under the Laws thereof, escaping into another, shall, in Consequence of any Law or Regulation therein, be discharged from such Service or Labour, but shall be delivered up on Claim of the Party to whom such Service or Labour may be due.

Section 3.   New States may be admitted by the Congress into this Union; but no new State shall be formed or erected within the Jurisdiction of any other State; nor any State be formed by the Junction of two or more States, or Parts of States, without the Consent of the Legislatures of the States concerned as well as of the Congress.

The Congress shall have Power to dispose of and make all needful Rules and Regulations respecting the Territory or other Property belonging to the United States; and nothing in this Constitution shall be so construed as to Prejudice any Claims of the United States, or of any particular State.

Section 4.   The United States shall guarantee to every State in this Union a Republican Form of Government, and shall protect each of them against

Invasion; and on Application of the Legislature, or of the Executive (when the Legislature cannot be convened) against domestic Violence.

Article V

The Congress, whenever two thirds of both Houses shall deem it necessary, shall propose Amendments to this Constitution, or, on the Application of the Legislatures of two thirds of the several States, shall call a Convention for proposing Amendments, which, in either Case, shall be valid to all Intents and Purposes, as Part of this Constitution, when ratified by the Legislatures of three fourths of the several States, or by Conventions in three fourths thereof, as the one or the other Mode of Ratification may be proposed by the Congress; provided that no Amendment which may be made prior to the Year One thousand eight hundred and eight shall in any Manner affect the first and fourth Clauses in the Ninth Section of the first Article; and that no State, without its Consent, shall be deprived of its equal Suffrage in the Senate.

Article VI

All Debts contracted and Engagements entered into, before the Adoption of this Constitution, shall be as valid against the United States under this Constitution, as under the Confederation.

This Constitution, and the Laws of the United States which shall be made in Pursuance thereof; and all Treaties made, or which shall be made, under the Authority of the United States, shall be the supreme Law of the Land; and the Judges in every State shall be bound thereby, any Thing in the Constitution or Laws of any State to the Contrary notwithstanding.

The Senators and Representatives before mentioned, and the Members of the several State Legislatures, and all executive and judicial Officers, both of the United States and of the several States, shall be bound by Oath or Affirmation, to support this Constitution; but no religious Test shall ever be required as a Qualification to any Office or public Trust under the United States.

Article VII

The Ratification of the Conventions of nine States, shall be sufficient for the Establishment of this Constitution between the States so ratifying the Same.

Done in Convention by the Unanimous Consent of the States present the Seventeenth Day of September in the Year of our Lord one thousand seven hundred and Eighty seven and of the Independence of the United States of

America the Twelfth. In witness thereof We have hereunto subscribed our Names,

GEORGE WASHINGTON—President
and Deputy from Virginia

New Hampshire	John Langdon Nicholas Gilman		George Read Gunning Bedford, Junior
Massachusetts	Nathaniel Gorham Rufus King	**Delaware**	John Dickinson Richard Bassett Jacob Broom

Connecticut	William Samuel
	  Johnson
	Roger Sherman
		Maryland	James McHenry
			Daniel of St. Tho.
			  Jenifer

New York	Alexander Hamilton		Daniel Carroll
New Jersey	William Livingston David A. Brearley William Paterson Jonathan Dayton	**Virginia**	John Blair James Madison Jr.
Pennsylvania	Benjamin Franklin Thomas Mifflin Robert Morris George Clymer Thomas FitzSimons Jared Ingersoll James Wilson Gouverneur Morris	**North Carolina**	William Blount Richard Dobbs Spaight Hugh Williamson
		South Carolina	John Rutledge Charles Cotesworth Pinckney Charles Pinckney Pierce Butler
		Georgia	William Few Abraham Baldwin

Articles in Addition to, and Amendment of, the Constitution of the United States of America, Proposed by Congress, and Ratified by the Several States, Pursuant to the Fifth Article of the Original Constitution.

Amendment I

Congress shall make no law respecting an establishment of religion, or prohibiting the free exercise thereof; or abridging the freedom of speech, or of the press; or the right of the people peaceably to assemble, and to petition the Government for a redress of grievances.

Amendment II

A well regulated Militia, being necessary to the security of a free State, the right of the people to keep and bear Arms, shall not be infringed.

Amendment III

No Soldier shall, in time of peace be quartered in any house, without the consent of the Owner, nor in time of war, but in a manner to be prescribed by law.

Amendment IV

The right of the people to be secure in their persons, houses, papers, and effects, against unreasonable searches and seizures, shall not be violated, and no Warrants shall issue, but upon probable cause, supported by Oath or affirmation, and particularly describing the place to be searched, and the persons or things to be seized.

Amendment V

No person shall be held to answer for a capital, or otherwise infamous crime, unless on a presentment or indictment of a Grand Jury, except in cases arising in the land or naval forces, or in the Militia, when in actual service in time of War or public danger; nor shall any person be subject for the same offence to be twice put in jeopardy of life or limb; nor shall be compelled in any criminal case to be a witness against himself, nor be deprived of life, liberty, or property, without due process of law; nor shall private property be taken for public use, without just compensation.

Amendment VI

In all criminal prosecutions, the accused shall enjoy the right to a speedy and public trial by an impartial jury of the State and district wherein the crime shall have been committed, which district shall have been previously ascertained by law, and to be informed of the nature and cause of the accusation; to be confronted with the witness against him; to have compulsory process for obtaining Witnesses in his favor, and to have the Assistance of Counsel for his defence.

Amendment VII

In Suits at common law, where the value in controversy shall exceed twenty dollars, the right of trial by jury shall be preserved, and no fact tried by a jury, shall be otherwise re-examined in any Court of the United States, than according to the rules of the common law.

Amendment VIII

Excessive bail shall not be required, nor excessive fines imposed, nor cruel and unusual punishments inflicted.

Amendment IX

The enumeration in the Constitution, of certain rights, shall not be construed to deny or disparage others retained by the people.

Amendment X

The powers not delegated to the United States by the Constitution, nor prohibited by it to the States, are reserved to the States respectively, or to the people. [The first ten amendments were ratified Dec. 15, 1791.]

Amendment XI

The Judicial power of the United States shall not be construed to extend to any suit in law or equity, commenced or prosecuted against one of the United States by Citizens of another State, or by Citizens or Subjects of any Foreign State. [Jan. 8, 1798]

Amendment XII

The Electors shall meet in their respective states and vote by ballot for President and Vice-President, one of whom, at least, shall not be an inhabitant of the same state with themselves; they shall name in their ballots the person voted for as President, and in distinct ballots the person voted for as Vice-President, and they shall make distinct lists of all persons voted for as President, and of all persons voted for as Vice-President, and of the number of votes for each, which lists they shall sign and certify, and transmit sealed to the seat of the government of the United States, directed to the President of the Senate;—The President of the Senate shall, in the presence of the Senate and House of Representatives, open all the certificates and the votes shall then be counted;—The person having the greatest number of votes for President, shall be the President, if such number be a majority of the whole number of Electors appointed; and if no person have such majority, then from the persons having the highest numbers not exceeding three on the list of those voted for as President, the House of Representatives shall choose immediately, by ballot, the President. But in choosing the President, the votes shall be taken by states, the representation from each state having one vote; a quorum for this purpose shall consist of a member or members from two-thirds of the states, and a majority of all the states shall be necessary to a choice. And if the House of Representatives shall not choose a President whenever the right of choice shall devolve upon them, before the fourth day of March next following, then the Vice-President shall act as President, as in the case of the death or other constitutional disability of the President—The person having the greatest number of votes as Vice-President, shall be the Vice-President, if such number be a majority of the whole number of Electors appointed, and if no person have a majority, then from the two highest numbers on the list, the Senate shall choose the Vice-President; a quorum for the purpose shall consist of two-thirds of the whole number of Senators, and a majority of the whole number shall be necessary to a choice. But no person constitutionally ineligible to the office of President shall be eligible to that of Vice-President of the United States. [Sept. 25, 1804]

Amendment XIII

Section 1.   Neither slavery nor involuntary servitude, except as a punishment for crime whereof the party shall have been duly convicted, shall exist within the United States, or any place subject to their jurisdiction.

Section 2.   Congress shall have power to enforce this article by appropriate legislation. [Dec. 18, 1865]

Amendment IV

Section 1.   All persons born or naturalized in the United States and subject to the jurisdiction thereof, are citizens of the United States and of the State wherein they reside. No State shall make or enforce any law which shall abridge the privileges or immunities of citizens of the United States; nor shall any State deprive any person of life, liberty, or property, without due process of law; nor deny any person within its jurisdiction the equal protection of the laws.

Section 2.   Representatives shall be apportioned among the several States according to their respective numbers, counting the whole number of persons in each State, excluding Indians not taxed. But when the right to vote at any election for the choice of electors for President and Vice President of the United States, Representatives in Congress, the Executive and Judicial officers of a State, or the members of the Legislature thereof, is denied to any of the male inhabitants of such State, being twenty-one years of age, and citizens of the United States, or in any way abridged, except for participation in rebellion, or other crime, the basis of representation therein shall be reduced in the proportion which the number of such male citizens shall bear to the whole number of male citizens twenty-one years of age in such State.

Section 3.   No person shall be a Senator or Representative in Congress, or elector of President and Vice President, or hold any office, civil or military, under the United States, or under any State, who, having previously taken an oath, as a member of Congress, or as an officer of the United States, or as a member of any State legislature, or as an executive or judicial officer of any State, to support the Constitution of the United States, shall have engaged in insurrection or rebellion against the same, or given aid or comfort to the enemies thereof. But Congress may by a vote of two-thirds of each House, remove such disability.

Section 4.   The validity of the public debt of the United States, authorized by law, including debts incurred for payment of pensions and bounties for services in suppressing insurrection or rebellion, shall not be questioned. But neither the United States nor any State shall assume or pay any debt or obligation incurred in aid of insurrection or rebellion against the United States, or any claim for the loss or emancipation of any slave; but all such debts, obligations and claims shall be held illegal and void.

Section 5.   The Congress shall have power to enforce by appropriate legislation, the provisions of this article. [July 28, 1868]

Amendment XV

Section 1.   The right of citizens of the United States to vote shall not be denied or abridged by the United States or by any State on account of race, color, or previous condition of servitude.

Section 2.   The Congress shall have power to enforce this article by appropriate legislation. [March 30, 1870]

Amendment XVI

The Congress shall have power to lay and collect taxes on incomes, from whatever source derived, without apportionment among the several States, and without regard to any census or enumeration. [Feb. 25, 1913]

Amendment XVII

The Senate of the United States shall be composed of two Senators from each State, elected by the people thereof, for six years; and each Senator shall have one vote. The electors in each State shall have the qualifications requisite for electors of the most numerous branch of the State legislatures.

When vacancies happen in the representation of any State in the Senate, the executive authority of such State shall issue writs of election to fill such vacancies: *Provided,* That the legislature of any State may empower the executive thereof to make temporary appointments until the people fill the vacancies by election as the legislature may direct.

This amendment shall not be so construed as to affect the election or term of any Senator chosen before it becomes valid as part of the Constitution. [May 31, 1913]

Amendment XVIII

Section 1.   After one year from the ratification of this article the manufacture, sale, or transportation of intoxicating liquors within, the importation thereof into, or the exportation thereof from the United States and all territory subject to the jurisdiction thereof for beverage purposes is hereby prohibited.

Section 2.   The Congress and the several States shall have concurrent power to enforce this article by appropriate legislation.

Section 3.   This article shall be inoperative unless it shall have been ratified as an amendment to the Constitution by the legislatures of the several States, as provided in the Constitution, within seven years from the date of the submission hereof to the States by the Congress. [Jan. 29, 1919]

Amendment XIX

The right of citizens of the United States to vote shall not be denied or abridged by the United States or by any State on account of sex.

Congress shall have power to enforce this article by appropriate legislation. [Aug. 26, 1920]

Amendment XX

Section 1.   The terms of the President and Vice President shall end at noon on the 20th day of January, and the terms of Senators and Representatives at noon on the 3d day of January, of the years in which such terms would have ended if this article had not been ratified; and the terms of their successors shall then begin.

Section 2.   The Congress shall assemble at least once in every year, and such meeting shall begin at noon on the 3d day of January, unless they shall by law appoint a different day.

Section 3.   If, at the time fixed for the beginning of the term of the President, the President elect shall have died, the Vice President elect shall become President. If a President shall not have been chosen before the time fixed for the beginning of his term, or if the President elect shall have failed to qualify, then the Vice President elect shall act as President until a President shall have qualified; and the Congress may by law provide for the case wherein neither a President elect nor a Vice President elect shall have qualified, declaring who shall then act as President, or the manner in which one who is to act shall be selected, and such person shall act accordingly until a President or Vice President shall have qualified.

Section 4.   The Congress may by law provide for the case of the death of any of the persons for whom the House of Representatives may choose a President whenever the right of choice shall have devolved upon them, and for the case of the death of any of the persons from whom the Senate may choose a Vice President whenever the right of choice shall have devolved upon them.

Section 5.   Sections 1 and 2 shall take effect on the 15th day of October following the ratification of this article.

Section 6.   This article shall be inoperative unless it shall have been ratified as an amendment to the Constitution by the legislatures of three-fourths of the several States within seven years from the date of its submission. [Feb. 6, 1933]

Amendment XXI

Section 1.   The eighteenth article of amendment to the Constitution of the United States is hereby repealed.

Section 2.   The transportation or importation into any State, Territory, or possession of the United States for delivery or use therein of intoxicating liquors, in violation of the laws thereof, is hereby prohibited.

Section 3.   This article shall be inoperative unless it shall have been ratified as an amendment to the Constitution by conventions in the several States, as provided in the Constitution, within seven years from the date of the submission hereof to the States by the Congress. [Dec. 5, 1933]

Amendment XXII

Section 1.   No person shall be elected to the office of the President more than twice, and no person who has held the office of President, or acted as President, for more than two years of a term to which some other person was elected President shall be elected to the office of the President more than once. But this Article shall not apply to any person holding the office of President when this Article was proposed by the Congress, and shall not prevent any person who may be holding the office of President, or acting as President, during the term within which this Article becomes operative from holding the office of President or acting as President during the remainder of such term.

Section 2.   This article shall be inoperative unless it shall have been ratified as an amendment to the Constitution by the legislatures of three-fourths of the several States within seven years from the date of its submission to the States by the Congress. [Feb. 27, 1951]

Amendment XXIII

Section 1.   The District constituting the seat of Government of the United States shall appoint in such manner as the Congress may direct:

A number of electors of President and Vice President equal to the whole number of Senators and Representatives in Congress to which the District would be entitled if it were a State, but in no event more than the least populous State; they shall be in addition to those appointed by the States, but they shall be considered, for the purposes of the election of President and Vice President, to be electors appointed by a State; and they shall meet in the District and perform such duties as provided by the twelfth article of amendment.

Section 2.   The Congress shall have power to enforce this article by appropriate legislation. [Mar. 29, 1961]

Amendment XXIV

Section 1.   The right of citizens of the United States to vote in any primary or other election for President or Vice President, for electors for President or Vice President, or for Senator or Representative in Congress, shall not be denied or abridged by the United States or any State by reason of failure to pay any poll tax or other tax.

Section 2.   The Congress shall have power to enforce this article by appropriate legislation. [Jan. 23, 1964]

Amendment XXV

Section 1.   In case of the removal of the President from office or of his death or resignation, the Vice President shall become President.

Section 2.   Whenever there is a vacancy in the office of the Vice President, the President shall nominate a Vice President who shall take office upon confirmation by a majority vote of both Houses of Congress.

Section 3.   Whenever the President transmits to the President pro tempore of the Senate and the Speaker of the House of Representatives his written declaration that he is unable to discharge the powers and duties of his office, and until he transmits to them a written declaration to the contrary, such powers and duties shall be discharged by the Vice President as Acting President.

Section 4.   Whenever the Vice President and a majority of either the principal officers of the executive departments or of such other body as Congress may by law provide, transmit to the President pro tempore of the Senate and the Speaker of the House of Representatives their written declaration that the President is unable to discharge the powers and duties of his office, the Vice President shall immediately assume the powers and duties of the office as Acting President.

Thereafter, when the President transmits to the President pro tempore of the Senate and the Speaker of the House of Representatives his written declaration that no inability exists, he shall resume the powers and duties of his office unless the Vice President and a majority of either the principal officers of the executive department or of such other body as Congress may by law provide, transmit within four days to the President pro tempore of the Senate and the Speaker of the House of Representatives their written declaration that the President is unable to discharge the powers and duties of his office. Thereupon Congress shall decide the issue, assembling within forty-eight hours for that purpose if not in session. If the Congress, within twenty-one days after receipt of the latter written declaration, or, if Congress is not in session, within twenty-one days after Congress is required to assemble, determines by two-thirds vote of both Houses that the President is unable to discharge the powers and duties of his office, the Vice President shall continue to discharge the same as Acting President; otherwise, the President shall resume the powers and duties of his office. [Feb. 10, 1967]

Amendment XXVI

Section 1.   The right of citizens of the United States, who are eighteen years of age or older, to vote shall not be denied or abridged by the United States or by any State on account of age.

Section 2.   The Congress shall have power to enforce this article by appropriate legislation. [June 30, 1971]

28

Objections to the Proposed Constitution (1787)

GEORGE MASON

Until recently, those opposed to the ratification of the Constitution, the anti-federalists, were dismissed as, in the words of one author, "men of little faith." Today there is a renewed appreciation of their political ideas and how they affected the future development of constitutional thought. George Mason had been one of the Virginia delegates to the Philadelphia convention, but he refused to sign the document primarily because it lacked a bill of rights. The following critique was drafted

Source: Lewis, ed., *Anti-Federalists versus Federalists* 65 (1967).

while he was still at Philadelphia, and then published afterward in opposition to ratification.

See H. J. Storing and M. Dry, eds., *The Complete Anti-Federalist* (7 vols., 1981); S. R. Boyd, *The Politics of Opposition: Antifederalists and the Acceptance of the Constitution* (1979); and J. H. Hutson, "Country, Court, and Constitution: Antifederalism and the Historians," 38 *W. and M.Q.* 337 (1981).

~~~~~~

There is no Declaration of Rights; and the Laws of the general Government being paramount to the Laws and Constitutions of the several States, the Declaration of Rights in the separate States are no Security. Nor are the people secured even in the Enjoyment of the Benefits of the common-Law: which stands here upon no other Foundation than its having been adopted by the respective Acts forming the Constitutions of the several States.

In the House of Representatives there is not the Substance, but the Shadow only of Representation; which can never produce proper Information in the Legislature, or inspire Confidence in the People: the Laws will therefore be generally made by Men little concern'd in, and unacquainted with their Effects and Consequences.*

The Senate have the Power of altering all Money-Bills, and of originating Appropriations of Money and the Sallerys of the Officers of their own Appointment in Conjunction with the President of the United States; altho' they are not the Representatives of the People, or amenable to them.

These with their other great Powers (vizt. their Power in the Appointment of Ambassadors and all public Officers, in making Treaties, and in trying all Impeachments) their Influence upon and Connection with the supreme Executive from these Causes, their Duration of Office, and their being a constant existing Body almost continually sitting, joined with their being one compleat Branch of the Legislature, will destroy any Balance in the Government, and enable them to accomplish what Usurpations they please upon the Rights and Libertys of the People.

The Judiciary of the United States is so constructed and extended, as to absorb and destroy the Judiciarys of the several States; thereby rendering Law as tedious[,] intricate and expensive, and Justice as unattainable, by a great part of the Community, as in England, and enabling the Rich to oppress and ruin the Poor.

The President of the United States has no constitutional Council (a thing unknown in any safe and regular Government) he will therefore be unsup-

*This Objection has been in some Degree lessened by an Amendment, often before refused, and at last made by an Erasure, after the Engrossment upon Parchment, of the word *forty,* and inserting *thirty,* in the 3d Clause of the 2d Section of the 1st Article.

ported by proper Information and Advice; and will generally be directed by Minions and Favourites—or He will become a Tool to the Senate—or a Council of State will grow out of the principal Officers of the great Departments; the worst and most dangerous of all Ingredients for such a Council, in a free Country; for they may be induced to join in any dangerous or oppressive Measures, to shelter themselves, and prevent an Inquiry into their own Misconduct in Office; whereas had a constitutional Council been formed (as was proposed) of six Members; vizt. two from the Eastern, two from the Middle, and two from the Southern States, to be appointed by Vote of the States in the House of Representatives, with the same Duration and Rotation of Office as the Senate, the Executive wou'd always have had safe and proper Information and Advice, the President of such a Council might have acted as Vice President of the United States, pro tempore, upon any Vacancy or Disability of the chief Magistrate; and long continued Sessions of the Senate wou'd in a great Measure have been prevented.

From this fatal Defect of a constitutional Council has arisen the improper Power of the Senate, in the Appointment of public Officers, and the alarming Dependence and Connection between that Branch of the Legislature, and the supreme Executive.

Hence also sprung that unnecessary and dangerous Officer, the Vice President; who for want of other Employment, is made President of the Senate; thereby dangerously blending the executive and legislative Powers; besides always' giving to some one of the States an unnecessary and unjust Pre-eminence over the others.

The President of the United States has the unrestrained Power of granting Pardon for Treason; which may be sometimes exercised to screen from Punishment those whom he had secretly instigated to commit the Crime, and thereby prevent a Discovery of his own Guilt.

By declaring all Treaties supreme Laws of the Land, the Executive and the Senate have in many Cases, an exclusive Power of Legislation; which might have been avoided by proper Distinctions with Respect to Treaties, and requiring the Assent of the House of Representatives, where it cou'd be done with Safety.

By requiring only a Majority to make all commercial and navigation Laws, the five Southern States (whose Produce and Circumstances are totally different from that of the eight Northern and Eastern States) will be ruined; for such rigid and premature Regulations may be made, as will enable the Merchants of the Northern and Eastern States not only to demand an exorbitant Freight, but to monopolize the Purchase of the Commodities at their own Price, for many years: to the great Injury of the landed Interest, and Impoverishment of the People: and the Danger is the greater, as the Gain on one Side will be in Proportion to the Loss on the other. Whereas requiring two thirds of the members present in both Houses wou'd have produced mutual moderation, promoted the general Interest, and removed an insuperable Objection to the Adoption of the Government.

Under their own Construction of the general Clause at the End of the enumerated powers the Congress may grant Monopolies in Trade and Commerce, constitute new Crimes, inflict unusual and severe Punishments, and extend their Power as far as they shall think proper; so that the State Legislatures have no Security for the Powers now presumed to remain to them; or the People for their Rights.

There is no Declaration of any kind for preserving the Liberty of the Press, the Tryal by Jury in civil Causes; nor against the Danger of standing Armys in time of Peace.

The State Legislatures are restrained from laying Export Duties on their own Produce.

The general Legislature is restrained from prohibiting the further Importation of Slaves for twenty odd Years; tho' such Importations render the United States weaker, more vulnerable, and less capable of Defence.

Both the general Legislature and the State Legislatures are expressly prohibited making ex post facto Laws; tho' there never was, or can be a Legislature but must and will make such Laws, when necessity and the public Safety require them; which will hereafter be a Breach of all the Constitutions in the Union, and afford precedents for other Innovations.

This Government will commence in a moderate Aristocracy; it is at present impossible to foresee whether it will, in its Operation, produce a Monarchy, or a corrupt oppressive Aristocracy; it will most probably vibrate some Years between the two, and then terminate in the one or the other.

29

The Federalist (1787–88)

Aside from the Constitution itself, no other source is considered as authoritative as *The Federalist* in determining the intent of the Framers. The eighty-five articles appeared in the New York press between October 1787 and May 1788 over the name "Publius." Of these, John Jay wrote five before illness forced him to withdraw from the project, James Madison of Virginia wrote thirty, and Alexander Hamilton of New York wrote most of the rest; the authorship of several remains in

Source: Rossiter, ed., *The Federalist Papers* 77, 464 (1961).

doubt. The essays explained and defended each section of the Constitution and the structure of each branch of government. Following are excerpts from Number 10, written by Madison, which argued that despite prior wisdom that a republic could only work in a small country, it was the best system for a large country as well; and from Number 78, by Hamilton, explaining the powers and necessity of a federal judiciary.

See G. Wills, *Explaining America: The Federalist* (1981); D. Adair, "The Tenth Federalist Revisited," 8 *W. and M.Q.* 48 (1951); and M. Diamond, "The Federalist," in L. Strauss et al., *History of Political Philosophy* (1963), pp. 573–93.

The Federalist No. 10 (Madison)

Among the numerous advantages promised by a well constructed Union, none deserves to be more accurately developed than its tendency to break and control the violence of faction. The friend of popular governments, never finds himself so much alarmed for their character and fate, as when he contemplates their propensity to this dangerous vice. He will not fail therefore to set a due value on any plan which, without violating the principles to which he is attached, provides a proper cure for it. The instability, injustice and confusion introduced into the public councils, have in truth been the mortal diseases under which popular governments have every where perished; as they continue to be the favorite and fruitful topics from which the adversaries to liberty derive their most specious declamations. The valuable improvements made by the American Constitutions on the popular models, both ancient and modern, cannot certainly be too much admired; but it would be an unwarrantable partiality, to contend that they have as effectually obviated the danger on this side as was wished and expected. Complaints are every where heard from our most considerate and virtuous citizens, usually the friends of public and private faith, and of public and personal liberty; that our governments are too unstable; that the public good is disregarded in the conflicts of rival parties; and that measures are too often decided, not according to the rules of justice, and the rights of the minor party; but by the superior force of an interested and over-bearing majority. However anxiously we may wish that these complaints had no foundation, the evidence of known facts will not permit us to deny that they are in some degree true. . . . These must be chiefly, if not wholly, effects of the unsteadiness and injustice, with which a factious spirit has tainted our public administrations.

By a faction I understand a number of citizens, whether amounting to a majority or minority of the whole, who are united and actuated by some common impulse of passion, or of interest, adverse to the rights of other citizens, or to the permanent and aggregate interests of the community.

There are two methods of curing the mischiefs of faction: the one, by removing its causes; the other, by controling its effects.

There are again two methods of removing the causes of faction: the one by destroying the liberty which is essential to its existence; the other, by giving to every citizen the same opinions, the same passions, and the same interests.

It could never be more truly said than of the first remedy, that it is worse than the disease. Liberty is to faction, what air is to fire, an aliment without which it instantly expires. But it could not be a less folly to abolish liberty, which is essential to political life, because it nourishes faction, than it would be to wish the annihilation of air, which is essential to animal life, because it imparts to fire its destructive agency.

The second expedient is as impracticable, as the first would be unwise. As long as the reason of man continues fallible, and he is at liberty to exercise it, different opinions will be formed. As long as the connection subsists between his reason and his self-love, his opinions and his passions will have a reciprocal influence on each other; and the former will be objects to which the latter will attach themselves. The diversity in the faculties of men from which the rights of property originate, is not less an insuperable obstacle to a uniformity of interests. The protection of these faculties is the first object of Government. From the protection of different and unequal faculties of acquiring property, the possession of different degrees and kinds of property immediately results: and from the influence of these on the sentiments and views of the respective proprietors, ensues a division of the society into different interests and parties. . . .

The inference to which we are brought is, that the *causes* of faction cannot be removed; and that relief is only to be sought in the means of controling its *effects*.

If a faction consists of less than a majority, relief is supplied by the republican principle, which enables the majority to defeat its sinister views by regular vote: It may clog the administration, it may convulse the society; but it will be unable to execute and mask its violence under the forms of the Constitution. When a majority is included in a faction, the form of popular government on the other hand enables it to sacrifice to its ruling passion or interest, both the public good and the rights of other citizens. To secure the public good, and private rights, against the danger of such a faction, and at the same time to preserve the spirit and the form of popular government, is then the great object to which our enquiries are directed: Let me add that it is the great desideratum, by which alone this form of government can be rescued from the opprobrium under which it has so long labored, and be recommended to the esteem and adoption of mankind.

By what means is this object attainable? Evidently by one of two only. Either the existence of the same passion or interest in a majority at the same time, must be prevented; or the majority, having such co-existent passion or interest, must be rendered, by their number and local situation, unable to concert and carry into effect schemes of oppression. If the impulse and the opportunity be suffered to coincide, we well know that neither moral nor religious motives can be relied on as an adequate control. They are not found to be such on the injustice and violence of individuals, and lose their efficacy in proportion to the number combined together; that is, in proportion as their efficacy becomes needful.

From this view of the subject, it may be concluded, that a pure Democracy, by which I mean, a Society, consisting of a small number of citizens, who assemble and administer the Government in person, can admit of no cure for the mischiefs of faction. A common passion or interest will, in almost every case, be felt by a majority of the whole; a communication and concert results from the form of Government itself; and there is nothing to check the inducements to sacrifice the weaker party, or an obnoxious individual. Hence it is, that such Democracies have ever been spectacles of turbulence and contention; have ever been found incompatible with personal security, or the rights of property; and have in general been as short in their lives, as they have been violent in their deaths. Theoretic politicians, who have patronized this species of Government, have erroneously supposed, that by reducing mankind to a perfect equality in their political rights, they would, at the same time, be perfectly equalized and assimilated in their possessions, their opinions, and their passions.

A Republic, by which I mean a Government in which the scheme of representation takes place, opens a different prospect, and promises the cure for which we are seeking. Let us examine the points in which it varies from pure Democracy, and we shall comprehend both the nature of the cure, and the efficacy which it must derive from the Union.

The two great points of difference between a Democracy and a Republic are, first, the delegation of the Government, in the latter, to a small number of citizens elected by the rest: secondly, the greater number of citizens, and greater sphere of country, over which the latter may be extended.

The effect of the first difference is, on the one hand to refine and enlarge the public views, by passing them through the medium of a chosen body of citizens, whose wisdom may best discern the true interest of their country, and whose patriotism and love of justice, will be least likely to sacrifice it to temporary or partial considerations. Under such a regulation, it may well happen that the public voice pronounced by the representatives of the people, will be more consonant to the public good, than if pronounced by the people themselves convened for the purpose. On the other hand, the effect may be inverted. Men of factious tempers, of local prejudices, or of sinister designs, may by intrigue, by corruption or by other means, first obtain the suffrages, and then betray the interests of the people. The question resulting is, whether small or extensive Republics are most favorable to the election of proper guardians of the public weal; and it is clearly decided in favor of the latter by two obvious considerations.

In the first place it is to be remarked that however small the Republic may be, the Representatives must be raised to a certain number, in order to guard against the cabals of a few; and that however large it may be, they must be limited to a certain number, in order to guard against the confusion of a multitude. Hence the number of Representatives in the two cases, not being in proportion to that of the Constituents, and being proportionally greatest in the small Republic, it follows, that if the proportion of fit characters, be not less, in the large than in the small Republic, the former will present a greater option, and consequently a greater probability of a fit choice.

In the next place, as each Representative will be chosen by a greater number of citizens in the large than in the small Republic, it will be more difficult for unworthy candidates to practise with success the vicious arts, by which elections are too often carried; and the suffrages of the people being more free, will be more likely to centre on men who possess the most attractive merit, and the most diffusive and established characters.

It must be confessed, that in this, as in most other cases, there is a mean, on both sides of which inconveniencies will be found to lie. By enlarging too much the number of electors, you render the representative too little acquainted with all their local circumstances and lesser interests; as by reducing it too much, you render him unduly attached to these, and too little fit to comprehend and pursue great and national objects. The Federal Constitution forms a happy combination in this respect; the great and aggregate interests being referred to the national, the local and particular, to the state legislatures.

The other point of difference is, the greater number of citizens and extent of territory which may be brought within the compass of Republican, than of Democratic Government; and it is this circumstance principally which renders factious combinations less to be dreaded in the former, than in the latter. The smaller the society, the fewer probably will be the distinct parties and interests composing it; the fewer the distinct parties and interests, the more frequently will a majority be found of the same party; and the smaller the number of individuals composing a majority, and the smaller the compass within which they are placed, the more easily will they concert and execute their plans of oppression. Extend the sphere, and you take in a greater variety of parties and interests; you make it less probable that a majority of the whole will have a common motive to invade the rights of other citizens; or if such a common motive exists, it will be more difficult for all who feel it to discover their own strength, and to act in unison with each other. Besides other impediments, it may be remarked, that where there is a consciousness of unjust or dishonorable purposes, a communication is always checked by distrust, in proportion to the number whose concurrence is necessary. . . .

The influence of factious leaders may kindle a flame within their particular States, but will be unable to spread a general conflagration through the other States: a religious sect, may degenerate into a political faction in a part of the Confederacy; but the variety of sects dispersed over the entire face of it, must secure the national Councils against any danger from that source: a rage for paper money, for an abolition of debts, for an equal division of property, or for any other improper or wicked project, will be less apt to pervade the whole body of the Union, than a particular member of it; in the same proportion as such a malady is more likely to taint a particular county or district, than an entire State.

In the extent and proper structure of the Union, therefore, we behold a Republican remedy for the diseases most incident to Republican Government. And according to the degree of pleasure and pride, we feel in being Republicans, ought to be our zeal in cherishing the spirit, and supporting the character of Federalists.

The Federalist No. 78 (Hamilton)

We proceed now to an examination of the judiciary department of the proposed government.

In unfolding the defects of the existing Confederation, the utility and necessity of a federal judicature have been clearly pointed out. It is the less necessary to recapitulate the considerations there urged, as the propriety of the institution in the abstract is not disputed; the only questions which have been raised being relative to the manner of constituting it, and to its extent. To these points, therefore, our observations shall be confined. . . .

According to the plan of the convention, all judges who may be appointed by the United States are to hold their offices *during good behavior;* which is conformable to the most approved of the State constitutions, and among the rest, to that of this State. Its propriety having been drawn into question by the adversaries of that plan, is no light symptom of the rage for objection, which disorders their imaginations and judgments. The standard of good behavior for the continuance in office of the judicial magistracy, is certainly one of the most valuable of the modern improvements in the practice of government. In a monarchy it is an excellent barrier to the despotism of the prince; in a republic it is a no less excellent barrier to the encroachments and oppressions of the representative body. And it is the best expedient which can be devised in any government, to secure a steady, upright, and impartial administration of the laws.

Whoever attentively considers the different departments of power must perceive, that, in a government in which they are separated from each other, the judiciary, from the nature of its functions, will always be the least dangerous to the political rights of the Constitution; because it will be least in a capacity to annoy or injure them. The Executive not only dispenses the honors, but holds the sword of the community. The legislature not only commands the purse, but prescribes the rules by which the duties and rights of every citizen are to be regulated. The judiciary, on the contrary, has no influence over either the sword or the purse; no direction either of the strength or of the wealth of the society; and can take no active resolution whatever. It may truly be said to have neither FORCE nor WILL, but merely judgment; and must ultimately depend upon the aid of the executive arm even for the efficacy of its judgments.

This simple view of the matter suggests several important consequences. It proves incontestably, that the judiciary is beyond comparison the weakest of the three departments of power; that it can never attack with success either of the other two; and that all possible care is requisite to enable it to defend itself against their attacks. It equally proves, that though individual oppression may now and then proceed from the courts of justice, the general liberty of the people can never be endangered from that quarter. . . .

The complete independence of the courts of justice is peculiarly essential in a limited Constitution. By a limited Constitution, I understand one which contains certain specified exceptions to the legislative authority; such, for instance, as that it shall pass no bills of attainder, no *ex-post-facto* laws, and the like. Limitations of this kind can be preserved in practice no other way than through the medium of courts of justice, whose duty it must be to declare all acts contrary to the manifest tenor of the Constitution void. Without this, all the reservations of particular rights or privileges would amount to nothing.

Some perplexity respecting the rights of the courts to pronounce legislative acts void, because contrary to the constitution, has arisen from an imagination that the doctrine would imply a superiority of the judiciary to the legislative power. It is urged that the authority which can declare the acts of another void, must necessarily be superior to the one whose acts may be declared void. As this doctrine is of great importance in all the American constitutions, a brief discussion of the ground on which it rests cannot be unacceptable.

There is no position which depends on clearer principles, than that every act of a delegated authority, contrary to the tenor of the commission under which it is exercised, is void. No legislative act, therefore, contrary to the Constitution, can be valid. To deny this would be to affirm, that the deputy is greater than his principal; that the servant is above his master; that the representatives of the people are superior to the people themselves; that men acting by virtue of powers, may do not only what their powers do not authorize, but what they forbid.

If it be said that the legislative body are themselves the constitutional judges of their own powers, and that the construction they put upon them is conclusive upon the other departments, it may be answered, that this cannot be the natural presumption, where it is not to be collected from any particular provisions in the Constitution. It is not otherwise to be supposed, that the Constitution could intend to enable the representatives of the people to substitute their *will* to that of their constituents. It is far more rational to suppose, that the courts were designed to be an intermediate body between the people and the legislature, in order, among other things, to keep the latter within the limits assigned to their authority. The interpretation of the laws is the proper and peculiar province of the courts. A constitution is, in fact, and must be regarded by the judges, as a fundamental law. It therefore belongs to them to ascertain its meaning, as well as the meaning of any particular act proceeding from the legislative body. If there should happen to be an irreconcilable variance between the two, that which has the superior obligation and validity ought, of course, to be preferred; or, in other words, the Constitution ought to be preferred to the statute, the intention of the people to the intention of their agents.

Nor does this conclusion by any means suppose a superiority of the judicial to the legislative power. It only supposes that the power of the people is superior to both; and that where the will of the legislature, declared in its statutes, stands in opposition to that of the people, declared in the Constitution, the judges ought to be governed by the latter rather than the former. They ought to regulate their decisions by the fundamental laws, rather than by those which are not fundamental. . . .

This independence of the judges is equally requisite to guard the Constitution and the rights of individuals from the effects of those ill humors, which the arts of designing men, or the influence of particular conjunctures, sometimes disseminate among the people themselves, and which, though they speedily give place to better information, and more deliberate reflection, have a tendency, in the meantime, to occasion dangerous innovations in the government, and serious oppressions of the minor party in the community.

Part IV

The New Nation

The administration of George Washington, the first president under the new Constitution, did not exactly have a blank slate to write upon, but in many areas it had very little precedent to guide its policies. There had, for example, been no federal judiciary under the Articles of Confederation, but the new Constitution called for the creation of a Supreme Court and such inferior courts as Congress chose to establish. Aside from the organizational structure of the court system, Congress also had to define the jurisdiction and powers of the federal courts. In doing so Congress relied in part on its experiences under British law, but it also wrote in its own ideas of how federalism should operate (Document 30).

The most pressing task confronting Washington at home was putting the government's financial house in order. The brilliant Secretary of the Treasury, Alexander Hamilton, came up with a daring proposal, which included chartering a national bank, a power not explicitly given to Congress in the Constitution. As was his custom, Washington sought advice from his chief ministers on the issue. Secretary of State Thomas Jefferson's strict construction of constitutional powers delineated one major strand of constitutional interpretation (Document 31); Hamilton's broad reading of Article I, Section 8, and especially of the elastic clause (Document 32), not only won the immediate case, but was ultimately adopted as the proper mode of interpretation (Document 55).

In foreign affairs, Washington sought neutrality, hoping to keep the young nation unembroiled in European affairs. But the Constitution said nothing about neutrality. It gave the power to declare war to the Congress; did that mean that only Congress had the power to declare neutrality as well? To Jefferson and his colleague James Madison, the strict construction of the Constitution meant that Congress alone had the power (Document 35), but once again Hamilton's broad reading of the document has proved the dominant interpretation (Document 34). The neutrality issue also raised one of the first questions of relations between the branches, a subject that has been the source of continuing discussion and controversy over the years. One aspect, however, the question of the courts' rendering advisory opinions, was definitely settled (Document 33).

The courts also began to explore other aspects of their role in a federal system. Could they entertain suits of citizens of one state against the governments of other states, a power apparently given in Article III (Document 36)? And could they review congressional legislation to determine if the statutes passed constitutional muster, a power not explicitly listed in the Constitution (Document 37)?

The exercise of power—any power—by the national government appeared alarming to a number of people. Many of the anti-federalists had opposed the Constitution because they believed the new government would undermine civil liberties and the powers of the states (Document 28). By the mid-1790s these worries had increased considerably, especially in light of the broad policies adopted by Washington and justified by Hamilton. When the Congress, utilizing old English standards of seditious libel, made it a crime to criticize the government, all of the old fears seemed justified, and aroused strong protest in the Virginia and Kentucky resolutions (Document 38). Similar fears of expanding federal power led to a protest against the idea of a federal criminal law (Document 40).

Despite the growing opposition, the Federalists had inaugurated the new government and gotten it off to a firm start. The criticism by the Jeffersonians alarmed conservatives, but it anticipated political developments in this country. Strong and vigorous protest and debate became a hallmark of democratic politics.

In this first decade of government under the Constitution one sees a transition from reliance upon older English traditions and the striking out on new and uniquely American paths. The arguments made by Hamilton, Madison, and Jefferson—all of whom were well-versed in British and continental political thought—are different from those of Otis, Henry, Dickinson, and the younger Jefferson. In the 1760s and 1770s the colonists based their appeals on British tradition and claimed that George III and his advisors had strayed from those ideals. After 1789, one hears little of English thought per se, and more about the intentions of the Framers and the nature of government and the federal system in America. The sources of authority become almost solely American as the new nation develops its own traditions and native writings.

30

Judiciary Act (1789)

One of the first acts of the Congress meeting under the Constitution was to establish the federal judiciary called for in Article III. Here Congress had little to follow from British practice, where the three court systems—Common Pleas (private law), King's Bench (criminal law), and Chancery (equity)—operated independently and derived their authority from the King's writ. By combining law and equity in one system, Congress took a giant step forward in simplifying the administration of justice as well as in striking out on an American path.

The debate in Congress centered on how much power the Constitution transferred from the states to the federal government. States rights activists opposed giving the new courts too much authority, while supporters argued that only a strong federal court system could overcome the weaknesses that had been so apparent during the Confederation period. Many hours were spent discussing Section 25, which defined the relationship between state and federal courts. For the most part the Judiciary Act of 1789 envisioned a strong and independent federal court system, and the statute established the basic framework of the federal courts and their powers for many years to come; sections of it are still in effect. One might note that Oliver Ellsworth, who would be the second Chief Justice, drafted much of the act.

See D. F. Henderson, *Courts for a New Nation* (1971); J. R. Saylor, "Creation of the Federal Judiciary," 8 *Baylor L. R.* 257 (1956); and C. Warren, "New Light on the History of the Federal Judiciary Act of 1789," 37 *Harv. L. R.* 49 (1923).

An Act to establish the Judicial Courts of the United States

Sec. 1. *Be it enacted,* That the supreme court of the United States shall consist of a chief justice and five associate justices, any four of whom shall be a quorum, and shall hold annually at the seat of government two sessions, the one commencing the first Monday of February, and the other the first Monday of August. That the associate justices shall have precedence according to the date of their commissions, or when the commissions of two or more of them bear date on the same day, according to their respective ages.

Source: 1 *Statutes at Large* 73 (1789).

Sec. 2.   That the United States shall be, and they hereby are, divided into thirteen districts, to be limited and called as follows, . . .

Sec. 3.   That there be a court called a District Court in each of the aforementioned districts, to consist of one judge, who shall reside in the district for which he is appointed, and shall be called a District Judge, and shall hold annually four sessions, . . .

Sec. 4.   That the beforementioned districts, except those of Maine and Kentucky, shall be divided into three circuits, and be called the eastern, the middle, and the southern circuit. . . . [T]hat there shall be held annually in each district of said circuits two courts which shall be called Circuit Courts, and shall consist of any two justices of the Supreme Court and the district judge of such districts, any two of whom shall constitute a quorum. *Provided,* That no district judge shall give a vote in any case of appeal or error from his own decision; but may assign the reasons of such his decision. . . .

Sec. 9.   That the district courts shall have, exclusively of the courts of the several States, cognizance of all crimes and offences that shall be cognizable under the authority of the United States, committed within their respective districts, or upon the high seas; where no other punishment than whipping, not exceeding thirty stripes, a fine not exceeding one hundred dollars, or a term of imprisonment not exceeding six months, is to be inflicted; and shall also have exclusive original cognizance of all civil cases of admiralty and maritime jurisdiction, including all seizures under laws of impost, navigation, or trade of the United States. . . . And shall also have cognizance, concurrent with the courts of the several States, or the circuit courts, as the case may be, of all causes where an alien sues for a tort only in violation of the law of nations or a treaty of the United States. And shall also have cognizance, concurrent as last mentioned, of all suits at common law where the United States sue, and the matter in dispute amounts, exclusive of costs, to the sum or value of one hundred dollars. And shall also have jurisdiction exclusively of the courts of the several States, of all suits against consuls or vice-consuls, except for offences above the description aforesaid. And the trial of issues in fact, in the district courts, in all cases except civil causes of admiralty and maritime jurisdiction, shall be by jury. . . .

Sec 11.   That the circuit courts shall have original cognizance, concurrent with the courts of the several States, of all suits of a civil nature at common law or in equity, where the matter in dispute exceeds, exclusive of costs, the sum or value of five hundred dollars, and the United States are plaintiffs or petitioners; or an alien is a party, or the suit is between a citizen of the State where the suit is brought and a citizen of another State. And shall have exclusive cognizance of all crimes and offences cognizable under the authority of the United States, except where this act otherwise provides, or the laws of the United States shall otherwise direct, and concurrent jurisdiction with the district courts of the crimes and offences cognizable therein. . . . And the circuit courts shall also have appellate jurisdiction from the district courts under the regulations and restrictions herinafter provided. . . .

Sec. 13.   That the Supreme Court shall have exclusive jurisdiction of all controversies of a civil nature, where a state is a party, except between a state and its citizens; and except also between a state and citizens of other states, or aliens, in which latter case it shall have original but not exclusive jurisdiction. And shall have exclusively all such jurisdiction of suits or proceedings against ambassadors or other public ministers, or their domestics, or domestic servants, as a court of law can have or exercise consistently with the law of nations; and original, but not exclusive jurisdiction of all suits brought by ambassadors or other public ministers, or in which a consul or vice-consul shall be a party. And the trial of issues in fact in the Supreme Court in all actions at law against citizens of the United States shall be by jury. The Supreme Court shall also have appellate jurisdiction from the circuit courts and courts of the several states in the cases hereinafter specially provided for; and shall have power to issue writs of prohibition to the district courts, when proceeding as courts of admiralty and maritime jurisdiction, and writs of *mandamus,* in cases warranted by the principle and usages of law, to any courts appointed, or persons holding office under the authority of the United States. . . .

Sec. 25.   That a final judgment or decree in any suit, in the highest court of law or equity of a State in which a decision in the suit could be had, where is drawn in question the validity of a treaty or statute of, or an authority exercised under, the United States, and the decision is against their validity; or where is drawn in question the validity of a statute of, or an authority exercised under, any State, on the ground of their being repugnant to the constitution, treaties, or laws of the United States, and the decision is in favour of such their validity, or where is drawn in question the construction of any clause of the constitution, or of a treaty, or statute of, or commission held under, the United States, and the decision is against the title, right, privilege, or exemption, specially set up or claimed by either party, under such clause of the said Constitution, treaty, statute, or commission, may be re-examined, and reversed or affirmed in the Supreme Court of the United States upon a writ of error, the citation being signed by the chief justice, or judge or chancellor of the court rendering or passing the judgment or decree complained of, or by a justice of the Supreme Court of the United States, in the same manner and under the same regulations, and the writ shall have the same effect as if the judgment or decree complained of had been rendered or passed in a circuit court, and the proceedings upon the reversal shall also be the same, except that the Supreme Court, instead of remanding the cause for a final decision as before provided, may, at their discretion, if the cause shall have been once remanded before, proceed to a final decision of the same, and award execution. But no other error shall be assigned or regarded as a ground of reversal in any such case as aforesaid, than such as appears on the face of the record, and immediately respects the before-mentioned questions of validity or construction of the said constitution, treaties, statutes, commissions, or authorities in dispute.

31

Opinion on the Constitutionality of a National Bank (1791)

THOMAS JEFFERSON

The first major constitutional controversy of the new government involved Hamilton's proposal for Congress to charter a "Bank of the United States." There is no specific power in Article I for Congress to charter banks or other corporations, and Jefferson put forward what has become known as a "strict construction" of the Constitution. He argued, in essence, that the Constitution provides for a government of limited powers, and that Congress has no authority other than what is explicitly spelled out in the Constitution. Jefferson, like many states rights advocates, feared that a strong central authority would usurp local authority and undermine the people's liberties. To prevent that from happening, he believed that one had to be ever on guard against the slightest expansion of federal power beyond that specifically permitted in the Constitution. Jefferson's views on governmental power would exert a powerful albeit minority influence for the next seventy years; see Documents 38, 40, 64, 66, 85, 86, and 100.

See D. Malone, *Jefferson and the Rights of Man* (1951), Chapter 20; C. Patterson, *The Constitutional Principles of Thomas Jefferson* (1953); and L. Banning, *The Jeffersonian Persuasion* (1978).

Source: Boyd, ed., 19 *Papers of Thomas Jefferson* 275 (1974).

I consider the foundation of the Constitution as laid on this ground that 'all powers not delegated to the U.S. by the Constitution, not prohibited by it to the states, are reserved to the states or to the people.' To take a single step beyond the boundaries thus specially drawn around the powers of Congress, is to take possession of a boundless feild of power, no longer susceptible of any definition.

The incorporation of a bank, and other powers assumed by this bill have not, in my opinion, been delegated to the U.S. by the Constitution.

I.   They are not among the powers specially enumerated, for these are

1.   A power to *lay taxes* for the purpose of paying the debts of the U.S. But no debt is paid by this bill, nor any tax laid. Were it a bill to raise money, it's origination in the Senate would condemn it by the constitution.

2.   'to borrow money.' But this bill neither borrows money, nor ensures the borrowing it. The proprietors of the bank will be just as free as any other money holders, to lend or not to lend their money to the public. The operation proposed in the bill, first to lend them two millions, and then borrow them back again, cannot change the nature of the latter act, which will still be a payment, and not a loan, call it by what name you please.

3.   'to regulate commerce with foreign nations, and among the states, and with the Indian tribes.' To erect a bank, and to regulate commerce, are very different acts. He who erects a bank creates a subject of commerce in it's bills: so does he who makes a bushel of wheat, or digs a dollar out of the mines. Yet neither of these persons regulates commerce thereby. To erect a thing which may be bought and sold, is not to prescribe regulations for buying and selling. Besides; if this was an exercise of the power of regulating commerce, it would be void, as extending as much to the internal commerce of every state, as to it's external. For the power given to Congress by the Constitution, does not extend to the internal regulation of the commerce of a state (that is to say of the commerce between citizen and citizen) which remains exclusively with it's own legislature; but to it's external commerce only, that is to say, it's commerce with another state, or with foreign nations or with the Indian tribes. Accordingly the bill does not propose the measure as a 'regulation of trade,' but as 'productive of considerable advantage to trade.'

Still less are these powers covered by any other of the special enumerations.

II.   Nor are they within either of the general phrases, which are the two following.

1.   'To lay taxes to provide for the general welfare of the U.S.' that is to say 'to lay taxes *for the purpose* of providing for the general welfare'. For the laying of taxes is the *power* and the general welfare the *purpose* for which the

power is to be exercised. They are not to lay taxes ad libitum *for any purpose they please;* but only to *pay the debts or provide for the welfare of the Union.* In like manner they are not *to do anything they please* to provide for the general welfare, but only *to lay taxes* for that purpose. To consider the latter phrase, not as describing the purpose of the first, but as giving a distinct and independent power to do any act they please, which might be for the good of the Union, would render all the preceding and subsequent enumerations of power completely useless. It would reduce the whole instrument to a single phrase, that of instituting a Congress with power to do whatever would be for the good of the U.S. and as they would be the sole judges of the good or evil, it would be also a power to do whatever evil they pleased. It is an established rule of construction, where a phrase will bear either of two meanings, to give it that which will allow some meaning to the other parts of the instrument, and not that which would render all the others useless. Certainly no such universal power was meant to be given them. It was intended to lace them up straitly within the enumerated powers, and those without which, as means, these powers could not be carried into effect. It is known that the very power now proposed *as a means,* was rejected *as an end,* by the Convention which formed the constitution. A proposition was made to them to authorize Congress to open canals, and an amendatory one to empower them to incorporate. But the whole was rejected, and one of the reasons of rejection urged in debate was that then they would have a power to erect a bank, which would render the great cities, where there were prejudices and jealousies on that subject adverse to the reception of the constitution.

2.   The second general phrase is 'to make all laws *necessary* and proper for carrying into execution the enumerated powers.' But they can all be carried into execution without a bank. A bank therefore is not *necessary,* and consequently not authorised by this phrase.

It has been much urged that a bank will give great facility, or convenience in the collection of taxes. Suppose this were true: yet the constitution allows only the means which are 'necessary' not those which are merely 'convenient' for effecting the enumerated powers. If such a latitude of construction be allowed to this phrase as to give any non-enumerated power, it will go to every one, for there is no one which ingenuity may not torture into a *convenience, in some way or other,* to *some one* of so long a list of enumerated powers. It would swallow up all the delegated powers, and reduce the whole to one phrase as before observed. Therefore it was that the constitution restrained them to the *necessary* means, that is to say, to those means without which the grant of the power would be nugatory.

But let us examine this *convenience,* and see what it is. The report on this subject, page 3. states the only *general* convenience to be the preventing the transportation and re-transportation of money between the states and the treasury. (For I pass over the increase of circulating medium ascribed to it as a merit, and which, according to my ideas of paper money is clearly a demerit.) Every state will have to pay a sum of tax-money into the treasury: and the treasury will have to pay, in every state, a part of the interest on the public debt, and salaries to the officers of government resident in that state. In most of the states there will still be a surplus of tax-money to come up to the seat of government for the officers residing there. The payments of interest and salary in each state may be made by treasury-orders on the state collector. This will take up the greater part of the money he has collected in his state, and consequently prevent the great mass of it from being drawn out of the state. If there be a balance of commerce in favour of that state against the one in which the government resides, the surplus of taxes will be remitted by the bills of exchange drawn for that commercial balance. And so it must be if there was a bank. But if there be no balance of commerce, either direct or circuitous, all the banks in the world could not bring up the surplus of taxes but in the form of money. Treasury orders then and bills of exchange may prevent the displacement of the main mass of the money collected, without the aid of any bank: and where these fail, it cannot be prevented even with that aid.

Perhaps indeed bank bills may be a more *convenient* vehicle than treasury orders. But a little *difference* in the degree of *convenience,* cannot constitute the necessity which the constitution makes the ground for assuming any non-enumerated power.

Besides; the existing banks will without a doubt, enter into arrangements for lending their agency: and the more favourable, as there will be a competition among them for it: whereas the bill delivers us up bound to the national bank, who are free to refuse all arrangement, but on their own terms, and the public not free, on such refusal, to employ any other bank. That of Philadelphia, I believe, now does this business, by their post-notes, which by an arrangement with the treasury, are paid by any state collector to whom they are presented. This expedient alone suffices to prevent the existence of that *necessity* which may justify the assumption of a non-enumerated power as a means for carrying into effect an enumerated one. The thing may be done, and has been done, and well done without this assumption; therefore it does not stand on that degree of *necessity* which can honestly justify it.

It may be said that a bank, whose bills would have a currency all over the states, would be more convenient than one whose currency is limited to a single state. So it would be still more convenient that there should be a bank whose bills should have a currency all over the world. But it does not follow from this superior conveniency that there exists anywhere a power to establish such a bank; or that the world may not go on very well without it.

Can it be thought that the Constitution intended that for a shade or two of *convenience,* more or less, Congress should be authorised to break down the most ancient and fundamental laws of the several states, such as those against Mortmain, the laws of alienage, the rules of descent, the acts of distribution, the laws of escheat and forfeiture, the laws of monopoly? Nothing but a necessity invincible by any other means, can justify such a prostration of laws which constitute the pillars of our whole system of jurisprudence. Will Congress be too strait-laced to carry the constitution into honest effect, unless they may pass over the foundation-laws of the state-governments for the slightest convenience to theirs?

The Negative of the President is the shield provided by the constitution to protect against the invasions of the legislature 1. the rights of the Executive 2. of the Judiciary 3. of the states and state legislatures. The present is the case of a right remaining exclusively with the states and is consequently one of those intended by the constitution to be placed under his protection.

It must be added however, that unless the President's mind on a view of every thing which is urged for and against this bill, is tolerably clear that it is unauthorised by the constitution, if the pro and the con hang so even as to balance his judgment, a just respect for the wisdom of the legislature would naturally decide the balance in favour of their opinion. It is chiefly for cases where they are clearly misled by error, ambition, or interest, that the constitution has placed a check in the negative of the President.

TH: JEFFERSON
Feb. 15. 1791.

32

Opinion as to the Constitutionality of the Bank of the United States (1791)

ALEXANDER HAMILTON

After receiving Jefferson's comments, Washington asked his Secretary of the Treasury, Alexander Hamilton, to reply. Hamilton did so in what has been characterized as one of the "great state papers" in American

Source: Syrett et al., eds., 8 *The Papers of Alexander Hamilton* 97 (1965).

political history. In his defense of the proposed bank charter, Hamilton set out a flexible interpretation of constitutional powers. The Constitution was an organic scheme of government, not a statute book, and the Framers left it to future generations to fill in the gaps. They provided ample power, not only in delegated authority, but also through implied powers as expressed in the "elastic clause." By this reasoning, Congress had not only the delegated powers, but all powers except those expressly prohibited. John Marshall accepted Hamilton's reasoning when the Supreme Court reviewed the bank issue (Document 56), but Andrew Jackson did not (Document 66). Over the years the Hamiltonian view has proved dominant, and although one occasionally hears talk about the idea of limited government, the major constitutional issues of the twentieth century have been the extent, and not the limit, of federal power.

See C. Rossiter, *Alexander Hamilton and the Constitution* (1964); J. C. Koritansky, "Alexander Hamilton's Philosophy of Government and Administration," 9 *Publius* 99 (1979); and G. Stourzh, *Alexander Hamilton and the Idea of Republican Government* (1970).

~~~~~~

The Secretary of the Treasury having perused with attention the papers containing the opinions of the Secretary of State and the Attorney-General, concerning the constitutionality of the bill for establishing a national bank, proceeds, according to the order of the President, to submit the reasons which have induced him to entertain a different opinion. . . .

In entering upon the argument, it ought to be premised that the objections of the Secretary of State and the Attorney-General are founded on a general denial of the authority of the United States to erect corporations. The latter, indeed, expressly admits, that if there be anything in the bill which is not warranted by the Constitution, it is the clause of incorporation.

Now it appears to the Secretary of the Treasury that this *general principle* is *inherent* in the very *definition* of government, and *essential* to every step of the progress to be made by that of the United States, namely: That every power vested in a government is in its nature *sovereign,* and includes, by *force* of the *term,* a right to employ all the *means* requisite and fairly applicable to the attainment of the *ends* of such power, and which are not precluded by restrictions and exceptions specified in the Constitution, or not immoral, or not contrary to the *essential ends* of political society.

This principle, in its application to government in general, would be admitted as an axiom; and it will be incumbent upon those who may incline to deny it, to prove a distinction, and to show that a rule which, in the general system of things, is essential to the preservation of the social order, is inapplicable to the United States.

The circumstance that the powers of sovereignty are in this country divided between the National and State governments, does not afford the distinction required. It does not follow from this, that each of the portion of *powers* delegated to the one or to the other, is not sovereign with *regard to its proper objects.* It will only *follow* from it, that each has sovereign power as to *certain things,* and not as to *other things.* To deny that the Government of the United States has sovereign power, as to its declared purposes and trusts, because its power does not extend to all cases, would be equally to deny that the State governments have sovereign power in any case, because their power does not extend to every case. The tenth section of the first article of the Constitution exhibits a long list of very important things which they may not do. And thus the United States would furnish the singular spectacle of a *political society* without *sovereignty,* or of a *people governed,* without *government.*

If it would be necessary to bring proof to a proposition so clear, as that which affirms that the powers of the Federal Government, as to *its objects,* were sovereign, there is a clause of its Constitution which would be decisive. It is that which declares that the Constitution, and the laws of the United States made in pursuance of it, and all treaties made, or which shall be made, under their authority, shall be the *supreme law of the land.* The power which can create the *supreme law of the land* in *any case,* is doubtless *sovereign* as to such case.

This general and indisputable principle puts at once an end to the *abstract* question, whether the United States have power to erect a corporation; that is to say, to give a *legal* or *artificial capacity* to one or more persons, distinct from the *natural.* For it is unquestionably incident to *sovereign power* to erect corporations, and consequently to *that* of the United States, in *relation* to the *objects* intrusted to the management of the government. The difference is this: where the authority of the government is general, it can create corporations in *all cases;* where it is confined to certain branches of legislation, it can create corporations *only* in those cases. . . .

Another argument made use of by the Secretary of State is, the rejection of a proposition by the Convention to empower Congress to make corporations, either generally, or for some special purpose.

What was the precise nature or extent of this proposition, or what the reasons for refusing it, is not ascertained by any authentic document, or even by accurate recollection. . . .

But whatever may have been the nature of the proposition, or the reasons for rejecting it, it includes nothing in respect to the real merits of the question. The Secretary of State will not deny that, whatever may have been the intention of the framers of a constitution or of a law, that intention is to be sought for in the instrument itself, according to the usual and established rules of construction. Nothing is more common than for laws to *express* and *effect* more or less than was intended. If, then, a power to erect a corporation in any case be deducible, by fair inference, from the whole or any part of the numerous provisions of the Constitution of the United States, arguments drawn from extrinsic circumstances, regarding the intention of the Convention, must be rejected. . . .

To establish such a right, it remains to show the relation of such an institution to one or more of the specified powers of the government. Accordingly it is affirmed that it has a relation, more or less direct, to the power of collecting taxes, to that of borrowing money, to that of regulating trade between the States, and to those of raising and maintaining fleets and armies. To the two former the relation may be said to be immediate; and in the last place it will be argued, that it is clearly within the provision which authorizes the making of all *needful rules and regulations* concerning the *property* of the United States, as the same has been practised upon by the government.

A bank relates to the collection of taxes in two ways—*indirectly,* by increasing the quantity of circulating medium and quickening circulation, which facilitates the means of paying directly, by creating a *convenient species* of medium in which they are to be paid.

To designate or appoint the *money* or *thing* in which taxes are to be paid, is not only a proper but a *necessary exercise* of the power of collecting them. Accordingly Congress, in the law concerning the collection of the duties on imports and tonnage, have provided that they shall be paid in gold and silver. But while it was an indispensable part of the work to say in what they should be paid, the choice of the specific thing was mere matter of discretion. . . .

The Secretary of State objects to the relation here insisted upon, by the following mode of reasoning: To erect a bank, says he, and to regulate commerce, are very different acts. He who creates a bank, creates a subject of commerce; so does he who makes a bushel of wheat, or digs a dollar out of the mines; yet neither of these persons regulates commerce thereby. To make a thing which may be bought and sold, is not to prescribe regulations for *buying* and *selling.*

This making the regulation of commerce to consist in prescribing rules for *buying* and *selling*—this, indeed, is a species of regulation of trade, but is one which falls more aptly within the province of the local jurisdictions than within that of the general government, whose care must be presumed to have been intended to be directed to those general political arrangements concerning trade on which its aggregate interests depend, rather than to the details of *buying* and *selling.* Accordingly, such only are the regulations to be found in the laws of the United States, whose objects are to give encouragement to the enterprise of our own merchants, and to advance our navigation and manufactures. And it is in reference to these general relations of commerce that an establishment which furnishes facilities to circulation, and a convenient medium of exchange and alienation, is to be regarded as a regulation of trade.

The Secretary of State further argues that if this was a regulation of commerce, it would be void, as *extending as much to the internal commerce of every State as to its external.* But what regulation of commerce does not extend to the internal commerce of every State? What are all the duties upon imported articles, amounting to prohibitions, but so many bounties upon domestic manufactures, affecting the interest of different classes of citizens, in different ways? What are all the provisions in the Coasting Act which relate to the trade between district and district of the same State? In short, what regulation of trade between the States but must affect the internal trade of each State? What can operate upon the whole but must extend to every part? . . .

A hope is entertained that it has, by this time, been made to appear, to the satisfaction of the President, that a bank has a natural relation to the power of collecting taxes—to that of regulating trade—to that of providing for the common defence—and that, as the bill under consideration contemplates the government in the light of a joint proprietor of the stock of the bank, it brings the case within the provision of the clause of the Constitution which immediately respects the property of the United States.

Under a conviction that such a relation subsists, the Secretary of the Treasury, with all deference, conceives that it will result as a necessary consequence from the position, that all the specified powers of government are sovereign, as to the proper objects; that the incorporation of a bank is a constitutional measure; and that the objections taken to the bill, in this respect, are ill-founded.

33

Reply to Washington (1793)

JOHN JAY

To avoid entanglement in the growing war between France and Great Britain, George Washington issued a Proclamation of Neutrality in 1793 (see next two documents). He realized that there might be some problems resulting from the proclamation that would require judicial resolution, and he sought an advisory opinion from the Supreme Court

Source: Johnston, ed., 3 *Correspondence and Public Papers of John Jay* 486 (1890–93).

on those questions. The Constitution does not specifically empower the Court to give advisory opinions, but neither does it forbid it to do so. A number of state courts then as now do give advisory opinions to the executive or legislative branches regarding the constitutionality of proposed orders or legislation, and if the Court had decided to do so few people would have considered it wrong. But Chief Justice John Jay took a very strict view of the responsibilities and functions of each branch, and in his reply to Washington's request reaffirmed and strengthened the idea of separation of powers.

See J. Goebel, *Antecedents and Beginnings to 1801* (1971), the first volume of the Holmes Device, P. Freund, gen. ed., *History of the Supreme Court of the United States;* and R. Morris, *John Jay, the Nation and the Court* (1967).

Thomas Jefferson to Chief-Justice Jay and Associate Justices, Philadelphia, July 18, 1793

GENTLEMEN:
 The war which has taken place among the powers of Europe produces frequent transactions within our ports and limits, on which questions arise of considerable difficulty, and of greater importance to the peace of the United States. These questions depend for their solution on the construction of our treaties, on the laws of nature and nations, and on the laws of the land, and are often presented under circumstances *which do not give a cognisance of them to the tribunals of the country.* Yet their decision is so little analogous to the ordinary functions of the executive, as to occasion much embarrassment and difficulty to them. The President therefore would be much relieved if he found himself free to refer questions of this description to the opinions of the judges of the Supreme Court of the United States, whose knowledge of the subject would secure us against errors dangerous to the peace of the United States, and their authority insure the respect of all parties. He has therefore asked the attendance of such of the judges as could be collected in time for the occasion, to know, in the first place, their opinion, whether the public may, with propriety, be availed of their *advice on these questions?* And if they may, to present, for their advice, the abstract questions which have already occurred, or may soon occur, from which they will themselves strike out such as any circumstances might, in their opinion, forbid them to pronounce on. I have the honour to be with sentiments of the most perfect respect, gentlemen,
 Your most obedient and humble servant,

THOS. JEFFERSON.

Chief-Justice Jay and Associate Justices to President Washington, Philadelphia, 8th August, 1793.

SIR:

We have considered the previous question stated in a letter written by your direction to us by the Secretary of State on the 18th of last month, [regarding] the lines of separation drawn by the Constitution between the three departments of the government. These being in certain respects checks upon each other, and our being judges of a court in the last resort, are considerations which afford strong arguments against the propriety of our extrajudicially deciding the questions alluded to, especially as the power given by the Constitution to the President, of calling on the heads of departments for opinions, seems to have been *purposely* as well as expressly united to the *executive* departments.

We exceedingly regret every event that may cause embarrassment to your administration, but we derive consolation from the reflection that your judgment will discern what is right, and that your usual prudence, decision, and firmness will surmount every obstacle to the preservation of the rights, peace, and dignity of the United States.

We have the honour to be, with perfect respect, sir, your most obedient and most humble servants.

34

Pacificus No. I (1793)

ALEXANDER HAMILTON

In 1778 the Continental Congress had signed a treaty of alliance with France, then under Bourbon rule. Following the 1789 Revolution, France had proclaimed itself a republic in 1792, and soon after declared war on Great Britain. The new French government dispatched "Citizen" Edmund Genet to the United States to secure American aid under the terms of the 1778 treaty. Washington sought advice from his cabi-

Source: Syrett et al., eds., 15 *Papers of Alexander Hamilton* 33 (1969).

net, all of whom urged that the United States remain neutral in the war. A difference of opinion arose, however, over which branch of government had the authority to issue a neutrality proclamation. Hamilton believed that the President could act on his own as chief magistrate. Congress had just adjourned and it would take several weeks to reconvene in special session, and since fighting between Great Britain and France had already begun, Washington followed his Treasury Secretary's advice.

The proclamation of neutrality by Washington without first consulting or securing the approval of Congress upset many who believed that the President had exceeded his constitutional authority. Since Congress had been specifically delegated the war power, they reasoned that Congress also had control over questions of neutrality, which were so closely tied to the war power. To defend Washington, Hamilton published a series of essays under the pseudonym of "Pacificus" beginning in late June 1793. As in his bank opinion, he took an expansive view of the powers of the presidency (see Document 35).

See F. McDonald, *The Presidency of George Washington* (1974); A. De Conde, *Entangling Alliance: Politics and Diplomacy Under George Washington* (1958); and P. A. Varg, *Foreign Policies of the Founding Fathers* (1963).

The objections which have been raised against the Proclamation of Neutrality lately issued by the President have been urged in a spirit of acrimony and invective, which demonstrates, that more was in view than merely a free discussion of an important public measure; that the discussion covers a design of weakening the confidence of the People in the author of the measure; in order to remove or lessen a powerful obstacle to the success of an opposition to the Government, which however it may change its form, according to circumstances, seems still to be adhered to and pursued with persevering Industry. . . .

The true nature & design of such an act is—to *make known* to the powers at War and to the Citizens of the Country, whose Government does the Act that such country is in the condition of a Nation at Peace with the belligerent parties, and under no obligations of Treaty, to become an *associate in the war* with either of them; that this being its situation its intention is to observe a conduct conformable with it and to perform towards each the duties of neutrality; and as a consequence of this state of things, to give warning to all within its jurisdiction to abstain from acts that shall contravene those duties, under the penalties which the laws of the land (of which the law of Nations is a part) annexes to acts of contravention.

This, and no more, is conceived to be the true import of a Proclamation of Neutrality. . . .

[W]hat department of the Government of the UStates is the proper one to make a declaration of Neutrality in the cases in which the engagements (of) the Nation permit and its interests require such a declaration.

A correct and well informed mind will discern at once that it can belong neither to the Legislative nor Judicial Department and of course must belong to the Executive.

The Legislative Department is not the *organ* of intercourse between the UStates and foreign Nations. It is charged neither with *making* nor *interpreting* Treaties. It is therefore not naturally that Organ of the Government which is to pronounce the existing condition of the Nation, with regard to foreign Powers, or to admonish the Citizens of their obligations and duties as founded upon that condition of things. Still less is it charged with enforcing the execution and observance of these obligations and those duties.

It is equally obvious that the act in question is foreign to the Judiciary Department of the Government. The province of that Department is to decide litigations in particular cases. It is indeed charged with the interpretation of treaties; but it exercises this function only in the litigated cases; that is where contending parties bring before it a specific controversy. It has no concern with pronouncing upon the external political relations of Treaties between Government and Government. This position is too plain to need being insisted upon.

It must then of necessity belong to the Executive Department to exercise the function in Question—when a proper case for the exercise of it occurs.

It appears to be connected with that department in various capacities, as the *organ* of intercourse between the Nation and foreign Nations—as the interpreter of the National Treaties in those cases in which the Judiciary is not competent, that is in the cases between Government and Government—as that Power, which is charged with the Execution of the Laws, of which Treaties form a part—as that Power which is charged with the command and application of the Public Force.

This view of the subject is so natural and obvious—so analogous to general theory and practice—that no doubt can be entertained of its justness, unless such doubt can be deduced from particular provisions of the Constitution of the UStates.

Let us see then if cause for such doubt is to be found in that constitution.

The second Article of the Constitution of the UStates, section 1st, establishes this general Proposition, That "The EXECUTIVE POWER shall be vested in a President of the United States of America."

The same article in a succeeding Section proceeds to designate particular cases of Executive Power. It declares among other things that the President shall be Commander in Chief of the army and navy of the UStates and of the Militia of the several states when called into the actual service of the UStates, that he shall have power by and with the advice of the senate to make treaties; that it shall be his duty to receive ambassadors and other public Ministers and to take care that the laws be faithfully executed.

It would not consist with the rules of sound construction to consider this enumeration of particular authorities as derogating from the more comprehensive grant contained in the general clause, further than as it may be coupled with express restrictions or qualifications; as in regard to the cooperation of the Senate in the appointment of Officers and the making of treaties; which are qualifica(tions) of the general executive powers of appointing officers and making treaties: Because the difficulty of a complete and perfect specification of all the cases of Executive authority would naturally dictate the use of general terms—and would render it improbable that a specification of certain particulars was designed as a substitute for those terms, when antecedently used. The different mode of expression employed in the constitution in regard to the two powers the Legislative and the Executive serves to confirm this inference. In the article which grants the legislative powers of the Governt. the expressions are—*"All Legislative powers herein granted shall be vested in a Congress of the UStates;"* in that which grants the Executive Power the expressions are, as already quoted "The EXECUTIVE PO[WER] shall be vested in a President of the UStates of America."

The enumeration ought rather therefore to be considered as intended by way of greater caution, to specify and regulate the principal articles implied in the definition of Executive Power; leaving the rest to flow from the general grant of that power, interpreted in conformity to other parts (of) the constitution and to the principles of free government.

The general doctrine then of our constitution is, that the EXECUTIVE POWER of the nation is vested in the President; subject only to the *exceptions* and *qu[a]lifications* which are expressed in the instrument.

Two of these have been already noticed—the participation of the Senate in the appointment of Officers and the making of Treaties. A third remains to be mentioned the right of the Legislature "to declare war and grant letters of marque and reprisal."

With these exceptions the EXECUTIVE POWER of the Union is completely lodged in the President. This mode of construing the Constitution has indeed been recognized by Congress in formal acts, upon full consideration and debate. The power of removal from office is an important instance.

And since upon general principles for reasons already given, the issuing of a proclamation of neutrality is merely an Executive Act; since also the general Executive Power of the Union is vested in the President, the conclusion is, that the step, which has been taken by him, is liable to no just exception on the score of authority. . . .

The President is the constitutional EXECUTOR of the laws. Our Treaties and the laws of Nations form a part of the law of the land. He who is to execute the laws must first judge for himself of their meaning. In order to the observance of that conduct, which the laws of nations combined with our treaties prescribed to this country, in reference to the present War in Europe, it was necessary for the President to judge for himself whether there was any thing in our treaties incompatible with an adherence to neutrality. Having judged that there was not, he had a right, and if in his opinion the interests of the Nation required it, it was his duty, as Executor of the laws, to proclaim the neutrality of the Nation, to exhort all persons to observe it, and to warn them of the penalties which would attend its non observance.

35

Helvidius No. I (1793)

JAMES MADISON

When Washington asked Jefferson for his views on neutrality, the Secretary of State argued that since only Congress could declare war, it also had sole authority to issue a neutrality proclamation. The President did not take Jefferson's advice, but the Secretary of State kept his silence until Hamilton published his "Pacificus" essays, justifying an expansive presidential authority. The essays alarmed Thomas Jefferson immensely, not only because of their implications for political and foreign policy, but also because they spoke to a broad interpretation of all executive powers. He wrote to his friend and disciple, James Madison, "For God's sake, my dear Sir, take up your pen, select the most striking heresies, and cut him to pieces in the face of the public." Madison took up the task reluctantly, and was not particularly satisfied with the results. Jefferson, on the other hand, was delighted and saw to their publication. In the essays, Madison used some of Hamilton's own words from *The Federalist* about the limits of executive power to argue that Washington had gone too far, and that the Congress had a far greater role to play in foreign policy than "Pacificus" conceded.

See works cited in previous document, as well as R. Loss, introduction to *The Letters of Pacificus and Helvidius* (1976), and A. Koch, *Jefferson and Madison: The Great Collaboration* (1950).

———

Source: Rutland et al., eds., 15 *Papers of James Madison* 66 (1985).

~~~~~~

Several pieces with the signature of PACIFICUS were lately published, which have been read with singular pleasure and applause, by the foreigners and degenerate citizens among us, who hate our republican government, and the French revolution; whilst the publication seems to have been too little regarded, or too much despised by the steady friends to both.

Had the doctrines inculcated by the writer, with the natural consequences from them, been nakedly presented to the public, this treatment might have been proper. Their true character would then have struck every eye, and been rejected by the feelings of every heart. But they offer themselves to the reader in the dress of an elaborate dissertation; they are mingled with a few truths that may serve them as a passport to credulity; and they are introduced with professions of anxiety for the preservation of peace, for the welfare of the government, and for the respect due to the present head of the executive, that may prove a snare to patriotism. . . .

The substance of the first piece, sifted from its inconsistencies and its vague expressions, may be thrown into the following propositions:

That the powers of declaring war and making treaties are, in their nature, executive powers:

That being particularly vested by the constitution in other departments, they are to be considered as exceptions out of the general grant to the executive department:

That being, as exceptions, to be construed strictly, the powers not strictly within them, remain with the executive:

That the executive consequently, as the organ of intercourse with foreign nations, and the interpreter and executor of treaties, and the law of nations, is authorised, to expound all articles of treaties, those involving questions of war and peace, as well as others; to judge of the obligations of the United States to make war or not, under any casus federis or eventual operation of the contract, relating to war; and, to pronounce the state of things resulting from the obligations of the United States, as understood by the executive:

That in particular the executive had authority to judge whether in the case of the mutual guaranty between the United States and France, the former were bound by it to engage in the war:

That the executive has, in pursuance of that authority, decided that the United States are not bound: And,

That its proclamation of the 22d of April last, is to be taken as the effect and expression of that decision.

The basis of the reasoning is, we perceive, the extraordinary doctrine, that the powers of making war and treaties, are in their nature executive; and therefore comprehended in the general grant of executive power, where not specially and strictly excepted out of the grant. . . .

2. If we consult for a moment, the nature and operation of the two powers to declare war and make treaties, it will be impossible not to see that

they can never fall within a proper definition of executive powers. The natural province of the executive magistrate is to execute laws, as that of the legislature is to make laws. All his acts therefore, properly executive, must pre-suppose the existence of the laws to be executed. A treaty is not an execution of laws: it does not pre-suppose the existence of laws. It is, on the contrary, to have itself the force of a *law,* and to be carried into *execution,* like all *other laws,* by the *executive magistrate.* To say then that the power of making treaties which are confessedly laws, belongs naturally to the department which is to execute laws, is to say, that the executive department naturally includes a legislative power. In theory, this is an absurdity—in practice a tyranny.

The power to declare war is subject to similar reasoning. A declaration that there shall be war, is not an execution of laws: it does not suppose pre-existing laws to be executed: it is not in any respect, an act merely executive. It is, on the contrary, one of the most deliberative acts that can be performed; and when performed, has the effect of *repealing* all the *laws* operating in a state of peace, so far as they are inconsistent with a state of war: and of *enacting* as *a rule for the executive,* a *new code* adapted to the relation between the society and its foreign enemy. In like manner a conclusion of peace *annuls* all the *laws* peculiar to a state of war, and *revives* the general *laws* incident to a state of peace.

These remarks will be strengthened by adding that treaties, particularly treaties of peace, have sometimes the effect of changing not only the external laws of the society, but operate also on the internal code, which is purely municipal, and to which the legislative authority of the country is of itself competent and compleat.

From this view of the subject it must be evident, that although the executive may be a convenient organ of preliminary communications with foreign governments, on the subjects of treaty or war; and the proper agent for carrying into execution the final determinations of the competent authority; yet it can have no pretensions from the nature of the powers in question compared with the nature of the executive trust, to that essential agency which gives validity to such determinations.

It must be further evident that, if these powers be not in their nature purely legislative, they partake so much more of that, than of any other quality, that under a constitution leaving them to result to their most natural department, the legislature would be without a rival in its claim.

Another important inference to be noted is, that the powers of making war and treaty being substantially of a legislative, not an executive nature, the rule of interpreting exceptions strictly, must narrow instead of enlarging executive pretensions on those subjects. . . .

Thus it appears that by whatever standard we try this doctrine, it must be condemned as no less vicious in theory than it would be dangerous in practice. It is countenanced neither by the writers on law; nor by the nature of the powers themselves; nor by any general arrangements or particular expressions, or plausible analogies, to be found in the constitution.

Whence then can the writer have borrowed it?

There is but one answer to this question.

The power of making treaties and the power of declaring war, are *royal prerogatives* in the *British government,* and are accordingly treated as Executive prerogatives by *British commentators.*

We shall be the more confirmed in the necessity of this solution of the problem, by looking back to the area of the constitution, and satisfying ourselves that the writer could not have been misled by the doctrines maintained by our own commentators on our own government. That I may not ramble beyond prescribed limits, I shall content myself with an extract from a work which entered into a systematic explanation and defence of the constitution, and to which there has frequently been ascribed some influence in conciliating the public assent to the government in the form proposed. Three circumstances conspire in giving weight to this cotemporary exposition. It was made at a time when no application to *persons* or *measures* could bias: The opinion given was not transiently mentioned, but formally and critically elucidated: It related to a point in the constitution which must consequently have been viewed as of importance in the public mind. The passage relates to the power of making treaties; that of declaring war, being arranged with such obvious propriety among the legislative powers, as to be passed over without particular discussion. . . .

It will not fail to be remarked on this commentary, that whatever doubts may be started as to the correctness of its reasoning against the legislative nature of the power to make treaties: it is *clear, consistent* and *confident,* in deciding that the power is *plainly* and *evidently* not an *executive power.*

HELVIDIUS.

36

Chisholm v. Georgia (1793)

The facts of this case are fairly simple: Chisholm, the executor of the estate of a South Carolina citizen and patriot, sued the state of Georgia to collect on goods supplied to the state during the Revolution. The issue is also simple: Did the federal courts, under the new Constitution, have jurisdiction if a citizen of one state sued the government of another state, or did a state's sovereignty place it beyond the reach of the federal courts? Only James Iredell believed that the Court lacked jurisdiction; all the other justices found the suit within the domain of the federal judiciary. The reaction to the decision led to the Eleventh Amendment, which specifically denied federal courts this jurisdiction, although in practice the courts have managed to nullify the intent of the amendment. The Supreme Court, before Chief Justice Marshall, followed the English practice of having all the justices deliver their opinions seriatum; Jay's was the last of five opinions.

See J. Goebel, Jr., *Antecedents and Beginnings to 1801* (1971), and C. Jacobs, *The Eleventh Amendment and Sovereign Immunity* (1972).

Chief Justice Jay

The question we are now to decide has been accurately stated, namely, is a State suable by individual citizens of another State?

It is said that Georgia refuses to appear and answer to the plaintiff in this action, because she is a sovereign State, and therefore not liable to such actions. . . .

Any one State in the Union may sue another State in this court, that is, all the people of one State may sue all the people of another State. It is plain, then, that a State may be sued, and hence it plainly follows that suability and state sovereignty are not incompatible. As one State may sue another State in this court, it is plain that no degradation to a State is thought to accompany her appearance in this court. It is not, therefore, to an appearance in this court that the objection points. To what does it point? It points to an appearance at the suit of one or more citizens. But why it should be more incompatible

Source: 2 Dallas 419 (1793).

that all the people of a State should be sued by one citizen, than by one hundred thousand, I cannot perceive, the process in both cases being alike, and the consequences of a judgment alike. Nor can I observe any greater inconveniences in the one case than in the other, except what may arise from the feelings of those who may regard a lesser number in an inferior light. But if any reliance be made on this inferiority, as an objection, at least one half of its force is done away by this fact, namely, that it is conceded that a State may appear in this court as plaintiff against a single citizen as defendant; and the truth is that the State of Georgia is at this moment prosecuting an action in this court against two citizens of South Carolina. . . .

Prior to the date of the constitution, the people had not any national tribunal to which they could resort for justice; the distribution of justice was then confined to State judicatories, in whose institution and organization the people of the other States had no participation, and over whom they had not the least control. There was then no general court of appellate jurisdiction by whom the errors of State courts, affecting either the nation at large or the citizens of any other State, could be revised and corrected. Each State was obliged to acquiesce in the measure of justice which another State might yield to her or to her citizens; and that even in cases where State considerations were not always favorable to the most exact measure. There was danger that from this source animosities would in time result; and as the transition from animosities to hostilities was frequent in the history of independent States, a common tribunal for the termination of controversies became desirable, from motives both of justice and of policy.

Prior also to that period the United States had, by taking a place among the nations of the earth, become amenable to the laws of nations, and it was their interest as well as their duty to provide that those laws should be respected and obeyed; in their national character and capacity the United States were responsible to foreign nations for the conduct of each State, relative to the laws of nations, and the performance of treaties; and there the inexpediency of referring all such questions to State courts, and particularly to the courts of delinquent States, became apparent. While all the States were bound to protect each, and the citizens of each, it was highly proper and reasonable that they should be in a capacity not only to cause justice to be done to each, and the citizens of each, but also to cause justice to be done by each, and the citizens of each; and that, not by violence and force, but in a stable, sedate, and regular course of judicial procedure.

These were among the evils against which it was proper for the nation, that is the people of all the United States, to provide by a national judiciary, to be instituted by the whole nation, and to be responsible to the whole nation. . . .

The question now before us renders it necessary to pay particular attention to that part of the second section which extends the judicial power "to controversies between a State and citizens of another State." It is contended that this ought to be construed to reach none of these controversies, excepting those in which a State may be plaintiff. The ordinary rules for construction will easily decide whether those words are to be understood in that limited sense.

This extension of power is remedial, because it is to settle controversies. It is, therefore, to be construed liberally. It is politic, wise, and good, that not only the controversies in which a State is plaintiff, but also those in which a State is defendant, should be settled; both cases, therefore, are within the reason of the remedy; and ought to be so adjudged, unless the obvious, plain, and literal sense of the words forbid it. If we attend to the words we find them to be express, positive, free from ambiguity, and without room for such implied expressions: "The judicial power of the United States shall extend to controversies between a State and citizens of another State." If the constitution really meant to extend these powers only to those controversies in which a State might be plaintiff, to the exclusion of those in which citizens had demands against a State, it is inconceivable that it should have attempted to convey that meaning in words not only so incompetent, but also repugnant to it; if it meant to exclude a certain class of these controversies, why were they not expressly excepted; on the contrary, not even an intimation of such intention appears in any part of the constitution. It cannot be pretended that where citizens urge and insist upon demands against a State, which the State refuses to admit and comply with, that there is no controversy between them. If it is a controversy between them, then it clearly falls not only within the spirit, but the very words of the constitution. What is it to the cause of justice, and how can it affect the definition of the word controversy, whether the demands which cause the dispute are made by a State against citizens of another State, or by the latter against the former? When power is thus extended to a controversy, it necessarily, as to all judicial purposes, is also extended to those between whom it subsists.

The exception contended for would contradict and do violence to the great and leading principles of a free and equal national government, one of the great objects of which is to insure justice to all. To the few against the many, as well as to the many against the few. It would be strange, indeed, that the joint and equal sovereigns of this country should, in the very constitution by which they professed to establish justice, so far deviate from the plain path of equality and impartiality, as to give to the collective citizens of one State a right of suing individual citizens of another State, and yet deny to those citizens a right of suing them. . . .

For the reasons before given, I am clearly of opinion that a State is suable by citizens of another State.

Hylton v. United States
(1796)

A 1794 statute imposed taxes on carriages kept by persons for their own use or let out to hire. During the debate in the House of Representatives, opponents of the tax argued that the measure violated the constitutional prohibition against direct taxes, since the tax had not been apportioned by population. Daniel Hilton refused to pay the tax, and as he told the Court, his object was "merely to ascertain a constitutional point." In order to meet the jurisdictional minimum of two thousand dollars, Hilton claimed to own 125 carriages, a fiction the government agreed to since it also wanted the law tested. The most forceful opinion came from Justice Paterson, who had been at the Philadelphia Convention, and he claimed that the Framers had intended Congress to have a broad taxing power. The case was the first in which the entire Court directly reviewed an act of Congress, and although the justices upheld the law, it is clear they assumed the Court had the power to void legislation it found in conflict with the Constitution.

See Goebel, cited for previous document, and C. Warren, *The Supreme Court in United States History* (1932), which has some useful insights on this early period.

Justice Paterson

Daniel Lawrence Hilton, on the 5th of *June,* 1794, and therefrom to the last day of *September* next following, owned, possessed, and kept one hundred and twenty-five chariots for the conveyance of persons, but exclusively for his own separate use, and not to let out to hire, or for the conveyance of persons for hire.

The question is, whether a tax upon carriages be a direct tax? If it be a direct tax, it is unconstitutional, because it has been laid pursuant to the rule of uniformity, and not to the rule of apportionment. In behalf of the Plaintiff in error, it has been urged, that a tax on carriages does not come within the description of a duty, impost, or excise, and therefore is a direct tax. It has, on the other hand, been contended, that as a tax on carriages is not a direct

---

Source: 3 Dallas 171 (1796).

tax; it must fall within one of the classifications just enumerated, and particularly must be a duty or excise. The argument on both sides turns in a circle; it is not a duty, impost, or excise, and therefore must be a direct tax; it is not tax, and therefore must be a duty or excise. What is the natural and common, or technical and appropriate, meaning of the words, duty and excise, it is not easy to ascertain. They present no clear and precise idea to the mind. Different persons will annex different significations to the terms. It was, however, obviously the intention of the framers of the Constitution, that Congress should possess full power over every species of taxable property, except exports. The term taxes, is generical, and was made use of to vest in Congress plenary authority in all cases of taxation. The general division of taxes is into direct and indirect. Although the latter term is not to be found in the Constitution, yet the former necessarily implies it. Indirect stands opposed to direct. There may, perhaps, be an indirect tax on a particular article, that cannot be comprehended within the description of duties, or imposts, or excises; in such case it will be comprised under the general denomination of taxes. For the term tax is the genus, and includes

1.   Direct taxes.
2.   Duties, imposts, and excises.
3.   All other classes of an indirect kind, and not within any of the classifications enumerated under the preceding heads.

The question occurs, how is such tax to be laid, uniformly or apportionately? The rule of uniformity will apply, because it is an indirect tax, and direct taxes only are to be apportioned. What are direct taxes within the meaning of the Constitution? The Constitution declares, that a capitation tax is a direct tax; and, both in theory and practice, a tax on land is deemed to be a direct tax. In this way, the terms direct taxes, and capitation and other direct tax, are satisfied. It is not necessary to determine, whether a tax on the product of land be a direct or indirect tax. Perhaps, the immediate product of land, in its original and crude state, ought to be considered as the land itself; it makes part of it; or else the provision made against taxing exports would be easily eluded. Land, independently of its produce, is of no value. When the produce is converted into a manufacture, it assumes a new shape; its nature is altered; its original state is changed; it becomes quite another subject, and will be differently considered. Whether direct taxes, in the sense of the Constitution, comprehend any other tax than a capitation tax, and tax on land, is a questionable point. If Congress, for instance, should tax, in the aggregate or mass, things that generally pervade all the states in the Union, then, perhaps, the rule of apportionment would be the most proper, especially if an assessment was to intervene. This appears by the practice of some of the states, to have been considered as a direct tax. Whether it be so under the Constitution of the *United States,* is a matter of some difficulty; but as it is not before the court, it would be improper to give any decisive opinion upon it. I never entertained a doubt, that the principal, I will not say, the only, objects, that the framers of the Constitution contemplated as falling within the rule of apportionment, were a capitation tax and a tax on land. Local considerations, and the particular circumstances, and relative situation of the states, naturally lead to this view of the subject. The provision was made in favor of the southern States. They possessed a large number of slaves; they had extensive tracts of territory, thinly settled, and not very productive. A majority of the states had but few slaves, and several of them a limited territory, well settled, and in a high state of cultivation. The southern states, if no provision had been introduced in the Constitution, would have been wholly at the mercy of the other states. Congress in such case, might tax slaves, at discretion or arbitrarily, and land in every part of the Union after the same rate or measure: so much a head in the first instance, and so much an acre in the second. To guard them against imposition in these particulars, was the reason of introducing the clause in the Constitution, which directs that representatives and direct taxes shall be apportioned among the states, according to their respective numbers.

On the part of the Plaintiff in error, it has been contended, that the rule of apportionment is to be favored rather than the rule of uniformity; and, of course, that the instrument is to receive such a construction, as will extend the former and restrict the latter. I am not of that opinion. The Constitution has been considered as an accommodating system; it was the effect of mutual sacrifices and concessions; it was the work of compromise. The rule of apportionment is of this nature; it is radically wrong; it cannot be supported by any solid reasoning. Why should slaves, who are a species of property, be represented more than any other property? The rule, therefore, ought not to be extended by construction.

Again, numbers do not afford a just estimate or rule of wealth. It is, indeed, a very uncertain and incompetent sign of opulence. There is another reason against the extension of the principle laid down in the Constitution.

The counsel on the part of the Plaintiff in error, have further urged, that an equal participation of the expense or burden by the several states in the Union, was the primary object, which the framers of the Constitution had in view; and that this object will be effected by the principle of apportionment, which is an operation upon states, and not on individuals; for, each state will be debited for the amount of its quota of the tax, and credited for its payments. This brings it to the old system of requisitions. An equal rule is doubtless the best. But how is this to be applied to states or to individuals? The latter are the objects of taxation, without reference to states, except in the case of direct taxes. The fiscal power is exerted certainly, equally, and effectually on individuals; it cannot be exerted on states. The history of the *United Netherlands,* and of our own country, will evince the truth of this position. The government of the *United States* could not go on under the confederation, because Congress were obliged to proceed in the line of requisition. Congress could not, under the old confederation, raise money by taxes, be the public exigencies ever so pressing and great. They had no coercive authority—if they had, it must have been exercised against the delinquent states, which would be ineffectual, or terminate in a separation. Requisitions were a dead letter, unless the state legislatures could be brought into action; and when they were, the sums raised were very disproportional. Unequal contributions or payments engendered discontent, and fomented state-jealousy. Whenever it shall be thought necessary or expedient to lay a direct tax on land, where the object is one and the same, it is to be apprehended, that it will be a fund not much more productive than that of requisition under the former government. Let us put the case. A given sum is to be raised from the landed property in the *United States.* It is easy to apportion this sum, or to assign to each state its quota. The Constitution gives the rule. Suppose the proportion of *North Carolina* to be eighty thousand dollars. This sum is to be laid on the landed property in the state, but by what rule, and by whom? Shall every acre pay the same sum, without regard to its quality, value, situation, or productiveness? This would be manifestly unjust. Do the laws of the different states furnish sufficient data for the purpose of forming one common rule, comprehending the quality, situation, and value of the lands? In some of the states there has been no land tax for several years, and where there has been, the mode of laying the tax is so various, and the diversity in the land is so great, that no common principle can be deduced, and carried into practice. Do the laws of each state furnish data, from whence to extract a rule, whose operation shall be equal and certain in the same state? Even this is doubtful. Besides, sub-divisions will be necessary; the apportionment of the state, and perhaps of a particular part of the state, is again to be apportioned among counties, townships, parishes, or districts. If the lands be classed, then a specific value must be annexed to each class. And there a question arises, how often are classifications and assessments to be made? Annually, triennially, septennially? The oftener they are made, the greater will be the expense; and the seldomer they are made, the greater will be the inequality, and injustice. In the process of the operation a number of persons will be necessary to class, to value, and assess the land; and after all the guards and provisions that can be devised, we must ultimately rely upon the discretion of the officers in the exercise of their functions. Tribunals of appeal must also be instituted to hear and decide upon unjust valuations, or the assessors will act *ad libitum* without check or control. The work, it is to be feared, will be operose and unproductive, and full of inequality, injustice, and oppression. Let us, however, hope, that a system of land taxation may be so corrected and matured by practice, as to become easy and equal in its operation, and productive and beneficial in its effects. But to return. A tax on carriages, if apportioned, would be oppressive and pernicious. How would it work? In some states there are many carriages, and in others but few. Shall the whole sum fall on one or two individuals in a state, who may happen to own and possess carriages? The thing would be absurd, and inequitable. In answer to this objection, it has been observed, that the sum, and not the tax, is to be apportioned; and that Congress may select in the different states different articles or objects from whence to raise the apportioned sum. The idea is novel. What, shall land be taxed in one state, slaves in another, carriages in a third, and horses in a fourth; or shall several of these be thrown together, in order to levy and make the quoted sum? The scheme is fanciful. It would not work well, and perhaps is utterly impracticable. It is easy to discern, that great, and perhaps insurmountable, obstacles must arise in forming the subordinate arrangements necessary to carry the system into effect; when formed, the operation would be slow and expensive, unequal and unjust. If a tax upon land, where the object is simple and uniform throughout the states, is scarcely practicable, what shall we say of a tax attempted to be apportioned among, and raised and collected from, a number of dissimilar objects. The difficulty will increase with the number and variety of the things proposed for taxation. We shall be obliged to resort to intricate and endless valuations and assessments, in which every thing will be arbitrary, and nothing certain. There will be no rule to walk by. The rule of uniformity, on the contrary, implies certainty, and leaves nothing to the will and pleasure of the assessor. In such case, the object and the sum coincide, the rule and the thing unite, and of course there can be no imposition. The truth is, that the articles taxed in one state should be taxed in another; in this way the spirit of jealousy is appeased, and tranquillity preserved; in this way the pressure on industry will be equal in the several states, and the relation between the different subjects of taxation duly preserved. Apportionment is an operation on states, and involves valuations and assessments, which are arbitrary, and should not be resorted to but in case of necessity. Uniformity is an instant operation on individuals, without the intervention of assessments, or any regard to states, and is at once easy, certain, and efficacious. All taxes on expences or consumption are indirect taxes. A tax on carriages is of this kind, and of course is not a direct tax. Indirect taxes are circuitous modes of reaching the revenue of individuals, who generally live according to their income.

Virginia and Kentucky
Resolutions (1798)

In the face of rising provocations from France, especially following the publication of the XYZ correspondence in the spring of 1798, the Hamiltonian faction seized upon the patriotic mood of the nation to push through the Alien and Sedition Laws in 1798. The three Alien laws certainly fell within Congress's power to regulate immigration and naturalization. The Sedition Law, however, made criticism of the government a crime, and was designed to silence the vociferous pamphleteers and newspaper editors critical of the Adams administration and its allegedly pro-British policies.

In many ways the Sedition Act evoked the old British law of seditious libel, which made the mere impugning the reputation of public officials an offense. Scholars have pointed out that following Zenger's case (Document 8), the law of seditious libel fell into disuse in the colonies but did not change except insofar as Americans now accepted truth as a full defense. In the prosecutions under the act, however, truth had little relevance. Luther Baldwin of New Jersey had to pay a one-hundred dollar fine for wishing out loud that the wad of a salute gun would hit President Adams in the rear, while Congressman Matthew Lyons spent four months in jail and paid a one-thousand dollar fine for ridiculing Adams's "unbounded thirst for ridiculous pomp, foolish adulation and selfish avarice."

Although critics charged that the law violated the First Amendment, the courts never adjudicated the constitutional issue. Moreover, it is not likely that the courts, given the views of free speech at the time, would have found it unconstitutional. It should also be noted that for all the opprobrium then and later heaped on the statute, it incorporated the idea of truth as a defense and thus was far advanced over the laws of seditious libel then in effect in the states or in Great Britain.

The laws evoked impassioned outcries from the Jeffersonians that they were the real targets of the Sedition Law, a claim justified by highly partisan prosecutions. In November 1798 the Kentucky legislature adopted a resolution secretly drafted by Thomas Jefferson, and the following month Virginia followed suit with one written by James Madison. Both complained about the substantive nature of the laws and also raised issues of states rights. They are remembered today for their

Source: *The Virginia Resolutions . . .* 22, 162 (1850).

defense of free speech, and also for their use by those who, in their opposition to policies of the national government, would have dissolved the Union.

See J. M. Smith, *Freedom's Fetters* (1956); A. Koch, *Jefferson and Madison* (1950); L. W. Levy, *Emergence of a Free Press* (1960); and W. Berns, "Freedom of the Press and the Alien and Sedition Laws: A Reappraisal," 1970 *Sup. Ct. Rev.* 109 (1971).

~~~~~~

Virginia Resolutions, December 21, 1798

1. *Resolved,* That the General Assembly of Virginia doth unequivocally express a firm resolution to maintain and defend the Constitution of the United States, and the Constitution of this State, against every aggression, either foreign or domestic, and that it will support the government of the United States in all measures warranted by the former.

2. That this Assembly most solemnly declares a warm attachment to the union of the States, to maintain which, it pledges all its powers; and that for this end it is its duty to watch over and oppose every infraction of those principles, which constitute the only basis of that union, because a faithful observance of them can alone secure its existence, and the public happiness.

3. That this Assembly doth explicitly and peremptorily declare that it views the powers of the Federal Government as resulting from the compact, to which the States are parties, as limited by the plain sense and intention of the instrument constituting that compact; as no further valid than they are authorized by the grants enumerated in that compact; and that in case of a deliberate, palpable, and dangerous exercise of other powers not granted by the said compact, the States, who are the parties thereto, have the right, and are in duty bound, to interpose for arresting the progress of the evil, and for maintaining within their respective limits, the authorities, rights, and liberties appertaining to them.

4. That the General Assembly doth also express its deep regret that a spirit has in sundry instances been manifested by the Federal Government, to enlarge its powers by forced constructions of the constitutional charter which defines them; and that indications have appeared of a design to expound certain general phrases (which, having been copied from the very limited grant of powers in the former articles of confederation, were the less liable to be misconstrued), so as to destroy the meaning and effect of the particular enumeration, which necessarily explains and limits the general phrases, and so as to consolidate the States by degrees into one sovereignty, the obvious tendency and inevitable result of which would be to transform the present

republican system of the United States into an absolute, or at best, a mixed monarchy.

5.   That the General Assembly doth particularly protest against the palpable and alarming infractions of the Constitution, in the two late cases of the "alien and sedition acts," passed at the last session of Congress, the first of which exercises a power nowhere delegated to the Federal Government; and which by uniting legislative and judicial powers to those of executive, subverts the general principles of free government, as well as the particular organization and positive provisions of the federal Constitution; and the other of which acts exercises in like manner a power not delegated by the Constitution, but on the contrary expressly and positively forbidden by one of the amendments thereto; a power which more than any other ought to produce universal alarm, because it is levelled against that right of freely examining public characters and measures, and of free communication among the people thereon, which has ever been justly deemed the only effectual guardian of every other right.

6.   That this State having by its convention which ratified the federal Constitution, expressly declared, "that among other essential rights, the liberty of conscience and of the press cannot be cancelled, abridged, restrained, or modified by any authority of the United States," and from its extreme anxiety to guard these rights from every possible attack of sophistry or ambition, having with other States recommended an amendment for that purpose, which amendment was in due time annexed to the Constitution, it would mark a reproachful inconsistency and criminal degeneracy, if an indifference were now shown to the most palpable violation of one of the rights thus declared and secured, and to the establishment of a precedent which may be fatal to the other. . . .

8.   That the Governor be desired to transmit a copy of the foregoing resolutions to the executive authority of each of the other States, with a request that the same may be communicated to the legislature thereof. And that a copy be furnished to each of the senators and representatives representing this state in the Congress of the United States.

Kentucky Resolutions, November 10, 1798

1.   *Resolved,* That the several states composing the United States of America, are not united on the principle of unlimited submission to their general government; but that by compact, under the style and title of a Constitution for the United States, and of amendments thereto, they constituted a general government for special purposes, delegated to that government certain definite powers, reserving, each state to itself, the residuary mass of right to their own self-government; and that whensoever the general government assumes undelegated powers, its acts are unauthoritative, void, and of no force: That

to this compact each state acceded as a state, and is an integral party, its co-states forming as to itself, the other party: That the government created by this compact was not made the exclusive or final *judge* of the extent of the powers delegated to itself; since that would have made its discretion, and not the Constitution, the measure of its powers; but that, as in all other cases of compact among parties having no common judge, each party has an equal right to judge for itself, as well of infractions, as of the mode and measure of redress.

2. *Resolved,* That the Constitution of the United States having delegated to Congress a power to punish treason, counterfeiting the securities and current coin of the United States, piracies and felonies committed on the high seas, and offences against the laws of nations, and no other crimes whatever, . . . all other [of] their acts which assume to create, define, or punish crimes other than those enumerated in the Constitution, are altogether void, and of no force, and that the power to create, define, and punish such other crimes is reserved, and of right appertains, solely and exclusively, to the respective states, each within its own territory.

3. *Resolved,* That it is true as a general principle, and is also expressly declared by one of the amendments to the Constitution, that "the powers not delegated to the United States by the Constitution, nor prohibited by it to the states, are reserved to the states respectively, or to the people;" and that no power over the freedom of religion, freedom of speech, or freedom of the press, being delegated to the United States by the Constitution, nor prohibited by it to the states, all lawful powers respecting the same did of right remain, and were reserved to the states, or to the people; that thus was manifested their determination to retain to themselves the right of judging how far the licentiousness of speech and of the press may be abridged without lessening their useful freedom, and how far those abuses which cannot be separated from their use, should be tolerated rather than the use be destroyed; and thus also they guarded against all abridgment by the United States of the freedom of religious opinions and exercises, and retained to themselves the right of protecting the same, as this state by a law passed on the general demand of its citizens, had already protected them from all human restraint or interference: and that in addition to this general principle and express declaration, another and more special provision has been made by one of the amendments to the Constitution, which expressly declares, that "Congress shall make no law respecting an establishment of religion, or prohibiting the free exercise thereof, or abridging the freedom of speech, or of the press," thereby guarding in the same sentence, and under the same words, the freedom of religion, of speech, and of the press, insomuch, that whatever violates either, throws down the sanctuary which covers the others, and that libels, falsehoods, and defamations, equally with heresy and false religion, are withheld from the cognizance of federal tribunals: that therefore the act of the Congress of the United States, passed on the 14th day of July, 1798, entitled, "an act in addition to the act for the punishment of certain

crimes against the United States," which does abridge the freedom of the press, is not law, but is altogether void and of no effect.

4. *Resolved,* That alien-friends are under the jurisdiction and protection of the laws of the state wherein they are; that no power over them has been delegated to the United States, nor prohibited to the individual states distinct from their power over citizens; and it being true as a general principle, and one of the amendments to the Constitution having also declared, that "the powers not delegated to the United States by the Constitution, nor prohibited by it to the states, are reserved to the states respectively, or to the people," the act of the Congress of the United States, passed on the 22d day of June, 1798, entitled "an act concerning aliens," which assumes power over alien-friends not delegated by the Constitution, is not law, but is altogether void and of no force. . . .

6. *Resolved,* That the imprisonment of a person under the protection of the laws of this commonwealth, on his failure to obey the simple *order* of the President, to depart out of the United States, as is undertaken by the said act, entitled "an act concerning aliens," is contrary to the Constitution, one amendment to which has provided, that "no person shall be deprived of liberty without due process of law," and that another having provided, "that in all criminal prosecutions, the accused shall enjoy the right to a public trial by an impartial jury, to be informed of the nature and cause of the accusation, to be confronted with the witnesses against him, to have compulsory process for obtaining witnesses in his favour, and to have the assistance of counsel for his defence," the same act undertaking to authorize the President to remove a person out of the United States, who is under the protection of the law, on his own suspicion, without accusation, without jury, without public trial, without confrontation of the witnesses against him, without having witnesses in his favour, without defence, without counsel, is contrary to these provisions, also, of the Constitution, is therefore not law, but utterly void and of no force.

That transferring the power of judging any person who is under the protection of the laws, from the courts to the President of the United States, as is undertaken by the same act, concerning aliens, is against the article of the Constitution which provides, that "the judicial power of the United States shall be vested in courts, the judges of which shall hold their offices during good behaviour," and that the said act is void for that reason also; and it is further to be noted, that this transfer of judiciary power is to that magistrate of the General Government, who already possesses all the executive, and a qualified negative in all the legislative powers. . . .

8. *Resolved,* That the preceding resolutions be transmitted to the senators and representatives in Congress from this commonwealth, who are hereby enjoined to present the same to their respective houses, and to use their best endeavours to procure, at the next session of Congress, a repeal of the aforesaid unconstitutional and obnoxious acts.

9. *Resolved, lastly,* That the Governor of this commonwealth be, and is hereby authorized and requested to communicate the preceding resolutions to the legislatures of the several states, to assure them that this commonwealth considers union for specified national purposes, and particularly for those specified in their late federal compact, to be friendly to the peace, happiness, and prosperity of all the states.

39

Georgia Judiciary Act (1799)

The complicated procedures that marked English common law had from the start proven far too complex for the frontier colonies. Americans had not the time, the money, the patience, or the skilled lawyers to engage in the subtle and lengthy business of pleadings that was at the heart of the English court system. Colonial procedures were for the most part freer than those in the Mother Country, but many English practices were adopted, especially in the courts of the more established and conservative colonies, such as New York.

Following the Revolution, a wave of reform swept the states, and although most kept the basic legal principles of English common law (see Document 21), at least in modified form, they did away with the convoluted pleadings and other complex procedures. The Georgia Judiciary Act of 1799 merged equity with law in a single court system, abolished many of the old forms, and allowed a plaintiff to initiate a suit by the simple action of filing a petition and stating the complaint, while a defendant could respond in an equally simple manner.

See R. W. Millar, *Civil Procedure of the Trial Court in Historical Perspective* (1952); L. M. Friedman, *A History of American Law* (1973); and W. E. Nelson, *Americanization of the Common Law* (1975).

Source: Cushing, ed., 2 *First Laws of . . . Georgia* 689 (1981).

VIII.   *And be it further enacted,* That all suits of a civil nature, cognizable in the said courts respectively, shall be by petition to the court, which petition shall contain the plaintiff's charge, allegation or demand, plainly, fully and distinctly set forth; and be signed by the plaintiff or his, her or their attorney, and to which petition the clerk shall annex a process signed by such clerk, and bear teste in the name of one of the judges, or justices of such court, directed to the sheriff, requiring the defendant or defendants to appear at the court to which the same shall be made returnable, and shall be served on the defendant or defendants at least *twenty* days before the return thereof, by delivering a copy of such petition and process to the defendant or defendants, or leaving such copy at his, her or their most notorious place or places of residence. And if any process shall be delivered to the sheriff or other officer whose duty it shall be to execute the same, so late that it cannot be served in manner aforesaid, *twenty* days before the sitting of the court to which it shall be returnable, such process shall not be executed, but the officer shall return the same with the truth of the case. And if any original civil process shall be taken out within *twenty* days of the next court, the same shall be made returnable to the next court to be held after the expiration of the said *twenty* days and not otherwise: And all process issued and returned in any other manner than that herein before directed, shall be, and the same is hereby declared to be null and void.

IX.   *And be it further enacted,* That all process issued by the clerks of the said courts respectively, where the sheriff, who ought to execute the same, shall be anywise interested, shall be directed to the coroner of such county, and served and returned by him in the same manner as is required of sheriffs: And for the more orderly and regular proceeding in the said courts, the following rules and methods shall be observed, to wit: The defendant or defendants shall appear at the court to which the petition and process shall be returnable, and on or before the last day of the said court, shall make his, her or their defence or answer in writing, which shall plainly, fully and distinctly set forth the cause of his defence, and be signed by the party making the same, or his, her or their attorney; which said answer may contain as many several matters as such defendant or defendants may think necessary for his, her or their defence: *Provided,* That no person shall be permitted to deny any deed, bond, bill, single or penal, note, draft, receipt, or order, unless he, she or they, shall make affidavit of the truth of such answer at the time of filing the same: And the said petition and answer shall be sufficient to carry the same to the jury, without any replication or other course of proceedings: And no petition, answer, return process, judgment, or other proceeding in any civil cause, shall be abated, arrested, quashed or reversed for any defect in matter of form, or for any clerical mistake or omission, not affecting the real merits of the cause; but the court on motion shall cause the same to be amended without any additional cost at the first term, and shall proceed to give judgment according to the right of the cause and matter of law, as it shall appear to the said court, without regard to such imperfections in matter of form, clerical mistake or omission; and no dilatory answer shall be received or admitted unless affidavit be made of the truth thereof.

X.   *And be it further enacted,* That where any defendant shall fail to appear and answer in manner aforesaid, the court on motion of the plaintiff, or his counsel, shall enter a judgment by default, and the plaintiff's claim, allegation or demand, shall be tried in all cases of judgment by default, by a jury; but no such trial shall in any case be had at the first term: And no cause whatsoever, depending in the said courts shall be continued more than one term at the instance of the same party.

XI.   *And be it further enacted,* That in all cases where a suit shall be instituted in any of the said courts, on any bond, note, or other written obligation, subscribed by several persons, who reside in different counties, the plaintiff shall have his option to institute his suit in either of the said counties, and the clerk shall issue the original petition and process and a copy or copies in such county, against the defendant or defendants who may reside therein, in manner directed by this act; and shall also issue another original and copy or copies thereof for the defendant or defendants, resident in other county or counties: and it shall be the duty of the plaintiff, his agent or attorney, to cause such original and copies to be delivered to the sheriff or other officer in such other county or counties, who shall execute and return the same to the court from whence they issued, in such manner as is herein before directed, and on such return the plaintiff may proceed as in other cases.

40

Instruction from Virginia Assembly to the Virginia Senators on Common Law (1800)

A major constitutional issue in the new republic was the extent to which English common law precedents still held sway in American law. For the most part, the more conservative Federalists tended to accede to English common law, while the Jeffersonian Republicans not only rejected the English precedent, but objected to judges making policy through common law decisions—a role they reserved solely to the legislature. Aside from these political considerations, some legal thinkers began to question the common law itself, terming it uncertain and capricious and arguing for the adoption of continental-style civil codes. The concern of the Virginia legislature stemmed in part from statements by Judge Peters in the Circuit Court case of United States v. Worrall, 28 Fed. Cases 774 (1798), that federal courts could exercise a federal criminal jurisdiction on the basis of their common law authority. The Supreme Court finally ruled on the matter in 1812; see Document 51.

See M. J. Horwitz, *The Transformation of American Law, 1780–1860* (1977); and R. E. Ellis, *The Jeffersonian Crisis: Courts and Politics in the Young Republic* (1971).

~~~~~~

The general assembly of Virginia would consider themselves unfaithful to the trust reposed in them, were they to remain silent, whilst a doctrine has been publicly advanced, novel in its principle, and tremendous in its consequences: That the common law of England is in force under the government of the United States. It is not at this time proposed to expose at large the monstrous pretentions resulting from the adoption of this principle. It ought never, however, to be forgotten, and can never be too often repeated, that it opens a new tribunal for the trial of crimes never contemplated by the

Source: St. George Tucker, ed. of Blackstone, 1 *Commentaries on the Laws of England* 438 (1803).

federal compact. It opens a new code of sanguinary criminal law, both obsolete and unknown, and either wholly rejected or essentially modified in almost all its parts by state institutions. It arrests, or supercedes, state jurisdictions, and innovates upon state laws. It subjects the citizen to punishment, according to the judiciary will, when he is left in ignorance of what this law enjoins as a duty, or prohibits as a crime. It assumes a range of jurisdiction for the federal courts, which defies limitation or definition. In short it is believed, that the advocates for the principle would, themselves, be lost in an attempt to apply it to the existing institutions of federal and state courts, by separating with precision their judiciary rights, and thus preventing the constant and mischievous interference of rival jurisdictions.

Deeply impressed with these opinions, the general assembly of Virginia, instruct the senators, and request the representatives from this state, in congress, to use their best efforts. . . .

To oppose the passing of any law, founded on, or recognizing the principle lately advanced, "that the common law of England, is in force under the government of the United States;" excepting from such opposition, such particular parts of the common law, as may have a sanction from the constitution, so far as they are necessarily comprehended in the technical phrases which express the powers delegated to the government; . . . and excepting, also, such other parts thereof as may be adopted by congress as necessary and proper for carrying into execution the powers expressly delegated.

Part V

Legal Foundations of Nationhood

The early nineteenth century saw the Supreme Court emerge not only as the coequal branch of government envisioned by the Framers, but also as the supreme arbiter of the Constitution. Much of the credit for this development goes to John Marshall, the great Chief Justice of the United States from 1801 to 1835, and to his colleague on the bench Joseph Story, who often provided the intellectual underpinnings for Marshall's sweepingly nationalistic opinions (Document 60).

The era started with the inauguration of Thomas Jefferson who, rather than attempting to overturn the policies of his Federalist predecessors, promised to maintain the new nation in all its constitutional vigor (Document 41). A few weeks before Jefferson took the oath of office, John Adams had appointed John Marshall as Chief Justice. There was little love lost between Jefferson and his cousin, and it was inevitable that they would be the foci of tensions between Republicans and Federalists. The first clash came over the appointment of midnight judges, and gave rise to one of the greatest opinions in Court history, Marshall's broad assertion that the Court was the premier interpreter of the Constitution (Document 42). While criticism of the Chief Justice's claims for judicial review have often come from those dissatisfied with the Court's rulings, there has, understandably, been little complaint from within the judiciary over this great power. One of the few such complaints came from the respected Pennsylvania jurist John Gibson (Document 43), and in recent years there have been some scholars who have given great attention to his views.

Tension within the government increased as Federalist judges such as Samuel Chase abused their judicial authority for partisan political purposes (Document 45), and Republicans tried to use the law against their political opponents (Document 47). But eventually the tensions passed as the Republicans grew more nationalistic, and the judiciary toned down some of its more extreme nationalist views. Jefferson, faced with the glorious prospect of acquiring the vast Louisiana Territory, had to agree to a Hamiltonian interpretation of the Constitution to justify his actions (Document 44), a view

169

ultimately validated by the Court (Document 45). And the Republicans were forced to uphold the authority of the federal courts over state tribunals in order to sustain their own foreign policy (Document 48).

Just as the Washington administration had shaped the contours of the federal government in its time, so the Marshall Court laid the foundation for national power under the Constitution in expansive interpretations of the Commerce Clause (Document 57), judicial authority (Documents 42, 48, and 51), and congressional powers to implement Article I powers (Document 54). These decisions did not always go unchallenged, and in Andrew Jackson's veto of the Bank bill (Document 55), one finds not only a repudiation of the Court's judgment, but an alternative view on the locus of power in constitutional interpretation. About this time, recognizing that neither public opinion nor the executive branch would support a Court decision, the state of Georgia successfully flouted a Marshall opinion (Document 58). States' rights proponents also won a victory of sorts in the Court's decision that the Bill of Rights applied only to the federal government (Document 59). In sum, though, these decisions of the Marshall Court established the foundations for the great economic and political expansion of the nation.

Through these early decades of the nineteenth century, significant changes were taking place in the nature of American commerce, as national markets replaced local markets and required a commercial law both more flexible and more reliable than older precepts. On the national level, the Marshall Court's interpretation of the Contract Clause protected businessmen from the threat of arbitrary state action (Documents 49, 51, and 52), while still allowing the states to enact appropriate legislation when Congress failed to act (Document 53). Some of the most creative judicial activity, however, took place in state courts, where judges used common law techniques to fit the changing nature of the marketplace; these cases are explored in Part VI.

41

First Inaugural (1801)

THOMAS JEFFERSON

The Republicans clearly won the election of 1800, and the Federalists prepared to turn over the reins of government on March 4, 1801. Many European observers believed that the United States would soon plunge into civil war, for history recorded no instance of one faction peacefully surrendering the power of government to another. Nonetheless, despite the temporary impasse in Congress caused by a tie in electoral votes between Jefferson and his running mate, Aaron Burr (a situation remedied by the Twelfth Amendment), the transition went peacefully.

For those who expected that Jefferson would repudiate all of the policies of the Federalists, policies he had bitterly criticized for several years, the speech must have seemed very disappointing. Rather, he urged reconciliation, and the free play of differing views in an atmosphere of freedom. In fact, he fulfilled Hamilton's prediction that once in office Jefferson would "temporize," that is, he would mute his more radical ideas and be sobered by responsibility and authority. Nonetheless, the election of 1800 did constitute a "revolution" of sorts, and Jefferson's masterful inaugural remains a hallmark of democratic thought.

See D. Malone, 3 and 4 *Jefferson and His Times* (1948–77); M. Peterson, *Thomas Jefferson and the New Nation* (1970); and D. Sisson, *The American Revolution of 1800* (1974).

Friends and Fellow Citizens:—

Called upon to undertake the duties of the first executive office of our country, I avail myself of the presence of that portion of my fellow citizens which is here assembled, to express my grateful thanks for the favor with which they have been pleased to look toward me, to declare a sincere consciousness that the task is above my talents, and that I approach it with those anxious and awful presentiments which the greatness of the charge and the weakness of my powers so justly inspire. A rising nation, spread over a wide and fruitful land, traversing all the seas with the rich productions of their

Source: Peterson, ed., *The Portable Thomas Jefferson* 290 (1975).

industry, engaged in commerce with nations who feel power and forget right, advancing rapidly to destinies beyond the reach of mortal eye—when I contemplate these transcendent objects, and see the honor, the happiness, and the hopes of this beloved country committed to the issue and the auspices of this day, I shrink from the contemplation, and humble myself before the magnitude of the undertaking. Utterly indeed, should I despair, did not the presence of many whom I here see remind me, that in the other high authorities provided by our constitution, I shall find resources of wisdom, of virtue, and of zeal, on which to rely under all difficulties. To you, then, gentlemen, who are charged with the sovereign functions of legislation, and to those associated with you, I look with encouragement for that guidance and support which may enable us to steer with safety the vessel in which we are all embarked amid the conflicting elements of a troubled world.

During the contest of opinion through which we have passed, the animation of discussion and of exertions has sometimes worn an aspect which might impose on strangers unused to think freely and to speak and to write what they think; but this being now decided by the voice of the nation, announced according to the rules of the constitution, all will, of course, arrange themselves under the will of the law, and unite in common efforts for the common good. All, too, will bear in mind this sacred principle, that though the will of the majority is in all cases to prevail, that will, to be rightful, must be reasonable; that the minority possess their equal rights, which equal laws must protect, and to violate which would be oppression. Let us, then, fellow citizens, unite with one heart and one mind. Let us restore to social intercourse that harmony and affection without which liberty and even life itself are but dreary things. And let us reflect that having banished from our land that religious intolerance under which mankind so long bled and suffered, we have yet gained little if we countenance a political intolerance as despotic, as wicked, and capable of as bitter and bloody persecutions. During the throes and convulsions of the ancient world, during the agonizing spasms of infuriated man, seeking through blood and slaughter his long-lost liberty, it was not wonderful that the agitation of the billows should reach even this distant and peaceful shore; that this should be more felt and feared by some and less by others; that this should divide opinions as to measures of safety. But every difference of opinion is not a difference of principle. We have called by different names brethren of the same principle. We are all republicans—we are all federalists. If there be any among us who would wish to dissolve this Union or to change its republican form, let them stand undisturbed as monuments of the safety with which error of opinion may be tolerated where reason is left free to combat it. I know, indeed, that some honest men fear that a republican government cannot be strong; that this government is not strong enough. But would the honest patriot, in the full tide of successful experiment, abandon a government which has so far kept us free and firm, on the theoretic and visionary fear that this government, the world's best hope, may by possibility want energy to preserve itself? I trust not. I believe this, on the contrary, the strongest government on earth. I believe it is the only one where every man, at the call of the laws, would fly to the standard of the law, and would meet invasions of the public order as his own personal concern. Sometimes it is said that man cannot be trusted with the government of himself. Can he, then, be trusted with the government of others? Or have we found angels in the forms of kings to govern him? Let history answer this question.

Let us, then, with courage and confidence pursue our own federal and republican principles, our attachment to our union and representative government. Kindly separated by nature and a wide ocean from the exterminating havoc of one quarter of the globe; too high-minded to endure the degradations of the others; possessing a chosen country, with room enough for our descendants to the thousandth and thousandth generation; entertaining a due sense of our equal right to the use of our own faculties, to the acquisitions of our industry, to honor and confidence from our fellow citizens, resulting not from birth but from our actions and their sense of them; enlightened by a benign religion, professed, indeed, and practiced in various forms, yet all of them including honesty, truth, temperance, gratitude, and the love of man; acknowledging and adoring an overruling Providence, which by all its dispensations proves that it delights in the happiness of man here and his greater happiness hereafter; with all these blessings, what more is necessary to make us a happy and prosperous people? Still one thing more, fellow citizens—a wise and frugal government, which shall restrain men from injuring one another, which shall leave them otherwise free to regulate their own pursuits of industry and improvement, and shall not take from the mouth of labor the bread it has earned. This is the sum of good government, and this is necessary to close the circle of our felicities.

About to enter, fellow citizens, on the exercise of duties which comprehend everything dear and valuable to you, it is proper that you should understand what I deem the essential principles of our government, and consequently those which ought to shape its administration. I will compress them within the narrowest compass they will bear, stating the general principle, but not all its limitations. Equal and exact justice to all men, of whatever state or persuasion, religious or political; peace, commerce, and honest friendship, with all nations—entangling alliances with none; the support of the state governments in all their rights, as the most competent administrations for our domestic concerns and the surest bulwarks against anti-republican tendencies; the preservation of the general government in its whole constitutional vigor, as the sheet anchor of our peace at home and safety abroad; a jealous care of the right of election by the people—a mild and safe corrective of abuses which are lopped by the sword of the revolution where peaceable remedies are unprovided; absolute acquiescence in the decisions of the majority—the vital principle of republics, from which there is no appeal but to force, the vital principle and immediate parent of despotism; a well-disciplined militia—our best reliance in peace and for the first moments of war, till regulars may relieve them; the supremacy of the civil over the military authority; economy in the public expense, that labor may be lightly burdened; the honest payment of our debts and sacred preservation of the public faith; encouragement of agriculture, and of commerce as its handmaid; the diffusion of information and the arraignment of all abuses at the bar of public reason; freedom of religion; freedom of the press; freedom of person under the protection of the *habeas corpus;* and trial by juries impartially selected—these principles form the bright constellation which has gone before us, and guided our steps through an age of revolution and reformation. The wisdom of our sages and the blood of our heroes have been devoted to their attainment. They should be the creed of our political faith—the text of civil instruction—the touchstone by which to try the services of those we trust; and should we wander from them in moments of error or alarm, let us hasten to retrace our steps and to regain the road which alone leads to peace, liberty, and safety.

I repair, then, fellow citizens, to the post you have assigned me. With experience enough in subordinate offices to have seen the difficulties of this, the greatest of all, I have learned to expect that it will rarely fall to the lot of imperfect man to retire from this station with the reputation and the favor which bring him into it. Without pretensions to that high confidence reposed in our first and great revolutionary character, whose preëminent services had entitled him to the first place in his country's love, and destined for him the fairest page in the volume of faithful history, I ask so much confidence only as may give firmness and effect to the legal administration of your affairs. I shall often go wrong through defect of judgment. When right, I shall often be thought wrong by those whose positions will not command a view of the whole ground. I ask your indulgence for my own errors, which will never be intentional; and your support against the errors of others, who may condemn what they would not if seen in all its parts. The approbation implied by your suffrage is a consolation to me for the past; and my future solicitude will be to retain the good opinion of those who have bestowed it in advance, to conciliate that of others by doing them all the good in my power, and to be instrumental to the happiness and freedom of all.

Relying, then, on the patronage of your good will, I advance with obedience to the work, ready to retire from it whenever you become sensible how much better choice it is in your power to make. And may that Infinite Power which rules the destinies of the universe, lead our councils to what is best, and give them a favorable issue for your peace and prosperity.

42

Marbury v. *Madison (1803)*

No other case in the history of the Court has had the significance of *Marbury*, for in it Chief Justice Marshall not only finessed a potentially dangerous political confrontation between the executive and judicial branches, but also claimed two important constitutional powers for the courts—the authority to declare statutes unconstitutional and the power to decide which branch of government would decide the merits of certain constitutional questions. William Marbury had been named a justice of the peace for the District of Columbia in the closing hours of John Adams's term, and the Secretary of State (John Marshall—now Chief Justice) had been unable to deliver the commission. The new president, Thomas Jefferson, chose to disregard these last-minute appointments, and refused to deliver the remaining commissions. Marbury and some of the other disappointed nominees then went to the Supreme Court seeking a writ of mandamus to force Secretary of State James Madison to deliver the commissions. Marshall understood that if he awarded the writ, Jefferson would ignore it; to refuse, however, would make it appear that the Court had acted out of fear.

As he did in all his cases, Marshall condensed the issues to a few direct questions. Did Marbury have a right to the commission? If he did, and his rights had been violated, did the law provide him with a remedy? Finally, if so, did a writ of mandamus from the Supreme Court constitute the proper remedy? This last question was the crucial one, and dealt with the jurisdictional authority of the Court. As such, it should have been answered first, since a negative response would have obviated the need to answer the first two issues. But, as can be seen, by answering the questions in this order, the Chief Justice could criticize the Jefferson administration and still avoid a direct confrontation with it.

See G. L. Haskins and H. A. Johnson, *Foundations of Power: John Marshall, 1801–1815* (1981); D. O. Dewey, *Marshall v. Jefferson: The Political Background of Marbury v. Madison* (1970); and M. Marcus and S. Bloch, "John Marshall's Selective Use of History . . . ," 1986 *Wis. L. R.* 301 (1986).

Source: 1 Cranch 137 (1803).

~~~~~~

Chief Justice Marshall delivered the opinion of the Court.

At the last term on the affidavits then read and filed with the clerk, a rule was granted in this case, requiring the Secretary of State to show cause why a mandamus should not issue, directing him to deliver to William Marbury his commission as a justice of the peace for the county of Washington, in the district of Columbia.

No cause has been shown, and the present motion is for a mandamus. The peculiar delicacy of this case, the novelty of some of its circumstances, and the real difficulty attending the points which occur in it, require a complete exposition of the principles on which the opinion to be given by the court is founded. . . .

In the order in which the court has viewed this subject, the following questions have been considered and decided:

1st. Has the applicant a right to the commission he demands?

2d. If he has a right, and that right has been violated, do the laws of his country afford him a remedy?

3d. If they do afford him a remedy, is it a mandamus issuing from this court?

The first object of inquiry is—1st. Has the applicant a right to the commission he demands? . . .

It [is] decidedly the opinion of the court, that when a commission has been signed by the president, the appointment is made; and that the commission is complete, when the seal of the United States has been affixed to it by the secretary of state. . . .

To withhold his commission, therefore, is an act deemed by the court not warranted by law, but violative of a vested legal right.

This brings us to the second inquiry; which is 2dly. If he has a right, and that right has been violated, do the laws of his country afford him a remedy?

The very essence of civil liberty certainly consists in the right of every individual to claim the protection of the laws, whenever he receives an injury. One of the first duties of government is to afford that protection. [The] government of the United States has been emphatically termed a government of laws, and not of men. It will certainly cease to deserve this high appellation, if the laws furnish no remedy for the violation of a vested legal right. . . .

By the constitution of the United States, the President is invested with certain important political powers, in the exercise of which he is to use his own discretion, and is accountable only to his country in his political character, and to his own conscience. To aid him in the performance of these duties, he is authorized to appoint certain officers, who act by his authority and in conformity with his orders.

In such cases, their acts are his acts; and whatever opinion may be entertained of the manner in which executive discretion may be used, still there exists, and can exist, no power to control that discretion. The subjects are political. They respect the nation, not individual rights, and being entrusted to the executive, the decision of the executive is conclusive. . . .

But when the legislature proceeds to impose on that officer other duties; when he is directed peremptorily to perform certain acts; when the rights of individuals are dependent on the performance of those acts; he is so far the officer of the law; is amenable to the laws for his conduct; and cannot at his discretion sport away the vested rights of others.

The conclusion from this reasoning is, that where the heads of departments are the political or confidential agents of the executive, merely to execute the will of the President, or rather to act in cases in which the executive possesses a constitutional or legal discretion, nothing can be more perfectly clear than that their acts are only politically examinable. But where a specific duty is assigned by law, and individual rights depend upon the performance of that duty, it seems equally clear, that the individual who considers himself injured, has a right to resort to the laws of his country for a remedy. . . .

It is, then, the opinion of the Court [that Marbury has a] right to the commission; a refusal to deliver which is a plain violation of that right, for which the laws of his country afford him a remedy.

It remains to be enquired whether,

3dly. He is entitled to the remedy for which he applies. This depends on—1st. The nature of the writ applied for, and,

2dly. The power of this court.

1st. The nature of the writ. . . .

This, then, is a plain case for a mandamus, either to deliver the commission, or a copy of it from the record; and it only remains to be enquired,

Whether it can issue from this court.

The act to establish the judicial courts of the United States authorizes the Supreme Court "to issue writs of mandamus in cases warranted by the principles and usages of law, to any courts appointed, or persons holding office, under the authority of the United States."

The Secretary of State, being a person holding an office under the authority of the United States, is precisely within the letter of the description; and if this court is not authorized to issue a writ of mandamus to such an officer, it must be because the law is unconstitutional, and therefore absolutely incapable of conferring the authority, and assigning the duties which its words purport to confer and assign.

The constitution vests the whole judicial power of the United States in one Supreme Court, and such inferior courts as congress shall, from time to time, ordain and establish. This power is expressly extended to all cases arising under the laws of the United States; and, consequently, in some form, may be exercised over the present case; because the right claimed is given by a law of the United States.

In the distribution of this power it is declared that "the Supreme Court shall have original jurisdiction in all cases affecting ambassadors, other public ministers and consuls, and those in which a state shall be a party. In all other cases, the Supreme Court shall have appellate jurisdiction."

It has been insisted, at the bar, that as the original grant of jurisdiction, to the supreme and inferior courts, is general, and the clause, assigning original jurisdiction to the Supreme Court, contains no negative or restrictive words, the power remains to the legislature, to assign original jurisdiction to that court in other cases than those specified in the article which has been recited; provided those cases belong to the judicial power of the United States.

If it had been intended to leave it in the discretion of the legislature to apportion the judicial power between the supreme and inferior courts according to the will of that body, it would certainly have been useless to have proceeded further than to have defined the judicial power, and the tribunals in which it should be vested. The subsequent part of the section is mere surplusage, is entirely without meaning, if such is to be the construction. If congress remains at liberty to give this court appellate jurisdiction, where the constitution has declared their jurisdiction shall be original; and original jurisdiction where the constitution has declared it shall be appellate; the distribution of jurisdiction, made in the constitution, is form without substance.

Affirmative words are often, in their operation, negative of other objects than those affirmed; and in this case, a negative or exclusive sense must be given to them or they have no operation at all.

It cannot be presumed that any clause in the constitution is intended to be without effect; and, therefore, such a construction is inadmissible, unless the words require it.

If the solicitude of the convention, respecting our peace with foreign powers, induced a provision that the supreme court should take original jurisdiction in cases which might be supposed to affect them; yet the clause would have proceeded no further than to provide for such cases, if no further restriction on the powers of congress had been intended. That they should have appellate jurisdiction in all other cases, with such exceptions as congress might make, is no restriction; unless the words be deemed exclusive of original jurisdiction.

When an instrument organizing fundamentally a judicial system, divides it into one supreme, and so many inferior courts as the legislature may ordain and establish; then enumerates its powers, and proceeds so far to distribute them, as to define the jurisdiction of the supreme court by declaring the cases in which it shall take original jurisdiction, and that in others it shall take appellate jurisdiction; the plain import of the words seems to be, that in one class of cases its jurisdiction is original, and not appellate; in the other it is appellate, and not original. If any other construction would render the clause inoperative, that is an additional reason for rejecting such other construction, and for adhering to their obvious meaning.

To enable this court, then, to issue a mandamus, it must be shown to be an exercise of appellate jurisdiction, or to be necessary to enable them to exercise appellate jurisdiction.

It has been stated at the bar that the appellate jurisdiction may be exercised in a variety of forms, and that if it be the will of the legislature that a mandamus should be used for that purpose, that will must be obeyed. This is true, yet the jurisdiction must be appellate, not original.

It is the essential criterion of appellate jurisdiction, that it revises and corrects the proceedings in a cause already instituted, and does not create that cause. Although, therefore, a mandamus may be directed to courts, yet to issue such a writ to an officer for the delivery of a paper, is in effect the same as to sustain an original action for that paper, and, therefore, seems not to belong to appellate, but to original jurisdiction. Neither is it necessary in such a case as this, to enable the court to exercise its appellate jurisdiction.

The authority, therefore, given to the Supreme Court, by the act establishing the judicial courts of the United States, to issue writs of mandamus to public officers, appears not to be warranted by the constitution; and it becomes necessary to enquire whether a jurisdiction, so conferred, can be exercised.

The question, whether an act, repugnant to the constitution, can become the law of the land, is a question deeply interesting to the United States; but, happily, not of an intricacy proportioned to its interest. It seems only necessary to recognize certain principles, supposed to have been long and well established, to decide it.

That the people have an original right to establish, for their future government, such principles as, in their opinion, shall most conduce to their own happiness, is the basis on which the whole American fabric has been erected. The exercise of this original right is a very great exertion; nor can it, nor ought it, to be frequently repeated. The principles, therefore, so established, are deemed fundamental. And as the authority from which they proceed is supreme, and can seldom act, they are designed to be permanent.

This original and supreme will organizes the government, and assigns to different departments their respective powers. It may either stop here, or establish certain limits not to be transcended by those departments.

The government of the United States is of the latter description. The powers of the legislature are defined and limited; and that those limits may not be mistaken, or forgotten, the constitution is written. To what purpose are powers limited, and to what purpose is that limitation committed to writing, if these limits may, at any time, be passed by those intended to be restrained? The distinction between a government with limited and unlimited powers is abolished, if those limits do not confine the persons on whom they are imposed, and if acts prohibited and acts allowed, are of equal obligation. It is a proposition too plain to be contested, that the constitution controls any legislative act repugnant to it; or, that the legislature may alter the constitution by an ordinary act.

Between these alternatives there is no middle ground. The constitution is either a superior, paramount law, unchangeable by ordinary means, or it is on a level with ordinary legislative acts, and, like other acts, is alterable when the legislature shall please to alter it.

If the former part of the alternative be true, then a legislative act contrary to the constitution is not law: if the latter part be true, then written constitutions are absurd attempts, on the part of the people, to limit a power in its own nature illimitable.

Certainly all those who have framed written constitutions contemplate them as forming the fundamental and paramount law of the nation, and consequently, the theory of every such government must be, that an act of the legislature, repugnant to the constitution, is void.

This theory is essentially attached to a written constitution, and is, consequently, to be considered, by this court, as one of the fundamental principles of our society. It is not therefore to be lost sight of in the further consideration of this subject.

If an act of the legislature, repugnant to the constitution, is void, does it, notwithstanding its invalidity, bind the courts, and oblige them to give it effect? Or, in other words, though it be not law, does it constitute a rule as operative as if it was a law? This would be to overthrow in fact what was established in theory; and would seem, at first view, an absurdity too gross to be insisted on. It shall, however, receive a more attentive consideration.

It is emphatically the province and duty of the judicial department to say what the law is. Those who apply the rule to particular cases, must of necessity expound and interpret that rule. If two laws conflict with each other, the courts must decide on the operation of each.

So if a law be in opposition to the constitution; if both the law and the constitution apply to a particular case, so that the court must either decide that case conformably to the law, disregarding the constitution; or conformably to the constitution, disregarding the law; the court must determine which of these conflicting rules governs the case. This is of the very essence of judicial duty.

If, then, the courts are to regard the constitution, and the constitution is superior to any ordinary act of the legislature, the constitution, and not such ordinary act, must govern the case to which they both apply.

Those then who controvert the principle that the constitution is to be considered, in court, as a paramount law, are reduced to the necessity of maintaining that courts must close their eyes on the constitution, and see only the law.

This doctrine would subvert the very foundation of all written constitutions. It would declare that an act which, according to the principles and theory of our government, is entirely void, is yet, in practice, completely obligatory. It would declare that if the legislature shall do what is expressly forbidden, such act, notwithstanding the express prohibition, is in reality effectual. It would be giving to the legislature a practical and real omnipotence, with the same breath which professes to restrict their powers within narrow limits. It is prescribing limits, and declaring that those limits may be passed at pleasure.

That it thus reduces to nothing what we have deemed the greatest improvement on political institutions—a written constitution—would of itself be sufficient, in America, where written constitutions have been viewed with so much reverence, for rejecting the construction. But the peculiar expressions of the constitution of the United States furnish additional arguments in favour of its rejection.

The judicial power of the United States is extended to all cases arising under the constitution.

Could it be the intention of those who gave this power, to say that in using it the constitution should not be looked into? That a case arising under the constitution should be decided without examining the instrument under which it arises?

This is too extravagant to be maintained.

In some cases, then, the constitution must be looked into by the judges. And if they can open it at all, what part of it are they forbidden to read or to obey?

There are many other parts of the constitution which serve to illustrate this subject. It is declared that "no tax or duty shall be laid on articles exported from any state." Suppose a duty on the export of cotton, of tobacco, or of flour; and a suit instituted to recover it. Ought judgment to be rendered in such a case? Ought the judges to close their eyes on the constitution, and only see the law?

The constitution declares that "no bill of attainder or ex post facto law shall be passed."

If, however, such a bill should be passed, and a person should be prosecuted under it; must the court condemn to death those victims whom the constitution endeavors to preserve?

"No person," says the constitution, "shall be convicted of treason unless on the testimony of two witnesses to the same overt act, or on confession in open court."

Here the language of the constitution is addressed especially to the courts. It prescribes, directly for them, a rule of evidence not to be departed from. If the legislature should change that rule, and declare *one* witness, or a confession *out* of court, sufficient for conviction, must the constitutional principle yield to the legislative act?

From these, and many other selections which might be made, it is apparent, that the framers of the constitution contemplated that instrument as a rule for the government of *courts,* as well as of the legislature.

Why otherwise does it direct the judges to take an oath to support it? This oath certainly applies, in an especial manner, to their conduct in their official character. How immoral to impose it on them, if they were to be used as the instruments, and the knowing instruments, for violating what they swear to support!

The oath of office, too, imposed by the legislature, is completely demonstrative of the legislative opinion on this subject. It is in these words: "I do solemnly swear that I will administer justice without respect to persons, and do equal right to the poor and to the rich; and that I will faithfully and impartially discharge all the duties incumbent on me as ____ , according to the best of my abilities and understanding, agreeably to *the constitution,* and laws of the United States."

Why does a judge swear to discharge his duties agreeably to the constitution of the United States, if that constitution forms no rule for his government? If it is closed upon him, and cannot be inspected by him?

If such be the real state of things, this is worse than solemn mockery. To prescribe, or to take this oath, becomes equally a crime.

It is also not entirely unworthy of observation that in declaring what shall be the *supreme* law of the land, the *constitution* itself is first mentioned; and not the laws of the United States generally, but those only which shall be made in *pursuance* of the constitution, have that rank.

Thus, the particular phraseology of the constitution of the United States confirms and strengthens the principle, supposed to be essential to all written constitutions, that a law repugnant to the constitution is void; and that *courts,* as well as other departments, are bound by that instrument.

The rule must be discharged.

43

Eakin v. *Raub (1825)*

Marshall's tour de force in *Marbury* has been the source of continual debate among legal scholars and opponents of the Court, but there has been little criticism of the idea of judicial review from the bench itself. The best-known critique is that of Judge John Bannister Gibson, who served on the Pennsylvania Supreme Court for thirty-seven years, first

Source: 12 Ser. and Rawle 330 (Pennsylvania 1825).

as associate and then as Chief Justice. A distinguished and creative jurist, Gibson was almost appointed to the United States Supreme Court. One should bear in mind, however, while reading this refutation of Marshall's assumptions and conclusions, that twenty years later Gibson publicly announced that he had changed his mind, at least regarding the practice in state courts. He had reached this conclusion, he explained, both because an intervening state constitutional convention had silently "sanctified the pretensions of the courts" and because of his "experience of the necessity of the case" (Norris v. Clymer, 2 Pa. 277 [1845]).

Even here Gibson carefully limited his criticism of *Marbury* to the issue of judicial review of the acts of a coordinate branch of state government. Near the end of his opinion he asserted that state courts have not only the power but also the obligation to invalidate state laws that conflict with federal obligations, since the states, in joining the Union, had agreed to the supremacy of federal over state powers.

See L. Hand, *The Bill of Rights* (1958); and H. Wechsler, "Toward Neutral Principles of Constitutional Law," 73 *Harv. L. R.* 1 (1959).

~~~~~~

Justice Gibson

I am aware, that a right to declare all unconstitutional acts void, without distinction as to either state or federal constitution, is generally held as a professional dogma; but I apprehend, rather as a matter of faith than of reason. It is not a little remarkable, that although the right in question has all along been claimed by the judiciary, no judge has ventured to discuss it, except Chief Justice Marshall; and if the argument of a jurist so distinguished for the strength of his ratiocinative powers be found inconclusive, it may fairly be set down to the weakness of the position which he attempts to defend. . . .

The constitution is said to be a law of superior obligation; and consequently, that if it were to come into collision with an act of the legislature, the latter would have to give way; this is conceded. But it is a fallacy, to suppose, that they can come into collision *before the judiciary.*

The constitution and the *right* of the legislature to pass the act, may be in collision; but is that a legitimate subject for judicial determination? If it be, the judiciary must be a peculiar organ, to revise the proceedings of the legislature, and to correct its mistakes; and in what part of the constitution are we to look for this proud preeminence? It is by no means clear, that to declare a law void, which has been enacted according to the forms prescribed in the constitution, is not a usurpation of legislative power. It is an act of sovereignty; and sovereignty and legislative power are said by Sir William *Blackstone* to be convertible terms. It is the business of the judiciary, to interpret the laws, not scan the authority of the lawgiver; and without the latter, it cannot take cognizance of a collision between a law and the constitution. So that, to affirm that the judiciary has a right to judge of the existence of such collision, is to take for granted the very thing to be proved.

But it has been said to be emphatically the business of the judiciary, to ascertain and pronounce what the law is; and that this necessarily involves a consideration of the constitution. It does so: but how far? If the judiciary will inquire into anything beside the form of enactment, where shall it stop? There must be some point of limitation to such an inquiry; for no one will pretend, that a judge would be justifiable in calling for the election returns, or scrutinizing the qualifications of those who composed the legislature.

It will not be pretended, that the legislature has not, at least, an equal right with the judiciary to put a construction on the constitution; nor that either of them is infallible; nor that either ought to be required to surrender its judgment to the other. Suppose, then, they differ in opinion as to the constitutionality of a particular law; if the organ whose business it first is to decide on the subject, is not to have its judgment treated with respect, what shall prevent it from securing the preponderance of its opinion by the strong arm of power? The soundness of any construction which would bring one organ of the government into collision with another, is to be more than suspected; for where collision occurs, it is evident, the machine is working in a way the framers of it did not intend. . . .

But the judges are sworn to support the constitution, and are they not bound by it as the law of the land? The oath to support the constitution is not peculiar to the judges, but is taken indiscriminately by every officer of the government, and is designed rather as a test of the political principles of the man, than to bind the officer in the discharge of his duty: otherwise, it were difficult to determine, what operation it is to have in the case of a recorder of deeds, for instance, who, in the execution of his office, has nothing to do with the constitution. But granting it to relate to the official conduct of the judge, as well as every other officer, and not to his political principles, still, it must be understood in reference to supporting the constitution, *only as far as that may be involved in his official duty;* and consequently, if his official duty does not comprehend an inquiry into the authority of the legislature, neither does his oath. . . .

But do not the judges do a *positive* act in violation of the constitution, when they give effect to an unconstitutional law? Not if the law has been passed according to the forms established in the constitution. The fallacy of the question is, in supposing that the judiciary adopts the acts of the legislature as its own; whereas, the enactment of a law and the interpretation of it are not concurrent acts, and as the judiciary is not required to concur in the enactment, neither is it in the breach of the constitution which may be the consequence of the enactment; the fault is imputable to the legislature, and on it the responsibility exclusively rests.

44

Memorandum on Louisiana Purchase (1803)

ALBERT GALLATIN

In early 1803 Napoleon Bonaparte, for a number of reasons, offered to sell the vast Louisiana Territory to the United States. Jefferson badly wanted Louisiana, but his belief in a narrow interpretation of the Constitution (see Document 31) created a severe problem for him. Nothing in the Constitution, he believed, explicitly granted the national government power to acquire additional territory, a view shared by his Attorney General, Levi Lincoln. For a while Jefferson thought he would have to secure a constitutional amendment in order to gain the vast western territory. But his Secretary of the Treasury, Albert Gallatin, realized that the time lost in seeking such an amendment could well lead the fickle Napoleon to withdraw his offer, and in a memorandum to Jefferson on January 13, 1803, laid out a constitutional basis for proceeding with the transaction. Gallatin, like Hamilton in the Bank dispute (Document 32), took a broad view of constitutional power and claimed that the treaty power included sovereign prerogatives such as acquiring new territory. Eager to secure Louisiana, Jefferson followed Gallatin's interpretation, which was later upheld by the Supreme Court (see next document).

See E. S. Brown, *Constitutional History of the Louisiana Purchase* (1920); R. Walters, Jr., *Albert Gallatin* (1957); and I. Brant, *James Madison, Secretary of State* (1953).

Source: H. Adams, 1 *Writings of Albert Gallatin* 111 (1879).

I have read Mr. Lincoln's observations, and cannot distinguish the difference between a power to acquire territory for the United States and the power to extend by treaty the territory of the United States; yet he contends that the first is unconstitutional, supposes that we may acquire East Louisiana and West Florida by annexing them to the Mississippi Territory. Nor do I think his other idea, that of annexation to a State, that, for instance, of East Florida to Georgia, as proposed by him, to stand on a better foundation. If the acquisition of territory is not warranted by the Constitution, it is not more legal to acquire for one State than for the United States; if the Legislature and Executive established by the Constitution are not the proper organs for the acquirement of new territory for the use of the Union, still less can they be so for the acquirement of new territory for the use of one State; if they have no power to acquire territory, it is because the Constitution has confined its views to the then existing territory of the Union, and *that* excludes a possibility of enlargement of one State as well as that of territory common to the United States. As to the danger resulting from the exercise of such power, it is as great on his plan as on the other. What could, on his construction, prevent the President and the Senate by treaty annexing Cuba to Massachusetts, or Bengal to Rhode Island, if ever the acquirement of colonies shall become a favorite object with governments, and colonies shall be acquired?

But does any constitutional objection really exist?

The 3d Section of the 4th Article of the Constitution provides:

1st.　That new States may be admitted by Congress into this Union.

2d.　That Congress shall have power to dispose of and make all needful rules and regulations respecting the territory or other property belonging to the United States.

Mr. Lincoln, in order to support his objections, is compelled to suppose, 1st, that the new States therein alluded to must be carved either out of other States, or out of the territory belonging to the United States; and, 2d, that the power given to Congress of making regulations respecting the territory belonging to the United States is expressly confined to the territory *then* belonging to the Union.

A general and perhaps sufficient answer is that the whole rests on a supposition, there being no words in the section which confine the authority given to Congress to those specific objects; whilst, on the contrary, the existence of the United States as a nation presupposes the power enjoyed by every nation of extending their territory by treaties, and the general power given to the President and Senate of making treaties designates the organs through which the acquisition may be made, whilst this section provides the proper authority (viz., Congress) for either admitting in the Union or governing as subjects the territory thus acquired. It may be further observed in relation to the power of admitting new States in the Union, that this section was substituted to the 11th Article of Confederation, which was in these words: "Canada acceding, &c., shall be admitted into, &c., but no other colony shall be admitted into the same, unless such admission be agreed to by nine (9) States." As the power was there explicitly given to nine (9) States, and as all the other powers given in the Articles of Confederation to nine (9) States were by the Constitution transferred to Congress, there is no reason to believe, as the words relative to the power of admission are, in the Constitution, general, that it was not the true intention of that Constitution to give the power generally and without restriction.

As to the other clause, that which gives the power of governing the territory of the United States, the limited construction of Mr. Lincoln is still less tenable; for if that power is limited to the territory belonging to the United States at the time when the Constitution was adopted, it would have precluded the United States from governing any territory acquired, since the adoption of the Constitution, by cession of one of the States, which, however, has been done in the case of the cessions of North Carolina and Georgia; and, as the words "other property" follow, and must be embraced by the same construction which will apply to the territory, it would result from Mr. L.'s opinion, that the United States could not, after the Constitution, either acquire or dispose of any personal property. To me it would appear:

1st.   That the United States as a nation have an inherent right to acquire territory.

2d.   That whenever that acquisition is by treaty, the same constituted authorities in whom the treaty-making power is vested have a constitutional right to sanction the acquisition.

3d.   That whenever the territory has been acquired, Congress have the power either of admitting into the Union as a new State, or of annexing to a State with the consent of that State, or of making regulations for the government of such territory.

The only possible objection must be derived from the 12th Amendment, which declares that powers not delegated to the United States, nor prohibited by it to the States, are reserved to the States or to the people. As the States are expressly prohibited from making treaties, it is evident that, if the power of acquiring territory by treaty is not considered within the meaning of the Amendment as delegated to the United States, it must be reserved to the people. If that be the true construction of the Constitution, it substantially amounts to this: that the United States are precluded from, and renounce altogether, the enlargement of territory, a provision sufficiently important and singular to have deserved to be expressly enacted. Is it not a more natural construction to say that the power of acquiring territory is delegated to the United States by the several provisions which authorize the several branches of government to make war, to make treaties, and to govern the territory of the Union?

American Insurance Co.
v. Canter (1828)

Eager to secure Louisiana, Jefferson adopted Gallatin's view, much to the distress of some of the constitutional purists within the Republican party; the issue, however, did not reach the Supreme Court for another quarter century. The facts of the case are as follows: The American Insurance Company sued to recover a cargo of cotton that it had insured, and that had been sold by order of the Florida territorial legislature. The insurer claimed that the territorial court that had directed the sale was not a duly authorized court, since the acquisition of Florida by the United States was unconstitutional. The Court completely dismissed this argument and ruled that the government, as part of its inherent sovereign powers, had the right to acquire territory through treaty or by military conquest. The opinion has been considered definitive ever since on the right of the nation to acquire, govern, and dispose of territory.

See L. Henkin, *Foreign Affairs and the Constitution* (1972).

Chief Justice Marshall delivered the opinion of the Court.

The plaintiffs filed their libel in this cause in the District Court of South Carolina, to obtain restitution of 356 bales of cotton, part of the cargo of the ship Point a Petre; which had been insured by them on a voyage from New-Orleans to Havre de Grace, in France. The Point a Petre was wrecked on the coast of Florida, the cargo saved by the inhabitants, and carried into Key West, where it was sold for the purpose of satisfying the salvors; by virtue of a decree of a Court, consisting of a notary and five jurors, which was erected by an Act of the territorial legislature of Florida. The owners abandoned to the underwriters, who having accepted the same, proceeded against the property; alleging that the sale was not made by order of a Court competent to change the property.

David Canter claimed the cotton as a *bona fide* purchaser, under the decree of a competent Court, which awarded seventy-six per cent. to the salvors, on the value of the property saved. . . .

Source: 1 Peters 511 (1828).

The tribunal was constituted by an Act of the territorial legislature of Florida, passed on the 4th July 1823, which is inserted in the record. That Act purports to give the power which has been exercised; consequently the sale is valid, if the territorial legislature was competent to enact the law.

The course which the argument has taken, will require, that, in deciding this question, the Court should take into view the relation in which Florida stands to the United States.

The Constitution confers absolutely on the government of the Union, the powers of making war, and of making treaties; consequently, that government possesses the power of acquiring territory, either by conquest or by treaty.

The usage of the world is, if a nation be not entirely subdued, to consider the holding of conquered territory as a mere military occupation, until its fate shall be determined at the treaty of peace. If it be ceded by the treaty, the acquisition is confirmed, and the ceded territory becomes a part of the nation to which it is annexed; either on the terms stipulated in the treaty of cession, or on such as its new master shall impose. On such transfer of territory, it has never been held, that the relations of the inhabitants with each other undergo any change. Their relations with their former sovereign are dissolved, and new relations are created between them and the government which has acquired their territory. The same Act which transfers their country, transfers the allegiance of those who remain in it; and the law, which may be denominated political, is necessarily changed, although that which regulates the intercourse, and general conduct of individuals, remains in force, until altered by the newly created power of the state.

On the 2d of February 1819, Spain ceded Florida to the United States. The 6th article of the treaty of cession, contains the following provision—"The inhabitants of the territories, which his Catholic majesty cedes to the United States by this treaty, shall be incorporated in the Union of the United States, as soon as may be consistent with the principles of the federal Constitution; and admitted to the enjoyment of the privileges, rights, and immunities of the citizens of the United States."

This treaty is the law of the land, and admits the inhabitants of Florida to the enjoyment of the privileges, rights, and immunities, of the citizens of the United States. It is unnecessary to inquire, whether this is not their condition, independent of stipulation. They do not, however, participate in political power; they do not share in the government, till Florida shall become a state. In the mean time, Florida continues to be a territory of the United States; governed by virtue of that clause in the Constitution, which empowers Congress "to make all needful rules and regulations, respecting the territory, or other property belonging to the United States."

Perhaps the power of governing a territory belonging to the United States, which has not, by becoming a state acquired the means of self-government, may result necessarily from the facts, that it is not within the jurisdiction of any particular state, and is within the power and jurisdiction of the United

States. The right to govern, may be the inevitable consequence of the right to acquire territory. Whichever may be the source whence the power is derived, the possession of it is unquestioned. In execution of it, Congress, in 1822, passed "an Act for the establishment of a territorial government in Florida;" and, on the 3d of March 1823, passed another Act to amend the Act of 1822. Under this Act, the territorial legislature enacted the law now under consideration.

The 5th section of the Act of 1823, creates a territorial legislature, which shall have legislative powers over all rightful objects of legislation; but no law shall be valid, which is inconsistent with the laws and Constitution of the United States. . . .

The 7th section of the Act of 1823, vests the whole judicial power of the territory "in two Superior Courts, and in such inferior Courts, and justices of the peace, as the legislative council of the territory may from time to time establish." This general grant is common to the superior and inferior Courts, and their jurisdiction is concurrent, except so far as it may be made exclusive in either, by other provisions of the statute. . . .

The 8th section extends the jurisdiction of the Superior Courts, in terms which admit of more doubt. The words are "That each of the said Superior Courts, shall moreover have and exercise the same jurisdiction, within its limits, in all cases arising under the laws and Constitution of the United States, which, by an Act to establish the judicial Courts of the United States, was vested in the Court of the Kentucky district." . . .

Is the admiralty jurisdiction of the District Courts of the United States vested in the Superior Courts of Florida under the words of the 8th section, declaring that each of the said Courts "shall moreover have and exercise the same jurisdiction within its limits, in all cases arising under the laws and Constitution of the United States," which was vested in the Courts of the Kentucky district?

It is observable, that this clause does not confer on the territorial Courts all the jurisdiction which is vested in the Court of the Kentucky district, but that part of it only which applies to "cases arising under the laws and Constitution of the United States." Is a case of admiralty of this description?

The Constitution and laws of the United States, give jurisdiction to the District Courts over all cases in admiralty; but jurisdiction over the case, does not constitute the case itself. We are therefore to inquire, whether cases in admiralty, and cases arising under the laws and Constitution of the United States, are identical.

If we have recourse to that pure fountain from which all the jurisdiction of the Federal Courts is derived, we find language employed which cannot well be misunderstood. The Constitution declares, that "the judicial power shall extend to all cases in law and equity, arising under this Constitution, the laws of the United States, and treaties made, or which shall be made, under their authority; to all cases affecting ambassadors, or other public ministers, and consuls; to all cases of admiralty and maritime jurisdiction."

The Constitution certainly contemplates these as three distinct classes of cases; and if they are distinct, the grant of jurisdiction over one of them does not confer jurisdiction over either of the other two. The discrimination made between them, in the Constitution, is, we think, conclusive against their identity. If it were not so, if this were a point open to inquiry, it would be difficult to maintain the proposition that they are the same. A case in admiralty does not, in fact, arise under the Constitution or laws of the United States. These cases are as old as navigation itself; and the law, admiralty and maritime as it has existed for ages, is applied by our Courts to the cases as they arise. It is not then to the 8th section of the territorial law that we are to look for the grant of admiralty and maritime jurisdiction, to the territorial Courts. Consequently, if that jurisdiction is exclusive, it is not made so by the reference to the District Court of Kentucky.

It has been contended, that by the Constitution the judicial power of the United States extends to all cases of admiralty and maritime jurisdiction; and that the whole of this judicial power must be vested "in one Supreme Court, and in such inferior Courts as Congress shall from time to time ordain and establish." Hence it has been argued, that Congress cannot vest admiralty jurisdiction in Courts created by the territorial legislature.

We have only to pursue this subject one step further, to perceive that this provision of the Constitution does not apply to it. The next sentence declares, that "the Judges both of the Supreme and inferior Courts, shall hold their offices during good behaviour." The Judges of the Superior Courts of Florida hold their offices for four years. These Courts, then, are not constitutional Courts, in which the judicial power conferred by the Constitution on the general government, can be deposited. They are incapable of receiving it. They are legislative Courts, created in virtue of the general right of sovereignty which exists in the government, or in virtue of that clause which enables Congress to make all needful rules and regulations, respecting the territory belonging to the United States. The jurisdiction with which they are invested, is not a part of that judicial power which is defined in the 3d article of the Constitution, but is conferred by Congress, in the execution of those general powers which that body possesses over the territories of the United States. Although admiralty jurisdiction can be exercised in the states in those Courts, only, which are established in pursuance of the third article of the Constitution; the same limitation does not extend to the territories. In legislating for them, Congress exercises the combined powers of the general, and of a state government.

We think, then, that the Act of the territorial legislature, erecting the Court by whose decree the cargo of the Point a Petre was sold, is not "inconsistent with the laws and Constitution of the United States," and is valid. Consequently, the sale made in pursuance of it changed the property, and the decree of the Circuit Court, awarding restitution of the property to the claimant, ought to be affirmed with costs.

46

Charge to Grand Jury (1803)

SAMUEL CHASE

Associate Justice Samuel Chase had signed the Declaration of Independence, but his subsequent long and often distinguished career had been marked by more than one blemish, and he had barely escaped impeachment while a Maryland state judge. Lawyers feared his frequent tirades from the bench, and he frequently used jury charges to vent his spleen on political figures and events he despised. His intemperate attacks on the expansion of the suffrage, which he claimed would lead to "mobocracy," provided the immediate cause for his impeachment by the Republican-controlled House of Representatives. But in a larger context, the impeachment stood for the battle between the Jeffersonians and what they viewed as the entrenched Federalist interests in the judiciary. So long as the Federalists controlled the courts, the Jeffersonians believed their democratic political ideals could never be fully realized. The following Chase charge to a Baltimore grand jury displays not only his political invective but why the Republicans sought to remove him.

See R. E. Ellis, *The Jeffersonian Crisis: Courts and Politics in the Young Republic* (1971); D. O. Dewey, *Marshall v. Jefferson* (1970); and R. B. Lillich, "The Chase Impeachment," 4 *A.J.L.H.* 49 (1960).

It is essentially necessary at all times, but more particularly at the present, that the public mind should be truly informed; and that our citizens should entertain correct principles of government, and fixed ideas of their social rights. It is a very easy task to deceive or mislead the great body of the people by propagating plausible, but false doctrines; for the bulk of mankind are governed by their passions and not by reason.

Falsehood can be more readily disseminated than truth, and the latter is heard with reluctance if repugnant to popular prejudice. From the year 1776, I have been a decided and avowed advocate for a representative or republican form of government, as since established by our state and national consti-

Source: Smith and Lloyd, *Trial of Samuel Chase . . . ,* Appendix v (1805).

tutions. It is my sincere wish that freemen should be governed by their representatives, fairly and freely elected by that class of citizens described in our bill of rights, who have property in, a common interest with, and an attachment to, the community.

. . . [T]he history of mankind (in ancient and modern times) informs us "that a monarchy may be free, and that a republic may be a tyranny." The true test of liberty is in the practical enjoyment of protection to the person and the property of the citizen, from all enquiry. Where the same laws govern the whole society without any distinction, and there is no power to dispense with the execution of the laws; where justice is impartially and speedily administered, and the poorest man in the community may obtain redress against the most wealthy and powerful, . . . in that country the people are free. This is our present situation.—Where law is uncertain, partial or arbitrary; where justice is not impartially administered to all; where property is insecure, and the person is liable to insult and violence without redress by law, the people are not free, whatever may be their form of government. To this situation, I greatly fear we are fast approaching.

. . . [T]he late alteration of the federal judiciary by the abolition of the office of the sixteenth circuit judges, and the recent change in our state constitution by the establishing of universal suffrage, . . . will, in my judgment, take away all security for property and personal liberty. The independence of the national judiciary is already shaken to its foundation, and the virtue of the people alone can restore it. The independence of the judges of this state will be entirely destroyed, if the bill for the abolition of the two supreme courts [is enacted]. The change of the state constitution, by allowing universal suffrage, will, in my opinion, certainly and rapidly destroy all protection to property, and all security to personal liberty; and our republican constitution will sink into a mobocracy, the worst of all possible governments. . . .

I cannot but remember the great and patriotic characters by whom your state constitution was framed. I cannot but recollect that attempts were then made in favor of universal suffrage; and to render the judges dependent upon the legislature. You may believe that the gentlemen who framed your constitution, possessed the full confidence of the people of Maryland, and that they were esteemed for their talents and patriotism, and for their public and private virtues. You must have heard that many of them held the highest civil and military stations, and that they, at every risk and danger, assisted to obtain and establish your independence. . . . With great concern I observe, that the sons of some of these characters have united to pull down the beautiful fabric of wisdom and republicanism that their fathers erected!

The declarations respecting the natural rights of man, which originated from the claim of the British parliament to make laws to bind America in all cases whatsoever; the publications since that period, of visionary and theoretical writers, asserting that men in a state of society, are entitled to exercise rights which they possessed in a state of nature; and the modern doctrines by our late reformers, that all men in a state of society, are entitled to enjoy equal liberty and equal rights, have brought this mighty mischief upon us; and I fear that it will rapidly progress, until peace and order, freedom and property shall be destroyed. . . .

I have long since subscribed to the opinion, that there could be no rights of man in a state of nature, previous to the institution of society; and that liberty properly speaking, could not exist in a state of nature. I do not believe that any number of men ever existed together in a state of nature, without some head, leader or chief, whose advice they followed, and whose precepts they obeyed. . . . The great object for which men establish any form of government, is to obtain security to their persons and property from violence, destroy the security to either and you tear up society by the roots. It appears to me that the institution of government is really no sacrifice made, as some writers contend, to natural liberty, for I think that previous to the formation of some species of government, a state of liberty could not exist. It seems to me that personal liberty and rights can only be acquired by becoming a member of a community, which gives the protection of the whole to every individual. . . . From hence I conclude that liberty and rights, (and also property) must spring out of civil society, and must be forever subject to the modification of particular governments. . . . I cheerfully subscribe to the doctrine of equal liberty and equal rights, if properly explained. I understand by equality of liberty and rights, only this, that every citizen, without respect to property or station, should enjoy an equal share of civil liberty; an equal protection from the laws, and an equal security for his person and property. Any other interpretation of these terms, is in my judgment, destructive of all government and all laws. . . . Will justice be impartially administered by judges dependant on the legislature for their continuance in office, and also for their support? Will liberty or property be protected or secured, by laws made by representatives chosen by electors, who have no property in, a common interest with, or attachment to the community?

Ex Parte Bollman (1807)

The details of the bizarre 1806 Burr conspiracy are still muddled, but it is clear that the former Vice-president was arrested and brought to Richmond to be tried for treason, and that a vindictive Jefferson wanted Burr convicted. John Marshall, in his role as circuit judge, presided over the trial, and in doing so imposed a very strict interpretation of what the Constitution meant by treason. Marshall was criticized then and later for having apparently changed his mind from the more expansive view of treason he had set forth in this earlier proceeding growing out of the Burr conspiracy, the arrest and allegedly unlawful detention of two of Burr's supposed co-conspirators, Samuel Swartwout and Dr. Erick Bollman. Although Marshall had no need to deal with the question of treason in this case, he hoped to depoliticize the matter and also establish a firm rule of law by defining what the Constitution meant by treason. It was an effort doomed to failure. The government used Marshall's definition in its case against Burr, and the Chief Justice had to modify his ruling, a decision that led to charges that he merely wanted to spite the administration. One element of Marshall's definition remained valid, however, and that was that treason could only take place within the context of war, that acts, even if hostile, by themselves did not necessarily meet the constitutional standard.

See M. Lomask, *Aaron Burr: Conspiracy and Years of Exile* (1982); B. Chapin, *The American Law of Treason* (1964); R. Faulkner, "John Marshall and the Burr Trial," 53 *J. Am. Hist.* 247 (1966).

Chief Justice Marshall delivered the opinion of the Court.

The prisoners having been brought before this court on a writ of *habeas corpus,* and the testimony on which they were committed having been fully examined and attentively considered, the court is now to declare the law upon their case. . . .

The specific charge brought against the prisoners is treason in levying war against the United States.

As there is no crime which can more excite and agitate the passions of men

Source: 4 Cranch 100 (1807).

than treason, no charge demands more from the tribunal before which it is made a deliberate and temperate inquiry. Whether this inquiry be directed to the fact or to the law, none can be more solemn, none more important to the citizen or to the government; none can more affect the safety of both.

To prevent the possibility of those calamities which result from the extension of treason to offences of minor importance, that great fundamental law which defines and limits the various departments of our government has given a rule on the subject both to the legislature and the courts of America, which neither can be permitted to transcend.

"Treason against the United States shall consist only in levying war against them, or in adhering to their enemies, giving them aid and comfort."

To constitute that specific crime for which the prisoners now before the court have been committed, war must be actually levied against the United States. However flagitious may be the crime of conspiring to subvert by force the government of our country, such conspiracy is not treason. To conspire to levy war, and actually to levy war, are distinct offences. The first must be brought into operation by the assemblage of men for a purpose treasonable in itself, or the fact of levying war cannot have been committed. So far has this principle been carried, that, in a case reported by Ventris, and mentioned in some modern treatises on criminal law, it has been determined that the actual enlistment of men to serve against the government does not amount to levying war. It is true that in that case the soldiers enlisted were to serve without the realm, but they were enlisted within it, and if the enlistment for a treasonable purpose could amount to levying war, then war had been actually levied.

It is not the intention of the court to say that no individual can be guilty of this crime who has not appeared in arms against his country. On the contrary, if war be actually levied, that is, if a body of men be actually assembled for the purpose of effecting by force a treasonable purpose, all those who perform any part, however minute, or however remote from the scene of action, and who are actually leagued in the general conspiracy, are to be considered as traitors. But there must be an actual assembling of men for the treasonable purpose, to constitute a levying of war.

Crimes so atrocious as those which have for their object the subversion by violence of those laws and those institutions which have been ordained in order to secure the peace and happiness of society, are not to escape punishment because they have not ripened into treason. The wisdom of the legislature is competent to provide for the case; and the framers of our constitution, who not only defined and limited the crime, but with jealous circumspection attempted to protect their limitation by providing that no person should be convicted of it, unless on the testimony of two witnesses to the same overt act, or on confession in open court, must have conceived it more safe that punishment in such cases should be ordained by general laws, formed upon deliberation, under the influence of no resentments, and without knowing on whom they were to operate, than that it should be inflicted under the influence of those passions which the occasion seldom fails to excite, and which a flexible definition of the crime, or a construction which would render it flexible, might bring into operation. It is therefore more safe as well as more consonant to the principles of our constitution, that the crime of treason should not be extended by construction to doubtful cases; and that crimes not clearly within the constitutional definition, should receive such punishment as the legislature in its wisdom may provide.

To complete the crime of levying war against the United States, there must be an actual assemblage of men for the purpose of executing a treasonable design. In the case now before the court, a design to overturn the government of the United States in New-Orleans by force, would have been unquestionably a design which, if carried into execution, would have been treason, and the assemblage of a body of men for the purpose of carrying it into execution would amount to levying of war against the United States; but no conspiracy for this object, no enlisting of men to effect it, would be an actual levying of war . . .

It is therefore the opinion of a majority of the court, that in the case of Samuel Swartwout there is not sufficient evidence of his levying war against the United States to justify his commitment on the charge of treason.

Against Erick Bollman there is still less testimony. Nothing has been said by him to support the charge that the enterprize in which he was engaged had any other object than was stated in the letter of Colonel Burr. Against him, therefore, there is no evidence to support a charge of treason.

That both of the prisoners were engaged in a most culpable enterprize against the dominions of a power at peace with the United States, those who admit the affidavit of General Wilkinson cannot doubt. But that no part of this crime was committed in the district of Columbia is apparent. It is therefore the unanimous opinion of the court that they cannot be tried in this district.

The law read on the part of the prosecution is understood to apply only to offences committed on the high seas, or in any river, haven, bason or bay, not within the jurisdiction of any particular state. In those cases there is no court which has particular cognizance of the crime, and therefore the place in which the criminal shall be apprehended, or, if he be apprehended where no court has exclusive jurisdiction, that to which he shall be first brought, is substituted for the place in which the offence was committed.

But in this case, a tribunal for the trial of the offence, wherever it may have been committed, had been provided by congress; and at the place where the prisoners were seized by the authority of the commander in chief, there existed such a tribunal. It would, too, be extremely dangerous to say, that because the prisoners were apprehended, not by a civil magistrate, but by the military power, there could be given by law a right to try the persons so seized in any place which the general might select, and to which he might direct them to be carried.

The act of congress which the prisoners are supposed to have violated, describes as offenders those who begin or set on foot, or provide, or prepare, the means for any military expedition or enterprize to be carried on from thence against the dominions of a foreign prince or state, with whom the United States are at peace.

There is a want of precision in the description of the offence which might produce some difficulty in deciding what cases would come within it. But several other questions arise which a court consisting of four judges finds itself unable to decide, and therefore, as the crime with which the prisoners stand charged has not been committed, the court can only direct them to be discharged. This is done with the less reluctance because the discharge does not acquit them from the offence which there is probable cause for supposing they have committed, and if those whose duty it is to protect the nation, by prosecuting offenders against the laws, shall suppose those who have been charged with treason to be proper objects for punishment, they will, when possessed of less exceptionable testimony, and when able to say at what place the offence has been committed, institute fresh proceedings against them.

48

United States v. Peters (1809)

A controversy between state sovereignty and national power had brewed in Pennsylvania since 1779, when the Continental Congress Committee on Appeals had reversed a decision of the state's admiralty court. A Gideon Olmstead had been attempting ever since to recover the proceeds from the sale of a prize ship, and in 1803, federal district judge Richard Peters had reaffirmed the committee ruling and directed that Olmstead be paid, but the state had reasserted its claim to paramount authority. Finally in 1808 a petition for mandamus to force

---

Source: 5 Cranch 115 (1809).

Peters to implement his decision reached the Supreme Court. Here was a potentially dangerous confrontation between state sovereignty and federal judicial power, and only a few years earlier the Court would have expected the executive and legislative branches to side with the states. But with the Jeffersonians committed to the embargo policy, they could not countenance a state defying federal authority; if Pennsylvania won, then the New England states could with equal temerity ignore the embargo. When the state did, in fact, attempt to block execution of the judgment, the Madison administration moved quickly to assert federal authority, and the opposition quickly collapsed.

See G. L. Haskins and H. A. Johnson, *Foundations of Power, 1801–1815* (1981); and S. B. Presser, "A Tale of Two Judges . . . ," 73 *Nw. U.L.R.* 26 (1978).

~~~~~~

Chief Justice Marshall delivered the opinion of the Court.

With great attention, and with serious concern, the court has considered the return made by the judge for the district of Pennsylvania to the *mandamus* directing him to execute the sentence pronounced by him in the case of *Gideon Olmstead and others* v. *Rittenhouse's Executrixes,* or to show cause for not so doing. The cause shown is an act of the legislature of Pennsylvania, passed subsequent to the rendition of his sentence. This act authorizes and requires the governor to demand, for the use of the state of Pennsylvania, the money which had been decreed to Gideon Olmstead and others; and which was in the hands of the executrixes of David Rittenhouse; and, in default of payment, to direct the attorney-general to institute a suit for the recovery thereof. This act further authorizes and requires the governor to use any further means he may think necessary for the protection of what it denominates "the just rights of the state," and also to protect the persons and properties of the said executrixes of David Rittenhouse, deceased, against any process whatever, issued out of any federal court in consequence of their obedience to the requisition of the said act.

If the legislatures of the several states may, at will, annul the judgments of the courts of the United States, and destroy the rights acquired under those judgments, the constitution itself becomes a solemn mockery; and the nation is deprived of the means of enforcing its laws by the instrumentality of its own tribunals. So fatal a result must be deprecated by all; and the people of Pennsylvania, not less than the citizens of every other state, must feel a deep interest in resisting principles so destructive of the union, and in averting consequences so fatal to themselves.

The act in question does not, in terms, assert the universal right of the state to interpose in every case whatever; but assigns, as a motive for its interposition in this particular case, that the sentence, the execution of which it prohibits, was rendered in a cause over which the federal courts have no jurisdiction.

If the ultimate right to determine the jurisdiction of the courts of the union is placed by the constitution in the several state legislatures, then this act concludes the subject; but if that power necessarily resides in the supreme judicial tribunal of the nation, then the jurisdiction of the district court of Pennsylvania, over the case in which that jurisdiction was exercised, ought to be most deliberately examined; and the act of Pennsylvania, with whatever respect it may be considered, cannot be permitted to prejudice the question. . . .

While this suit was depending, the state of Pennsylvania forbore to assert its title, and, in January, 1803, the court decreed in favour of the libellants; soon after which, the legislature passed the act which has been stated.

It is contended that the federal courts were deprived of jurisdiction, in this cause, by that amendment of the constitution which exempts states from being sued in those courts by individuals. This amendment declares, "that the judicial power of the United States shall not be construed to extend to any suit, in law or equity, commenced or prosecuted against one of the United States by citizens of another state, or by citizens or subjects of any foreign state."

The right of a state to assert, as plaintiff, any interest it may have in a subject, which forms the matter of controversy between individuals, in one of the courts of the United States, is not affected by this amendment; nor can it be so construed as to oust the court of its jurisdiction, should such claim be suggested. The amendment simply provides, that no suit shall be commenced or prosecuted against a state. The state cannot be made a defendant to a suit brought by an individual; but it remains the duty of the courts of the United States to decide all cases brought before them by citizens of one state against citizens of a different state, where a state is not necessarily a defendant. In this case, the suit was not instituted against the state or its treasurer, but against the executrixes of David Rittenhouse, for the proceeds of a vessel condemned in the court of admiralty, which were admitted to be in their possession. If these proceeds had been the actual property of Pennsylvania, however wrongfully acquired, the disclosure of that fact would have presented a case on which it was unnecessary to give an opinion; but it certainly can never be alleged, that a mere suggestion of title in a state to property, in possession of an individual, must arrest the proceedings of the court, and prevent their looking into the suggestion, and examining the validity of the title.

If the suggestion in this case be examined, it is deemed perfectly clear that no title whatever to the certificates in question was vested in the state of Pennsylvania. . . .

Since, then, the state of Pennsylvania had neither possession of, nor right to, the property on which the sentence of the district court was pronounced, and since the suit was neither commenced nor prosecuted against that state, there remains no pretext for the allegation that the case is within that amendment of the constitution which has been cited; and, consequently, the state of Pennsylvania can possess no constitutional right to resist the legal process which may be directed in this cause.

It will be readily conceived that the order which this court is enjoined to make by the high obligations of duty and of law, is not made without extreme regret at the necessity which has induced the application. But it is a solemn duty, and therefore must be performed. *A peremptory mandamus must be awarded.*

49

Fletcher v. Peck (1810)

In 1795 the Georgia legislature granted 35 million acres of the so-called Yazoo tract (in what is now Mississippi and Alabama) to four companies for 1.5 cents an acre. The entire transaction was marked with fraud and bribery, and the following year a newly elected legislature rescinded the grant. The four companies in the meantime had sold off several million acres, and questions now rose as to who owned title to the land—the legislature, the companies, or people who had purchased the land from the companies. Because of the Eleventh Amendment, the purchasers could not sue Georgia to clear the title, so a suit was arranged between citizens of two states who had interests in the land, in order that the issue could be brought into the federal courts under the diversity of citizenship rule. Given the general antagonism to the Court, as well as the fact that a subsequent arrangement between the federal government and Georgia had made many of the issues moot, Marshall might well have dismissed the suit. But with so many Americans engaged in land speculation, he used the occasion to uphold the

Source: 6 Cranch 87 (1810).

sanctity of a state's pledge, even when made under fraudulent circumstances.

See C. P. Magrath, *Yazoo: Land and Politics in the New Republic, the Case of Fletcher v. Peck* (1966); R. K. Newmyer, *The Supreme Court under Marshall and Taney* (1968); and B. F. Wright, *The Contract Clause of the Constitution* (1938).

~~~~~~

Chief Justice Marshall

The suit was instituted on several covenants contained in a deed made by John Peck, the defendant in error, conveying to Robert Fletcher, the plaintiff in error, certain lands which were part of a large purchase made by James Gunn and others, in the year 1795, from the state of Georgia, the contract for which was made in the form of a bill passed by the legislature of that state. . . .

That the legislature of Georgia, unless restrained by its own constitution, possesses the power of disposing of the unappropriated lands within its own limits, in such manner as its own judgment shall dictate, is a proposition not to be controverted. The only question, then, presented by this demurrer, for the consideration of the court, is this, did the then constitution of the state of Georgia prohibit the legislature to dispose of the lands, which were the subject of this contract, in the manner stipulated by the contract?

The question, whether a law be void for its repugnancy to the constitution, is, at all times, a question of much delicacy, which ought seldom, if ever, to be decided in the affirmative, in a doubtful case. The court, when impelled by duty to render such a judgment, would be unworthy of its station, could it be unmindful of the solemn obligations which that station imposes. But it is not on slight implication and vague conjecture that the legislature is to be pronounced to have transcended its powers, and its acts to be considered as void. The opposition between the constitution and the law should be such that the judge feels a clear and strong conviction of their incompatibility with each other. . . .

That corruption should find its way into the governments of our infant republics, and contaminate the very source of legislation, or that impure motives should contribute to the passage of a law, or the formation of a legislative contract, are circumstances most deeply to be deplored. How far a court of justice would, in any case, be competent, on proceedings instituted by the state itself, to vacate a contract thus formed, and to annul rights acquired, under that contract, by third persons having no notice of the improper means by which it was obtained, is a question which the court would approach with much circumspection. It may well be doubted how far the validity of a law depends upon the motives of its framers, and how far the particular inducements, operating on members of the supreme sovereign power of a state, to the formation of a contract by that power, are examinable in a court of justice. If the principle be conceded, that an act of the supreme sovereign power might be declared null by a court, in consequence of the means which procured it, still would there be much difficulty in saying to what extent those means must be applied to produce this effect. Must it be direct corruption, or would interest or undue influence of any kind be sufficient? Must the vitiating cause operate on a majority, or on what number of the members? Would the act be null, whatever might be the wish of the nation, or would its obligation or nullity depend upon the public sentiment?

If the majority of the legislature be corrupted, it may well be doubted, whether it be within the province of the judiciary to control their conduct, and, if less than a majority act from impure motives, the principle by which judicial interference would be regulated, is not clearly discerned.

Whatever difficulties this subject might present, when viewed under aspects of which it may be susceptible, this court can perceive none in the particular pleadings now under consideration.

This is not a bill brought by the state of Georgia, to annul the contract, nor does it appear to the court, by this count, that the state of Georgia is dissatisfied with the sale that has been made. The case, as made out in the pleadings, is simply this. One individual who holds lands in the state of Georgia, under a deed convenanting that the title of Georgia was in the grantor, brings an action of covenant upon this deed, and assigns, as a breach, that some of the members of the legislature were induced to vote in favour of the law, which constituted the contract, by being promised an interest in it, and that therefore the act is a mere nullity.

This solemn question cannot be brought thus collaterally and incidentally before the court. It would be indecent, in the extreme, upon a private contract, between two individuals, to enter into an inquiry respecting the corruption of the sovereign power of a state. If the title be plainly deduced from a legislative act, which the legislature might constitutionally pass, if the act be clothed with all the requisite forms of a law, a court, sitting as a court of law, cannot sustain a suit brought by one individual against another founded on the allegation that the act is a nullity, in consequence of the impure motives which influenced certain members of the legislature which passed the law. . . .

The lands in controversy vested absolutely in James Gunn and others, the original grantees, by the conveyance of the governor, made in pursuance of an act of assembly to which the legislature was fully competent. Being thus in full possession of the legal estate, they, for a valuable consideration, conveyed portions of the land to those who were willing to purchase. If the original transaction was infected with fraud, these purchasers did not participate in it, and had no notice of it. They were innocent. Yet the legislature of Georgia has involved them in the fate of the first parties to the transaction, and, if the act be valid, has annihilated their rights also.

The legislature of Georgia was a party to this transaction; and for a party to pronounce its own deed invalid, whatever cause may be assigned for its invalidity, must be considered as a mere act of power which must find its vindication in a train of reasoning not often heard in courts of justice.

But the real party, it is said, are the people, and when their agents are unfaithful, the acts of those agents cease to be obligatory.

It is, however, to be recollected that the people can act only by these agents, and that, while within the powers conferred on them, their acts must be considered as the acts of the people. If the agents be corrupt, others may be chosen, and, if their contracts be examinable, the common sentiment, as well as common usage of mankind, points out a mode by which this examination may be made, and their validity determined.

If the legislature of Georgia was not bound to submit its pretensions to those tribunals which are established for the security of property, and to decide on human rights, if it might claim to itself the power of judging in its own case, yet there are certain great principles of justice, whose authority is universally acknowledged, that ought not to be entirely disregarded.

If the legislature be its own judge in its own case, it would seem equitable that its decision should be regulated by those rules which would have regulated the decision of a judicial tribunal. The question was, in its nature, a question of title, and the tribunal which decided it was either acting in the character of a court of justice, and performing a duty usually assigned to a court, or it was exerting a mere act of power in which it was controlled only by its own will.

If a suit be brought to set aside a conveyance obtained by fraud, and the fraud be clearly proved, the conveyance will be set aside, as between the parties; but the rights of third persons, who are purchasers without notice, for a valuable consideration, cannot be disregarded. Titles, which, according to every legal test, are perfect, are acquired with that confidence which is inspired by the opinion that the purchaser is safe. If there be any concealed defect, arising from the conduct of those who had held the property long before he acquired it, of which he had no notice, that concealed defect cannot be set up against him. He has paid his money for a title good at law, he is innocent, whatever may be the guilt of others, and equity will not subject him to the penalties attached to that guilt. All titles would be insecure, and the intercourse between man and man would be very seriously obstructed, if this principle be overturned.

A court of chancery, therefore, had a bill been brought to set aside the conveyance made to James Gunn and others, as being obtained by improper practices with the legislature, whatever might have been its decision as respected the original grantees, would have been bound, by its own rules, and by the clearest principles of equity, to leave unmolested those who were purchasers, without notice, for a valuable consideration.

If the legislature felt itself absolved from those rules of property which are common to all the citizens of the United States, and from those principles of equity which are acknowledged in all our courts, its act is to be supported by its power alone, and the same power may devest any other individual of his lands, if it shall be the will of the legislature so to exert it.

It is not intended to speak with disrespect of the legislature of Georgia, or of its acts. Far from it. The question is a general question, and is treated as one. For although such powerful objections to a legislative grant, as are alleged against this, may not again exist, yet the principle, on which alone this rescinding act is to be supported, may be applied to every case to which it shall be the will of any legislature to apply it. The principle is this; that a legislature may, by its own act, devest the vested estate of any man whatever, for reasons which shall, by itself, be deemed sufficient.

In this case the legislature may have had ample proof that the original grant was obtained by practices which can never be too much reprobated, and which would have justified its abrogation so far as respected those to whom crime was imputable. But the grant, when issued, conveyed an estate in fee-simple to the grantee, clothed with all the solemnities which law can bestow. This estate was transferrable; and those who purchased parts of it were not stained by that guilt which infected the original transaction. Their case is not distinguishable from the ordinary case of purchasers of a legal estate without knowledge of any secret fraud which might have led to the emanation of the original grant. According to the well known course of equity, their rights could not be affected by such fraud. Their situation was the same, their title was the same, with that of every other member of the community who holds land by regular conveyances from the original paten-tee.

Is the power of the legislature competent to the annihilation of such title, and to a resumption of the property thus held?

The principle asserted is, that one legislature is competent to repeal any act which a former legislature was competent to pass; and that one legislature cannot abridge the powers of a succeeding legislature.

The correctness of this principle, so far as respects general legislation, can never be controverted. But, if an act be done under a law, a succeeding legislature cannot undo it. The past cannot be recalled by the most absolute power. Conveyances have been made, those conveyances have vested legal estates, and, if those estates may be seized by the sovereign authority, still, that they originally vested is a fact, and cannot cease to be a fact.

When, then, a law is in its nature a contract, when absolute rights have vested under that contract, a repeal of the law cannot devest those rights; and the act of annulling them, if legitimate, is rendered so by a power applicable to the case of every individual in the community. . . .

The validity of this rescinding act, then, might well be doubted, were

Georgia a single sovereign power. But Georgia cannot be viewed as a single, unconnected, sovereign power, on whose legislature no other restrictions are imposed than may be found in its own constitution. She is a part of a large empire; she is a member of the American union; and that union has a constitution the supremacy of which all acknowledge, and which imposes limits to the legislatures of the several states, which none claim a right to pass. The constitution of the United States declares that no state shall pass any bill of attainder, *ex post facto* law, or law impairing the obligation of contracts.

Does the case now under consideration come within this prohibitory section of the constitution?

In considering this very interesting question, we immediately ask ourselves what is a contract? Is a grant a contract? . . .

. . . [A] grant is a contract executed, the obligation of which still continues, and since the constitution uses the general term contract, without distinguishing between those which are executory and those which are executed, it must be construed to comprehend the latter as well as the former. A law annulling conveyances between individuals, and declaring that the grantors should stand seised of their former estates, notwithstanding those grants, would be as repugnant to the constitution as a law discharging the vendors of property from the obligation of executing their contracts by conveyances. It would be strange if a contract to convey was secured by the constitution, while an absolute conveyance remained unprotected.

If, under a fair construction of the constitution, grants are comprehended under the term contracts, is a grant from the state excluded from the operation of the provision? Is the clause to be considered as inhibiting the state from impairing the obligation of contracts between two individuals, but as excluding from that inhibition contracts made with itself? . . .

It is, then, the unanimous opinion of the court, that, in this case, the estate having passed into the hands of a purchaser for a valuable consideration, without notice, the state of Georgia was restrained, either by general principles which are common to our free institutions, or by the particular provisions of the constitution of the United States, from passing a law whereby the estate of the plaintiff in the premises so purchased could be constitutionally and legally impaired and rendered null and void.

50

United States v. Hudson and Goodwin (1812)

As noted in Document 40, the question of whether a federal common law existed excited state jealousies in the early years of the Republic. Justice Samuel Chase, on circuit in United States v. Worrall, 2 Dallas 384 (1798), had held that the entire common law had never been adopted in the United States, and that since common law differed from one state to another, there could be no general common law. As to criminal law, only "Congress should define the offense to be tried, and apportion the punishments to be inflicted." In the following case, the entire Court affirmed Chase's earlier holding that no federal common law crimes existed, and that the only federal crimes were those defined by Congress. The decision was considered to be definitive on the issue. See also Document 59, another affirmation by the Court that the Constitution did in fact reserve rights and powers to the states.

See G. L. Haskins and H. A. Johnson, *Foundations of Power, 1801–1815* (1981).

Justice Johnson

The only question which this case presents is, whether the Circuit Courts of the United States can exercise a common law jurisdiction in criminal cases. We state it thus broadly because a decision on a case of libel will apply to every case in which jurisdiction is not vested in those Courts by statute.

Although this question is brought up now for the first time to be decided by this Court, we consider it as having been long since settled in public opinion. In no other case for many years has this jurisdiction been asserted; and the general acquiescence of legal men shews the prevalence of opinion in favor of the negative of the proposition.

The course of reasoning which leads to this conclusion is simple, obvious, and admits of but little illustration. The powers of the general Government are made up of concessions from the several states—whatever is not expressly given to the former, the latter expressly reserve. The judicial power of the

---

Source: 7 Cranch 32 (1812).

United States is a constituent part of those concessions—that power is to be exercised by Courts organized for the purpose, and brought into existence by an effort of the legislative power of the Union. Of all the Courts which the United States may, under their general powers, constitute, one only, the Supreme Court, possesses jurisdiction derived immediately from the constitution, and of which the legislative power cannot deprive it. All other Courts created by the general Government possess no jurisdiction but what is given them by the power that creates them, and can be vested with none but what the power ceded to the general Government will authorize them to confer.

It is not necessary to inquire whether the general Government, in any and what extent, possesses the power of conferring on its Courts a jurisdiction in cases similar to the present; it is enough that such jurisdiction has not been conferred by any legislative act, if it does not result to those Courts as a consequence of their creation.

And such is the opinion of the majority of this Court: For, the power which congress possess to create Courts of *inferior jurisdiction,* necessarily implies the power to limit the jurisdiction of those Courts to particular objects; and when a Court is created, and its operations confined to certain specific objects, with what propriety can it assume to itself a jurisdiction—much more extended— in its nature very indefinite—applicable to a great variety of subjects—varying in every state in the Union—and with regard to which there exists no definite criterion of distribution between the district and Circuit Courts of the same district?

The only ground on which it has ever been contended that this jurisdiction could be maintained is, that, upon the formation of any political body, an implied power to preserve its own existence and promote the end and object of its creation, necessarily results to it. But, without examining how far this consideration is applicable to the peculiar character of our constitution, it may be remarked that it is a principle by no means peculiar to the common law. It is coeval, probably, with the first formation of a limited Government; belongs to a system of universal law, and may as well support the assumption of many other powers as those more peculiarly acknowledged by the common law of England.

But if admitted as applicable to the state of things in this country, the consequence would not result from it which is here contended for. If it may communicate certain implied powers to the general Government, it would not follow that the Courts of that Government are vested with jurisdiction over any particular act done by an individual in supposed violation of the peace and dignity of the sovereign power. The legislative authority of the Union must first make an act a crime, affix a punishment to it, and declare the Court that shall have jurisdiction of the offence.

Certain implied powers must necessarily result to our Courts of justice from the nature of their institution. But jurisdiction of crimes against the state is not among those powers. To fine for contempt—imprison for contumacy—

inforce the observance of order, &c. are powers which cannot be dispensed with in a Court, because they are necessary to the exercise of all others: and so far our Courts no doubt possess powers not immediately derived from statute; but all exercise of criminal jurisdiction in common law cases we are of opinion is not within their implied powers.

51

Martin v. Hunter's Lessee (1816)

In this, Justice Joseph Story's first great opinion, we can see his devotion to developing a strong national authority and devaluing the power of the states. Originally, the case involved a prosaic question of whether common law rights of property and inheritance had been adopted by Virginia during and after the Revolution. The property at issue was the large estate of Lord Fairfax, a loyalist who had fled to England and bequeathed the land to his nephew. Virginia confiscated the property during the war, but under the terms of Jay's Treaty, titles of lands confiscated from loyalists were to be restored to the original holders. The Virginia high court had ruled against the Fairfax interests, and by taking the appeal the Supreme Court was asserting the authority over state courts granted to it by Section 25 of the 1789 Judiciary Act (Document 30).

John Marshall did not participate in the case because his brother was involved in the suit, but there is no doubt Marshall agreed with Story, who upheld the treaty terms over state law, although Marshall's political sensitivity might have winced at Story's arrogance.

See R. K. Newmyer, *Supreme Court Justice Joseph Story: Statesman of the Old Republic* (1985).

Source: 1 Wheaton 304 (1816).

~~~~~~

Justice Story

. . . But, even admitting that the language of the constitution is not manda-tory, and that congress may constitutionally omit to vest the judicial power in courts of the United States, it cannot be denied that when it is vested, it may be exercised to the utmost constitutional extent.

This leads us to the consideration of the great question, as to the nature and extent of the appellate jurisdiction of the United States. We have already seen, that appellate jurisdiction is given by the constitution to the supreme court, in all cases where it has not original jurisdiction; subject, however, to such exceptions and regulations as congress may prescribe. It is, therefore, capable of embracing every case enumerated in the constitution, which is not exclusively to be decided by way of original jurisdiction. What is there to restrain its exercise over state tribunals, in the enumerated cases? The appel-late power is not limited by the terms of the third article to any particular courts. It is the *case,* then, and not the *court,* that gives the jurisdiction. If the judicial power extends to the case, it will be in vain to search in the letter of the constitution for any qualification as to the tribunal where it depends. It is incumbent, then, upon those who assert such a qualification, to show its existence, by necessary implication. If the text be clear and distinct, no restriction upon its plain and obvious import ought to be admitted, unless the inference be irresistible. . . .

It must be conceded that the constitution not only contemplated, but meant to provide for cases within the scope of the judicial power of the United States, which might yet depend before state tribunals. It was foreseen that in the exercise of their ordinary jurisdiction, state courts would incidentally take cognisance of cases arising under the constitution, the laws and treaties of the United States. Yet, to all these cases, the judicial power, by the very terms of the constitution, is to extend. It cannot extend by original jurisdiction if that was already rightfully and exclusively attached in the state courts, which (as has been already shown) may occur; it must, therefore, extend by appel-late jurisdiction, or not at all. It would seem to follow that the appellate power of the United States must, in such cases, extend to state tribunals; and if in such cases, there is no reason why it should not equally attach upon all others within the purview of the constitution.

It has been argued that such an appellate jurisdiction over state courts is inconsistent with the genius of our governments, and the spirit of the consti-tution. That the latter was never designed to act upon state sovereignties, but only upon the people, and that if the power exists, it will materially im-pair the sovereignty of the states, and the independence of their courts. We cannot yield to the force of this reasoning; it assumes principles which we cannot admit, and draws conclusions to which we do not yield our as-sent.

It is a mistake that the constitution was not designed to operate upon states, in their corporate capacities. It is crowded with provisions which restrain or annul the sovereignty of the states in some of the highest branches of their prerogatives. The tenth section of the first article contains a long list of disabilities and prohibitions imposed upon the states. Surely, when such essential portions of state sovereignty are taken away, or prohibited to be exercised, it cannot be correctly asserted that the constitution does not act upon the states. When, therefore, the states are stripped of some of the highest attributes of sovereignty, it is certainly difficult to support the argument that the appellate power over the decisions of state courts is contrary to the genius of our institutions. The courts of the United States can, without question, revise the proceedings of the executive and legislative authorities of the states, and if they are found to be contrary to the constitution, may declare them to be of no legal validity. Surely, the exercise of the same right over judicial tribunals is not a higher or more dangerous act of sovereign power.

Nor can such a right be deemed to impair the independence of state judges. It is assuming the very ground in controversy to assert that they possess an absolute independence of the United States. In respect to the powers granted to the United States, they are not independent; they are expressly bound to obedience, by the letter of the constitution; and if they should unintentionally transcend their authority, or misconstrue the constitution, there is no more reason for giving their judgments an absolute and irresistible force, than for giving it to the acts of the other co-ordinate departments of state sovereignty.

The argument urged from the possibility of the abuse of the revising power, is equally unsatisfactory. It is always a doubtful course, to argue against the use or existence of a power, from the possibility of its abuse. It is still more difficult by such an argument, to ingraft upon a general power a restriction which is not to be found in the terms in which it is given. From the very nature of things, the absolute right of decision, in the last resort, must rest somewhere—wherever it may be vested, it is susceptible of abuse. In all questions of jurisdiction, the inferior, or appellate court, must pronounce the final judgment; and common sense, as well as legal reasoning, has conferred it upon the latter. . . .

It is further argued, that no great public mischief can result from a construction which shall limit the appellate power of the United States to cases in their own courts: first, because state judges are bound by an oath to support the constitution of the United States, and must be presumed to be men of learning and integrity; and secondly, because congress must have an unquestionable right to remove all cases within the scope of the judicial power from the state courts to the courts of the United States, at any time before final judgment, though not after final judgment. As to the first reason—admitting that the judges of the state courts are, and always will be, of as much learning, integrity and wisdom, as those of the courts of the United States, (which we very cheerfully admit,) it does not aid the argument. It is manifest that the constitution has proceeded upon a theory of its own, and given or withheld powers according to the judgment of the American people, by whom it was adopted. We can only construe its powers, and cannot inquire into the policy or principles which induced the grant of them. The constitution has presumed (whether rightly or wrongly we do not inquire) that state attachments, state prejudices, state jealousies, and state interests, might sometimes obstruct, or control, or be supposed to obstruct or control, the regular administration of justice. Hence, in controversies between states; between citizens of different states; between citizens claiming grants under different states; between a state and its citizens, or foreigners, and between citizens and foreigners, it enables the parties, under the authority of congress, to have the controversies heard, tried and determined before the national tribunals. No other reason than that which has been stated can be assigned, why some, at least, of those cases should not have been left to the cognizance of the state courts. In respect to the other enumerated cases—the cases arising under the constitution, laws and treaties of the United States, cases affecting ambassadors and other public ministers, and cases of admiralty and maritime jurisdiction—reasons of a higher and more extensive nature, touching the safety, peace and sovereignty of the nation, might well justify a grant of exclusive jurisdiction.

This is not all. A motive of another kind, perfectly compatible with the most sincere respect for state tribunals, might induce the grant of appellate power over their decisions. That motive is the importance, and even necessity of *uniformity* of decisions throughout the whole United States, upon all subjects within the purview of the constitution. Judges of equal learning and integrity, in different states, might differently interpret a statute, or a treaty of the United States, or even the constitution itself: if there were no revising authority to control these jarring and discordant judgments, and harmonize them into uniformity, the laws, the treaties and the constitution of the United States would be different in different states, and might, perhaps, never have precisely the same construction, obligation, or efficacy, in any two states. The public mischiefs that would attend such a state of things would be truly deplorable; and it cannot be believed that they could have escaped the enlightened convention which formed the constitution. What indeed, might then have been only prophecy, has now become fact; and the appellate jurisdiction must continue to be the only adequate remedy for such evils.

The power of Congress to remove suits from state courts to the national courts forms the second ground upon which the argument we are considering has been attempted to be sustained. This power of removal is not to be found in express terms in any part of the constitution; if it be given, it is only given by implication, as a power necessary and proper to carry into effect some express power. If the right of removal from state courts exist before judgment because it is included in the appellate power, it must, for the same reason, exist after judgment. And if the appellate power by the constitution does not include cases pending in state courts, the right of removal, which is but a mode of exercising that power, cannot be applied to them. Precisely the same objections, therefore, exist as to the right of removal before judgment, as after, and both must stand or fall together. Nor, indeed, would the force of the arguments on either side materially vary, if the right of removal were an exercise of original jurisdiction. It would equally trench upon the jurisdiction and independence of state tribunals. . . .

On the whole, the court are of opinion, that the appellate power of the United States does extend to cases pending in the state courts; and that the 25th section of the judiciary act, which authorizes the exercise of this jurisdiction in the specified cases, by a writ of error, is supported by the letter and spirit of the constitution. We find no clause in that instrument which limits this power; and we dare not interpose a limitation where the people have not been disposed to create one.

Strong as this conclusion stands upon the general language of the constitution, it may still derive support from other sources. It is an historical fact, that this exposition of the constitution, extending its appellate power to state courts, was, previous to its adoption, uniformly and publicly avowed by its friends, and admitted by its enemies, as the basis of their respective reasonings, both in and out of the state conventions. It is an historical fact, that at the time when the judiciary act was submitted to the deliberations of the first congress, composed as it was, not only of men of great learning and ability, but of men who had acted a principal part in framing, supporting or opposing that constitution, the same exposition was explicitly declared and admitted by the friends and by the opponents of that system. It is an historical fact, that the supreme court of the United States have, from time to time, sustained this appellate jurisdiction in a great variety of cases, brought from the tribunals of many of the most important states in the Union, and that no state tribunal has ever breathed a judicial doubt on the subject, or declined to obey the mandate of the supreme court, until the present occasion. This weight of contemporaneous exposition by all parties, this acquiescence of enlightened state courts, and these judicial decisions of the supreme court through so long a period, do, as we think, place the doctrine upon a foundation of authority which cannot be shaken, without delivering over the subject to perpetual and irremediable doubts.

Dartmouth College v. Woodward (1819)

In 1815 Dartmouth College became embroiled in a political controversy after a dispute between the president of the school, John Wheelock (son of the founder), and the trustees. The Republicans controlling the state sided with Wheelock, and in 1816 the legislature annulled the royal charter granted in 1769, and placed Dartmouth University, as it would be called, under state control. The old trustees, however, declined to recognize the legality of this action, and the secretary, William Woodward, refused to turn over the school's records and seal to the new state-appointed trustees. The state court found for the new trustees, holding the school to be a public corporation and therefore subject to state regulation. On appeal, the Supreme Court held for the old trustees. Marshall's audacious opinion supported a vested rights interpretation of the Contract Clause, but it was poorly reasoned.

Story's concurring opinion is the more important, in that he not only supported vested rights and sanctity of contract but also informed the states how and under what conditions they could regulate corporations—namely, by reserving the right at the time a corporate charter was issued. At this time most states did not have general incorporation laws but issued special charters tailored to the needs of individual enterprises. Many states would have refused to issue any more charters of any kind if Marshall's opinion had been taken literally, and that would have created a serious obstacle to economic development. Story in effect said to the states that once you make a promise, you must keep that promise, but if you believe that in the future you may need to change some terms, you will be able to do so if you take the simple precaution of preserving that power as part of the terms of the grant. The states quickly adopted this device, and in response to the growing need for corporate charters, soon adopted the notion of general, generic charters, all of which had this "safety device" embedded in them.

See Newmyer, *Story,* cited in previous document; F. N. Stites, *Private Interest and Public Gain: The Dartmouth College Case, 1819* (1972); and B. F. Wright, *The Contract Clause of the Constitution* (1938).

Source: 4 Wheaton 518 (1819).

Chief Justice Marshall delivered the opinion of the Court.

. . . [T]his Court has . . . declared, that, in no doubtful case, would it pronounce a legislative act to be contrary to the constitution. But the American people have said, in the constitution of the United States, that "no State shall pass any bill of attainder, *ex post facto* law, or law impairing the obligation of contracts." In the same instrument they have also said, "that the judicial power shall extend to all cases in law and equity arising under the constitution." On the judges of this Court, then, is imposed the high and solemn duty of protecting, from even legislative violation, those contracts which the constitution of our country has placed beyond legislative control; and, however irksome the task may be, this is a duty from which we dare not shrink. . . .

It can require no argument to prove, that the circumstances of this case constitute a contract. An application is made to the crown for a charter to incorporate a religious and literary institution. In the application, it is stated that large contributions have been made for the object, which will be conferred on the corporation, as soon as it shall be created. The charter is granted, and on its faith the property is conveyed. Surely in this transaction every ingredient of a complete and legitimate contract is to be found.

The points for consideration are,

1.   Is this contract protected by the constitution of the United States? . . .

2.   On the first point it has been argued, that the word "contract," in its broadest sense, would comprehend the political relations between the government and its citizens, would extend to offices held within a State for State purposes, and to many of those laws concerning civil institutions, which must change with circumstances, and be modified by ordinary legislation; which deeply concern the public, and which, to preserve good government, the public judgment must control. That even marriage is a contract, and its obligations are affected by the laws respecting divorces. That the clause in the constitution, if construed in its greatest latitude, would prohibit these laws. . . . That as the framers of the constitution could never have intended to insert in that instrument a provision so unnecessary, so mischievous, and so repugnant to its general spirit, the term "contract" must be understood in a more limited sense. That it must be understood as intended to guard against a power of at least doubtful utility, the abuse of which had been extensively felt; and to restrain the legislature in future from violating the right to property. That anterior to the formation of the constitution, a course of legislation had prevailed in many, if not in all, of the States, which weakened the confidence of man in man, and embarrassed all transactions between individuals, by dispensing with a faithful performance of engagements. To correct this mischief, by restraining the

power which produced it, the State legislatures were forbidden "to pass any law impairing the obligation of contracts," that is, of contracts respecting property, under which some individual could claim a right to something beneficial to himself; and that since the clause in the constitution must in construction receive some limitation, it may be confined, and ought to be confined, to cases of this description. . . .

The general correctness of these observations cannot be controverted. That the framers of the constitution did not intend to restrain the States in the regulation of their civil institutions, adopted for internal government, and that the instrument they have given us, is not to be so construed, may be admitted. The provision of the constitution never has been understood to embrace other contracts, than those which respect property, or some object of value, and confer rights which may be asserted in a court of justice. . . .

The parties in this case differ less on general principles, less on the true construction of the constitution in the abstract, than on the application of those principles to this case, and on the true construction of the charter of 1769. This is the point on which the cause essentially depends. If the act of incorporation be a grant of political power, if it create a civil institution to be employed in the administration of the government, or if the funds of the college be public property, or if the State of New Hampshire, as a government, be alone interested in its transactions, the subject is one in which the legislature of the State may act according to its own judgment, unrestrained by any limitation of its power imposed by the constitution of the United States.

But if this be a private eleemosynary institution, endowed with a capacity to take property for objects unconnected with government, whose funds are bestowed by individuals on the faith of the charter; if the donors have stipulated for the future disposition and management of those funds in the manner prescribed by themselves; there may be more difficulty in the case. . . . Those who are no longer interested in the property, may yet retain such an interest in the preservation of their own arrangements, as to have a right to insist, that those arrangements shall be held sacred. Or, if they have themselves disappeared, it becomes a subject of serious and anxious inquiry, whether those whom they have legally empowered to represent them forever, may not assert all the rights which they possessed, while in being. . . .

[Marshall here reviewed the history of Dartmouth and its original grant, to show that all along it had been a private eleemosynary institution.]

That education is an object of national concern, and a proper subject of legislation, all admit. That there may be an institution founded by government, and placed entirely under its immediate control, the officers of which would be public officers, amenable exclusively to government, none will deny. But is Dartmouth College such an institution? Is education altogether in the hands of government? Does every teacher of youth become a public officer, and do donations for the purpose of education necessarily become public property, so far that the will of the legislature, not the will of the donor, becomes the law of the donation? . . .

Doctor Wheelock, as the keeper of his charity school, instructing the Indians in the art of reading, and in our holy religion; sustaining them at his own expense, and on the voluntary contributions of the charitable, could scarcely be considered as a public officer, exercising any portion of those duties which belong to government; nor could the legislature have supposed, that his private funds, or those given by others, were subject to legislative management, because they were applied to the purposes of education. . . .

A corporation is an artificial being, invisible, intangible, and existing only in contemplation of law. Being the mere creature of law, it possesses only those properties which the charter of its creation confers upon it, either expressly, or as incidental to its very existence. These are such as are supposed best calculated to effect the object for which it was created. Among the most important are immortality, and, if the expression may be allowed, individuality; properties, by which a perpetual succession of many persons are considered as the same, and may act as a single individual. They enable a corporation to manage its own affairs, and to hold property without the perplexing intricacies, the hazardous and endless necessity, of perpetual conveyances for the purpose of transmitting it from hand to hand. It is chiefly for the purpose of clothing bodies of men, in succession, with these qualities and capacities, that corporations were invented, and are in use. By these means, a perpetual succession of individuals are capable of acting for the promotion of the particular object, like one immortal being. But this being does not share in the civil government of the country, unless that be the purpose for which it was created. Its immortality no more confers on it political power, or a political character, than immortality would confer such power or character on a natural person. It is no more a State instrument, than a natural person exercising the same powers would be. If, then, a natural person, employed by individuals in the education of youth . . . would not become a public officer, or be considered as a member of the civil government, how is it, that this artificial being, created by law, for the purpose of being employed by the same individuals for the same purposes, should become a part of the civil government of the country? Is it because its existence, its capacities, its powers, are given by law? Because the government has given it the power to take and to hold property in a particular form, and for particular purposes, has the government a consequent right substantially to change that form, or to vary the purposes to which the property is to be applied? This principle has never been asserted or recognized, and is supported by no authority. Can it derive aid from reason?

The objects for which a corporation is created are universally such as the government wishes to promote. They are deemed beneficial to the country; and this benefit constitutes the consideration, and, in most cases, the sole consideration of the grant. In most eleemosynary institutions, the object would be difficult, perhaps unattainable, without the aid of a charter of incorporation. Charitable, or public spirited individuals, desirous of making permanent appropriations for charitable or other useful purposes, find it impossible to effect their design securely, and certainly, without an incorporating act. They apply to the government, state their beneficent object, and offer to advance the money necessary for its accomplishment. . . . The proposition is considered and approved. The benefit to the public is considered as an ample compensation for the faculty it confers, and the corporation is created. If the advantages to the public constitute a full compensation for the faculty it gives, there can be no reason for exacting a further compensation, by claiming a right to exercise over this artificial being a power which changes its nature, and touches the fund, for the security and application of which it was created. There can be no reason for implying in a charter, given for a valuable consideration, a power which is not only not expressed, but is in direct contradiction to its express stipulations. . . .

. . . It requires no very critical examination of the human mind to enable us to determine, that one great inducement to these gifts is the conviction felt by the giver, that the disposition he makes of them is immutable. It is probable, that no man ever was, and that no man ever will be, the founder of a college, believing at the time, that an act of incorporation constitutes no security for the institution; believing, that it is immediately to be deemed a public institution, whose funds are to be governed and applied, not by the will of the donor, but by the will of the legislature. . . . If every man finds in his own bosom strong evidence of the universality of this sentiment, there can be but little reason to imagine, that the framers of our constitution were strangers to it, and that, feeling the necessity and policy of giving permanence and security to contracts, of withdrawing them from the influence of legislative bodies, whose fluctuating policy, and repeated interferences, produced the most perplexing and injurious embarrassments, they still deemed it necessary to leave these contracts subject to those interferences. The motives for such an exception must be very powerful, to justify the construction which makes it. . . .

The opinion of the Court, after mature deliberation, is, that this is a contract, the obligation of which cannot be impaired, without violating the constitution of the United States. . . .

Justice Story's Opinion

. . . Eleemosynary corporations are such as are constituted for the perpetual distribution of the free alms and bounty of the founder, in such manner as he has directed; and in this class are ranked hospitals for the relief of poor and impotent persons, and colleges for the promotion of learning and piety, and the support of persons engaged in literary pursuits.

Another division of corporations is into public and private. Public corporations are generally esteemed such as exist for public political purposes only, such as towns, cities, parishes, and counties; and in many respects they are so, although they involve some private interests; but strictly speaking, public corporations are such only as are founded by the government for public purposes, where the whole interests belong also to the government. If, therefore, the foundation be private, though under the charter of the government, the corporation is private. . . . For instance, a bank created by the government for its own uses, whose stock is exclusively owned by the government, is, in the strictest sense, a public corporation. . . . But a bank, whose stock is owned by private persons, is a private corporation, although it is erected by the government, and its objects and operations partake of a public nature. The same doctrine may be affirmed of insurance, canal, bridge, and turnpike companies. In all these cases, the uses may, in a certain sense, be called public, but the corporations are private. . . .

This reasoning applies in its full force to eleemosynary corporations. A hospital founded by a private benefactor is, in point of law, a private corporation, although dedicated by its charter to general charity. So a college, founded and endowed in the same manner, although, being for the promotion of learning and piety, it may extend its charity to scholars from every class in the community, and thus acquire the character of a public institution. . . .

When, then, the argument assumes, that because the charity is public, the corporation is public, it manifestly confounds the popular, with the strictly legal sense of the terms. . . . But it is on this foundation, that a superstructure is erected, which is to compel a surrender of the cause. When the corporation is said at the bar to be public, it is merely meant, that the whole community may be the proper objects of the bounty, but that the government have the sole right, as trustees of the public interests, to regulate, control, and direct the corporation, and its funds and its franchises, at its own good will and pleasure. Now, such an authority does not exist in the government, except where the corporation is in the strictest sense public; that is, where its whole interests and franchises are the exclusive property and domain of the government itself. If it had been otherwise, Courts of law would have been spared many laborious adjudications in respect to eleemosynary corporations. . . . Nay, more, private trustees for charitable purposes would have been liable to have the property confided to their care taken away from them without any assent or default on their part, and the administration submitted, not to the control of law and equity, but to the arbitrary discretion of the government. Yet, who ever thought before, that the munificent gifts of private donors for general charity became instantaneously the property of the government; and that the trustees appointed by the donors, whether corporate or unincorporated, might be compelled to yield up their rights to whomsoever the government might appoint to administer them? If we were to establish such a principle, it would extinguish all future eleemosynary endowments. . . .

When a private eleemosynary corporation is . . . created by the charter of the crown, it is subject to no other control on the part of the crown, than what is expressly or implicitly reserved by the charter itself. Unless a power be reserved for this purpose, the crown cannot, in virtue of its prerogative, without the consent of the corporation, alter or amend the charter, or divest the corporation of any of its franchises, or add to them, or add to, or diminish, the number of the trustees, or remove any of the members, or change, or control the administration of the charity, or compel the corporation to receive a new charter. This is the uniform language of the authorities, and forms one of the most stubborn, and well settled doctrines of the common law.

The remaining inquiry is, whether the acts of the legislature of New Hampshire now in question, or any of them, impair the obligations of the charter of Dartmouth College. . . .

[Justice Story then reviewed the struggle between the state and the college.]

If these are not essential changes, impairing the rights and authorities of the trustees, and vitally affecting the interests and organization of Dartmouth College under its old charter, it is difficult to conceive what acts, short of an unconditional repeal of the charter, could have that effect. If a grant of land or franchises be made to A., in trust for special purposes, can the grant be revoked, and a new grant thereof be made to A., B., and C., in trust for the same purposes, without violating the obligation of the first grant? If property be vested by grant in A. and B., for the use of a college, or a hospital, of private foundation, is not the obligation of that grant impaired when the estate is taken from their exclusive management, and vested in them in common with ten other persons? . . . If a bank, or insurance company, by the terms of its charter, be under the management of directors, elected by the stockholders, would not the rights acquired by the charter be impaired if the legislature should take the right of election from the stockholders, and appoint directors unconnected with the corporation? These questions carry their own answers along with them. The common sense of mankind will teach us, that all these cases would be direct infringements of the legal obligations of the grants to which they refer; and yet they are, with no essential distinction, the same as the case now at the bar.

In my judgment it is perfectly clear, that any act of a legislature which takes away any powers or franchises vested by its charter in a private corporation or its corporate officers, or which restrains or controls the legitimate exercise of them, or transfers them to other persons, without its assent, is a violation of the obligations of that charter. If the legislature mean to claim such an authority, it must be reserved in the grant. The charter of Dartmouth College contains no such reservation; and I am, therefore, bound to declare, that the acts of the legislature of New Hampshire, now in question, do impair the obligations of that charter, and are, consequently, unconstitutional and void.

In pronouncing this judgment, it has not for one moment escaped me how delicate, difficult, and ungracious is the task devolved upon us. The predicament in which this Court stands in relation to the nation at large, is full of perplexities and embarrassments. It is called to decide on causes between citizens of different States, between a State and its citizens, and between different States. It stands, therefore, in the midst of jealousies and rivalries of conflicting parties, with the most momentous interests confided to its care. Under such circumstances, it never can have a motive to do more than its duty; and, I trust, it will always be found to possess firmness enough to do that.

Under these impressions I have pondered on the case before us with the most anxious deliberation. I entertain great respect for the legislature, whose acts are in question. I entertain no less respect for the enlightened tribunal whose decision we are called upon to review. In the examination, I have endeavoured to keep my steps *super antiquas vias* of the law, under the guidance of authority and principle. It is not for judges to listen to the voice of persuasive eloquence or popular appeal. We have nothing to do but to pronounce the law as we find it; and having done this, our justification must be left to the impartial judgment of our country.

53

Sturges v. *Crowninshield (1819)*

The Constitution (Article I, Section 8) gives Congress the power to enact bankruptcy legislation, but Congress had failed to exercise this power, and in order to meet the needs of the commercial community, the states had passed a variety of measures. In 1811 Richard Crownin-

Source: 4 Wheaton 122 (1819).

shield filed for bankruptcy under a recently enacted New York law, returned to Massachusetts, and recouped his fortune. Josiah Sturges now sued to recover a loan made to Crowninshield a few weeks before the enactment of the New York statute. The question was whether a bankruptcy law applied to debts made before its passage, and there had been conflicting opinions on this issue in the circuit courts. The Supreme Court ruled unanimously that the Constitution did not forbid state laws, but the Contract Clause did set limits on what the states could do, and a state could not affect contracts made before enactment of its law. The decision was welcomed by commercial interests, who in an era of expanding economic opportunities badly needed some mechanism to handle debts and debtors unable to meet their obligations. Congress still had the power, but the Court opened the door for states to act in this and other matters when Congress, for whatever reason, refused to do so.

See C. Warren, *Bankruptcy in the United States* (1935); and P. J. Coleman, *Debtors and Creditors in America . . .* (1974).

Chief Justice Marshall delivered the opinion of the Court.

This case is adjourned from the Court of the United States, for the first circuit and the district of Massachusetts, on several points on which the judges of that Court were divided, which are stated in the record for the opinion of this Court. The first is,

Whether, since the adoption of the constitution of the United States, any State has authority to pass a bankrupt law, or whether the power is exclusively vested in the Congress of the United States? . . .

In considering this question, it must be recollected that, previous to the formation of the new constitution, we were divided into independent States, united for some purposes, but, in most respects, sovereign. These States could exercise almost every legislative power, and, among others, that of passing bankrupt laws. When the American people created a national legislature, with certain enumerated powers, it was neither necessary nor proper to define the powers retained by the States. These powers proceed, not from the people of America, but from the people of the several States; and remain, after the adoption of the constitution, what they were before, except so far as they may be abridged by that instrument. In some instances, as in making treaties, we find an express prohibition; and this shows the sense of the Convention to have been, that the mere grant of a power to Congress, did not imply a prohibition on the States to exercise the same power. But it has never been supposed, that this concurrent power of legislation extended to every possible case in which its exercise by the States has not been expressly prohibited. The confusion resulting from such a practice would be endless. The principle laid down by the counsel for the plaintiff, in this respect, is undoubtedly correct. Whenever the terms in which a power is granted to Congress, or the nature of the power, require that it should be exercised exclusively by Congress, the subject is as completely taken from the State Legislatures, as if they had been expressly forbidden to act on it.

Is the power to establish uniform laws on the subject of bankruptcies, throughout the United States, of this description?

The peculiar terms of the grant certainly deserve notice. Congress is not authorized merely to pass laws, the operation of which shall be uniform, but to *establish* uniform laws on the subject throughout the United States. This *establishment* of *uniformity* is, perhaps, incompatible with State legislation, on that part of the subject to which the acts of Congress may extend. . . .

The power granted to Congress may be exercised or declined, as the wisdom of that body shall decide. If, in the opinion of Congress, uniform laws concerning bankruptcies ought not to be established, it does not follow that partial laws may not exist, or that State legislation on the subject must cease. It is not the mere existence of the power, but its exercise, which is incompatible with the exercise of the same power by the States. It is not the right to establish these uniform laws, but their actual establishment, which is inconsistent with the partial acts of the States.

It has been said, that Congress has exercised this power; and, by doing so, has extinguished the power of the States, which cannot be revived by repealing the law of Congress.

We do not think so. If the right of the States to pass a bankrupt law is not taken away by the mere grant of that power to Congress, it cannot be extinguished; it can only be suspended, by the enactment of a general bankrupt law. The repeal of that law cannot, it is true, confer the power on the States; but it removes a disability to its exercise, which was created by the act of Congress.

Without entering farther into the delicate inquiry respecting the precise limitations which the several grants of power to Congress, contained in the constitution, may impose on the State Legislatures, than is necessary for the decision of the question before the Court, it is sufficient to say, that until the power to pass uniform laws on the subject of bankruptcies be exercised by Congress, the States are not forbidden to pass a bankrupt law, provided it contain no principle which violates the 10th section of the first article of the constitution of the United States. . . .

We proceed to the great question on which the cause must depend. Does the law of New-York, which is pleaded in this case, impair the obligation of contracts, within the meaning of the constitution of the United States?

This act liberates the person of the debtor, and discharges him from all liability for any debt previously contracted, on his surrendering his property in the manner it prescribes.

In discussing the question whether a State is prohibited from passing such a law as this, our first inquiry is into the meaning of words in common use, What is the obligation of a contract? and what will impair it?

It would seem difficult to substitute words which are more intelligible, or less liable to misconstruction, than those which are to be explained. A contract is an agreement in which a party undertakes to do, or not to do, a particular thing. The law binds him to perform his undertaking, and this is, of course, the obligation of his contract. In the case at bar, the defendant has given his promissory note to pay the plaintiff a sum of money on or before a certain day. The contract binds him to pay that sum on that day; and this is its obligation. Any law which releases a part of this obligation, must, in the literal sense of the word, impair it. Much more must a law impair it which makes it totally invalid, and entirely discharges it.

The words of the constitution, then, are express, and incapable of being misunderstood. They admit of no variety of construction, and are acknowledged to apply to that species of contract, an engagement between man and man for the payment of money, which has been entered into by these parties. Yet the opinion that this law is not within the prohibition of the constitution has been entertained by those who are entitled to great respect, and has been supported by arguments which deserve to be seriously considered.

It has been contended, that as a contract can only bind a man to pay to the full extent of his property, it is an implied condition that he may be discharged on surrendering the whole of it.

But it is not true that the parties have in view only the property in possession when the contract is formed, or that its obligation does not extend to future acquisitions. Industry, talents, and integrity, constitute a fund which is as confidently trusted as property itself. Future acquisitions are, therefore, liable for contracts; and to release them from this liability impairs their obligation.

It has been argued, that the States are not prohibited from passing bankrupt laws, and that the essential principle of such laws is to discharge the bankrupt from all past obligations; that the States have been in the constant practice of passing insolvent laws, such as that of New-York, and if the framers of the constitution had intended to deprive them of this power, insolvent laws would have been mentioned in the prohibition; that the prevailing evil of the times, which produced this clause in the constitution, was the practice of emitting paper money, of making property which was useless to the creditor a discharge of his debt, and of changing the time of payment by authorizing distant instalments. Laws of this description, not insolvent laws, constituted, it is said, the mischief to be remedied; and laws of this description, not insolvent laws, are within the true spirit of the prohibition.

The constitution does not grant to the States the power of passing bankrupt laws, or any other power; but finds them in possession of it, and may either prohibit its future exercise entirely, or restrain it so far as national policy may require. It has so far restrained it as to prohibit the passage of any law impairing the obligation of contracts. Although, then, the States may, until that power shall be exercised by Congress, pass laws concerning bankrupts; yet they cannot constitutionally introduce into such laws a clause which discharges the obligations the bankrupt has entered into. It is not admitted that, without this principle, an act cannot be a bankrupt law; and if it were, that admission would not change the constitution, nor exempt such acts from its prohibitions.

54

McCulloch v. Maryland (1819)

The charter of the Bank of the United States had expired in 1811, and the Republican administration had refused to renew it, since Madison still adhered to the views set forth in Jefferson's denunciation of the measure (Document 31). The War of 1812, however, had shown Madison how essential a central bank was to the effective management of the government's resources, and in his annual message to Congress in December 1815, Madison urged a number of nationalistic measures, including a new bank.

In 1816 Congress chartered the Second Bank of the United States, which quickly established branches in several states. Local banks objected to the Bank's influence, and passed a variety of statutes designed to curb its power. Maryland enacted a law that imposed a tax on all banks "not chartered by the Legislature" and operating "without authority from the State." It also imposed personal liability on the officers of such banks for failure to pay the tax. James McCulloch, the cashier of the Baltimore branch of the Bank, refused to pay the tax, and the state courts found him guilty of violating the Maryland statute. The Bank then took an appeal to the Supreme Court. The issues in the case were hardly new; in many ways, it was a replay of the debate between Jefferson and Hamilton over the constitutionality of the first Bank (see Documents 31 and 32). Marshall's strong endorsement of national sovereignty did not end the debate; the scope of the national authority to reach local affairs is a characteristic and continuing problem of our

Source: 4 Wheaton 316 (1819).

federal system of government. When the charter of the Second Bank came up for renewal, it found its legitimacy challenged despite this strong opinion (see the next document).

See B. Hammond, *Banks and Politics in America—From the Revolution to the Civil War* (1957); Plous and Baker, "*McCulloch* v. *Maryland:* Right Principle, Wrong Case," 9 *Stan. L. R.* 710 (1957); and G. Gunther, ed., *John Marshall's Defense of McCulloch v. Maryland* (1969).

~~~~~~

Chief Justice Marshall delivered the opinion of the Court.

In the case now to be determined, the defendant, a sovereign State, denies the obligation of a law enacted by the legislature of the Union, and the plaintiff, on his part, contests the validity of an act which has been passed by the legislature of that State. The constitution of our country, in its most interesting and vital parts, is to be considered; the conflicting powers of the government of the Union and of its members, as marked in that constitution, are to be discussed; and an opinion given, which may essentially influence the great operations of the government. No tribunal can approach such a question without a deep sense of its importance, and of the awful responsibility involved in its decision. But it must be decided peacefully, or remain a source of hostile legislation, perhaps of hostility of a still more serious nature; and if it is to be so decided, by this tribunal alone can the decision be made. On the Supreme Court of the United States has the constitution of our country devolved this important duty.

The first question made in the cause is, has Congress power to incorporate a bank?

It has been truly said that this can scarcely be considered as an open question, entirely unprejudiced by the former proceedings of the nation respecting it. The principle now contested was introduced at a very early period of our history, has been recognised by many successive legislatures, and has been acted upon by the judicial department, in cases of peculiar delicacy, as a law of undoubted obligation. . . .

The power now contested was exercised by the first Congress elected under the present constitution. The bill for incorporating the bank of the United States did not steal upon an unsuspecting legislature, and pass unobserved. Its principle was completely understood, and was opposed with equal zeal and ability. After being resisted, first in the fair and open field of debate, and afterwards in the executive cabinet, with as much persevering talent as any measure has ever experienced, and being supported by arguments which convinced minds as pure and as intelligent as this country can boast, it became a law. The original act was permitted to expire; but a short experience of the embarrassments to which the refusal to revive it exposed the government, convinced those who were most prejudiced against the measure of its necessity, and induced the passage of the present law. It would require no ordinary share of intrepidity to assert that a measure adopted under these circumstances was a bold and plain usurpation, to which the constitution gave no countenance.

These observations belong to the cause; but they are not made under the impression that, were the question entirely new, the law would be found irreconcilable with the constitution.

In discussing this question, the counsel for the State of Maryland have deemed it of some importance, in the construction of the constitution, to consider that instrument not as emanating from the people, but as the act of sovereign and independent States. The powers of the general government, it has been said, are delegated by the States, who alone are truly sovereign; and must be exercised in subordination to the States, who alone possess supreme dominion.

It would be difficult to sustain this proposition. The Convention which framed the constitution was indeed elected by the State legislatures. But the instrument, when it came from their hands, was a mere proposal, without obligation, or pretensions to it. It was reported to the then existing Congress of the United States, with a request that it might "be submitted to a convention of delegates, chosen in each State by the people thereof, under the recommendation of its legislature, for their assent and ratification." This mode of proceeding was adopted; and by the convention, by Congress, and by the State legislatures, the instrument was submitted to the people. They acted upon it in the only manner in which they can act safely, effectively, and wisely, on such a subject, by assembling in convention. It is true, they assembled in their several States—and where else should they have assembled? No political dreamer was ever wild enough to think of breaking down the lines which separate the States, and of compounding the American people into one common mass. Of consequence, when they act, they act in their States. But the measures they adopt do not, on that account, cease to be the measures of the people themselves, or become the measures of the State governments.

From these conventions the constitution derives its whole authority. The government proceeds directly from the people; is "ordained and established" in the name of the people; and is declared to be ordained, "in order to form a more perfect union, establish justice, ensure domestic tranquility, and secure the blessings of liberty to themselves and to their posterity." The assent of the States, in their sovereign capacity, is implied in calling a convention, and thus submitting that instrument to the people. But the people were at perfect liberty to accept or reject it; and their act was final. It required not the affirmance, and could not be negatived, by the State governments. The constitution, when thus adopted, was of complete obligation, and bound the State sovereignties. . . .

The government of the Union, then (whatever may be the influence of this fact on the case), is, emphatically, and truly, a government of the people. In form and in substance it emanates from them. Its powers are granted by them, and are to be exercised directly on them, and for their benefit.

This government is acknowledged by all to be one of enumerated powers. The principle, that it can exercise only the powers granted to it, [is] now universally admitted. But the question respecting the extent of the powers actually granted, is perpetually arising, and will probably continue to arise, as long as our system shall exist. . . .

Among the enumerated powers, we do not find that of establishing a bank or creating a corporation. But there is no phrase in the instrument which, like the articles of confederation, excludes incidental or implied powers; and which requires that everything granted shall be expressly and minutely described. Even the 10th amendment, which was framed for the purpose of quieting the excessive jealousies which had been excited, omits the word "expressly," and declares only that the powers "not delegated to the United States, nor prohibited to the States, are reserved to the States or to the people"; thus leaving the question, whether the particular power which may become the subject of contest has been delegated to the one government, or prohibited to the other, to depend on a fair construction of the whole instrument. The men who drew and adopted this amendment had experienced the embarrassments resulting from the insertion of this word in the articles of confederation, and probably omitted it to avoid those embarrassments. A constitution, to contain an accurate detail of all the subdivisions of which its great powers will admit, and of all the means by which they may be carried into execution, would partake of the prolixity of a legal code, and could scarcely be embraced by the human mind. It would probably never be understood by the public. Its nature, therefore, requires, that only its great outlines should be marked, its important objects designated, and the minor ingredients which compose those objects be deduced from the nature of the objects themselves. That this idea was entertained by the framers of the American constitution, is not only to be inferred from the nature of the instrument, but from the language. Why else were some of the limitations, found in the ninth section of the 1st article, introduced? It is also, in some degree, warranted by their having omitted to use any restrictive term which might prevent its receiving a fair and just interpretation. In considering this question, then, we must never forget that it is *a constitution* we are expounding.

Although, among the enumerated powers of government, we do not find the word "bank," or "incorporation," we find the great powers to lay and collect taxes; to borrow money; to regulate commerce; to declare and conduct a war; and to raise and support armies and navies. The sword and the purse, all the external relations, and no inconsiderable portion of the industry of the nation, are entrusted to its government. It can never be pretended that these vast powers draw after them others of inferior importance, merely because they are inferior. Such an idea can never be advanced. But it may with great reason be contended, that a government, entrusted with such ample powers, on the due execution of which the happiness and prosperity of the nation so vitally depends, must also be entrusted with ample means for their execution. The power being given, it is the interest of the nation to facilitate its execution. It can never be their interest, and cannot be presumed to have been their intention, to clog and embarrass its execution by withholding the most appropriate means. . . . Can we adopt that construction (unless the words imperiously require it) which would impute to the framers of that instrument, when granting these powers for the public good, the intention of impeding their exercise by withholding a choice of means? If, indeed, such be the mandate of the constitution, we have only to obey; but that instrument does not profess to enumerate the means by which the powers it confers may be executed; nor does it prohibit the creation of a corporation, if the existence of such a being be essential to the beneficial exercise of those powers. It is, then, the subject of fair inquiry, how far such means may be employed.

It is not denied, that the powers given to the government imply the ordinary means of execution. That, for example, of raising revenue, and applying it to national purposes, is admitted to imply the power of conveying money from place to place, as the exigencies of the nation may require, and of employing the usual means of conveyance. But it is denied that the government has its choice of means; or, that it may employ the most convenient means, if, to employ them, it be necessary to erect a corporation. . . .

The government which has a right to do an act, and has imposed on it the duty of performing that act, must, according to the dictates of reason, be allowed to select the means; and those who contend that it may not select any appropriate means, that one particular mode of effecting the object is excepted, take upon themselves the burden of establishing that exception. The power of creating a corporation, though appertaining to sovereignty, is not, like the power of making war, or levying taxes, or of regulating commerce, a great substantive and independent power, which cannot be implied as incidental to other powers, or used as a means of executing them. It is never the end for which other powers are exercised, but a means by which other objects are accomplished. The power of creating a corporation is never used for its own sake, but for the purpose of effecting something else. No sufficient reason is, therefore, perceived, why it may not pass as incidental to those powers which are expressly given, if it be a direct mode of executing them.

But the constitution of the United States has not left the right of Congress to employ the necessary means, for the execution of the powers conferred on the government, to general reasoning. To its enumeration of powers is added that of making "all laws which shall be necessary and proper for carrying into execution the foregoing powers, and all other powers vested by this constitution, in the government of the United States, or in any department thereof."

The counsel for the State of Maryland have urged various arguments, to prove that this clause, though in terms a grant of power, is not so in effect;

but is really restrictive of the general right, which might otherwise be implied, of selecting means for executing the enumerated powers. . . .

. . . Almost all compositions contain words, which, taken in their rigorous sense, would convey a meaning different from that which is obviously intended. It is essential to just construction, that many words which import something excessive should be understood in a more mitigated sense—in that sense which common usage justifies. The word "necessary" is of this description. It has not a fixed character peculiar to itself. It admits of all degrees of comparison; and is often connected with other words, which increase or diminish the impression the mind receives of the urgency it imports. A thing may be necessary, very necessary, absolutely or indispensably necessary. To no mind would the same idea be conveyed by these several phrases. This comment on the word is well illustrated by the passage cited at the bar, from the 20th section of the 1st article of the constitution. It is, we think, impossible to compare the sentence which prohibits a State from laying "imposts, or duties on imports or exports, except what may be *absolutely* necessary for executing its inspection laws," with that which authorizes Congress "to make all laws which shall be necessary and proper for carrying into execution" the powers of the general government, without feeling a conviction that the convention understood itself to change materially the meaning of the word "necessary," by prefixing the word "absolutely." This word, then, like others, is used in various senses; and, in its construction, the subject, the context, the intention of the person using them, are all to be taken into view.

Let this be done in the case under consideration. The subject is the execution of those great powers on which the welfare of a nation essentially depends. It must have been the intention of those who gave these powers, to insure, as far as human prudence could insure, their beneficial execution. This could not be done by confiding the choice of means to such narrow limits as not to leave it in the power of Congress to adopt any which might be appropriate, and which were conducive to the end. This provision is made in a constitution intended to endure for ages to come, and, consequently, to be adapted to the various *crises* of human affairs. To have prescribed the means by which government should, in all future time, execute its powers, would have been to change, entirely, the character of the instrument, and give it the properties of a legal code. It would have been an unwise attempt to provide, by immutable rules, for exigencies which, if foreseen at all, must have been seen dimly, and which can be best provided for as they occur. To have declared that the best means shall not be used, but those alone without which the power given would be nugatory, would have been to deprive the legislature of the capacity to avail itself of experience, to exercise its reason, and to accommodate its legislation to circumstances. If we apply this principle of construction to any of the powers of the government, we shall find it so pernicious in its operation that we shall be compelled to discard it. . . .

The result of the most careful and attentive consideration bestowed upon this clause is, that if it does not enlarge, it cannot be construed to restrain the powers of Congress, or to impair the right of the legislature to exercise its best judgment in the selection of measures to carry into execution the constitutional powers of the government. If no other motive for its insertion can be suggested, a sufficient one is found in the desire to remove all doubts respecting the right to legislate on that vast mass of incidental powers which must be involved in the constitution, if that instrument be not a splendid bauble.

We admit, as all must admit, that the powers of the government are limited, and that its limits are not to be transcended. But we think the sound construction of the constitution must allow to the national legislature that discretion, with respect to the means by which the powers it confers are to be carried into execution, which will enable that body to perform the high duties assigned to it, in the manner most beneficial to the people. Let the end be legitimate, let it be within the scope of the constitution, and all means which are appropriate, which are plainly adapted to that end, which are not prohibited, but consist with the letter and spirit of the constitution, are constitutional. . . .

. . . Should Congress, in the execution of its powers, adopt measures which are prohibited by the constitution; or should Congress, under the pretext of executing its powers, pass laws for the accomplishment of objects not entrusted to the government; it would become the painful duty of this tribunal, should a case requiring such a decision come before it, to say that such an act was not the law of the land. But where the law is not prohibited, and is really calculated to effect any of the objects entrusted to the government, to undertake here to inquire into the degree of its necessity, would be to pass the line which circumscribes the judicial department, and to tread on legislative ground. This court disclaims all pretensions to such a power.

After this declaration, it can scarcely be necessary to say that the existence of State banks can have no possible influence on the question. No trace is to be found in the constitution of an intention to create a dependence of the government of the Union on those of the States, for the execution of the great powers assigned to it. Its means are adequate to its ends; and on those means alone was it expected to rely for the accomplishment of its ends. To impose on it the necessity of resorting to means which it cannot control, which another government may furnish or withhold, would render its course precarious, the result of its measures uncertain, and create a dependence on other governments, which might disappoint its most important designs, and is incompatible with the language of the constitution. But were it otherwise, the choice of means implies a right to choose a national bank in preference to State banks, and Congress alone can make the election.

After the most deliberate consideration, it is the unanimous and decided opinion of this Court, that the act to incorporate the Bank of the United States is a law made in pursuance of the constitution, and is a part of the supreme law of the land. . . .

It being the opinion of the Court, that the act incorporating the bank is constitutional; and that the power of establishing a branch in the State of Maryland might be properly exercised by the bank itself, we proceed to inquire—

2.   Whether the State of Maryland may, without violating the constitution, tax that branch?

That the power of taxation is one of vital importance; that it is retained by the States; that it is not abridged by the grant of a similar power to the government of the Union; that it is to be concurrently exercised by the two governments: are truths which have never been denied. But, such is the paramount character of the constitution, that its capacity to withdraw any subject from the action of even this power, is admitted. The States are expressly forbidden to lay any duties on imports or exports, except what may be absolutely necessary for executing their inspection laws. If the obligation of this prohibition must be conceded, the same paramount character would seem to restrain, as it certainly may restrain, a State from such other exercise of this power; as is in its nature incompatible with, and repugnant to, the constitutional laws of the Union. . . .

On this ground the counsel for the bank place its claim to be exempted from the power of a State to tax its operations. There is no express provision for the case, but the claim has been sustained on a principle which so entirely pervades the constitution, is so intermixed with the materials which compose it, so interwoven with its web, so blended with its texture, as to be incapable of being separated from it, without rending it into shreds.

This great principle is, that the constitution and the laws made in pursuance thereof are supreme; that they control the constitution and laws of the respective States, and cannot be controlled by them. From this, which may be almost termed an axiom, other propositions are deduced as corollaries, on the truth or error of which, and on their application to this case, the cause has been supposed to depend. These are, 1st. that a power to create implies a power to preserve. 2nd. That a power to destroy, if wielded by a different hand, is hostile to, and incompatible with these powers to create and to preserve. 3d. That where this repugnancy exists, that authority which is supreme must control, not yield to that over which it is supreme. . . .

That the power of taxing by the States may be exercised so as to destroy it, is too obvious to be denied. But taxation is said to be an absolute power, which acknowledges no other limits than those expressly prescribed in the constitution, and like sovereign power of every other description, is trusted to the discretion of those who use it. But the very terms of this argument admit that the sovereignty of the State, in the article of taxation itself, is subordinate to, and may be controlled by, the constitution of the United States. How far it has been controlled by that instrument must be a question of construction. In making this construction, no principle not declared, can be admissible, which would defeat the legitimate operations of a supreme government. It is of the very essence of supremacy to remove all obstacles to its action within its own sphere, and so to modify every power vested in subordinate governments, as to exempt its own operations from their own influence. This effect need not be stated in terms. It is so involved in the declaration of supremacy, so necessarily implied in it, that the expression of it could not make it more certain. We must, therefore, keep it in view while construing the constitution.

The argument on the part of the State of Maryland is, not that the States may directly resist a law of Congress, but that they may exercise their acknowledged powers upon it, and that the constitution leaves them this right in the confidence that they will not abuse it.

Before we proceed to examine this argument, and to subject it to the test of the constitution, we must be permitted to bestow a few considerations on the nature and extent of this original right of taxation, which is acknowledged to remain with the States. It is admitted that the power of taxing the people and their property is essential to the very existence of government, and may be legitimately exercised on the objects to which it is applicable, to the utmost extent to which the government may choose to carry it. The only security against the abuse of this power, is found in the structure of the government itself. In imposing a tax the legislature acts upon its constituents. . . .

The sovereignty of a State extends to everything which exists by its own authority, or is introduced by its permission; but does it extend to those means which are employed by Congress to carry into execution powers conferred on that body by the people of the United States? We think it demonstrable that it does not. Those powers are not given by the people of a single State. They are given by the people of the United States, to a government whose laws, made in pursuance of the constitution, are declared to be supreme. Consequently, the people of a single State cannot confer a sovereignty which will extend over them.

If we measure the power of taxation residing in a State, by the extent of sovereignty which the people of a single State possess, and can confer on its government, we have an intelligible standard, applicable to every case to which the power may be applied. We have a principle which leaves the power of taxing the people and property of a State unimpaired; which leaves to a State the command of all its resources, and which places beyond its reach, all those powers which are conferred by the people of the United States on the government of the Union, and all those means which are given for the purpose of carrying those powers into execution. We have a principle which is safe for the States, and safe for the Union. We are relieved, as we ought to be, from clashing sovereignty; from interfering powers; from a repugnancy between a right in one government to pull down what there is an acknowledged right in another to build up; from the incompatibility of a right in one government to destroy what there is a right in another to preserve. We are not driven to the perplexing inquiry, so unfit for the judicial department, what degree of taxation is the legitimate use, and what degree may amount to the abuse of the power. The attempt to use it on the means employed by the government of the Union, in pursuance of the constitution, is itself an abuse, because it is the usurpation of a power which the people of a single State cannot give.

We find, then, on just theory, a total failure of this original right to tax the means employed by the government of the Union, for the execution of its powers. The right never existed, and the question whether it has been surrendered, cannot arise.

But, waiving this theory for the present, let us resume the inquiry, whether this power can be exercised by the respective States, consistently with a fair construction of the constitution?

That the power to tax involves the power to destroy; that the power to destroy may defeat and render useless the power to create; that there is a plain repugnance, in conferring on one government a power to control the constitutional measures of another, which other, with respect to those very measures, is declared to be supreme over that which exerts the control, are propositions not to be denied. But all inconsistencies are to be reconciled by the magic of the word CONFIDENCE. Taxation, it is said, does not necessarily and unavoidably destroy. To carry it to the excess of destruction would be an abuse, to presume which, would banish that confidence which is essential to all government.

But is this a case of confidence? Would the people of any one State trust those of another with a power to control the most insignificant operations of their State government? We know they would not. Why, then, should we suppose that the people of any one State should be willing to trust those of another with a power to control the operations of a government to which they have confided their most important and most valuable interests? In the legislature of the Union alone, are all represented. The legislature of the Union alone, therefore, can be trusted by the people with the power of controlling measures which concern all, in the confidence that it will not be abused. This, then, is not a case of confidence, and we must consider it as it really is.

If we apply the principle for which the State of Maryland contends, to the constitution generally, we shall find it capable of changing totally the character of that instrument. We shall find it capable of arresting all the measures of the government, and of prostrating it at the foot of the States. The American people have declared their constitution, and the laws made in pursuance thereof, to be supreme; but this principle would transfer the supremacy, in fact, to the States.

If the States may tax one instrument, employed by the government in the execution of its powers, they may tax any and every other instrument. They may tax the mail; they may tax the mint; they may tax patent rights; they may tax the papers of the custom-house; they may tax judicial process; they may tax all the means employed by the government, to an excess which would defeat all the ends of government. This was not intended by the American people. They did not design to make their government dependent on the States. . . .

The Court has bestowed on this subject its most deliberate consideration. The result is a conviction that the States have no power, by taxation or otherwise, to retard, impede, burden, or in any manner control, the operations of the constitutional laws enacted by Congress to carry into execution the powers vested in the general government. This is, we think, the unavoidable consequence of that supremacy which the constitution has declared.

We are unanimously of opinion, that the law passed by the legislature of Maryland, imposing a tax on the Bank of the United States, is unconstitutional and void.

This opinion does not deprive the States of any resources which they originally possessed. It does not extend to a tax paid by the real property of the bank, in common with the other real property within the State, nor to a tax imposed on the interest which the citizens of Maryland may hold in this institution, in common with other property of the same description throughout the State. But this is a tax on the operations of the bank, and is, consequently, a tax on the operation of an instrument employed by the government of the Union to carry its powers into execution. Such a tax must be unconstitutional.

55

Veto of Bank Bill (1832)

ANDREW JACKSON

Andrew Jackson had no understanding of banks; he instinctively distrusted them, and especially distrusted the Bank of the United States. Like most westerners, he objected to the Bank's conservative policies, which limited credit for land speculation. The charter of the Second Bank was not due to expire until 1836, but its friends hit upon the strategem of petitioning Congress for a renewal in 1832, an election year, confident that Jackson would not dare to antagonize commercial interests by vetoing the measure. They were wrong, and Jackson's veto message tapped a wellspring of popular support and widespread anti-

Source: Richardson, ed., 2 *Messages and Papers of the Presidents* 576 (1897).

Bank sentiment in much of the nation. Despite the Supreme Court's ruling that Congress had the power to charter banks, Jackson believed otherwise. Moreover, in this message (drafted in part by future Chief Justice Roger B. Taney) Jackson argued that each constituent branch of government had independent power to interpret the Constitution, and that no branch had to be bound by the opinions of others, even of the Supreme Court. Although Jackson's views never gained acceptance, this message constituted the greatest challenge in the nineteenth century to the Court's assumption of the power as final arbiter of the Constitution.

See R. V. Remini, *Andrew Jackson and the Bank War* (1967); and B. Hammond, *Banks and Politics . . .* (1957).

To the Senate:

The bill "to modify and continue" the act entitled "An act to incorporate the subscribers to the Bank of the United States" was presented to me on the 4th July instant. Having considered it with that solemn regard to the principles of the Constitution which the day was calculated to inspire, and come to the conclusion that it ought not to become a law, I herewith return it to the Senate, in which it originated, with my objections.

A bank of the United States is in many respects convenient for the Government and useful to the people. Entertaining this opinion, and deeply impressed with the belief that some of the powers and privileges possessed by the existing bank are unauthorized by the Constitution, subversive of the rights of the States, and dangerous to the liberties of the people, I felt it my duty at an early period of my Administration to call the attention of Congress to the practicability of organizing an institution combining all its advantages and obviating these objections. I sincerely regret that in the act before me I can perceive none of those modifications of the bank charter which are necessary, in my opinion, to make it compatible with justice, with sound policy, or with the Constitution of our country. . . .

It is maintained by the advocates of the bank that its constitutionality in all its features ought to be considered as settled by precedent and by the decision of the Supreme Court. To this conclusion I can not assent. Mere precedent is a dangerous source of authority, and should not be regarded as deciding questions of constitutional power except where the acquiescence of the people and the States can be considered as well settled. So far from this being the case on this subject, an argument against the bank might be based on precedent. One Congress, in 1791, decided in favor of a bank; another, in 1811, decided against it. One Congress, in 1815, decided against a bank;

another, in 1816, decided in its favor. Prior to the present Congress, therefore, the precedents drawn from that source were equal. If we resort to the States, the expressions of legislative, judicial, and executive opinions against the bank have been probably to those in its favor as 4 to 1. There is nothing in precedent, therefore, which, if its authority were admitted, ought to weigh in favor of the act before me.

If the opinion of the Supreme Court covered the whole ground of this act, it ought not to control the coordinate authorities of this Government. The Congress, the Executive, and the Court must each for itself be guided by its own opinion of the Constitution. Each public officer who takes an oath to support the Constitution swears that he will support it as he understands it, and not as it is understood by others. It is as much the duty of the House of Representatives, of the Senate, and of the President to decide upon the constitutionality of any bill or resolution which may be presented to them for passage or approval as it is of the supreme judges when it may be brought before them for judicial decision. The opinion of the judges has no more authority over Congress than the opinion of Congress has over the judges, and on that point the President is independent of both. The authority of the Supreme Court must not, therefore, be permitted to control the Congress or the Executive when acting in their legislative capacities, but to have only such influence as the force of their reasoning may deserve.

But in the case relied upon the Supreme Court have not decided that all the features of this corporation are compatible with the Constitution. It is true that the court have said that the law incorporating the bank is a constitutional exercise of power by Congress; but taking into view the whole opinion of the court and the reasoning by which they have come to that conclusion, I understand them to have decided that inasmuch as a bank is an appropriate means for carrying into effect the enumerated powers of the General Government, therefore the law incorporating it is in accordance with that provision of the Constitution which declares that Congress shall have power "to make all laws which shall be necessary and proper for carrying those powers into execution." Having satisfied themselves that the word *"necessary"* in the Constitution means *"needful," "requisite," "essential," "conducive to,"* and that "a bank" is a convenient, a useful, and essential instrument in the prosecution of the Government's "fiscal operations," they conclude that to "use one must be within the discretion of Congress" and that "the act to incorporate the Bank of the United States is a law made in pursuance of the Constitution;" "but," say they, *"where the law is not prohibited and is really calculated to effect any of the objects intrusted to the Government, to undertake here to inquire into the degree of its necessity would be to pass the line which circumscribes the judicial department and to tread on legislative ground."*

The principle here affirmed is that the "degree of its necessity," involving all the details of a banking institution, is a question exclusively for legislative consideration. A bank is constitutional, but it is the province of the Legislature to determine whether this or that particular power, privilege, or exemption is "necessary and proper" to enable the bank to discharge its duties to the Government, and from their decision there is no appeal to the courts of justice. Under the decision of the Supreme Court, therefore, it is the exclusive province of Congress and the President to decide whether the particular features of this act are *necessary* and *proper* in order to enable the bank to perform conveniently and efficiently the public duties assigned to it as a fiscal agent, and therefore constitutional, or *unnecessary* and *improper,* and therefore unconstitutional.

Without commenting on the general principle affirmed by the Supreme Court, let us examine the details of this act in accordance with the rule of legislative action which they have laid down. It will be found that many of the powers and privileges conferred on it cannot be supposed necessary for the purpose for which it is proposed to be created, and are not, therefore, means necessary to attain the end in view, and consequently not justified by the Constitution. . . .

On two subjects only does the Constitution recognize in Congress the power to grant exclusive privileges or monopolies. It declares that "Congress shall have power to promote the progress of science and useful arts by securing for limited times to authors and inventors the exclusive right to their respective writings and discoveries." Out of this express delegation of power have grown our laws of patents and copyrights. As the Constitution expressly delegates to Congress the power to grant exclusive privileges in these cases as the means of executing the substantive power "to promote the progress of science and useful arts," it is consistent with the fair rules of construction to conclude that such a power was not intended to be granted as a means of accomplishing any other end. On every other subject which comes within the scope of Congressional power there is an ever-living discretion in the use of proper means, which can not be restricted or abolished without an amendment of the Constitution. Every act of Congress, therefore, which attempts by grants of monopolies or sale of exclusive privileges for a limited time, or a time without limit, to restrict or extinguish its own discretion in the choice of means to execute its delegated powers is equivalent to a legislative amendment of the Constitution, and palpably unconstitutional.

This act authorizes and encourages transfers of its stock to foreigners and grants them an exemption from all State and national taxation. So far from being *"necessary and proper"* that the bank should possess this power to make it a safe and efficient agent of the Government in its fiscal operations, it is calculated to convert the Bank of the United States into a foreign bank, to impoverish our people in time of peace, to disseminate a foreign influence through every section of the Republic, and in war to endanger our independence.

The several States reserved the power at the formation of the Constitution to regulate and control titles and transfers of real property, and most, if not all, of them have laws disqualifying aliens from acquiring or holding lands within their limits. But this act, in disregard of the undoubted right of the

States to prescribe such disqualifications, gives to aliens stockholders in this bank an interest and title, as members of the corporation, to all the real property it may acquire within any of the States of this Union. This privilege granted to aliens is not *"neccessary"* to enable the bank to perform its public duties, nor in any sense *"proper,"* because it is vitally subversive of the rights of the States.

The Government of the United States have no constitutional power to purchase lands within the States except "for the erection of forts, magazines, arsenals, dockyards, and other needful buildings," and even for these objects only "by the consent of the legislature of the State in which the same shall be." By making themselves stockholders in the bank and granting to the corporation the power to purchase lands for other purposes they assume a power not granted in the Constitution and grant to others what they do not themselves possess. It is not *neccessary* to the receiving, safe-keeping, or transmission of the funds of the Government that the bank should possess this power, and it is not *proper* that Congress should thus enlarge the powers delegated to them in the Constitution. . . .

The Government is the only *"proper"* judge where its agents should reside and keep their offices, because it best knows where their presence will be *"necessary."* It can not, therefore, be *"necessary"* or *"proper"* to authorize the bank to locate branches where it pleases to perform the public service, without consulting the Government, and contrary to its will. The principle laid down by the Supreme Court concedes that Congress can not establish a bank for purposes of private speculation and gain, but only as a means of executing the delegated powers of the General Government. By the same principle a branch bank can not constitutionally be established for other than public purposes. The power which this act gives to establish two branches in any State, without the injunction or request of the Government and for other than public purposes, is not *"neccessary"* to the due *execution* of the powers delegated to Congress. . . .

It is maintained by some that the bank is a means of executing the constitutional power "to coin money and regulate the value thereof." Congress have established a mint to coin money and passed laws to regulate the value thereof. The money so coined, with its value so regulated, and such foreign coins as Congress may adopt are the only currency known to the Constitution. But if they have other power to regulate the currency, it was conferred to be exercised by themselves, and not to be transferred to a corporation. If the bank be established for that purpose, with a charter unalterable without its consent, Congress have parted with their power for a term of years, during which the Constitution is a dead letter. It is neither necessary nor proper to transfer its legislative power to such a bank, and therefore unconstitutional.

By its silence, considered in connection with the decision of the Supreme Court in the case of McCulloch against the State of Maryland, this act takes from the States the power to tax a portion of the banking business carried on within their limits, in subversion of one of the strongest barriers which secured them against Federal encroachments. Banking, like farming, manufacturing, or any other occupation or profession, is *a business,* the right to follow which is not originally derived from the laws. Every citizen and every company of citizens in all of our States possessed the right until the State legislatures deemed it good policy to prohibit private banking by law. If the prohibitory State laws were now repealed, every citizen would again possess the right. The State banks are a qualified restoration of the right which has been taken away by the laws against banking, guarded by such provisions and limitations as in the opinion of the State legislatures the public interest requires. These corporations, unless there be an exemption in their charter, are, like private bankers and banking companies, subject to State taxation. The manner in which these taxes shall be laid depends wholly on legislative discretion. It may be upon the bank, upon the stock, upon the profits, or in any other mode which the sovereign power shall will.

Upon the formation of the Constitution the States guarded their taxing power with peculiar jealousy. They surrendered it only as it regards imports and exports. In relation to every other object within their jurisdiction, whether persons, property, business, or professions, it was secured in as ample a manner as it was before possessed. All persons, though United States officers, are liable to a poll tax by the States within which they reside. The lands of the United States are liable to the usual land tax, except in the new States, from whom agreements that they will not tax unsold lands are exacted when they are admitted into the Union. Horses, wagons, any beasts or vehicles, tools, or property belonging to private citizens, though employed in the service of the United States, are subject to State taxation. Every private business, whether carried on by an officer of the General Government or not, whether it be mixed with public concerns or not, even if it be carried on by the Government of the United States itself, separately or in partnership, falls within the scope of the taxing power of the State. Nothing comes more fully within it than banks and the business of banking, by whomsoever instituted and carried on. Over this whole subject-matter it is just as absolute, unlimited, and uncontrollable as if the Constitution had never been adopted, because in the formation of that instrument it was reserved without qualification.

The principle is conceded that the States can not rightfully tax the operations of the General Government. They can not tax the money of the Government deposited in the State banks, nor the agency of those banks in remitting it; but will any man maintain that their mere selection to perform this public service for the General Government would exempt the State banks and their ordinary business from State taxation? Had the United States, instead of establishing a bank at Philadelphia, employed a private banker to keep and transmit their funds, would it have deprived Pennsylvania of the right to tax his bank and his usual banking operations? It will not be pretended. Upon what principle, then, are the banking establishments of the Bank of the United States and their usual banking operations to be exempted from taxation? It is not their public agency or the deposits of the Government which the States claim a right to tax, but their banks and their banking powers, instituted and exercised within State jurisdiction for their private emolument—those powers and privileges for which they pay a bonus, and which the States tax in their own banks. The exercise of these powers within a State, no matter by whom or under what authority, whether by private citizens in their original right, by corporate bodies created by the States, by foreigners or the agents of foreign governments located within their limits, forms a legitimate object of State taxation. From this and like sources, from the persons, property, and business that are found residing, located, or carried on under their jurisdiction, must the States, since the surrender of their right to raise a revenue from imports and exports, draw all the money necessary for the support of their governments and the maintenance of their independence. There is no more appropriate subject of taxation than banks, banking, and bank stocks, and none to which the States ought more pertinaciously to cling.

It can not be *necessary* to the character of the bank as a fiscal agent of the Government that its private business should be exempted from that taxation to which all the State banks are liable, nor can I conceive it *"proper"* that the substantive and most essential powers reserved by the States shall be thus attacked and annihilated as a means of executing the powers delegated to the General Government. It may be safely assumed that none of those sages who had an agency in forming or adopting our Constitution ever imagined that any portion of the taxing power of the States not prohibited to them nor delegated to Congress was to be swept away and annihilated as a means of executing certain powers delegated to Congress.

If our power over means is so absolute that the Supreme Court will not call in question the constitutionality of an act of Congress the subject of which "is not prohibited, and is really calculated to effect any of the objects intrusted to the Government," although, as in the case before me, it takes away powers expressly granted to Congress and rights scrupulously reserved to the States, it becomes us to proceed in our legislation with the utmost caution. Though not directly, our own powers and the rights of the States may be indirectly legislated away in the use of means to execute substantive powers. We may not enact that Congress shall not have the power of exclusive legislation over the District of Columbia, but we may pledge the faith of the United States that as a means of executing other powers it shall not be exercised for twenty years or forever. We may not pass an act prohibiting the States to tax the banking business carried on within their limits, but we may, as a means of executing our powers over other objects, place that business in the hands of our agents and then declare it exempt from State taxation in their hands. Thus may our own powers and the rights of the States, which we can not directly curtail or invade, be frittered away and extinguished in the use of means employed by us to execute other powers. That a bank of the United States, competent to all the duties which may be required by the

Government, might be so organized as not to infringe on our own delegated powers or the reserved rights of the States I do not entertain a doubt. Had the Executive been called upon to furnish the project of such an institution, the duty would have been cheerfully performed. In the absence of such a call it was obviously proper that he should confine himself to pointing out those prominent features in the act presented which in his opinion make it incompatible with the Constitution and sound policy. . . .

The bank is professedly established as an agent of the executive branch of the Government, and its constitutionality is maintained on that ground. Neither upon the propriety of present action nor upon the provisions of this act was the Executive consulted. It has had no opportunity to say that it neither needs nor wants an agent clothed with such powers and favored by such exemptions. There is nothing in its legitimate functions which makes it necessary or proper. Whatever interest or influence, whether public or private, has given birth to this act, it can not be found either in the wishes or necessities of the executive department, by which present action is deemed premature, and the powers conferred upon its agent not only unnecessary, but dangerous to the Government and country. . . .

Nor is our Government to be maintained or our Union preserved by invasions of the rights and powers of the several States. In thus attempting to make our General Government strong we make it weak. Its true strength consists in leaving individuals and States as much as possible to themselves— in making itself felt, not in its power, but in its beneficence; not in its control, but in its protection; not in binding the States more closely to the center, but leaving each to move unobstructed in its proper orbit.

Experience should teach us wisdom. Most of the difficulties our Government now encounters and most of the dangers which impend over our Union have sprung from an abandonment of the legitimate objects of Government by our national legislation, and the adoption of such principles as are embodied in this act. Many of our rich men have not been content with equal protection and equal benefits, but have besought us to make them richer by act of Congress. By attempting to gratify their desires we have in the results of our legislation arrayed section against section, interest against interest, and man against man, in a fearful commotion which threatens to shake the foundations of our Union. It is time to pause in our career to review our principles, and if possible revive that devoted patriotism and spirit of compromise which distinguished the sages of the Revolution and the fathers of our Union. If we can not at once, in justice to interests vested under improvident legislation, make our Government what it ought to be, we can at least take a stand against all new grants of monopolies and exclusive privileges, against any prostitution of our Government to the advancement of the few at the expense of the many, and in favor of compromise and gradual reform in our code of laws and system of political economy.

I have now done my duty to my country. If sustained by my fellow-citizens, I shall be grateful and happy; if not, I shall find in the motives which impel me ample grounds for contentment and peace. In the difficulties which surround us and the dangers which threaten our institutions there is cause for neither dismay nor alarm. For relief and deliverance let us firmly rely on that kind Providence which I am sure watches with peculiar care over the destinies of our Republic, and on the intelligence and wisdom of our country-men. Through *His* abundant goodness and *their* patriotic devotion our liberty and Union will be preserved.

56

Cohens v. Virginia (1821)

The Cohen brothers had been convicted in a Virginia court for selling District of Columbia lottery tickets in violation of state law. They claimed that under the Supremacy Clause they were immune from state laws if they sold congressionally authorized lottery tickets. Virginia maintained that the Supreme Court had no jurisdiction to review a state criminal law case without the state's permission. The Court ruled that in issuing the lottery tickets Congress had not granted any immunity against state prohibitions, thus technically upholding the Virginia stat-ute. More important, Chief Justice Marshall finally got his say on Sec-tion 25 of the Judiciary Act, the same section Justice Story had upheld in *Martin* (Document 51), and which gave the Supreme Court appellate review over state court decisions. The judicial power, he claimed, "as originally given, extends to all cases arising under the constitution or a law of the United States, whoever may be the party." Marshall wrote an extensive opinion, from which the following is taken, upholding the Court's power to hear the case. That point made, he then issued a brief ruling supporting Virginia's claim that the District Lottery law did not preempt a state's prohibition against lotteries.

See C. Warren, "Legislative and Judicial Attacks on the Supreme Court of the United States—A History of the Twenty-fifth Section of the Judiciary Act," 47 *Am. L. R.* 1 (1913).

Source: 6 Wheaton 264 (1821).

~~~~~~

Chief Justice Marshall delivered the opinion of the Court.

The first question to be considered is, whether the jurisdiction of this court is excluded by the character of the parties, one of them being a State, and the other a citizen of that State?

The 2d section of the third article of the constitution defines the extent of the judicial power of the United States. Jurisdiction is given to the courts of the Union in two classes of cases. In the first, their jurisdiction depends on the character of the cause, whoever may be the parties. This class comprehends "all cases in law and equity arising under this constitution, the laws of the United States, and treaties made, or which shall be made, under their authority." This clause extends the jurisdiction of the court to all the cases described, without making in its terms any exception whatever, and without any regard to the condition of the party. If there be any exception, it is to be implied against the express words of the article.

In the second class, the jurisdiction depends entirely on the character of the parties. In this are comprehended "controversies between two or more States, between a State and citizens of another State," "and between a State and foreign states, citizens, or subjects." If these be the parties, it is entirely unimportant what may be the subject of controversy. Be it what it may, these parties have a constitutional right to come into the courts of the Union. . . .

The jurisdiction of the court, then, being extended by the letter of the constitution to all cases arising under it, or under the laws of the *United* States, it follows that those would withdraw any case of this description from that jurisdiction, must sustain the exemption they claim on the spirit and true meaning of the constitution, which spirit and true meaning must be so apparent as to overrule the words which its framers have employed.

The counsel for the defendant in error have undertaken to do this; and have laid down the general proposition, that a sovereign independent State is not suable, except by its own consent.

This general proposition will not be controverted. But its consent is not requisite in each particular case. It may be given in a general law. And if a State has surrendered any portion of its sovereignty, the question whether a liability to suit be a part of this portion, depends on the instrument by which the surrender is made. If upon a just construction of that instrument, it shall appear that the State has submitted to be sued, then it has parted with this sovereign right of judging in every case on the justice of its own pretensions, and has intrusted that power to a tribunal in whose impartiality it confides.

The American States, as well as the American people, have believed a close and firm Union to be essential to their liberty and to their happiness. They have been taught by experience, that this Union cannot exist without a government for the whole; and they have been taught by the same experience that this government would be a mere shadow, that must disappoint all their hopes, unless invested with large portions of that sovereignty which belongs to independent States. Under the influence of this opinion, and thus instructed by experience, the American people, in the conventions of their respective States, adopted the present constitution.

If it could be doubted whether, from its nature, it were not supreme in all cases where it is empowered to act, that doubt would be removed by the declaration that "this constitution, and the laws of the United States which shall be made in pursuance thereof, and all treaties made, or which shall be made, under the authority of the United States, shall be the supreme law of the land; and the judges in every State shall be bound thereby, any thing in the constitution or laws of any State to the contrary notwithstanding."

This is the authoritative language of the American people; and, if gentlemen please, of the American States. It marks with lines too strong to be mistaken, the characteristic distinction between the government of the Union and those of the States. The general government, though limited as to its objects, is supreme with respect to those objects. This principle is a part of the constitution; and if there be any who deny its necessity, none can deny its authority. . . .

With the ample powers confided to this supreme government, for these interesting purposes, are connected many express and important limitations on the sovereignty of the States, which are made for the same purposes. The powers of the Union, on the great subjects of war, peace, and commerce, and on many others, are in themselves limitations of the sovereignty of the States; but in addition to these, the sovereignty of the States is surrendered in many instances where the surrender can only operate to the benefit of the people, and where, perhaps, no other power is conferred on congress than a conservative power to maintain the principles established in the constitution. The maintenance of these principles in their purity, is certainly among the great duties of the government. One of the instruments by which this duty may be peaceably performed, is the judicial department. It is authorized to decide all cases, of every description, arising under the constitution or laws of the United States. From this general grant of jurisdiction, no exception is made of those cases in which a State may be a party. . . . We think a case arising under the constitution or laws of the United States, is cognizable in the courts of the Union, whoever may be the parties to that case. . . .

. . . The constitution gave to every person having a claim upon a State, a right to submit his case to the court of the nation. However unimportant his claim might be, however little the community might be interested in its decision, the framers of our constitution thought it necessary for the purposes of justice, to provide a tribunal as superior to influence as possible, in which that claim might be decided. Can it be imagined, that the same persons considered a case involving the constitution of our country and the majesty of the laws, questions in which every American citizen must be deeply interested, as withdrawn from this tribunal, because a State is a party? . . .

The mischievous consequences of the construction contended for on the part of Virginia, are also entitled to great consideration. It would prostrate, it has been said, the government and its laws at the feet of every State in the Union. And would not this be its effect? What power of the government could be executed by its own means, in any State disposed to resist its execution by a course of legislation? The laws must be executed by individuals acting within the several States. If these individuals may be exposed to penalties, and if the courts of the Union cannot correct the judgments by which these penalties may be enforced, the course of the government may be, at any time, arrested by the will of one of its members. Each member will possess a veto on the will of the whole. . . .

These collisions may take place in times of no extraordinary commotion. But a constitution is framed for ages to come, and is designed to approach immortality as nearly as human institutions can approach it. Its course cannot always be tranquil. It is exposed to storms and tempests, and its framers must be unwise statesmen, indeed, if they have not provided it, as far as its nature will permit, with the means of self-preservation from the perils it may be destined to encounter. No government ought to be so defective in its organization, as not to contain within itself the means of securing the execution of its own laws against other dangers than those which occur every day. Courts of justice are the means most usually employed; and it is reasonable to expect that a government should repose on its own courts, rather than on others. There is certainly nothing in the circumstances under which our constitution was formed; nothing in the history of the times, which would justify the opinion that the confidence reposed in the States was so implicit as to leave in them and their tribunals the power of resisting or defeating, in the form of law, the legitimate measures of the Union. The requisitions of congress, under the confederation, were as constitutionally obligatory as the laws enacted by the present congress. That they were habitually disregarded, is a fact of universal notoriety. With the knowledge of this fact, and under its full pressure, a convention was assembled to change the system. Is it so improbable that they should confer on the judicial department the power of construing the constitution and laws of the Union in every case, in the last resort, and of preserving them from all violation from every quarter, so far as judicial decisions can preserve them, that this improbability should essentially affect the construction of the new system? We are told, and we are truly told, that the great change which is to give efficacy to the present system, is its ability to act on individuals directly, instead of acting through the instrumentality of state governments. But, ought not this ability, in reason and sound policy, to be applied directly to the protection of individuals employed in the execution of the laws, as well as to their coercion? Your laws reach the individual without the aid of any other power; why may they not protect him from punishment for performing his duty in executing them? . . .

It is very true that, whenever hostility to the existing system shall be come universal, it will be also irresistible. The people made the constitution, and the people can unmake it. It is the creature of their will, and lives only by their will. But this supreme and irresistible power to make or to unmake resides only in the whole body of the people; not in any subdivision of them. The attempt of any of the parts to exercise it is usurpation, and ought to be repelled by those to whom the people have delegated their power of repelling it. . . .

. . . The framers of the constitution were, indeed, unable to make any provisions which should protect that instrument against a general combination of the States, or of the people, for its destruction; and, conscious of this inability, they have not made the attempt. But they were able to provide against the operation of measures adopted in any one State, whose tendency might be to arrest the execution of the laws; and this it was the part of true wisdom to attempt. We think they have attempted it.

It has been also urged, as an additional objection to the jurisdiction of the court, that cases between a State and one of its own citizens, do not come within the general scope of the constitution; and were obviously never intended to be made cognizable in the federal courts. The state tribunals might be suspected of partiality in cases between itself or its citizens and aliens, or the citizens of another State, but not in proceedings by a State against its own citizens. That jealousy which might exist in the first case, could not exist in the last, and therefore the judicial power is not extended to the last. This is very true, so far as jurisdiction depends on the character of the parties; and the argument would have great force if urged to prove that this court could not establish the demand of a citizen upon his State, but is not entitled to the same force when urged to prove that this court cannot inquire whether the constituion or laws of the United States protect a citizen from a prosecution instituted against him by a State. If jurisdiction depended entirely on the character of the parties, and was not given where the parties have not an original right to come into court, that part of the 2d section of the third article, which extends the judicial power to all cases arising under the constitution and laws of the United States, would be mere surplusage. It is to give jurisdiction where the character of the parties would not give it, that this very important part of the clause was inserted. It may be true, that the partiality of the state tribunals, in ordinary controversies between a State and its citizens, was not apprehended, and therefore the judicial power of the Union was not extended to such cases; but this was not the sole nor the greatest object for which this department was created. A more important, a much more interesting object, was the preservation of the constitution and laws of the United States, so far as they can be preserved by judicial authority; and therefore the jurisdiction of the courts of the Union was expressly extended to all cases arising under that constitution and those laws. If the constitution or laws may be violated by proceedings instituted by a State against its own citizens, and if that violation may be such as essentially to affect the constitution and the laws, such as to arrest the progress of government in its constitutional course, why should these cases be excepted from that provision which expressly extends the judicial power of the Union to all cases arising under the constitution and laws? . . .

When, then, the constitution declares the jurisdiction, in cases where a State shall be a party, to be original, and in all cases arising under the constitution or a law, to be appellate—the conclusion seems irresistible, that its framers designed to include in the first class those cases in which jurisdiction is given, because a State is a party; and to include in the second, those in which jurisdiction is given, because the case arises under the constitution or a law.

This reasonable construction is rendered necessary by other considerations.

That the constitution or a law of the United States is involved in a case, and makes a part of it, may appear in the progress of a cause, in which the courts of the Union, but for that circumstance, would have no jurisdiction, and which of consequence could not originate in the supreme court. In such a case the jurisdiction can be exercised only in its appellate form. To deny its exercise in this form, is to deny its existence, and would be to construe a clause dividing the power of the supreme court, in such manner as in a considerable degree to defeat the power itself. All must perceive that this construction can be justified only where it is absolutely necessary. We do not think the article under consideration presents that necessity. . . .

It is most true that this court will not take jurisdiction if it should not; but it is equally true, that it must take jurisdiction if it should. The judiciary cannot, as the legislature may, avoid a measure because it approaches the confines of the constitution. We cannot pass it by because it is doubtful. With whatever doubts, with whatever difficulties, a case may be attended, we must decide it, if it be brought before us. We have no more right to decline the exercise of jurisdiction which is given, than to usurp that which is not given. The one or the other would be treason to the constitution. Questions may occur which we would gladly avoid; but we cannot avoid them. All we can do is, to exercise our best judgment, and conscientiously to perform our duty. In doing this on the present occasion, we find this tribunal invested with appellate jurisdiction in all cases arising under the constitution and laws of the United States. We find no exception to this grant, and we cannot insert one. . . .

It is, then, the opinion of the court, that the defendant who removes a judgment rendered against him by a state court into this court, for the purpose of reëxamining the question whether that judgment be in violation of the constitution or laws of the United States, does not commence or prosecute a suit against the State, whatever may be its opinion where the effect of the writ may be to restore the party to the possession of a thing which he demands. . . .

The second objection to the jurisdiction of the court is, that its appellate power cannot be exercised, in any case, over the judgment of a state court.

This objection is sustained chiefly by arguments drawn from the supposed total separation of the judiciary of a State from that of the Union, and their entire independence of each other. The argument considers the federal judiciary as completely foreign to that of a State; and as being no more connected with it, in any respect whatever, than the court of a foreign state. If this hypothesis be just, the argument founded on it is equally so; but if the hypothesis be not supported by the constitution, the argument fails with it. . . .

That the United States form, for many, and for most important purposes, a single nation, has not yet been denied. In war, we are one people. In making peace, we are one people. In all commercial regulations, we are one and the same people. In many other respects, the American people are one; and the government which is alone capable of controlling and managing their interests, in all these respects, is the government of the Union. It is their government, and in that character they have no other. America has chosen to be, in many respects, and to many purposes, a nation; and for all these purposes her government is complete; to all these objects, it is competent. The people have declared, that in the exercise of all powers given for these objects, it is supreme. It can, then, in effecting these objects, legitimately control all individuals or governments within the American territory. The constitution and laws of a State, so far as they are repugnant to the constitution and laws of the United States, are absolutely void. These States are constituent parts of the United States. They are members of one great empire—for some purposes sovereign, for some purposes subordinate.

In a government so constituted, is it unreasonable that the judicial power should be competent to give efficacy to the constitutional laws of the legislature? That department can decide on the validity of the constitution or law of a State, if it be repugnant to the constitution or to a law of the United States. Is it unreasonable that it should also be empowered to decide on the judgment of a state tribunal enforcing such unconstitutional law? Is it so very unreasonable as to furnish a justification for controlling the words of the constitution?

We think it is not. We think that in a government acknowledgedly supreme, with respect to objects of vital interest to the nation, there is nothing inconsistent with sound reason, nothing incompatible with the nature of government, in making all its departments supreme, so far as respects those objects, and so far as is necessary to their attainment. The exercise of the appellate power over those judgments of the state tribunals which may contravene the constitution or laws of the United States, is, we believe, essential to the attainment of those objects.

Gibbons v. *Ogden (1824)*

Unlike *McCulloch,* in which Marshall explicated an implied power of the national government, the steamboat case gave the Chief Justice an opportunity to expound an explicit power—to regulate interstate and foreign commerce. The New York legislature had granted the Fulton-Livingston interests a monopoly on steamboat navigation on all state waters as well as on adjacent coastal waters and the Hudson River between New York and New Jersey, and Aaron Ogden was a licensee of the monopoly. A would-be competitor, Thomas Gibbons, unable to break the monopoly in state courts, secured a federal coasting license under the Coasting Act of 1793 and then claimed that the federal license took precedence over New York's power to regulate the lower Hudson River. The decision, in which Marshall took a very broad view of what constituted interstate commerce and the national power to regulate it, had immediate and long-term effects. It broke up an unpopular monopoly, but more important, permitted the national government to adapt its policies to new technologies in transportation and commerce, a flexibility that would have great importance in the twentieth century.

See M. G. Baxter, *The Steamboat Monopoly: Gibbons v. Ogden* (1972); F. Frankfurter, *The Commerce Clause under Marshall, Taney, and Waite* (1937); and E. S. Corwin, *Commerce Power Versus States Rights* (1936).

Chief Justice Marshall delivered the opinion of the Court.

The appellant contends that this decree is erroneous, because the laws which purport to give the exclusive privilege it sustains, are repugnant to the constitution and laws of the United States.

They are said to be repugnant—

1st. To that clause in the constitution which authorizes congress to regulate commerce. . . .

This Constitution contains an enumeration of powers expressly granted by the people to their government. It has been said, that these powers ought to be construed strictly. But why ought they to be so construed? Is there one

---

Source: 9 Wheaton 1 (1824).

sentence in the constitution which gives countenance to this rule? What do gentlemen mean, by a strict construction? If they contend only against that enlarged construction, which would extend words beyond their natural and obvious import, we might question the application of the term, but should not controvert the principle. If they contend for that narrow construction which, in support of some theory not to be found in the constitution, would deny to the government those powers which the words of the grant, as usually understood, import, and which are consistent with the general views and objects of the instrument; for that narrow construction, which would cripple the government, and render it unequal to the objects for which it is declared to be instituted, and to which the powers given, as fairly understood, render it competent; then we cannot perceive the propriety of this strict construction, nor adopt it as the rule by which the constitution is to be expounded. If, from the imperfection of human language, there should be serious doubts respecting the extent of any given power, it is a well settled rule, that the objects for which it was given, especially when those objects are expressed in the instrument itself, should have great influence in the construction. . . .

The words are, "Congress shall have power to regulate commerce with foreign nations, and among the several States, and with the Indian tribes."

The subject to be regulated is commerce; and to ascertain the extent of the power, it becomes necessary to settle the meaning of the word. The counsel for the appellee would limit it to traffic, to buying and selling, or the interchange of commodities, and do not admit that it comprehends navigation. This would restrict a general term, applicable to many objects, to one of its significations. Commerce, undoubtedly, is traffic, but it is something more: it is intercourse. It describes the commercial intercourse between nations, and parts of nations, in all its branches, and is regulated by prescribing rules for carrying on that intercourse. . . . All America understands, and has uniformly understood, the word "commerce" to comprehend navigation. It was so understood, and must have been so understood, when the constitution was framed. The power over commerce, including navigation, was one of the primary objects for which the people of America adopted their government, and must have been contemplated in forming it. . . .

To what commerce does this power extend? The constitution informs us, to commerce "with foreign nations, and among the several States, and with the Indian tribes." It has been universally admitted that these words comprehend every species of commercial intercourse between the United States and foreign nations. No sort of trade can be carried on between this country and any other, to which this power does not extend. . . .

The subject to which the power is next applied, is to commerce "among the several States." The word "among" means intermingled with. A thing which is among others, is intermingled with them. Commerce among the States, cannot stop at the external boundary line of each State, but may be introduced into the interior.

It is not intended to say that these words comprehend that commerce which is completely internal, which is carried on between man and man in a State, or between different parts of the same State, and which does not extend to or affect other States. Such a power would be inconvenient, and is certainly unnecessary.

Comprehensive as the word "among" is, it may very properly be restricted to that commerce which concerns more States than one. The phrase is not one which would probably have been selected to indicate the completely interior traffic of a State, because it is not an apt phrase for that purpose; and the enumeration of the particular classes of commerce to which the power was to be extended, would not have been made, had the intention been to extend the power to every description. The enumeration presupposes something not enumerated; and that something, if we regard the language or the subject of the sentence, must be the exclusively internal commerce of a State. The genius and character of the whole government seem to be, that its action is to be applied to all the external concerns of the nation, and to those internal concerns which affect the States generally; but not to those which are completely within a particular State, which do not affect other States, and with which it is not necessary to interfere, for the purpose of executing some of the general powers of the government. The completely internal commerce of a State, then, may be considered as reserved for the State itself. . . .

We are now arrived at the inquiry—What is this power [of Congress]?

It is the power to regulate; that is, to prescribe the rule by which commerce is to be governed. This power, like all others vested in Congress, is complete in itself, may be exercised to its utmost extent, and acknowledges no limitations, other than are prescribed in the constitution. These are expressed in plain terms, and do not affect the questions which arise in this case, or which have been discussed at the bar. If, as has always been understood, the sovereignty of Congress, though limited to specified objects, is plenary as to those objects, the power over commerce with foreign nations, and among the several States, is vested in Congress as absolutely as it would be in a single government, having in its constitution the same restrictions on the exercise of the power as are found in the constitution of the United States. The wisdom and the discretion of Congress, their identity with the people, and the influence which their constituents possess at elections, are, in this, as in many other instances, as that, for example, of declaring war, the sole restraints on which they have relied, to secure them from its abuse. They are the restraints on which the people must often rely solely, in all representative governments.

The power of Congress, then, comprehends navigation, within the limits of every State in the Union; so far as that navigation may be, in any manner, connected with "commerce with foreign nations, or among the several States, or with the Indian tribes." It may, of consequence, pass the jurisdictional line of New York, and act upon the very waters to which the prohibition now under consideration applies. . . .

Powerful and ingenious minds, taking, as postulates, that the powers expressly granted to the government of the Union, are to be contracted by construction, into the narrowest possible compass, and that the original powers of the States are retained, if any possible construction will retain them, may, by a course of well digested, but refined and metaphysical reasoning, founded on these premises, explain away the constitution of our country, and leave it, a magnificent structure, indeed, to look at, but totally unfit for use. They may so entangle and perplex the understanding, as to obscure principles, which were before thought quite plain, and induce doubts where, if the mind were to pursue its own course, none would be perceived. In such a case, it is peculiarly necessary to recur to safe and fundamental principles to sustain those principles, and, when sustained, to make them the tests of the arguments to be examined. . . .

It has been urged with great earnestness, that although the power of Congress to regulate commerce with foreign nations, and among the several States, be co-extensive with the subject itself, and have no other limits than are prescribed in the constitution, yet the States may severally exercise the same power, within their respective jurisdictions. In support of this argument, it is said, that they possessed it as an inseparable attribute of sovereignty, before the formation of the constitution, and still retain it, except so far as they have surrendered it by that instrument; that this principle results from the nature of the government, and is secured by the tenth amendment; that an affirmative grant of power is not exclusive, unless in its own nature it be such that the continued exercise of it by the former possessor is inconsistent with the grant, and that this is not of that description.

The appellant, conceding these postulates, except the last, contends that full power to regulate a particular subject, implies the whole power, and leaves no residuum; that a grant of the whole is incompatible with the existence of a right in another to any part of it. . . .

The grant of the power to lay and collect taxes is, like the power to regulate commerce, made in general terms, and has never been understood to interfere with the exercise of the same power by the States; and hence has been drawn an argument which has been applied to the question under consideration. But the two grants are not, it is conceived, similiar in their terms or their nature. Although many of the powers formerly exercised by the States, are transferred to the government of the Union, yet the State governments remain, and constitute a most important part of our system. The power of taxation is indispensable to their existence, and is a power which, in its own nature, is capable of residing in, and being exercised by, different authorities at the same time. A power in one to take what is necessary for certain purposes, is not, in its nature, incompatible with a power in another to take what is necessary for other purposes. When, then, each government exercises the power of taxation, neither is exercising the power of the other. But, when a State proceeds to regulate commerce, it is exercising the very power that is granted to Congress, and is doing the very thing which Congress, is authorized to do. There is no analogy, then, between the power of taxation and the power of regulating commerce. . . .

. . . If the legislative power of the Union can reach [certain objects], it must be for national purposes; it must be where the power is expressly given for a special purpose, or is clearly incidental to some power which is expressly given. It is obvious, that the government of the Union, in the exercise of its express powers, that, for example, of regulating commerce with foreign nations and among the States, may use means that may also be employed by a State, in the exercise of its acknowledged powers; that, for example, of regulating commerce within the State. If a State, in passing laws on subjects acknowledged to be within its control, and with a view to those subjects, shall adopt a measure of the same character with one which Congress may adopt, it does not derive its authority from the particular power which has been granted, but from some other, which remains with the State, and may be executed by the same means. All experience shows, that the same measures, or measures scarcely distinguishable from each other, may flow from distinct powers; but this does not prove that the powers themselves are identical. Although the means used in their execution may sometimes approach each other so nearly as to be confounded, there are other situations in which they are sufficiently distinct to establish their individuality.

In our complex system, presenting the rare and difficult scheme of one general government, whose action extends over the whole, but which possesses only certain enumerated powers; and of numerous State governments, which retain and exercise all powers not delegated to the Union, contests respecting power must arise. Were it even otherwise, the measures taken by the respective governments to execute their acknowledged powers, would often be of the same description, and might, sometimes, interfere. This, however, does not prove that the one is exercising, or has a right to exercise, the powers of the other. . . .

It has been contended by counsel for the appellant, that, as the word "to regulate" implies in its nature, full power over the thing to be regulated, it excludes, necessarily, the action of all others that would perform the same operation on the same thing. That regulation is designed for the entire result, applying in those parts which remain as they were, as well as to those which are altered. It produces a uniform whole, which is as much disturbed and deranged by changing what the regulating power designs to leave untouched, as that on which it has operated.

There is great force in this argument, and the Court is not satisfied that it has been refuted.

Since, however, in exercising the power of regulating their own purely internal affairs, whether of trading or police, the States may sometimes enact laws, the validity of which depends on their interfering with, and being contrary to, an act of Congress passed in pursuance of the constitution, the Court will enter upon the inquiry, whether the laws of New-York [have], in their application to this case, come into collision with an act of Congress, and deprived a citizen of a right to which that act entitles him. Should this collision exist, it will be immaterial whether those laws were passed in virtue of a concurrent power "to regulate commerce with foreign nations and among the several States," or in virtue of a power to regulate their domestic trade and police. In one case and the other, the acts of New-York must yield to the law of Congress; and the decision sustaining the privilege they confer, against a right given by a law of the Union, must be erroneous.

58

Worcester v. *Georgia (1832)*

In 1830 Georgia defied a federal treaty with the Cherokees by extending its jurisdiction over all Indians living within the state. The first test of this state law had reached the Supreme Court in Cherokee Nation v. Georgia, 5 Peters 1 (1831), in which an aging John Marshall had carefully skirted the major issues, implying that the state was in the wrong. The following year the issue came back to the Court in this case of Samuel Worcester, a missionary arrested for inhabiting Indian land without a license from the state. Annoyed at Georgia's contempt of his previous decision, Marshall this time spelled out explicitly the state's lack of jurisdiction over the Indians and their land, and suggested that the President had an obligation to protect Indian rights. Supposedly Andrew Jackson, on hearing of this opinion, said: "John Marshall has made his decision, now let him enforce it." Jackson, aside from sharing the frontiersman's disdain of the Indians and any obligation the government might have to them, also believed in strict separation of powers. He rejected the idea that one branch of government could direct another coequal branch to act in any particular manner (see Document 55). The Court could not enforce its deci-

Source: 6 Peters 515 (1832).

sion, Jackson pointedly ignored it, and Georgia successfully flouted the Court's authority.

See R. Satz, *American Indian Policy in the Jacksonian Era* (1975); J. Burke, "The Cherokee Cases: A Study in Law, Politics and Morality," 21 *Stan. L. R.* 500 (1969); and E. A. Niles, "After John Marshall's Decision . . . ," 39 *J. So. His.* 519 (1973).

~~~~~~

Chief Justice Marshall delivered the opinion of the Court.

This cause, in every point of view in which it can be placed, is of the deepest interest.

The defendant is a state, a member of the union, which has exercised the powers of government over a people who deny its jurisdiction, and are under the protection of the United States.

The plaintiff is a citizen of the state of Vermont, condemned to hard labour for four years in the penitentiary of Georgia; under colour of an act which he alleges to be repugnant to the constitution, laws, and treaties of the United States.

The legislative power of a state, the controlling power of the constitution and laws of the United States, the rights, if they have any, the political existence of a once numerous and powerful people, the personal liberty of a citizen, are all involved in the subject now to be considered.

It behoves this court, in every case, more especially in this, to examine into its jurisdiction with scrutinizing eyes; before it proceeds to the exercise of a power which is controverted. . . .

The indictment and plea in this case draw in question, we think, the validity of the treaties made by the United States with the Cherokee Indians; if not so, their construction is certainly drawn in question; and the decision has been, if not against their validity, "against the right, privilege or exemption, specially set up and claimed under them." They also draw into question the validity of a statute of the state of Georgia, "on the ground of its being repugnant to the constitution, treaties and laws of the United States, and the decision is in favour of its validity."

It is, then, we think, too clear for controversy, that the act of congress, by which this court is constituted, has given it the power, and of course imposed on it the duty, of exercising jurisdiction in this case. This duty, however unpleasant, cannot be avoided. Those who fill the judicial department have no discretion in selecting the subjects to be brought before them. We must examine the defence set up in this plea. We must inquire and decide whether the act of the legislature of Georgia, under which the plaintiff in error has been prosecuted and condemned, be consistent with, or repugnant to, the constitution, laws and treaties of the United States. . . .

It has been said at the bar, that the acts of the legislature of Georgia seize on the whole Cherokee country, parcel it out among the neighbouring counties of the state, extend her code over the whole country, abolish its institutions and its laws, and annihilate its political existence.

If this be the general effect of the system, let us inquire into the effect of the particular statute and section on which the indictment is founded.

It enacts that "all white persons, residing within the limits of the Cherokee nation on the 1st day of March next, or at any time thereafter, without a license or permit from his excellency the governor, or from such agent as his excellency the governor shall authorise to grant such permit or license, and who shall not have taken the oath hereinafter required, shall be guilty of a high misdemeanour, and, upon conviction thereof, shall be punished by confinement to the penitentiary, at hard labour, for a term not less than four years."

The eleventh section authorises the governor, should he deem it necessary for the protection of the mines, or the enforcement of the laws in force within the Cherokee nation, to raise and organize a guard, &c.

The thirteenth section enacts, "that the said guard or any member of them, shall be, and they are hereby authorised and empowered to arrest any person legally charged with or detected in a violation of the laws of this state, and to convey, as soon as practicable, the person so arrested, before a justice of the peace, judge of the superior, or justice of inferior court of this state, to be dealt with according to law."

The extra-territorial power of every legislature being limited in its action, to its own citizens or subjects, the very passage of this act is an assertion of jurisdiction over the Cherokee nation, and of the rights and powers consequent on jurisdiction.

The first step, then, in the inquiry, which the constitution and laws impose on this court, is an examination of the rightfulness of this claim. . . .

The early journals of congress exhibit the most anxious desire to conciliate the Indian nations. Three Indian departments were established; and commissioners appointed in each, "to treat with the Indians in their respective departments, in the name and on the behalf of the United Colonies, in order to preserve peace and friendship with the said Indians, and to prevent their taking any part in the present commotions."

The most strenuous exertions were made to procure those supplies on which Indian friendships were supposed to depend; and every thing which might excite hostility was avoided. . . .

During the war of the revolution, the Cherokees took part with the British. After its termination, the United States, though desirous of peace, did not feel its necessity so strongly as while the war continued. Their political situation being changed, they might very well think it advisable to assume a higher tone, and to impress on the Cherokees the same respect for congress which was before felt for the king of Great Britain. This may account for the language of the treaty of Hopewell. There is the more reason for supposing that the Cherokee chiefs were not very critical judges of the language, from the fact that every one makes his mark; no chief was capable of signing his name. It is probable the treaty was interpreted to them.

The treaty is introduced with the declaration, that "the commissioners plenipotentiary of the United States give peace to all the Cherokees, and receive them into the favour and protection of the United States of America, on the following conditions." . . .

The treaty of Hopewell seems not to have established a solid peace. To accommodate the differences still existing between the state of Georgia and the Cherokee nation, the treaty of Holston was negotiated in July 1791. The existing constitution of the United States had been then adopted, and the government, having more intrinsic capacity to enforce its just claims, was perhaps less mindful of high sounding expressions, denoting superiority. We hear no more of giving peace to the Cherokees. The mutual desire of establishing permanent peace and friendship, and of removing all causes of war, is honestly avowed, and, in pursuance of this desire, the first article declares, that there shall be perpetual peace and friendship between all the citizens of the United States of America and all the individuals composing the Cherokee nation.

The second article repeats the important acknowledgement, that the Cherokee nation is under the protection of the United States of America, and of no other sovereign whosoever. . . .

This relation was that of a nation claiming and receiving the protection of one more powerful: not that of individuals abandoning their national character, and submitting as subjects to the laws of a master. . . .

This treaty, thus explicitly recognizing the national character of the Cherokees, and their right of self government; thus guarantying their lands; assuming the duty of protection, and of course pledging the faith of the United States for that protection; has been frequently renewed, and is now in full force.

To the general pledge of protection have been added several specific pledges, deemed valuable by the Indians. Some of these restrain the citizens of the United States from encroachments on the Cherokee country, and provide for the punishment of intruders.

From the commencement of our government, congress has passed acts to regulate trade and intercourse with the Indians; which treat them as nations, respect their rights, and manifest a firm purpose to afford that protection which treaties stipulate. All these acts, and especially that of 1802, which is still in force, manifestly consider the several Indian nations as distinct political communities, having territorial boundaries, within which their authority is exclusive, and having a right to all the lands within those boundaries, which is not only acknowledged, but guaranteed by the United States.

In 1819, congress passed an act for promoting those humane designs of civilizing the neighbouring Indians, which had long been cherished by the executive. It enacts, "that, for the purpose of providing against the further decline and final extinction of the Indian tribes adjoining to the frontier settlements of the United States, and for introducing among them the habits and arts of civilization, the president of the United States shall be, and he is hereby authorized, in every case where he shall judge improvement in the habits and condition of such Indians practicable, and that the means of instruction can be introduced *with their own consent,* to employ capable persons, of good moral character, to instruct them in the mode of agriculture suited to their situation; and for teaching their children in reading, writing and arithmetic; and for performing such other duties as may be enjoined, according to such instructions and rules as the president may give and prescribe for the regulation of their conduct in the discharge of their duties."

This act avowedly contemplates the preservation of the Indian nations as an object sought by the United States, and proposes to effect this object by civilizing and converting them from hunters into agriculturists. Though the Cherokees had already made considerable progress in this improvement, it cannot be doubted that the general words of the act comprehend them. Their advance in the "habits and arts of civilization," rather encouraged perseverance in the laudable exertions still farther to meliorate their condition. This act furnishes strong additional evidence of a settled purpose to fix the Indians in their country by giving them security at home.

The treaties and laws of the United States contemplate the Indian territory as completely separated from that of the states; and provide that all intercourse with them shall be carried on exclusively by the government of the union. . . .

Georgia, herself, has furnished conclusive evidence that her former opinions on this subject concurred with those entertained by her sister states, and by the government of the United States. Various acts of her legislature have been cited in the argument, including the contract of cession made in the year 1802, all tending to prove her acquiescence in the universal conviction that the Indian nations possessed a full right to the lands they occupied, until that right should be extinguished by the United States, with their consent: that their territory was separated from that of any state within whose chartered limits they might reside, by a boundary line, established by treaties: that, within their boundary, they possessed rights with which no state could interfere: and that the whole power of regulating the intercourse with them, was vested in the United States. A review of these acts, on the part of Georgia, would occupy too much time, and is the less necessary, because they have been accurately detailed in the argument at the bar. Her new series of laws, manifesting her abandonment of these opinions, appears to have commenced in December 1828.

In opposition to this original right, possessed by the undisputed occupants of every country; to this recognition of that right, which is evidenced by our history, in every change through which we have passed; is placed the charters granted by the monarch of a distant and distinct region, parcelling out a territory in possession of others whom he could not remove and did not attempt to remove, and the cession made of his claims by the treaty of peace.

The actual state of things at the time, and all history since, explain these charters; and the king of Great Britain, at the treaty of peace, could cede only what belonged to his crown. These newly asserted titles can derive no aid from the articles so often repeated in Indian treaties; extending to them, first, the protection of Great Britain, and afterwards that of the United States. These articles are associated with others, recognizing their title to self government. The very fact of repeated treaties with them recognizes it; and the settled doctrine of the law of nations is, that a weaker power does not surrender its independence—its right to self government, by associating with a stronger, and taking its protection. A weak state, in order to provide for its safety, may place itself under the protection of one more powerful, without stripping itself of the right of government, and ceasing to be a state. Examples of this kind are not wanting in Europe. "Tributary and feudatory states," says Vattel, "do not thereby cease to be sovereign and independent states, so long as self government and sovereign and independent authority are left in the administration of the state." At the present day, more than one state may be considered as holding its right of self government under the guarantee and protection of one or more allies.

The Cherokee nation, then, is a distinct community occupying its own territory, with boundaries accurately described, in which the laws of Georgia can have no force, and which the citizens of Georgia have no right to enter, but with the assent of the Cherokees themselves, or in conformity with treaties, and with the acts of congress. The whole intercourse between the United States and this nation, is, by our constitution and laws, vested in the government of the United States.

The act of the state of Georgia, under which the plaintiff in error was prosecuted, is consequently void, and the judgment a nullity. Can this court revise, and reverse it?

If the objection to the system of legislation, lately adopted by the legislature of Georgia, in relation to the Cherokee nation, was confined to its extra-territorial operation, the objection, though complete, so far as respected mere right, would give this court no power over the subject. But it goes much further. If the review which has been taken be correct, and we think it is, the acts of Georgia are repugnant to the constitution, laws, and treaties of the United States.

They interfere forcibly with the relations established between the United States and the Cherokee nation, the regulation of which, according to the settled principles of our constitution, are committed exclusively to the government of the union.

They are in direct hostility with treaties, repeated in a succession of years, which mark out the boundary that separates the Cherokee country from Georgia; guaranty to them all the land within their boundary; solemnly pledge the faith of the United States to restrain their citizens from trespassing on it; and recognize the pre-existing power of the nation to govern itself.

They are in equal hostility with the acts of congress for regulating th' intercourse, and giving effect to the treaties.

The forcible seizure and abduction of the plaintiff in error, who was residing in the nation with its permission, and by authority of the president of the United States, is also a violation of the acts which authorise the chief magistrate to exercise this authority.

Will these powerful considerations avail the plaintiff in error? We think they will. He was seized, and forcibly carried away, while under guardianship of treaties guarantying the country in which he resided, and taking it under the protection of the United States. He was seized while performing, under the sanction of the chief magistrate of the union, those duties which the humane policy adopted by congress had recommended. He was apprehended, tried, and condemned, under colour of a law which has been shown to be repugnant to the constitution, laws, and treaties of the United States. Had a judgment, liable to the same objections, been rendered for property, none would question the jurisdiction of this court. It cannot be less clear when the judgment affects personal liberty, and inflicts disgraceful punishment, if punishment could disgrace when inflicted on innocence. The plaintiff in error is not less interested in the operation of this unconstitutional law than if it affected his property. He is not less entitled to the protection of the constitution, laws, and treaties of his country. . . .

It is the opinion of this court that the judgment of the superior court for the county of Gwinnett, in the state of Georgia, condemning Samuel A. Worcester to hard labour, in the penitentiary of the state of Georgia, for four years, was pronounced by that court under colour of a law which is void, as being repugnant to the constitution, treaties, and laws of the United States, and ought, therefore, to be reversed and annulled.

59

Barron v. Baltimore (1833)

A major argument of the anti-federalists against the Constitution had been the absence of a Bill of Rights (Document 28), and they had reasoned that the great powers conferred upon the new national govern-

Source: 7 Peters 243 (1833).

ment could threaten individual liberties unless specifically restrained. At that time, men like Jefferson, Mason, and Madison believed that no similar provisions were required for the states. Their reasons included belief in a federal system, the expectation that state bills of rights would limit local governments, and a faith that the states provided the best line of protection for personal liberty.

The assumption that the first eight amendments to the Constitution did not apply to the states was not tested in the federal courts until this case, which arose on appeal from a Maryland court. The city of Baltimore had, in the course of repairing and improving its streets, damaged Barron's wharf, and in fact made it useless. He sued on the basis that the Fifth Amendment's prohibition against deprivation of property without due process or just compensation applied against the states as well as the federal government. The Marshall Court did not accept the argument, and while some critics claimed that this decision went against his earlier and more expansive view of national power, there is valid evidence that the opinion correctly interprets the intentions of the Framers. The Bill of Rights continued to apply only to the national government until the twentieth century, when the Supreme Court used the Due Process Clause of the Fourteenth Amendment to "incorporate" the protections of the first eight amendments against the states.

Chief Justice Marshall, delivered the opinion of the Court.

The judgment brought up by this writ of error having been rendered by the court of a state, this tribunal can exercise no jurisdiction over it, unless it be shown to come within the provisions of the twenty-fifth section of the judicial act.

The plaintiff in error contends that it comes within that clause in the fifth amendment to the constitution, which inhibits the taking of private property for public use, without just compensation. He insists that this amendment, being in favour of the liberty of the citizen, ought to be so construed as to restrain the legislative power of a state, as well as that of the United States. If this proposition be untrue, the court can take no jurisdiction of the cause.

The question thus presented is, we think, of great importance, but not of much difficulty.

The constitution was ordained and established by the people of the United States for themselves, for their own government, and not for the government of the individual states. Each state established a constitution for itself, and, in that constitution, provided such limitations and restrictions on the powers of its particular government as its judgment dictated. The people of the United States framed such a government for the United States as they supposed best adapted to their situation and best calculated to promote their interests. The powers they conferred on this government were to be exercised by itself; and the limitations on power, if expressed in general terms, are naturally, and, we think, necessarily applicable to the government created by the instrument. They are limitations of power granted in the instrument itself; not of distinct governments, framed by different persons and for different purposes.

If these propositions be correct, the fifth amendment must be understood as restraining the power of the general government, not as applicable to the states. In their several constitutions they have imposed such restrictions on their respective governments as their own wisdom suggested; such as they deemed most proper for themselves. It is a subject on which they judge exclusively, and with which others interfere no farther than they are supposed to have a common interest.

The counsel for the plaintiff in error insists that the constitution was intended to secure the people of the several states against the undue exercise of power by their respective state governments; as well as against that which might be attempted by their general government. In support of this argument he relies on the inhibitions contained in the tenth section of the first article.

We think that section affords a strong if not a conclusive argument in support of the opinion already indicated by the court.

The preceding section contains restrictions which are obviously intended for the exclusive purpose of restraining the exercise of power by the departments of the general government. Some of them use language applicable only to congress: others are expressed in general terms. The third clause, for example, declares that "no bill of attainder or ex post facto law shall be passed." No language can be more general; yet the demonstration is complete that it applies solely to the government of the United States. In addition to the general arguments furnished by the instrument itself, some of which have been already suggested, the succeeding section, the avowed purpose of which is to restrain state legislation, contains in terms the very prohibition. It declares that "no state shall pass any bill of attainder or ex post facto law." This provision, then, of the ninth section, however comprehensive its language, contains no restriction on state legislation.

The ninth section having enumerated, in the nature of a bill of rights, the limitations intended to be imposed on the powers of the general government, the tenth proceeds to enumerate those which were to operate on the state legislatures. These restrictions are brought together in the same section, and are by express words applied to the states. . . .

If the original constitution, in the ninth and tenth sections of the first article, draws this plain and marked line of discrimination between the limitations it imposes on the powers of the general government, and on those of the state; if in every inhibition intended to act on state power, words are employed which directly express that intent; some strong reason must be assigned for departing from this safe and judicious course in framing the amendments, before that departure can be assumed.

We search in vain for that reason.

Had the people of the several states, or any of them, required changes in their constitutions; had they required additional safeguards to liberty from the apprehended encroachments of their particular governments: the remedy was in their own hands, and would have been applied by themselves. A convention would have been assembled by the discontented state, and the required improvements would have been made by itself. The unwieldy and cumbrous machinery of procuring a recommendation from two-thirds of congress, and the assent of three-fourths of their sister states, could never have occurred to any human being as a mode of doing that which might be effected by the state itself. Had the framers of these amendments intended them to be limitations on the powers of the state governments, they would have imitated the framers of the original constitution, and have expressed that intention. Had congress engaged in the extraordinary occupation of improving the constitutions of the several states by affording the people additional protection from the exercise of power by their own governments in matters which concerned themselves alone, they would have declared this purpose in plain and intelligible language.

But it is universally understood, it is a part of the history of the day, that the great revolution which established the constitution of the United States, was not effected without immense opposition. Serious fears were extensively entertained that those powers which the patriot statesmen, who then watched over the interests of our country, deemed essential to union, and to the attainment of those invaluable objects for which union was sought, might be exercised in a manner dangerous to liberty. In almost every convention by which the constitution was adopted, amendments to guard against the abuse of power were recommended. These amendments demanded security against the apprehended encroachments of the general government—not against those of the local governments.

In compliance with a sentiment thus generally expressed, to quiet fears thus extensively entertained, amendments were proposed by the required majority in congress, and adopted by the states. These amendments contain no expression indicating an intention to apply them to the state governments. This court cannot so apply them.

We are of opinion that the provision in the fifth amendment to the constitution, declaring that private property shall not be taken for public use without just compensation, is intended solely as a limitation on the exercise of power by the government of the United States, and is not applicable to the legislation of the states. We are therefore of opinion that there is no repugnancy between the several acts of the general assembly of Maryland, given in evidence by the defendants at the trial of this cause, in the court of that state, and the constitution of the United States. This court, therefore, has no jurisdiction of the cause; and it is dismissed.

Rules of Constitutional Interpretation (1833)

JOSEPH STORY

The strongly nationalistic opinions that issued from the Marshall Court seemed to confirm some of the Jeffersonians' earlier fears regarding abuse of judicial power. In part to refute these charges, as well as to reconfirm the Court's role as supreme arbiter of the Constitution, Joseph Story claimed that judges did not decide cases arbitrarily or on the basis of political prejudice, but were bound by fixed standards of interpretation. In his *Commentaries,* he set out to establish rules of construction, the first in a long series of such efforts, and in many ways the most daring, since he had few precedents on which to base his work. All told, Story listed nineteen rules, some specific and some general, by which judges could interpret a Constitution that was not always clear in its language or intent. Story's *Commentaries,* the product of the greatest legal mind of the early nineteenth century, have been adjudged as the logical successor to *The Federalist,* and the work remained authoritative for more than a century. It also had the intent of making constitutional law more formal and technical, and thus turning it into a monopoly of lawyers.

See R. K. Newmyer, *Supreme Court Justice Joseph Story* (1985), esp. Chapter 5; A. McLaughlin, "Social Compact and Constitutional Construction," 5 *A.H.R.* 467 (1900); and G. T. Dunne, *Justice Joseph Story and the Rise of the Supreme Court* (1970).

In this view of the matter, let us now proceed to consider the rules, by which it ought to be interpreted; for, if these rules are correctly laid down, it will save us from many embarrassments in examining and defining its powers. Much of the difficulty, which has arisen in all the public discussions on this subject, has had its origin in the want of some uniform rules of interpretation, expressly or tacitly agreed on by the disputants. Very different doctrines on this point have been adopted by different commentators; and not unfrequently very different language held by the same parties at different periods.

Source: Story, 1 *Commentaries on the Constitution of the United States* 382 (1833)

In short, the rules of interpretation have often been shifted to suit the emergency; and the passions and prejudices of the day, or the favor and odium of a particular measure, have not unfrequently furnished a mode of argument, which would, on the one hand, leave the constitution crippled and inanimate, or, on the other hand, give it an extent and elasticity, subversive of all rational boundaries.

Let us, then, endeavor to ascertain, what are the true rules of interpretation applicable to the constitution; so that we may have some fixed standard, by which to measure its powers, and limit its prohibitions, and guard its obligations, and enforce its securities of our rights and liberties.

I.   The first and fundamental rule in the interpretation of all instruments is, to construe them according to the sense of the terms, and the intention of the parties. Mr. Justice Blackstone has remarked, that the intention of a law is to be gathered from the words, the context, the subject-matter, the effects and consequence, or the reason and spirit of the law. . . .

Where the words are plain and clear, and the sense distinct and perfect arising on them, there is generally no necessity to have recourse to other means of interpretation. It is only, when there is some ambiguity or doubt arising from other sources, that interpretation has its proper office. There may be obscurity, as to the meaning, from the doubtful character of the words used, from other clauses in the same instrument, or from an incongruity or repugnancy between the words, and the apparent intention derived from the whole structure of the instrument, or its avowed object. In all such cases interpretation becomes indispensable. . . .

II.   In construing the constitution of the United States, we are, in the first instance, to consider, what are its nature and objects, its scope and design, as apparent from the structure of the instrument, viewed as a whole, and also viewed in its component parts. Where its words are plain, clear, and determinate, they require no interpretation; and it should, therefore, be admitted, if at all, with great caution, and only from necessity, either to escape some absurd consequence, or to guard against some fatal evil. Where the words admit of two senses, each of which is conformable to common usage, that sense is to be adopted, which, without departing from the literal import of the words, best harmonizes with the nature and objects, the scope and design of the instrument. Where the words are unambiguous, but the provision may cover more or less ground according to the intention, which is yet subject to conjecture; or where it may include in its general terms more or less, than might seem dictated by the general design, as that may be gathered from other parts of the instrument, there is much more room for controversy; and the argument from inconvenience will probably have different influences upon different minds. Whenever such questions arise, they will probably be settled, each upon its own peculiar grounds; and whenever it is a question of power, it should be approached with infinite caution, and affirmed only upon the most persuasive reasons. In examining the constitution, the antecedent situation of the country, and its institutions, the existence and operations of the state governments, the powers and operations of the confederation, in short all the circumstances, which had a tendency to produce, or to obstruct its formation and ratification, deserve a careful attention. Much also, may be gathered from contemporary history and contemporary interpretation, to aid us in just conclusions. . . .

It is obvious, however, that contemporary interpretation must be resorted to with much qualification and reserve. In the first place, the private interpretation of any particular man, or body of men, must manifestly be open to much observation. The constitution was adopted by the people of the United States; and it was submitted to the whole upon a just survey of its provisions, as they stood in the text itself. In different states and in different conventions, different and very opposite objections are known to have prevailed; and might well be presumed to prevail. Opposite interpretations, and different explanations of different provisions, may well be presumed to have been presented in different bodies, to remove local objections, or to win local favor. . . . The known diversity of construction of different parts of it, as well as of the mass of its powers, in the different state conventions; the total silence upon many objections, which have since been started; and the strong reliance upon others, which have since been universally abandoned, add weight to these suggestions. Nothing but the text itself was adopted by the people. And it would certainly be a most extravagant doctrine to give to any commentary then made, and, *à fortiori,* to any commentary since made under a very different posture of feeling and opinion, an authority, which should operate as an absolute limit upon the text, or should supersede its natural and just interpretation. . . .

But to return to the rules of interpretation arising *ex directo* from the text of the constitution. And first the rules to be drawn from the nature of the instrument. It is to be construed, as a *frame,* or *fundamental law* of government, established by the PEOPLE of the United States, according to their own free pleasure and sovereign will. In this respect it is in nowise distinguishable from the constitutions of the state governments. Each of them is established by the people for their own purposes, and each is founded on their supreme authority. The powers, which are conferred, the restrictions, which are imposed, the authorities, which are exercised, the organization and distribution thereof, which are provided, are in each case for the same object, the common benefit of the governed, and not for the profit or dignity of the rulers.

And yet it has been a very common mode of interpretation to insist upon a diversity of rules in construing the state constitutions, and that of the general government. Thus, in the Commentaries of Mr. Tucker upon Blackstone, we find it laid down, as if it were an incontrovertible doctrine in regard to the constitution of the United States, that "as federal, it is to be construed *strictly,* in all cases, where the antecedent rights of a state may be drawn in question. As a social compact, it ought likewise "to receive the same strict construction, wherever the right of personal liberty, or of personal security, or of private property may become the object of dispute; because every person, whose liberty or property was thereby rendered subject to the new government, *was antecedently a member of a civil society, to whose regulations he had submitted himself, and under whose authority and protection he still remains, in all cases not expressly submitted to the new government."*

We here see, that the whole reasoning is founded, not on the notion, that the rights of the *people* are concerned, but the rights of the *states.* And by strict construction is obviously meant the most limited sense belonging to the words. And the learned author relies, for the support of his reasoning, upon some rules laid down by Vattel in relation to the interpretation of treaties in relation to *odious* things. It would seem, then, that the constitution of the United States is to be deemed an odious instrument. And why, it may be asked? Was it not framed for the good of the people, and by the people? . . .

. . . The state governments have no right to assume, that the power is more safe or more useful with them, than with the general government; that they have a higher capacity and a more honest desire to preserve the rights and liberties of the people, than the general government; that there is no danger in trusting them; but that all the peril and all the oppression impend on the other side. The people have not so said, or thought; and they have the exclusive right to judge for themselves on the subject. They avow, that the constitution of the United States was adopted by them, "in order to form a more perfect union, establish justice, ensure domestic tranquillity, provide for the common defence, promote the general welfare, and secure the blessings of liberty to themselves and their posterity." It would be a mockery to ask if these are odious objects. If these require every grant of power, withdrawn from the state governments, to be deemed *strictissimi juris,* and construed in the most limited sense, even if it should defeat these objects. What peculiar sanctity have the state governments in the eyes of the people beyond these objects? Are they not framed for the same general ends? Was not the very inability of the state governments suitably to provide for our national wants, and national independence, and national protection, the very groundwork of the whole system? . . .

IV.   From the foregoing considerations we deduce the conclusion, that as a frame or fundamental law of government, The constitution of the United States is to receive a reasonable interpretation of its language, and its powers, keeping in view the objects and purposes, for which those powers were conferred. By a reasonable interpretation, we mean, that in case the words are susceptible of two different senses, the one strict, the other more enlarged, that should be adopted, which is most consonant with the apparent objects and intent of the constitution; that, which will give it efficacy and force, as a *government,* rather than that, which will impair its operations, and reduce it to a state of imbecility. Of course we do not mean, that the words for this purpose are to be strained beyond their common and natural sense;

but keeping within that limit, the exposition is to have a fair and just latitude, so as on the one hand to avoid obvious mischief, and on the other hand to promote the public good. . . .

If, then, we are to give a reasonable construction to this instrument, as a constitution of government established for the common good, we must throw aside all notions of subjecting it to a strict interpretation, as if it were subversive of the great interests of society, or derogated from the inherent sovereignty of the people. And this will naturally lead us to some other rules properly belonging to the subject.

V. Where the power is granted in general terms, the power is to be construed, as coextensive with the terms, unless some clear restriction upon it is deducible from the context. We do not mean to assert, that it is necessary, that such restriction should be expressly found in the context. It will be sufficient, if it arise by necessary implication. But it is not sufficient to show, that there was, or might have been, a sound or probable motive to restrict it. A restriction founded on conjecture is wholly inadmissible. The reason is obvious: the text was adopted by the people in its obvious, and general sense. We have no means of knowing, that any particular gloss, short of this sense, was either contemplated, or approved by the people; and such a gloss might, though satisfactory in one state, have been the very ground of objection in another. It might have formed a motive to reject it in one, and to adopt it in another. The sense of a part of the people has no title to be deemed the sense of the whole. Motives of state policy, or state interest, may properly have influence in the question of ratifying it; but the constitution itself must be expounded, as it stands; and not as that policy, or that interest may seem now to dictate. We are to construe, and not to frame the instrument.

VI.   A power, given in general terms, is not to be restricted to particular cases, merely because it may be susceptible of abuse, and, if abused, may lead to mischievous consequences. This argument is often used in public debate; and in its common aspect addressed itself so much to popular fears and prejudices, that it insensibly acquires a weight in the public mind, to which it is nowise entitled. The argument *ab inconvenienti* is sufficiently open to question, from the laxity of application, as well as of opinion, to which it leads. But the argument from a possible abuse of a power against its existence or use, is, in its nature, not only perilous, but in respect to governments, would shake their very foundation. Every form of government unavoidably includes a grant of some discretionary powers. It would be wholly imbecile without them. It is impossible to foresee all the exigencies, which may arise in the progress of events, connected with the rights, duties, and operations of a government. If they could be foreseen, it would be impossible *ab ante* to provide for them. The means must be subject to perpetual modification, and change; they must be adapted to the existing manners, habits, and institutions of society, which are never stationary; to the pressure of dangers, or necessities; to the ends in view; to general and permanent operations, as well as to fugitive and extraordinary emergencies. In short, if the whole society is not to be revolutionized at every critical period, and remodelled in every generation, there must be left to those, who administer the government, a very large mass of discretionary powers, capable of greater or less actual expansion according to circumstances, and sufficiently flexible not to involve the nation in utter destruction from the rigid limitations imposed upon it by an improvident jealousy. Every power, however limited, as well as broad, is in its own nature susceptible of abuse. No constitution can provide perfect guards against it. Confidence must be reposed some where; and in free governments, the ordinary securities against abuse are found in the responsibility of rulers to the people, and in the just exercise of their elective franchise; and ultimately in the sovereign power of change belonging to them, in cases requiring extraordinary remedies. Few cases are to be supposed, in which a power, however general, will be exerted for the permanent oppression of the people. And yet, cases may easily be put, in which a limitation upon such a power might be found in practice to work mischief; to incite foreign aggression; or encourage domestic disorder. The power of taxation, for instance, may be carried to a ruinous excess; and yet, a limitation upon that power might, in a given case, involve the destruction of the independence of the country.

VII.   On the other hand, a rule of equal importance is, not to enlarge the construction of a given power beyond the fair scope of its terms, merely because the restriction is inconvenient, impolitic, or even mischievous. If it be mischievous, the power of redressing the evil lies with the people by an exercise of the power of amendment. If they do not choose to apply the remedy, it may fairly be presumed, that the mischief is less than what would arise from a further extension of the power; or that it is the least of two evils. Nor should it ever be lost sight of, that the government of the United States is one of limited and enumerated powers; and that a departure from the true import and sense of its powers is, *pro tanto,* the establishment of a new constitution. It is doing for the people, what they have not chosen to do for themselves. It is usurping the functions of a legislator, and deserting those of an expounder of the law. Arguments drawn from impolicy or inconvenience ought here to be of no weight. The only sound principle is to declare, *ita lex scripta est,* to follow, and to obey. Nor, if a principle so just and conclusive could be overlooked, could there well be found a more unsafe guide in practice, than mere policy and convenience. Men on such subjects complexionally differ from each other. The same men differ from themselves at different times. Temporary delusions, prejudices, excitements, and objects have irresistible influence in mere questions of policy. And the policy of one age may ill suit the wishes or the policy of another. The constitution is not to be subject to such fluctuations. It is to have a fixed, uniform, permanent construction. It should be, so far at least as human infirmity will allow, not dependent upon the passions or parties of particular times, but the same yesterday, to-day, and for ever. . . .

VIII.   No construction of a given power is to be allowed, which plainly defeats, or impairs its avowed objects. If, therefore, the words are fairly susceptible of two interpretations, according to their common sense and use, the one of which would defeat one, or all of the objects, for which it was obviously given, and the other of which would preserve and promote all, the former interpretation ought to be rejected, and the latter be held the true interpretation. This rule results from the dictates of mere common sense; for every instrument ought to be so construed, *ut magis valeat, quam pereat.* For instance, the constitution confers on congress the power to declare war. Now the word *declare* has several senses. It may mean to proclaim, or publish. But no person would imagine, that this was the whole sense, in which the word is used in this connection. It should be interpreted in the sense, in which the phrase is used among nations, when applied to such a subject-matter. A power to declare war is a power to make, and carry on war. It is not a mere power to make known an existing thing, but to give life and effect to the thing itself. The true doctrine has been expressed by the supreme court: "If from the imperfection of human language there should be any serious doubts respecting the extent of any given power, the objects, for which it was given, especially when those objects are expressed in the instrument itself, should have great influence in the construction."

IX.   Where a power is remedial in its nature, there is much reason to contend, that it ought to be construed liberally. That was the doctrine of Mr. Chief Justice Jay, in *Chisholm* v. *Georgia;* and it is generally adopted in the interpretation of laws. But this liberality of exposition is clearly inadmissible, if it extends beyond the just and ordinary sense of the terms.

X.   In the interpretation of a power, all the ordinary and appropriate means to execute it are to be deemed a part of the power itself. This results from the very nature and design of a constitution. In giving the power, it does not intend to limit it to any one mode of exercising it, exclusive of all others. It must be obvious, (as has been already suggested,) that the means of carrying into effect the objects of a power may, nay, must be varied, in order to adapt themselves to the exigencies of the nation at different times. A mode efficacious and useful in one age, or under one posture of circumstances, may be wholly vain, or even mischievous at another time. Government presupposes the existence of a perpetual mutability in its own operations on those, who are its subjects; and a perpetual flexibility in adapting itself to their wants, their interests, their habits, their occupations, and their infirmities . . .

In the practical application of government, then, the public functionaries must be left at liberty to exercise the powers, with which the people by the constitution and laws have entrusted them. They must have a wide discretion, as to the choice of means; and the only limitation upon that discretion would seem to be, that the means are appropriate to the end. And this must naturally admit of considerable latitude; for the relation between the action and the end (as has been justly remarked) is not always so direct and palpable, as to strike the eye of every observer. If the end be legitimate and within the scope of the constitution, all the means, which are appropriate, and which are plainly adapted to that end, and which are not prohibited, may be constitutionally employed to carry it into effect. When, then, it is asked, who is to judge of the necessity and propriety of the laws to be passed for executing the powers of the union, the true answer is, that the national government, like every other, must judge in the first instance of the proper exercise of its powers; and its constituents in the last. If the means are within the reach of the power, no other department can inquire into the policy or convenience of the use of them. If there be an excess by overleaping the just boundary of the power, the judiciary may generally afford the proper relief; and in the last resort the people, by adopting such measures to redress it, as the exigency may suggest, and prudence may dictate.

XI.   And this leads us to remark, in the next place, that in the interpretation of the constitution there is no solid objection to implied powers. Had the faculties of man been competent to the framing of a system of government which would leave nothing to implication, it cannot be doubted, that the effort would have been made by the framers of our constitution. The fact, however, is otherwise. There is not in the whole of that admirable instrument a grant of powers, which does not draw after it others, not expressed, but vital to their exercise; not substantive and independent, indeed, but auxiliary and subordinate. There is no phrase in it, which like the articles of confederation, excludes incidental and implied powers, and which requires, that every thing granted shall be expressly and minutely described. Even the tenth amendment, which was framed for the purpose of quieting the excessive jealousies, which had been excited, omits the word "expressly," (which was contained in the articles of confederation,) and declares only, that "the powers, not delegated to the United States, nor prohibited by it to the states, are reserved to the states respectively, or to the people;" thus leaving the question, whether the particular power, which may become the subject of contest, has been delegated to the one government, or prohibited to the other, to depend upon a fair construction of the whole instrument. . . .

We may, however, lay down some few rules, deducible from what has been already said, in respect to cases of implied prohibitions upon the existence or exercise of powers by the states, as guides to aid our inquiries. (1.) Wherever the power given to the general government requires, that, to be efficacious and adequate to its end, it should be exclusive, there arises a just implication for deeming it exclusive. Whether exercised, or not, in such a case makes no difference. (2.) Wherever the power in its own nature is not incompatible with a concurrent power in the states, either in its nature or exercise, there the power belongs to the states. (3.) But in such a case, the concurrency of the power may admit of restrictions or qualifications in its nature, or exercise. In its nature, when it is capable from its general character of being applied to objects or purposes, which would control, defeat, or destroy the powers of the general government. In its exercise, when there arises a conflict in the actual laws and regulations made in pursuance of the power by the general and state governments. In the former case there is a qualification engrafted upon the generality of the power, excluding its application to such objects and purposes. In the latter, there is (at least generally) a qualification, not upon the power itself, but only upon its exercise, to the extent of the actual conflict in the operations of each. (4.) In cases of implied limitations or prohibitions of power, it is not sufficient to show a possible, or potential inconvenience. There must be a plain incompatibility, a direct repugnancy, or an extreme practical inconvenience, leading irresistibly to the same conclusion. (5.) If such incompatibility, repugnancy, or extreme inconvenience would result, it is no answer, that in the actual exercise of the power, each party may, if it chooses, avoid a positive interference with the other. The objection lies to the power itself, and not to the exercise of it. If it exist, it may be applied to the extent of controlling, defeating, or destroying the other. It can never be presumed, that the framers of the constitution, declared to be supreme, could intend to put its powers at hazard upon the good wishes, or good intentions, or discretion of the states in the exercise of their acknowledged powers. (6.) Where no such repugnancy, incompatibility, or extreme inconvenience would result, then the power in the states is restrained, not in its nature, but in its operations, and then only to the extent of the actual interference. In fact, it is obvious, that the same means may often be applied to carry into operation different powers. And a state may use the same means to effectuate an acknowledged power in itself, which congress may apply for another purpose in the acknowledged exercise of a very different power. Congress may make that a regulation of commerce, which a state may employ as a guard for its internal policy, or to preserve the public health or peace, or to promote its own peculiar interests. These rules seem clearly deducible from the nature of the instrument; and they are confirmed by the positive injunctions of the tenth amendment of the constitution. . . .

XVIII.   And this leads us to remark, in the next place, that it is by no means a correct rule of interpretation to construe the same word in the same sense, wherever it occurs in the same instrument. It does not follow, either logically or grammatically, that because a word is found in one connexion in the constitution, with a definite sense, therefore the same sense is to be adopted in every other connexion, in which it occurs. This would be to suppose, that the framers weighed only the force of single words, as philologists or critics, and not whole clauses and objects, as statesmen, and practical reasoners. And yet nothing has been more common, than to subject the constitution to this narrow and mischievous criticism. Men of ingenious and subtle minds, who seek for symmetry and harmony in language, having found in the constitution a word used in some sense, which falls in with their favorite theory of interpreting it, have made that the standard, by which to measure its use in every other part of the instrument. They have thus stretched it, as it were, on the bed of Procrustes, lopping off its meaning, when it seemed too large for their purposes, and extending it, when it seemed too short. They have thus distorted it to the most unnatural shapes, and crippled, where they have sought only to adjust its proportions according to their own opinions. It was very justly observed by Mr. Chief Justice Marshall, in *The Cherokee Nation* v. *The State of Georgia,* that "it has been said, that the same words have not necessarily the same meaning attached to them, when found in different parts of the same instrument. Their meaning is controlled by the context. This is undoubtedly true. In common language, the same word has various meanings; and the peculiar sense, in which it is used in any sentence, is to be determined by the context." A very easy example of this sort will be found in the use of the word "establish," which is found in various places in the constitution. Thus, in the preamble, one object of the constitution is avowed to be "to establish justice," which seems here to mean to settle firmly, to fix unalterably, or rather, perhaps, as justice, abstractedly considered, must be considered as forever fixed and unalterable, to dispense or administer justice. Again, the constitution declares, that congress shall have power "to establish an uniform rule of naturalization, and uniform laws on the subject of bankruptcies," where it is manifestly used as equivalent to make, or form, and not to fix or settle unalterably and forever. Again, "congress shall have power to establish post-offices and post-roads," where the appropriate sense would seem to be to create, to found, and to regulate, not so much with a view to permanence of form, as to convenience of action. Again, it is declared, that "congress shall make no law respecting an establishment of religion," which seems to prohibit any laws, which shall recognize, found, confirm, or patronize any particular religion, or form of religion, whether permanent or temporary, whether already existing, or to arise in future. In this clause, establishment seems equivalent in meaning to settlement, recognition, or support. . . .

XIX.   But the most important rule, in cases of this nature, is, that a constitution of government does not, and cannot, from its nature, depend in any great degree upon mere verbal criticism, or upon the import of single words. Such criticism may not be wholly without use; it may sometimes illustrate, or unfold the appropriate sense; but unless it stands well with the context and subject-matter, it must yield to the latter. While, then, we may well resort to the meaning of single words to assist our inquiries, we should never forget, that it is an instrument of government we are to construe; and, as has been already stated, that must be the truest exposition, which best harmonizes with its design, its objects, and its general structure.

The remark of Mr. Burke may, with a very slight change of phrase be addressed as an admonition to all those, who are called upon to frame, or to interpret a constitution. Government is a practical thing made for the happiness of mankind, and not to furnish out a spectacle of uniformity to gratify the schemes of visionary politicians. The business of those, who are called to administer it, is to rule, and not to wrangle. It would be a poor compensation, that one had triumphed in a dispute, whilst we had lost an empire; that we had frittered down a power, and at the same time had destroyed the republic.

Part VI ~~~~~~~~~~~~~~~~~

A Nation Bursting
with Energy

The noted legal historian J. Willard Hurst has described the interaction between the law, the economy, and the society in the nineteenth century as a "release of energy." Certainly the young nation exuded vitality, with people flocking westward, building canals and railroads, populating new cities, and embarking upon new economic ventures.

All of this put enormous strain on the legal system, which had to adjust to the new demands of an expanding and changing society. American law in 1800, with minor exceptions, still relied primarily on established English rules and maxims that had for the most part fit the needs of the colonial society and even the young republic (Document 21). But the changes that took place in the Jeffersonian and Jacksonian eras required a rethinking of the law, and in fine common law tradition, the necessary changes occurred.

Most of the cases in this section are from state courts, because for the majority of Americans local law affected their daily lives far more than did the decisions of the Supreme Court, whose jurisdiction extended only to "cases and controversies" arising under the constitution. State courts made new rules on contractual obligations (Document 63), liability for damages to property (Documents 66 and 71), custody of children (Documents 70 and 72), employer liability (Document 74), labor practices (Documents 62 and 75), and the state police powers (Document 78). Significant reforms in legal procedure also took place at the local level (Document 76).

A major development of this period was the creation of national markets, in which producers and buyers no longer negotiated at arm's length across a stall. Now deals could be struck involving parties in two or more states, with middlemen as well as producer and consumer, and all had to rely upon specific rules that would be honored in all markets. Some issues did go before federal courts, since they involved multiple jurisdictions, or in some cases, because the necessity for new law raised federal issues. Thus federal courts handed down decisions on rules for water use (Document 65), approved state powers in the absence of federal action (Documents 68 and 79), allowed old contracts to be superseded by new state charters for the public good (Document 69), and established a federal commercial common law (Document 73). But these federal rules did not operate in a vacuum, especially in commercial matters, and federal judges remained keenly aware that state courts would have the primary responsibility for enforcing private law matters.

The dynamic changes in the legal system can be seen as paralleling political change as well. This is the era of Jacksonian democracy, when more people became involved in the political process. Not everyone approved of these developments (Document 64), and for some, the pace of reform proved agonizingly slow (Document 77). How far the country had come can be seen in the constitutional revision of one state at midcentury (Document 80).

61

Palmer v. *Mulligan*
(1805)

Legal historian Morton J. Horwitz sees this New York case as one of the first to display what he terms the emerging legal mentality of the nineteenth century, an "instrumental" conception of the law. Instead of being totally bound by common law precedent, judges began to frame their opinions in terms of the developmental and commercial needs of the time. In this New York Supreme Court case, the plaintiff, a downstream mill owner, sued the defendant for obstructing the water flow by a new upstream dam. English common law had always protected the flow of water downstream, and thus effectively prevented any developmental use upstream of existing dams. The court here abandoned precedent, and did so by reference to the contemporary needs of society. One might keep in mind J. Willard Hurst's distinction between "static" and "dynamic" property. In England the law had attempted to preserve property, especially land, intact; Americans, on the other hand, looked at land as commercial raw material, to be used and developed so as to make a profit. With land so plentiful, there seemed little need to preserve it inviolate.

See M. J. Horwitz, *The Tranformation of American Law, 1780–1860* (1977); W. E. Nelson, *The Americanization of the Common Law . . . 1760–1830* (1975); and J. W. Hurst, *Law and the Conditions of Freedom in the Nineteenth-Century United States* (1956).

Judge Livingston

In determining this cause, I am willing to admit that the erection of the plaintiffs' mills and dam is not only no nuisance or obstruction to the river, but a public as well as private benefit. Still I am not satisfied of their right to recover. Whatever their pretensions to build a dam and mills adjoining their own land may have been, it must be conceded that, as far as the public are concerned, the defendants had the same right opposite their ground, provided it could be done without injury to the navigation of the river. This is not pretended to be the case; but as the plaintiffs' mills were first erected,

Source: 3 Caines R. 307 (New York 1805).

it is said, that if the defendants have any right of this kind, they must so use it as not to injure their neighbours. Without denying this position, which is indeed become a familiar maxim, its operation must be restrained within reasonable bounds so as not to deprive a man of the enjoyment of his property, merely because of some trifling inconvenience or damage to others; of this nature is the injury now complained of, so far at least as it is supported by proof. It is not pretended that the water is diverted, or that less business can be now done at the plaintiffs' mills than formerly, but they are obliged to bring their logs a very little farther round in the river, (in order to get them into the dam,) which is the principal, if not only inconvenience they are exposed to by the defendants' conduct. Were the law to regard little inconveniences of this nature, he who could first build a dam or mill on any public or navigable river, would acquire an exclusive right, at least for some distance, whether he owned the contiguous banks or not; for it would not be easy to build a second dam or mound in the same river on the same side, unless at a considerable distance, without producing some mischief or detriment to the owner of the first. Were this not permitted for fear of some inconsiderable damage to other persons, the public, whose advantage is always to be regarded, would be deprived of the benefit which always attends competition and rivalry. As well, therefore, to secure to individuals the free and undisturbed enjoyment of their property, as to the public the benefits which must frequently redound to it from such use, the operation of the maxim *sic utere tuo ut alienum non lœldas* should be limited to such cases only where a manifest and serious damage is the result of such use or enjoyment, and where it is very clear indeed that the party had no right to use it in that way. Hence it becomes impossible, and, indeed, improper, to attempt to define every case which may occur of this kind. Each must depend on its own circumstances; and the fewer precedents of this kind which are set, the better. Confining myself, therefore, strictly to the case before us, my opinion is, and the jury probably proceeded on that ground, that the plaintiffs proved no injury, or one so remote and insignificant, as not to justify their insisting on an abatement of the defendants' dam, or damages for its erection.

If this view of the subject be correct, it will account for my passing over some points which were made on the argument without giving an opinion on them. This I avoid doing, because experience has already convinced me that it is always best in a judge to be silent on every point which he does not regard important and necessary in the decision of a cause.

Commonwealth v. Pullis (1806)

Also known as the Philadelphia Cordwainers case, this is one of the first instances in which efforts to unionize labor ran afoul of the law. In 1794 Philadelphia shoemakers organized the "Federal Society of Journey-man Cordwainers" (the name came from the cordovan leather they worked with) in an effort to secure stable wages. Over the next decade the union secured some wage increases, and in 1805 struck for higher rates. The strike collapsed after the indictment of the union leaders for the common law crime of conspiracy. The trial took place in the Phila-delphia Mayor's Court, which was not a court of record, so the report we have consists of shorthand notes taken by Thomas Lloyd, a young Republican printer who later published the proceedings. The follow-ing excerpt is the charge of the judge, known in the court as the "recorder," and his attitude toward a free market economy is very indicative of the times (compare this to Document 75).

See D. Montgomery, "The Working Class of the Preindustrial American City, 1780–1830." 9 *Labor His.* 1 (1968) and W. Nelles, "The First American Labor Case," 41 *Yale L. J.* 165 (1931).

Recorder Levy, Instructing the Jury

It is proper to consider, is such a combination consistent with the principles of our law, and injurious to the public welfare? The usual means by which the prices of work are regulated, are the demand for the article and the excellence of its fabric. . . . To make an artificial regulation, is not to regard the excellence of the work or quality of the material, but to fix a positive and arbitrary price, governed by no standard, controlled by no impartial person, but dependent on the will of the few who are interested. . . . It is an unnatural, artificial means of raising the price of work beyond its standard, and taking an undue advantage of the public. Is the rule of law bottomed upon such principles, as to permit or protect such conduct? . . . Is there any man who can calculate (if this is tolerated) at what price he may safely contract to

Source: J. R. Commons et al., 3 *Documentary History of American Industrial Society* 60 (1910).

deliver articles, for which he may receive orders, if he is to be regulated by the journeymen in an arbitrary jump from one price to another? . . . What then is the operation of this kind of conduct upon the commerce of the city? It exposes it to inconveniences, if not to ruin; therefore, it is against the public welfare. How does it operate upon the defendants? We see that those who are in indigent circumstances, and who have families to maintain, and who get their bread by their daily labour, have declared here upon oath, that it was impossible for them to hold out . . . and it has been admitted by the witnesses for the defendants, that such persons, however sharp and pressing their necessities, were obliged to stand to the turn-out, or never afterwards to be employed. . . . Can such a regulation be just and proper? Does it not tend to involve necessitous men in the commission of crimes? If they are prevented from working for six weeks, it might induce those who are thus idle, and have not the means of maintenance, to take other courses for the support of their wives and children. It might lead them to procure it by crimes—by burglary, larceny, or highway robbery! A father cannot stand by and see, without agony, his children suffer; if he does, he is an inhuman monster; he will be driven to seek bread for them, either by crime, by beggary, or a removal from the city. . . . Does this measure tend to make good workmen? No: it puts the botch incapable of doing justice to his work, on a level with the best tradesman. The master must give the same wages to each. Such a practice would take away all the excitement to excel in workmanship or industry. . . . In every point of view, this measure is pregnant with public mischief and private injury. . . .

What has been the conduct of the defendants in this instance? They belong to an association, the object of which is, that every person who follows the trade of a journeyman shoemaker, must be a member of their body. . . . If they do not join the body, a term of reproach is fixed upon them. The members of the body will not work with them, and they refuse to board or lodge with them. . . . If the purpose of the association is well understood, it will be found they leave no individual at liberty to join the society or reject it. . . . Is there any reason to suppose that the laws are not competent to redress an evil of this magnitude? . . .

It is in the volumes of the common law we are to seek for information in the far greater number, as well as the most important causes that come before our tribunals. That invaluable code has ascertained and defined, with a critical precision, and with a consistency that no fluctuating political body could or can attain, not only the civil rights of property, but the nature of all crimes from treason to trespass, has pointed out the rules of evidence and the mode of proof, and has introduced and perpetuated, for their investigation, that admirable institution, the freeman's-boast, the trial by jury. . . . Its rules are the result of the wisdom of ages. It says there may be cases in which what one man may do without offence, many combined may not do with impunity. . . .

. . . A combination of workmen to raise their wages may be considered in a two fold point of view: one is to benefit themselves . . . the other is to injure those who do not join their society. The rule of law condemns both. If the rule be clear, we are bound to conform to it even though we do not comprehend the principle upon which it is founded. . . . It is enough, that it is the will of the majority. . . . But the rule in this case is pregnant with sound sense and all the authorities are clear upon the subject. . . .

. . . In the turn-out of last fall, if each member of the body had stood alone, fettered by no promises to the rest, many of them might have changed their opinion as to the price of wages and gone to work. . . . The continuance in improper conduct may therefore well be attributed to the combination. The good sense of those individuals was prevented by this agreement, from having its free exercise. . . . Is this like the formation of a society for the promotion of the general welfare of the community, such as to advance the interests of religion, or to accomplish acts of charity and benevolence? . . . These are for the benefit of third persons, the society in question to promote the selfish purposes of the members. . . . How can these cases be considered on an equal footing? The journeymen shoemakers . . . could not go farther than saying, no one should work unless they all got the wages demanded by the majority; is this freedom? . . . Was it the spirit of '76 that either masters or journeymen, in regulating the prices of their commodities should set up a rule contrary to the law of their country? General and individual liberty was the spirit of '76. It is our first blessing. It has been obtained and will be maintained . . . . It is not a question, whether we shall have an imperium in imperio, whether we shall have, besides our state legislature a new legislature consisting of journeymen shoemakers. . . . [T]hough we acknowledge it is the hard hand of labour that promises the wealth of a nation, though we acknowledge the usefulness of such a large body of tradesmen and agree they should have every thing to which they are legally entitled; yet we conceive they ought to ask nothing more. They should neither be the slaves nor the governors of the community. . . .

. . . [The court has] given you the rule as they have found it in the book, and it is now for you to say, whether the defendants are guilty or not. The rule they consider as fixed, they cannot change it. . . . If you can reconcile it to your consciences, to find the defendants not guilty, you will do so; if not, the alternative that remains, is a verdict of guilty.

63

~~~~~~

Sands v. *Taylor (1810)*

English contract law at the end of the eighteenth century relied on title theory; the ownership of a particular item changed hands when title to that item passed from seller to buyer. The law assumed that both parties bargained at arm's length and were knowledgeable about the goods involved, and that the sale involved specific items; for example, a particular horse or cow. For breach of contract, the law allowed the aggrieved party to recover only the consideration tendered. The title theory of contract made sense in local markets where buyer and seller did in fact deal face to face and haggle over a specific item. It made no sense, however, in larger markets where buyer and seller were primarily interested in whether the price of fungible goods would rise or fall.

In this case, the buyer refused to accept a shipment of wheat he had ordered. Rather than let the wheat rot and then sue for breach, the seller disposed of the wheat at the current market price, and then sued the buyer for the difference between the contract price and what he had been able to get on the market. Judge Spencer's decision in the New York Supreme Court is a wonderful example of the common law at its best, recognizing and adapting to new situations.

See L. M. Friedman, *A History of American Law* (1973); G. Gilmore, *Death of Contract* (1974); and M. J. Horwitz, *The Transformation of American Law, 1780–1860* (1977) and "Historical Foundations of Modern Contract Law," 87 *Harv. L. R.* 917 (1974).

~~~~~~

Judge Spencer

The questions arising from the case are, 1st. What was the nature of the sale of the wheat; is it to be considered a sale by sample and a warranty that the cargo would answer every purpose, which the sample would? and

2d. Was the subsequent sale of the wheat at public auction, such a dissolution of the contract, as to take away the plaintiffs' right to the difference between the sale to the defendants and that at auction?

In considering this case, I shall take it for granted that the sale of the wheat was by *Pearsall,* the plaintiffs' agent; that it was by sample; that he knew the defendants' object in purchasing, was to malt the wheat, and that the sample

---

Source: 5 Johns. 39 (New York 1810).

malted, but the residue of the cargo would not. These admissions must, however, be connected with other facts warranted by the case, such as that the cargo was southern wheat, known to be so, by the defendants, when they purchased it; that the difference between the sample and the cargo consisted in a part of the latter being heated; but that it was not more, nor so much heated, as southern cargoes usually are, and that the defendants are brewers and maltsters.

It has been frequently decided here, that on the sale of a commodity, no action can be sustained for any difference in quality between the thing contracted for and the thing delivered, unless there be fraud or a warranty; I am disposed to confine this rule to the case of a sale where the thing sold is exhibited, and am ready to admit, that on sales by sample, there is an implied warranty that the sample, taken in the usual way, is a fair specimen of the thing sold. It appears to me that the sample by which the defendants purchased, was a fair exhibition of the quality of wheat, of which the cargo consisted; it was taken out in the usual manner, by the plaintiffs' agent running his arm down and drawing out the sample; and there is no pretence that there was any difference between the sample and the cargo, except that the latter was heated in a manner incident to every cargo of southern wheat. This deterioration of the cargo, and which undoubtedly prevented its malting, was a fact against which the exhibition of the sample did not warrant, and it is a fact with which the defendants must be presumed acquainted; for the law will presume every dealer in articles brought to market acquainted with all the circumstances usually attendant on cargoes composed of those articles. It seems to me to result necessarily from these facts, that the defendants' ground of refusal to receive the residue of the cargo, after a part had been delivered, is not that there has been any thing represented, by the exhibition of the sample, unfair in itself and deceptive; but that the defendants themselves made the purchase without a competent knowledge of the usual and customary course of the trade. This, I think, is what they cannot be permitted to take advantage of.

Although I have not adopted the same course of reasoning which was used by the judge, at the circuit, the result is the same, and the evidence which he overruled, I have considered as having been given.

The contract between the parties, and its part execution, produced a change of property; the defendants became entitled to the wheat, and the plaintiffs to the price stipulated to be given for it. After the defendants refused to accept the residue of the cargo, it was thrown on the plaintiffs' hands; and they were, by necessity, made the defendants' trustees, to manage it; and being thus constituted trustees, or agents, for the defendants, they must either abandon the property to destruction, by refusing to have any concern with it, or take a course more for the advantage of the defendants, by selling it. There is a strong analogy between this case and that of the assured, in case of an abandonment, when a loss has happened within the terms of the policy, and the assurer refuses to accept the abandonment. In both cases, the party in possession is to be considered an agent to the other party, from necessity: and his exercise of the right to sell ought not to be viewed as a waiver of his rights on the contract. This rule operates justly, as respects both parties; for the reasons which induced the one party to refuse the acceptance of the property, will induce the other to act fairly, and to sell it to the best advantage. It is a much fitter rule, than to require it of the party, on whom the possession of the thing is thrown, against his will, and contrary to the duty of the other party, to suffer the property to perish, as a condition on which his right to damages is to depend.

There are no adjudications, in the books, which either establish or deny the rule adopted in this case; but it appears to me to be founded on principles dictated by good sense and justice. . . . On the whole, I think the rule now established by the court is a safe one, and conducive to the attainment of justice between the parties.

64

Against Universal Suffrage (1821)

JAMES KENT

Between 1800 and 1860, every state revised its constitution at least once, and some altered their basic documents several times. Most states adopted the constitutional convention as the basic mode for change, with the electorate choosing delegates to represent them as a committee of the whole. These conventions dealt with a variety of topics, but in the early part of the century the democratization of the political process was a major issue in nearly every state.

Apportionment and suffrage proved persistent themes, since changes in electoral distribution and who could vote determined who would rule. In general, the western states proved more liberal in granting the

Source: Commager, ed., *Documents of American History* 232 (1958 6th ed.).

franchise than did the older seaboard states. The proposal to abolish the property qualification for voting in New York aroused fierce opposition from conservatives, who continued to insist that only those with a stake in society (a property interest) should have a voice in electing its government. Chancellor James Kent opposed the extension of suffrage at the 1821 New York constitutional convention, but despite his appeal the move to liberalize the franchise succeeded.

See J. T. Horton, *James Kent* (1939); M. G. Chute, *First Liberty: Right to Vote in America, 1619–1850* (1969); and M. Peterson, ed., *Democracy, Liberty and Property: The State Constitutional Conventions of the 1820s* (1966).

These are some of the fruits of our present government; and yet we seem to be dissatisfied with our present condition, and we are engaged in the bold and hazardous experiment of remodelling the constitution. Is it not fit and discreet: I speak as to wise men; is it not fit and proper that we should pause in our career, and reflect well on the immensity of the innovation in contemplation? Discontent in the midst of so much prosperity, and with such abundant means of happiness, looks like ingratitude, and as if we were disposed to arraign the goodness of Providence. Do we not expose ourselves to the danger of being deprived of the blessings we have enjoyed? . . .

The senate has hitherto been elected by the farmers of the state—by the free and independent lords of the soil, worth at least $250 in freehold estate, over and above all debts charged thereon. The governor has been chosen by the same electors, and we have hitherto elected citizens of elevated rank and character. Our assembly has been chosen by freeholders, possessing a freehold of the value of $50, or by persons renting a tenement of the yearly value of $5, and who have been rated and actually paid taxes to the state. By the report before us, we propose to annihilate, at one stroke, all those property distinctions and to bow before the idol of universal suffrage. That extreme democratic principle, when applied to the legislative and executive departments of the government, has been regarded with terror, by the wise men of every age, because in every European republic, ancient and modern, in which it has been tried, it has terminated disastrously, and been productive of corruption, injustice, violence, and tyranny. And dare we flatter ourselves that we are a peculiar people, who can run the career of history, exempted from the passions which have disturbed and corrupted the rest of mankind? If we are like other races of men, with similar follies and vices, then I greatly fear that our posterity will have reason to deplore in sackcloth and ashes, the delusion of the day. . . .

Now, sir, I wish to preserve our senate as the representative of the landed interest. I wish those who have an interest in the soil, to retain the exclusive possession of a branch in the legislature, as a strong hold in which they may find safety through all the vicissitudes which the state may be destined, in the course of Providence, to experience. I wish them to be always enabled to say that their freeholds cannot be taxed without their consent. The men of no property, together with the crowds of dependents connected with great manufacturing and commercial establishments, and the motley and undefinable population of crowded ports, may, perhaps, at some future day, under skilful management predominate in the assembly, and yet we should be perfectly safe if no laws could pass without the free consent of the owners of the soil. That security we at present enjoy; and it is that security which I wish to retain.

The apprehended danger from the experiment of universal suffrage applied to the whole legislative department, is no dream of the imagination. It is too mighty an excitement for the moral constitution of men to endure. The tendency of universal suffrage, is to jeopardize the rights of property, and the principles of liberty. There is a constant tendency in human society, and the history of every age proves it; there is a tendency in the poor to covet a share in the plunder of the rich; in the debtor to relax or avoid the obligation of contracts; in the majority to tyrannize over the minority, and trample down their rights; in the indolent and profligate, to cast the whole burthens of society upon the industrious and the virtuous; and *there is a tendency in ambitious and wicked men, to inflame these combustible materials.* It requires a vigilant government, and a firm administration of justice, to counteract that tendency. Thou shalt not covet; thou shalt not steal; are divine injunctions induced by this miserable depravity of our nature. Who can undertake to calculate with any precision, how many millions of people, this great state will contain in the course of this and the next century, and who can estimate the future extent and magnitude of our commercial ports? The disproportion between the men of property, and the men of no property, will be in every society in a ratio to its commerce, wealth, and population. We are no longer to remain plain and simple republics of farmers, like the New-England colonists, or the Dutch settlements on the Hudson. We are fast becoming a great nation, with great commerce, manufactures, population, wealth, luxuries, and with the vices and miseries that they engender. One seventh of the population of the city of Paris at this day subsists on charity, and one third of the inhabitants of that city die in the hospitals; what would become of such a city with universal suffrage? France has upwards of four, and England upwards of five millions of manufacturing and commercial labourers without property. Could these Kingdoms sustain the weight of universal suffrage? The radicals in England, with the force of that mighty engine, would at once sweep away the property, the laws, and the liberties of that island like a deluge.

The growth of the city of New-York is enough to startle and awaken those who are pursuing the IGNIS FATUUS of universal suffrage.

Tyler v. *Wilkinson*
(1827)

The common law had traditionally opposed all diversion or obstruction of the natural flow of water, and as late as 1824, Joseph Angell had reaffirmed this view in his treatise, *Watercourses.* But the developmental needs of new commercial enterprises often required obstruction and diversion of water in order to power mills or create navigable channels. As a result, by the time Joseph Story decided this landmark case on circuit, he was faced on the one hand with numerous cases and arguments like those of Angell supporting the traditional view, and on the other by a growing number of cases and writers championing development (see Document 61). Morton J. Horwitz has described *Tyler* as "the classically transitional judicial opinion, filled with ambiguities sufficient to make any future legal developments possible." Story seemed to reaffirm the traditional view, and in fact upheld the plaintiff's claim to the use of the water, but then insisted that the true test of water law should be "reasonable use," a phrase that could be expanded to mean almost any utilitarian use.

See M. J. Horwitz, *Transformation of American Law* (1977); and J. W. Hurst, *Law and the Conditions of Freedom in the Nineteenth-Century United States* (1956).

Circuit Justice Story

This is a very important case, complicated in facts, and voluminous in testimony. It will not, however, be necessary to go over the details of the proofs, or even of the arguments, urged at the bar, further than may serve to explain the opinion of the court, and give a clear understanding of the points in controversy.

The river Pawtucket forms a boundary line between the states of Massachusetts and Rhode Island, in that part of its course where it separates the town of North Providence from the town of Seekonk. It is a fresh water river, above the lower falls between these towns, and is there unaffected by the ebb or flow of the tide. At these falls there is an ancient dam, called the lower dam, extending quite across the river, and several mills are built near

---

Source: 24 Fed. Cases 472 (C.C.D.R.I. 1827).

it, as well on the eastern as on the western side of the river. The plaintiffs, together with some of the defendants, are the proprietors in fee of the mills and adjacent land on the eastern bank, and either by themselves or their lessees are occupants of the same. The mills and land adjacent, on the western bank, are owned by some of the defendants. The lower dam was built as early as the year 1718, by the proprietors on both sides of the river, and is indispensable for the use of their mills respectively. . . . About thirty years before the filing of the bill, to wit, in 1792, another dam was built across the river at a place above the head of the trench, and about 20 rods above the lower dam; and the mills on the upper dam, as well as those on Sergeant's trench, are now supplied with water by proper flumes, &c. from the pond formed by the upper dam. The proprietors of this last dam are also made defendants. . . .

. . . The bill charges, that the owners of Sergeant's trench are entitled, as against the owners of the lower dam, only to what is called a wastewater privilege, that is, to a right to use only such surplus water, as is not wanted by the owners of the lower dam and lands for any purposes whatever. In other words, that the right of the owners of Sergeant's trench is a subservient right to that of the plaintiffs, and takes place only as to any water which the plaintiffs may not, from time to time, have any occasion to use for any mills erected, or to be erected, by them. It charges a fraudulent combination between the owners of the upper dam and Sergeant's trench, injuriously to appropriate and use the water, and that the latter appropriate a great deal more water than they are entitled to by ancient usage, and waste the water to the injury of the plaintiffs. The object of the bill is to establish the right of the plaintiffs, and to obtain an injunction and for general relief.

The principal points, which have been discussed at the bar, are, first, what is the nature and extent of the right of the owners of Sergeant's trench; and, secondly, whether that right has been exceeded by them to the injury of the plaintiffs.

Before proceeding to an examination of these points, it may be proper to ascertain the nature and extent of the right, which riparian proprietors generally possess, to the waters of rivers flowing through their lands. Unless I am mistaken, this will relieve us from a great portion of the difficulties which incumber this cause, and lead us to a satisfactory conclusion upon its merits. . . . I have, however, read over all the cases on this subject, which were cited at the bar, or which are to be found in Mr. Angell's valuable work on water courses, or which my own auxiliary researches have enabled me to reach. The general principles, which they contain and support, I do not say in every particular instance, but with a very strong and controlling current of authority, appear to me to be the following.

Primá facie every proprietor upon each bank of a river is entitled to the land, covered with water, in front of his bank, to the middle thread of the stream, or, as it is commonly expressed, usque ad filum aquae. In virtue of this ownership he has a right to the use of the water flowing over it in its natural current, without diminution or obstruction. But, strictly speaking, he has no property in the water itself; but a simple use of it, while it passes along. The consequence of this principle is, that no proprietor has a right to use the water to the prejudice of another. It is wholly immaterial, whether the party be a proprietor above or below, in the course of the river; the right being common to all the proprietors on the river, no one has a right to diminish the quantity which will, according to the natural current, flow to a proprietor below, or to throw it back upon a proprietor above. This is the necessary result of the perfect equality of right among all the proprietors of that, which is common to all. The natural stream, existing by the bounty of Providence for the benefit of the land through which it flows, is an incident annexed, by operation of law, to the land itself. When I speak of this common right, I do not mean to be understood, as holding the doctrine, that there can be no diminution whatsoever, and no obstruction or impediment whatsoever, by a riparian proprietor, in the use of the water as it flows; for that would be to deny any valuable use of it. There may be, and there must be allowed of that, which is common to all, a reasonable use. The true test of the principle and extent of the use is, whether it is to the injury of the other proprietors or not. There may be a diminution in quantity, or a retardation or acceleration of the natural current indispensable for the general and valuable use of the water, perfectly consistent with the existence of the common right. The diminution, retardation, or acceleration, not positively and sensibly injurious by diminishing the value of the common right, is an implied element in the right of using the stream at all. The law here, as in many other cases, acts with a reasonable reference to public convenience and general good, and it is not betrayed into a narrow strictness, subversive of common sense, nor into an extravagant looseness, which would destroy private rights. The maxium is applied, "Sic utere tuo, ut non allenum lædas."

But of a thing, common by nature, there may be an appropriation by general consent or grant. Mere priority of appropriation of running water, without such consent or grant, confers no exclusive right. It is not like the case of mere occupancy, where the first occupant takes by force of his priority of occupancy. That supposes no ownership already existing, and no right to the use already acquired. But our law annexes to the riparian proprietors the right to the use in common, as an incident to the land; and whoever seeks to found an exclusive use, must establish a rightful appropriation in some manner known and admitted by the law. Now, this may be, either by a grant from all the proprietors, whose interest is affected by the particular appropriation, or by a long exclusive enjoyment, without interruption, which affords a just presumption of right. By our law, upon principles of public convenience, the term of twenty years of exclusive uninterrupted enjoyment has been held a conclusive presumption of a grant or right. . . .

With these principles in view, the general rights of the plaintiffs cannot admit of much controversy. They are riparian proprietors, and, as such, are entitled to the natural flow of the river without diminution to their injury. . . . Their rights, as riparian proprietors, are general; and it is incumbent on the parties, who seek to narrow these rights, to establish by competent proofs their own title to divert and use the stream.

And this leads me to the consideration of the nature and extent of the rights of the trench owners. There is no doubt, that in point of law or fact, there may be a right to water of a very limited nature, and subservient to the more general right of the riparian proprietors. . . . The doctrine of subservient rights and uses is probably as old as the common law itself. But in questions of usage, the fact, how much water has been actually used, is not always decisive of the nature and extent of the right. Nor are occasional interruptions of the use, under peculiar circumstances, conclusive of a superior right to control and limit the entire use, to suspend it at pleasure, or destroy it at discretion. The nature and object and value of the use are very material ingredients to explain and qualify the effect of such interruptions. It is not, for instance, to be presumed, that valuable mills will be erected to be fed by an artificial canal from a river, and the stream be indispensable for the support of such mills, and yet, that the right to the stream is so completely lodged in another, that it may be cut off or diminished, or suspended at pleasure; but, if there should not be water enough for the progressive wants of all, the riparian proprietor should reserve to himself the power of future appropriation for his own exclusive use. In such cases, reasonable presumption must be made from acts in their own nature somewhat equivocal and susceptible of different interpretations. . . . Men who build mills, and invest valuable capital in them, cannot be presumed, without the most conclusive evidence, to give their deliberate assent to the acceptance of such ruinous conditions. . . .

The conclusion, to which my mind has arrived on this point, is that the owners on Sergeant's trench have a right to the flow of the quantity of water which was accustomed to flow therein antecedent to 1796; that this right is general, and not qualified by any pre-eminent right in the plaintiffs or the other owners of the lower dam, either as riparian proprietors or otherwise, to the use of the water, in case of a deficiency; that, if there be a deficiency, it must be borne by all parties, as a common loss, wherever it may fall, according to existing rights; that the trench proprietors have no right to appropriate more water than belonged to them in 1796, and ought to be restrained from any further appropriation; and that the plaintiffs to this extent are entitled to have their general right established, and an injunction granted.

It is impracticable for the court to do more, in this posture of the case, than to refer it to a master to ascertain, as near as may be, and in conformity with the suggestions in the opinion of the court, the quantity to which the trench owners are entitled, and to report a suitable mode and arrangement permanently to regulate and adjust the flow of the water, so as to preserve the rights of all parties.

In respect to the question of damages for any excess of the use of the water by the trench owners, beyond their right, within six years next before the filing of the bill, I have not thought it my duty to go into a consideration of the evidence. It is a fit subject, either for reference to a master, or for an issue of quantum damnificatus, if either party shall desire it.

The decree of the court is to be drawn up accordingly; and all further directions are reserved to the further hearing upon the master's report, &c. Decree accordingly.

66

~~~~~~

Lansing v. *Smith* *(1828)*

Economic advances, however beneficial, involve costs. The building of the Erie Canal, for example, gave rise to hundreds of suits by landowners whose traditional rights to the undisturbed use of their property had been violated. In response to the question, "Who will pay?" the common law had always answered, "The trespasser," and took no account of the social utility of the act. In the early nineteenth century, American courts abandoned this doctrine because, as one judge noted, the older rules "are much modified by the exigencies of the social state." Courts first immunized the state from suits for alleged damage to property resulting from socially useful undertakings, as well as for damage resulting from takings under eminent domain. They then immunized entrepreneurs acting under authority of the state from liability for most injuries to land resulting from developmental activity. In the following case, the New York Supreme Court ruled that when the state undertook to improve navigation through public works, it would not be liable for the tradtional injuries to land such as overflowing of riparian lands and obstruction of access to private docks. In effect, the courts gave developmental forces in the economy a free hand (see also Document 81).

Source: 4 Wendall 9 (New York 1828).

~~~~~~

By the Chancellor

The plaintiff claims to recover in this case on two distinct grounds. The first is that the act of 1823, authorizing the construction of the Albany basin, was unconstitutional so far as it authorized the defendants to do any acts injurious to his property. The other relates to their conduct in the erection of the temporary bridges; which the plaintiff insists was not within the powers conferred by the act. The first question arises both under the special pleadings and the bill of exceptions; the latter arises under the general issue only. The first ground, the main question in this cause, I shall now proceed to consider.

In deciding upon the constitutionality of the act of 1823, it will be necessary to ascertain what were the rights of the plaintiff as against the state, previous to the passage of that act. The people of this state, as the successors of its former sovereign, are entitled to all the rights which formerly belonged to the king by his prerogative. Through the medium of their legislature they may exercise all the powers which previous to the revolution could have been exercised either by the king alone, or by him in conjunction with his parliament; subject only to those restrictions which have been imposed by the constitution of this state or of the United States.

By the common law, the king as *parens patriæ* owned the soil under all the waters of all navigable rivers or arms of the sea where the tide regularly ebbs and flows, including the shore or bank to high water mark. . . . He held these rights, not for his own benefit, but for the benefit of his subjects at large; who were entitled to the free use of the sea, and all tide waters, for the purposes of navigation, fishing, &c., subject to such regulations and restrictions as the crown or the parliament might prescribe. By *magna charta,* and many subsequent statutes, the powers of the king are limited, and he can not now deprive his subjects of these rights by granting the public navigable waters to individuals. But there can be no doubt of the right of parliament in England, or the legislature of this state, to make such grants, when they do not interfere with the vested rights of particular individuals. The right to navigate the public waters of the state and to fish therein, and the right to use the public highways, are all *public* rights belonging to the people at large. They are not the *private* unalienable rights of each individual. Hence the legislature as the representatives of the public may restrict and regulate the exercise of those rights in such manner as may be deemed most beneficial to the public at large; provided they do not interfere with vested rights which have been granted to individuals.

What then were the rights of the owner of the land adjacent to this wharf before the patent from the commissioners of the land office, and what new rights did he acquire under that patent? Before the patent was granted, the bank of the Hudson between high and low water mark belonged to the people, and he had no better right to the use of it than any other person. If he built on it, or erected a wharf there, it would be a purpresture which the legislature might direct to be demolished or to be seized for the use of the public. . . . Or the legislature might authorize erections in front thereof, as in the case of Smith's wharf on the Thames. . . . If it was calculated in any manner to impede or injure the navigation of the river, it might also be abated as a common nuisance. . . . So long as the constituted authorities of the state did not think proper to interfere, persons navigating the river might come to the wharf, subject to the payment of such wharfage as the state allowed the owner to take. But even the taking of a common wharfage, or toll at a ferry, is a franchise, subject to the control and regulation of the legislature, and can not be lawfully exercised without their permission. . . . It is evident from what has been said that the plaintiff had no vested rights previous to his patent which could deprive the legislature of the power to construct this basin. It remains to be seen whether he acquired any such rights under the patent. If a legislative grant or a grant by authority of the government is made to any individual, it is in the nature of a contract executed. And the constitution of the United States has prohibited the state legislatures from passing any law impairing the obligation of contracts. The state constitution has also provided that private property shall not be taken for public uses without just compensation.

There is nothing in the act under which the patent in this case was granted which gives to the owner of the adjacent lands the exclusive right to a water grant so as to deprive the legislature of the power of granting it to another. The object of the act was to authorize the commissioners of the land office, in their discretion, to make such grants in certain cases for the promotion of commerce. It was to prevent the necessity of frequent applications to the legislature for that purpose. And the prohibition against granting to any others than the owners of the adjacent land was a proper and salutary limitation of the power given to the commissioners. It never could have been intended as a restriction upon the power of the legislature. . . . The true question is whether, by authorizing the commissioners of the land office to make the grant to the plaintiff, they have precluded themselves from making a great public improvement for the benefit of commerce. I can see nothing in the constitution of this state, or of the United States which can give such an effect to the grant. On the contrary, the act itself, under which the patent issued, authorized the grant to be made only where it was deemed beneficial to commerce; and it would be directly in opposition to the spirit of the law to give a construction to this grant which would deprive the state of the power to regulate the wharves, ports, harbors, and navigable waters within its boundaries for the benefit of commerce. If that patent is to be considered a grant of a right to erect a wharf, there is an implied reservation of the right of the legislature to regulate the use of that wharf and the waters adjacent, and to fix and determine the amount of wharfage. By the common law, such a reservation was implied in every grant of that description. The basin was in fact constructed for the benefit of the public, for the safety and protection of boats navigating the canal, although individuals have acquired rights under the law in consequence of their expenditures for the public benefit. The wharf of the plaintiff, as well as the adjacent lot, might have been more valuable if the canal had terminated where it now does, and the basin had not been made; but whether it would have terminated there if the act of 1823 had not been passed, is a question which can not now be determined. The plaintiff still retains the privilege of a wharfinger, although the nature of the business is materially changed by the making of the canal and the construction of the basin. His private property has not been taken for the public use, and there has been no violation of any contract on the part of the state, either expressed or implied, in the patent. I am satisfied the act of 1823 was valid and constitutional, and that the loss of the plaintiff, if any has been sustained by him in consequence of the building of the pier and lock, or the construction of the basin, is *damnum absque injuria,* for which no action lies against the defendants.

As to the alleged injury in consequence of the erection of the temporary bridges, I have arrived at the conclusion that there was no evidence in this case which could have authorized the jury to find the defendants guilty of erecting those bridges. . . . Some injury must necessarily have been sustained by all the owners of property on the west side of the basin during the erection of the pier, whether these bridges had been there or not; and it is doubtful whether any other mode of getting earth to the pier could have been devised, which in its effect would not have been more injurious to the wharf owners generally. . . .

But I think the whole ground of the plaintiff's suit in this case has failed, and that the judgment of the supreme court should be affirmed.

67

Veto of Maysville Road Bill (1830)

ANDREW JACKSON

"Internal improvements," a variation on the Federalist-Republican debate over the limits of the national government's power, constituted one of the major political issues in the first half of the nineteenth

Source: Richardson, ed., 2 *Messages and Papers of the Presidents* 483 (1897).

century. Those who favored a strong national government committed to assisting the economic development of the nation argued on behalf of the government spending money to develop roads, canals, and railroads that would facilitate the flow of interstate commerce. Opponents claimed these items were the sole responsibility of the states, and that federal funds should not be spent on them. In practice both sides often tailored their arguments to political exigencies, with opponents supporting expenditures in their own areas, and proponents voting against improvements in districts controlled by the other party (whichever party that might be). In 1830 Congress appropriated money to buy stock in a road from Maysville, Kentucky, to Henry Clay's hometown of Lexington. Twenty miles long, the road lay entirely within Kentucky, but its advocates claimed it made up part of the National Road through the Cumberland Gap. Jackson had signed other bills supporting local projects, and despite the constitutional arguments made in his veto, which received wide popular approval, his action was as much a slap at Clay as a statement of high principle.

See G. R. Taylor, *The Transportation Revolution, 1815–1860* (1951); and C. Goodrich, *Government Promotion of Canals and Railroads, 1800–1900* (1960).

To the House of Representatives.

Gentlemen: I have maturely considered the bill proposing to authorize "a subscription of stock in the Maysville, Washington, Paris, and Lexington Turnpike Road Company," and now return the same to the House of Representatives, in which it originated, with my objections to its passage. . . .

The constitutional power of the Federal Government to construct or promote works of internal improvement presents itself in two points of view— the first as bearing upon the sovereignty of the States within whose limits their execution is contemplated, if jurisdiction of the territory which they may occupy be claimed as necessary to their preservation and use; the second as asserting the simple right to appropriate money from the National Treasury in aid of such works when undertaken by State authority, surrendering the claim of jurisdiction. In the first view the question of power is an open one, and can be decided without the embarrassments attending the other, arising from the practice of the Government. Although frequently and strenuously attempted, the power to this extent has never been exercised by the Government in a single instance. It does not, in my opinion, possess it; and no bill, therefore, which admits it can receive my official sanction.

But in the other view of the power the question is differently situated. The ground taken at an early period of the Government was "that whenever money has been raised by the general authority and is to be applied to a particular measure, a question arises whether the particular measure be within the enumerated authorities vested in Congress. If it be, the money requisite for it may be applied to it; if not, no such application can be made." The document in which this principle was first advanced is of deservedly high authority, and should be held in grateful remembrance for its immediate agency in rescuing the country from much existing abuse and for its conservative effect upon some of the most valuable principles of the Constitution. The symmetry and purity of the Government would doubtless have been better preserved if this restriction of the power of appropriation could have been maintained without weakening its ability to fulfill the general objects of its institution, an effect so likely to attend its admission, notwithstanding its apparent fitness, that every subsequent Administration of the Government, embracing a period of thirty out of the forty-two years of its existence, has adopted a more enlarged construction of the power. It is not my purpose to detain you by a minute recital of the acts which sustain this assertion, but it is proper that I should notice some of the most prominent in order that the reflections which they suggest to my mind may be better understood. . . .

The bill before me does not call for a more definite opinion upon the particular circumstances which will warrant appropriations of money by Congress to aid works of internal improvement, for although the extension of the power to apply money beyond that of carrying into effect the object for which it is appropriated has, as we have seen, been long claimed and exercised by the Federal Government, yet such grants have always been professedly under the control of the general principle that the works which might be thus aided should be "of a general, not local, national, not State," character. A disregard of this distinction would of necessity lead to the subversion of the federal system. That even this is an unsafe one, arbitrary in its nature, and liable, consequently, to great abuses, is too obvious to require the confirmation of experience. It is, however, sufficiently definite and imperative to my mind to forbid my approbation of any bill having the character of the one under consideration. I have given to its provisions all the reflection demanded by a just regard for the interests of those of our fellow-citizens who have desired its passage, and by the respect which is due to a coördinate branch of the Government, but I am not able to view it in any other light than as a measure of purely local character; or, if it can be considered national, that no further distinction between the appropriate duties of the General and State Governments need be attempted, for there can be no local interest that may not with equal propriety be denominated national. It has no connection with any established system of improvements; is exclusively within the limits of a State, starting at a point on the Ohio River and running out 60 miles to an interior town, and even as far as the State is interested conferring partial instead of general advantages. . . .

In the other view of the subject, and the only remaining one which it is my intention to present at this time, is involved the expediency of embarking in a system of internal improvement without a previous amendment of the Constitution explaining and defining the precise powers of the Federal Government over it. Assuming the right to appropriate money to aid in the construction of national works to be warranted by the contemporaneous and continued exposition of the Constitution, its insufficiency for the successful prosecution of them must be admitted by all candid minds. If we look to usage to define the extent of the right, that will be found so variant and embracing so much that has been overruled as to involve the whole subject in great uncertainty and to render the execution of our respective duties in relation to it replete with difficulty and embarrassment. It is in regard to such works and the acquisition of additional territory that the practice obtained its first footing. In most, if not all, other disputed questions of appropriation the construction of the Constitution may be regarded as unsettled if the right to apply money in the enumerated cases is placed on the ground of usage. . . .

If it be the wish of the people that the construction of roads and canals should be conducted by the Federal Government, it is not only highly expedient, but indispensably necessary, that a previous amendment of the Constitution, delegating the necessary power and defining and restricting its exercise with reference to the sovereignty of the States, should be made. Without it nothing extensively useful can be effected.

68

City of New York v. Miln (1837)

New York required that all ships docking in New York harbor provide a list of passengers and post security against any becoming public charges. Miln, the master of the ship *Emily,* failed to do so, and the state imposed the statutory penalty. Miln claimed that the state had no power to pass such a law, since it encroached on congressional authority over interstate and foreign commerce. Justice Philip Barbour avoided the Commerce Clause issue and invoked, for the first time, what would

Source: 8 Peters 122 (1837).

later be called the state police power—the right of a government to take necessary steps to protect the health, safety, and welfare of its citizens. The state therefore had the right to protect itself against unwanted paupers. Common law, it should be noted, had sanctioned restrictions on paupers for centuries, and over the next century many states, relying on *Miln,* enacted laws restricting indigents. The Supreme Court finally overruled this aspect of *Miln* in Edwards v. California, 314 U.S. 160 (1941).

The Court also had a hidden agenda. Abolitionists at this time were protesting southern laws regulating the movement of free blacks within their borders, especially the free black seamen who manned ships that made stops at southern ports. In many states such free blacks were practically imprisoned while their ships were in port. The Court could hardly strike down the New York law and sustain the southern statutes, which certainly would have been challenged had *Miln* been decided otherwise.

See E. Freund, *The Police Power* (1904).

***

Justice Barbour delivered the opinion of the Court.

This case comes before this Court upon a certificate of division of the circuit court of the United States for the southern district of New York.

It was an action of debt brought in that court by the plaintiff, to recover of the defendant, as consignee of the ship called the Emily, the amount of certain penalties imposed by a statute of New York, passed February 11th, 1824; entitled, An act concerning passengers in vessels coming to the port of New York.

The statute, amongst other things, enacts, that every master or commander of any ship, or other vessel, arriving at the port of New York, from any country out of the United States, or from any other of the United States than the state of New York, shall, within twenty-four hours after the arrival of such ship or vessel in the said port, make a report in writing, on oath or affirmation, to the mayor of the city of New York, or, in case of his sickness, or absence, to the recorder of the said city, of the name, place of birth, and last legal settlement, age and occupation, of every person who shall have been brought as a passenger in such ship or vessel, on her last voyage from any country out of the United States into the port of New York, or any of the United States, and from any of the United States other than the state of New York, to the city of New York. . . .

It is contended by the counsel for the defendant, that the act in question is a regulation of commerce; that the power to regulate commerce is, by the constitution of the United States, granted to congress; that this power is exclusive, and that consequently, the act is a violation of the constitution of the United States.

On the part of the plaintiff it is argued, that an affirmative grant of power previously existing in the states to congress, is not exclusive; except 1st, where it is so expressly declared in terms, by the clause giving the power; or 2dly, where a similar power is prohibited to the states; or 3dly, where the power in the states would be repugnant to, and incompatible with, a similar power in congress: that this power falls within neither of these predicaments; that it is not, in terms, declared to be exclusive; that it is not prohibited to the states; and that it is not repugnant to, or incompatible with, a similar power in congress; and that having pre-existed in the states, they therefore have a concurrent power in relation to the subject; and that the act in question would be valid, even if it were a regulation of commerce, it not contravening any regulation made by congress.

But they deny that it is a regulation of commerce: on the contrary, they assert that it is a mere regulation of internal police, a power over which is not granted to congress; and which therefore, as well upon the true construction of the constitution, as by force of the tenth amendment to that instrument, is reserved to, and resides in the several states.

We shall not enter into any examination of the question whether the power to regulate commerce, be or be not exclusive of the states, because the opinion which we have formed renders it unnecessary: in other words, we are of opinion that the act is not a regulation of commerce, but of police; and that being thus considered, it was passed in the exercise of a power which rightfully belonged to the states.

That the state of New York possessed power to pass this law before the adoption of the constitution of the United States, might probably be taken as a truism, without the necessity of proof. . . .

The power then of New York to pass this law having undeniably existed at the formation of the constitution, the simple inquiry is, whether by that instrument it was taken from the states, and granted to congress; for if it were not, it yet remains with them.

If, as we think, it be a regulation, not of commerce, but police; then it is not taken from the states. To decide this, let us examine its purpose, the end to be attained, and the means of its attainment.

It is apparent, from the whole scope of the law, that the object of the legislature was, to prevent New York from being burdened by an influx of persons brought thither in ships, either from foreign countries, or from any other of the states; and for that purpose a report was required of the names, places of birth, &c. of all passengers, that the necessary steps might be taken by the city authorities, to prevent them from becoming chargeable as paupers.

Now, we hold that both the end and the means here used, are within the competency of the states, since a portion of their powers were surrendered to the federal government. . . .

. . . Whilst a state is acting within the legitimate scope of its power as to the end to be attained, it may use whatsoever means, being appropriate to that end, it may think fit; although they may be the same, or so nearly the same, as scarcely to be distinguishable from those adopted by congress acting under a different power: subject, only, say the Court, to this limitation, that in the event of collision, the law of the state must yield to the law of congress. The Court must be understood, of course, as meaning that the law of congress is passed upon a subject within the sphere of its power.

Even then, if the section of the act in question could be considered as partaking of the nature of a commercial regulation, the principle here laid down would save it from condemnation, if no such collision exist. . . .

Now in relation to the section in the act immediately before us, that is obviously passed with a view to prevent her citizens from being oppressed by the support of multitudes of poor persons, who come from foreign countries without possessing the means of supporting themselves. There can be no mode in which the power to regulate internal police could be more appropriately exercised. New York, from her particular situation, is, perhaps more than any other city in the Union, exposed to the evil of thousands of foreign emigrants arriving there, and the consequent danger of her citizens being subjected to a heavy charge in the maintenance of those who are poor. It is the duty of the state to protect its citizens from this evil; they have endeavoured to do so, by passing, amongst other things, the section of the law in question. We should, upon principle, say that it had a right to do so. . . .

We think it as competent and as necessary for a state to provide precautionary measures against the moral pestilence of paupers, vagabonds, and possibly convicts; as it is to guard against the physical pestilence, which may arise from unsound and infectious articles imported, or from a ship, the crew of which may be labouring under an infectious disease.

As to any supposed conflict between this provision and certain treaties of the United States, by which reciprocity as to trade and intercourse is granted to the citizens of the governments, with which those treaties were made; it is obvious to remark, that the record does not show that any person in this case was a subject or citizen of a country to which treaty stipulation applies: but, moreover, those which we have examined, stipulate that the citizens and subjects of the contracting parties shall submit themselves to the laws, decrees, and usages to which native citizens and subjects are subjected. . . .

We express no opinion on any other part of the act of the legislature of New York; because no question could arise in the case in relation to any part of the act, except that declared upon.

There is, then, no collision between the law in question, and the acts of congress just commented on; and, therefore, if the state law were to be considered as partaking of the nature of a commercial regulation; it would stand the test of the most rigid scrutiny, if tried by the standard laid down in the reasoning of the Court, quoted from the case of Gibbons against Ogden.

But we do not place our opinion on this ground. We choose rather to plant ourselves on what we consider impregnable positions. They are these: That a state has the same undeniable and unlimited jurisdiction over all persons and things, within its territorial limits, as any foreign nation; where that jurisdiction is not surrendered or restrained by the constitution of the United States. That, by virtue of this, it is not only the right, but the bounden and solemn duty of a state, to advance the safety, happiness and prosperity of its people, and to provide for its general welfare, by any and every act of legislation, which it may deem to be conducive to these ends; where the power over the particular subject, or the manner of its exercise is not surrendered or restrained, in the manner just stated. That all those powers which relate to merely municipal legislation, or what may perhaps, more properly be called *internal police,* are not thus surrendered or restrained; and that, consequently, in relation to these, the authority of a state is complete, unqualified, and exclusive.

We are aware, that it is at all times difficult to define any subject with proper precision and accuracy; if this be so in general, it is emphatically so in relation to a subject so diversified and multifarious as the one which we are now considering.

If we were to attempt it, we should say, that every law came within this description which concerned the welfare of the whole people of a state, or any individual within it; whether it related to their rights, or their duties; whether it respected them as men, or as citizens of the state; whether in their public or private relations; whether it related to the rights of persons, or of property, of the whole people of a state, or of any individual within it; and whose operation was within the territorial limits of the state, and upon the persons and things within its jurisdiction. . . .

Justice Story, dissenting.

[Justice Story first reviewed the expansive definition of commerce set out by Chief Justice Marshall in *Gibbons* v. *Ogden.*]

I admit, in the most unhesitating manner, that the states have a right to pass health laws and quarantine laws, and other police laws, not contravening the laws of congress rightfully passed under their constitutional authority. I admit, that they have a right to pass poor laws, and laws to prevent the introduction of paupers into the state, under the like qualifications. I go further, and admit, that in the exercise of their legitimate authority over any particular subject, the states may generally use the same means which are used by congress, if these means are suitable to the end. But I cannot admit that the states have authority to enact laws, which act upon subjects beyond their territorial limits, or within those limits, and which trench upon the authority of congress in its power to regulate commerce. It was said by this Court in the case of Brown v. The State of Maryland, 12 Wheat 419, that even the acknowledged power of taxation by a state, cannot be so exercised as to interfere with any regulation of commerce by congress.

It has been argued, that the act of New York is not a regulation of commerce, but is a mere police law upon the subject of paupers and it has been likened to the cases of health laws, quarantine laws, ballast laws, gunpowder laws, and others of a similar nature. The nature and character of these laws were fully considered, and the true answer given to them in the case of Gibbons v. Ogden, 9 Wheat. R. 1; and though the reasoning there given might be expanded, it cannot in its grounds and distinctions be more pointedly illustrated, or better expounded. I have already said that I admit the power of the states to pass such laws, and to use the proper means to effectuate the objects of them; but it is with this reserve, that these means are not exclusively vested in congress. A state cannot make a regulation of commerce to enforce its health laws, because it is a means withdrawn from its authority. It may be admitted that it is a means adapted to the end; but it is quite a different question whether it be a means within the competency of the state jurisdiction. The states have a right to borrow money; and borrowing by the issue of bills of credit, would certainly be an appropriate means: but we all know, that the emission of bills of credit by a state is expressly prohibited by the constitution. If the power to regulate commerce be exclusive in congress, then there is no difference between an express and an implied prohibition upon the states.

But how can it be truly said, that the act of New York is not a regulation of commerce? No one can well doubt, that if the same act had been passed by congress it would have been a regulation of commerce; and in that way, and in that only, would it be a constitutional act of congress. The right of congress to pass such an act has been expressly conceded at the argument. The act of New York purports on its very face to regulate the conduct of masters, and owners, and passengers, in foreign trade; and in foreign ports and places. Suppose the act had required, that the master and owner of ships should make report of all goods taken on board or landed in foreign ports, and of the nature, qualities, and value of such goods; could there be a doubt that it would have been a regulation of commerce? If not, in what essential respect does the requirement of a report of the passengers taken or landed in a foreign port or place, differ from the case put? I profess not to be able to see any. I listened with great attention to the argument, to ascertain upon what ground the act of New York was to be maintained, not to be a regulation of commerce. I confess that I was unable to ascertain any, from the reasoning of either of the learned counsel who spoke for the plaintiff. Their whole argument on this point seemed to me to amount to this: that if it were a regulation of commerce, still it might also be deemed a regulation of police, and a part of the system of poor laws; and therefore justifiable as a means to attain the end. In my judgment, for the reasons already suggested, that is not a just consequence, or a legitimate deduction. If the act is a regulation of commerce, and that subject belongs exclusively to congress; it is a means cut off from the range of state sovereignty and state legislation.

And this leads me more distinctly to the consideration of the other point in question; and that is, whether if the act of New York be a regulation of commerce, it is void and unconstitutional? If the power of congress to regulate commerce be an exclusive power; or if the subject matter has been constitutionally regulated by congress, so as to exclude all additional or conflicting legislation by the states; then, and in either case, it is clear, that the act of New York is void and unconstitutional. . . .

Such is a brief view of the grounds upon which my judgment is, that the act of New York is unconstitutional and void. In this opinion I have the consolation to know that I had the entire concurrence, upon the same grounds, of that great constitutional jurist, the late Mr. Chief Justice Marshall. Having heard the former arguments, his deliberate opinion was, that the act of New York was unconstitutional; and that the present case fell directly within the principles established in the case of Gibbons v. Ogden, . . . and Brown v. The State of Maryland.

69

Proprietors of the Charles River Bridge v. *Proprietors of the Warren Bridge (1837)*

The bridge case marked a major shift of emphasis between the Marshall and Taney courts. The Charles River Bridge had been built in 1785 by a state-chartered private company to connect Boston with Charleston, and

Source: 11 Peters 420 (1837).

it enjoyed a monopoly status. By 1827, however, population growth led the legislature to authorize another company to build a second bridge. The Warren Bridge could charge tolls until its costs had been recovered, and the bridge would then revert to the state and be operated toll-free. The company earned back its investment in six years, and the now toll-free Warren Bridge, of course, destroyed the profitability of the Charles River Bridge. The owners of the latter claimed that their charter implied a monopoly, and that the new bridge undermined their property rights. No doubt John Marshall would have agreed, as did Joseph Story in his dissent. But the majority opinion by the new Chief Justice, Roger Brooke Taney, reflected the Jacksonian sentiment against monopoly, as well as the belief—already prevalent in state law—that the states had the power to encourage new and dynamic capital investment for the benefit of its citizenry. Legislative sovereignty could not be bound by old technology to restrain needed development.

See S. I. Kutler, *Privilege and Creative Destruction: The Charles River Bridge Case* (1971); and R. K. Newmyer, "Justice Joseph Story, the Charles River Bridge Case and the Crisis of Republicanism," 17 *Am. J. Leg. Hist.* 232 (1973).

Chief Justice Taney delivered the opinion of the Court.

The questions involved in this case are of the gravest character, and the court have given to them the most anxious and deliberate consideration. The value of the right claimed by the plaintiffs is large in amount; and many persons may no doubt be seriously affected in their pecuniary interests by any decision which the court may pronounce; and the questions which have been raised as to the power of the several States, in relation to the corporations they have charted, are pregnant with important consequences; not only to the individuals who are concerned in the corporate franchises, but to the communities in which they exist. The court are fully sensible that it is their duty, in exercising the high powers conferred on them by the constitution of the United States, to deal with these great and extensive interests with the utmost caution; guarding, as far as they have the power to do so, the rights of property, and at the same time carefully abstaining from any encroachment on the rights reserved to the States. . . .

Borrowing, as we have done, our system of jurisprudence from the English law; and having adopted, in every other case, civil and criminal, its rules for the construction of statutes; is there any thing in our local situation, or in the nature of our political institutions, which should lead us to depart from the principle where corporations are concerned? . . . We think not; and it would present a singular spectacle, if, while the courts in England are restraining, within the strictest limits, the spirit of monopoly, and exclusive privileges in nature of monopolies, and confining corporations to the privileges plainly given to them in their charter; the courts of this country should be found enlarging these privileges by implication; and construing a statute more unfavorably to the public, and to the rights of the community, than would be done in a case in an English court of justice.

But we are not now left to determine, for the first time, the rules by which public grants are to be construed in this country. The subject has already been considered in this court; and the rule of construction, above stated, fully established. . . .

. . . The case most analogous to this, and in which the question came more directly before the court, is the case of the Providence Bank *v.* Billings. . . .

It may, perhaps, be said, that in the case of the Providence Bank, this court were speaking of the taxing power; which is of vital importance to the very existence of every government. But the object and end of all government is to promote the happiness and prosperity of the community by which it is established; and it can never be assumed, that the government intended to diminish its power of accomplishing the end for which it was created. And in a country like ours, free, active, and enterprising, continually advancing in numbers and wealth, new channels of communication are daily found necessary, both for travel and trade; and are essential to the comfort, convenience, and prosperity of the people. A State ought never to be presumed to surrender this power, because, like the taxing power, the whole community have an interest in preserving it undiminished. And when a corporation alleges, that a State has surrendered for seventy years, its power of improvement and public accommodation, in a great and important line of travel, along which a vast number of its citizens must daily pass; the community have a right to insist, in the language of this court above quoted, "that its abandonment ought not to be presumed, in a case, in which the deliberate purpose of the State to abandon it does not appear." . . . While the rights of private property are sacredly guarded, we must not forget that the community also have rights, and that the happiness and well being of every citizen depends on their faithful preservation.

Adopting the rule of construction above stated as the settled one, we proceed to apply it to the charter of 1785, to the proprietors of the Charles River Bridge. This act of incorporation is in the usual form, and the privileges such as are commonly given to corporations of that kind. It confers on them the ordinary faculties of a corporation, for the purpose of building the bridge; and establishes certain rates of toll, which the company are authorized to take. This is the whole grant. There is no exclusive privilege given to them over the waters of Charles River, above or below their bridge. No right to erect another bridge themselves, nor to prevent other persons from erecting one. No engagement from the State that another shall not be erected; and no undertaking not to sanction competition, nor to make improvements that may diminish the amount of its income. Upon all these subjects the charter is silent; and nothing is said in it about a line of travel, so much insisted on in the argument, in which they are to have exclusive privileges. No words are used, from which an intention to grant any of these rights can be inferred. If the plaintiff is entitled to them, it must be implied, simply, from the nature of the grant; and cannot be inferred from the words by which the grant is made.

The relative position of the Warren Bridge has already been described. It does not interrupt the passage over the Charles River Bridge, nor make the way to it or from it less convenient. None of the faculties or franchises granted to that corporation have been revoked by the legislature, and its right to take the tolls granted by the charter remains unaltered. In short, all the franchises and rights of property enumerated in the charter, and there mentioned to have been granted to it, remain unimpaired. But its income is destroyed by the Warren Bridge; which, being free, draws off the passengers and property which would have gone over it, and renders their franchise of no value. This is the gist of the complaint. For it is not pretended that the erection of the Warren Bridge would have done them any injury, or in any degree affected their right of property, if it had not diminished the amount of their tolls. In order then to entitle themselves to relief, it is necessary to show that the legislature contracted not to do the act of which they complain, and that they impaired, or, in other words, violated that contract by the erection of the Warren Bridge.

The inquiry then is, Does the charter contain such a contract on the part of the State? Is there any such stipulation to be found in that instrument? It must be admitted on all hands that there is none,—no words that even relate to another bridge, or to the diminution of their tolls, or to the line of travel. If a contract on that subject can be gathered from the charter, it must be by implication, and cannot be found in the words used. Can such an agreement be implied? The rule of construction before stated is an answer to the question. In charters of this description, no rights are taken from the public, or given to the corporation, beyond those which the words of the charter, by their natural and proper construction, purport to convey. There are no words which import such a contract as the plaintiffs in error contend for, and none can be implied; and the same answer must be given to them that was given by this court to the Providence Bank. 4 Pet. 514. The whole community are interested in this inquiry, and they have a right to require that the power of promoting their comfort and convenience, and of advancing the public prosperity, by providing safe, convenient, and cheap ways for the transportation of produce and the purposes of travel, shall not be construed to have been surrendered or diminished by the State, unless it shall appear by plain words that it was intended to be done. . . .

And what would be the fruits of this doctrine of implied contracts on the part of the States, and of property in a line of travel by a corporation, if it should now be sanctioned by this court? To what results would it lead us? If it is to be found in the charter to this bridge, the same process of reasoning must discover it in the various acts which have been passed, within the last forty years, for turnpike companies. And what is to be the extent of the privileges of exclusion on the different sides of the road? The counsel who have so ably argued this case, have not attempted to define it by any certain boundaries. How far must the new improvement be distant from the old one? How near may you approach without invading its rights in the privileged line? If this court should establish the principles now contended for, what is to become of the numerous railroads established on the same line of travel with turnpike companies; and which have rendered the franchises of the turnpike corporations of no value? Let it once be understood that such charters carry with them these implied contracts, and give this unknown and undefined property in a line of travelling, and you will soon find the old turnpike corporations awakening from their sleep, and calling upon this court to put down the improvements which have taken their place. The millions of property which have been invested in railroads and canals, upon lines of travel which had been before occupied by turnpike corporations, will be put in jeopardy. We shall be thrown back to the improvements of the last century, and obliged to stand still, until the claims of the old turnpike corporations shall be satisfied, and they shall consent to permit these States to avail themselves of the lights of modern science, and to partake of the benefit of those improvements which are now adding to the wealth and prosperity, and the convenience and comfort of every other part of the civilized world. Nor is this all. This court will find itself compelled to fix, by some arbitrary rule, the width of this new kind of property in a line of travel; for if such a right of property exists, we have no lights to guide us in marking out its extent, unless, indeed, we resort to the old feudal grants, and to the exclusive rights of ferries, by prescription, between towns; and are prepared to decide that when a turnpike road from one town to another had been made, no railroad or canal, between these two points, could afterwards be established. This court are not prepared to sanction principles which must lead to such results.

70

Nickerson's Case (1837)

Family law, like land and contract law, derived from English custom, and the traditional legal view was patriarchal and authoritarian. Although a single woman had substantial legal rights, she lost nearly all

---

Source: 19 Wendall 16 (New York 1837).

of them after marriage. Two, as the wedding rites proclaimed, became one, but in law that one was the husband, who had extensive powers over the person and property of his wife and of their children. Children, in fact, had no legal rights, and were considered the property of their fathers. The state, as a result, tended to interfere very little in family matters, and when it did, it gave great weight to the father's presumptive claims.

Some transitions did take place in the Jacksonian era, and one should compare this case to Document 72. In this case the wife had separated from her husband, and the court, showing an unusually heavy reliance on English precedent at this late date, upheld a traditional patriarchal view of the family, with the child as the father's "property." While this is nominally a dispute over custody of the child, the judge's opinion is best understood as a commentary on the status of women.

See C. N. Degler, *At Odds: Women and Family in America* (1980); and N. Basch, *In the Eyes of the Law: Women, Marriage and Property in Nineteenth Century New York* (1982).

Chief Justice Nelson

The father is the natural guardian of his infant children, and in the absence of good and sufficient reasons shown to the court, such as ill usage, grossly immoral principles or habits, want of ability, &c. is entitled to their custody, care and education. All the authorities concur on this point. . . .

Many of the cases are very strong and decisive in vindication of this paternal authority. In *The King* v. *De Manneville,* 5 East, 221, the child was only eight months old, and had been forcibly taken from the mother, and there was some ground of apprehension that the father intended to carry it out of the kingdom. But the court refused to interfere. Lord Ellenborough observed, that the father was the person entitled by law to the custody of his child: that if he abused the right to the detriment of the child, the court would protect it. Having the legal right, and not having abused it in that case, he was entitled to have it restored to him. The case of Mr. *Lytton* and *Sir W. Murray,* referred to by Lawrence, J. in the same case, were equally decisive upon the point. In the case of De Manneville, the mother had separated from her husband on an allegation of ill usage, and taken the child with her. This same case afterwards came before Lord Eldon, 10 Vesey, 51, who also refused the mother the custody of the child, as she had withdrawn herself from the protection of her husband; but restrained him from removing the child out of the kingdom. . . . In the great case of *Wellesley* v. *The Duke of Beaufort,* 2 Russell, 9, Lord Eldon, in vindicating the power of the court of chancery to control the authority of the father over his infant children, concedes that "the law makes the father the guardian of his children by nature and by nurture;" and places the right of the court to interfere upon the abuse of the trust, or special interest of the child. The same ground is stated in *Lyons* v. *Blenkin,* Jacob, 245, 4 Cond. Ch. R. 120. So fully does the law recognize the authority of the father on this subject, that he is permitted to perpetuate it beyond his own life; for he may by deed, or will duly executed, "dispose of the custody and tuition of such (his) child, during his minority or for any less time to any person or persons in possession or remainder." . . .

In one specified case, the revised statutes have enlarged the power of this court over the subject beyond that which it appears from the authorities above referred to existed at common law; and provide, that on the application of the mother, being an inhabitant of this state, in case the husband and wife live in a state of separation without being divorced, "the court on due consideration may award the charge and custody of the child so brought before it (on *habeas corpus*) to the mother, for such time, under such regulations and restrictions, and with such provisions and directions as the case may require." . . . It may be well doubted, I think, whether this statute was intended to apply where the wife withdraws from the protection of the husband and lives separate from him without any reasonable excuse; because then the separation would be unauthorized, and in violation of the law of the land. It was probably designed to remove the difficulty that existed at common law in denying or restraining the authority of the father in the case of an authorized separation, such as for ill usage, or by consent, where no ground existed for impeaching that authority upon common law principles. The legislature could not have intended that the court should ever award to the mother the care and education of her minor children, when she had wilfully and without pretence of excuse, abandoned her family and the protection of her husband, if he was in a situation to take care of them, and no well founded objection existed in the case.

The interference of the court with the relation of father and child, by withdrawing the latter from the natural affection, kindness and obligations of the former, is a delicate and strong measure; and the power should never be exerted except for the most sound and solid reasons. In this country, the hopes of the child in respect to its education and future advancement, is mainly dependent upon the father; for this he struggles and toils through life; the desire of its accomplishment operating as one of the most powerful incentives to industry and thrift. The violent abruption of this relation would not only tend to wither these motives to action, but necessarily in time, alienate the father's natural affections; and if property should be accumulated, the child under such circumstances could hardly expect to inherit it.

In view of the foregoing rights of the father, and duty of the court, I have diligently and carefully examined the facts disclosed in the affidavits, and feel myself bound to say that upon the whole, nothing appears that can justify the conclusion that the father is not a fit and proper person to have the care and education of his child, or that it would be for the interest of the child pecuniarily or otherwise, to commit its custody to the mother, according to the principles of the common law, and the numerous adjudged cases already referred to. I must also say, that unless the case can be materially varied, Mrs. Nickerson has greatly mistaken the obligations and duties which devolved upon her by the marriage vow; and that she is now living in a state unauthorized by the law of the land. The statute . . . enumerates the cases in which a separation may be legalized, either by a dissolution of the marriage contract or by a divorce from bed and board. The course of the decisions of the court of chancery clearly show that no divorce or separation could be decreed upon the facts before me.

It is, no doubt, possible that the home of the wife may be made intolerable without any actual violence committed upon her person; harsh and cruel usage that would justify a separation, may be practised towards her short of this by an unkind husband, and this is what seems intended to be *intimated* in the affidavits opposing this motion. Upon questions, however, involving such solemn considerations, and so deeply affecting the future condition and character of the parties we cannot act upon *insinuations.* We regard only the facts. The character of the husband in this case, is very strongly supported by his neighbors and acquaintances who have known him from infancy. They declared upon oath that he is a young man of sober, moral and industrious habits, and express the belief that he has ever conducted towards his wife with kindness and affection. . . . Under all this weight of evidence, it is difficult for us to conclude that he has meanly and secretly outraged her affections, or sought the privacy of the conjugal relations to torture her feelings and thus render her life wretched and insupportable with him, at the same time concealing from his neighbors and even intimate friends any apparent unkindness or want of affection.

71

Parker v. *Foote (1838)*

An essential element of English property law had been the idea of prescription, whereby long usage endowed the property with certain rights. The common law rule of "ancient lights" enabled the owner of

Source: 19 Wendell 309 (New York 1838).

a building to prevent his neighbor from erecting any structure that would interfere with his enjoyment of the sunlight that had tradition-ally shone on his building. Again, a rule that made sense in a relatively static society poved anachronistic in a dynamic economy in which growth was considered an essential element of progress. In this case, the New York court, following the arguments of Judge James Gould of Connecticut regarding water rights, did away with the notion of pre-scriptive rights. This case must be seen along with Documents 61, 65, 69, and 81 as illustrative of the developmental concept of property adopted by American state courts as opposed to the traditional, static concept embedded in English precedents.

See M. J. Horwitz, *The Transformation of American Law, 1780–1860* (1977).

Judge Bronson

The modern doctrine of presuming a right, by grant or otherwise, to ease-ments and incorporeal hereditaments after 20 years of uninterrupted adverse enjoyment, exerts a much wider influence in quieting possession, than the old doctrine of title by prescription, which depended on immemorial usage. The period of 20 years has been adopted by the courts in analogy to the statute limiting an entry into lands; but as the statute does not apply to incorporeal rights, the adverse user is not regarded as a legal bar, but only as a ground for presuming a right, either by grant or in some other form. . . .

To authorize the presumption, the enjoyment of the easement must not only be uninterrupted for the period of 20 years, but it must be adverse, not by leave or favor, but under a claim or assertion of right; and it must be with the knowledge and acquiescence of the owner. . . . To this doctrine I cannot subscribe. . . . I think it sufficient at this time to say, that in whatever manner the water may be appropriated or enjoyed, it must, of necessity, be either rightful or wrongful. The use of the stream must be such as is authorized by the title of the occupant to the soil over which the water flows, or it must be a usurpation on the rights of another. If the enjoyment is rightful, there can be no occasion for presuming a grant. The title of the occupant is as perfect at the outset, as it can be after the lapse of a century. If the user be wrongful, a usurpation to any extent upon the rights of another, it is then adverse; and if acquiesced in for 20 years, a reasonable foundation is laid for presuming a grant. If the enjoyment is not according to the title of the occupant, the injured party may have redress by action. His remedy does not depend on the question whether he has built on his mill site or otherwise appropriated the stream to his own use. It is enough that his right has been invaded; and although in a particular case he may be entitled to recover only nominal damages, that will be a sufficient vindication of his title, and will put an end to all ground for presuming a grant. . . .

The presumption we are considering is a mixed one of law and fact. The inference that the right is in him who has the enjoyment, so long as nothing appears to the contrary, is a natural one—it is a presumption of fact. But adverse enjoyment, when left to exert only its natural force as mere presumptive evidence, can never conclude the true owner. No length of possession could work such a consequence. Hence the necessity of fixing on some definite period of enjoyment, and making that operate as a presumptive bar to the rightful owner. This part of the rule is wholly artificial; it is a presumption of mere law. In general, questions depending upon mixed presumptions of this description must be submitted to the jury, under proper instructions from the court. The difference between length of time which operates as a bar to a claim and that which is only used by way of evidence was very clearly stated by Ld. Mansfield, in the Mayor, etc., v. Horner, Cowp., 102. "A jury is concluded," he says, "by length of time that operates as a bar, as where the Statute of Limitations is pleaded in bar to a debt; although the jury is satisfied that the debt is due and unpaid, it is still a bar. So in the case of prescription, if it be time out of mind, a jury is bound to conclude the right from that prescription, if there could be a legal commencement of the right. But length of time used merely by way of evidence may be left to the consideration of a jury to be credited or not, and to draw their inference one way or the other, according to circumstances." In Darwin v. Upton, 2 Saund. 175, n. 2, the question related to lights, and it was said by the same learned judge that "Acquiescence for 20 years is such decisive presumption of a right by grant or otherwise, that unless contradicted or explained, the jury ought to believe it; but it is impossible that length of time can be said to be an absolute bar, like a Statute of Limitations; it is certainly a presumptive bar which ought to go to the jury." . . .

In a plain case, where there is no evidence to repeal the presumption arising from 20 years' uninterrupted adverse user of an incorporeal right, the judge may very properly instruct the jury that it is their duty to find in favor of the party who has had the enjoyment; but still it is a question for the jury. The judge erred in this case in wholly withdrawing that question from the consideration of the jury. On this ground, if no other, the verdict must be set aside.

The bill of exceptions presents another question which may probably arise on a second trial, and it seems proper, therefore, to give it some examination.

As neither light, air nor prospect can be the subject of a grant, the proper presumption, if any, to be made in this case, is that there was some covenant or agreement not to obstruct the lights. . . .

Most of the cases on the subject we have been considering relate to ways, commons, markets, water-courses, and the like, where the user or enjoyment, if not rightful, has been an immediate and continuing injury to the person against whom the presumption is made. His property has either been invaded, or his beneficial interest in it has been rendered less valuable. The injury has been of such a character that he might have immediate redress by action. But in the case of windows overlooking the land of another, the injury, if any, is merely ideal or imaginary. The light and air which they admit are not the subjects of property beyond the moment of actual occupancy; and for overlooking one's privacy no action can be maintained. The party has no remedy but to build on the adjoining land, opposite the offensive window. . . . Upon what principle the courts in England have applied the same rule of presumption to two classes of cases so essentially different in character, I have been unable to discover. If one commit a daily trespass on the land of another, under a claim of right to pass over, or feed his cattle upon it; or divert the water from his mill, or throw it back upon his land or machinery; in these and the like cases long continued acquiescence affords strong presumptive evidence of right. But in the case of lights there is no adverse user, nor, indeed, any use whatever of another's property; and no foundation is laid for indulging any presumption against the rightful owner.

The learned judges who have laid down this doctrine have not told us upon what principle or analogy in the law it can be maintained. They tell us that a man may build at the extremity of his own land, and that he may lawfully have windows looking out upon the lands of his neighbor. . . . The reason why he may lawfully have such windows must be because he does his neighbor no wrong; and, indeed, so it is adjudged, as we have already seen; and yet, somehow or other, by the exercise of a lawful right in his own land for 20 years, he acquires a beneficial interest in the land of his neighbor. The original proprietor is still seised of the fee, with the privilege of paying taxes and assessments; but the right to build on the land, without which city and village lots are of little or no value, has been destroyed by a lawful window. How much land can thus be rendered useless to the owner remains yet to be settled. . . . Now what is the acquiescence which concludes the owner? . . . How, then, has he forfeited the beneficial interest in his property? He has neglected to incur the expense of building a wall 20 or 50 feet high, as the case may be—not for his own benefit, but for the sole purpose of annoying his neighbor. That was his only remedy. A wanton act of this kind, although done in one's own land, is calculated to render a man odious. Indeed, an attempt has been made to sustain an action for erecting such a wall. Mahan v. Brown, 13 Wend., 261.

There is, I think, no principle upon which the modern English doctrine on the subject of lights can be supported. It is an anomaly in the law. It may do well enough in England; and I see that it has recently been sanctioned with some qualification, by an Act of Parliament. Stat. 2 & 3 Wm. IV., ch. 71, sec. 3. But it cannot be applied in the growing cities and villages of this country, without working the most mischievous consequences. It has never, I think, been deemed a part of our law. 3 Kent, Com., 446, n. a. Nor do I find that it has been adopted in any of the States. . . . It cannot be necessary to cite cases to prove that those portions of the common law of England which are hostile to the spirit of our institutions, or which are not adapted to the existing state of things in this country, form no part of our law. And besides, it would be difficult to prove that the rule in question was known to the common law previous to Apr. 19, 1775.

72

Mercein v. *People ex. rel. Barry (1840)*

It is amazing to see a case like this appear in New York just a few years after *Nickerson* (Document 70), for it completely abandoned the traditional paternalism and espoused what we would consider a modern rule in awarding custody of children; namely, trying to determine the best interests of the child. As in *Nickerson,* the parents lived apart and evidently could not divorce. The child is under three, delicate and sickly, and one sees the assumption here that young children had especial need for maternal care. For the next 125 years there would be a presumption in favor of the mother in custody suits.

See materials cited for Document 70, as well as a case decided soon after this, *Gilkeson* v. *Gilkeson* (1851), in Zainaldin, *Law in Antebellum Society* (1983).

Senator Paige

. . . The father's right to his child is not absolute and inalienable. In those American cases which uphold to the greatest extent the right of the father, it is conceded that it may be lost by his ill usage, immoral principles or habits, or by his inability to provide for his children. But the great principle which runs through nearly all the American and the earlier English cases, is that which is stated by *Thompson, Ch. J. in the matter of Waldron,* 13 *Johns.* 418,

---

Source: 22 Wendall 65 (New York 1840).

when speaking of the custody of the infant, in the case of the claim made by the father, to such custody, viz: "It is the benefit and welfare of the infant to which the attention of the court ought principally to be directed." As a necessary result of this principle, it follows that the custody of infant children must always be regulated by judicial discretion, exercised in reference to their best interests. Where an infant is brought up on habeas corpus, the court will not decide upon the right of guardianship, and if there is no improper restraint, the court will not deliver over the infant to the custody of another. If the infant is competent to form a judgment and declare his election, the court will after examination allow him to go where he pleases, otherwise will exercise its judgment for him; and this judgment is to be exercised (being in lieu of the judgment of the infant) with reference to the interest and welfare of the infant. . . . The interest of the infant is deemed paramount to the claims of both parents. This is the predominant question which is to be considered by the court or tribunal before whom the infant is brought. The rights of the parents must in all cases yield to the interests and welfare of the infant. These principles were recognized and adjudged as a part of the law of this state, in the cases last referred to. And if the cases of *The People* v. *Chegaray,* 18 *Wen.* 640, and of *Nickerson,* 19 *Wen.* 16, conflict with these authorities, they are in my judgment, to the extent of such conflict, a departure from the law as established in the state. But even in the case of *Nickerson,* relied on by the relator, *Nelson, Ch. J.,* admits the general rule above stated. He says, "Nothing appears to show that the father is not a fit and proper person to have the care and education of his child, or that it would be for the interest of the child pecuniarily or otherwise, to commit its custody to the mother." It will be found that in a great variety of cases, courts have, in the exercise of a judicial discretion as to the custody of infant children, committed them to the custody of the mother, or of some third person notwithstanding, and in opposition to the claims of the father to such custody.

By the law of nature, the father has no paramount right to the custody of his child. By that law the wife and child are equal to the husband and father; but inferior and subject to their sovereign. The head of a family, in his character of husband and father, has no authority over his wife and children; but in his character of sovereign he has. On the establishment of civil societies, the power of the chief of a family as sovereign, passes to the chief or government of the nation. And the chief or magistrate of the nation not possessing the requisite knowledge necessary to a judicious discharge of the duties of guardianship and education of children, such portion of the sovereign power as relates to the discharge of their duties, is transferred to the parents, subject to such restrictions and limitations as the sovereign power of the nation think proper to prescribe. There is no parental authority independent of the supreme power of the state. But the former is derived altogether from the latter. In the civil state there is no inequality between the father and mother. Ordinarily a child, during infancy, is entirely under the discipline of its mother; and very frequently wives discharge the duty of education of their children better than the husbands. *De Felice, Lectures on*

Natural Rights—Lecture 30. It seems then, that by the law of nature, the father has no paramount inalienable right to the custody of his child. And the civil or municipal law in setting bounds to his parental authority, and in entirely or partially depriving him of it in cases where the interests and welfare of his child require it, does not come in conflict with or subvert any of the principles of the natural law. The moment a child is born, it owes allegiance to the government of the country of its birth, and is entitled to the protection of that government. And such government is obligated by its duty of protection, to consult the welfare, comfort and interests of such child in regulating its custody during the period of its minority. By the civil code of *Austria,* where husband and wife are separated, and cannot agree which shall have the charge of the education of the children, the mother has the custody of *males* until they arrive at the full age of *four years,* and of *females* until the full age of *seven years.*

The law of England at the time of the American revolution and even until after the year 1800, in relation to the custody of infant children, was the same as I understand it to be in this state. I refer to the speech of *Lord Lyndhurst* in the house of lords on the 30th July, 1838, on the bill in relation to the custody of infants, 44 *vol. Parl. Debates, 3 Series, p.* 771, he says: "As the law now stood, the father of a child born in lawful wedlock was entitled to the entire and absolute control and custody of that child, and to exclude from any share in that control and custody the mother of that child. The mother might be the most virtuous woman that ever lived, amiable in her manners, fond and attached to her children; the father, on the other hand, might be profligate in character, brutal in manner, living in adultery, and yet would have the right, under the existing law, to the custody of the children of his marriage, to the exclusion of even access to them of his wife, their mother." *Lord Denman,* the chief justice of the queen's bench, in a speech on the same subject in the house of lords, on the 18th July, 1839, 49 *vol. Parl. Debates, p.* 494, says: "In the case of *The King* vs. *Greenhill,* which had been decided in 1836, before himself and the other judges of the king's bench, he believed that there was not one judge who had not felt ashamed of the state of the law, and that it was such as to render it odious in the eyes of the country. The effect in that case was to enable the father to take his children from his young and blameless wife, and place them in the charge of a woman with whom he then cohabited."

If such was the state of the English law, Lord Denman might well say he was ashamed of it, and that it was odious in the eyes of the country. This state has never been disgraced by laws so subversive of the welfare of infant children, of the rights of mothers, and of the morals of the people. In 1839, through the untiring and praiseworthy exertions of Serjeant *Talfourd,* the British parliament modified the relation to the custody of infants, by an act which authorizes the lord chancellor and master of the rolls, to make an order for the access of the mother to her infant children, and if the infant be within the age of seven years, to make an order that it be delivered to and remain in the custody of the mother until attaining such age.

Upon a review of all the authorities binding upon the courts of this state, I have come to the undoubting conclusion, that the right of the father to the custody of his child is not absolute, and that such custody is referrable to its interest and welfare, and is to be selected by the court in the exercise of a sound judicial discretion, irrespective of the claims of either parent. This conclusion I believe is warranted by the law of this state, as well as by the law of nature. A sense of parental duty ought ever to withhold a parent from pressing his or her claims to the custody of a child, whenever the true interests of such child forbid it; and whenever this parental obligation fails to influence the conduct of the parent, it is fortunate that the enlightened principles of our law authorize our courts to interpose in behalf of the child.

If then a judicial discretion is to be exercised in relation to the welfare, comfort and interest of the infant, as connected with her custody, was this discretion improperly exercised in this case by Judge Inglis? The infant was under three years of age; was delicate and sickly, requiring peculiarly a mother's care and attention. The mother possessed every qualification to bestow this care and attention. Ought the judge to have delivered this infant, under such circumstances, over to the father, or to have allowed it to remain in the custody of the mother? I confess I have no hesitation in saying that I entirely concur in the position of the chancellor, viz: that all other things being equal, the mother is the most proper person to be entrusted with the custody of a child of this tender age. He says, "the law of nature has given to her an attachment for her infant offspring which no other relative will be likely to possess in an equal degree. And where no sufficient reasons exist for depriving her of the care and nurture of her child, it would not be a proper exercise of discretion in any court to violate the law of nature in this respect." I am, therefore, in favor of reversing the judgment of the supreme court.

73

Swift v. Tyson (1842)

Although the Court had declared in 1812 that no federal common law existed (Document 50), the different commercial rules in the various states proved burdensome in the face of growing national markets. No

Source: 16 Peters 1 (1842)

member of the Supreme Court at this time was more sensitive to the demands upon the legal system of a rapidly expanding economy than Joseph Story, whose various treatises on several aspects of commercial law were considered definitive through much of the nineteenth century. He had never accepted *United States* v. *Hudson and Goodwin,* and throughout his career on the bench he attempted to achieve uniformity of decisional rules in federal courts.

In *Swift* the Court had to decide whether a federal district court in New York should follow that state's common law in a question of commercial law, or whether it could look elsewhere. For a unanimous bench, Story ruled that federal courts under Section 34 of the Judiciary Act were bound only by local *statutory* rules, and in the absence of specific laws, could apply a generalized federal commercial common law. Following "Old Swifty," as it came to be called, federal courts did help fashion a somewhat uniform national business law, but the case also led to problems in forum shopping, as commercial litigants would seek to have their cases shifted from state to federal courts to evade stringent state regulations. The demise of Old Swifty came in Erie Railroad v. Tompkins, 304 U.S. 64 (1938).

See R. Birdwell and R. U. Whitten, *The Constitution and the Common Law* (1977); T. Freyer, *Harmony and Dissonance: The Swift and Erie Cases . . .* (1981); and C. A. Heckman, "The Relationship of *Swift* v. *Tyson* to the Status of Commercial Law in the Nineteenth Century . . ." 17 *Am. J. Leg. His.* 246 (1973).

~~~~~~

Justice Story delivered the opinion of the Court.

There is no doubt, that a bonâ fide holder of a negotiable instrument for a valuable consideration, without any notice of facts which impeach its validity as between the antecedent parties, if he takes it under an endorsement made before the same becomes due, holds the title unaffected by these facts, and may recover thereon, although as between the antecedent parties the transaction may be without any legal validity. . . .

In the present case, the plaintiff is a bonâ fide holder without notice for what the law deems a good and valid consideration, that is, for a pre-existing debt; and the only real question in the cause is, whether, under the circumstances of the present case, such a pre-existing debt constitutes a valuable consideration in the sense of the general rule applicable to negotiable instruments. We say, under the circumstances of the present case, for the acceptance having been made in New York, the argument on behalf of the defendant is, that the contract is to be treated as a New York contract, and therefore to be governed by the laws of New York, as expounded by its

Courts, as well upon general principles, as by the express provisions of the thirty-fourth section of the judiciary act of 1789, ch. 20. And then it is further contended, that by the law of New York, as thus expounded by its Courts, a pre-existing debt does not constitute, in the sense of the general rule, a valuable consideration applicable to negotiable instruments. . . .

But, admitting the doctrine to be fully settled in New York, it remains to be considered, whether it is obligatory upon this Court, if it differs from the principles established in the general commercial law. It is observable that the Courts of New York do not found their decisions upon this point upon any local statute, or positive, fixed, or ancient local usage: but they deduce the doctrine from the general principles of commercial law. It is, however, contended, that the thirty-fourth section of the judiciary act of 1789, ch. 20, furnishes a rule obligatory upon this Court to follow the decisions of the state tribunals in all cases to which they apply. That section provides "that the laws of the several states, except where the Constitution, treaties, or statutes of the United States shall otherwise require or provide, shall be regarded as rules of decision in trials at common law in the Courts of the United States, in cases where they apply." In order to maintain the argument, it is essential, therefore, to hold, that the word "laws," in this section, includes within the scope of its meaning the decisions of the local tribunals. In the ordinary use of language it will hardly be contended that the decisions of Courts constitute laws. They are, at most, only evidence of what the laws are; and are not of themselves laws. They are often reexamined, reversed, and qualified by the Courts themselves, whenever they are found to be either defective, or ill-founded, or otherwise incorrect. The laws of a state are more usually understood to mean the rules and enactments promulgated by the legislative authority thereof, or long established local customs having the force of laws. In all the various cases which have hitherto come before us for decision, this Court have uniformly supposed, that the true interpretation of the thirty-fourth section limited its application to state laws strictly local, that is to say, to the positive statutes of the state, and the construction thereof adopted by the local tribunals, and to rights and titles to things having a permanent locality, such as the rights and titles to real estate, and other matters immovable and intraterritorial in their nature and character. It never has been supposed by us, that the section did apply, or was designed to apply, to questions of a more general nature, not at all dependent upon local statutes or local usages of a fixed and permanent operation, as, for example, to the construction of ordinary contracts or other written instruments, and especially to questions of general commercial law, where the state tribunals are called upon to perform the like functions as ourselves, that is, to ascertain upon general reasoning and legal analogies, what is the true exposition of the contract or instrument, or what is the just rule furnished by the principles of commercial law to govern the case. And we have not now the slightest difficulty in holding, that this section, upon its true intendment and construction, is strictly limited to local statutes and local usages of the character before stated, and does not extend to contracts and other instruments of a commercial nature, the true interpretation and effect whereof are to be sought, not in the decisions of the local tribunals, but in the general principles and doctrines of commercial jurisprudence. Undoubtedly, the decisions of the local tribunals upon such subjects are entitled to, and will receive, the most deliberate attention and respect of this Court; but they cannot furnish positive rules, or conclusive authority, by which our own judgments are to be bound up and governed. The law respecting negotiable instruments may be truly declared in the language of Cicero, adopted by Lord Mansfield in Luke v. Lyde, 2 Burr.R. 883, 887, to be in a great measure, not the law of a single country only, but of the commercial world.

74

Farwell v. *Boston & Worcester Railroad (1842)*

Labor law in the early nineteenth century derived almost entirely from English common law rules of master and servant. While the master had liability for any damage inflicted by his servant on a third party, three rules practically immunized employers from liability for injuries sustained by a servant in his employ. The fellow servant doctrine had developed at a time when most workingmen labored in small shops, and it could be expected that they would learn the foibles of their fellow workers and take precautions against them. Thus, if one were injured by the clumsiness of a another worker, the fault lay not with the master but with the injured worker for failing to take the necessary precautions.

The rule of contributory negligence held that if the injured worker had been in the least bit responsible, no liability attached to the employer. The third rule, assumption of risk, assumed that when an em-

Source: 45 Mass. 49 (1842).

ployer and an employee negotiated their labor agreement, the employer would inform the applicant of any unusual conditions or dangers. The employee would then bargain with the employer, and in return for higher wages, would assume all the risks involved.

Under these three rules it would be practically impossible for an injured employee in a large modern factory to win an injury award from his employer. Although Chief Justice Shaw is justly recognized as one of the most humane and creative state judges of his time, in this case he stood squarely for the traditional rules, ignoring the changes in industrial employment that had already made them obsolete. Shortly after this case, some states began to statutorily change some of the rules, especially as they applied to railroads.

See L. W. Levy, *The Law of the Commonwealth and Chief Justice Shaw* (1957); G. E. White, *Tort Law in America* (1980); and L. M. Friedman and J. Ladinsky, "Social Change and the Law of Industrial Accidents," 67 *Col. L. R.* 50 (1967).

<hr />

Chief Justice Shaw

This is an action of new impression in our courts, and involves a principle of great importance. It presents a case, where two persons are in the service and employment of one company, whose business it is to construct and maintain a rail road, and to employ their trains of cars to carry persons and merchandise for hire. They are appointed and employed by the same company to perform separate duties and services, all tending to the accomplishment of one and the same purpose—that of the safe and rapid transmission of the trains; and they are paid for their respective services according to the nature of their respective duties, and the labor and skill required for their proper performance. The question is, whether, for damages sustained by one of the persons so employed, by means of the carelessness and negligence of another, the party injured has a remedy against the common employer. It is an argument against such an action, though certainly not a decisive one, that no such action has before been maintained.

It is laid down by Blackstone, that if a servant, by his negligence, does any damage to a stranger, the master shall be answerable for his neglect. . . . This rule is obviously founded on the great principle of social duty, that every man, in the management of his own affairs, whether by himself or by his agents or servants, shall so conduct them as not to injure another; and if he does not, and another thereby sustains damage, he shall answer for it. . . . But this presupposes that the parties stand to each other in the relation of strangers, between whom there is no privity; and the action, in such case, is an action sounding in tort. . . .

But this does not apply to the case of a servant bringing his action against his own employer to recover damages for an injury arising in the course of that employment, where all such risks and perils as the employer and the servant respectively intend to assume and bear may be regulated by the express or implied contract between them, and which, in contemplation of law, must be presumed to be thus regulated.

The same view seems to have been taken by the learned counsel for the plaintiff in the argument. . . . The claim, therefore, is placed, and must be maintained, if maintained at all, on the ground of contract. As there is no express contract between the parties, applicable to this point, it is placed on the footing of an implied contract of indemnity, arising out of the relation of master and servant. It would be an implied promise, arising from the duty of the master to be responsible to each person employed by him . . . to pay for all damage occasioned by the negligence of every other person employed in the same service. If such a duty were established by law . . . it would be a rule of frequent and familiar occurrence, and its existence and application, with all its qualifications and restrictions, would be settled by judicial precedents. But we are of opinion that no such rule has been established, and the authorities, as far as they go, are opposed to the principle. . . .

The general rule, resulting from considerations as well of justice as of policy, is, that he who engages in the employment of another for the performance of specified duties and services, for compensation, takes upon himself the natural and ordinary risks and perils incident to the performance of such services, and in legal presumption, the compensation is adjusted accordingly. And we are not aware of any principle which should except the perils arising from the carelessness and negligence of those who are in the same employment. These are perils which the servant is as likely to know, and against which he can as effectually guard, as the master. They are perils incident to the service, and which can be as distinctly foreseen and provided for in the rate of compensation as any others. . . .

. . . In considering the rights and obligations arising out of particular relations, it is competent for courts of justice to regard considerations of policy and general convenience, and to draw from them such rules as will, in their practical application, best promote the safety and security of all parties concerned. This is, in truth, the basis on which implied promises are raised, being duties legally inferred from a consideration of what is best adapted to promote the benefit of all persons concerned, under given circumstances. To take the well known and familiar cases, . . . a common carrier, without regard to actual fault or neglect in himself or his servants, is made liable for all losses of goods confided to him for carriage, except those caused by the act of God or of a public enemy, because he can best guard them against all minor dangers, and because, in case of actual loss, it would be extremely difficult for the owner to adduce proof of embezzlement, or other actual fault or neglect on the part of the carrier. . . . The risk is therefore thrown upon the carrier, and he receives, in the form of payment for the carriage, a premium for the risk which he thus assumes. So of an innkeeper; he can best secure the attendance of honest and faithful servants, and guard his house against thieves. Whereas, if he were responsible only upon proof of actual negligence, he might connive . . . and even participate in the embezzlement of the property of the guests, during the hours of their necessary sleep, and yet it would be difficult, and often impossible, to prove these facts. . . .

We are of opinion that these considerations apply strongly to the case in question. Where several persons are employed in the conduct of one common enterprise or undertaking, and the safety of each depends much on the care and skill with which each other shall perform his appropriate duty, each is an observer of the conduct of the others, can give notice of any misconduct, incapacity or neglect of duty, and leave the service, if the common employer will not take such precautions, and employ such agents as the safety of the whole party may require. By these means, the safety of each will be much more effectually secured, than could be done by a resort to the common employer for indemnity in case of loss by the negligence of each other. . . .

In applying these principles to the present case, it appears that the plaintiff was employed by the defendants as an engineer, at the rate of wages usually paid in that employment, being a higher rate than the plaintiff had before received as a machinist. It was a voluntary undertaking on his part, with a full knowledge of the risks incident to the employment; and the loss was sustained by means of an ordinary casualty, caused by the negligence of another servant of the company. Under these circumstances, the loss must be deemed to be the result of a pure accident, . . . and . . . it must rest where it first fell, unless the plaintiff has a remedy against the person actually in default; of which we give no opinion.

It was strongly pressed in the argument, that [this rule] could not apply where two or more are employed in different departments of duty, at a distance from each other, and where one can in no degree control or influence the conduct of another. But we think this is founded upon a supposed distinction, on which it would be extremely difficult to establish a practical rule. When the object to be accomplished is one and the same, when the employers are the same, and the several persons employed derive their authority and their compensation from the same source, it would be extremely difficult to distinguish, what constitutes one department and what a distinct department of duty. . . . If it were made to depend upon the nearness or distance of the persons from each other, the question would immediately arise, how near or how distant must they be, to be in the same or different departments. . . .

Besides, it appears to us, that the argument rests upon an assumed principle of responsibility which does not exist. The master, in the case supposed, is not exempt from liability, because the servant has better means of providing for his safety, when he is employed in immediate connexion with those from whose negligence he might suffer; but because the *implied contract* of the master does not extend to indemnify the servant against the negligence of any one but himself; and he is not liable in tort, as for the negligence of his servant, because the person suffering does not stand towards him in the relation of a stranger, but is one whose rights are regulated by contract express or implied. . . .

In coming to the conclusion that the plaintiff, in the present case, is not entitled to recover, considering it as in some measure a nice question, we would add a caution against any hasty conclusion as to the application of this rule to a case not fully within the same principle. . . . We are far from intending to say that there are no implied warranties and undertakings arising out of the relation of master and servant. Whether, for instance, the employer would be responsible to an engineer for a loss arising from a defective or ill-constructed steam engine: Whether this would depend upon an implied warranty of its goodness and sufficiency, or upon the fact of wilful misconduct, or gross negligence on the part of the employer . . . are questions on which we give no opinion. In the present case, the claim of the plaintiff is not put on the ground that the defendants did not furnish a sufficient engine, a proper rail road track, a well constructed switch, and a person of suitable skill and experience to attend it; the gravamen of the complaint is, that that person was chargeable with negligence in not changing the switch. . . . Upon this question, supposing the accident to have occurred, and the loss to have been caused, by the negligence of the person employed to attend to and change the switch, in his not doing so in the particular case, the court are of opinion that it is a loss for which the defendants are not liable, and that the action cannot be maintained.

Plaintiff nonsuit.

75

Commonwealth v. Hunt (1842)

Most state courts continued to view labor unions, even during the Jacksonian era, as proscribed by common law rules against conspiracy. The Whig Party had a definite antilabor bias, and in this case the Whig district attorney of Boston brought an indictment charging conspiracy

Source: 45 Mass. 11 (1842).

against the Journeymen Bootmakers' Society. At the trial, Judge Peter
O. Thacher, who had on more than one occasion ruled unions to be
conspiracies, practically ordered the jury to find the labor leaders
guilty. But Chief Justice Shaw, hardly a radical, overturned the conviction on appeal, and ruled that unions were not by themselves illegal,
nor were their demands that only union members be hired. Most state
courts ignored *Hunt* and continued to follow the antiunion holding of
the Cordwainers' case (Document 62).

See E. E. Pessen, *Most Uncommon Jacksonians* (1967); J. G. Rayback, *A History
of American Labor* (1966); and W. E. Hugins, *Jacksonian Democracy and the
Working Class* (1960).

Chief Justice Shaw

We have no doubt, that by the operation of the constitution of this Commonwealth, the general rules of the common law, making conspiracy an indictable offence, are in force here. . . . Still, it is proper in this connexion to
remark, that although the common law in regard to conspiracy in this Commonwealth is in force, yet it will not necessarily follow that every indictment
at common law for this offence is a precedent for a similar indictment in this
State. The general rule of the common law is, that it is a criminal and
indictable offence, for two or more to confederate and combine together, by
concerted means, to do that which is unlawful or criminal, to the injury of
the public, or portions or classes of the community, or even to the rights of
an individual. This rule of law may be equally in force as a rule of the
common law, in England, and in this Commonwealth; and yet it must depend
upon the local laws of each country to determine, whether the purpose to
be accomplished by the combination, or the concerted means of accomplishing it, be unlawful or criminal in the respective countries. All those laws of
the parent country, whether rules of the common law, or early English
statutes, which were made for the purpose of regulating the wages of laborers, the settlement of paupers, and making it penal for any one to use a trade
or handicraft to which he had not served a full apprenticeship—not being
adapted to the circumstances of our colonial condition—were not adopted,
used or approved, and therefore [are not in force here.] . . .
 . . . It appears to us to follow, as a necessary legal conclusion, that when
the criminality of a conspiracy consists in an unlawful agreement of two or
more persons to compass or promote some criminal or illegal purpose, that
purpose must be fully and clearly stated in the indictment; and if the criminality of the offence, which is intended to be charged, consists in the agreement
to compass or promote some purpose, not of itself criminal or unlawful, by
the use of fraud, force, falsehood, or other criminal or unlawful means, such

intended use of fraud, falsehood, or other criminal or unlawful means, must be set out in the indictment. . . .

With these general views of the law, it becomes necessary to consider the circumstances of the present case, as they appear from the indictment itself, and from the bill of exceptions filed and allowed.

One of the exceptions, though not the first in the order of time, yet by far the most important, was this:

The counsel for the defendants contended, and requested the court to instruct the jury, that the indictment did not set forth any agreement to do a criminal act, or to do any lawful act by any specified criminal means, and that the agreements therein set forth did not constitute a conspiracy indictable by any law of this Commonwealth. But the judge refused so to do. . . .

We are here carefully to distinguish between the confederacy set forth in the indictment, and the confederacy or association contained in the constitution of the Boston Journeymen Bootmakers' Society, as stated in the little printed book, which was admitted as evidence on the trial. Because, though it was thus admitted as evidence, it would not warrant a conviction for any thing not stated in the indictment. It was proof, as far as it went to support the averments in the indictment. If it contained any criminal matter not set forth in the indictment, it is of no avail. . . .

Now it is to be considered, that the preamble and introductory matter in the indictment—such as unlawfully and deceitfully designing and intending unjustly to extort great sums, &c.—is mere recital, and not traversable, and therefore cannot aid an imperfect averment of the facts constituting the description of the offence. The same may be said of the concluding matter, which follows the averment, as to the great damage and oppression not only of their said masters, employing them in said art and occupation, but also of divers other workmen in the same art, mystery and occupation, to the evil example, &c. If the facts averred constitute the crime, these are properly stated as the legal inferences to be drawn from them. If they do not constitute the charge of such an offence, they cannot be aided by these alleged consequences.

Stripped then of these introductory recitals and alleged injurious consequences, and of the qualifying epithets attached to the facts, the averment is this; that the defendants and others formed themselves into a society, and agreed not to work for any person, who should employ any journeyman or other person, not a member of such society, after notice given him to discharge such workman.

The manifest intent of the association is, to induce all those engaged in the same occupation to become members of it. Such a purpose is not unlawful. It would give them a power which might be exerted for useful and honorable purposes, or for dangerous and pernicious ones. If the latter were the real and actual object, and susceptible of proof, it should have been specially charged. Such an association might be used to afford each other assistance in times of poverty, sickness and distress; or to raise their intellectual, moral and social condition; or to make improvement in their art; or for other proper purposes. Or the association might be designed for purposes of oppression and injustice. But in order to charge all those, who become members of an association, with the guilt of a criminal conspiracy, it must be averred and proved that the actual, if not the avowed object of the association, was criminal. . . .

Nor can we perceive that the objects of this association whatever they may have been, were to be attained by criminal means. The means which they proposed to employ . . . were, that they would not work for a person, who, after due notice, should employ a journeyman not a member of their society. Supposing the object of the association to be laudable and lawful, or at least not unlawful, are these means criminal? The case supposes that these persons are not bound by contract, but free to work for whom they please, or not to work, if they so prefer. In this state of things, we cannot perceive, that it is criminal for men to agree together to exercise their own acknowledged rights, in such a manner as best to subserve their own interests. One way to test this is, to consider the effect of such an agreement, where the object of the association is acknowledged on all hands to be a laudable one. Suppose a class of workmen, impressed with the manifold evils of intemperance, should agree with each other not to work in a shop in which ardent spirit was furnished, or not to work in a shop with any one who used it, or not to work for an employer, who should, after notice, employ a journeyman who habitually used it. The consequences might be the same. A workman, who, should still persist in the use of ardent spirit, would find it more difficult to get employment; a master employing such an one might, at times, experience inconvenience in his work, in losing the services of a skilful but intemperate workman. Still it seems to us, that as the object would be lawful, and the means not unlawful, such an agreement could not be pronounced a criminal conspiracy.

. . . If a large number of men, engaged for a certain time, should combine together to violate their contract, and quit their employment together, it would present a very different question. Suppose a farmer, employing a large number of men, engaged for the year, at fair monthly wages, and suppose that just at the moment that his crops were ready to harvest, they should all combine to quit his service, unless he would advance their wages, at a time when other laborers could not be obtained. It would surely be a conspiracy to do an unlawful act, though of such a character, that if done by an individual, it would lay the foundation of a civil action only, and not of a criminal prosecution. . . .

The second count . . . alleges that the defendants . . . did assemble, conspire, confederate and agree together, not to work for any master or person who should employ any workman not being a member of a certain club, society or combination, called the Boston Journeymen Bootmaker's Society, or who should break any of their by-laws [and to] compel one Isaac

B. Wait, a master cordwainer, to turn out of his employ one Jeremiah Horne. . . . So far as the averment of a conspiracy is concerned, all the remarks made in reference to the first count are equally applicable to this. . . . It was an agreement, as to the manner in which they would exercise an acknowledged right to contract with others for their labor. It does not aver a conspiracy or even an intention to raise their wages; and it appears by the bill of exceptions, that the case was not put upon the footing of a conspiracy to raise their wages. Such an agreement, as set forth in this count, would be perfectly justifiable under the recent English statute, by which this subject is regulated. . . .

Suppose a baker in a small village had the exclusive custom of his neighborhood, and was making large profits by the sale of his bread. Supposing a number of those neighbors, believing the price of his bread too high, should propose to him to reduce his prices, or if he did not, that they would introduce another baker; and on his refusal, such other baker should, under their encouragement, set up a rival establishment, and sell his bread at lower prices; the effect would be to diminish the profit of the former baker, and to the same extent to impoverish him. And it might be said and proved, that the purpose of the associates was to diminish his profits, and thus impoverish him, though the ultimate and laudable object of the combination was to reduce the cost of bread to themselves and their neighbors. The same thing may be said of all competition in every branch of trade and industry; and yet it is through that competition, that the best interests of trade and industry are promoted. It is scarcely necessary to allude to the familiar instances of opposition lines of conveyance, rival hotels, and the thousand other instances, where each strives to gain custom to himself, by ingenious improvements, by increased industry, and by all the means by which he may lessen the price of commodities, and thereby diminish the profits of others.

We think, therefore, that associations may be entered into, the object of which is to adopt measures that may have a tendency to impoverish another, that is, to diminish his gains and profits, and yet so far from being criminal or unlawful, the object may be highly meritorious and public spirited. The legality of such an association will therefore depend upon the means to be used for its accomplishment. If it is to be carried into effect by fair or honorable and lawful means, it is, to say the least, innocent; if by falsehood or force, it may be stamped with the character of conspiracy. It follows as a necessary consequence, that if criminal and indictable, it is so by reason of the criminal means intended to be employed for its accomplishment; and as a further legal consequence, that as the criminality will depend on the means, those means must be stated in the indictment. . . .

. . . [L]ooking solely at the indictment, disregarding the qualifying epithets, recitals and immaterial allegations, and confining ourselves to facts so averred as to be capable of being traversed and put in issue, we cannot perceive that it charges a criminal conspiracy punishable by law. The exceptions must, therefore, be sustained, and the judgment arrested.

What Shall Be Done with the Practice of the Courts? (1847)

DAVID FIELD

The common law and its system of special pleadings had grown enormously complex by the 1830s, and reformers began urging a complete revision of the common law and of court procedure. Law, they believed, should be clear, so that a layman could understand it; it should be embodied in a statute (positive law), and not subject to judicial whim; and the rules of court should be streamlined, abandoning the cumbersome writ system, which by then seemed to retard rather than advance justice. All of this, of course, fit in with the political reforms of the Jacksonian era, which strove to do away with special privilege—in this case, the special privileges enjoyed by lawyers through their expertise in the common law writ system.

In 1846, New York established a commission "to revise, reform, simplify, and abridge the rules and practices, pleadings, forms and proceedings" of the state's courts. The outstanding figure on the commission proved to be David Dudley Field, and thanks to his efforts the resulting New York Code of 1848, often called the Field Code, emphasized statutory law and streamlined courtroom procedure. Although conservative eastern lawyers opposed the Field reforms, western states, which lacked long traditions, soon adopted the new ideas.

See C. M. Cook, *The American Codification Movement* (1981); M. Bloomfield, "William Sampson and the Codifiers . . ." 11 *Am. J. Legal His.* 234 (1967); and R. W. Miller, *Civil Procedure . . . in Historical Perspective* (1952).

The profession stands at this time in a position in which it has not before been placed. Shall it set itself in opposition to the demands of a radical reform? shall it be indifferent to it? or shall it unite heartily in its prosecution? None can reform so well as we, as none would be benefited so much. We can not remain motionless. We must either take part in the changes or set our-

---

Source: Sprague, ed., *Papers of David Dudley Field* (1884).

selves in opposition to them, and then, as I think, be overwhelmed by them. . . .

Every consideration, as it seems to me, makes it expedient for us all now to enter heartily upon the work of amendment. Those of us who have long been laboring for a radical reformation of the law, and those who have felt less inclination for it, should find this an occasion to act together in the common pursuit of thorough and wise reforms. We feel the inconvenience of the present state of things. We know that the technicality and the drudgery of legal proceedings are discreditable to our profession. Justice is entangled in the net of forms. . . .

For all reasons, therefore, it appears to me the wiser and safer plan, when we are about it, to make a radical reform; in short, to go back to first principles, break up the present system, and reconstruct a simple and natural scheme of legal procedure. . . .

Such a reform, I am persuaded, should have in view nothing less than a uniform course of proceeding, in all cases, legal and equitable. . . .

What is meant by a uniform course of proceeding? Not that precisely the same shall take place, for all demands, and all kinds of relief. That is not possible, so long as the cases themselves differ from each other. . . .

. . . Is it practicable to abolish all the forms of action now in use in common law cases, and to substitute in their place a complaint and answer, according to the fact . . .? By practicable, I mean not possible only, but capable of being done, without failing of any of the purposes subserved by the present forms of pleading. Are these forms necessary? Are they useful? . . .

In the earliest periods of our law, every cause was commenced by an original writ, issuing out of the Court of Chancery, describing briefly the cause of action, and returnable before some of the courts of law. It was this writ which gave jurisdiction of the cause to those Courts, the writ combining the two qualities of a summons to the defendant and a commission to the Judges to hear and determine the controversy. . . . They were conceived in certain fixed forms, and, unless an original writ could be found or devised for the case, the suitor was without remedy in the courts of law.

The writs, being thus confined within certain established forms, were soon classified, and all actions at common law were accordingly divided into a certain number of classes, fifty-nine in all, according to some enumerations; the more common of which were the writ of right, dower, ejectment, debt, covenant, detinue, trespass, trespass on the case, and replevin.

These actions were all known in the time of Edward I, and, though some of them have been modified and made more comprehensive, no new action has been devised within the last three hundred years, although property has taken many new shapes, and the business of mankind has undergone a complete revolution. . . .

On the return of the original writ into the Court of Common Law, the pleadings there commenced. The plaintiff repeated the original writ, the defendant answered it. The answers also soon fell into set forms. At first the allegations were made orally, and taken down by the clerk. About the middle of the fourteenth century oral pleadings were discontinued, but the same forms were used as before, and to this day the record is framed as though the parties or their attorneys actually made their allegations in open court. . . .

The narrow spirit in which the Courts construed the language, and required the proof to correspond with the allegation, in the strictest literal sense, led to repetitions, pleonasms, and to the introduction of different counts as different ways of stating the same case. For these reasons the pleadings came in process of time to be long, overloaded with verbiage, uncouth phrases, and endless repetitions. Many rules have been established by the Courts and pleaders together, prescribing the manner of pleading and the forms of the allegations. These rules, and the commentaries upon them, form, as every lawyer knows, one of the most technical and abstruse branches of the law. They are ingenious, everybody will admit; the principal ones are founded on sound logic; others are founded on distinctions purely verbal; and many of them tend to shut out the truth, and embarrass the party in a labyrinth of forms. . . .

Of what real utility is this system? . . . There can not be any good reason why the story should not be told in the ordinary language of life, in the only language intelligible to the juries who are to decide the causes; and if that were done, the distinction of actions would cease, of course. . . .

What I propose, then, in respect to cases of legal cognizance, is this: that the present forms of action be abolished, and in their stead a complaint and answer required, each setting forth the real claim and defense of the parties. . . .

Let the plaintiff set forth his cause of action in his complaint briefly, in ordinary language, and without repetition; and let the defendant make his answer in the same way. . . . The disputed facts will be sifted from the undisputed, and the parties will go to trial knowing what they have to answer. The plaintiff will state his case as he believes it, and as he expects to prove it. The defendant, on his part, will set forth what he believes and expects to establish, and he need set forth no more. He will not be likely to aver what he does not believe. His answer will disclose the whole of his defense, because he will not be allowed to prove anything which the answer does not contain. . . .

. . . But suppose the answer to set up new facts, which the plaintiff can not deny, but which he can answer by new matter, explaining away the effect of the new facts of the answer, how, it may be asked, is the plaintiff to bring the new matter out? I answer, he may bring it out in his proof in answer to the proof on the defendant's part. . . . How will the question appear upon the pleadings? So far as the record is concerned, it will appear thus: The allegations of the complaint are admitted; a new fact is alleged on the part of the defendant; this new fact the plaintiff is considered as opposing, either by a positive denial or as capable of being explained away by other facts, and therefore not having the effect claimed for it.

Either this may be done, or the course now pursued in equity cases may be followed, of amending the complaint when new facts are brought forward by the answer. Or still another mode may be adopted—that of requiring the parties respectively to give notice to each other of their points before the trial. Something of the sort now prevails in the Court of Admiralty of this district, and in the common-law Courts of Massachusetts.

The most ample power of amendment should likewise be given to the Courts. They should be enabled to amend the pleadings, in furtherance of justice, either when they are not sufficiently precise, or when they vary from the proofs; taking care to guard the parties against injury from surprise. . . .

The legitimate end of every administration of law is to do justice, with the least possible delay and expense. Every system of pleading is useful only as it tends to this end. This it can do but in one of two ways: either by enabling the parties the better to prepare for trial, or by assisting the jury and the Court in judging the cause. Let us consider it, then, in these two aspects:

First, as it enables the parties to prepare for trial. This it can only do by informing them of each other's case. To make them settle beforehand wherein they disagree, so as to enable them to dispense with unnecessary proofs, and to be prepared with those which are necessary, is the legitimate end of pleadings, so far as the parties are concerned. Now, no system could accomplish this more effectually than the one proposed. . . .

Is not this a certain way of apprising the parties of what they have to try? And is it not a simpler and easier way of doing it, than by the long labyrinth of replications, rejoinders, and the like? All this excessive subtlety and refinement on the one hand, and this monstrous jargon and prolixity on the other, can not be necessary to inform the parties of the points in dispute between them. . . .

Second, as it assists the jury and the Court in performing their functions. An opinion prevails that nothing but common-law issues are fit for a jury. Many lawyers are wedded to the system of pleading according to the ancient rules, though they admit and deplore the imperfections of our present practice. It is said that the production of the issue disentangles the case, lessens the number of questions of fact, and separates them from the questions of law.

Now, I deny, in the first place, that the production of an issue, according to the course of the common law, does really lessen the number of questions of fact. The declaration may contain any number of counts, each setting forth different causes of action, or the same cause of action in different forms. If the same plea is put into all the counts, there will be as many issues as there are counts. But the defendant may plead as many pleas to each count as he likes; and the plaintiff, with leave of the Court, may put in as many replications to each plea as he may happen to have answers to it. . . .

But, apart from this, is it possible for any system of pleading to lessen the number of real questions without doing injustice? The jury must pass upon all the disputed questions of fact in a cause, or it must be imperfectly understood. No pleading can lessen the number of questions really disputed; it may lessen the number apparently disputed but the apparent dispute disappears the moment the trial is opened. . . .

The attempt to reduce questions to all their elements before trial, must commonly fail. What subordinate ones may arise can scarcely be known till the evidence is all disclosed. The greatest diligence and skill will lead only to an approximation, greater or less according to the nature of the original questions. The first one is always this: Has the plaintiff the right, or the defendant? This depends upon others. . . .

The most accurate analysis of a cause takes place at the trial, and then there really is something analogous to the ancient oral pleading. Indeed, we must not forget that our system of pleading had its origin in a practice which no longer exists. Being carried on orally by the parties, in the presence of the Court, it rested always under its supervision. It was, in fact, nothing more than the forming of an issue, by the Court, from the respective allegations of the parties.

When the presence of the Judge was withdrawn it lost an essential part of its original character. The substitute for that now is the trial. First, the plaintiff opens his case, and calls his witnesses; the defendant then does the same. After the testimony is finished, the defendant goes over his case again, and makes his analysis of the points and of the evidence. The plaintiff follows with his analysis and arguments, and upon this the Judge charges the jury. Then comes the true analysis of the case—the fullest development of all the points in the controversy, which no system of special pleading can dispense with. . . .

So far we have considered the question without reference to the expense and delay of the old system of pleading. These are, however, important elements in the question. To do justice with the least expense and delay is, I repeat, the object of every administration of law. It has been said that it is better to have a Judge decide wrong, than not to decide soon. Without going so far as this, I must think time one of the most important elements in the proper administration of justice. Suppose it were certain that a cause would be better decided if the parties were allowed five years to get their proofs, and the Court five years to decide: Who would think of allowing any such thing? The expensiveness of lawsuits is also a consideration of immense consequence. Dear justice is no justice to the largest class of litigants. . . .

Six sections like the following, incorporated into the new code of procedure, with a few forms annexed, would contain all the provisions necessary to establish the course of pleading, which I propose in all civil cases:

1.   The first proceeding shall be a complaint filed with the Clerk of the Court, setting forth briefly, in ordinary language, and without repetition, the

nature and particulars of the cause of suit, and praying for the relief to which the complainant thinks himself entitled. . . .

2.   Within ten days after the day of appearance, the defendant shall file with the Clerk of the Court his answer to the complaint, setting forth briefly, in ordinary language, and without repetition, the nature and particulars of his defense. But further time to answer may be granted by a Judge of the Court, for good cause shown. . . .

3.   No other pleading shall be allowed than the complaint and answer aforesaid, and, upon the filing of the answer, the cause shall be deemed at issue. If the defendant shall neglect to file his answer within the time aforesaid, the allegations of the complaint shall, for the purposes of that suit, be taken to be true. And when an answer is filed containing new matter, not responsive to the complaint, the Court may require from either party notice of any other facts, intended to be proved on the trial, relating to such new matter.

4.   The defendant shall not be required to make any discovery by answer, nor shall the answer, in any cases, be deemed evidence against the complainant. But any party to the suit may be examined as a witness at the instance of the opposite party, and for that purpose he shall be subject, like any other witness, to subpoena, to examination conditionally, or upon commission.

5.   The Court shall have power at any time, in its discretion, to amend any process, pleading, or proceeding in furtherance of justice, taking care to guard the parties against injury from surprise, by correcting any mistake in the name of any complainant or defendant, or by adding or striking out the name of any complainant or defendant, or by conforming any pleading or proceeding to the facts proved, whenever the variance between the allegation and the proof is not material to the right of the case. And the Court may also compel the parties respectively to amend the complaint or answer for want of sufficient precision therein; and the defendant may be allowed, in the discretion of the Court, and after notice to the complainant, to file a supplemental answer containing any new defense occurring after the former answer. And the Court may, also, upon the trial, disregard any variance between the allegation and the proof not material in substance.

6.   All suits shall be brought in the name of the real party in interest, and against the party as to whom relief is prayed. . . .

I lay out of view the advantage that this change would be to the profession itself. This is altogether too narrow a view of the question, although I think it quite apparent that the real usefulness and dignity of the profession would be increased by it. The practice is now too technical. It requires a vast amount of drudgery to be performed; too many and too long papers; too many steps to be taken; too many motions to be made. In short, instead of a straight path to an object in sight, we have to grope our way through a labyrinth of old passages, some of them in decay, some of them dark, many of them blocked up, and quite uncertain when we shall emerge to the light. Most fervently do I hope that the year 1847 will see this labyrinth uncovered and demolished.

77

Declaration of Seneca Falls Convention (1848)

One of the reform movements that arose during the "freedom's ferment" of the early nineteenth century was a drive for greater rights for women, especially in the political arena. Although women often were the daily workers of the antislavery movement, they found that while they were allowed to do the drudge work, they could not take leadership roles nor lobby openly for abolition. The drudgery of daily housework and its deadening impact on the mind also struck some women as unfair. Several of these factors came together in the life of Elizabeth Cady Stanton, who then took the lead in the effort to secure for women the basic right to vote. At a meeting of suffrage sympathizers (including men) at Seneca Falls, New York, in July 1848, the following declaration, deliberately modeled on the Declaration of Independence, was adopted, as well as a series of resolutions that called for women's suffrage and a reform of laws that kept women in an inferior status. Very little in the way of progress came from the Seneca Falls statement, although it would serve for the next seventy years as the goal for which the suffrage movement strove. In the country as a whole, nearly all reform energy soon focused on the single issue of slavery and its abolition.

See E. C. Stanton, *Eighty Years & More* (1898); E. Griffith, *In Her Own Right* (1984); and E. Flexner, *Century of Struggle* (1968).

Source: E. C. Stanton, S. B. Anthony, and M. J. Gage, eds., 1 *History of Women's Suffrage* 70 (1887).

When, in the course of human events, it becomes necessary for one portion of the family of man to assume among the people of the earth a position different from that which they have hitherto occupied, but one to which the laws of nature and of nature's God entitle them, a decent respect to the opinions of mankind requires that they should declare the causes that impel them to such a course.

We hold these truths to be self-evident: that all men and women are created equal; that they are endowed by their Creator with certain inalienable rights; that among these are life, liberty, and the pursuit of happiness; that to secure these rights governments are instituted, deriving their just powers from the consent of the governed. Whenever any form of government becomes destructive of these ends, it is the right of those who suffer from it to refuse allegiance to it, and to insist upon the institution of a new government, laying its foundation on such principles, and organizing its powers in such form, as to them shall seem most likely to effect their safety and happiness. Prudence, indeed, will dictate that governments long established should not be changed for light and transient causes; and accordingly all experience hath shown that mankind are more disposed to suffer, while evils are sufferable, than to right themselves by abolishing the forms to which they were accustomed. But when a long train of abuses and usurpations, pursuing invariably the same object, evinces a design to reduce them under absolute despotism, it is their duty to throw off such government, and to provide new guards for their future security. Such has been the patient sufferance of the women under this government, and such is now the necessity which constrains them to demand the equal station to which they are entitled.

The history of mankind is a history of repeated injuries and usurpations on the part of man toward woman, having in direct object the establishment of an absolute tyranny over her. To prove this, let facts be submitted to a candid world.

He has never permitted her to exercise her inalienable right to the elective franchise.

He has compelled her to submit to laws, in the formation of which she had no voice.

He has withheld from her rights which are given to the most ignorant and degraded men—both natives and foreigners.

Having deprived her of this first right of a citizen, the elective franchise, thereby leaving her without representation in the halls of legislation, he has oppressed her on all sides.

He has made her, if married, in the eye of the law, civilly dead.

He has taken from her all right in property, even to the wages she earns.

He has made her, morally, an irresponsible being, as she can commit many crimes with impunity, provided they be done in the presence of her husband.

In the covenant of marriage, she is compelled to promise obedience to her husband, he becoming to all intents and purposes, her master—the law giving him power to deprive her of her liberty, and to administer chastisement.

He has so framed the laws of divorce, as to what shall be the proper causes, and in case of separation, to whom the guardianship of the children shall be given, as to be wholly regardless of the happiness of women—the law, in all cases, going upon a false supposition of the supremacy of man, and giving all power into his hands.

After depriving her of all rights as a married woman, if single, and the owner of property, he has taxed her to support a government which recognizes her only when her property can be made profitable to it.

He has monopolized nearly all the profitable employments, and from those she is permitted to follow, she receives but a scanty remuneration. He closes against her all the avenues to wealth and distinction which he considers most honorable to himself. As a teacher of theology, medicine, or law, she is not known.

He has denied her the facilities for obtaining a thorough education, all colleges being closed against her.

He allows her in Church, as well as State, but a subordinate position, claiming Apostolic authority for her exclusion from the ministry, and, with some exceptions, from any public participation in the affairs of the Church.

He has created a false public sentiment by giving to the world a different code of morals for men and women, by which moral delinquencies which exclude women from society, are not only tolerated, but deemed of little account in man.

He has usurped the prerogative of Jehovah himself, claiming it as his right to assign for her a sphere of action, when that belongs to her conscience and to her God.

He has endeavored, in every way that he could, to destroy her confidence in her own powers, to lessen her self-respect, and to make her willing to lead a dependent and abject life.

Now, in view of this entire disfranchisement of one-half the people of this country, their social and religious degradation—in view of the unjust laws above mentioned, and because women do feel themselves aggrieved, oppressed, and fraudulently deprived of their most sacred rights, we insist that they have immediate admission to all the rights and privileges which belong to them as citizens of the United States.

In entering upon the great work before us, we anticipate no small amount of misconception, misrepresentation, and ridicule; but we shall use every instrumentality within our power to effect our object. We shall employ agents, circulate tracts, petition the State and National legislatures, and endeavor to enlist the pulpit and the press in our behalf. We hope this Convention will be followed by a series of Conventions embracing every part of the country.

78

Commonwealth v. Alger (1851)

In the *Charles River Bridge* case (Document 69), Chief Justice Taney declared that the courts could not take from the state "any portion of that power over their own internal police and improvements, which is so necessary to their well being and prosperity." The police power, as it has come to be called, could thus be used as a balance to the vested rights theory used to protect property rights, and to advance the needs of a changing society. The police power remained primarily a state power in the nineteenth century (see Document 68), and although rarely provided for in a constitutional manner, was recognized by courts as implicit in sovereignty. Governments by definition had the power to look after the health, safety, and welfare of their citizens. Perhaps the best exposition of the police power came from Chief Justice Lemuel Shaw of Massachusetts, in a case involving state restrictions on building docks on private property into Boston harbor. For the next ninety years a major legal and constitutional issue in the United States involved determining the line between the power of the state to regulate private property for the good of society on the one hand and the rights of private property on the other.

See E. Freund, *The Police Power* (1904); and L. W. Levy, *The Law of the Commonwealth and Chief Justice Shaw* (1957).

Chief Justice Shaw

In proceeding to give judgment in the present case, the court are deeply impressed with the importance of the principles which it involves, and the magnitude and extent of the great public interests, and the importance and value of the private rights, directly or indirectly to be affected by it. It affects the relative rights of the public and of individual proprietors, in the soil lying on tide waters, between high and low water mark, over which the sea ebbs and flows, in the ordinary action of the tides.

The defendant has been indicted for having erected and built a wharf over and beyond certain lines, described as the commissioners' lines, into the

---

Source: 61 Mass. 53 (1851)

harbor of Boston. The case comes before this court, upon a report of the judge of the municipal court, who, deeming the questions of law involved in the case doubtful and important, with the consent of the defendant, pursuant to the statute, reported the same for the consideration of this court. . . .

. . . The uncontested facts in the present case are, that the defendant was owner of land, bounded on a cove or arm of the sea, in which the tide ebbed and flowed, that he built the wharf complained of, on the flats before his said land, between high and low water mark, and within one hundred rods of his upland, but below the commissioners' line as fixed by one of these statutes; although it was so built as not to obstruct or impede navigation. This certainly presents the case most favorably for the defendant.

We may, perhaps, better embrace the several subjects involved in the inquiry, by considering,

First, What are the rights of owners of land, bounding on salt water, whom it is convenient to designate as riparian proprietors, to the flats over which the tide ebbs and flows, as such rights are settled and established by the laws of Massachusetts; and,

Second, What are the just powers of the legislature to limit, control, or regulate the exercise and enjoyment of these rights.

I.   By the common law of England, as it stood long before the emigration of our ancestors to this country and the settlement of the colony of Massachusetts, the title to the land or property in the soil, under the sea, and over which the tide waters ebbed and flowed, including flats, or the sea-shore, lying between high and low water mark, was in the king, as the representative of the sovereign power of the country. But it was held by a rule equally well settled, that this right of property was held by the king in trust, for public uses, established by ancient custom or regulated by law, the principal of which were for fishing and navigation. These uses were held to be public, not only for all the king's subjects, but for foreigners, being subjects of states at peace with England, and coming to the ports and havens of England, with their ships and vessels for the purposes of trade and commerce. . . .

Assuming that by the common law of England, as above stated, the right of riparian proprietors, bounding upon tide waters, extending to high water mark only, and assuming that the first settlers of Massachusetts regarded the law of England as their law, and governed themselves by it, it follows that the earliest grants of land bounding on tide waters would be to the high water line and not below it, and would have so remained, but for the colony ordinance, now to be considered. . . .

The great purpose of the 16th article of the "Body of Liberties" [1647] was to declare a great principle of public right, to abolish the forest laws, the game laws, and the laws designed to secure several and exclusive fisheries, and to make them all free. It expressly extended this right to places in which the tide ebbs and flows, then public domain, open to all. But when there afterwards came a provision, in effect declaring this territory, between high and low water mark, the private property of the riparian proprietor or owner of the upland; this would seem to take away or abridge the right to the use of the shores, previously given; but this was accompanied by another, that, for fowling and fishing, persons may pass over another man's property, of course including these shores thus made private property; this restores the public right to pass on foot over flats or places over which the sea ebbs and flows, so long as they are not actually reclaimed and converted into tillage or mowing land. . . .

Taking the terms of the ordinance, with a long course of judicial decisions upon its construction, nearly if not quite uniform, the court are of opinion that the antecedent law limiting the right of private proprietors of land bounding on the sea or salt water, to the line of high water, was changed by it; that, after this ordinance, the grant of lands, so situated, by the colonial government to individuals, or to proprietors of townships or companies of settlers, through whom they came to individuals, vested in such grantees an estate in fee in the land lying between high and low water mark, subject to the restriction expressed in the proviso, "so as not to stop or hinder the passage of boats and vessels," &c., and subject to all such restraints and limitations of absolute dominion over it, in its use and appropriation, as other real estate is subject to, for the security and benefit of other proprietors, and of the public, in the enjoyment of their rights. . . .

II.   Assuming, then, that the defendant was owner in fee of the soil and flats upon which the wharf in question was built, it becomes necessary to inquire whether it was competent for the legislature to pass the acts establishing the harbor lines, and what is the legal validity and effect of those acts.

There is now no occasion and no ground to deny or question the full and sovereign power of the commonwealth, within its limits, by legislative acts, to exercise dominion over the sea and the shores of the sea, and all its arms and branches, and the lands under them, and all other lands flowed by tide water, subject to the rights of riparian ownership. . . .

Supposing, then, that the commonwealth does hold all the power which exists anywhere, to regulate and dispose of the sea-shores, and tide waters, and all lands under them, and all public rights connected with them, whether this power be traced to the right of property or right of sovereignty as its principal source, it must be regarded as held in trust for the best interest of the public, for commerce and navigation, and for all the legitimate and appropriate uses to which it may be made subservient. Assuming, then, that the commonwealth does hold this power, within certain limits, the question recurs, whether the acts under consideration are within its just and legitimate exercise. . . .

We think it is a settled principle, growing out of the nature of well ordered civil society, that every holder of property, however absolute and unqualified may be his title, holds it under the implied liability that his use of it may be so regulated, that it shall not be injurious to the equal enjoyment of others having an equal right to the enjoyment of their property, nor injurious to the rights of the community. All property in this commonwealth, as well that in the interior as that bordering on tide waters, is derived directly or indirectly from the government, and held subject to those general regulations, which are necessary to the common good and general welfare. Rights of property, like all other social and conventional rights, are subject to such reasonable limitations in their enjoyment, as shall prevent them from being injurious, and to such reasonable restraints and regulations established by law, as the legislature, under the governing and controlling power vested in them by the constitution, may think necessary and expedient.

This is very different from the right of eminent domain, the right of a government to take and appropriate private property to public use, whenever the public exigency requires it; which can be done only on condition of providing a reasonable compensation therefor. The power we allude to is rather the police power, the power vested in the legislature by the constitution, to make, ordain and establish all manner of wholesome and reasonable laws, statutes and ordinances, either with penalties or without, not repugnant to the constitution, as they shall judge to be for the good and welfare of the commonwealth, and of the subjects of the same.

It is much easier to perceive and realize the existence and sources of this power, than to mark its boundaries, or prescribe limits to its exercise. There are many cases in which such a power is exercised by all well ordered governments, and where its fitness is so obvious, that all well regulated minds will regard it as reasonable. Such are the laws to prohibit the use of warehouses for the storage of gunpowder near habitations or highways; to restrain the height to which wooden buildings may be erected in populous neighborhoods, and require them to be covered with slate or other incombustible matérial; to prohibit buildings from being used for hospitals for contagious diseases, or for the carrying on of noxious or offensive trades; to prohibit the raising of a dam, and causing stagnant water to spread over meadows, near inhabited villages, thereby raising noxious exhalations, injurious to health and dangerous to life.

Nor does the prohibition of such noxious use of property, a prohibition imposed because such use would be injurious to the public, although it may diminish the profits of the owner, make it an appropriation to a public use, so as to entitle the owner to compensation. If the owner of a vacant lot in the midst of a city could erect thereon a great wooden building, and cover it with shingles, he might obtain a larger profit of his land, than if obliged to build of stone or brick, with a slated roof. If the owner of a warehouse in a cluster of other buildings could store quantities of gunpowder in it for himself and others, he might be saved the great expense of transportation. If a landlord could let his building for a smallpox hospital, or a slaughterhouse, he might obtain an increased rent. But he is restrained; not because the public have occasion to make the like use, or to make any use of the property, or to take any benefit or profit to themselves from it; but because it would be a noxious use, contrary to the maxim, *sic utere tuo, ut alienum non lœdas.* It is not an appropriation of the property to a public use, but the restraint of an injurious private use by the owner, and is therefore not within the principle of property taken under the right of eminent domain. The distinction, we think, is manifest in principle, although the facts and circumstances of different cases are so various, that it is often difficult to decide whether a particular exercise of legislation is properly attributable to the one or the other of these two acknowledged powers. . . .

But in reference to the present case, and to the act of the legislature, establishing lines in the harbor, beyond which private proprietors are prohibited from building wharves, it is urged that such a restraint upon the estate of an individual, debarring him to some extent from the most beneficial use of it, is in effect taking his estate. If such restraint were in fact imposed upon the estate of one proprietor only, or on several estates on the same line of shore, the objection would be much more formidable. But we are to consider the subject matter, to which such restraint applies. The value of this species of estate, that of shore and flats, consists mainly in the means it affords of building wharves from the upland towards deep water, to place merchandise and build wharves upon, and principally to afford access, to vessels requiring considerable depth of water, from the sea to suitable landings. Now, if along a shore where there are flats of considerable extent, one were restrained to a certain length, whilst others were allowed to extend further, the damage might be great. So if one were allowed to extend, and the coterminous proprietors adjacent were restrained, it would be obviously more injurious. The one extended would stop or check the current along the others, cause mud to accumulate near them, and thus render the water shoal at those wharves. But where all are permitted to extend alike, and all are restrained alike, by a line judiciously adapted to the course of the current, so that all have the benefit of access to their wharves, with the same depth of water, and the same strength of current at their heads, the damage must be comparatively less.

But of this the legislature must judge. Having once come to the conclusion that a case exists, in which it is competent for the legislature to make a law on the subject, it is for them, under a high sense of duty to the public and to individuals, with a sacred regard to the rights of property and all other private rights, to make such reasonable regulations as they may judge necessary to protect public and private rights, and to impose no larger restraints upon the use and enjoyment of private property, than are in their judgment strictly necessary to preserve and protect the rights of others. . . .

On the whole, the court are of opinion that the act fixing a line within the harbor of Boston, beyond which no riparian proprietor should erect a wharf or other permanent structure, although to some extent it prohibited him from building such structure on flats of which he owned the fee, was a constitutional law, and one which it was competent for the legislature to make; that it was binding on the defendant, and rendered him obnoxious to its penalties, if he violated its provisions.

79

Cooley v. Board of Wardens of the Port of Philadelphia (1851)

An 1803 Pennsylvania law required ships entering or leaving the Philadelphia port to engage a local pilot to guide them through the harbor and imposed a fine for failure to do so. Cooley protested the law, arguing that the power to regulate the harbor fell under the interstate commerce power of the Congress. Although there was no doubt, after the steamboat case (Document 57), that Congress did have this power, the issue was whether states could, in the absence of an exercise of federal power, regulate commerce that, while interstate in nature, directly affected them. The Court had a precedent in Willson v. Black Bird Creek Marsh Co., 2 Pet. 245 (1829), in which Chief Justice Marshall had sustained a Delaware law authorizing the damming of a creek to keep out marsh waters, even though the creek was navigable and thus fell under the federal commerce reach. But since Congress had not acted specifically, silence could be interpreted to give the states permission to act.

A majority of the Court took this very commonsense approach in this situation, that until Congress acted, states remained free to regulate matters primarily local in nature. The opinion neither restricted nor expanded federal power, but provided a rule of thumb for future gray-area cases.

See F. Frankfurter, *The Commerce Clause under Marshall, Taney and Waite* (1937).

Source: 12 Howard 299 (1851).

~~~~~~

Justice Curtis delivered the opinion of the Court.

The regulation of the qualifications of pilots, of the modes and times of offering and rendering their services, of the responsibilities which shall rest upon them, of the powers they shall possess, of the compensation they may demand, and of the penalties by which their rights and duties may be enforced, do constitute regulations of navigation, and consequently of commerce, within the just meaning of Art. I, § 8. . . .

It becomes necessary, therefore, to consider whether this law of Pennsylvania, being a regulation of commerce, is valid.

The act of Congress of the 7th of August, 1789, sect. 4, is as follows: "That all pilots in the bays, inlets, rivers, harbors, and ports of the United States shall continue to be regulated in conformity with the existing laws of the States, respectively, wherein such pilots may be, or with such laws as the States may respectively hereafter enact for the purpose, until further legislative provision shall be made by Congress." If the law of Pennsylvania, now in question, had been in existence at the date of this act of Congress, we might hold it to have been adopted by Congress, and thus made a law of the United States, and so valid. But the law on which these actions were founded was not enacted till 1803. What effect then can be attributed to so much of the act of 1789, as declares, that pilots shall continue to be regulated in conformity, "with such laws as the States may respectively hereafter enact for the purpose, until further legislative provision shall be made by Congress"?

If the States were divested of the power to legislate on this subject by the grant of the commercial power to Congress, it is plain this act could not confer upon them power thus to legislate. If the Constitution excluded the States from making any law regulating commerce, certainly Congress cannot regrant, or in any manner reconvey to the States that power. And yet this act of 1789 gives its sanction only to laws enacted by the States. This necessarily implies a constitutional power to legislate. Holding these views we are brought directly and unavoidably to the consideration of the question, whether the grant of the commercial power to Congress, did per se deprive the States of all power to regulate pilots. This question has never been decided by this court, nor, in our judgment, has any case depending upon all the considerations which must govern this one, come before this court. . . .

The diversities of opinion, which have existed on this subject, have arisen from the different views taken of the nature of this power. But when the nature of a power like this is spoken of, when it is said that the nature of the power requires that it should be exercised exclusively by Congress, it must be intended to refer to the subjects of that power, and to say they are of such a nature as to require exclusive legislation by Congress. Now the power to regulate commerce, embraces a vast field, containing not only many, but exceedingly various subjects, quite unlike in their nature; some imperatively demanding a single uniform rule, operating equally on the commerce of the United States in every port; and some, like the subject now in question, as imperatively demanding that diversity, which alone can meet the local necessities of navigation.

Either absolutely to affirm, or deny that the nature of this power requires exclusive legislation by Congress, is to lose sight of the nature of the subjects of this power, and to assert concerning all of them, what is really applicable but to a part. Whatever subjects of this power are in their nature national, or admit only of one uniform system, or plan of regulation, may justly be said to be of such a nature as to require exclusive legislation by Congress. That this cannot be affirmed of laws for the regulation of pilots and pilotage is plain. The act of 1789 contains a clear and authoritative declaration by the first Congress, that the nature of this subject is such, that until Congress should find it necessary to exert its power, it should be left to the legislation of the States; that it is local and not national; that it is likely to be the best provided for, not by one system, or plan of regulations, but by as many as the legislative discretion of the several States should deem applicable to the local peculiarities of the ports within their limits.

Viewed in this light, so much of this act of 1789 as declares that pilots shall continue to be regulated "by such laws as the States may respectively hereafter enact for that purpose," instead of being held to be inoperative, as an attempt to confer on the States a power to legislate, of which the Constitution had deprived them, is allowed an appropriate and important signification. It manifests the understanding of Congress, at the outset of the government, that the nature of this subject is not such as to require its exclusive legislation. The practice of the States, and of the national government, has been in conformity with this declaration, from the origin of the national government to this time; and the nature of the subject when examined, is such as to leave no doubt of the superior fitness and propriety, not to say the absolute necessity, of different systems of regulation, drawn from local knowledge and experience, and conformed to local wants. How then can we say, that by the mere grant of power to regulate commerce, the States are deprived of all the power to legislate on this subject, because from the nature of the power the legislation of Congress must be exclusive? . . .

It is the opinion of a majority of the court that the mere grant to Congress of the power to regulate commerce, did not deprive the States of power to regulate pilots, and that although Congress has legislated on this subject, its legislation manifests an intention, with a single exception, not to regulate this subject, but to leave its regulation to the several states. To these precise questions, which are all we are called on to decide, this opinion must be understood to be confined. It does not extend to the question what other subjects, under the commercial power, are within the exclusive control of Congress, or may be regulated by the States in absence of all congressional legislation; nor to the general question, how far any regulation on a subject by Congress may be deemed to operate as an exclusion of all legislation by the States upon the same subject. We decide the precise questions before us, applicable to this particular subject in the state in which the legislation of Congress has left it. We go no further. . . .

Affirmed.

[Justices McLean and Wayne dissented; Justice Daniel concurred on other grounds.]

80

Ohio Constitution of 1851

In the decades between 1800 and 1860 every state in the Union revised its constitution at least once, usually through the device of a popularly elected state convention. An analysis of the changes in these documents shows a steady democratization of the political system, greater awareness (at least in the North) of the need for written protections of individual liberties, and especially from 1840 onward, prohibitions against the use of state monies to subsidize private economic development. Moreover, many states wrote support of public education and eleemosynary institutions into the constitution. These trends are clearly discernible in the Ohio Constitution of 1851.

It should be noted that states did not write their constitutions on blank slates, but borrowed heavily from their own experience as well as from that of sister states. The expansion of democracy in any one area, either through extension of the suffrage, elimination of office-holding requirements, or elaboration of Bill of Rights protections, soon would be copied by other states.

See H. Walker, *An Analysis and Appraisal of the Ohio State Constitution, 1851–1951* (1951).

Source: *Report of Debates . . . for the Revision of the Constitution of the State of Ohio, 1850–51* 856 (1851).

We the people of the State of Ohio grateful to Almighty God for our freedom, to secure its blessings and promote our common welfare, do establish this Constitution.

Article I.   Bill of Rights

Sec. 1.   All men are, by nature, free and independent, and have certain inalienable rights, among which are those of enjoying and defending life and liberty, acquiring, possessing, and protecting property, and seeking and obtaining happiness and safety.

Sec. 2.   All political power is inherent in the people. Government is instituted for their equal protection and benefit, and they have the right to alter, reform, or abolish the same, whenever they may deem it necessary; and no special privileges or immunities shall ever be granted, that may not be altered, revoked, or repeated by the General Assembly.

Sec. 3.   The people have the right to assemble together, in a peaceable manner, to consult for their common good; to instruct their Representatives, and to petition the General Assembly for the redress of grievances.

Sec. 4.   The people have the right to bear arms for their defense and security; but standing armies, in time of peace, are dangerous to liberty, and shall not be kept up; and the military shall be in strict subordination to the civil power.

Sec. 5.   The right of trial by jury shall be inviolate.

Sec. 6.   There shall be no slavery in this State; nor involuntary servitude, unless for the punishment of crime.

Sec. 7.   All men have a natural and indefeasible right to worship Almighty God according to the dictates of their own conscience. No person shall be compelled to attend, erect, or support any place of worship, or maintain any form of worship, against his consent; and no preference shall be given, by law, to any religious society; nor shall any interference with the rights of conscience be permitted. No religious test shall be required as a qualification for office, nor shall any person be incompetent to be a witness on account of his religious belief; but nothing herein shall be construed to dispense with oaths and affirmations. Religion, morality and knowledge, however, being essential to good government, it shall be the duty of the General Assembly to pass suitable laws, to protect every religious denomination in the peaceable enjoyment of its own mode of public worship, and to encourage schools, and the means of instruction.

Sec. 8.   The privilege of the writ of habeas corpus shall not be suspended, unless, in cases of rebellion or invasion, the public safety require it.

Sec. 9.   All persons shall be bailable by sufficient sureties, except for capital offences where the proof is evident, or the presumption great. Excessive bail shall not be required; nor excessive fines imposed; nor cruel and unusual punishments inflicted.

Sec. 10.   Except in cases of impeachment and cases arising in the army and navy, or in the militia, when in actual service, in time of war, or public danger, and in cases of petit larceny and other inferior offences, no person shall be held to answer for a capital, or otherwise infamous crime, unless on presentment or indictment of a grand jury. In any trial, in any court, the party accused shall be allowed to appear and defend in person and with counsel; to demand the nature and cause of the accusation against him and to have a copy thereof; to meet the witnesses face to face, and to have compulsory process to procure the attendance of witnesses in his behalf, and a speedy public trial by an impartial jury of the county or district in which the offence is alleged to have been committed; nor shall any person be compelled in any criminal case, to be a witness against himself, or be twice put in jeopardy for the same offence.

Sec. 11.   Every citizen may freely speak, write, and publish his sentiments on all subjects, being responsible for the abuse of the right; and no law shall be passed to restrain or abridge the liberty of speech or of the press. In all criminal prosecutions for libel, the truth may be given in evidence to the jury, and if it shall appear to the jury that the matter charged as libelous is true, and was published with good motives and for justifiable ends, the party shall be acquitted.

Sec. 12.   No person shall be transported out of the state, for any offence committed within the same; and no conviction shall work corruption of blood, or forfeiture of estate.

Sec. 13.   No soldier shall, in time of peace, be quartered in any house, without the consent of the owner nor, in time of war, except in the manner prescribed by law.

Sec. 14.   The right of the people to be secure in their persons, houses, papers, and possessions, against unreasonable searches and seizures, shall not be violated; and no warrant shall issue, but upon probable cause, supported by oath or affirmation, particularly describing the place to be searched, and the person and things to be seized.

Sec. 15.   No person shall be imprisoned for debt in any civil action, on mesne or final process, unless in cases of fraud.

Sec. 16.   All courts shall be open, and every person, for an injury done him in his land, goods, person or reputation, shall have remedy by due course of law, and justice administered without denial or delay.

Sec. 17. No hereditary emoluments, honors, or privileges, shall ever be granted or conferred by this State.

Sec. 18. No power of suspending laws shall ever be exercised, except by the General Assembly.

Sec. 19. Private property shall ever be held inviolate, but subservient to the public welfare. When taken in time of war, or other public exigency, imperatively requiring its immediate seizure, or for the purpose of making or repairing roads, which shall be open to the public, without charge, a compensation shall be made to the owner, in money; and in all other cases, where private property shall be taken for public use, a compensation therefor shall first be made in money, or first secured by a deposit of money; and such compensation shall be assessed by a jury, without deduction for benefits to any property of the owner.

Sec. 20. This enumeration of rights shall not be construed to impair or deny others retained by the people; and all powers, not herein delegated, remain with the people. . . .

Article IV. Judicial

Sec. 1. The judicial power of the State shall be vested in a Supreme Court, in District Courts, Courts of Common Pleas, Courts of Probate, Justices of the Peace and in such other Courts inferior to the Supreme Court, in one or more counties, as the General Assembly, may, from time to time, establish.

Sec. 2. The Supreme Court shall consist of five judges, a majority of whom shall be necessary to form a quorum or to pronounce a decision. It shall have original jurisdiction in quo warranto, mandamus, habeas corpus, and procedendo, and such appellate jurisdiction as may be provided by law. It shall hold at least one term, in each year, at the seat of government, and such other terms, at the seat of government or elsewhere as may be provided by law. The Judges of the Supreme Court shall be elected by the electors of the State at large. . . .

Sec. 4. The jurisdiction of the courts of common pleas and of the Judges thereof, shall be fixed by law. . . .

Sec. 14. The Judges of the Supreme Court and of the Court of Common Pleas shall, at stated times, receive for their services such compensation as may be provided by law, which shall not be diminished, or increased, during their term of office, but they shall receive no fees or perquisites, nor hold any other office of profit or trust under the authority of this State, or the United States. All votes for either of them, for any elective office, except a judicial office under the authority of this State, given by the General Assembly, or the people, shall be void.

Sec. 15.   The General Assembly may increase or diminish the number of the Judges of the Supreme Court, the number of the districts of the Court of Common Pleas, the number of Judges in any district, change the districts or the subdivisions thereof, or establish other courts, whenever two-thirds of the members elected to each house shall concur therein but, no such change, addition, or diminution, shall vacate the office of any Judge. . . .

Sec. 17.   Judges may be removed from office by concurrent resolution of both Houses of the General Assembly, if two-thirds of the members elected to each House concur therein; but no such removal shall be made, except upon complaint, the substance of which shall be entered on the journal, nor until the party charged shall have had notice thereof, and an opportunity to be heard.

Sec. 18.   The several Judges of the Supreme Court of the Common Pleas, and of such other Courts as may be created, shall respectively have and exercise such power and jurisdiction, at chambers, or otherwise, as may be directed by law.

Sec. 19.   The General Assembly may establish Courts of Conciliation, and prescribe their powers and duties; but such Courts shall not render final judgment in any case, except upon submission by the parties of the matter in dispute, and their agreement to abide such judgment. . . .

Article V.   Elective Franchise

Sec. 1.   Every white male citizen of the United States, of the age of twenty one years, who shall have been a resident of the State one year next preceding the election, and of the county, township or ward, in which he resides, such time as may be provided by law, shall have the qualifications of an elector, and be entitled to vote at all elections.

Sec. 2.   All elections shall be by ballot.

Sec. 3.   Electors, during their attendance at elections, and in going to and returning therefrom, shall be privileged from arrest in all cases, except treason, felony, and breach of the peace.

Sec. 4.   The General Assembly shall have the power to exclude from the privilege of voting, or of being eligible to office, any person convicted of bribery, perjury, or other infamous crime.

Sec. 5.   No person in the military, naval or marine service of the United States, shall, by being stationed in any garrison or military or naval station within the State, be considered a resident of this State.

Sec. 6.   No idiot or insane person, shall be entitled to the privileges of an elector.

Article VI.   Education

Sec. 1.   The principal of all funds arising from the sale or other disposition of lands, or other property granted or entrusted to this State for educational and religious purposes, shall forever be preserved inviolate, and undiminished; and, the income arising therefrom shall be faithfully applied to the specific objects of the original grants or appropriations.

Sec. 2.   The General Assembly shall make such provisions by taxation, or otherwise, as with the income arising from the school trust fund, will secure a thorough and efficient system of common schools throughout the State, but no religious or other sect or sects shall have any exclusive right to, or control of, any part of the school funds of this State.

Article VII.   Public Institutions

Sec. 1.   Institutions for the benefit of the insane, blind, and deaf and dumb, shall always be fostered and supported by the State; and be subject to such regulations as may be prescribed by the General Assembly.

Sec. 2.   The Directors of the Penitentiary shall be appointed or elected in such a manner as the General Assembly may direct; and the Trustees of the benevolent and, other State institutions, now elected by the General Assembly, and of such other State institutions as may be hereafter created, shall be appointed by the Governor, by and with the advice and consent of the Senate, and upon all nominations made by the Governor, the question shall be taken by the yeas and nays, and entered upon the journals of the Senate.

Sec. 3.   The Governor shall have power to fill all vacancies that may occur in the office aforesaid, until the next session of the General Assembly, and, until a successor to his appointee shall be confirmed and qualified. . . .

Article VIII.   Public Debt and Public Works . . .

Sec. 4.   The credit of the State shall not, in any manner, be given or loaned to, or in aid of, any individual, association or corporation whatever; nor shall the State ever hereafter become a joint owner, or stockholder, in any company or association in this State or elsewhere, formed for any purpose whatever.

Sec. 5.   The State shall never assume the debts of any county, city, town, or township, or of any corporation whatever, unless such debt shall have been created to repel invasion, suppress insurrection, or defend the State in war.

Sec. 6.   The General Assembly shall never authorize any county, city, town or township, by vote of its citizens, or otherwise, to become a stockholder in any joint stock company, corporation, or association whatever; or to raise money for or loan its credit to, or in aid of, any such company, corporation, or association. . . .

Article XI.   *Apportionment*

Sec. 1.   The apportionment of this State for members of the General Assembly, shall be made every ten years, after the year one thousand eight hundred and fifty-one, in the following manner: The whole population of the State, as ascertained by the federal census, or in such other mode as the General Assembly may direct, shall be divided by the number "one hundred," and the quotient shall be the ratio of representation in the House of Representatives, for ten years next succeeding such apportionment. . . .

Article XII.   *Finance and Taxation*

Sec. 1.   The levying of taxes by the poll, is grievous and oppressive; therefore, the General Assembly shall never levy a poll tax, for county or State purposes.

Sec. 2.   Laws shall be passed, taxing, by a uniform rule, all moneys, credits, investments in bonds, stocks, joint stock companies, or otherwise; and also all real and personal property, according to its true value in money; but burying grounds, public school houses, houses used exclusively for public worship; institutions of purely public charity, public property used exclusively for any public purpose; and personal property to an amount not exceeding in value two hundred dollars for each individual, may by general laws, be exempted from taxation: but, all such laws shall be subject to alteration or repeal; and the value of all property, so exempted, shall from time to time, be ascertained and published as may be directed by law.

Sec. 3.   The General Assembly shall provide, by law, for taxing the notes and bills discounted or purchased, moneys loaned, and all other property, effects, or dues, of every description, (without deduction,) of all banks, now existing, or hereafter created, and of all bankers, so that all property employed in banking, shall always bear a burden of taxation equal to that imposed on the property of individuals.

Sec. 4.   The General Assembly shall provide for raising revenue, sufficient to defray the expense of the State, for each year, and also a sufficient sum to pay the interest on the State debt.

Sec. 5.   No tax shall be levied, except in pursuance of law; and every law imposing a tax shall state, distinctly, the object of the same, to which only, it shall be applied.

Sec. 6.   The State shall never contract any debt for purposes of internal improvement.

Article XIII.   Corporations

Sec. 1.   The General Assembly shall pass no special act conferring corporate powers.

Sec. 2.   Corporations may be formed under general laws; but all such laws may, from time to time, be altered, or repealed. . . .

Sec. 4.   The Property of corporations, now existing, or hereafter created, shall forever be subject to taxation, the same as the property of individuals.

Sec. 5.   No right of way shall be appropriated to the use of any corporation until full compensation therefor be first made in money, or first secured by a deposit of money, to the owner, irrespective of any benefit from any improvement proposed by such corporation; which compensation shall be ascertained by a jury of twelve men, in a court of record, as shall be prescribed by law.

81

Hentz v. Long Island Railroad Co. (1852)

Traditional English law, as we have noted in a number of previous cases, held property practically inviolate, guaranteeing to a property owner full and quiet enjoyment of his estate. Anyone or anything intruding into that enjoyment violated the right of property, and could

Source: 13 Barb. 646 (New York 1852).

be enjoined or made to pay damages. The advent of the railroad obviously affected the traditional right of quiet enjoyment, and under the old common law, the roads with their noisy engines would have been considered nuisances, and enjoined from operating. That law, however, would have prevented commercial progress and development, avidly sought after by Americans in the nineteenth century. And so in the best common law manner, judges revised the law to meet the needs of the time.

See M. J. Horwitz, *The Transformation of American Law, 1780–1860* (1977); and L. W. Levy, *The Law of the Commonwealth and Chief Justice Shaw* (1957).

Judge S. B. Strong

The plaintiff alleges in his complaint that he has been for the last five years, and is, lawfully possessed of a lot in the village of Hempstead, in the county of Queens comprising half an acre; on which there are a dwelling house and shop fronting on Main-street, and a barn and other out buildings on Fulton-street. That while he has been so possessed of the said premises, the defendants having previously, and in or about the year 1837, laid down and along Main-street, and upon such premises, certain timbers and iron rails, constituting their railroad track, continued them thereon, running over the same with passenger and freight cars drawn by horses, greatly to his injury. . . . That about the 5th of last August, the defendants took up the old timbers and rails and tore up the soil of his land, and laid down in their place other timbers and iron rails, and have at various times since run upon the said rails with their locomotives, propelled by steam; that "by the coming of the said locomotives upon and running the same over his said close, the health and lives of his family, tenants and inmates, are prejudiced and endangered, and the value of his property lessened; that an offensive smoke has filled his dwelling house; that the same is a nuisance of the most flagrant character," and that the continuance thereof would be an irreparable injury to his said property and the enjoyment thereof; and that his tenants are likely to abandon the same. That the defendants have since such 5th of August last, run upon and over the said premises certain freight cars loaded with manure and merchandise, propelling the same by means of their steam engine and horses, often without agents to watch and conduct them, and to the danger, nuisance and inconvenience of himself and family; and that from the contiguity of his land to the depot, the locomotives frequently stop opposite to his premises, and he is thus injured more than the rest of mankind.

He therefore claims two thousand dollars damages, and prays for an order of injunction restraining the defendants during the pendency of this suit from running their locomotives or cars of any description upon or over his said premises, and that a judgment may be given him for his damages, and for a perpetual injunction. . . .

The only remaining question is whether the road where it passes the plaintiff's premises is a nuisance. . . . The legislature has expressly authorized various companies to lay and use their track through many of our cities and villages, and cars are now drawn by locomotives propelled by steam through Albany, Schenectady, Utica, Syracuse, Rochester, Buffalo, Poughkeepsie, Brooklyn, Jamaica, and many other cities and villages. It was held in the case of Drake v. The Hudson River Railroad Company, (7 Barb. 509,) that a road passing through the streets in the city of New York, and when the cars are drawn by steam-power into a crowded part of the city (although not to the terminus of the road) was not a nuisance. . . . Is there then any thing peculiar to Main-street, or in the management of the defendants, which makes the railroad where it passes the plaintiff's house a nuisance? It is not averred in the complaint that the railroad constitutes any serious impediment to the travel, along the highway. It no where appears that the rails are badly laid down, so as to create any obstruction on the surface, and it is apparent that the street is of sufficient width for carriages to pass each other without danger or difficulty, on either side of the railway. Besides, a number of respectable inhabitants of the place deposed that the condition of the street as a passway has been considerably improved by the defendants' works upon it.

Is there any thing in the management of the road and its appendages which renders it offensive to the plaintiff, to such an extent as to justify the interposition of this court by way of restraint upon the action of the defendants? One of the causes of complaint is that the steam locomotive passes as far south as Fulton-street, and occasionally below it. It is apparent that many of those who have favored the introduction of the road into the village have acted on the supposition that the locomotive was not to proceed below Fulton-street, but there is no evidence of any definite agreement with the defendants to that effect; and as their charter does not restrict them as to the means of transportation on any part of their route, I am not authorized to interfere, but must leave the matter to the good sense of those who may be intrusted with the management of the affairs of the company. It is manifestly for their interest to conduct its operations in such a manner as to gratify the reasonable wishes of that part of the community which gives to the company an efficient support. The plaintiff complains that about two years ago, and for about a year, the track was disused and suffered "to go to ruin," its shattered state embarrassing the travel upon the highway, causing the breaking of vehicles, and hindering their passage to and from his premises. There were no doubt serious grievances at the time, but they resulted from the then impaired condition of the track. The cause has since been removed, and the papers furnish us no reasons to apprehend a recurrence of the same or similar evils. None of the papers mention any serious accidents since the track has been relaid and the locomotive has passed over it, and if there had been any, they would no doubt have been discovered by the plaintiff, or the learned member of the bar who has resided during the past summer with him, who acts as one of his counsel in this action, and has shown a laudable zeal, and made strenuous exertions in behalf of his client. The plaintiff complains also of the smoke from the locomotive, on the ground that it is prejudicial to the health and comfort of himself and his family, and he alleges that the establishment as now conducted is a "nuisance of the most flagrant character," and the lives of his family, tenants and inmates are endangered. The general charge that it is a flagrant nuisance, cannot be taken into consideration, any further than as it may be supported by the facts. In this case there are none except those which I have mentioned. The smoke must undoubtedly be annoying to some extent, but not more disagreeable or prejudicial than what may proceed from many lawful establishments in the village, nor is the inconvenience so constant or continuous. There may be some danger to human life from the rapid passage of a railroad train, but in the opinion of many, not more than what results from the passage of ordinary carriages. Accidents to children, or to adults who are not grossly careless, from the locomotives when passing through our most populous cities, are very rare. The times of their passage are generally known, and the noise made by the movement over the rails, and the engineer's whistle, give timely notice of the approach of the train. When the usual precautions are practiced the danger is very slight, and when there is any carelessness or mismanagement the company and its officers are very properly held to a rigid accountability. It is true that there can be no satisfaction for the loss of life, nor any adequate remuneration for the deprivation of a limb, but the strong probability that the company will encounter a serious loss of property, and that a careless or notoriously incompetent conductor, or engineer, will undergo a disgraceful punishment where serious injuries are inflicted, must necessarily lead to great caution and to consequent security. The evils of which the plaintiff complains are by no means peculiar to himself. They are the necessary concomitants of this species of locomotion, whether in the city or in the country. They cannot be prevented without an entire suspension of one of the greatest improvements of modern times.

Private rights should undoubtedly be effectually guarded, but the courts cannot extend the protection of the interest of any one so far as to restrict the lawful pursuits of another. The maxim *sic uteri tuo ut non alienum laedas* is true when correctly construed. It extends to all damages for which the law gives redress, but no further. If it should be applied literally, it would deprive us to a great extent of the legitimate use of our property, and impair, if not destroy its value. A man who sets up a new store or hotel in the vicinity of an old one, or who discovers and makes a new machine which wholly supersedes a prior invention, or who erects a new dwelling house so near that of his neighbor as to endanger it from the cinders which may escape from the chimney, or as to interrupt some fine prospect, or who plants a grove so near the boundary line of another as to shade a valuable garden, or prevent the free circulation of air around a dwelling house, inflicts an injury for which the law gives no redress, and which cannot be averted by the tribunals intrusted with its administration. So too there are some useful employments which endanger the lives of human beings which cannot and ought not to be prohibited. Lives are sometimes destroyed by an omnibus, a carman's cart, a stage or a steamboat, but so long as they are not imminently dangerous they cannot be prohibited. We cannot enjoy our private rights, nor can we avail ourselves of the many advantages resulting from modern discoveries, without encountering some risk to our lives, or our property, or to some extent endangering the lives or injuring the property of others. The questions in all such cases are, is the business a lawful one, and is the injury or danger to others by or from its legitimate pursuit inevitable? If they are, the law furnishes no remedy either by way of indemnity or prevention. . . .

Upon the whole I am satisfied that the case presented in behalf of the plaintiff does not call for, or warrant, the interposition of this court by way of restriction upon the future action of the defendants.

The motion for an injunction must therefore be denied, and the order temporarily restraining the defendants must be vacated.

Part VII

Slavery and the
Dissolving Union

I n 1619, a Dutch cargo ship brought African Negroes to Virginia, and sold them to the settlers for labor. Historians believe that, at least in the beginning, the English colonists did not distinguish between the blacks and white indentured servants, but that within three to four decades, black status had been determined: They would be slaves for life, as would their issue (Document 82). The problem of slavery, although quiescent for the next two centuries, became an ever more troublesome question for Americans. At the Continental Congress that wrote the Declaration of Independence and at the Philadelphia Constitutional Convention, opponents of slavery held their tongues or went along with southern demands in order to achieve the immediate goals of independence or nationhood.

But by the early nineteenth century, the issue could no longer be ignored. Abolitionists became more vocal (Document 87), while slaveholders worried about the growing power of the federal government (Document 84). The various mechanisms for dealing with runaway slaves came under attack in northern courts (Documents 88, 89, 90), while at the same time southerners tightened their grip on what they considered their "chattels personal" (Documents 92, 93).

Slavery became a cancer, eating away at the nation. The South demanded a stronger Fugitive Slave Law to enforce what it believed to be the North's constitutional obligations (Document 95); in return, states enacted personal liberty laws designed to thwart the remanding of runaways (Document 96), or refused to obey federal court orders (Document 99). The Supreme Court, in a gross error of judgment, tried to resolve the issue through judicial fiat (Document 97), only to find its decision attacked throughout the North (Document 98).

Finally the South, believing itself and its "peculiar institution" under attack, decided to withdraw from the Union, relying on constitutional arguments that had been circulating for more than four decades (Documents 85, 86, 87). The moribund Buchanan administration in Washington seemed unable to act (Document 100), and stood by helplessly as the Union dissolved (Document 101).

82

Maryland Statute on Negroes and Other Slaves (1664)

The first boatload of African Negroes arrived in Virginia in 1619, and for the next several decades the status of blacks in the Chesapeake region remained unclear. Some served a term of years, similar to that of indentured servants, and then went free; others were enslaved for life. By the time the Maryland legislature acted, the debate had been resolved: All blacks and their children, as well as the products of racially mixed liaisons, would be slaves *durante vita*—for life. Statutes such as this one marked a major shift in the southern labor system from white servants indentured for a set term of years to black slaves owned perpetually as property. But the analogy to property, while used so often in southern rhetoric, could not hide the fact that this was a special type of property, and special rules eventually developed around the slaveholding system (Document 93).

See W. D. Jordan, *White Over Black* (1968), Pts. 1 and 2; A. L. Higginbotham, *In the Matter of Color: Race and the American Legal Process, the Colonial Period* (1978); O. Handlin and M. Handlin, "The Origins of the Southern Labor System," 7 *W. & M. Q.* 199 (1950); and W. M. Wiecek, "The Statutory Law of Slavery and Race in the Thirteen Mainland Colonies of British America," 34 *W. & M. Q.* 258 (1977).

Bee itt Enacted by the Right Honourable the Lord Proprietary, by the advice and Consent of the upper and lower house of this present Generall Assembly, That all Negroes or other slaves already within the Province And all Negroes and other slaves to bee hereafter imported into the Province shall serve Durante Vita. And all Children born of any Negro or other slave shall be Slaves as their ffathers were for the terme of their lives. And forasmuch as divers freeborne English women forgettfull of their free Condition and to the disgrace of our Nation doe intermarry with Negro Slaves, by which alsoe divers suites may arise touching the Issue of such woemen and a great damage doth befall the Masters of such Negros—for prevention whereof and for deterring such freeborne women from such shamefull Matches, Bee itt

---

Source: Rose, ed., *Documentary History of Slavery in North America* 24 (1976).

further Enacted by the Authority advice and Consent aforesaid, That whatsoever free borne woman shall inter marry with any slave from and after the Last day of this present Assembly shall Serve the master of such slave dureing the life of her husband, And that all the Issue of such freeborne woemen soe marryed shall be Slaves as their fathers were. And Bee itt further Enacted that all the Issues of English or other freeborne woemen that have already marryed Negroes shall serve the Masters of their Parents till they be Thirty years of age and noe longer.

83

Somerset v. *Stewart* *(1772)*

By the time of the Revolution slavery was a fixed part of the American legal and economic system. Opposition to slavery had been growing in England, however, and a decision on the King's Bench, the country's highest common law court, provided a lever later used by abolitionists in the United States. An American slave, brought to England by his master, had run away; Somerset had been recaptured and consigned to be sold to Jamaica. English emancipationists secured a writ of habeas corpus to free Somerset, and hoped to have slavery declared illegal in Great Britain. William Murray, Baron Mansfield, the Chief Justice of King's Bench, freed Somerset, but did so on narrow though important legal grounds. First, when confronted by competing laws, a court should choose the law of its own jurisdiction; second, slavery was held so odious that only positive law, that is, a specific statute, could support it. *Somerset* became part of American law, and served as a basis in numerous suits to free slaves (Document 88).

See W. M. Wiecek, "*Somerset:* Lord Mansfield and the Legitimacy of Slavery . . . ," 42 *U. Chi. L. R.* 86 (1974), and *The Sources of Antislavery Constitutionalism in America, 1760–1848* (1977); and E. Fiddes, "Lord Mansfield and the Sommersett Case," 50 *Law Q. R.* 499 (1934).

———

Source: 99 Eng. Rep. 499 (K. B. 1772).

~~~~~~

Lord Mansfield

The question is, if the owner had a right to detain the slave, for the sending of him over to be sold in Jamaica. In five or six cases of this nature, I have known it to be accommodated by agreement between the parties: on its first coming before me, I strongly recommended it here. But if the parties will have it decided, we must give our opinion. Compassion will not, on the one hand, nor inconvenience on the other, be to decide; but the law: in which the difficulty will be principally from the inconvenience on both sides. Contract for sale of a slave is good here; the sale is a matter to which the law properly and readily attaches, and will maintain the price according to the agreement. But here the person of the slave himself is immediately the object of enquiry; which makes a very material difference. The now question is, whether any dominion, authority or coercion can be exercised in this country, on a slave according to the American laws? The difficulty of adopting the relation, without adopting it in all its consequences, is indeed extreme; and yet, many of those consequences are absolutely contrary to the municipal law of England. We have no authority to regulate the conditions in which law shall operate. On the other hand, should we think the coercive power cannot be exercised: 'tis now about fifty years since the opinion given by two of the greatest men of their own or any times, (since which no contract has been brought to trial, between the masters and slaves;) the service performed by the slaves without wages, is a clear indication they did not think themselves free by coming hither. The setting 14,000 or 15,000 men at once free loose by a solemn opinion, is much disagreeable in the effects it threatens. . . .

. . . On the part of Somerset, the case which we gave notice should be decided this day, the Court now proceeds to give its opinion. I shall recite the return to the writ of habeas corpus, as the ground of our determination; omitting only words of form. The captain of the ship on board of which the negro was taken, makes his return to the writ in terms signifying that there have been, and still are, slaves to a great number in Africa; and that the trade in them is authorized by the laws and opinions of Virginia and Jamaica; that they are goods and chattels; and, as such, saleable and sold. That James Somerset, is a negro of Africa, and long before the return of the King's writ was brought to be sold, and was sold to Charles Stewart, Esq. then in Jamaica, and has not been manumitted since; that Mr. Stewart, having occasion to transact business, came over hither, with an intention to return; and brought Somerset, to attend and abide with him, and to carry him back as soon as the business should be transacted. That such intention has been, and still continues; and that the negro did remain till the time of his departure, in the service of his master Mr. Stewart, and quitted it without his consent; and thereupon, before the return of the King's writ, the said Charles Stewart did commit the slave on board the "Ann and Mary," to save custody, to be kept till he should set sail, and then to be taken with him to Jamaica, and there sold as a slave. And this is the cause why he, Captain Knowles, who was then and now is, commander of the above vessel, then and now lying in the river of Thames, did the said negro, committed to his custody, detain; and on which he now renders him to the orders of the Court. We pay all due attention to the opinion of Sir Philip Yorke, and Lord Chief Justice Talbot, whereby they pledged themselves to the British planters, for all the legal consequences of slaves coming over to this kingdom or being baptized, recognized by Lord Hardwicke, sitting as Chancellor on the 19th of October 1749, that trover would lie: that a notion had prevailed, if a negro came over, or became a Christian, he was emancipated, but no ground in law; that he and Lord Talbot, when Attorney and Solicitor-General, were of opinion, that no such claim for freedom was valid; that tho' the Statute of Tenures had abolished villains regardant to a manor, yet he did not conceive but that a man might still become a villain in gross, by confessing himself such in open Court. We are so well agreed, that we think there is no occasion of having it argued (as I intimated an intention at first,) before all the Judges, as is usual, for obvious reasons, on a return to a habeas corpus; the only question before us is, whether the cause on the return is sufficient? If it is, the negro must be remanded; if it is not, he must be discharged. Accordingly, the return states, that the slave departed and refused to serve; whereupon he was kept, to be sold abroad. So high an act of dominion must be recognized by the law of the country where it is used. The power of a master over his slave has been extremely different, in different countries. The state of slavery is of such a nature, that it is incapable of being introduced on any reasons, moral or political; but only positive law, which preserves its force long after the reasons, occasion, and time itself from whence it was created, is erased from memory: it's so odious, that nothing can be suffered to support it, but positive law. Whatever inconveniences, therefore, may follow from a decision, I cannot say this case is allowed or approved by the law of England; and therefore the black must be discharged.

84

Defense of States' Rights (1820)

JOHN TAYLOR

The impact of *McCulloch* v. *Maryland* (Document 54) lay less in its specific holding—there could not have been much surprise at the Court's vindication of the Bank—than in the bold manner in which Chief Justice Marshall had interpreted national power, and the broad, expansive reading he gave to the Constitution. To many Republicans, the decision sounded an alarm; they saw in Marshall's abstractions the legitimation of an all-encompassing national power against which they had fought for decades. Probably no purer statement of an extreme agrarian, states' rights doctrine can be found than that in the attack on *McCulloch* by John Taylor of Caroline. The Virginian sounded an alarm sure to alert Southerners to the danger: If Congress could incorporate a bank, then would it not also have the power to interfere in local matters and free slaves? Taylor's concerns were far from hypothetical, for Congress had already started to debate the Missouri question when he wrote.

See K. M. Bailor, "John Taylor of Caroline, 1790–1820," 75 *Va. Mag. Hist. & Biog.* 290 (1967).

The constitution gives no authority to the federal government to exercise such powers over the state governments. Can it then be true, as the position of the court declares, that the federal government have a right so *to modify every power vested in the state governments, as to exempt its own operations from their influence?* Upon the ground of this doctrine, the supreme court of the federal government has attempted so to modify the concurrent right of taxation reserved to the states, as to exempt the incorporating power assumed by congress, from its influence. This is one of the enumerated powers invested in the states, by which it was certainly foreseen and intended, that they might influence the operations of the federal government; and if in this case such an influence justifies a modification of the state power of taxation by the federal government, and even by one of its departments, the same reason will

---

Source: Taylor, *Construction Construed and Constitutions Vindicated* (1820).

justify a modification of all the rest of the enumerated influencing state powers. The supreme court might by the same principle, appoint senators, electors, and militia officers, should the states neglect to do it; in order, by modifying these powers of the state governments, as being subordinate to the supposed supremacy of the federal government, *to exempt the latter from their influence.*

If, therefore, it should have been proved, that the federal government is not invested with a power of modifying the powers bestowed by the people on the state governments, the pretended supremacy, supposed to bestow a right so unlimited, does not exist; the modification on the state power of taxation was of course unconstitutional; and the question would seem to be settled. But it starts up again in a new form; and though it should be allowed that the entire federal government do not possess a right to modify the state constitutions, yet it is still contended, that one of its subordinate departments does possess it; and its supreme court have accordingly modified and restricted the power of internal taxation bestowed by the state constitutions on their governments. This power under the state constitutions was unlimited. It is not limited by the federal constitution. But the federal court have adjudged, that it is either necessary or convenient that it should be limited; and for that reason they have modified it by a precedent sufficient to justify other modifications of state powers to any extent, upon the ground of possessing an unlimited supremacy over the legislative and judicial power of the states.

The supremacy we have examined is confined to the constitution, the laws, and treaties. It is not extended to judicial decisions. Suppose congress should pass a law declaring such state laws as they pleased, to be unconstitutional and void. An excessive interpretation of the word "supreme," might give some countenance to so evident an usurpation; and as one branch of the federal legislature is elected by the people, it would afford some security, however imperfect, against such a prostration of the state governments at the feet of the federal legislative power. But neither this excessive supremacy, nor this defective security, plead for lodging the same unlimited power in the federal courts. Were they to possess it, they might modify the state governments, in a mode, contrary to the will of congress, as is exemplified in the case under consideration. In creating the bank of the United States, congress did not endeavour to prohibit the states from taxing the property employed in that speculation. Had the state right to do so been considered in that body, its constitutionality might have been decided in the affirmative. The court, therefore, in assuming a power to restrain this state right, may have violated the will both of the federal and state legislature, and modified the state constitutions, contrary to the judgment of both. The state law asserted the right, the federal law is silent, and the court imposes a constitutional rule on both (as if it were itself a constituent or elemental power,) objected to by one, and never assented to by the other. This outstrips even the arbitrary principle laid down by the court itself "that the supreme government may modify every power vested in subordinate governments, to exempt its own operations from their influence." It will not be asserted that the federal court is the supreme government, or that it has operations to carry on, which ought to be exempted from the influence of the subordinate state governments. If these governments are not subordinate to that court, it cannot modify their powers, even under its own principle; and if the federal government possesses this modifying power, it ought to be exercised by congress, before it can be enforced by the court. The court at most can only execute, and have no power to pronounce the modification. Congress might have intended, that the power of taxing the United States bank, like that of taxing state banks, should remain as a concurrent power, like the other concurrent powers of taxation. If that body conceived itself possessed of a power to modify the state power of taxation, it could only do so by its own act, and that act ought to have been explicit, that the people might, by election, have expressed their opinion concerning it. But when the modification is expressed by the court, the chief remedy for deciding spherical collisions, and for restraining each division of power within its own orbit, is wholly evaded, and completely transferred from the people to the judges.

But, though it should be allowed, that the court derives no supremacy from that clause of the constitution, which bestows it upon the constitution itself, the laws and treaties, yet it has been claimed under another. "The judicial *power of the United States* shall be vested in *one supreme court,* and in *inferior courts.* The judges, both of the *supreme* and *inferior* courts shall hold their offices during good behaviour." And in the next clause, this *"judicial power of the United States"* is defined and limited. By this clause, a judicial power is vested. Was it a limited or an unlimited power? It is expressed to be *"the judicial power of the United States."* In the second section of the same article, the judicial power of the United States is expressly defined and limited; and this defined and limited judicial power, is that which is vested in *the supreme and such inferior courts as congress may from time to time establish.* The word "supreme" is evidently used in reference to "inferior." The supremacy bestowed is over the inferior courts *to be established by congress,* and not *over the state courts,* either supreme or inferior. This is manifested by the division of jurisdiction between the supreme and inferior courts. In cases "affecting ambassadors, publick ministers and consuls, and where a state shall be a party, the supreme court shall have original jurisdiction. In all other cases *before mentioned* the supreme court shall have appellate jurisdiction." "Before mentioned." Thus expressly limiting the jurisdiction of the supreme court of the United States, to the subjects defined in the preceding article. If, therefore, any thing in the federal constitution is plain enough to be understood, I think we may certainly conclude, that the word "supreme" was not intended to extend the power of the federal court in any degree whatsoever. That court by declaring every local or internal law of congress constitutional, would extend its own jurisdiction; a limitation of which, attended with a power to extend it without controul, by a supreme power over the state courts, would be no limitation at all; since the power of supremacy would destroy the co-ordinate right of construing the constitution, in which resides the power of enforcing the limitation. A jurisdiction, limited by its own will, is an unlimited jurisdiction. . . .

The federal constitution does not say, "that the legislative power shall consist of one supreme and inferior legislatures;" because it considered the state and federal legislatures as independent of each other, within their respective spheres. Had it considered the state legislatures as subordinate to the federal legislature, the supremacy of the latter would have been declared, and the subordination of the former expressed, as objects upon which this supremacy was to operate. If one federal court only had been allowed by the constitution, the word "supreme" would have been unnecessary. In creating and specifying the objects, namely, the inferior federal courts, upon which the supremacy was to operate, all other objects are excluded. The judicial federal power therefore stands in the same relation to the state judicial power, as the federal legislative power does to the state legislative power; and if either be independent of the other whilst acting within its own sphere, both must be also independent of the other. If congress cannot repeal or injoin state laws, the supreme federal court cannot injoin or abrogate state judgments or decrees. If the federal legislative power be limited, the federal judicial power must also be limited. . . .

It is objected, that if the supreme federal court do not possess an unlimited or unchecked supremacy in construing the constitution, clashing constructions will ensue. This is truth and yet it is not a good reason for overturning our system of dividing, limiting and checking power, if that system be a good one; and if it be even a bad one, the people only, and neither one of their departments separately, nor all united, can alter or amend it. The objection applies as strongly to the other departments of our government, as to the judicial. If the federal legislature and executive do not possess an absolute supremacy over the state legislatures and executives, clashing constitutional constructions will ensue. The jurisdiction on the federal judicial power is as expressly limited, as the legislative and executive federal powers. There is no judicial supremacy recognized in the supreme federal court, except that over inferior federal courts. And, if the supremacy of the constitution bestows upon any federal department a supremacy over the correspondent state department, it must bestow upon every federal department, a similar supremacy over the other correspondent state departments.

85

South Carolina Exposition (1828)

JOHN C. CALHOUN

Although the *Exposition* was written in response to the so-called Tariff of Abominations of 1828, the constitutional theory it espoused took on greater significance as the debate over slavery heated up between 1830 and 1860. Calhoun, formerly an ardent nationalist, wrote the document secretly, since he was the nationalistic Andrew Jackson's running mate in the presidential election of that year. The *Exposition* did not call for the breakup of the Union; rather, it proposed the idea of nullification, whereby a state could protect its interests against a hostile majority. Calhoun also took issue with the idea that the Constitution derived its authority directly from the people. He held that the Union was a compact of states, and ultimate sovereignty remained in the states. Since sovereignty was indivisible, it could never be ceded. This argument, in the hands of slavery's defenders, developed into the axiom that states could secede from the Union to protect their vital interests, such as slavery.

See A. O. Spain, *The Political Theory of John C. Calhoun* (1950); W. S. Jenkins, *Pro-Slavery Thought in the Old South* (1935); and W. W. Freehling, *Prelude to Civil War: The Nullification Controversy in South Carolina, 1816–1836* (1966).

The Committee do not propose to enter into an elaborate, or refined argument on the question of the constitutionality of the Tariff system.

The General Government is one of specific powers, and it can rightfully exercise only the powers expressly granted, and those that may be "necessary and proper" to carry them into effect; all others being reserved expressly to the States, or to the people. It results necessarily, that those who claim to exercise a power under the Constitution, are bound to shew, that it is expressly granted, or that it is necessary and proper, as a means to some of the granted powers. The advocates of the Tariff have offered no such proof. It is true, that the third [*sic*] section of the first article of the Constitution of the United States authorizes Congress to lay and collect an impost duty, but it

Source: Wilson and Hemphill, eds., 10 *Papers of John C. Calhoun* 445 (1977).

is granted as a tax power, for the sole purpose of revenue; a power in its nature essentially different from that of imposing protective or prohibitory duties. The two are incompatable [*sic*]; for the prohibitory system must end in destroying the revenue from impost. It has been said that the system is a violation of the spirit and not the letter of the Constitution. The distinction is not material. The Constitution may be as grossly violated by acting against its meaning as against its letter; but it may be proper to dwell a moment on the point, in order to understand more fully the real character of the acts, under which the interest of this, and other States similarly situated, has been sacrificed. The facts are few and simple. The Constitution grants to Congress the power of imposing a duty on imports for revenue; which power is abused by being converted into an instrument for rearing up the industry of one section of the country on the ruins of another. The violation then consists in using a power, granted for one object, to advance another, and that by the sacrifice of the original object. It is, in a word, *a violation of perversion,* the most dangerous of all, because the most insidious, and difficult to resist. Others cannot be perpetrated without the aid of the judiciary; this may be, by the executive and legislative alone. The courts by their own decisions cannot look into the motives of legislators—they are obliged to take acts by their titles and professed objects, and if *they* be constitutional they cannot interpose their power, however grossly the acts may violate the Constitution. The proceedings of the last session sufficiently prove, that the House of Representatives are aware of the distinction, and determined to avail themselves of the advantage. . . .

If there be a political proposition universally true, one which springs directly from the nature of man, and is independent of circumstances, it is, that irresponsible power is inconsistent with liberty and must corrupt those who exercise it. On this great principle our political system rests. We consider all powers as delegated from the people and to be controlled by those who are interested in their just and proper exercise; and our governments, both State and General, are but a system of judicious contrivances to bring this fundamental principle into fair practical operation. . . . From diversity of interest in the several classes of the people and sections of the country, laws act differently, so that the same law, though couched in general terms and apparently fair, shall in reality transfer the power and prosperity of one class or section to another; in such case responsibility to constituents, which is but the means of enforcing the fidelity of representatives to them, must prove wholly insufficient to preserve the purity of public agents, or the liberty of the country. It would in fact be inapplicable to the evil. The disease would be in the community itself; in the constituents, not in the representatives. The opposing interest of the community would engender necessarily opposing hostile parties, organized in this very diversity of interest; the stronger of which, if the government provided no efficient check, would exercise unlimited and unrestrained power over the weaker. The relations of equality between them would thus be destroyed, and in its place there would be substituted the relation of sovereign and subject, between the stronger and the weaker interest, in its most odious and oppressive form. . . . On the great and vital point, the industry of the country, which comprehends nearly all the other interests, two great sections of the Union are opposed. We want free trade; they, restrictions. We want moderate taxes, frugality in the government, economy, accountability, and a rigid application of the public money, to the payment of the public debt, and the objects authorized by the Constitution; in all these particulars, if we may judge by experience, their views of their interest are the opposite. They act and feel on all questions connected with the American System, as sovereigns; as those always do who impose burdens on others for their own benefit; and we, on the contrary, like those on whom such burdens are imposed. In a word, to the extent stated, the country is divided and organized into two great opposing parties, one sovereign and the other subject; marked by all the characteristics which must ever accompany that relation, under whatever form it may exist. That our industry is controlled by the many, instead of one, by a majority in Congress elected by a majority in the community having an opposing interest, instead of hereditary rulers, forms not the slightest mitigation of the evil. In fact, instead of mitigating, it aggravates. In our case one opposing branch of industry cannot prevail without associating others, and thus instead of a single act of oppression we must bear many. . . . Liberty comprehends the idea of *responsible power,* that those who make and execute the laws should be controlled by those on whom they operate; that the governed should govern. Thus to prevent rulers from abusing their trust, constituents must controul [*sic*] them through elections; and so to prevent the major from oppressing the minor interests of society, the constitution must provide . . . a check founded on the same principle, and equally efficacious. In fact the abuse of delegated power, and the tyranny of the greater over the less interests of society, are the two great dangers, and the only two, to be guarded against; and if *they* be effectually guarded liberty must be *eternal.* . . . No government based on the naked principle, that the majority ought to govern, however true the maxim in its proper sense and under proper restrictions, ever preserved its liberty, even for a single generation. The history of all has been the same, injustice, violence and anarchy, succeeded by the government of one, or a few, under which the people seek refuge, from the more oppressive despotism of the majority. Those governments only, which provide checks, which limit and restrain within proper bounds the power of the majority, have had a prolonged existence, and been distinguished for virtue, power and happiness. Constitutional government, and the government of a majority, are utterly incompatible, it being the sole purpose of a constitution to impose limitations and checks upon the majority. An unchecked majority, is a despotism—and government is free, and will be permanent in proportion to the number, complexity and efficiency of the checks, by which its powers are controlled. . . .

Our system, then consists of two distinct and independent sovereignties.

The general powers conferred on the General Government, are subject to its sole and separate control, and the States cannot, without violating the Constitution, interpose their authority to check, or in any manner counteract its movements, so long, as they are confined to its proper sphere; so also the peculiar and local powers, reserved to the States, are subject to their exclusive control, nor can the General Government interfere with them, without on its part, also violating the Constitution. In order to have a full and clear conception of our institutions, it will be proper to remark, that there is in our system a striking distinction between the government and the sovereign power. Whatever may be the true doctrine in regard to the sovereignty of the States individually, it is unquestionably clear that while the government of the union is vested in its legislative, executive and political departments, the actual sovereign power, resides in the several States, who created it, in their separate and distinct political character. . . .

. . . The constitutional power to protect their rights as members of the confederacy, results necessarily, by the most simple and demonstrable arguments, from the very nature of the relation subsisting between the States and General Government. If it be conceded, as it must by every one who is the least conversant with our institutions, that the sovereign power is divided between the States and General Government, and that the former holds its reserved rights, in the same high sovereign capacity, which the latter does its delegated rights; it will be impossible to deny to the States the right of deciding on the infraction of their rights, and the proper remedy to be applied for the correction. The right of judging, in such cases, is an essential attribute of sovereignty of which the States cannot be divested, without losing their sovereignty itself; and being reduced to a subordinate corporate condition. In fact, to divide power, and to give to one of the parties the exclusive right of judging of the portion allotted to each, is in reality not to divide at all; and to reserve such exclusive right to the General Government, (it matters not by what department it be exercised,) is in fact to constitute it one great consolidated government, with unlimited powers, and to reduce the States to mere corporations. It is impossible to understand the force of terms, and to deny these conclusions. The opposite opinion can be embraced only on hasty and imperfect views of the relation existing between the States and the General Government. But the existence of the right of judging of their powers, clearly established from the sovereignty of the States, as clearly implies a veto, or controul on the action of the General Government on contested points of authority; and this very controul is the remedy, which the Constitution has provided to prevent the encroachment of the General Government on the reserved right of the States; and by the exercise of which, the distribution of power between the General and State Governments, may be preserved forever inviolate, as is established by the Constitution; and thus afford effectual protection to the great minor interest of the community, against the oppression of the majority.

South Carolina Ordinance of Nullification (1832)

Although the protests against the high rates of the 1828 tariff led to some reductions, by 1832 the actual level of the tariffs mattered less to some people than the principle. Ardent states' rights advocates began to develop Calhoun's theories of state sovereignty, and claimed that the states had the right to nullify federal laws. In the election of 1832, the "Nullies" swept every county in South Carolina, and Governor James Hamilton called for a special legislative session, which in turn called for a popular convention. Controlled entirely by the "Nullies," the convention adopted an ordinance declaring the tariffs of 1828 and 1832 void and prohibiting federal enforcement of collection. The vehemence of the South Carolina action dismayed even sympathetic southern states, and not one went along. Andrew Jackson easily outflanked the nullifiers by calling for further reductions, and warned the people of the state that their actions could lead to armed conflict. The constitutional argument of the ordinance, however, did not disappear, but gained increasing strength in the South. Its advocates believed that only such a doctrine would protect the southern states from northern efforts to use the national government to do away with slavery.

See items listed for previous document, as well as M. D. Peterson, *Olive Branch and Sword: The Compromise of 1833* (1982).

Whereas the Congress of the United States, by various acts, purporting to be acts laying duties and imposts on foreign imports, but in reality intended for the protection of domestic manufactures, and the giving of bounties to classes and individuals engaged in particular employments, at the expense and to the injury and oppression of other classes and individuals, and by wholly exempting from taxation certain foreign commodities, such as are not produced or manufactured in the United States, to afford a pretext for imposing higher and excessive duties on articles similar to those intended to be protected, hath exceeded its just powers under the Constitution, which confers on it no authority to afford such protection, and hath violated the true meaning and intent of the Constitution, which provides for equality in imposing the bur-

Source: 1 *S. C. Statutes at Large* 329 (1832).

thens of taxation upon the several States and portions of the Confederacy: *And whereas* the said Congress, exceeding its just power to impose taxes and collect revenue for the purpose of effecting and accomplishing the specific objects and purposes which the Constitution of the United States authorizes it to effect and accomplish, hath raised and collected unnecessary revenue for objects unauthorized by the Constitution:—

We, therefore, the people of the State of South Carolina in Convention assembled, do declare and ordain, . . . That the several acts and parts of acts of the Congress of the United States, purporting to be laws for the imposing of duties and imposts on the importation of foreign commodities, . . . are unauthorized by the Constitution of the United States, and violate the true meaning and intent thereof, and are null, void, and no law, nor binding upon this State, its officers or citizens; and all promises, contracts, and obligations, made or entered into, or to be made or entered into, with purpose to secure the duties imposed by the said acts, and all judicial proceedings which shall be hereafter had in affirmance thereof, are and shall be held utterly null and void.

And it is further Ordained, That it shall not be lawful for any of the constituted authorities, whether of this State or of the United States, to enforce the payment of duties imposed by the said acts within the limits of this State; but it shall be the duty of the Legislature to adopt such measures and pass such acts as may be necessary to give full effect to this Ordinance, and to prevent the enforcement and arrest the operation of the said acts and parts of acts of the Congress of the United States within the limits of this State, from and after the 1st day of February next, . . .

And it is further Ordained, That in no case of law or equity, decided in the courts of this State, wherein shall be drawn in question the authority of this ordinance, or the validity of such act or acts of the Legislature as may be passed for the purpose of giving effect thereto, or the validity of the aforesaid acts of Congress, imposing duties, shall any appeal be taken or allowed to the Supreme Court of the United States, nor shall any copy of the record be printed or allowed for that purpose; and if any such appeal shall be attempted to be taken, the courts of this State shall proceed to execute and enforce their judgments, according to the laws and usages of the State, without reference to such attempted appeal, and the person or persons attempting to take such appeal may be dealt with as for a contempt of the court.

And it is further Ordained, That all persons now holding any office of honor, profit, or trust, civil or military, under this State, (members of the Legislature excepted), shall, within such time, and in such manner as the Legislature shall prescribe, take an oath well and truly to obey, execute, and enforce, this Ordinance, and such act or acts of the Legislature as may be passed in pursuance thereof, according to the true intent and meaning of the same; and on the neglect or omission of any such person or persons so to do, his or their office or offices shall be forthwith vacated, . . . and no person hereafter elected to any office of honor, profit, or trust, civil or military, (members of the Legislature excepted), shall, until the Legislature shall otherwise provide and direct, enter on the execution of his office, . . . until he shall, in like manner, have taken a similar oath; and no juror shall be empannelled in any of the courts of this State, in any cause in which shall be in question this Ordinance, or any act of the Legislature passed in pursuance thereof, unless he shall first, in addition to the usual oath, have taken an oath that he will well and truly obey, execute, and enforce this Ordinance, and such act or acts of the Legislature as may be passed to carry the same into operation and effect, according to the true intent and meaning thereof.

And we, the People of South Carolina, to the end that it may be fully understood by the Government of the United States, and the people of the co-States, that we are determined to maintain this, our Ordinance and Declaration, at every hazard, *Do further Declare* that we will not submit to the application of force, on the part of the Federal Government, to reduce this State to obedience; but that we will consider the passage, by Congress, of any act . . . to coerce the State, shut up her ports, destroy or harass her commerce, or to enforce the acts hereby declared to be null and void, otherwise than through the civil tribunals of the country, as inconsistent with the longer continuance of South Carolina in the Union: and that the people of this State will thenceforth hold themselves absolved from all further obligation to maintain or preserve their political connexion with the people of the other States, and will forthwith proceed to organize a separate Government, and do all other acts and things which sovereign and independent States may of right to do.

87

Declaration of American Anti-Slavery Society (1833)

The furor over slavery aroused by the Missouri debate of 1819 died down somewhat in the 1820s, but then suddenly came back to life. Debates in Virginia over abolition in 1829 and 1831, talk in the North

Source: Ruchames, ed., *The Abolitionists* 78 (1963)

about colonization, the publication of David Walker's *Appeal to the Colored Citizens of the World* (1829), Nat Turner's rebellion (1831), and the nullification crisis brought southern fears to the fore. Anxiety increased in 1833 with the founding of the American Anti-Slavery Society, led by the fiery abolitionist William Lloyd Garrison and pledged to ending slavery. The sentiments adopted at the founding meeting established the basic argument of the Society for the next three decades, namely, the illegality of slavery, if not under the Constitution (which Garrison had damned as a "covenant with hell") then certainly under natural law.

The growing strength of the abolition movement over the next three decades put a severe strain on the Constitution and on the legal system. Southerners were correct in asserting that the Constitution recognized and protected slavery, and that northern states had agreed to respect their "peculiar institution" as part of the price of Union. Abolitionists therefore divided on the appropriate means by which they could challenge the legal basis of slavery, a debate ultimately fought out on a national stage.

See R. M. Cover, *Justice Accused: Antislavery and the Judicial Process* (1975); and R. B. Nye, *William Lloyd Garrison and Humanitarian Reformers* (1955).

We have met together for the achievement of an enterprise, without which that of our fathers is incomplete; and which, for its magnitude, solemnity, and probable results upon the destiny of the world, as far transcends theirs as moral truth does physical force.

In purity of motive, in earnestness of zeal, in decision of purpose, in intrepidity of action, in steadfastness of faith, in sincerity of spirit, we would not be inferior to them. . . .

Their grievances, great as they were, were trifling in comparison with the wrongs and sufferings of those for whom we plead. Our fathers were never slaves—never bought and sold like cattle—never shut out from the light of knowledge and religion—never subjected to the lash of brutal taskmasters.

But those, for whose emancipation we are striving—constituting at the present time at least one-sixth part of our countrymen—are recognized by law, and treated by their fellow-beings, as brute beasts; are plundered daily of the fruits of their toil without redress; really enjoy no constitutional nor legal protection from licentious and murderous outrages upon their persons; and are ruthlessly torn asunder—the tender babe from the arms of its frantic mother—the heartbroken wife from her weeping husband—at the caprice or pleasure of irresponsible tyrants. For the crime of having a dark complexion, they suffer the pangs of hunger, the infliction of stripes, the ignominy of brutal servitude. They are kept in heathenish darkness by laws expressly enacted to make their instruction a criminal offence.

These are the prominent circumstances in the condition of more than two million people, the proof of which may be found in thousands of indisputable facts, and in the laws of the slave-holding States.

Hence we maintain—that, in view of the civil and religious privileges of this nation, the guilt of its oppression is unequalled by any other on the face of the earth; and, therefore, that it is bound to repent instantly, to undo the heavy burdens, and to let the oppressed go free. . . .

It is piracy to buy or steal an native African, and subject him to servitude. Surely, the sin is as great to enslave an American as an African.

Therefore we believe and affirm—that there is no difference, in principle, between the African slave trade and American slavery:

That every American citizen, who detains a human being in involuntary bondage as his property, is, according to Scripture, (Ex. xxi, 16,) a man-stealer.

That the slaves ought instantly to be set free, and brought under the protection of law:

That if they had lived from the time of Pharaoh down to the present period, and had been entailed through successive generations, their right to be free could never have been alienated, but their claims would have constantly risen in solemnity:

That all those laws which are now in force, admitting the right of slavery, are therefore, before God, utterly null and void; being an audacious usurpation of the Divine prerogative, a daring infringement on the law of nature, a base overthrow of the very foundations of the social compact, a complete extinction of all the relations, endearments and obligations of mankind, and a presumptuous transgression of all the holy commandments; and that therefore they ought instantly to be abrogated.

We further believe and affirm—that all persons of color, who possess the qualifications which are demanded of others, ought to be admitted forwith to the enjoyment of the same privileges, and the exercise of the same prerogatives, as others; and that the paths of preferment, of wealth and of intelligence, should be opened as widely to them as to persons of a white complexion.

We maintain that no compensation should be given to the planters emancipating their slaves:

Because it would be a surrender of the great fundamental principle, that man cannot hold property in man:

Because slavery is a crime, and therefore is not an article to be sold:

Because the holders of slaves are not the just proprietors of what they claim; freeing the slave is not depriving them of property, but restoring it to its rightful owner; it is not wronging the master, but righting the slave— restoring him to himself:

Because immediate and general emancipation would only destroy nominal, not real property; it would not amputate a limb or break a bone of the slaves, but by infusing motives into their breasts, would make them doubly valuable to the masters as free laborers; and

Because, if compensation is to be given at all, it should be given to the outraged and guiltless slaves, and not to those who have plundered and abused them.

We regard as delusive, cruel and dangerous, any scheme of expatriation which pretends to aid, either directly or indirectly, in the emancipation of the slaves, or to be a substitute for the immediate and total abolition of slavery.

We fully and unanimously recognise the sovereignty of each State, to legislate exclusively on the subject of the slavery which is tolerated within its limits; we concede that Congress, under the present national compact, has no right to interfere with any of the slave States, in relation to this momentous subject:

But we maintain that Congress has a right, and is solemnly bound, to suppress the domestic slave trade between the several States, and to abolish slavery in those portions of our territory which the Constitution has placed under its exclusive jurisdiction.

We also maintain that there are, at the present time, the highest obligations resting upon the people of the free States to remove slavery by moral and political action, as prescribed in the Constitution of the United States. They are now living under a pledge of their tremendous physical force, to fasten the galling fetters of tyranny upon the limbs of millions in the Southern States; they are liable to be called at any moment to suppress a general insurrection of the slaves; they authorize the slave owner to vote for three-fifths of his slaves as property, and thus enable him to perpetuate his oppression; they support a standing army at the South for its protection; and they seize the slave, who has escaped into their territories, and send him back to be tortured by an enraged master or a brutal driver. This relation to slavery is criminal, and full of danger: IT MUST BE BROKEN UP.

These are our views and principles—these our designs and measures. With entire confidence in the overruling justice of God, we plant ourselves upon the Declaration of our Independence and the truths of Divine Revelation, as upon the Everlasting Rock.

88

Commonwealth v. *Aves*
(1836)

This celebrated case, also known as *Med's Case,* gave antislavery advocates one of their few victories in the courts. Med, a six-year-old slave
girl, was accompanying her mistress on a vacation. She was not a runaway (which would have brought her under federal law) but a "so-
journer," a slave brought into a free state or in temporary residence
there. Lawyers for the abolitionists argued that under Massachusetts
law there could be no slavery of any sort, and even sojourners had to
be freed. Chief Justice Shaw recognized the political dangers of the
case, but also understood the enormous public sympathy for the little
girl. He found his solution in the famous English case of *Somerset* v.
Stewart (Document 83), in which Baron Mansfield, facing a similar
situation, resorted to a choice of law rule stating that when a court had
to choose between different codes regarding slavery, it should follow
the laws of its own jurisdiction. Although few other states followed the
Mansfield and Shaw reasoning, the case did give a major impetus to
abolitionist argument that slavery could not exist except where positive
(statutory) law supported it.

See R. M. Cover, *Justice Accused: Antislavery and the Judicial Process* (1975); and
L. W. Levy, *The Law of the Commonwealth and Chief Justice Shaw* (1957).

Chief Justice Shaw delivered the opinion of the court.

The question now before the Court arises upon a return to a habeas corpus
. . . for the purpose of bringing up the person of a colored child named Med,
and instituting a legal inquiry into the fact of her detention, and the causes
for which she was detained. . . .

The precise question presented by the claim of the respondent is, whether
a citizen of any one of the United States, where negro slavery is established
by law, coming into this State, for any temporary purpose of business or
pleasure, staying some time, but not acquiring a domicil here, who brings a
slave with him as a personal attendant, may restrain such slave of his liberty

Source: 35 Mass. 193 (1836).

during his continuance here, and convey him out of this State on his return, against his consent. . . .

It is now to be considered as an established rule, that by the constitution and laws of this Commonwealth, before the adoption of the constitution of the United States, in 1789, slavery was abolished, as being contrary to the principles of justice, and of nature, and repugnant to the provisions of the declaration of rights, which is a component part of the constitution of the State. . . .

Without pursuing this inquiry farther, it is sufficient for the purposes of the case before us, that by the constitution adopted in 1780, slavery was abolished in Massachusetts, upon the ground that it is contrary to natural right and the plain principles of justice. The terms of the first article of the declaration of rights are plain and explicit. "All men are born free and equal, and have certain natural, essential, and unalienable rights, which are, the right of enjoying and defending their lives and liberties, that of acquiring, possessing, and protecting property." It would be difficult to select words more precisely adapted to the abolition of negro slavery. According to the laws prevailing in all the States, where slavery is upheld, the child of a slave is not deemed to be born free, a slave has no right to enjoy and defend his own liberty, or to acquire, possess, or protect property. That the description was broad enough in its terms to embrace negroes, and that it was intended by the framers of the constitution to embrace them, is proved by the earliest contemporaneous construction, by an unbroken series of judicial decisions, and by a uniform practice from the adoption of the constitution to the present time. The whole tenor of our policy, of our legislation and jurisprudence, from that time to the present, has been consistent with this construction, and with no other.

Such being the general rule of law, it becomes necessary to inquire how far it is modified or controlled in its operation; either,

1. By the law of other nations and states, as admitted by the comity of nations to have a limited operation within a particular state; or

2. By the constitution and laws of the United States.

In considering the first, we may assume that the law of this State is analogous to the law of England, in this respect; that while slavery is considered as unlawful and inadmissible in both, and this because contrary to natural right and to laws designed for the security of personal liberty, yet in both, the existence of slavery in other countries is recognized, and the claims of foreigners, growing out of that condition, are, to a certain extent, respected. Almost the only reason assigned by Lord *Mansfield* in Sommersett's case was, that slavery is of such a nature, that it is incapable of being introduced on any reasons moral or political, but only by positive law; and, it is so odious, that nothing can be suffered to support it but positive law.

The same doctrine is clearly stated in the full and able opinion of Marshall C. J., in the case of the *Antelope,* 10 Wheat. 120. He is speaking of the slave trade, but the remark itself shows that it applies to the state of slavery. "That it is contrary to the law of nature will scarcely be denied. That every man has a natural right to the fruits of his own labor, is generally admitted, and that no other person can rightfully deprive him of those fruits, and appropriate them against his will, seems to be the necessary result of the admission."

But although slavery and the slave trade are deemed contrary to natural right, yet it is settled by the judicial decisions of this country and of England, that it is not contrary to the law of nations. . . . The consequence is, that each independent community, in its intercourse with every other, is bound to act on the principle, that such other country has a full and perfect authority to make such laws for the government of its own subjects, as its own judgment shall dictate and its own conscience approve, provided the same are consistent with the law of nations; and no independent community has any right to interfere with the acts or conduct of another state, within the territories of such state, or on the high seas, which each has an equal right to use and occupy; and that each sovereign state, governed by its own laws, although competent and well authorized to make such laws as it may think most expedient to the extent of its own territorial limits, and for the government of its own subjects, yet beyond those limits, and over those who are not her own subjects, has no authority to enforce her own laws, or to treat the laws of other states as void, although contrary to its own views of morality.

This view seems consistent with most of the leading cases on the subject. . . .

This view of the law applicable to slavery, marks strongly the distinction between the relation of master and slave, as established by the local law of particular states, and in virtue of that sovereign power and independent authority which each independent state concedes to every other, and those natural and social relations, which are everywhere and by all people recognized, and which, though they may be modified and regulated by municipal law, are not founded upon it, such as the relation of parent and child, and husband and wife. Such also is the principle upon which the general right of property is founded, being in some form universally recognized as a natural right, independently of municipal law.

This affords an answer to the argument drawn from the maxim, that the right of personal property follows the person, and therefore, where by the law of a place a person there domiciled acquires personal property, by the comity of nations the same must be deemed his property everywhere. It is obvious, that if this were true, in the extent in which the argument employs it, if slavery exists anywhere, and if by the laws of any place a property can be acquired in slaves, the law of slavery must extend to every place where such slaves may be carried. The maxim, therefore, and the argument can apply only to those commodities which are everywhere, and by all nations, treated and deemed subjects of property. But it is not speaking with strict accuracy to say, that a property can be acquired in human beings, by local laws. Each state may, for its own convenience, declare that slaves shall be deemed property, and that the relations and laws of personal chattels shall be deemed to apply to them. . . . But it would be a perversion of terms to say, that such local laws do in fact make them personal property generally; they can only determine, that the same rules of law shall apply to them as are applicable to property, and this effect will follow only so far as such laws *proprio vigore* can operate. . . .

The conclusion to which we come from this view of the law is this:

That by the general and now well established law of this Commonwealth, bond slavery cannot exist, because it is contrary to natural right, and repugnant to numerous provisions of the constitution and laws, designed to secure the liberty and personal rights of all persons within its limits and entitled to the protection of the laws. . . .

That, as a general rule, all persons coming within the limits of a state, become subject to all its municipal laws, civil and criminal, and entitled to the privileges which those laws confer; that this rule applies as well to blacks as whites, except in the case of fugitives, to be afterwards considered; that if such persons have been slaves, they become free, not so much because any alteration is made in their *status,* or condition, as because there is no law which will warrant, but there are laws, if they choose to avail themselves of them, which prohibit, their forcible detention or forcible removal.

That the law arising from the comity of nations cannot apply; because if it did, it would follow as a necessary consequence, that all those persons, who, by force of local laws, and within all foreign places where slavery is permitted, have acquired slaves as property, might bring their slaves here, and exercise over them the rights and power which an owner of property might exercise, and for any length of time short of acquiring a domicil; that such an application of the law would be wholly repugnant to our laws, entirely inconsistent with our policy and our fundamental principles, and is therefore inadmissible. . . .

The constitution and laws of the United States, then, are confined to cases of slaves escaping from other States and coming within the limits of this State without the consent and against the will of their masters, and cannot by any sound construction extend to a case where the slave does not escape and does not come within the limits of this State against the will of the master, but by his own act and permission. The provision is to be construed according to its plain terms and import, and cannot be extended beyond this, and where the case is not that of an escape, the general rule shall have its effect. It is upon these grounds we are of opinion, that an owner of a slave in another State where slavery is warranted by law, voluntarily bringing such slave into this State, has no authority to detain him against his will, or to carry him out of the State against his consent, for the purpose of being held in slavery.

Prigg v. *Pennsylvania* (1842)

By this time growing abolitionist sentiment had led to a number of questions over the reach and legitimacy of the Fugitive Slave Law of 1793. To settle the issue of constitutionality, Pennsylvania and Maryland entered into a collusive prosecution against a Maryland slave catcher. Edward Prigg was indicted for violating the Pennsylvania personal liberty law by catching a runaway slave and her children and taking them back to Maryland without securing the necessary Pennsylvania authorization. As an effort to settle the controversy, *Prigg* failed miserably, and the seven separate opinions ranged over the entire spectrum of pro- and antislavery thought. A majority of the judges held the 1793 federal Fugitive Slave Act constitutional, and held the Pennsylvania law unconstitutional since it interfered with a master's right to his property, and reinforced the master's right to recapture slaves in states other than his domicile. In a unique dictum, Joseph Story suggested that states could negate the federal law by prohibiting their officials from cooperating in its enforcement, a stratagem quickly adopted in the North.

See R. M. Cover, *Justice Accused . . .* , (1975); P. Finkelman, "*Prigg* v. *Pennsylvania* and the Northern State Courts: Anti-Slavery uses of a Pro-Slavery Decision," 25 *Civ. War Hist.* 5 (1979); J. C. Burke, "What Did the Prigg Decision Really Decide?" 93 *Pa. Mag. His. & Bio.* 73 (1969); and S. Campbell, *The Slave Catchers . . .* (1970).

Justice Story delivered the opinion of the Court.

Before proceeding to discuss the very important and interesting questions involved in this record, it is fit to say, that the cause has been conducted in the Court below, and has been brought here by the co-operation and sanction, both of the state of Maryland, and the state of Pennsylvania, in the most friendly and courteous spirit, with a view to have those questions finally disposed of by the adjudication of this Court; so that the agitations on this subject in both states, which have had a tendency to interrupt the

Source: 16 Peters 539 (1842).

harmony between them, may subside, and the conflict of opinion be put at rest. . . .

There are two clauses in the Constitution upon the subject of fugitives, . . . They are both contained in the second section of the fourth article, and are in the following words: "A person charged in any state with treason, felony, or other crime, who shall flee from justice, and be found in another state, shall, on demand of the executive authority of the state from which he fled, be delivered up, to be removed to the state having jurisdiction of the crime."

"No person held to service or labour in one state under the laws thereof, escaping into another, shall in consequence of any law or regulation therein, be discharged from such service or labour; but shall be delivered up, on claim of the party to whom such service or labour may be due."

The last clause is that, the true interpretation whereof is directly in judgment before us. Historically, it is well known, that the object of this clause was to secure to the citizens of the slaveholding states the complete right and title of ownership in their slaves, as property, in every state in the Union into which they might escape from the state where they were held in servitude. The full recognition of this right and title was indispensable to the security of this species of property in all the slaveholding states; and, indeed, was so vital to the preservation of their domestic interests and institutions, that it cannot be doubted that it constituted a fundamental article, without the adoption of which the Union could not have been formed. Its true design was to guard against the doctrines and principles prevalent in the non-slaveholding states, by preventing them from intermeddling with, or obstructing, or abolishing the rights of the owners of slaves.

By the general law of nations, no nation is bound to recognise the state of slavery, as to foreign slaves found within its territorial dominions, when it is in opposition to its own policy and institutions, in favour of the subjects of other nations where slavery is recognised. If it does it, it is a matter of comity, and not as a matter of international right. The state of slavery is deemed to be a mere municipal regulation, founded upon and limited to the range of the territorial laws. . . .

It is manifest from this consideration, that if the Constitution had not contained this clause, every non-slaveholding state in the Union would have been at liberty to have declared free all runaway slaves coming within its limits, and to have given them entire immunity and protection against the claims of their masters; a course which would have created the most bitter animosities, and engendered perpetual strife between the different states. . . .

The clause manifestly contemplates the existence of a positive, unqualified right on the part of the owner of the slave, which no state law or regulation can in any way qualify, regulate, control, or restrain. The slave is not to be discharged from service or labour, in consequence of any state law or regulation. Now, certainly, without indulging in any nicety of criticism upon words, it may fairly and reasonably be said, that any state law or state regulation, which interrupts, limits, delays, or postpones the right of the owner to the immediate possession of the slave, and the immediate command of his service and labour, operates, pro tanto, a discharge of the slave therefrom. The question can never be, how much the slave is discharged from; but whether he is discharged from any, by the natural or necessary operation of state laws or state regulations. . . .

We have said, that the clause contains a positive and unqualified recognition of the right of the owner in the slave, unaffected by any state law or regulation whatsoever, because there is no qualification or restriction of it to be found therein; and we have no right to insert any which is not expressed, and cannot be fairly implied. . . . If this be so, then all the incidents to that right attach also. The owner must, therefore, have the right to seize and repossess the slave, which the local laws of his own state confer upon him as property; and we all know that this right of seizure and recaption is universally acknowledged in all the slaveholding states. . . . Upon this ground we have not the slightest hesitation in holding, that, under and in virtue of the Constitution, the owner of a slave is clothed with entire authority, in every state in the Union, to seize and recapture his slave, whenever he can do it without any breach of the peace, or any illegal violence. In this sense, and to this extent this clause of the Constitution may properly be said to execute itself, and to require no aid from legislation, state or national.

But the clause of the Constitution does not stop here. . . . Many cases must arise in which, if the remedy of the owner were confined to the mere right of seizure and recaption, he would be utterly without any adequate redress. He may not be able to lay his hands upon the slave. . . . He may be restricted by local legislation as to the mode of proofs of his ownership; as to the Courts in which he shall sue, and as to the actions which he may bring; or the process he may use to compel the delivery of the slave. Nay, the local legislation may be utterly inadequate to furnish the appropriate redress, by authorizing no process in rem, or no specific mode of repossessing the slave, but a mere remedy in damages; and that perhaps against persons utterly insolvent or worthless. . . .

And this leads us to the consideration of the other part of the clause, which implies at once a guaranty and duty. It says, "But he (the slave) shall be delivered up on claim of the party to whom such service or labour may be due." Now, we think it exceedingly difficult, if not impracticable, to read this language and not to feel, that it contemplated some farther remedial redress than that, which might be administered at the hands of the owner himself. . . . If, indeed, the Constitution guarantees the right . . . the natural inference certainly is, that the national government is clothed with the appropriate authority and functions to enforce it. . . . The clause is found in the national Constitution, and not in that of any state. It does not point out any state functionaries, or any state action to carry its provisions into effect. The states cannot, therefore, be compelled to enforce them; and it might well be deemed an unconstitutional exercise of the power of interpretation, to insist that the states are bound to provide means to carry into effect the duties of the national government, nowhere delegated or intrusted to them by the Constitution. . . .

Congress has taken this very view of the power and duty of the national government. As early as the year 1791, the attention of Congress was drawn to it. . . . The result of their deliberations, was the passage of the act of the 12th of February, 1793. . . .

But it has been argued, that the act of Congress is unconstitutional, because it does not fall within the scope of any of the enumerated powers of legislation confided to that body; and therefore it is void. Stripped of its artificial and technical structure, the argument comes to this, that although rights are exclusively secured by, or duties are exclusively imposed upon, the national government, yet, unless the power to enforce these rights, or to execute these duties can be found among the express powers of legislation enumerated in the Constitution, they remain without any means of giving them effect by any act of Congress; . . . even although, in a practical sense, they may become a nullity from the want of a proper remedy to enforce them, or to provide against their violation. . . . Such a limited construction of the Constitution has never yet been adopted as correct, either in theory or practice. No one has ever supposed that Congress could, constitutionally, by its legislation, exercise powers, or enact laws beyond the powers delegated to it by the Constitution. But it has, on various occasions, exercised powers which were necessary and proper as means to carry into effect rights expressly given, and duties expressly enjoined thereby. The end being required, it has been deemed a just and necessary implication, that the means to accomplish it are given also. . . .

The same uniformity of acquiescence in the validity of the act of 1793, upon the other part of the subject-matter, that of fugitive slaves, has prevailed throughout the whole Union until a comparatively recent period. . . . So far as the judges of the Courts of the United States have been called upon to enforce it, and to grant the certificate required by it, it is believed that it has been uniformly recognised as a binding and valid law, and as imposing a constitutional duty. Under such circumstances, if the question were one of doubtful construction, such long acquiescence in it, such contemporaneous expositions of it, and such extensive and uniform recognition of its validity, would in our judgment entitle the question to be considered at rest. . . .

But we do not wish to rest our present opinion upon the ground either of contemporaneous exposition, or long acquiescence. . . . On the contrary, our judgment would be the same, if the question were entirely new, and the act of Congress were of recent enactment. We hold the act to be clearly constitutional in all its leading provisions, and, indeed, with the exception of that part, which confers authority upon state magistrates, to be free from reasonable doubt and difficulty upon the grounds already stated. As to the authority so conferred upon state magistrates, while a difference of opinion has existed, and may exist still on the point, in different states, whether state magistrates are bound to act under it, none is entertained by this Court, that state magistrates may, if they choose, exercise that authority, unless prohibited by state legislation. . . .

In the next place, the nature of the provision and the objects to be attained by it, require that it should be controlled by one and the same will, and act uniformly by the same system of regulations throughout the Union. If, then, the states have a right, in the absence of legislation by Congress, to act upon the subject, each state is at liberty to prescribe just such regulations as suit its own policy, local convenience, and local feelings. . . . One state may require the owner to sue in one mode, another in a different mode. One state may make a statute of limitations as to the remedy, in its own tribunals, short and summary; another may prolong the period, and yet restrict the proofs. . . . The duty might be enforced in some states; retarded, or limited in others; and denied, as compulsory in many, if not in all. Consequences like these must have been foreseen as very likely to occur in the non-slaveholding states, where legislation, if not silent on the subject, and purely voluntary, could scarcely be presumed to be favorable to the exercise of the rights of the owner.

It is scarcely conceivable, that the slaveholding states would have been satisfied with leaving to the legislation of the non-slaveholding states, a power of regulation, in the absence of that of Congress, which would or might practically amount to a power to destroy the rights of the owner. . . . Surely such a state of things never could have been intended, under such a solemn guarantee of right and duty. On the other hand, construe the right of legislation as exclusive in Congress, and every evil, and every danger vanishes. The right and the duty are then co-extensive and uniform in remedy and operation throughout the whole Union. The owner has the same security, and the same remedial justice, and the same exemption from state regulation and control, through however many states he may pass with his fugitive slave in his possession, in transitu, to his own domicile. . . .

These are some of the reasons, but by no means all, upon which we hold the power of legislation on this subject to be exclusive in Congress. To guard, however, against any possible misconstruction of our views, it is proper to state, that we are by no means to be understood in any manner whatsoever to doubt or to interfere with the police power belonging to the states in virtue of their general sovereignty. . . . We entertain no doubt whatsoever, that the states, in virtue of their general police power, possess full jurisdiction to arrest and restrain runaway slaves, and remove them from their borders, and otherwise to secure themselves against their depredations and evil example, as they certainly may do in cases of idlers, vagabonds, and paupers. . . . But such regulations can never be permitted to interfere with or to obstruct the just rights of the owner to reclaim his slave, derived from the Constitution of the United States, or with the remedies prescribed by Congress to aid and enforce the same.

Upon these grounds, we are of opinion that the act of Pennsylvania upon which this indictment is founded, is unconstitutional and void. It purports to punish as a public offence against that state, the very act of seizing and removing a slave by his master, which the Constitution of the United States was designed to justify and uphold.

90

Jones v. *Van Zandt* *(1847)*

Despite the ruling in *Prigg* upholding the constitutionality of the Fugitive Slave law, abolitionists continued to attack it in the courts. In this case Salmon P. Chase updated the *Somerset* argument regarding positive law and adapted it to American conditions. Slavery, he claimed, was contrary to natural law, and therefore could only be supported by positive local law, which could not extend beyond jurisdictional lines. Once a slave left such a jurisdiction, he became free. Chase also attacked the Fugitive Slave Act as unconstitutional, because the Constitution did not give the federal government the power to enslave anyone. The act, he claimed, violated the due process, search, and seizure provisions of the Fourth, Fifth and Seventh amendments. The Court, speaking through Justice Levi Woodbury (who had succeeded Story), dismissed the challenge, upheld the law, and declared that slavery was a "political question," which each state had the right to settle for itself. He went on to argue that the Fugitive Slave Act was a condition for the South's ratifying the Constitution—a charge that the abolitionists had broadcast—and therefore one of the "sacred compromises" that had to be enforced in order to preserve the Union.

See Cover, *Justice Accused* (1975); and M. V. Tushnet, *The American Law of Slavery, 1810–1860* (1984).

Source: 5 Howard 215 (1847).

Justice Woodbury delivered the opinion of the Court.

It remains to consider the fifth and sixth divisions of opinion under this head. They are, whether the act of Congress, under which the action is brought, is repugnant either to the constitution, or the ordinance "for the government of the territory northwest of the river Ohio."

This court has already, after much deliberation, decided that the act of February 12th, 1793, was not repugnant to the constitution. The reasons for their opinion are fully explained by Justice Story in Prigg *v.* Pennsylvania. . . .

In coming to that conclusion they were fortified by the idea, that the constitution itself, in the clause before cited, flung its shield, for security, over such property as is in controversy in the present case, and the right to pursue and reclaim it within the limits of another State.

This was only carrying out, in our confederate form of government, the clear right of every man at common law to make fresh suit and recapture of his own property within the realm. . . .

But the power by national law to pursue and regain most kinds of property, in the limits of a foreign government, is rather an act of comity than strict right; and hence, as the property in persons might not thus be recognized in some of the States in the Union, and its reclamation not be allowed through either courtesy or right, this clause was undoubtedly introduced into the constitution, as one of its compromises, for the safety of that portion of the Union which did permit such property, and which otherwise might often be deprived of it entirely by its merely crossing the line of an adjoining State. . . .

This was thought to be too harsh a doctrine in respect to any title to property,—of a friendly neighbour, not brought nor placed in another State, under its laws, by the owner himself, but escaping there against his consent, and often forthwith pursued in order to be reclaimed.

The act of Congress, passed only four years after the constitution was adopted, was therefore designed merely to render effective the guaranty of the constitution itself; and a course of decisions since, in the courts of the States and general government, has for half a century exhibited great uniformity in favor of the validity as well as expediency of the act. . . .

While the compromises of the constitution exist, it is impossible to do justice to their requirements, or fulfil the duty incumbent on us towards all the members of the Union, under its provisions, without sustaining such enactments as those of the statute of 1793.

We do not now propose to review at length the reasoning on which this act has been pronounced constitutional. All of its provisions have been found necessary to protect private rights, under the clause in the constitution relating to this subject, and to execute the duties imposed on the general government to aid by legislation in enforcing every constitutional provision, whether in favor of itself or others. This grows out of the position and nature of such a government, and is as imperative on it in cases not enumerated specially, in respect to such legislation, as in others.

That this act of Congress, then, is not repugnant to the constitution, must be considered as among the settled adjudications of this court.

The last question on which a division is certified relates to the ordinance of 1787, and the supposed repugnancy to it of the act of Congress of 1793.

The ordinance prohibited the existence of slavery in the territory northwest of the river Ohio among only its own people. Similar prohibitions have from time to time been introduced into many of the old States. But this circumstance does not affect the domestic institution of slavery, as other States may choose to allow it among their people, nor impair their rights of property under it, when their slaves happen to escape to other States. These other States, whether northwest of the river Ohio, or on the eastern side of the Alleghenies, if out of the Union, would not be bound to surrender fugitives, even for crimes, it being, as before remarked, an act of comity, or imperfect obligation. . . . But while within the Union, and under the obligations of the constitution and laws of the Union, requiring that this kind of property in citizens of other States—the right to "service or labor"—be not discharged or destroyed, they must not interfere to impair or destroy it, but, if one so held to labor escape into their limits, should allow him to be retaken and returned to the place where he belongs. In all this there is no repugnance to the ordinance. Wherever that existed, States still maintain their own laws, as well as the ordinance, by not allowing slavery to exist among their own citizens. . . . But in relation to inhabitants of other States, if they escape into the limits of States within the ordinance, and if the constitution allow them, when fugitives from labor, to be reclaimed, this does not interfere with their own laws as to their own people, nor do acts of Congress interfere with them, which are rightfully passed to carry these constitutional rights into effect there, as fully as in other portions of the Union.

Before concluding, it may be expected by the defendant that some notice should be taken of the argument, urging on us a disregard of the constitution and the act of Congress in respect to this subject, on account of the supposed inexpediency and invalidity of all laws recognizing slavery or any right of property in man. But that is a political question, settled by each State for itself; and the federal power over it is limited and regulated by the people of the States in the constitution itself, as one of its sacred compromises, and which we possess no authority as a judicial body to modify or overrule.

Whatever may be the theoretical opinions of any as to the expediency of some of those compromises, or of the right of property in persons which they recognize, this court has no alternative, while they exist, but to stand by the constitution and laws with fidelity to their duties and their oaths. Their path is a strait and narrow one, to go where that constitution and the laws lead, and not to break both, by travelling without or beyond them.

Let our opinion on the several points raised be certified to the Circuit Court of Ohio in conformity to these views.

91

Luther v. *Borden (1849)*

Although this case did not deal directly with slavery, it explicated the idea of a "political question," a doctrine many scholars believe the Court should have invoked when confronted with the political compromises on slavery (see Document 97).

The case arose in Rhode Island, the only state that had not adopted a new constitution after independence; it continued to be governed under the royal charter issued by Charles II in 1663. By the 1840s the inequities in this document had led to widespread discontent and the so-called Dorr Rebellion, in which opponents drafted a new constitution and elected a rump government before being put down by the state militia. Martin Luther, a Dorrite leader, sued Luther Borden and others who had searched his house without a warrant, but his real purpose was to publicize Dorrite grievances.

The case is a landmark for its exposition of the so-called "political question doctrine," which holds that some issues are beyond the judicial capacity to resolve within the normal bounds of constitutional authority and separation of powers. The nature of these problems may vary, but all have a common undercurrent—the recognition by judges that in certain areas, other branches of government may refuse to enforce their rulings. Chief Justice Taney did not invent this idea, but he is generally credited with raising it to the level of a constitutional doctrine. Had he followed his own advice in *Dred Scott* the Court might have avoided what a later Chief Justice called its great "self-inflicted wound."

Source: 7 Howard 1 (1849).

In recent years the Supreme Court has vitiated the doctrine considerably, and there are some who question whether it remains a viable jurisprudential concept.

See W. M. Wiecek, *The Guaranty Clause of the U.S. Constitution* (1972); J. S. Shuchman, "The Political Background of the Political Question Doctrine," 16 *A.J.L.H.* 111 (1972); and A. Bickel, *The Least Dangerous Branch* (1962).

Chief Justice Taney delivered the opinion of the Court.

This case has arisen out of the unfortunate political differences which agitated the people of Rhode Island in 1841 and 1842.

It is an action of trespass brought by Martin Luther, the plaintiff in error, against Luther M. Borden and others, the defendants, in the Circuit Court of the United States for the District of Rhode Island, for breaking and entering the plaintiff's house. The defendants justify upon the ground that large numbers of men were assembled in different parts of the State for the purpose of overthrowing the government by military force, and were actually levying war upon the State; that, in order to defend itself from this insurrection, the State was declared by competent authority to be under martial law; that the plaintiff was engaged in the insurrection; and that the defendants, being in the military service of the State, by command of their superior officer, broke and entered the house and searched the rooms for the plaintiff, who was supposed to be there concealed, in order to arrest him, doing as little damage as possible. The plaintiff replied, that the trespass was committed by the defendants of their own proper wrong, and without any such cause; and upon the issue joined on this replication, the parties proceeded to trial.

The evidence offered by the plaintiff and the defendants is stated at large in the record; and the questions decided by the Circuit Court, and brought up by the writ of error, are not such as commonly arise in an action of trespass. The existence and authority of the government under which the defendants acted was called in question; and the plaintiff insists, that, before the acts complained of were committed, that government had been displaced and annulled by the people of Rhode Island, and that the plaintiff was engaged in supporting the lawful authority of the State, and the defendants themselves were in arms against it.

This is a new question in this court, and certainly a very grave one; and at the time when the trespass is alleged to have been committed it had produced a general and painful excitement in the State, and threatened to end in bloodshed and civil war. . . .

[The Chief Justice here reviewed the history of the government of Rhode Island and the facts leading up to and the conclusion of Dorr's Rebellion.]

The Circuit Court . . . instructed the jury that the charter government and laws under which the defendants acted were, at the time the trespass is alleged to have been committed, in full force and effect as the form of government and paramount law of the State, and constituted a justification of the acts of the defendants as set forth in their pleas.

It is this opinion of the Circuit Court that we are now called upon to review. It is set forth more at large in the exception, but is in substance as above stated; and the question presented is certainly a very serious one: For, if this court is authorized to enter upon this inquiry as proposed by the plaintiff, and it should be decided that the charter government had no legal existence during the period of time above mentioned,—if it had been annulled by the adoption of the opposing government,—then the laws passed by its legislature during that time were nullities; its taxes wrongfully collected; its salaries and compensation to its officers illegally paid; its public accounts improperly settled; and the judgments and sentences of its courts in civil and criminal cases null and void, and the officers who carried their decisions into operation answerable as trespassers, if not in some cases as criminals.

When the decision of this court might lead to such results, it becomes its duty to examine very carefully its own powers before it undertakes to exercise jurisdiction.

Certainly, the question which the plaintiff proposed to raise by the testimony he offered has not heretofore been recognized as a judicial one in any of the State courts. In forming the constitutions of the different States, after the Declaration of Independence, and in the various changes and alterations which have since been made, the political department has always determined whether the proposed constitution or amendment was ratified or not by the people of the State, and the judicial power has followed its decision. In Rhode Island, the question has been directly decided. Prosecutions were there instituted against some of the persons who had been active in the forcible opposition to the old government. And in more than one of the cases evidence was offered on the part of the defence similar to the testimony offered in the Circuit Court, and for the same purpose; that is, for the purpose of showing that the proposed constitution had been adopted by the people of Rhode Island, and had, therefore, become the established government, and consequently that the parties accused were doing nothing more than their duty in endeavouring to support it.

But the courts uniformly held that the inquiry proposed to be made belonged to the political power and not to the judicial; that it rested with the political power to decide whether the charter government had been displaced or not; and when that decision was made, the judicial department would be bound to take notice of it as the paramount law of the State, without the aid of oral evidence or the examination of witnesses; that, according to the laws and institutions of Rhode Island, no such change had been recognized by the political power; and that the charter government was the lawful and established government of the State during the period in contest, and that those who were in arms against it were insurgents, and liable to punishment. This doctrine is clearly and forcibly stated in the opinion of the Supreme Court of the State in the trial of Thomas W. Dorr, who was the governor elected under the opposing constitution, and headed the armed force which endeavoured to maintain its authority. . . .

The point, then, raised here has been already decided by the courts of Rhode Island. The question relates, altogether, to the constitution and laws of that State; and the well settled rule in this court is, that the courts of the United States adopt and follow the decisions of the State courts in questions which concern merely the constitution and laws of the State.

Upon what ground could the Circuit Court of the United States which tried this case have departed from this rule, and disregarded and overruled the decisions of the courts of Rhode Island? Undoubtedly the courts of the United States have certain powers under the Constitution and laws of the United States which do not belong to the State courts. But the power of determining that a State government has been lawfully established, which the courts of the State disown and repudiate, is not one of them. Upon such a question the courts of the United States are bound to follow the decisions of the State tribunals, and must therefore regard the charter government as the lawful and established government during the time of this contest.

Besides, if the Circuit Court had entered upon this inquiry, by what rule could it have determined the qualification of voters upon the adoption or rejection of the proposed constitution, unless there was some previous law of the State to guide it? It is the province of a court to expound the law, not to make it. And certainly it is no part of the judicial functions of any court of the United States to prescribe the qualification of voters in a State, giving the right to those to whom it is denied by the written and established constitution and laws of the State, or taking it away from those to whom it is given; nor has it the right to determine what political privileges the citizens of a State are entitled to, unless there is an established constitution or law to govern its decision. . . .

Moreover, the Constitution of the United States, as far as it has provided for an emergency of this kind, and authorized the general government to interfere in the domestic concerns of a State, has treated the subject as political in its nature, and placed the power in the hands of that department.

The fourth section of the fourth article of the Constitution of the United States provides that the United States shall guarantee to every State in the Union a republican form of government, and shall protect each of them against invasion; and on the application of the legislature or of the executive (when the legislature cannot be convened) against domestic violence.

Under this article of the Constitution it rests with Congress to decide what government is the established one in a State. For as the United States guaran-

tee to each State a republican government, Congress must necessarily decide
what government is established in the State before it can determine whether
it is republican or not. And when the senators and representatives of a State
are admitted into the councils of the Union, the authority of the government
under which they are appointed, as well as its republican character, is recognized by the proper constitutional authority. And its decision is binding on
every other department of the government, and could not be questioned in
a judicial tribunal. It is true that the contest in this case did not last long
enough to bring the matter to this issue; and as no senators or representatives
were elected under the authority of the government of which Mr. Dorr was
the head, Congress was not called upon to decide the controversy. Yet the
right to decide is placed there, and not in the courts. . . .

The remaining question is whether the defendants, acting under military
orders issued under the authority of the government, were justified in breaking and entering the plaintiff's house. In relation to the act of the legislature
declaring martial law, it is not necessary in the case before us to inquire to
what extent, nor under what circumstances, that power may be exercised by
a State. Unquestionably a military government, established as the permanent
government of the State, would not be a republican government, and it
would be the duty of Congress to overthrow it. But the law of Rhode Island
evidently contemplated no such government. It was intended merely for the
crisis, and to meet the peril in which the existing government was placed by
the armed resistance to its authority. It was so understood and construed by
the State authorities. And, unquestionably, a State may use its military power
to put down an armed insurrection, too strong to be controlled by the civil
authority. The power is essential to the existence of every government,
essential to the preservation of order and free institutions, and is as necessary
to the States of this Union as to any other government. The State itself must
determine what degree of force the crisis demands. And if the government
of Rhode Island deemed the armed opposition so formidable, and so ramified
throughout the State, as to require the use of its military force and the
declaration of martial law, we see no ground upon which this court can
question its authority. It was a state of war; and the established government
resorted to the rights and usages of war to maintain itself, and to overcome
the unlawful opposition. And in that state of things the officers engaged in
its military service might lawfully arrest any one, who, from the information
before them, they had reasonable grounds to believe was engaged in the
insurrection; and might order a house to be forcibly entered and searched,
when there were reasonable grounds for supposing he might be there concealed. Without the power to do this, martial law and the military array of
the government would be mere parade, and rather encourage attack than
repel it. No more force, however, can be used than is necessary to accomplish
the object. And if the power is exercised for the purposes of oppression, or
any injury wilfully done to person or property, the party by whom, or by
whose order it is committed would undoubtedly be answerable. . . .

Much of the argument on the part of the plaintiff turned upon political rights and political questions, upon which the court has been urged to express an opinion. We decline doing so. The high power has been conferred on this court of passing judgment upon the acts of the State sovereignties, and of the legislative and executive branches of the federal government, and of determining whether they are beyond the limits of power marked out for them respectively by the Constitution of the United States. This tribunal, therefore, should be the last to overstep the boundaries which limit its own jurisdiction. And while it should always be ready to meet any question confided to it by the Constitution, it is equally its duty not to pass beyond its appropriate sphere of action, and to take care not to involve itself in discussions which properly belong to other forums. No one, we believe, has ever doubted the proposition, that, according to the institutions of this country, the sovereignty in every State resides in the people of the State, and that they may alter and change their form of government at their own pleasure. But whether they have changed it or not by abolishing an old government, and establishing a new one in its place, is a question to be settled by the political power. And when that power has decided, the courts are bound to take notice of its decision, and to follow it.

The judgment of the Circuit Court must therefore be affirmed.

92

~~~~~~~~~~~~~~~~~~~~~~~~~~~~~~~~~~~~~~~

State v. *Caesar (a slave) (1849)*

Slave codes (see Document 93) regulated the daily life of the slaves, but if they broke the law, they also had to contend with the state's criminal code, which often punished slaves far more harshly than it did white men for the same crime. In this case, a slave killed a white man in self-defense. The majority noted that under similar circumstances, the charge against a white man would have been reduced to manslaughter, and ordered a new trial. Chief Justice Ruffin's dissent is notable for his

Source: 9 Iredell 391 (North Carolina 1849).

bluntness in demanding a harsher standard for blacks, lest they lose their fear and awe of whites. This view should be understood in light of the role law has always played in social control. Although modern law in Western democracies is far more lenient than the law of one or two centuries ago, dissident elements in society are still subject to harsh penalties if they stray too far from accepted norms. The slave, of course, was considered a deviant who had to be kept under strict control.

See M. V. Tushnet, *The American Law of Slavery, 1810–1860* (1984); A. E. K. Nash, "Fairness and Formalism in the Treatment of Blacks in the State Supreme Courts of the Old South," 56 *Va. L. R.* 64 (1970); M. S. Hindus, "Black Justice under White Law . . . ," 63 *J.A.H.* 575 (1976); and P. J. Schwarz, *Twice Condemned: Slaves and the Criminal Laws of Virginia, 1705–1865* (1988).

Justice Pearson delivered the opinion of the court.

The prisoner, a slave, is convicted of murder in killing a *white man.* The case presents the question, whether the rules of law, by which manslaughter is distinguished from murder, as between white men, are applicable, when the party killing is a slave. If not, then to what extent a difference is to be made? . . .

These being only two cases in this Court, where it was necessary to discuss the question, while it renders our duty the more difficult, cannot fail to strike every mind, as a convincing proof of the due subordination and good conduct of our slave population, and to suggest, that, if any departure from the known and ordinary rules of the law of homicide is to be made, it is called for to a very limited extent. . . .

To present the general question by itself, and prevent confusion, it will be well to ascertain, what would have been the offence, if all the parties had been white men? Two friends are quietly talking together at night—two strangers come up—one strikes each of the friends several blows with a board; the blows are slight, but calculated to irritate—a third friend comes up—one of the strangers seizes him, and orders one of the former to go and get a whip that he might whip him. Upon his refusing thus to become an aider in their unlawful act, the two strangers set upon him—one holds his hands, while the other beats him with his fist upon the head and breast, he not venturing to make resistance and begging for mercy—his friend yielding to a burst of generous indignation, exclaims, "I can't stand this," takes up a fence rail, knocks one down, and then knocks the other down, and without a *repetition of the blow,* the three friends make their escape. The blow given to one proves fatal. Is not the bare statement sufficient? Does it require argument, or a reference to adjudged cases to show, that this is not a case of *murder?* or, "of

a black," diabolical heart, regardless of social duty and fatally bent on mischief? It is clearly a case of manslaughter in its most mitigated form. The
provocation was grievous. The blow was inflicted with the first thing that
could be laid hold of: it was *not repeated* and must be attributed, *not to malice,*
but to a generous impulse, excited by witnessing injury done to a friend. The
adjudged cases fully sustain this conclusion. In 12 *Coke. Rep.* 87, "two are
playing at bowls; they quarrel and engage in a fight: a friend of one, standing
by, seizes a bowl and strikes a blow, whereof the man dies. This is manslaughter, because of the *passion,* which is excited, when one *sees his friend assaulted."*
This is the leading case; it is referred to and approved by all the subsequent
authorities. . . .

As this would have been a case of manslaughter, if the parties had been
white men; are the same rules applicable, the party killing being a slave? The
lawmaking power has not expressed its will, but has left the law to be
declared by the "Courts, as it may be deduced from the primary principles
of the doctrine of homicide." The task is no easy one, yet it is the duty of
the Court to ascertain and declare what the law is.

I think the same rules are not applicable; for, from the nature of the
institution of slavery, a provocation, which, given by one white man to
another, would excite the passions, and "dethrone reason for a time,"
would not and ought not to produce this effect, when given by a white man
to a slave. Hence, although, if a white man, receiving a slight blow, kills
with a deadly weapon, it is but manslaughter; if a slave, for such a blow,
should kill a white man, it would be *murder;* for, accustomed as he is to
constant humiliation, it would not be calculated to excite to such a degree
as to "dethrone reason," and must be ascribed to a "wicked heart, regardless of social duty. . . ."

The announcement of this proposition, now directly made for the first
time, may have somewhat the appearance of a law, *made after the fact.* It is,
however, not a *new law,* but merely a new application of a well settled
principle of the common law. The analogy holds in the other relations of
life—parent and child, tutor and pupil, master and apprentice, master and
slave. A blow, given to the child, pupil, apprentice, or slave, is less apt to
excite passion, than when the parties are two white men "free and equal;"
hence, a blow, given to persons, filling these relations, is not, under ordinary
circumstances, a legal provocation. So, a blow, given by a white man to a
slave, is not, under ordinary circumstances, a legal provocation, because it
is less apt to excite passion, than between equals. The analogy fails only in
this: in the cases above put, the law *allows* of the *infliction of blows.* A master
is *not indictable* for a battery upon his slave; a parent, tutor, master of an
apprentice, is *not* indictable, except there be an excess of force; whereas the
law *does not allow a white man to inflict* blows upon a slave, who is *not his
property*—he is liable to indictment for so doing. In other words, in this last
case, the blow *is not* a legal provocation, although the party, giving it, *is liable*
to indictment; while in the other cases, whenever the blow subjects one party

to an indictment, it is a legal provocation for the other party. This is a departure from the legal analogy, to the prejudice of the slave. It is supposed, a regard to due subordination makes it necessary, but the application of the *new principle,* by which this departure is justified, should, I think, be made with great caution, because it adds to the list of constructive murders, or murders by "malice implied."

Assuming that there is a difference, to what extent is the difference to be carried? In prosecuting this enquiry, it should be borne in mind, that the reason of the difference is, that a blow inflicted upon a white man carries with it a feeling of degradation, as well as bodily pain, and a sense of injustice; all, or either of which are calculated to excite passion: whereas, a blow inflicted upon a slave is not attended with any feeling of degradation, by reason of his lowly condition, and is only calculated to excite passion from bodily pain and a sense of wrong; for, in the language of Chief Justice TAYLOR, in *Hale's case,* 2 Hawks, 582, "the instinct of a slave may be, and generally is, turned into subserviency to his master's will, and from him he receives chastisement, whether it be merited or not, with perfect submission, for, he knows the extent of the dominion assumed over him, and the law ratifies the claim. But when the same authority is wantonly usurped by a stranger, nature is disposed to assert her rights, and prompt the slave to resistance." . . .

I think it clearly deducible from *Hale's case,* and analogies of the common law, that, if a white man wantonly inflicts upon a slave, over whom he has no authority, a severe blow, or repeated blows under unusual circumstances, and the slave *at the instant* strikes and kills, without evincing, by the means used, great wickedness or cruelty, he is only guilty of manslaughter, giving due weight to motives of policy and the necessity for subordination.

This latter consideration, perhaps, requires the killing should be *at the instant;* for, it may not be consistent with due subordination to allow a slave, after he is extricated from his difficulty and is no longer receiving blows or in danger, to return and seek a combat. A wild beast wounded or in danger will turn upon a man, but he seldom so far forgets his sense of inferiority as to seek a combat. Upon this principle, which man has in common with the beast, a slave may, without losing sight of his inferiority, strike a white man, when in danger or suffering wrong; but he will not seek a combat after he is extricated. . . .

The prisoner was the associate or friend of Dick—his general character was shown to be that of an obedient slave, submissive to white men—he had himself received several slight blows, without offence on his part, to which he quietly submitted—he was present from the beginning—saw the wanton injury and suffering inflicted upon his helpless, unoffending and unresisting associate—he must either run away and leave him at the mercy of two drunken ruffians, to suffer, he knew not how much, from their fury and disappointed lust—the hour of the night forbade the hope of aid from white men—or he must yield to a generous impulse and come to the rescue. He used force enough to release his associate and they made their escape, without a *repetition* of the *blow.* Does this show he has the heart of a murderer? On the contrary, are we not forced, in spite of stern policy, to admire, even in a slave, the generosity, which incurs danger to save a friend? The law requires a slave to tame down his feelings to suit his lowly condition, but it would be savage, to allow him, under no circumstances, to yield to a generous impulse.

I think his Honor erred in charging the jury, that, under the circumstances, the prisoner was guilty of murder, and that there was no legal provocation. For this error the prisoner is entitled to a new trial. He cannot, in my opinion, be convicted of murder, without overruling *Hale's case* and *Will's case.* It should be borne in mind, that in laying down rules upon this subject, they must apply to white men as a class, and not as individuals; must be suited to the most *degraded,* as well as the most orderly. Hence great caution is required to protect slave property from wanton outrages, while, at the same time, due subordination is preserved.

It should also be borne in mind, that a conviction of manslaughter is far from being an acquittal; it extenuates on account of human infirmity, but does not justify or excuse. Manslaughter is felony. For the second offence life is forfeited.

I think there ought to be a new trial.

Chief Justice Ruffin dissented.

I am unable to concur in the judgment of the Court, and, upon a point of such general consequence, I conceive it to be a duty to state my dissent, and the grounds of it. . . .

It is very clear, that the question turns on the difference in the condition of the free white men and negro slaves. For, there is no doubt, if all the persons had been white men, that the conduct of the deceased would have palliated the killing by the person assaulted, or by his comrade, to manslaughter. It may also be assumed, that if all the parties had been slaves, the homicide would have been of the same degree. But it has been repeatedly declared by the highest judicial authorities, and it is felt by every person, lay as well as legal, that the rule for determining what is a mitigating provocation cannot, in the nature of things, be the same between persons who are in *equali jure,* as two freemen, and those who stand in the very great disparity of free whites and black slaves. Thus in *Hale's case,* 2 Hawks, 582, the point was, whether a battery by a white man on the slave of another was indictable, and the language of the Court was, "that, as there was no positive law decisive of the question, a solution of it must be deduced from general principles, from reasonings founded on the common law, adapted to the existing condition and circumstances of our society, and indicating that result, which is best adapted to general expedience." Hence the Court held, that such a battery was a breach of the peace and as such indictable: but explicitly declared further, "that, at the same time, it is undeniable, that such offence must be considered with a view to the actual condition of society, and the difference between a white man and a slave, securing the first from injury or insult, and the other from needless violence and outrage; and that from that difference it arises, that many circumstances, which would not constitute a legal provocation for a battery by one white man on another, would justify it, if committed on a slave, provided it were not excessive." . . . The dissimilarity in the condition of slaves from any thing known at the common law cannot be denied; and, therefore, as it appears to me, the rules upon this, as upon all other kinds of intercourse between white men and slaves, must vary from those applied by the common law, between persons so essentially differing in their relations, education, rights, principles of action, habits, and motives for resentment. Judges cannot, indeed, be too sensible of the difficulty and delicacy of the task of adjusting the rules of law to new subjects; and therefore they should be and are proportionally cautious against rash expositions, not suited to the actual state of things, and not calculated to promote the security of persons, the stability of national institutions, and the common welfare. It was but an instance of the practical wisdom, which is characteristic of the common law and its judicial ministers as a body, that the Courts should, in those cases, have shown themselves so explicit in stating the general principle, on which the rules of law on this subject must ultimately be placed, and yet so guarded in respect to the rules themselves in detail. Yet it is of the utmost importance, nay, of the most pressing necessity, that there should be rules, which, as rules of law, should be known; so that all persons, of whatever race or condition, may understand their rights and responsibilities in respect to acts, by which blood is shed and life taken, and for which the slayer may be called to answer at the peril of his own life. . . .

If, however, that rule were not to be deemed law in virtue of an adjudication, its intrinsic correctness is sufficient to sustain it. As has been already stated, it is founded on the difference of condition of free white men and slaves, according to our institutions and habits. There is nothing analogous to it in the relations recognised by the common law. . . . It involves a necessity, not only for the discipline on the part of the owner requisite to procure productive labor from them, but for enforcing a subordination to the white race, which alone is compatible with the contentment of the slaves with their destiny, the acknowledged superiority of the whites, and the public quiet and security. The whites forever feel and assert a superiority, and exact an humble submission from the slaves; and the latter, in all they say and do, not only profess, but plainly exhibit a corresponding deep and abiding sense of legal and personal inferiority. Negroes—at least the great mass of them—born with deference to the white man, take the most contumelious language without answering again, and generally submit tamely to his buffets, though unlawful and unmerited. Such are the habits of the country. It is not now the question, whether these things are naturally right and proper to exist. They do exist actually, legally, and inveterately. Indeed, they are inseparable from the state of slavery; and are only to be deemed wrong upon the admission that slavery is fundamentally wrong. . . . The law holds, that, when one free person is smitten by another and kills him on the sudden, it is not murder; because the act is not fairly and generally attributable to malignity of heart, but to that infirmity which is common to men in general in that condition; and, therefore it is fit, that there should be a compassionate consideration for it. That principle is as applicable to contests arising between the white and slave castes, as to the whites by themselves. The cases of children and apprentices, at the common law, do not rest upon an independent arbitrary rule, but are examples merely of the principle under consideration. It is found that, when fathers and mothers correct those under their tutelage, they are not ordinarily prone to resent by violent retaliation, much less to attempt to kill; but that, on the contrary, the young do the elder reverence. If, then, a child under punishment slays his parent, the conclusion is, that he was not moved to it by heat of blood on the sudden, but by a malignant and diabolical spirit of vengeance. That is the effect of applying that test of common experience between persons in those relations. What will be the effect of applying it by a calm observer between free whites and negro slaves? Why, as laid down in the cases of *Tackett* and *Mann,* in respect to a provocation from a slave to a white man, upon which death takes place, "every individual in the community feels and understands, that the homicide of a slave may be extenuated by acts, which would not constitute a legal provocation, if done by a white person"; and that "many circumstances, which would not constitute such a provocation for a battery by one white man upon another, would justify it, if committed on a slave." That, we see, is the result of an application of the principle of the common law to the homicide of a slave by a white man—of that fruit of "the wisdom and experience of many ages of wise and discreet men, adapted to the habits, institutions, and actual condition of our citizens." And I think a Judge in this country will find himself compelled to adhere to that rule, whenever he is called to consider, whether the offence of a white man, whom he is trying for killing a slave, is or is not extenuated by the abusive and insolent reproaches of the slave and his trespass on his property before his face. So, it follows, as certainly as day follows night, that many things, which drive a white man to madness, will not have the like effect, if done by a white man to a slave; and, particularly, it is true, that slaves are not ordinarily moved to kill a white man for a common beating. For, it is an incontestable fact, that the great mass of slaves—nearly all of them—are the least turbulent of all men; that, when sober, they never attack a white man; and seldom, very seldom, exhibit any temper or sense of provocation at even gross and violent injuries from white men. They sometimes deliberately murder; oftener at the instigation of others, than on their own motive. They sometimes kill each other in heat of blood, being sensible to the dishonor in their own caste of crouching in submission to one of themselves. That, however, is much less frequent than among whites; for they have a duller sensibility to degradation. But hardly such a thing is known, as that a slave turns in retaliation on a white man, and, especially, that he attempts to take life for even a wanton battery, unless it be carried to such extremity as to render resistance proper in defence of his own life. . . . Such being the real state of things, it is a just conclusion of reason, when a slave kills a white man for a battery not likely to kill, maim, or do permanent injury, nor accompanied by unusual cruelty, that the act did not flow from generous and uncontrollable resentment, but from a bad heart— one, intent upon the assertion of an equality, social and personal, with the white, and bent on mortal mischief in support of the assertion. It is but the pretence of a provocation, not usually felt. Therefore, it cannot be tolerated in the law, though acted on in this particular instance by the prisoner—just as the law will not allow any provocation of words, gestures, or trespass on land or goods from one *in equali jure*—however grievous sometimes to be borne, and however they may have actually transported a particular individual—to exten- uate a homicide, because, as it holds, a rational being is not too infirm to withstand such acts of provocation. Therefore we concluded in *Jarrott's case,* as I would now hold, "that the law will not permit the slave to resist"—that is, in a case of an ordinary assault and battery on him—"but that it is his duty to submit, or flee, or seek the protection of his master": as in almost every instance he would in fact do. . . .

All the foregoing reasons apply with yet more force against the prisoner; as he was not engaged in any way, but was a mere looker on. I believe, this is the very first instance in which a slave has ventured to interpose, either between white men, or between a white man and a slave, taking part against the white man. Why should he intermeddle upon the plea of resisting the unlawful power, or redressing the wanton wrong, of a white man, when he, to whom the wrong was done, is admitted to have been unresisting? Shall one slave be the arbiter of the quarrels witnessed by him between another slave and the whites? It seems to me to be dangerous to the last degree to hold the doctrine, that negro slaves may assume to themselves the judgment as to the right or propriety of resistance, by one of his own race, to the authority taken over them by the whites, and, upon the notion of a generous sympathy with their oppressed fellow servants, may step forward to secure them from the hands of a white man, and much less to avenge their wrongs. First denying their general subordination to the whites, it may be ap- prehended that they will end in denouncing the injustice of slavery itself, and, upon that pretext, band together to throw off their common bondage entirely. The rule, which extenuates the assistance given by a white man to his friend, in a conflict between him and another white man—all being *in equali jure*—cannot, I think, be safely or fairly extended, so as to allow a slave, upon supposed generous impulses, to do the noble duty of killing a white man, because he tyrannizes over a negro man, so far as to give him a rap with a ratan and a few blows with his fists. I have never heard such a position advanced before, either as a doctrine of our law or as an opinion of any portion of our people.

For these reasons, the judgment, I think, ought to be affirmed.

93

Slave Code of Virginia (1860)

Strict laws regulated the behavior and the legal status of black slaves in the South, and also reflected the ambivalence of whites toward their bondsmen. On the one hand, the codes defined the slaves as property, usually as "chattels personal," and confirmed the owners' rights to "time, labor and services"; on the other, the codes also viewed the slaves as persons, and required masters to treat them humanely, furnish them with adequate food, clothing, and shelter, and take care of them in sickness and old age. The codes also placed severe restrictions on the slaves in terms of legal rights or, more precisely, the total lack of any rights. Above all, the codes tried to prevent rebelliousness in slaves in order to avoid any outward manifestations of discontent, either individually or by groups, and required public officials and whites to take all steps necessary to capture runaways and put down discontent. The sections of the Virginia slave code were passed at various times, and some dated back to the early eighteenth century, but they are representative of codes throughout the slave states. This selection is taken from the last codification before the Civil War, and represents the code at its fullest development.

See K. M. Stampp, *The Peculiar Institution* (1956); and E. J. Clark, Jr., "Aspects of North Carolina Slave Code, 1715–1860," 39 *No. Car. His. Rev.* 148 (1862).

Source: *Code of Virginia,* Titles 30, 54, 55 (1860 ed.).

~~~~~~

Free Persons May Become Slaves

It shall be lawful for any free person of color, resident within this common-wealth, of the age of eighteen years if a female, and of the age of twenty-one years if a male, to choose his or her master, upon the terms and conditions herein after mentioned.

When any free person as aforesaid desires to choose a master, such person shall file a petition in the circuit court of the county or corporation in which such free person of color resides, setting forth his desire to choose an owner, and setting forth the name of such person as he or she desires to select as an owner; which petition shall be signed by such free person of color in the presence of at least two subscribing witnesses. . . .

Definition of Mulatto; Estates

Every person who has one-fourth part or more of negro blood shall be deemed a mulatto, and the word "negro" in any other section of this or in any future statute, shall be construed to mean mulatto as well as negro.

No free negro shall be capable of acquiring (except by descent) any slave.

Slaves shall be deemed personal estate.

Any person who shall permit an insane, aged or infirm slave owned by him or under his control, to go at large without adequate provision for his support, shall be punished by fine not exceeding fifty dollars, and the over-seers of the poor of the county or corporation, in which such slave may be found, shall provide for his maintenance, and may charge such person quar-terly or annually with a sufficient sum therefore and recover it from time to time, by motion in the court of such county or corporation. . . .

Emancipation

Any person may emancipate any of his slaves by last will in writing, or by deed, recorded in the court of his county or corporation.

The increase of any female so emancipated by deed or will hereafter made, born between the death of the testator, or the record of the deed, and the time when her right to the enjoyment of her freedom arrives, shall also be free at that time, unless the deed or will otherwise provides.

All slaves emancipated as aforesaid, shall be liable for any debt contracted, by the person emancipating them, before such emancipation is made. . . .

Sale of Poisons to Negroes Prohibited

It shall not be lawful for any apothecary, druggist or other person to sell to any free negro, or to any slave without the written permission of the owner or master of such slave, any poisonous drug. Any person violating the provisions of this *section* shall forfeit five hundred dollars one-half to the commonwealth, and the remainder to the informer, and shall be confined in the county or corporation jail for not less than one nor more than two years. . . .

Special Court, How Convened and Constituted to Hear Proof of Escape of Slaves; What Officers to Attend; Their Fees.

Whenever a slave shall escape from his owner or person having him in possession, if the county or corporation court of the county wherein such owner or person resides be not in session, it shall be the duty of the sheriff or sergeant, upon request in writing of such owner or other person, or his agent, to summon a court to meet forthwith at the courthouse of such county or corporation, to hear proof of the escape of such slave and that he owed service or labor to the owner or person aforesaid, and to order such proof to be entered on the records of such court, together with a general description of the slave so escaping, with such convenient certainty as may be, pursuant to the provisions of the tenth section of the act of congress concerning persons escaping from the service of their masters, passed eighteenth September eighteen hundred and fifty.

The clerk of such county court and the sheriff of the county shall then and there attend upon said court, which may consist of two or more justices of such county; and the said court, when so organized shall be a court of record, and may be adjourned from time to time until its proceedings are closed. The sheriff, sergeant and clerk aforesaid shall be authorized to charge the owner or person aforesaid such fees as are allowed by law for like services, and collect the same as other fees are collected by them respectively.

Runaways Apprehended

Every slave arrested as a runaway, shall be taken before a justice and if there be reasonable cause to suspect that such slave is a runaway, the justice shall give a certificate thereof, stating therein, as near as may be, if the same be known, the distance of the place of arrest from that from which the slave may be supposed to have fled, and the sum of money demandable therefor by the person making the arrest, including mileage. If the arrest be made without the state, the slave shall be taken before a justice of the county or corporation into which he may be first brought, and such justice shall give the proper certificate.

The justice giving the certificate, by his precept endorsed thereon shall command the person, applying for the same, forthwith to deliver the slave for safe keeping (together with the said certificate) to the jailor of his county or corporation, who shall give his receipt therefor, or if the owner of the slave or his agent be known, the precept may command the delivery to be made to such owner or agent, upon the payment of the sum of money demandable for the arrest and mileage, and, upon default of such payment, to the jailor of the county or corporation in which such default is made.

Any person confined in jail, on suspicion of being a runaway slave may be discharged by the county or corporation court, in which case, or if he die in jail, the prison fees and other lawful charges shall be chargeable upon such person (if he be a free negro), upon the owner (if he be a slave), upon the person making the arrest, or upon the county or corporation, as the court may deem proper. . . .

Free Negroes

No negro, emancipated since the first day of May eighteen hundred and six, or hereafter, or claiming his right to freedom under a negro so emancipated, shall, after being twenty-one years of age, remain in this state more than one year without lawful permission.

Any such negro may be permitted by the court of any county or corporation to remain in this state, and reside in such county or corporation only, but the order granting the permission shall be void, unless it show that all the acting justices were summoned, and a majority of them present and voting on the question of permitting said negro to remain in the state; that notice of the application for such permission was posted at the courthouse door for at least two months immediately preceding and the attorney for the commonwealth, or in his absence some other attorney appointed by the court for the purpose, represented the state as counsel in the case, and that the applicant produced satisfactory proof of his being of good character, sober, peaceable, orderly and industrious. But permission shall not be granted to any person who, having removed from this state, shall have returned into it. Nor shall any such permission granted to a female negro, be deemed a permission to the issue of such female, whether born before or after it was granted.

The court granting such permission may, for any cause which seems to it sufficient, revoke the same, first summoning the negro to whom it was granted to appear and show cause, if any he can, against the revocation; and such negro shall not remain in the state more than one year thereafter.

If any negro, so permitted to remain, be sentenced for felony by any court of this state or the United States, such permission shall, by the sentence aforesaid, and at the termination of his imprisonment under such sentence, if he be imprisoned within this state, be ipso facto revoked. . . .

Every free negro shall, every five years, be registered and numbered in a book to be kept by the clerk of the court of the county or corporation where such free negro resides; which register shall specify his name, age, color and stature, with any apparent mark or scar on his face, head or hands, by what instrument he was emancipated, and when and where it was recorded; or that he was born free, and in what county or place. In the case of a negro emancipated since the first day of May eighteen hundred and six, or any descendant of a female negro so emancipated, born after such emancipation, the register shall state whether or not permission has been granted him to reside in this state, and if granted, when and by what court. . . .

Insurrection

If a free person advise or conspire with a slave to rebel or make insurrection, or with any person, to induce a slave to rebel or make insurrection, he shall be punished with death, whether such rebellion or insurrection be made or not. . . .

Assembling of Negroes; Trading by Free Negroes

If any person, knowingly, permit a slave, not belonging to him to remain on his plantation, lot or tenement above four hours at one time without leave of the owner or manager of such slave, he shall be fined three dollars; and any person who shall so permit more than five such slaves to be at one time on his plantation, lot or tenement, shall be fined one dollar for each slave above that number, and such assemblage shall be an unlawful assembly.

Every assemblage of negroes for the purpose of religious worship when such worship is conducted by a negro, and every assemblage of negroes for the purpose of instruction in reading or writing, or in the night time for any purpose, shall be an unlawful assembly. Any justice may issue his warrant to any officer or other person, requiring him to enter any place where such assemblage may be, and seize any negro therein; and he, or any other justice, may order such negro to be punished with stripes.

If a white person assemble with negroes for the purpose of instructing them to read or write, or if he associate with them in an unlawful assembly, he shall be confined in jail not exceeding six months and fined not exceeding one hundred dollars; and any justice may require him to enter into a recognizance, with sufficient security, to appear before the circuit, county or corporation court, of the county or corporation where the offence was committed, at its next term, to answer therefor, and in the mean time to keep the peace and be of good behavior.

If a free negro sell or barter, or offer to sell or barter, any agricultural products, without having a certificate in writing, from one respectable white person of the county or neighborhood, of his belief, that he raised, or otherwise came honestly by the same, such products shall be forfeited and the negro be punished with stripes. And any white person who shall purchase, or receive in trade, agricultural products, of a free negro, who has not such certificate, shall be deemed guilty of a misdemeanor. . . .

Offences by Negroes

If a slave plot or conspire to rebel or make insurrection, or commit an offence for the commission of which a free negro, at the time of committing the same, is punishable with death or by confinement in the penitentiary for not less three years, he shall be punished with death. But unless it be an offence for which a free white person, if he had committed it, might have been punished with death, such slave, instead of being punished with death, may, at the discretion of the court, be punished by sale and transportation beyond the limits of the United States.

If a slave commit an offence for which a free negro, if he had committed it, might be punished by confinement in the penitentiary for a period less than three years, such slave shall be punished by stripes, but if, having been once sentenced for such offence, he afterwards commits an offence for which a free negro, if he had committed it, might be punished by such confinement, he shall be punished with death, or, at the discretion of the court, by sale and transportation as aforesaid.

If a slave be sentenced to sale and transportation, under either of the next two preceding sections, the same proceedings shall be had in the case of a slave under sentence of death, whose punishment is commuted by the governor to sale and transportation.

If a slave commit an offence, the commission whereof by a free person, is punishable as a misdemeanor, he shall be punished by stripes.

A negro shall be punished with stripes:

First, If he use provoking language or menacing gestures to a white person:

Secondly, If he furnish a slave, without the consent of his master or manager, any pass, permit or token of his being from home with authority.

Thirdly, If he keep or carry fire arms, sword or other weapon or knife or ammunition; besides forfeiting to the state, any such articles in his possession:

Fourthly, If he be guilty of being in a riot, rout, unlawful assemblage or making seditious speeches:

Fifthly, If he sell or attempt to sell, or prepare or administer, any medicine; except a slave administering medicine by his master's order, in his family, or the family of another, with the consent of such other, and except a free negro administering medicine in his own family, or the family of another person with the consent of such other.

Whenever, by statute, punishment with stripes is prescribed, the number of stripes shall be in the discretion of the court or justice by whom the offence is tried, so as not to exceed thirty-nine at one time.

What Negroes Tried as Slaves; How Negroes Tried for Felony

A negro who is a slave for a term of years, or for the life of another, shall be prosecuted, tried and punished, for an offence, as a slave. A negro detained as a slave, but suing for his freedom, shall be prosecuted and tried for an offence as a free negro.

The county and corporation courts, consisting of five justices thereof, at the least, shall be courts of oyer and terminer for the trial of negroes charged with felony, except in the case of free negroes charged with felonious homicide, or an offence punishable with death. Such trial shall be on a charge entered of record stating the offence, but without a jury or a presentment, information or indictment. The justice, who committed or recognized the accused, shall not sit on his trial.

No justice interested in a slave shall sit on his trial for felony.

The court, on the trial of a slave for felony, shall assign him counsel, and allow such counsel a fee not exceeding twenty-five dollars, which shall be paid by the owner of the slave.

No slave shall be condemned to death, nor a free negro to the penitentiary, unless all the justices sitting on his trial agree in the sentence.

When a slave is condemned to death, or a free negro to the penitentiary, the court shall cause the testimony given on his trial to be committed to writing and filed of record, and the clerk shall forthwith transmit a copy of the whole record to the executive.

The court, for good cause, may continue such trial from term to term, and, if a trial be commenced at any term, such term may be extended until the trial is concluded. But if any such case be continued until the end of the third regular term after the commitment of the accused, or a recognizance for his appearance for trial, he shall be discharged, unless such continuance was on his own application, or because of his insanity or his escape from custody or failure to appear, or by reason of the witnesses for the commonwealth being enticed or kept away, or prevented from attending by sickness or some inevitable accident.

On a charge against a negro, for felony, in a county or corporation court, the court may adjudge the accused not to be guilty of the offence charged, but guilty of an offence, of which a free white person might be found guilty, on an indictment against him for such felony, and ascertain the punishment so far as it is not fixed by law, and give judgment accordingly.

Of Slaves Condemned to Death

The value of a slave condemned and executed, or sentenced to or reprieved for, sale and transportation, shall be paid to the owner out of the treasury; such value shall be the cash price for which he would sell at public sale, with a knowledge of his condemnation. It shall be fixed by the court, and entered of record.

If such slave be a slave only for a term of years, or for the life of another person, he shall be valued accordingly.

A slave brought into this state contrary to law, or who, in passing through it, or temporarily sojourning in it, committed the offence for which he is condemned, shall not be valued by the court or paid for out of the treasury; nor shall a slave be so paid for, who may be condemned for an offence, in the commission of which his owner was either principal or accessory and convicted thereof.

If a slave, condemned to death, escape before his execution, and be retaken, the jailor of the court, by which the slave was condemned, shall, as soon as may be, inform the said court of the fact; and the said court, five justices at least sitting, on being satisfied of his identity, shall cause the sentence to be carried into effect on a day appointed by said court.

Negroes Tried for Misdemeanor; Appeals in Such Cases

A slave shall be tried, for a misdemeanor, by a justice of the county or corporation in which the offence is committed.

A free negro shall be tried by such justice, for a misdemeanor, punishable by stripes; for any other misdemeanor, he may be tried as other free persons. But a justice before whom a free negro is charged with a misdemeanor, punishable by fine and imprisonment, or either may either try him, and inflict on him such punishment, as he would inflict on a slave for the same offence, or commit or recognize him for trial at the next court of the county or corporation, at which a grand jury will be impaneled.

In the case of a negro, convicted of a misdemeanor, by a justice there may be an appeal from the decision to the county or corporation court, by the negro, if free, or if he be a slave, by his owner. Such negro shall, unless let to bail, be committed by the justice to jail until the next term of such court, and the witnesses shall also be recognized to appear then.

Every such appeal shall be tried without pleadings in writing, and without a continuance, except for good cause; the court shall hear all the evidence produced on either side, and give such judgment as seems to it proper, and enforce the execution thereof.

Roberts v. *City of Boston* (1849)

Although we tend to emphasize the plight of bondsmen in the prewar South, the life of free blacks in the North was only marginally better. Many state laws regulated the behavior of free blacks, and racial prejudice informed many aspects of society even in those areas, like Massachusetts, that strongly opposed slavery. Boston, for example, had long maintained a segregated school system, and when the quality of the lone black school deteriorated, a suit was entered challenging the constitutionality of segregation under the provisions of the Massachusetts constitution. Charles Sumner argued that segregation violated the state's equal protection clause, and psychologically harmed black children. Chief Justice Shaw nonetheless upheld the school board's power to take race into consideration and interpreted the equal protection clause to mean only that the state had to treat each person according to his or her circumstances. Six years later, the legislature overturned Shaw's ruling by statutorily prohibiting racial segregation in public schools.

See L. F. Litwak, *North of Slavery: The Negro in the Free States, 1790–1860* (1961); L. W. Levy and H. B. Phillips, "The *Roberts* Case: Source of the 'Separate but Equal' Doctrine," 56 *A.H.R.* 510 (1951); and L. W. Levy, *The Law of the Commonwealth and Chief Justice Shaw* (1957).

Chief Justice Shaw delivered the opinion of the court.

The plaintiff, a colored child of five years of age, has commenced this action, by her father and next friend, against the city of Boston, upon the statute of 1845, *c.* 214, which provides, that any child unlawfully excluded from public school instruction, in this commonwealth, shall recover damages therefor, in an action against the city or town, by which such public school instruction is supported. The question therefore is, whether, upon the facts agreed, the plaintiff has been unlawfully excluded from such instruction.

By the agreed statement of facts, it appears, that the defendants support a class of schools called primary schools, to the number of about one hundred

Source: 5 Cushing 198 (Massachusetts 1849).

and sixty, designed for the instruction of children of both sexes, who are between the ages of four and seven years. Two of these schools are appropriated by the primary school committee, having charge of that class of schools, to the exclusive instruction of colored children, and the residue to the exclusive instruction of white children.

The plaintiff, by her father, took proper measures to obtain admission into one of these schools appropriated to white children, but pursuant to the regulations of the committee, and in conformity therewith, she was not admitted. Either of the schools appropriated to colored children was open to her; the nearest of which was about a fifth of a mile or seventy rods more distant from her father's house than the nearest primary school. It further appears, by the facts agreed, that the committee having charge of that class of schools had, a short time previously to the plaintiff's application, adopted a resolution, upon a report of a committee, that in the opinion of that board, the continuance of the separate schools for colored children, and the regular attendance of all such children upon the schools, is not only legal and just, but is best adapted to promote the instruction of that class of the population. . . .

. . . The plaintiff had access to a school, set apart for colored children, as well conducted in all respects, and as well fitted, in point of capacity and qualification of the instructors, to advance the education of children under seven years old, as the other primary schools; the objection is, that the schools thus open to the plaintiff are exclusively appropriated to colored children, and are at a greater distance from her home. Under these circumstances, has the plaintiff been unlawfully excluded from public school instruction? Upon the best consideration we have been able to give the subject, the court are all of opinion that she has not.

It will be considered, that this is a question of power, or of the legal authority of the committee intrusted by the city with this department of public instruction; because, if they have the legal authority, the expediency of exercising it in any particular way is exclusively with them.

The great principle, advanced by the learned and eloquent advocate of the plaintiff, is, that by the constitution and laws of Massachusetts, all persons without distinction of age or sex, birth or color, origin or condition, are equal before the law. This, as a broad general principle, such as ought to appear in a declaration of rights, is perfectly sound; it is not only expressed in terms, but pervades and animates the whole spirit of our constitution of free government. But, when this great principle comes to be applied to the actual and various conditions of persons in society, it will not warrant the assertion, that men and women are legally clothed with the same civil and political powers, and that children and adults are legally to have the same functions and be subject to the same treatment; but only that the rights of all, as they are settled and regulated by law, are equally entitled to the paternal consideration and protection of the law, for their maintenance and security. What those rights are, to which individuals, in the infinite variety of circumstances by which they are surrounded in society, are entitled, must depend on laws adapted to their respective relations and conditions.

Conceding, therefore, in the fullest manner, that colored persons, the descendants of Africans, are entitled by law, in this commonwealth, to equal rights, constitutional and political, civil and social, the question then arises, whether the regulation in question, which provides separate schools for colored children, is a violation of any of these rights. . . .

The power of general superintendence vests a plenary authority in the committee to arrange, classify, and distribute pupils, in such a manner as they think best adapted to their general proficiency and welfare. If it is thought expedient to provide for very young children, it may be, that such schools may be kept exclusively by female teachers, quite adequate to their instruction, and yet whose services may be obtained at a cost much lower than that of more highly-qualified male instructors. So if they should judge it expedient to have a grade of schools for children from seven to ten, and another for those from ten to fourteen, it would seem to be within their authority to establish such schools. So to separate male and female pupils into different schools. It has been found necessary, that is to say, highly expedient, at times, to establish special schools for poor and neglected children, who have passed the age of seven, and have become too old to attend the primary school, and yet have not acquired the rudiments of learning, to enable them to enter the ordinary schools. If a class of youth, of one or both sexes, is found in that condition, and it is expedient to organize them into a separate school, to receive the special training, adapted to their condition, it seems to be within the power of the superintending committee, to provide for the organization of such special school.

A somewhat more specific rule, perhaps, on these subjects, might be beneficially provided by the legislature; but yet, it would probably be quite impracticable to make full and precise laws for this purpose, on account of the different condition of society in different towns. . . .

In the absence of special legislation on this subject, the law has vested the power in the committee to regulate the system of distribution and classification; and when this power is reasonably exercised, without being abused or perverted by colorable pretences, the decision of the committee must be deemed conclusive. The committee, apparently upon great deliberation, have come to the conclusion, that the good of both classes of schools will be best promoted, by maintaining the separate primary schools for colored and for white children, and we can perceive no ground to doubt, that this is the honest result of their experience and judgment.

It is urged, that this maintenance of separate schools tends to deepen and perpetuate the odious distinction of caste, founded in a deep-rooted prejudice in public opinion. This prejudice, if it exists, is not created by law, and probably cannot be changed by law. Whether this distinction and prejudice, existing in the opinion and feelings of the community, would not be as effectually fostered by compelling colored and white children to associate together in the same schools, may well be doubted; at all events, it is a fair and proper question for the committee to consider and decide upon, having in view the best interests of both classes of children placed under their superintendence, and we cannot say, that their decision upon it is not founded on just grounds of reason and experience, and in the results of a discriminating and humane judgment.

The increased distance to which the plaintiff was obliged to go to school from her father's house, is not such, in our opinion, as to render the regulation in question unreasonable, much less illegal.

On the whole the court are of opinion, that upon the facts stated, the action cannot be maintained.

95

Fugitive Slave Act (1850)

Article IV, Section 2 of the Constitution called for states to surrender back escaped slaves to their owners, but northern states had, through personal liberty laws (see Document 96) and other devices, thwarted efforts to recapture and return runaways. As tensions between North and South escalated in the 1840s, this issue often appeared as the major southern complaint. In an effort to reconcile differences and save the Union, the Compromise of 1850 included a strengthened federal Fugitive Slave Act, which so one-sidedly favored slaveowners that it became a major propaganda weapon of the abolitionists. The constitutional arguments against the act emphasized that Article IV placed the primary obligation on the states and did not give Congress a separate power, and that the act violated several rights guaranteed under the Constitution, including trial by jury, cross-examination of witnesses and accusers, and habeas corpus.

See H. Hamilton, *Prologue to Crisis: The Compromise of 1850* (1964); P. Finkelman, *An Imperfect Union: Slavery, Federalism, and Comity* (1981); S. W. Campbell, *The Slave Catchers: Enforcement of the Fugitive Slave Law, 1850–1860* (1970); and A. Johnson, "Constitutionality of Fugitive Slave Acts," 31 *Yale L. J.* 161 (1921).

Source: 9 *Statutes at Large* 462 (1850).

Be it enacted by the Senate and House of Representatives of the United States of America in congress assembled, That the persons who have been, or may hereafter be, appointed commissioners, in virtue of any act of Congress, by the Circuit Courts of the United States, and who, in consequence of such appointment, are authorized to exercise the powers that any justice of the peace, or other magistrate of any of the United States, may exercise in respect to offenders for any crime or offence against the United States, by arresting, imprisoning or bailing the same under and by virtue of the thirty-third section of the act of the twenty-fourth of September seventeen hundred and eighty-nine, entitled "An Act to establish the judicial courts of the United States," shall be, and are hereby, authorized and required to exercise and discharge all the powers and duties conferred by this act.

SEC. 2. *And be it further enacted,* That the Superior Court of each organized Territory of the United States shall have the same power to appoint commissioners to take acknowledgements of bail and affidavits, and to take depositions of witnesses in civil causes, which is now possessed by the Circuit Court of the United States; and all commissioners who shall hereafter be appointed for such purposes by the Superior Court of any organized Territory of the United States, shall possess all the powers, and exercise all the duties, conferred by law upon the commissioners appointed by the Circuit Courts of the United States for similar purposes, and shall moreover exercise and discharge all the powers and duties conferred by this act. . . .

SEC. 4. *And be it further enacted,* That the commissioners above named shall have concurrent jurisdiction with the judges of the Circuit and District Courts of the United States, in their respective circuits and districts within the several States, and the judges of the Superior Courts of the Territories, severally and collectively, in term-time and vacation; and shall grant certificates to such claimants, upon satisfactory proof being made, with authority to take and remove such fugitives from service or labor, under the restrictions herein contained, to the State or Territory from which such persons may have escaped or fled.

SEC. 5. *And be it further enacted,* That it shall be the duty of all marshals and deputy marshals to obey and execute all warrants and precepts issued under the provisions of this act, when to them directed; and should any marshal or deputy marshal refuse to receive such warrant, or other process, when tendered, or to use all proper means diligently to execute the same, he shall, on conviction thereof, be fined in the sum of one thousand dollars, to the use of such claimant, on the motion of such claimant, by the Circuit or District Court for the district of such marshal; and after arrest of such fugitive, by such marshal or his deputy, or whilst at any time in his custody under the provisions of this act, should such fugitive escape, whether with or without the assent of such marshal or his deputy, such marshal shall be liable on his official bond, to be prosecuted for the benefit of such claimant, for the full value of the service or labor of said fugitive in the State, Territory, or District whence he escaped: and the better to enable the said commissioners, when thus appointed, to execute their duties faithfully and efficiently, in conformity with the requirements of the Constitution of the United States and of this act, they are hereby authorized and empowered, within their counties respectively, to appoint, in writing under their hands, any one or more suitable persons, from time to time, to execute all such warrants and other process as may be issued by them in the lawful performance of their respective duties; with authority to such commissioners, or the persons to be appointed by them, to execute process as aforesaid, to summon and call to their aid the bystanders, or *posse comitatus* of the proper county, when necessary to ensure a faithful observance of the clause of the Constitution referred to, in conformity with the provisions of this act; and all good citizens are hereby commanded to aid and assist in the prompt and efficient execution of this law, whenever their services may be required, as aforesaid, for that purpose; and said warrants shall run, and be executed by said officers, any where in the State within which they are issued.

SEC. 6.   *And be it further enacted,* That when a person held to service or labor in any State or Territory of the United States, has heretofore or shall hereafter escape into another State or Territory of the United States, the person or persons to whom such service or labor may be due, or his, her, or their agent or attorney, duly authorized, by power of attorney, in writing, acknowledged and certified under the seal of some legal officer or court of the State or Territory in which the same may be executed, may pursue and reclaim such fugitive person, either by procuring a warrant from some one of the courts, judges, or commissioners aforesaid, of the proper circuit, district, or county, for the apprehension of such fugitive from service or labor, or by seizing and arresting such fugitive, where the same can be done without process, and by taking, or causing such person to be taken, forthwith before such court, judge, or commissioner, whose duty it shall be to hear and determine the case of such claimant in a summary manner. . . . In no trial or hearing under this act shall the testimony of such alleged fugitive be admitted in evidence; and the certificates in this and the first [fourth] section mentioned, shall be conclusive of the right of the person or persons in whose favor granted, to remove such fugitive to the State or Territory from which he escaped, and shall prevent all molestation of such person or persons by any process issued by any court, judge, magistrate, or other person whomsoever.

SEC. 7.   *And be it further enacted,* That any person who shall knowingly and willingly obstruct, hinder, or prevent such claimant, his agent or attorney, or any person or persons lawfully assisting him, her, or them, from arresting such a fugitive from service or labor, either with or without process as aforesaid, or shall rescue, or attempt to rescue, such fugitive from service or labor, from the custody of such claimant, his or her agent or attorney, or other person or persons lawfully assisting as aforesaid, when so arrested, pursuant to the authority herein given and declared; or shall aid, abet, or assist such person so owing service or labor as aforesaid, directly or indirectly, to escape from such claimant, his agent or attorney, or other person or persons legally authorized as aforesaid; or shall harbor or conceal such fugitive, so as to prevent the discovery and arrest of such person, after notice or knowledge of the fact that such person was a fugitive from service or labor as aforesaid, shall, for either of said offences, be subject to a fine not exceeding one thousand dollars, and imprisonment not exceeding six months, by indictment and conviction before the District Court of the United States for the district in which such offence may have been committed, or before the proper court of criminal jurisdiction, if committed within any one of the organized Territories of the United States; and shall moreover forfeit and pay, by way of civil damages to the party injured by such illegal conduct, the sum of one thousand dollars, for each fugitive so lost as aforesaid, to be recovered by action of debt, in any of the District or Territorial Courts aforesaid, within whose jurisdiction the said offence may have been committed. . . .

SEC. 9. *And be it further enacted,* That, upon affidavit made by the claimant of such fugitive, his agent or attorney, after such certificate has been issued, that he has reason to apprehend that such fugitive will be rescued by force from his or their possession before he can be taken beyond the limits of the State in which the arrest is made, it shall be the duty of the officer making the arrest to retain such fugitive in his custody, and to remove him to the State whence he fled, and there to deliver him to said claimant, his agent, or attorney. And to this end, the officer aforesaid is hereby authorized and required to employ so many persons as he may deem necessary to overcome such force, and to retain them in his service so long as circumstances may require. The said officer and his assistants, while so employed, to receive the same compensation, and to be allowed the same expenses, as are now allowed by law for transportation of criminals, to be certified by the judge of the district within which the arrest is made, and paid out of the treasury of the United States.

Massachusetts Personal Liberty Act (1855)

Dissatisfaction with the Fugitive Slave Law of 1793 led several northern states to enact so-called "personal liberty" laws, guaranteeing jury trial, habeas corpus, and other procedural safeguards to blacks caught in the recapture scheme. The early laws were not meant to prevent rendition of captured slaves, but to make sure that fairness prevailed and that free blacks were not sent back to slavery. Following the 1850 Compromise, however, many northern states enacted new personal liberty laws, which were, in fact, designed to sabotage the operation of the new Fugitive Slave Act (Document 95). The following law resulted from the uproar over the capture and rendition of a slave named Anthony Burns in 1854. A hostile mob attempted a rescue, a guard was killed in the uproar, and Burns was ultimately marched back to Virginia under massive federal and state escort. United States Commissioner Edward Loring upheld the constitutionality of the act, and at almost the same time Congress passed the Kansas-Nebraska Act, causing even further uproar. The Massachusetts legislature passed the 1855 law, with the defiant title of "An Act to Protect the Rights and Liberties of the People of the Commonwealth of Massachusetts," and following Story's suggestion in *Prigg* (Document 89), provided for removal of state officials aiding rendition. Loring, who was also a probate judge, was promptly removed from office.

J. H. Pease and W. H. Pease, *The Fugitive Slave Law and Anthony Burns* (1975); and J. Parker, *Personal Liberty Laws* (1861)

Sec. 2. The meaning of the one hundred and eleventh chapter of the Revised Statutes is hereby declared to be, that every person imprisoned or restrained of his liberty is entitled, as of right and of course, to the writ of *habeas corpus,* except in the cases mentioned in the second section of that chapter.

Sec. 3. The writ of *habeas corpus* may be issued by the supreme judicial court, the court of common pleas, by any justice's court or police court of

---

Source: Massachusetts, *Acts and Resolves . . . 1855, 924.*

any town or city, by any court of record, or by any justice of either of said courts, or by any judge of probate; and it may be issued by any justice of the peace, if no magistrate above named is known to said justice of the peace to be within five miles of the place where the party is imprisoned or restrained, and it shall be returnable before the supreme judicial court, or any one of the justices thereof, whether the court may be in session or not, and in term time or vacation. . . .

Sec. 6.   If any claimant shall appear to demand the custody or possession of the person for whose benefit such writ is sued out, such claimant shall state in writing the facts on which he relies, with precision and certainty; and neither the claimant of the alleged fugitive, nor any person interested in his alleged obligation to service or labor, nor the alleged fugitive, shall be permitted to testify at the trial of the issue; and no confessions, admissions or declarations of the alleged fugitive against himself shall be given in evidence. Upon every question of fact involved in the issue, the burden of proof shall be on the claimant, and the facts alleged and necessary to be established, must be proved by the testimony of at least two credible witnesses, or other legal evidence equivalent thereto, and by the rules of evidence known and secured by the common law; and no *ex parte* deposition or affidavit shall be received in proof in behalf of the claimant, and no presumption shall arise in favor of the claimant from any proof that the alleged fugitive or any of his ancestors had actually been held as a slave, without proof that such holding was legal.

Sec. 7.   If any person shall remove from the limits of this Commonwealth, or shall assist in removing therefrom, or shall come into the Commonwealth with the intention of removing or of assisting in the removing therefrom, or shall procure or assist in procuring to be so removed, any person being in the peace thereof who is not "held to service or labor" by the "party" making "claim," or who has not "escaped" from the "party" making "claim," within the meaning of those words in the constitution of the United States, on the pretence that such person is so held or has so escaped, or that his "service or labor" is so "due," or with the intent to subject him to such "service or labor," he shall be punished by a fine of not less than one thousand, nor more than five thousand dollars, and by imprisonment in the State Prison not less than one, nor more than five years. . . .

Sec. 9.   No person, while holding any office of honor, trust, or emolument, under the laws of this Commonwealth, shall, in any capacity, issue any warrant or other process, or grant any certificate, under or by virtue of an act of congress . . . or shall in any capacity, serve any such warrant or other process.

Sec. 10.   Any person who shall grant any certificate under or by virtue of the acts of congress, mentioned in the preceding section, shall be deemed to have resigned any commission from the Commonwealth which he may possess, his office shall be deemed vacant, and he shall be forever thereafter ineligible to any office of trust, honor or emolument under the laws of this Commonwealth.

Sec. 11.   Any person who shall act as counsel or attorney for any claimant of any alleged fugitive from service or labor, under or by virtue of the acts of congress mentioned in the ninth section of this act, shall be deemed to have resigned any commission from the Commonwealth that he may possess, and he shall be thereafter incapacitated from appearing as counsel or attorney in the courts of this Commonwealth. . . .

Sec. 14.   Any person holding any judicial office under the constitution or laws of this Commonwealth, who shall continue, for ten days after the passage of this act, to hold the office of United States commissioner, or any office . . . which qualifies him to issue any warrant or other process . . . under the [Fugitive Slave Acts] shall be deemed to have violated good behavior, to have given reason for the loss of public confidence, and furnished sufficient ground either for impeachment or for removal by address.

Sec. 15.   Any sheriff, deputy sheriff, jailer, coroner, constable, or other officer of this Commonwealth, or the police of any city or town, or any district, county, city or town officer, or any officer or other member of the volunteer militia of this Commonwealth, who shall hereafter arrest . . . any person for the reason that he is claimed or adjudged to be a fugitive from service or labor, shall be punished by fine . . . and by imprisonment. . . .

Sec. 16.   The volunteer militia of the Commonwealth shall not act in any manner in the seizure . . . of any person for the reason that he is claimed or adjudged to be a fugitive from service or labor. . . .

Sec. 19.   No jail, prison, or other place of confinement belonging to, or used by, either the Commonwealth of Massachusetts or any county therein, shall be used for the detention or imprisonment of any person accused or convicted of any offence created by [the Federal Fugitive Slave Acts] . . . or accused or convicted of obstructing or resisting any process, warrant, or order issued under either of said acts, or of rescuing, or attempting to rescue, any person arrested or detained under any of the provisions of either of the said acts.

Dred Scott v. Sandford (1857)

Dred Scott's case holds a unique place in constitutional history as an example of the Supreme Court trying to impose a judicial solution on a political problem (compare Document 91). It called down enormous criticism on the Court and Chief Justice Taney; a later Chief Justice, Charles Evans Hughes, described it as a great "self-inflicted wound." Scott, born a slave, had been taken by his master into free territory, and upon the argument that "once free always free," later sued for his freedom. Scott and his supporters managed to get the case into federal courts, and a major question existed whether a slave had standing to sue in federal court. Before the Court could decide the merits of the case, it had to decide whether it had jurisdiction.

Taney, in a dense and convoluted argument, denied that slaves could enter federal court. Having determined the Court had no jurisdiction, he should have just dismissed the suit. But Taney, determined to settle the issue of slavery in the territories, went on to the merits, holding that slaves were property and could never be citizens. Other justices disagreed with the reasoning, but a majority seemed to support his conclusion. Despite widespread approval in the South, the North ignored the decision, and indeed, it became another steppingstone on the road to war.

See D. E. Fehrenbacher, *The Dred Scott Case* (1978); W. Ehrlich, *They Have No Rights: Dred Scott's Struggle for Freedom* (1979); W. M. Wiecek, "Slavery and Abolition Before the United States Supreme Court, 1820–1860," 65 *J. Am. His.* 34 (1978); S. Kutler, *The Dred Scott Decision* (1967); and W. Mendelson, "Dred Scott's Case," 38 *Minn. L. R.* 16 (1953).

Chief Justice Taney delivered the opinion of the Court.

The question is simply this: Can a negro, whose ancestors were imported into this country, and sold as slaves, become a member of the political community formed and brought into existence by the constitution of the United States, and as such become entitled to all the rights, and privileges, and immunities,

Source: 19 Howard 393 (1857).

guarantied by that instrument to the citizen? One of which rights is the privilege of suing in a court of the United States in the cases specified in the constitution. . . .

The words "people of the United States" and "citizens" are synonymous terms, and mean the same thing. They both describe the political body who, according to our republican institutions, form the sovereignty, and who hold the power and conduct the government through their representatives. They are what we familiarly call the "sovereign people," and every citizen is one of this people, and a constituent member of this sovereignty. The question before us is, whether the class of persons described in the plea in abatement compose a portion of this people, and are constituent members of this sovereignty? We think they are not, and that they are not included, and were not intended to be included, under the word "citizens" in the constitution, and can therefore claim none of the rights and privileges which that instrument provides for and secures to citizens of the United States. On the contrary, they were at that time considered as a subordinate and inferior class of beings, who had been subjugated by the dominant race, and, whether emancipated or not, yet remained subject to their authority, and had no rights or privileges but such as those who held the power and the government might choose to grant them.

It is not the province of the court to decide upon the justice or injustice, the policy or impolicy, of these laws. The decision of that question belonged to the political or law-making power; to those who formed the sovereignty and framed the constitution. The duty of the court is, to interpret the instrument they have framed, with the best lights we can obtain on the subject, and to administer it as we find it, according to its true intent and meaning when it was adopted.

In discussing this question, we must not confound the rights of citizenship which a State may confer within its own limits, and the rights of citizenship as a member of the Union. It does not by any means follow, because he has all the rights and privileges of a citizen of a State, that he must be a citizen of the United States. He may have all of the rights and privileges of the citizen of a State, and yet not be entitled to the rights and privileges of a citizen in any other State. For, previous to the adoption of the constitution of the United States, every State had the undoubted right to confer on whomsoever it pleased the character of citizen, and to endow him with all its rights. But this character of course was confirmed to the boundaries of the State, and gave him no rights or privileges in other States beyond those secured to him by the laws of nations and the comity of States. Nor have the several States surrendered the power of conferring these rights and privileges by adopting the constitution of the United States. . . .

It is very clear, therefore, that no State can, by any act or law of its own, passed since the adoption of the constitution, introduce a new member into the political community created by the constitution of the United States. It cannot make him a member of this community by making him a member of its own. And for the same reason it cannot introduce any person, or description of persons, who were not intended to be embraced in this new political family, which the constitution brought into existence, but were intended to be excluded from it.

The question then arises, whether the provisions of the constitution, in relation to the personal rights and privileges to which the citizen of a State should be entitled, embraced the negro African race, at that time in this country, or who might afterwards be imported, who had then or should afterwards be made free in any State; and to put it in the power of a single State to make him a citizen of the United States, and endue him with the full rights of citizenship in every other State without their consent? Does the constitution of the United States act upon him whenever he shall be made free under the laws of a State, and raised there to the rank of a citizen, and immediately clothe him with all the privileges of a citizen in every other State, and in its own courts?

The court think the affirmative of these propositions cannot be maintained. And if it cannot, the plaintiff in error could not be a citizen of the State of Missouri, within the meaning of the constitution of the United States, and, consequently, was not entitled to sue in its courts.

It is true, every person, and every class and description of persons, who were at the time of the adoption of the constitution recognized as citizens in the several States, became also citizens of this new political body; but none other; it was formed by them, and for them and their posterity, but for no one else. And the personal rights and privileges guaranteed to citizens of this new sovereignty were intended to embrace those only who were then members of the several State communities, or who should afterwards by birthright or otherwise become members, according to the provisions of the constitution and the principles on which it was founded. It was the union of those who were at that time members of distinct and separate political communities into one political family, whose power, for certain specified purposes, was to extend over the whole territory of the United States. And it gave to each citizen rights and privileges outside of his State which he did not before possess, and placed him in every other State upon a perfect equality with its own citizens as to rights of person and rights of property; it made him a citizen of the United States. . . .

In the opinion of the court, the legislation and histories of the times, and the language used in the declaration of independence, show, that neither the class of persons who had been imported as slaves, nor their descendants, whether they had become free or not, were then acknowledged as a part of the people, nor intended to be included in the general words used in that memorable instrument. . . .

It is too clear for dispute, that the enslaved African race were not intended to be included, and formed no part of the people who framed and adopted this declaration; for if the language, as understood in that day, would embrace them, the conduct of the distinguished men who framed the declaration of independence would have been utterly and flagrantly inconsistent with the principles they asserted; and instead of the sympathy of mankind, to which they so confidently appealed, they would have deserved and received universal rebuke and reprobation. . . .

But there are two clauses in the constitution which point directly and specifically to the negro race as a separate class of persons, and show clearly that they were not regarded as a portion of the people or citizens of the government then formed.

One of these clauses reserves to each of the thirteen States the right to import slaves until the year 1808, if it thinks proper. . . . And by the other provision the States pledge themselves to each other to maintain the right of property of the master, by delivering up to him any slave who may have escaped from his service, and be found within their respective territories. . . .

The only two provisions which point to them and include them, treat them as property, and make it the duty of the government to protect it; no other power, in relation to this race, is to be found in the constitution; and as it is a government of special, delegated, powers, no authority beyond these two provisions can be constitutionally exercised. The government of the United States had no right to interfere for any other purpose but that of protecting the rights of the owner, leaving it altogether with the several States to deal with this race, whether emancipated or not, as each State may think justice, humanity, and the interests and safety of society, require. The States evidently intended to reserve this power exclusively to themselves. . . .

Upon a full and careful consideration of the subject, the court is of opinion, that, upon the facts stated . . . , Dred Scott was not a citizen of Missouri within the meaning of the constitution of the United States, and not entitled as such to sue in its courts; and, consequently, that the circuit court had no jurisdiction of the case, and that the judgment on the plea in abatement is erroneous. . . .

We proceed . . . to inquire whether the facts relied on by the plaintiff entitled him to his freedom. . . .

The act of Congress, upon which the plaintiff relies, declares that slavery and involuntary servitude, except as a punishment for crime, shall be forever prohibited in all that part of the territory ceded by France, under the name of Louisiana, which lies north of thirty-six degrees thirty minutes north latitude and not included within the limits of Missouri. And the difficulty which meets us at the threshold of this part of the inquiry is whether Congress was authorized to pass this law under any of the powers granted to it by the Constitution; for, if the authority is not given by that instrument, it is the duty of this Court to declare it void and inoperative and incapable of conferring freedom upon anyone who is held as a slave under the laws of any one of the states.

The counsel for the plaintiff has laid much stress upon that article in the Constitution which confers on Congress the power "to dispose of and make all needful rules and regulations respecting the territory or other property belonging to the United States"; but, in the judgment of the Court, that provision has no bearing on the present controversy, and the power there given, whatever it may be, is confined, and was intended to be confined, to the territory which at that time belonged to, or was claimed by, the United States and was within their boundaries as settled by the treaty with Great Britain and can have no influence upon a territory afterward acquired from a foreign government. It was a special provision for a known and particular territory, and to meet a present emergency, and nothing more. . . .

We do not mean, however, to question the power of Congress in this respect. The power to expand the territory of the United States by the admission of new states is plainly given; and in the construction of this power by all the departments of the government, it has been held to authorize the acquisition of territory, not fit for admission at the time, but to be admitted as soon as its population and situation would entitle it to admission. . . .

. . . It may be safely assumed that citizens of the United States who migrate to a territory belonging to the people of the United States cannot be ruled as mere colonists, dependent upon the will of the general government, and to be governed by any laws it may think proper to impose. The principle upon which our governments rest, and upon which alone they continue to exist, is the union of states, sovereign and independent within their own limits in their internal and domestic concerns, and bound together as one people by a general government, possessing certain enumerated and restricted powers, delegated to it by the people of the several states, and exercising supreme authority within the scope of the powers granted to it, throughout the dominion of the United States. A power, therefore, in the general government to obtain and hold colonies and dependent territories, over which they might legislate without restriction, would be inconsistent with its own existence in its present form. Whatever it acquires, it acquires for the benefit of the people of the several states who created it. It is their trustee acting for them and charged with the duty of promoting the interests of the whole people of the Union in the exercise of the powers specifically granted. . . .

But the power of Congress over the person or property of a citizen can never be a mere discretionary power under our Constitution and form of government. The powers of the government and the rights and privileges of the citizen are regulated and plainly defined by the Constitution itself. And, when the territory becomes a part of the United States, the federal government enters into possession in the character impressed upon it by those who created it. It enters upon it with its powers over the citizen strictly defined and limited by the Constitution, from which it derives its own existence, and by virtue of which alone it continues to exist and act as a government and sovereignty. It has no power of any kind beyond it; and it cannot, when it enters a territory of the United States, put off its character and assume discretionary or despotic powers which the Constitution has denied to it. It cannot create for itself a new character separated from the citizens of the United States and the duties it owes them under the provisions of the Constitution. The territory, being a part of the United States, the government and the citizen both enter it under the authority of the Constitution, with their respective rights defined and marked out; and the federal government can exercise no power over his person or property, beyond what that instrument confers, nor lawfully deny any right which it has reserved. . . .

These powers, and others, in relation to rights of person, which it is not necessary here to enumerate, are, in express and positive terms, denied to the general government; and the rights of private property have been guarded with equal care. Thus the rights of property are united with the rights of person and placed on the same ground by the Fifth Amendment to the Constitution, which provides that no person shall be deprived of life, liberty, and property without due process of law. And an act of Congress which deprives a citizen of the United States of his liberty or property, without due process of law, merely because he came himself or brought his property into a particular territory of the United States, and who had committed no offense against the laws, could hardly be dignified with the name of due process of law. . . .

It seems, however, to be supposed that there is a difference between property in a slave and other property and that different rules may be applied to it in expounding the Constitution of the United States. And the laws and usages of nations, and the writings of eminent jurists upon the relation of master and slave and their mutual rights and duties, and the powers which governments may exercise over it, have been dwelt upon in the argument.

But, in considering the question before us, it must be borne in mind that there is no law of nations standing between the people of the United States and their government and interfering with their relation to each other. The powers of the government and the rights of the citizen under it are positive and practical regulations plainly written down. The people of the United States have delegated to it certain enumerated powers and forbidden it to exercise others. It has no power over the person or property of a citizen but what the citizens of the United States have granted. And no laws or usages of other nations, or reasoning of statesmen or jurists upon the relations of master and slave, can enlarge the powers of the government or take from the citizens the rights they have reserved. And if the Constitution recognizes the right of property of the master in a slave, and makes no distinction between that description of property and other property owned by a citizen, no tribunal, acting under the authority of the United States, whether it be legislative, executive, or judicial, has a right to draw such a distinction or deny to it the benefit of the provisions and guaranties which have been provided for the protection of private property against the encroachments of the government.

Now, as we have already said in an earlier part of this opinion, upon a different point, the right of property in a slave is distinctly and expressly affirmed in the Constitution. The right to traffic in it, like an ordinary article of merchandise and property, was guaranteed to the citizens of the United States, in every state that might desire it, for twenty years. And the government in express terms is pledged to protect it in all future time if the slave escapes from his owner. That is done in plain words—too plain to be misunderstood. And no word can be found in the Constitution which gives Congress a greater power over slave property or which entitles property of that kind to less protection than property of any other description. The only power conferred is the power coupled with the duty of guarding and protecting the owner in his rights.

Upon these considerations it is the opinion of the Court that the act of Congress which prohibited a citizen from holding and owning property of this kind in the territory of the United States north of the line therein mentioned is not warranted by the Constitution and is therefore void; and that neither Dred Scott himself, nor any of his family, were made free by being carried into this territory; even if they had been carried there by the owner with the intention of becoming a permanent resident.

98

Lincoln-Douglas Debates (1858)

The *Dred Scott* case raised fears in the North that the decision would impose slavery on the free states, and indeed, some Southerners argued that the Constitution now allowed them to take their slaves anywhere, even for sale in the North. In the debate between Illinois senatorial candidates Abraham Lincoln and the incumbent Stephen A. Douglas, Lincoln several times suggested the possibility that the Court, following its reasoning in *Dred Scott,* might nationalize slavery by forbidding the states to exclude it. At Freeport, he posed a series of questions to Douglas regarding the case, hoping to trap Douglas into a position that would be anathema to either proslavery or abolitionist elements: How

Source: P. Crawford, *Lincoln-Douglas Debate at Freeport* (1958).

could Douglas square the decision with popular sovereignty, in which the people decided if there was to be slavery in the territories? Douglas fell into the trap, claiming that without local police ordinances, slavery could not exist. This angered proslavery forces, who wanted a strong endorsement of the decision, as well as abolitionists, who wanted a strong condemnation. Although Lincoln lost the senatorial election, Douglas's so-called "Freeport doctrine" probably cost him unified Democratic support in the 1860 presidential election. Note also Lincoln's careful answers to Douglas's questions, in which he tried to reassure the South that he did not oppose slavery where it currently exists.

See R. W. Johannsen, ed., *Lincoln Douglas Debates of 1858* (1965); D. E. Fehrenbacher, *Prelude to Greatness: Lincoln in the 1850's* (1962); and R. A. Heckman, *Lincoln versus Douglas* (1967).

Lincoln's Opening Speech

As to the first one, in regard to the fugitive slave law, I have never hesitated to say, and I do not now hesitate to say, that I think, under the Constitution of the United States, the people of the southern states are entitled to a congressional fugitive slave law. Having said that, I have had nothing to say in regard to the existing fugitive slave law further than that I think it should have been framed so as to be free from some of the objections that pertain to it, without lessening its efficiency. And inasmuch as we are not now in an agitation in regard to an alteration or modification of that law, I would not be the man to introduce it as a new subject of agitation upon the general question of slavery.

In regard to the other question of whether I am pledged to the admission of any more slave states into the Union, I state to you very frankly that I would be exceedingly sorry ever to be put in a position of having to pass upon that question. I should be exceedingly glad to know that there would never be another slave state admitted into the Union; . . . but I must add, that if slavery shall be kept out of the territories during the territorial existence of any one given territory, and then the people shall, having a fair chance and a clear field, when they come to adopt the constitution, do such an extraordinary thing as to adopt a slave constitution, uninfluenced by the actual presence of the institution among them, I see no alternative, if we own the country, but to admit them into the Union. . . .

The fourth one is in regard to the abolition of slavery in the District of Columbia. In relation to that, I have my mind very distinctly made up. I should be exceedingly glad to see slavery abolished in the District of Columbia. . . . I believe that Congress possesses the constitutional power to abolish it. Yet as a member of Congress, I should not with my present views, be in favor of *endeavoring* to abolish slavery in the District of Columbia, unless it would be upon these conditions. *First,* that the abolition should be gradual. *Second,* that it should be on a vote of the majority of qualified voters in the District, and *third,* that compensation should be made to unwilling owners. With these three conditions, I confess I would be exceedingly glad to see Congress abolish slavery in the District of Columbia, and, in the language of Henry Clay, "sweep from our Capital that foul blot upon our nation." . . .

In regard to the fifth interrogatory, I must say here, that as to the question of the abolition of the slave trade between the different states, I can truly answer, as I have, that I am *pledged* to nothing about it. It is a subject to which I have not given that mature consideration that would make me feel authorized to state a position so as to hold myself entirely bound by it. In other words, that question has never been prominently enough before me to induce me to investigate whether we really have the constitutional power to do it. I could investigate it if I had sufficient time, to bring myself to a conclusion upon that subject, but I have not done so, and I say so frankly to you here, and to Judge Douglas. I must say, however, that if I should be of opinion that Congress does possess the constitutional power to abolish the slave trade among the different states, I should still not be in favor of the exercise of that power unless upon some conservative principle as I conceive it, akin to what I have said in relation to the abolition of slavery in the District of Columbia.

My answer as to whether I desire that slavery should be prohibited in all the territories of the United States is full and explicit within itself, and cannot be made clearer by any comments of mine. So I suppose in regard to the question whether I am opposed to the acquisition of any more territory unless slavery is first prohibited therein, my answer is such that I could add nothing by way of illustration, or making myself better understood, than the answer which I have placed in writing.

Now in all this, the Judge has me and he has me on the record. I suppose he had flattered himself that I was really entertaining one set of opinions for one place and another set for another place—that I was afraid to say at one place what I uttered at another. What I am saying here I suppose I say to a vast audience as strongly tending to Abolitionism as any audience in the state of Illinois, and I believe I am saying that which, if it would be offensive to any persons and render them enemies to myself, would be offensive to persons in this audience.

I now proceed to propound to the Judge the interrogatories, as far as I have framed them. I will bring forward a new installment when I get them ready. . . . I will bring them forward now, only reaching to number four.

The first one is—

Question 1.   If the people of Kansas shall, by means entirely unobjectionable in all other respects, adopt a state constitution, and ask admission into the Union under it, *before* they have the requisite number of inhabitants according to the English Bill—some ninety-three thousand—will you vote to admit them? . . .

Q. 2.   Can the people of a United States territory, in any lawful way, against the wish of any citizen of the United States, exclude slavery from its limits prior to the formation of a state constitution? . . .

Q. 3.   If the Supreme Court of the United States shall decide that states can not exclude slavery from their limits, are you in favor of acquiescing in, adopting and following such decision as a rule of political action? . . .

Q. 4.   Are you in favor of acquiring additional territory, in disregard of how such acquisition may affect the nation on the slavery question? . . .

Douglas's Reply

In a few moments I will proceed to review the answers which he has given to these interrogatories; but in order to relieve his anxiety I will first respond to those which he has presented to me. Mark you, he has not presented interrogatories which have ever received the sanction of the party with which I am acting, and hence he has no other foundation for them than his own curiosity. . . .

First, he desires to know if the people of Kansas shall form a constitution by means entirely proper and unobjectionable and ask admission into the Union as a state, before they have the requisite population for a member of Congress, whether I will vote for that admission. Well, now, I regret exceedingly that he did not answer that interrogatory himself before he put it to me, in order that we might understand, and not be left to infer, on which side he is. . . . Mr. Trumbull, during the last session of Congress, voted from the beginning to the end against the admission of Oregon, although a free state, because she had not the requisite population for a member of Congress. . . . Mr. Trumbull would not consent, under any circumstances, to let a state, free or slave, come into the Union until it had the requisite population. As Mr. Trumbull is in the field, fighting for Mr. Lincoln, I would like to have Mr. Lincoln answer his own question and tell me whether he is fighting Trumbull on that issue or not. . . . But I will answer his question. In reference to Kansas; it is my opinion, that as she has population enough to constitute a slave state, she has people enough for a free state. . . . I will not make Kansas an exceptional case to the other states of the Union. ("Sound," and "hear, hear.") I hold it to be a sound rule of universal application to require a territory to contain the requisite population for a member of Congress, before it is admitted as a state into the Union. I made that proposition in the Senate in 1856, and I renewed it during the last session, in a bill providing that no territory of the United States should form a constitution and apply for admission until it had the requisite population. . . .

The next question propounded to me by Mr. Lincoln is, can the people of a territory in any lawful way against the wishes of any citizen of the United States; exclude slavery from their limits prior to the formation of a state constitution? I answer emphatically, as Mr. Lincoln has heard me answer a hundred times from every stump in Illinois, that in my opinion the people of a territory can, by lawful means, exclude slavery from their limits prior to the formation of a state constitution. . . . Mr. Lincoln knew that I had answered that question over and over again. He heard me argue the Nebraska Bill on that principle all over the state in 1854, in 1855 and in 1856, and he has no excuse for pretending to be in doubt as to my position on that question. It matters not what way the Supreme Court may hereafter decide as to the abstract question whether slavery may or may not go into a territory under the Constitution, the people have the lawful means to introduce it or exclude it as they please, for the reason that slavery cannot exist a day or an hour anywhere, unless it is supported by local police regulations. . . . Those police regulations can only be established by the local legislature, and if the people are opposed to slavery they will elect representatives to that body who will by unfriendly legislation effectually prevent the introduction of it into their midst. If, on the contrary, they are for it, their legislation will favor its extension. Hence, no matter what the decision of the Supreme Court may be on that abstract question, still the right of the people to make a slave territory or a free territory is perfect and complete under the Nebraska Bill. I hope Mr. Lincoln deems my answer satisfactory on that point. . . .

The third question which Mr. Lincoln presented is, if the Supreme Court of the United States shall decide that a state of this Union cannot exclude slavery from its own limits will I submit to it? I am amazed that Lincoln should ask such a question. . . . Yes, a school boy does know better. Mr. Lincoln's object is to cast an imputation upon the Supreme Court. He knows that there never was but one man in America, claiming any degree of intelligence or decency, who ever for a moment pretended such a thing. It is true that the Washington *Union,* in an article published on the 17th of last December, did put forth that doctrine, and I denounced the article on the floor of the Senate. . . .

The fourth question of Mr. Lincoln is, are you in favor of acquiring additional territory in disregard as to how such acquisition may affect the Union on the slavery question. This question is very ingeniously and cunningly put. . . .

The Black Republican creed lays it down expressly, that under no circumstances shall we acquire any more territory unless slavery is first prohibited in the country. I ask Mr. Lincoln whether he is in favor of that proposition. Are you (addressing Mr. Lincoln) opposed to the acquisition of any more territory, under any circumstances, unless slavery is prohibited in it? That he does not like to answer. When I ask him whether he stands up to that article in the platform of his party, he turns, Yankee-fashion, and without answering it, asks me whether I am in favor of acquiring territory without regard to how it may affect the Union on the slavery question. . . . I answer that whenever it becomes necessary, in our growth and progress to acquire more territory, that I am in favor of it, without reference to the question of slavery, and when we have acquired it, I will leave the people free to do as they please, either to make it slave or free territory, as they prefer. . . . It is idle to tell me or you that we have territory enough. Our fathers supposed that we had enough when our territory extended to the Mississippi River, but a few years' growth and expansion satisfied them that we needed more, and the Louisiana territory, from the west branch of the Mississippi, to the British possessions, was acquired. Then we acquired Oregon, then California and New Mexico. We have enough now for the present, but this is a young and a growing nation. It swarms as often as a hive of bees, and as new swarms are turned out each year, there must be hives in which they can gather and make their honey. . . . So it would be with this great nation. With our natural increase, growing with a rapidity unknown in any other part of the globe, with the tide of emigration that is fleeing from despotism in the old world to seek a refuge in our own, there is a constant torrent pouring into this country that requires more land, more territory upon which to settle, and just as fast as our interests and our destiny require additional territory in the north, in the south, or on the islands of the ocean, I am for it, and when we acquire it will leave the people, according to the Nebraska Bill, free to do as they please on the subject of slavery and every other question. . . .

99

Ableman v. Booth (1859)

In 1854 a mob led by Sherman Booth rescued a slave from a jail in Wisconsin. Federal marshals arrested Booth and charged him with violating the 1850 Fugitive Slave Law, but he secured a writ of habeas corpus from the Wisconsin Supreme Court. After he had been arrested a second time and convicted, the same court freed him, and ruled the federal statute unconstitutional. Attorney General Jeremiah Black secured a writ of error from the United States Supreme Court directed

Source: 21 Howard 506 (1859).

against the Wisconsin court, which refused to accept it. The Supreme Court nonetheless accepted jurisdiction, even though both Booth and the Wisconsin judges refused to appear.

Whatever their feelings on slavery or states' rights, the justices could not ignore so blatant an attack on the high court's authority, and Chief Justice Taney wrote a decision every bit as nationalistic as any written by Marshall or Story. The case has been somewhat stigmatized because Taney upheld the Fugitive Slave Law in dicta, but the crux of the decision, the supremacy of the federal government, has withstood the test of time.

See T. D. Morris, *Free Men All: The Personal Liberty Laws of the North, 1780–1861* (1974); P. Finkelman, *An Imperfect Union: Slavery, Federalism and Comity* (1981); and A. Bestor, "State Sovereignty and Slavery: A Reinterpretation of Proslavery Constitutional Doctrine, 1846–1860," 54 *J. Ill. St. His. Soc.* 117 (1961).

~~~~~~

Chief Justice Taney delivered the opinion of the Court.

[The Chief Justice first reviewed in detail the two cases of the arrest and release of Sherman M. Booth.]

It will be seen, from the foregoing statement of facts, that a judge of the Supreme Court of the State of Wisconsin in the first of these cases, claimed and exercised the right to supervise and annul the proceedings of a commissioner of the United States, and to discharge a prisoner, who had been committed by the commissioner for an offence against the laws of this Government, and that this exercise of power by the judge was afterwards sanctioned and affirmed by the Supreme Court of the State.

In the second case, the State court has gone a step further, and claimed and exercised jurisdiction over the proceedings and judgment of a District Court of the United States, and upon a summary and collateral proceeding, by *habeas corpus,* has set aside and annulled its judgment, and discharged a prisoner who had been tried and found guilty of an offence against the laws of the United States, and sentenced to imprisonment by the District Court.

And it further appears that the State court have not only claimed and exercised this jurisdiction, but have also determined that their decision is final and conclusive upon all the courts of the United States, and ordered their clerk to disregard and refuse obedience to the writ of error issued by this court, pursuant to the act of Congress of 1789, to bring here for examination and revision the judgment of the State court.

These propositions are new in the jurisprudence of the United States, as well as of the States; and the supremacy of the State courts over the courts of the United States, in cases arising under the Constitution and laws of the United States, is now for the first time asserted and acted upon in the Supreme Court of a State. . . .

If the judicial power exercised in this instance has been reserved to the States, no offence against the laws of the United States can be punished by their own courts, without the permission and according to the judgment of the courts of the State in which the party happens to be imprisoned; for, if the Supreme Court of Wisconsin possessed the power it has exercised in relation to offences against the act of Congress in question, it necessarily follows that they must have the same judicial authority in relation to any other law of the United States; and, consequently, their supervising and controlling power would embrace the whole criminal code of the United States, and extend to offences against our revenue laws, or any other law intended to guard the different departments of the General Government from fraud or violence. And it would embrace all crimes, from the highest to the lowest; including felonies, which are punished with death, as well as misdemeanors, which are punished by imprisonment. And, moreover, if the power is possessed by the Supreme Court of the State of Wisconsin, it must belong equally to every other State in the Union, when the prisoner is within its territorial limits; and it is very certain that the State courts would not always agree in opinion; and it would often happen, that an act which was admitted to be an offence, and justly punished, in one State, would be regarded as innocent, and indeed as praiseworthy, in another.

It would seem to be hardly necessary to do more than state the result to which these decisions of the State courts must inevitably lead. It is, of itself, a sufficient and conclusive answer; for no one will suppose that a Government which has now lasted nearly seventy years, enforcing its laws by its own tribunals, and preserving the union of the States, could have lasted a single year, or fulfilled the high trusts committed to it, if offences against its laws could not have been punished without the consent of the State in which the culprit was found.

The judges of the Supreme Court of Wisconsin do not distinctly state from what source they suppose they have derived this judicial power. There can be no such thing as judicial authority, unless it is conferred by a Government or sovereignty; and if the judges and courts of Wisconsin possess the jurisdiction they claim, they must derive it either from the United States or the State. It certainly has not been conferred on them by the United States; and it is equally clear it was not in the power of the State to confer it, even if it had attempted to do so; for no State can authorize one of its judges or courts to exercise judicial power, by *habeas corpus* or otherwise, within the jurisdiction of another and independent Government. And although the State of Wisconsin is sovereign within its territorial limits to a certain extent, yet that sovereignty is limited and restricted by the Constitution of the United States. And the powers of the General Government, and of the State, although both exist and are exercised within the same territorial limits, are yet separate and distinct sovereignties, acting separately and independently of each other, within their respective spheres. And the sphere of action appropriated to the United States is as far beyond the reach of the judicial process issued by a State judge or a State court, as if the line of division was traced by landmarks and monuments visible to the eye. And the State of Wisconsin had no more power to authorize these proceedings of its judges and courts, than it would have had if the prisoner had been confined in Michigan, or in any other State of the Union, for an offence against the laws of the State in which he was imprisoned. . . .

. . . The Constitution was not formed merely to guard the States against danger from foreign nations, but mainly to secure union and harmony at home; for if this object could be attained, there would be but little danger from abroad; and to accomplish this purpose, it was felt by the statesmen who framed the Constitution, and by the people who adopted it, that it was necessary that many of the rights of sovereignty which the States then possessed should be ceded to the General Government; and that, in the sphere of action assigned to it, it should be supreme, and strong enough to execute its own laws by its own tribunals, without interruption from a State or from State authorities. And it was evident that anything short of this would be inadequate to the main objects for which the Government was established; and that local interests, local passions or prejudices, incited and fostered by individuals for sinister purposes, would lead to acts of aggression and injustice by one State upon the rights of another, which would ultimately terminate in violence and force, unless there was a common arbiter between them, armed with power enough to protect and guard the rights of all, by appropriate laws, to be carried into execution peacefully by its judicial tribunals.

The language of the Constitution, by which this power is granted, is too plain to admit of doubt or to need comment. It declares that "this Constitution, and the laws of the United States which shall be passed in pursuance thereof, and all treaties made, or which shall be made, under the authority of the United States, shall be the supreme law of the land, and the judges in every State shall be bound thereby, anything in the Constitution or laws of any State to the contrary notwithstanding."

But the supremacy thus conferred on this Government could not peacefully be maintained, unless it was clothed with judicial power, equally paramount in authority to carry it into execution; for if left to the courts of justice of the several States, conflicting decisions would unavoidably take place, and the local tribunals could hardly be expected to be always free from the local influences of which we have spoken. And the Constitution and laws and treaties of the United States, and the powers granted to the Federal Government, would soon receive different interpretations in different States, and the

Government of the United States would soon become one thing in one State and another thing in another. It was essential, therefore, to its very existence as a Government, that it should have the power of establishing courts of justice, altogether independent of State power, to carry into effect its own laws; and that a tribunal should be established in which all cases which might arise under the Constitution and laws and treaties of the United States, whether in a State court or a court of the United States, should be finally and conclusively decided. Without such a tribunal, it is obvious that there would be no uniformity of judicial decision; and that the supremacy, (which is but another name for independence,) so carefully provided in the clause of the Constitution above referred to, could not possibly be maintained peacefully, unless it was associated with this paramount judicial authority.

Accordingly, it was conferred on the General Government, in clear, precise, and comprehensive terms. It is declared that its judicial power shall (among other subjects enumerated) extend to all cases in law and equity arising under the Constitution and laws of the United States, and that in such cases, as well as the others there enumerated, this court shall have appellate jurisdiction both as to law and fact, with such exceptions and under such regulations as Congress shall make. The appellate power, it will be observed, is conferred on this court in all cases or suits in which such a question shall arise. It is not confined to suits in the inferior courts of the United States, but extends to all cases where such a question arises, whether it be in a judicial tribunal of a State or of the United States. And it is manifest that this ultimate appellate power in a tribunal created by the Constitution itself was deemed essential to secure the independence and supremacy of the General Government in the sphere of action assigned to it; to make the Constitution and laws of the United States uniform, and the same in every State; and to guard against evils which would inevitably arise from conflicting opinions between the courts of a State and of the United States, if there was no common arbiter authorized to decide between them.

The importance which the framers of the Constitution attached to such a tribunal, for the purpose of preserving internal tranquillity, is strikingly manifested by the clause which gives this court jurisdiction over the sovereign States which compose this Union, when a controversy arises between them. Instead of reserving the right to seek redress for injustice from another State by their sovereign powers, they have bound themselves to submit to the decision of this court, and to abide by its judgment. And it is not out of place to say, here, that experience has demonstrated that this power was not unwisely surrendered by the States; for in the time that has already elapsed since this Government came into existence, several irritating and angry controversies have taken place between adjoining States, in relation to their respective boundaries, and which have sometimes threatened to end in force and violence, but for the power vested in this court to hear them and decide between them. . . .

. . . This tribunal, therefore, was erected, and the powers of which we have spoken conferred upon it, not by the Federal Government, but by the people of the States, who formed and adopted that Government, and conferred upon it all the powers, legislative, executive, and judicial, which it now possesses. And in order to secure its independence, and enable it faithfully and firmly to perform its duty, it engrafted it upon the Constitution itself, and declared that this court should have appellate power in all cases arising under the Constitution and laws of the United States. So long, therefore, as this Constitution shall endure, this tribunal must exist with it, deciding in the peaceful forms of judicial proceeding the angry and irritating controversies between sovereignties, which in other countries have been determined by the arbitrament of force. . . .

We are sensible that we have extended the examination of these decisions beyond the limits required by any intrinsic difficulty in the questions. But the decisions in question were made by the supreme judicial tribunal of the State; and when a court so elevated in its position has pronounced a judgment which, if it could be maintained, would subvert the very foundations of this Government, it seemed to be the duty of this court, when exercising its appellate power, to show plainly the grave errors into which the State court has fallen, and the consequences to which they would inevitably lead.

But it can hardly be necessary to point out the errors which followed their mistaken view of the jurisdiction they might lawfully exercise; because, if there was any defect of power in the commissioner, or in his mode of proceeding, it was for the tribunals of the United States to revise and correct it, and not for a State court. And as regards the decision of the District Court, it had exclusive and final jurisdiction by the laws of the United States; and neither the regularity of its proceedings nor the validity of its sentence could be called in question in any other court, either of a State or the United States, by *habeas corpus* or any other process.

But although we think it unnecessary to discuss these questions, yet, as they have been decided by the State court, and are before us on the record, and we are not willing to be misunderstood, it is proper to say that, in the judgment of this court, the act of Congress commonly called the fugitive slave law is, in all of its provisions, fully authorized by the Constitution of the United States; that the commissioner had lawful authority to issue the warrant and commit the party, and that his proceedings were regular and conformable to law. We have already stated the opinion and judgment of the court as to the exclusive jurisdiction of the District Court, and the appellate powers which this court is authorized and required to exercise. And if any argument was needed to show the wisdom and necessity of this appellate power, the cases before us sufficiently prove it, and at the same time emphatically call for its exercise.

The judgment of the Supreme Court of Wisconsin must therefore be reversed in each of the cases now before the court.

100

Limits of Federal Power (1860)

JEREMIAH S. BLACK

As the Union tottered toward secession in the fall of 1860, President James Buchanan sought the advice of his Attorney General on the powers of the federal government to deal with the crisis. The proslavery Jeremiah S. Black of Pennsylvania, in an official opinion, declared that aside from fairly limited and well-defined areas, such as the preservation and protection of governmental property, the President had few powers other than those of a "defensive" nature (see Document 106). If a state seceded, Black opined, the President could make no response. Congress or the states might have the power, but if they exercised it in a coercive manner, then a state would be justified in seceding. Buchanan relied on this opinion in his annual State of the Union message, and while he asserted that the Constitution did not permit secession, there was little he could do to stop it. As Senator William Seward interpreted the speech and Black's opinion: "It is the duty of the President to execute the laws—unless somebody opposes him—and that no state has the right to go out of the Union—unless it wants to."

See K. L. Stampp, *And the War Came: The North and the Secession Crisis, 1860–1861* (1950); P. S. Paludan, "The American Civil War Considered as a Crisis in Law and Order," 77 *A.H.R.* 1013 (1972); H. Adams, *The Great Secession Winter . . .* (G. Hochfield, ed., 1958); and W. N. Brigance, *Jeremiah Sullivan Black* (1934).

Attorney General's Office, November 20, 1860

SIR: I have had the honor to receive your note of the 17th, and I now reply to the grave questions therein propounded as fully as the time allowed me will permit.

Within their respective spheres of action, the Federal Government, and the Government of a State, are both of them independent and supreme; but each is utterly powerless beyond the limits assigned to it by the Constitution. If Congress would attempt to change the law of descents, to make a new rule of personal succession, or to dissolve the family relations existing in any State,

---

Source: 9 *Opinions of the Attorney Generals* 517 (1860).

the act would be simply void; but not more void than would be a State law to prevent the recapture of fugitives from labor, to forbid the carrying of the mails, or to stop the collection of duties on imports. The will of a State, whether expressed in its constitution or laws, cannot, while it remains in the confederacy, absolve her people from the duty of obeying the just and constitutional requirements of the Central Government. Nor can any act of the Central Government displace the jurisdiction of a State; because the laws of the United States are supreme and binding only so far as they are passed *in pursuance of the Constitution.* I do not say what might be effected by mere revolutionary force. I am speaking of legal and constitutional right.

This is the view always taken by the judiciary, and so universally adopted, that the statement of it may seem common-place. The Supreme Court of the United States has declared it in many cases. . . .

The duty which these principles devolve not only upon every officer, but every citizen, is that which Mr. Jefferson expressed so compendiously in his first inaugural, namely: "To support the State governments in all their rights, as the most competent administrators for their domestic concerns, and the surest bulwarks against anti-republican tendencies," combined with "the preservation of the General Government in its whole constitutional vigor, as the sheet-anchor of our peace at home and safety abroad."

To the chief executive magistrate of the Union is confided the solemn duty of seeing the laws faithfully executed. That he may be able to meet this duty with a power equal to its performance, he nominates his own subordinates, and removes them at his pleasure. For the same reason the land and naval forces are under his orders as their commander-in-chief. But his power is to be used only in the manner prescribed by the legislative department. He cannot accomplish a legal purpose by illegal means, or break the laws himself to prevent them from being violated by others.

The acts of Congress sometimes give the President a broad discretion in the use of the means by which they are to be executed, and sometimes limit his power so that he can exercise it only in a certain prescribed manner. Where the law directs a thing to be done without saying how, that implies the power to use such means as may be necessary and proper to accomplish the end of the legislature. But where the mode of performing a duty is pointed out by statute, that is the exclusive mode, and no other can be followed. The United States have no common law to fall back upon when the written law is defective. If, therefore, an act of Congress declares that a certain thing shall be done by a particular officer, it cannot be done by a different officer. The agency which the law furnishes for its own execution must be used to the exclusion of all others. . . .

Your right to take such measures as may seem to be necessary for the protection of the public property is very clear. It results from the proprietary rights of the Government as owner of the forts, arsenals, magazines, dock yards, navy yards, custom houses, public ships, and other property which the United States have bought, built, and paid for. Besides, the Government of the United States is authorized by the Constitution (art. 1, sec. 8) to "exercise exclusive legislation in all cases whatsoever . . . over all places purchased by the consent of the Legislature of the State in which the same shall be, for the erection of forts, magazines, arsenals, dock yards, and other needful buildings." It is believed that no important public building has been bought or erected on ground where the Legislature of the State in which it is has not passed a law consenting to the purchase of it, and ceding the exclusive jurisdiction. This Government, then, is not only the owner of those buildings and grounds, but, by virtue of the supreme and paramount law, it regulates the action and punishes the offences of all who are within them. If any one of an owner's rights is plainer than another, it is that of keeping exclusive possession and repelling intrusion. The right of defending the public property includes also the right of recapture after it has been unlawfully taken by another. President Jefferson held the opinion, and acted upon it, that he could order a military force to take possession of any land to which the United States had title, though they had never occupied it before, though a private party claimed and held it, and though it was not then needed nor proposed to be used for any purpose connected with the operations of the Government. This may have been a stretch of executive power, but the right of retaking public property in which the Government has been carrying on its lawful business, and from which its officers have been unlawfully thrust out, cannot well be doubted; and when it was exercised at Harper's Ferry, in October, 1859, every one acknowledged the legal justice of it.

I come now to the point in your letter which is probably of the greatest practical importance. By the act of 1807, you may employ such parts of the land and naval forces as you may judge necessary, for the purpose of causing the laws to be duly executed, in all cases where it is lawful to use the militia for the same purpose. By the act of 1795, the militia may be called forth "whenever the laws of the United States shall be opposed, or the execution thereof obstructed in any State, by combinations too powerful to be suppressed by the ordinary course of judicial proceedings, or by the power vested in the marshals." This imposes upon the President the sole responsibility of deciding whether the exigency has arisen which requires the use of military force, and in proportion to the magnitude of that responsibility will be his care not to overstep the limits of his legal and just authority.

The laws referred to in the act of 1795 are manifestly those which are administered by the judges and executed by the ministerial officers of the courts for the punishment of crime against the United States, for the protection of rights claimed under the federal Constitution and laws, and for the enforcement of such obligations as come within the cognizance of the federal judiciary. To compel obedience to these laws the courts have authority to punish all who obstruct their regular administration, and the marshals and their deputies have the same powers as sheriffs and their deputies in the several States in executing the laws of the States. These are the ordinary means provided for the execution of the laws, and the whole spirit of our system is opposed to the employment of any other, except in cases of extreme necessity, arising out of great and unusual combinations against them. Their agency must continue to be used until their incapacity to cope with the power opposed to them shall be plainly demonstrated. It is only upon clear evidence to that effect that a military force can be called into the field. Even then, its operations must be purely defensive. It can suppress only such combinations as are found directly opposing the laws and obstructing the execution thereof. It can do no more than what might and ought to be done by a civil *posse,* if a civil *posse* could be raised large enough to meet the same opposition. On such occasions especially, the military power must be kept in strict subordination to the civil authority, since it is only in aid of the latter that the former can act at all.

But what if the feeling in any State against the United States should become so universal that the federal officers themselves (including judges, district attorneys, and marshals) would be reached by the same influences and resign their places? Of course the first step would be to appoint others in their stead, if others could be got to serve. But in such an event, it is more than probable that great difficulty would be found in filling the offices. We can easily conceive how it might become altogether impossible. We are, therefore, obliged to consider what can be done in case we have no courts to issue judicial process, and no ministerial officers to execute it. In that event, troops would certainly be out of place, and their use wholly illegal. If they are sent to aid the courts and marshals, there must be courts and marshals to be aided. Without the exercise of those functions which belong exclusively to the civil service, the laws cannot be executed in any event, no matter what may be the physical strength which the Government has at its command. Under such circumstances, to send a military force into any State, with orders to act against the people, would be simply making war upon them.

The existing laws put and keep the Federal Government strictly on the defensive. You can use force only to repel an assault on the public property, and aid the courts in the performance of their duty. If the means given you to collect the revenue and execute the other laws be insufficient for that purpose, Congress may extend and make them more effectual to those ends.

If one of the States should declare her independence, your action cannot depend upon the rightfulness of the cause upon which such declaration is based. Whether the retirement of a State from the Union be the exercise of a right reserved in the Constitution, or a revolutionary movement, it is certain that you have not in either case the authority to recognize the independence or to absolve her from her federal obligations. Congress, or the other States in convention assembled, must take such measures as may be necessary and proper. In such an event, I see no course for you but to go straight onward in the path you have hitherto trodden—that is, execute the laws to the extent of the defensive means placed in your hands, and act generally upon the assumption that the present constitutional relations between the States and the Federal Government continue to exist, until a new order of things shall be established either by law or force.

Whether Congress has the constitutional right to make war against one or more States, and require the Executive of the Federal Government to carry it on by means of force to be drawn from the other States, is a question for Congress itself to consider. It must be admitted that no such power is expressly given, nor are there any words in the Constitution which imply it. Among the powers enumerated in article 1, section 8, is that "to declare war, grant letters of marque and reprisal, and to make rules concerning captures on land and water." This certainly means nothing more than the power to commence and carry on hostilities against the foreign enemies of the nation. Another clause in the same section gives Congress the power "to provide for calling forth the militia," and to use them within the limits of the State. But this power is so restricted by the words which immediately follow, that it can be exercised only for one of the following purposes: 1. To execute the laws of the Union; that is, to aid the federal officers in the performance of their regular duties. 2. To suppress insurrections against the State; but this is confined by article 4, section 4, to cases in which the State herself shall apply for assistance against her own people. 3. To repel the invasion of a State by enemies who come from abroad to assail her in her own territory. All these provisions are made to protect the States, not to authorize an attack by one part of the country upon another; to preserve the peace, and not to plunge them into civil war. Our forefathers do not seem to have thought that war was calculated "to form a more perfect union, establish justice, insure domestic tranquillity, provide for the common defence, promote the general welfare, and secure the blessings of liberty to ourselves and our posterity." There was undoubtedly a strong and universal conviction among the men who framed and ratified the Constitution, that military force would not only be useless, but pernicious, as a means of holding the States together.

If it be true that war cannot be declared, nor a system of general hostilities carried on by the Central Government against a State, then it seems to follow that an attempt to do so would be *ipso facto* an expulsion of such State from the Union. Being treated as an alien and an enemy, she would be compelled to act accordingly. And if Congress shall break up the present Union, by unconstitutionally putting strife and enmity and armed hostility between different sections of the country, instead of the domestic tranquillity which the Constitution was meant to insure, will not all the States be absolved from their federal obligations? Is any portion of the people bound to contribute their money or their blood to carry on a contest like that?

The right of the General Government to preserve itself in its whole constitutional vigor, by repelling a direct and positive aggression upon its property or its officers, cannot be denied. But this is a totally different thing from an offensive war, to punish the people for the political misdeeds of their State Government, or to prevent a threatened violation of the Constitution, or to enforce an acknowledgment that the Government of the United States is supreme. The States are colleagues of one another, and if some of them shall conquer the rest and hold them as subjugated provinces, it would totally destroy the whole theory upon which they are now connected.

If this view of the subject be correct, as I think it is, then the Union must utterly perish at the moment when Congress shall arm one part of the people against another for any purpose beyond that of merely protecting the General Government in the exercise of its proper constitutional functions.

I am, very respectfully, yours,

J. S. Black

101

South Carolina Ordinance of Secession (1860)

Throughout the presidential election campaign of 1860, Southerners had warned that the election of Lincoln would threaten the continuation of slavery, despite denials by the Republicans that they had any intention of attacking slavery where it already existed. Immediately upon Lincoln's election, the South Carolina legislature called a convention to meet in December to discuss dissolving the state's ties to the Union. The state, which had always been a hotbed of states' rights sentiment (Documents 85, 86), elected a bevy of fire-eaters to the convention, which on December 20 unanimously voted an Ordinance of Secession. Six other states—Georgia, Florida, Alabama, Mississippi, Louisiana, and Texas—followed suit in the next few weeks.

The idea of secession had by this time been discussed for so long in the South that in Southern eyes it had already acquired a patina of legitimacy. Calhoun had argued that sovereignty could never be surrendered, so the states in entering the Union had never given up their sovereign powers. By this view, the federal government constituted

Source: R. Scott, ed., 1 *War of the Rebellion* 110 (1880).

little more than a convenient arrangement that could be discarded when it ceased to be convenient.

See J. A. May and J. R. Faunt, eds., *South Carolina Secedes* (1960); R. A. Wooster, *The Secession Conventions of the South* (1962); D. L. Smiley, "Revolutionary Origins of South's Constitutional Defenses," 44 *N. Car. His. R.* 256 (1967).

~~~~~~

THE STATE OF SOUTH CAROLINA:

At a Convention of the People of the State of South Carolina, begun and holden at Columbia on the seventeenth day of December, in the year of our Lord one thousand eight hundred and sixty, and thence continued by adjournment to Charleston, and there, by divers adjournments, to the twentieth of December in the same year:

AN ORDINANCE to dissolve the union between the State of South Carolina and other States united with her under the compact entitled "The Constitution of the United States of America":

We, the People of the State of South Carolina in convention assembled, do declare and ordain, and it is hereby declared and ordained, that the ordinance adopted by us in convention on the twenty-third day of May, in the year of our Lord one thousand seven hundred and eighty-eight, whereby the Constitution of the United States of America was ratified, and also all acts and parts of acts of the general assembly of this State ratifying amendments of the said Constitution, are hereby repealed; and that the union now subsisting between South Carolina and other States, under the name of the "United States of America," is hereby dissolved.

Done at Charleston the twentieth day of December, in the year of our Lord one thousand eight hundred and sixty.

Part VIII

Civil War and Reconstruction

The Civil War, aside from all its other aspects, must be seen as the great constitutional crisis of American history. The Framers had never made provision for a civil war, and it was accepted by nearly everyone that the national government had only limited powers. Confronted by civil strife, many believed, either the Constitution would have to be abandoned or the Union sundered. Had the federal government been in the hands of ideologically rigid men, it is likely that the Union would have failed. Lincoln and his lieutenants, but especially Lincoln, understood the Constitution as a flexible document that had within it the powers necessary to preserve the Union. This flexibility—in constitutional thought as well as in political dealings—made Lincoln the true genius of preserving the republic.

Such flexibility was not present everywhere. The Confederacy adopted the 1787 Constitution almost verbatim (Document 102) but interpreted it in a narrow and constricted manner. Chief Justice Roger Taney spent his last years bitterly attacking Lincoln for what he claimed were violations of the Constitution in support of an illegal war (Document 103). Other members of the Court fortunately recognized that in wartime national preservation took precedence over some legal niceties (Documents 105, 109) and were willing to wait until the Union had been preserved before exploring the limits of governmental power.

What did emerge during the war years was a philosophy Harold Hyman has called the "adequacy-of-the-Constitution" theory, which enphasized that the Constitution, by definition, had to have sufficient explicit or implicit powers to meet challenges to the survival of the Union. This theory emerged in the writings of legal experts (Document 106), and in some private musings by Lincoln himself (Document 108). It is quite clear in the Emancipation Proclamation (Document 104) and in the early plans for Reconstruction (Document 107).

Unfortunately, Andrew Johnson lacked his predecessor's political skills and broad view of the Constitution. In light of southern efforts to deny freedmen their rights (Document 110), Congress passed the first Civil Rights

Act (Document 111), which Johnson vetoed, claiming that the government had no power to meddle in these affairs (Document 112). It made very little sense to Congress, or to most of the North, that there had been sufficient constitutional power to prosecute a civil war to preserve the Union, but not enough to successfully reconstruct it. The continued political tension between president and Congress paralyzed the government and led to the only incident of impeachment of a chief executive (Document 114).

The Supreme Court, as during most wars, kept a low profile, but with the hostilities ended, it gradually reasserted its powers as chief interpreter of the Constitution. It declared that the national government could not impose military rule where the civil courts were open (Document 113), and resisted congressional efforts to limit its jurisdiction (Documents 115, 116). The Court had relatively little to do with the Reconstruction, although it did, in some ways, pass on the legitimacy of the war and the government's efforts (Documents 117, 118). And in one of the first cases it heard on the Fourteenth Amendment (Document 119), the Court narrowly split over the meaning of the Due Process Clause, and thus set the stage for the great debate over substantive due process in the next sixty years.

Sections of the Confederate Constitution (1861)

Throughout the decades leading up to the Civil War, Southerners had argued that they were the true adherents to the Constitution, and that the North had broken the original bargain in which the states had joined. When secession occurred, the Confederacy essentially adopted the federal Constitution, and made only a few changes. These focused on those matters that Southerners believed had been most distorted, including slavery, of course, but also internal improvements (Document 67) and the compact nature of the Union (Document 85). Interestingly enough, however, the wording of the Confederate constitution would have allowed as nationalistic an interpretation as John Marshall ever took; it did not, for example, envisage a state seceding from the Confederacy. Following are those clauses that differ in some way from the federal Constitution, as well as a few to show the similarities; the Bill of Rights, for example, is incorporated into the body of the Confederate constitution.

See C. R. Lee, *The Confederate Constitution* (1963); F. L. Owsley, *State Rights in the Confederacy* (1925); E. Thomas, *The Confederate Nation, 1861–1865* (1979); and C. A. Amlund, *Federalism in the Southern Confederacy* (1966).

We, the people of the Confederate States, each State acting in its sovereign and independent character, in order to form a permanent federal government, establish justice, insure domestic tranquility and secure the blessings of liberty to ourselves and our posterity—invoking the favor and guidance of Almighty God—do ordain and establish this Constitution for the Confederate States of America.

Article 1

Section 2

5. The House of Representatives shall choose their speaker and other officers, and shall have the sole power of impeachment; except that any

---

Source: *Constitution of the Confederate States of America* (1861).

judicial or other federal officer, resident and acting solely within the limits of any State, may be impeached by a vote of two-thirds of both branches of the Legislature thereof.

Section 6

2.   No Senator or Representative shall, during the time for which he was elected, be appointed to any civil office under the authority of the Confederate States, which shall have been created, or the emoluments whereof shall have been increased during such time; and no person holding any office under the Confederate States shall be a member of either House during his continuance in office. But Congress may, by law, grant to the principal officers in each of the Executive Departments a seat upon the floor of either House, with the privilege of discussing any measures appertaining to his department.

Section 7

2.   . . . The President may approve any appropriation and disapprove any other appropriation in the same bill. In such case he shall, in signing the bill, designate the appropriations disapproved; and shall return a copy of such appropriations, with his objections, to the House in which the bill shall have originated; and the same proceedings shall then be had as in case of other bills disapproved by the President.

Section 8

The Congress shall have power—

1.   To lay and collect taxes, duties, imposts and excises, for revenue necessary to pay the debts, provide for the common defence, and carry on the Government of the Confederate States; but no bounties shall be granted from the treasury; nor shall any duties or taxes on importations from foreign nations be laid to promote or foster any branch of industry; and all duties, imposts and excises shall be uniform throughout the Confederate States:

2.   To borrow money on the credit of the Confederate States.

3.   To regulate commerce with foreign nations, and among the several States, and with the Indian tribes; but neither this, nor any other clause contained in the constitution, shall ever be construed to delegate the power to Congress to appropriate money for any internal improvement intended to facilitate commerce; except for the purpose of furnishing lights, beacons and buoys, and other aids to navigation upon the coasts, and the improvement of harbors, and the removing of obstructions in river navigation, in all which cases, such duties shall be laid on the navigation facilitated thereby, as may be necessary to pay the costs and expenses thereof.

Section 9

1.   The importation of negroes of the African race, from any foreign country, other than the slaveholding States or Territories of the United States of America, is hereby forbidden; and Congress is required to pass such laws as shall effectually prevent the same.

2.   Congress shall also have power to prohibit the introduction of slaves from any State not a member of, or Territory not belonging to, this Confederacy.

3.   The privilege of the writ of habeas corpus shall not be suspended, unless when in cases of rebellion or invasion, the public safety may require it.

4.   No bill of attainder, *ex post facto* law, or law denying or impairing the right of property in negro slaves, shall be passed.

12.   Congress shall make no law respecting an establishment of religion, or prohibiting the free exercise thereof, or abridging the freedom of speech, or of the press; or the right of the people peaceably to assemble and petition the government for a redress of grievances.

13.   A well regulated militia being necessary to the security of a free State, the right of the people to keep and bear arms shall not be infringed.

14.   No soldier shall, in time of peace, be quartered in any house without the consent of the owner; nor in time of war, but in a manner to be prescribed by law.

15.   The right of the people to be secure in their persons, houses, papers and effects against unreasonable searches and seizures, shall not be violated; and no warrants shall issue but upon probable cause, supported by oath or affirmation, and particularly describing the place to be searched, and the persons or things to be seized.

16.   No person shall be held to answer for a capital or otherwise infamous crime, unless on a presentment or indictment of a grand jury, except in cases arising in the land or naval forces, or in the militia, when in actual service, in time of war or public danger; nor shall any person be subject for the same offence, to be twice put in jeopardy of life or limb; nor be compelled, in any criminal case, to be a witness against himself; nor be deprived of life, liberty, or property, without due process of law; nor shall private property be taken for public use, without just compensation.

17.   In all criminal prosecutions the accused shall enjoy the right to a speedy and public trial, by an impartial jury of the State and district wherein the crime shall have been committed, which district shall have been previously ascertained by law, and to be informed of the nature and cause of the accusation; to be confronted with the witnesses against him; to have compul-

sory process for obtaining witnesses in his favor; and to have the assistance of counsel for his defence.

18.   In suits at common law, where the value in controversy shall exceed twenty dollars, the right of trial by jury shall be preserved; and no fact so tried by a jury shall be otherwise re-examined in any court of the Confederacy, than according to the rules of the common law.

19.   Excessive bail shall not be required, nor excessive fines imposed, nor cruel and unusual punishments inflicted.

20.   Every law, or resolution having the force of law, shall relate to but one subject, and that shall be expressed in the title.

Article II

Section 1

1.   The executive power shall be vested in a President of the Confederate States of America. He and the Vice-President shall hold their offices for the term of six years: but the President shall not be re-eligible. . . .

Section 2

3.   The principal officer in each of the Executive Departments, and all persons connected with the diplomatic service, may be removed from office at the pleasure of the President. All other civil officers of the Executive Department may be removed at any time by the President, or other appointing power, when their services are unnecessary, or for dishonesty, incapacity, inefficiency, misconduct or neglect of duty; and when so removed, the removal shall be reported to the Senate, together with the reasons therefor.

Article IV

Section 2

3.   No slave or other person held to service or labor in any State or Territory of the Confederate States, under the laws thereof, escaping or lawfully carried into another, shall, in consequence of any law or regulation therein, be discharged from such service or labor; but shall be delivered up on claim of the party to whom such slave belongs, or to whom such service or labor may be due.

Section 3

1.   Other States may be admitted into this Confederacy by a vote of two-thirds of the whole House of Representatives, and two-thirds of the Senate,

the Senate voting by States; but no new State shall be formed or erected within the jurisdiction of any other State; nor any State be formed by the junction of two or more States, or parts of States, without the consent of the Legislatures of the States concerned as well as of the Congress.

3. The Confederate States may acquire new territory, and Congress shall have power to legislate and provide governments for the inhabitants of all territory belonging to the Confederate States, lying without the limits of the several States; and may permit them, at such times, and in such manner as it may by law provide, to form States to be admitted into the Confederacy. In all such territory, the institution of negro slavery as it now exists in the Confederate States, shall be recognized and protected by Congress, and by the territorial government; and the inhabitants of the several Confederate States and Territories, shall have the right to take to such territory any slaves, lawfully held by them in any of the States or Territories of the Confederate States.

4. The Confederate States shall guaranty to every State that now is or hereafter may become a member of this Confederacy, a republican form of government, and shall protect each of them against invasion; and on application of the Legislature (or of the Executive when the legislature is not in session) against domestic violence.

Article V

Section 1

1. Upon the demand of any three States, legally assembled in their several conventions, the Congress shall summon a convention of all the States, to take into consideration such amendments to the Constitution as the said States shall concur in suggesting at the time when the said demand is made; and should any of the proposed amendments to the Constitution be agreed on by the said convention—voting by States—and the same be ratified by the Legislatures of two-thirds of the several States, or by conventions in two-thirds thereof—as the one or the other mode of ratification may be proposed by the general convention—they shall thenceforward form a part of this Constitution. But no State shall, without its consent, be deprived of its equal representation in the Senate.

Article VI

1. The government established by this Constitution is successor of the Provisional Government of the Confederate States of America; and all the laws passed by the latter shall continue in force until the same shall be repealed or modified; and all the officers appointed by the same shall remain in office until their successors are appointed and qualified, or the offices abolished.

2.   All debts contracted and engagements entered into before the adoption of this Constitution shall be as valid against the Confederate States under this Constitution as under the Provisional Government.

3.   This Constitution, and the laws of the Confederate States, made in pursuance thereof, and all treaties made, or which shall be made, under the authority of the Confederate States, shall be the supreme law of the land; and the judges in every State shall be bound thereby, anything in the constitution or laws of any State to the contrary notwithstanding.

4.   The Senators and Representatives before mentioned, and the members of the several State Legislatures, and all executive and judicial officers, both of the Confederate States and of the several States, shall be bound by oath or affirmation, to support this Constitution; but no religious test shall ever be required as a qualification to any office or public trust under the Confederate States.

5.   The enumeration, in the Constitution, of certain rights shall not be construed to deny or disparage others retained by the people of the several States.

6.   The powers not delegated to the Confederate States by the Constitution, nor prohibited by it to the States, are reserved to the States, respectively, or the people thereof.

Article VII

1.   The ratification of the conventions of five States shall be sufficient for the establishment of this Constitution between the States so ratifying the same.

103

Ex Parte Merryman (1861)

Prosecession riots in Baltimore led to the arrest of John Merryman, a prominent socialite who was trying to train recruits for the Confederacy. No one was quite sure if treason applied to a civil war; if so, would

Source: 17 Fed. Cases 144 (C.C.D.Md. 1861).

all of the rebels have to be charged? If not, what crime did Confederate allies commit? Merryman, lodged in Fort McHenry, had access to his lawyer, who appealed to Chief Justice Taney as circuit judge for Maryland. Taney issued a writ of habeas corpus aware that it would not be obeyed, but he intended his circuit opinion to be an open challenge to the President, who, in his opinion, was conducting an illegal war. Although Taney's opinion received wide circulation in the South, his brethren on the Supreme Court refused to go along, in part because they understood the political realities of a nation at war, and also because Taney's assertions regarding the supposed widespread use of habeas corpus were historically inaccurate. In terms of national jurisdiction, the limited number of federal crimes occasioned few appeals for habeas; state habeas was the important writ, especially in criminal trials. Taney did, however, focus attention on whether Congress or the President had the power, granted in the Constitution, of suspending habeas during rebellions.

See R. M. Spector, "Lincoln and Taney: A Study in Constitutional Polarization," 15 *Am. J. Leg. His.* 199 (1971); C. B. Swisher, *The Taney Period, 1836–1864* (1974); and W. F. Duker, *A Constitutional History of Habeas Corpus* (1980).

~~~~~~

Chief Justice Taney on Circuit

The application in this case for a writ of habeas corpus is made to me under the 14th section of the judiciary act of 1789, which renders effectual for the citizen the constitutional privilege of the writ of habeas corpus. That act gives to the courts of the United States, as well as to each justice of the supreme court, and to every district judge, power to grant writs of habeas corpus for the purpose of an inquiry into the cause of commitment. The petition was presented to me, at Washington, under the impression that I would order the prisoner to be brought before me there, but as he was confined in Fort McHenry, in the city of Baltimore, which is in my circuit, I resolved to hear it in the latter city, as obedience to the writ, under such circumstances, would not withdraw General Cadwalader, who had him in charge, from the limits of his military command. . . .

The case, then, is simply this: a military officer, residing in Pennsylvania, issues an order to arrest a citizen of Maryland, upon vague and indefinite charges, without any proof, so far as appears; under this order, his house is entered in the night, he is seized as a prisoner, and conveyed to Fort McHenry, and there kept in close confinement; and when a habeas corpus is served on the commanding officer, requiring him to produce the prisoner before a justice of the supreme court, in order that he may examine into the legality of the imprisonment, the answer of the officer, is that he is authorized by the president to suspend the writ of habeas corpus at his discretion, and in the exercise of that discretion, suspends it in this case, and on that ground refuses obedience to the writ.

As the case comes before me, therefore, I understand that the president not only claims the right to suspend the writ of habeas corpus himself, at his discretion, but to delegate that discretionary power to a military officer, and to leave it to him to determine whether he will or will not obey judicial process that may be served upon him. No official notice has been given to the courts of justice, or to the public, by proclamation or otherwise, that the president claimed this power, and had exercised it in the manner stated in the return. And I certainly listened to it with some surprise, for I had supposed it to be one of those points of constitutional law upon which there was no difference of opinion, and that it was admitted on all hands, that the privilege of the writ could not be suspended, except by act of congress. . . .

The clause of the constitution, which authorizes the suspension of the privilege of the writ of habeas corpus, is in the 9th section of the first article. This article is devoted to the legislative department of the United States, and has not the slightest reference to the executive department. It begins by providing "that all legislative powers therein granted, shall be vested in a congress of the United States, which shall consist of a senate and house of representatives." And after prescribing the manner in which these two branches of the legislative department shall be chosen, it proceeds to enumerate specifically the legislative powers which it thereby grants [and legislative powers which it expressly prohibits); and at the conclusion of this specification, a clause is inserted giving congress "the power to make all laws which shall be necessary and proper for carrying into execution the foregoing powers, and all other powers vested by this constitution in the government of the United States, or in any department or officer thereof."

The power of legislation granted by this latter clause is, by its words, carefully confined to the specific objects before enumerated. But as this limitation was unavoidably somewhat indefinite, it was deemed necessary to guard more effectually certain great cardinal principles, essential to the liberty of the citizen, and to the rights and equality of the states, by denying to congress, in express terms, any power of legislation over them. It was apprehended, it seems, that such legislation might be attempted, under the pretext that it was necessary and proper to carry into execution the powers granted; and it was determined, that there should be no room to doubt, where rights of such vital importance were concerned; and accordingly, this clause is immediately followed by an enumeration of certain subjects, to which the powers of legislation shall not extend. The great importance which the framers of the constitution attached to the privilege of the writ of habeas corpus, to protect the liberty of the citizen, is proved by the fact, that its suspension, except in cases of invasion or rebellion, is first in the list of prohibited powers; and even in these cases the power is denied, and its exercise prohibited, unless the public safety shall require it.

It is true, that in the cases mentioned, congress is, of necessity, the judge of whether the public safety does or does not require it; and their judgment is conclusive. But the introduction of these words is a standing admonition to the legislative body of the danger of suspending it, and of the extreme caution they should exercise, before they give the government of the United States such power over the liberty of a citizen.

It is the second article of the constitution that provides for the organization of the executive department, enumerates the powers conferred on it, and prescribes its duties. And if the high power over the liberty of the citizen now claimed, was intended to be conferred on the president, it would undoubtedly be found in plain words in this article; but there is not a word in it that can furnish the slightest ground to justify the exercise of the power. . . .

So too, his powers in relation to the civil duties and authority necessarily conferred on him are carefully restricted, as well as those belonging to his military character. He cannot appoint the ordinary officers of government, nor make a treaty with a foreign nation or Indian tribe, without the advice and consent of the senate, and cannot appoint even inferior officers, unless he is authorized by an act of congress to do so. He is not empowered to arrest any one charged with an offence against the United States, and whom he may, from the evidence before him, believe to be guilty; nor can he authorize any officer, civil or military, to exercise this power, for the fifth article of the amendments to the constitution expressly provides that no person "shall be deprived of life, liberty or property, without due process of law"—that is, judicial process.

Even if the privilege of the writ of habeas corpus were suspended by act of congress, and a party not subject to the rules and articles of war were afterwards arrested and imprisoned by regular judicial process, he could not be detained in prison, or brought to trial before a military tribunal, for the article in the amendments to the constitution immediately following the one above referred to (that is, the sixth article) provides, that "in all criminal prosecutions, the accused shall enjoy the right to a speedy and public trial by an impartial jury of the state and district wherein the crime shall have been committed, which district shall have been previously ascertained by law; and to be informed of the nature and cause of the accusation; to be confronted with the witnesses against him; to have compulsory process for obtaining witnesses in his favor; and to have the assistance of counsel for his defence."

The only power, therefore, which the president possesses, where the "life, liberty or property" of a private citizen is concerned, is the power and duty prescribed in the third section of the second article, which requires "that he shall take care that the laws shall be faithfully executed." He is not authorized to execute them himself, or through agents or officers, civil or military, appointed by himself, but he is to take care that they be faithfully carried into execution, as they are expounded and adjudged by the co-ordinate branch of the government to which that duty is assigned by the constitution. It is thus made his duty to come in aid of the judicial authority, if it shall be resisted by a force too strong to be overcome without the assistance of the executive arm; but in exercising this power he acts in subordination to judicial authority, assisting it to execute its process and enforce its judgments.

With such provisions in the constitution, expressed in language too clear to be misunderstood by any one, I can see no ground whatever for supposing that the president, in any emergency, or in any state of things, can authorize the suspension of the privileges of the writ of habeas corpus, or the arrest of a citizen, except in aid of the judicial power. He certainly does not faithfully execute the laws, if he takes upon himself legislative power, by suspending the writ of habeas corpus, and the judicial power also, by arresting and imprisoning a person without due process of law.

Nor can any argument be drawn from the nature of sovereignty, or the necessity of government, for self-defence in times of tumult and danger. The government of the United States is one of delegated and limited powers; it derives its existence and authority altogether from the constitution, and neither of its branches, executive, legislative or judicial, can exercise any of the powers of government beyond those specified and granted; for the tenth article of the amendments to the constitution, in express terms, provides that "the powers not delegated to the United States by the constitution, nor prohibited by it to the states, are reserved to the states, respectively, or to the people."

Indeed, the security against imprisonment by executive authority, provided for in the fifth article of the amendments to the constitution, which I have before quoted, is nothing more than a copy of a like provision in the English constitution, which had been firmly established before the declaration of independence. Blackstone states it in the following words: "To make imprisonment lawful, it must be either by process of law from the courts of judicature, or by warrant from some legal officer having authority to commit to prison." 1 Bl. Comm. 137.

The people of the United Colonies, who had themselves lived under its protection, while they were British subjects, were well aware of the necessity of this safeguard for their personal liberty. And no one can believe that, in framing a government intended to guard still more efficiently the rights and liberties of the citizen, against executive encroachment and oppression, they would have conferred on the president a power which the history of England had proved to be dangerous and oppressive in the hands of the crown; and which the people of England had compelled it to surrender, after a long and obstinate struggle on the part of the English executive to usurp and retain it. . . .

But the documents before me show, that the military authority in this case has gone far beyond the mere suspension of the privilege of the writ of habeas corpus. It has, by force of arms, thrust aside the judicial authorities and officers to whom the constitution has confided the power and duty of interpreting and administering the laws, and substituted a military government in its place, to be administered and executed by military officers. For, at the time these proceedings were had against John Merryman, the district judge of Maryland, the commissioner appointed under the act of congress, the district attorney and the marshal, all resided in the city of Baltimore, a few miles only from the home of the prisoner. Up to that time, there had never been the slightest resistance or obstruction to the process of any court or judicial officer of the United States, in Maryland, except by the military authority. And if a military officer, or any other person, had reason to believe that the prisoner had committed any offence against the laws of the United States, it was his duty to give information of the fact and the evidence to support it, to the district attorney; it would then have become the duty of that officer to bring the matter before the district judge or commissioner, and if there was sufficient legal evidence to justify his arrest, the judge or commissioner would have issued his warrant to the marshal to arrest him; and upon the hearing of the case, would have held him to bail, or committed him for trial, according to the character of the offence, as it appeared in the testimony, or would have discharged him immediately, if there was not sufficient evidence to support the accusation. There was no danger of any obstruction or resistance to the action of the civil authorities, and therefore no reason whatever for the interposition of the military.

Yet, under these circumstances, a military officer, stationed in Pennsylvania, without giving any information to the district attorney, and without any application to the judicial authorities, assumes to himself the judicial power in the district of Maryland; undertakes to decide what constitutes the crime of treason or rebellion; what evidence (if indeed he required any) is sufficient to support the accusation and justify the commitment; and commits the party, without a hearing, even before himself, to close custody, in a strongly garrisoned fort, to be there held, it would seem, during the pleasure of those who committed him.

The constitution provides, as I have before said, that "no person shall be deprived of life, liberty or property, without due process of law." It declares that "the right of the people to be secure in their persons, houses, papers and effects, against unreasonable searches and seizures, shall not be violated; and no warrant shall issue, but upon probable cause, supported by oath or affirmation, and particularly describing, the place to be searched, and the persons or things to be seized." It provides that the party accused shall be entitled to a speedy trial in a court of justice.

These great and fundamental laws, which congress itself could not suspend, have been disregarded and suspended, like the writ of habeas corpus, by a military order, supported by force of arms. Such is the case now before me, and I can only say that if the authority which the constitution has confided to the judiciary department and judicial officers, may thus, upon any pretext or under any circumstances, be usurped by the military power, at its discretion, the people of the United States are no longer living under a government of laws, but every citizen holds life, liberty and property at the will and pleasure of the army officer in whose military district he may happen to be found.

In such a case, my duty was too plain to be mistaken. I have exercised all the power which the constitution and laws confer upon me, but that power has been resisted by a force too strong for me to overcome. It is possible that the officer who has incurred this grave responsibility may have misunderstood his instructions, and exceeded the authority intended to be given him; I shall, therefore, order all the proceedings in this case, with my opinion, to be filed and recorded in the circuit court of the United States for the district of Maryland, and direct the clerk to transmit a copy, under seal, to the president of the United States. It will then remain for that high officer, in fulfilment of his constitutional obligation to "take care that the laws be faithfully executed," to determine what measures he will take to cause the civil process of the United States to be respected and enforced.

104

The Emancipation Proclamation (1863)

Lincoln and the North entered the war to preserve the Union rather than to free the slaves, but within a relatively short time emancipation became an accepted war aim. Neither Congress nor the President knew exactly what constitutional powers they had in this area. Congress passed a few desultory confiscation laws that had a limited impact. Then in the fall of 1862 Lincoln issued his preliminary proclamation, warning that on January 1, 1863, he would free all the slaves in those states still in rebellion. Intended as a war and propaganda measure, the Emancipation Proclamation had far more symbolic than real impact, because the federal government had no means to enforce it at that time. Moreover, aside from a sweeping interpretation of the powers of the Commander-in-Chief, there is no textual basis for such an expression of presidential power. But Lincoln believed strongly in what has been called the "adequacy-of-the-Constitution" theory (see Documents 106,

Source: Nicolay and Hay, 9 *Complete Works of Abraham Lincoln* 161 (1905).

108), and the Proclamation did at least give some basis for determining the freedmen's status until the adoption of the Thirteenth Amendment.

See J. G. Randall, *Constitutional Problems under Lincoln* (rev. ed., 1951); J. H. Franklin, *The Emancipation Proclamation* (1963); H. Belz, *Emancipation and Equal Rights: Politics and Constitutionalism in the Civil War Era* (1978); and L. Cox, *Lincoln and Black Freedom: A Study in Presidential Leadership* (1981).

~~~~~~

Whereas, on the twenty-second day of September, in the year of our Lord one thousand eight hundred and sixty-two, a proclamation was issued by the President of the United States, containing, among other things, the following, to wit:

"That on the first day of January, in the year of our Lord one thousand eight hundred and sixty-three, all persons held as slaves within any State, or designated part of a State, the people whereof shall then be in rebellion against the United States, shall be then, thenceforward, and forever free; and the Executive Government of the United States, including the military and naval authority thereof, will recognize and maintain the freedom of such persons, and will do no act or acts to repress such persons, or any of them, in any efforts they may make for their actual freedom.

"That the Executive will, on the first day of January aforesaid, by proclamation, designate the States and parts of States, if any, in which the people thereof respectively shall then be in rebellion against the United States; and the fact that any State, or the people thereof, shall on that day be in good faith represented in the Congress of the United States by members chosen thereto at elections wherein a majority of the qualified voters of such State shall have participated, shall in the absence of strong countervailing testimony be deemed conclusive evidence that such State and the people thereof are not then in rebellion against the United States."

Now, therefore, I, Abraham Lincoln, President of the United States, by virtue of the power in me vested as commander-in-chief of the army and navy of the United States, in time of actual armed rebellion against the authority and government of the United States, and as a fit and necessary war measure for suppressing said rebellion, do, on this first day of January, in the year of our Lord one thousand eight hundred and sixty-three, and in accordance with my purpose so to do, publicly proclaimed for the full period of 100 days from the day first above mentioned, order and designate as the States and parts of States wherein the people thereof, respectively, are this day in rebellion against the United States, the following, to wit:

Arkansas, Texas, Louisiana (except the parishes of St. Bernard, Plaquemines, Jefferson, St. John, St. Charles, St. James, Ascension, Assumption, Terre Bonne, Lafourche, St. Mary, St. Martin, and Orleans, including the city of New Orleans), Mississippi, Alabama, Florida, Georgia, South Carolina,

North Carolina, and Virginia (except the forty-eight counties designated as West Virginia, and also the counties of Berkeley, Accomac, Northampton, Elizabeth City, York, Princess Anne, and Norfolk, including the cities of Norfolk and Portsmouth), and which excepted parts are for the present left precisely as if this proclamation were not issued.

And by virtue of the power and for the purpose aforesaid, I do order and declare that all persons held as slaves within said designated States and parts of States are, and henceforward shall be, free; and that the Executive Government of the United States, including the military and naval authorities thereof, will recognize and maintain the freedom of said persons.

And I hereby enjoin upon the people so declared to be free to abstain from all violence, unless in necessary self-defense; and I recommend to them that, in all cases where allowed, they labor faithfully for reasonable wages.

And I further declare and make known that such persons of suitable condition will be received into the armed service of the United States to garrison forts, positions, stations, and other places, and to man vessels of all sorts in said service.

And upon this act, sincerely believed to be an act of justice, warranted by the Constitution upon military necessity, I invoke the considerate judgment of mankind and the gracious favor of Almighty God.

In witness whereof, I have hereunto set my hand and caused the seal of the United States to be affixed.

Done at the city of Washington, this first day of January, in the year of our Lord one thousand eight hundred and sixty-three, and of the independence of the United States of America the eighty-seventh.

ABRAHAM LINCOLN.

105

Prize Cases (1863)

Approximately a dozen suits deriving from Lincoln's orders blockading Southern ports were grouped together, and they raised two major questions—whether the United States was engaged in a formal war in which

---

Source: 2 Black 635 (1863).

a blockade was a permissible tool, and if so, whether the blockade had been imposed in a constitutionally correct manner. If the Court ruled that the hostilities constituted war rather than insurrection, then a blockade was appropriate, but the Confederacy was sovereign; if it ruled that an insurrection existed, then the Union had no right to blockade part of its own country. Opponents of the blockade also argued that only Congress, and not the President, had war powers, and therefore only Congress could impose a blockade.

By a bare five-to-four vote, the Court sustained the Lincoln administration and essentially said that with a great war going on, the courts would defer to the political branches to determine how best to preserve the Union. The minority, all Democrats, said that the war against the South was neither legal nor constitutional, and that the President had no independent war powers. The careful ruling by the majority pleased few people. It did not give the administration the full endorsement it had sought, but neither did it pose the confrontation Taney had sought in *Merryman* (Document 103). The definition also did not threaten Lincoln's careful effort to avoid having the conflict declared a war between two sovereign nations.

See C. B. Swisher, *The Taney Period, 1836–1864* (1974); and S. L. Bernath, *Squall Across the Atlantic: American Civil War Prize Cases and Diplomacy* (1970).

Justice Grier delivered the opinion of the Court.

There are certain propositions of law which must necessarily affect the ultimate decision of these cases, and many others, which it will be proper to discuss and decide before we notice the special facts peculiar to each.

They are, 1st. Had the President a right to institute a blockade of ports in possession of persons in armed rebellion against the Government, on the principles of international law, as known and acknowledged among civilized States?

2d. Was the property of persons domiciled or residing within those States a proper subject of capture on the sea as "enemies' property?"

I. Neutrals have a right to challenge the existence of a blockade *de facto,* and also the authority of the party exercising the right to institute it. They have a right to enter the ports of a friendly nation for the purposes of trade and commerce, but are bound to recognize the rights of a belligerent engaged in actual war, to use this mode of coercion, for the purpose of subduing the enemy.

That a blockade *de facto* actually existed, and was formally declared and notified by the President on the 27th and 30th of April, 1861, is an admitted fact in these cases.

That the President, as the Executive Chief of the Government and Commander-in-chief of the Army and Navy, was the proper person to make such notification, has not been, and cannot be disputed.

The right of prize and capture has its origin in the *"jus belli,"* and is governed and adjudged under the law of nations. To legitimate the capture of a neutral vessel or property on the high seas, a war must exist *de facto,* and the neutral must have a knowledge or notice of the intention of one of the parties belligerent to use this mode of coercion against a port, city, or territory, in possession of the other.

Let us enquire whether, at the time this blockade was instituted, a state of war existed which would justify a resort to these means of subduing the hostile force.

War has been well defined to be, "That state in which a nation prosecutes its right by force."

The parties belligerent in a public war are independent nations. But it is not necessary to constitute war, that both parties should be acknowledged as independent nations or sovereign States. A war may exist where one of the belligerents claims sovereign rights as against the other.

Insurrection against a government may or may not culminate in an organized rebellion, but a civil war always begins by insurrection against the lawful authority of the Government. A civil war is never solemnly declared; it becomes such by its accidents—the number, power, and organization of the persons who originate and carry it on. When the party in rebellion occupy and hold in a hostile manner a certain portion of territory; have declared their independence; have cast off their allegiance; have organized armies; have commenced hostilities against their former sovereign, the world acknowledges them as belligerents, and the contest a *war. They* claim to be in arms to establish their liberty and independence, in order to become a sovereign State, while the sovereign party treats them as insurgents and rebels who owe allegiance, and who should be punished with death for their treason.

The laws of war, as established among nations, have their foundation in reason, and all tend to mitigate the cruelties and misery produced by the scourge of war. Hence the parties to a civil war usually concede to each other belligerent rights. They exchange prisoners, and adopt the other courtesies and rules common to public or national wars. . . .

As a civil war is never publicly proclaimed, *eo nomine* against insurgents, its actual existence is a fact in our domestic history which the Court is bound to notice and to know. . . .

By the Constitution, Congress alone has the power to declare a national or foreign war. It cannot declare war against a State, or any number of States, by virtue of any clause in the Constitution. The Constitution confers on the President the whole Executive power. He is bound to take care that the laws be faithfully executed. He is Commander-in-chief of the Army and Navy of the United States, and of the militia of the several States when called into the actual service of the United States. He has no power to initiate or declare a war either against a foreign nation or a domestic State. But by the Acts of Congress of February 28th, 1795, and 3d of March, 1807, he is authorized to call out the militia and use the military and naval forces of the United States in case of invasion by foreign nations, and to suppress insurrection against the government of a State or of the United States. . . .

This greatest of civil wars was not gradually developed by popular commotion, tumultuous assemblies, or local unorganized insurrections. However long may have been its previous conception, it nevertheless sprung forth suddenly from the parent brain, a Minerva in the full panoply of *war.* The President was bound to meet it in the shape it presented itself, without waiting for Congress to baptize it with a name; and no name given to it by him or them could change the fact.

It is not the less a civil war, with belligerent parties in hostile array, because it may be called an "insurrection" by one side, and the insurgents be considered as rebels or traitors. It is not necessary that the independence of the revolted province or State be acknowledged in order to constitute it a party belligerent in a war according to the law of nations. Foreign nations acknowledge it as war by a declaration of neutrality. The condition of neutrality cannot exist unless there be two belligerent parties. . . .

As soon as the news of the attack on Fort Sumter, and the organization of a government by the seceding States, assuming to act as belligerents, could become known in Europe, to wit, on the 13th of May, 1861, the Queen of England issued her proclamation of neutrality, "recognizing hostilities as existing between the Government of the United States of America and *certain States* styling themselves the Confederate States of America." This was immediately followed by similar declarations or silent acquiescence by other nations.

After such an official recognition by the sovereign, a citizen of a foreign State is estopped to deny the existence of a war with all its consequences as regards neutrals. They cannot ask a Court to affect a technical ignorance of the existence of a war, which all the world acknowledges to be the greatest civil war known in the history of the human race, and thus cripple the arm of the Government and paralyze its power by subtle definitions and ingenious sophisms.

The law of nations is also called the law of nature; it is founded on the common consent as well as the common sense of the world. It contains no such anomalous doctrine as that which this Court are now for the first time desired to pronounce, to wit: That insurgents who have risen in rebellion against their sovereign, expelled her Courts, established a revolutionary government, organized armies, and commenced hostilities, are not *enemies* because they are *traitors;* and a war levied on the Government by traitors, in order to dismember and destroy it, is not a *war* because it is an "insurrection."

Whether the President in fulfilling his duties, as Commander in-chief, in suppressing an insurrection, has met with such armed hostile resistance, and a civil war of such alarming proportions as will compel him to accord to them the character of belligerents, is a question to be decided *by him,* and this Court must be governed by the decisions and acts of the political department of the Government to which this power was entrusted. "He must determine what degree of force the crisis demands." The proclamation of blockade is itself official and conclusive evidence to the Court that a state of war existed which demanded and authorized a recourse to such a measure, under the circumstances peculiar to the case. . . .

If it were necessary to the technical existence of a war, that it should have a legislative sanction, we find it in almost every act passed at the extraordinary session of the Legislature of 1861, which was wholly employed in enacting laws to enable the Government to prosecute the war with vigor and efficiency. And finally, in 1861, we find Congress *"ex majore cautela"* and in anticipation of such astute objections, passing an act "approving, legalizing, and making valid all the acts, proclamations, and orders of the President, &c., as if they had been *issued and done under the previous express authority* and direction of the Congress of the United States." . . .

On this first question therefore we are of the opinion that the President had a right, *jure belli,* to institute a blockade of ports in possession of the States in rebellion, which neutrals are bound to regard.

II.   We come now to the consideration of the second question. What is included in the term *"enemies' property?"*

Is the property of all persons residing within the territory of the States now in rebellion, captured on the high seas, to be treated as "enemies' property" whether the owner be in arms against the Government or not?

The right of one belligerent not only to coerce the other by direct force, but also to cripple his resources by the seizure or destruction of his property, is a necessary result of a state of war. Money and wealth, the products of agriculture and commerce, are said to be the sinews of war, and as necessary in its conduct as numbers and physical force. Hence it is, that the laws of war recognize the right of a belligerent to cut these sinews of the power of the enemy, by capturing his property on the high seas.

The appellants contend that the term "enemy" is properly applicable to those only who are subjects or citizens of a foreign State at war with our own. They quote from the pages of the common law, which say, "that persons who wage war against the King may be of two kinds, subjects or citizens. The former are not proper enemies, but rebels and traitors; the latter are those that come properly under the name of enemies." . . .

They contend, also, that insurrection is the act of individuals and not of a government or sovereignty; that the individuals engaged are subjects of law. That confiscation of their property can be effected only under a municipal law. That by the law of the land such confiscation cannot take place without the conviction of the owner of some offence, and finally that the secession ordinances are nullities and ineffectual to release any citizen from his allegiance to the national Government, and consequently that the Constitution and Laws of the United States are still operative over persons in all the States for punishment as well as protection.

This argument rests on the assumption of two propositions each of which is without foundation on the established law of nations. It assumes that where a civil war exists, the party belligerent claiming to be sovereign, cannot, for some unknown reason, exercise the rights of belligerents, although the revolutionary party may. Being sovereign, he can exercise only sovereign rights over the other party. The insurgent may be killed on the battle-field or by the executioner; his property on land may be confiscated under the municipal law; but the commerce on the ocean, which supplies the rebels with means to support the war, cannot be made the subject of capture under the laws of war, because it is *"unconstitutional!!!"* Now, it is a proposition never doubted, that the belligerent party who claims to be sovereign, may exercise both belligerent and sovereign rights. . . . Treating the other party as a belligerent and using only the milder modes of coercion which the law of nations has introduced to mitigate the rigors of war, cannot be a subject of complaint by the party to whom it is accorded as a grace or granted as a necessity. We have shown that a civil war such as that now waged between the Northern and Southern States is properly conducted according to the humane regulations of public law as regards capture on the ocean.

Under the very peculiar Constitution of this Government, although the citizens owe supreme allegiance to the Federal Government, they owe also a qualified allegiance to the State in which they are domiciled. Their persons and property are subject to its laws. . . .

. . . Several of these States have combined to form a new confederacy, claiming to be acknowledged by the world as a sovereign State. Their right to do so is now being decided by wager of battle. The ports and territory of each of these States are held in hostility to the General Government. It is no loose, unorganized insurrection, having no defined boundary or possession. It has a boundary marked by lines of bayonets, and which can be crossed only by force—south of this line is enemies' territory, because it is claimed and held in possession by an organized, hostile and belligerent power.

All persons residing within this territory whose property may be used to increase the revenues of the hostile power are, in this contest, liable to be treated as enemies, though not foreigners. They have cast off their allegiance and made war on their Government, and are none the less enemies because they are traitors.

But in defining the meaning of the term "enemies' property," we will be led into error if we refer to Fleta and Lord Coke for their definition of the word "enemy." It is a technical phrase peculiar to prize courts, and depends upon principles of public policy as distinguished from the common law.

Whether property be liable to capture as "enemies' property" does not in any manner depend on the personal allegiance of the owner. "It is the il-legal traffic that stamps it as 'enemies' property.' It is of no consequence whether it belongs to an ally or a citizen. . . . The owner, *pro hac vice,* is an enemy." . . .

The produce of the soil of the hostile territory, as well as other property engaged in the commerce of the hostile power, as the source of its wealth and strength, are always regarded as legitimate prize, without regard to the domicil of the owner, and much more so if he reside and trade within their territory.

[Having determined these general principles, the Court then disposed of the particular cases according to the circumstances surrounding each ship.]

106

Adequacy of the Constitution (1863)

WILLIAM WHITING

Before the Civil War, Southerners had argued vociferously that the national government had narrowly defined and strictly limited powers, and even John Marshall had accepted the notion of a government of limited powers, although his parameters stretched further than those of John Taylor of Caroline (Document 84). Few people, even in the North, accepted the radical Hamiltonian view that the national government had all powers except those specifically denied to it. The Framers, however, had not contemplated a civil war, and many people worried that a government of limited powers would not be able to fight such a war and survive. Either the Constitution would have to be scrapped, or the government would fail. William Whiting, Timothy Farrar, and

Source: W. Whiting, *War Powers under the Constitution of the United States* . . . (43d ed., 1871).

others who developed the "adequacy-of-the-Constitution" theory argued that common sense dictated that the Constitution contained all powers necessary for its preservation. Lincoln accepted and used this theory, as would Woodrow Wilson and Franklin D. Roosevelt in the twentieth century. Whiting, a constitutional scholar, joined the War Department and wrote what essentially became a constitutional manual for officers explaining the army's powers in war and in reconstruction.

See H. Hyman, *A More Perfect Union . . .* (1973); A. Bestor, "The American Civil War Considered as a Constitutional Crisis," 69 *Am. His. R.* 327 (1964); and J. G. Randall, *Constitutional Problems Under Lincoln* (rev. ed. 1951).

Powers we should expect to find

If the ground-plan of our government was intended to be more than a temporary expedient,—if it was designed, according to the declaration of its authors, for a *perpetual* Union,—then it will doubtless be found, upon fair examination, to contain whatever is essential to carry that design into effect. Accordingly, in addition to provisions for adapting it to great changes in the situation and circumstances of the people by *amendments,* we find that powers essential to its own perpetuity are vested in the executive and legislative departments, to be exercised *according to their discretion,* for the good of the country—powers which, however dangerous, must be intrusted to every government, to enable it to maintain its own existence, and to protect the rights of the people. Those who founded a government for themselves intended that it should never be overthrown; nor even altered, except by those under whose authority it was established. Therefore they gave to the President, and to Congress, the means essential to the preservation of the republic, but none for its dissolution.

Laws for peace, and laws for war

Times of peace have required the passage of numerous statutes for the protection and development of agricultural, manufacturing, and commercial industry, and for the suppression and punishment of ordinary crimes and offences. A state of general civil war in the United States is, happily, new and unfamiliar. These times have demanded new and unusual legislation to call into action those powers which the constitution provides for times of war.

Leaving behind us the body of laws regulating the rights, liabilities, and duties of citizens, in time of public tranquillity, we must now turn our attention to the RESERVED and HITHERTO UNUSED powers contained in the constitution, which enable Congress to pass a body of laws to regulate the rights, liabilities, and duties of citizens in time of war. We must enter and explore the arsenal and armory, with all their engines of defence, enclosed, by our wise forefathers for the safety of the republic, within the old castle walls of that constitution; for now the garrison is summoned to surrender; and if there be any cannon, it is time to unlimber and run them out the port-holes, to fetch up the hot shot, to light the match, and "hang out our banners on the *outer* walls."

The Union is gone forever if the Constitution denies the power to save it.

The question whether republican constitutional government shall now cease in America, must depend upon the construction given to these *hitherto unused powers.* Those who desire to see an end of this government will deny that it has the ability to save itself. Many new inquiries have arisen in relation to the existence and limitation of its powers. Must the successful prosecution of war against rebels, the preservation of national honor, and securing of permanent peace,—if attainable only by rooting out the evil which caused and maintains the rebellion,—be effected by destroying rights solemnly guaranteed by the constitution we are defending? If so, the next question will be, whether the law of self-defence and overwhelming necessity will not justify the country in denying to rebels and traitors in arms whatever rights they or their friends may claim under a charter which they have repudiated, and have armed themselves to overthrow and destroy? Can one party break the contract, and justly hold the other party bound by it? Is the constitution to be so interpreted that rebels and traitors cannot be put down? Are we so hampered, as some have asserted, that even if war end in reëstablishing the Union, and enforcing the laws over all the land, the results of victory can be turned against us, and the conquered enemy may then treat us as though they had been victors? Will vanquished criminals be able to resume their rights to the same political superiority over the citizens of free States, which, as the only privileged class, they have hitherto enjoyed? Have they who are now engaged in this rebellion, and have committed treason and other high crimes against the republic, a protection against punishment for these offences, by reason of any rights, privileges, or immunities guaranteed to peaceful citizens by the constitution? Cannot government, the people's agent, wage genuine and effectual war against the people's enemy? Must the soldier of the Union, when in action, keep one eye upon his rifle, and the other upon the constitutional rights of rebels? Is the power to make war, when once lawfully brought into action, to be controlled, baffled, and emasculated by any obligation to guard or respect rights set up by or for belligerent traitors? . . .

Civil rights of loyal citizens in loyal districts are modified by the existence of war.

While war is raging, many of the rights held sacred by the constitution—rights which cannot be violated by any acts of Congress—may and must be suspended and held in abeyance. If this were not so, the government might itself be destroyed; the army and navy might be sacrificed, and one part of the constitution would NULLIFY the rest.

If *freedom of speech* cannot be suppressed, spies cannot be caught, imprisoned, and hung.

If *freedom of the press* cannot be interfered with, all our military plans may be betrayed to the enemy.

If no man can be *deprived of life without trial by jury,* a soldier cannot slay the enemy in battle.

If *enemy's property* cannot be taken without "due process of law," how can the soldier disarm his foe and seize his weapons?

If no person can be arrested, sentenced, and shot, without *trial by jury* in the county or State where his crime is alleged to have been committed, how can a *deserter be shot,* or a *spy be hung,* or an *enemy be taken prisoner?*

It has been said that *"amidst arms* the *laws are silent."* It would be more just to say, that while war rages, the *rights,* which in peace are sacred, must and do give way to the higher right, the right of public safety, the right which the country, the whole country, claims to protection from its enemies, domestic and foreign, from spies, from conspirators, and from traitors. The sovereign and almost dictatorial military powers, existing only in actual war, ending when war ends, to be used in self-defence, and to be laid down when no longer necessary, are, while they last, as lawful, as constitutional, as sacred, as the administration of justice by judicial courts in time of peace. They may be dangerous; war itself is dangerous; but danger does not make them *unconstitutional.* If the commander-in-chief orders his soldiers to seize the arms and ammunition of the rebels; to capture their persons; to shell out their batteries; to hang spies or shoot deserters; to destroy insurgents waging open battle; to send traitors to forts and prisons; to stop the press from aiding and comforting the enemy by betraying our military plans; to arrest within our lines, or wherever they can be seized, persons against whom there is reasonable evidence of their having aided or abetted the rebels, or of intending so to do, the pretension that he thereby violates the constitution is not only erroneous, but it is a plea in behalf of treason. To set up the rules of civil administration as overriding and controlling the laws of war, is to aid and abet the enemy. It falsifies the clear meaning of the constitution, which not only gives the power, but makes it the plain duty of the President, to wage war, when lawfully declared or recognized, against the public enemy of his country. The restraints to which he is subject, when in war, are not found in municipal regulations, which can be administered only in peace, but in the laws and usages of nations regulating the conduct of war.

107

~~~~~~

Early Plans for Reconstruction (1863–1864)

Plans for reconstructing the sundered Union began to be discussed relatively early in the war. Northern leaders understood that political conditions would not automatically return to normal once the fighting stopped, and beyond that, provisions had to be made for the freed slaves and to ensure that the conditions that had led to war would not be recreated.

Like the Emancipation Proclamation (Document 104), Lincoln's Ten Percent Reconstruction program should be seen as a war measure. In December of 1863 Union victory was still far from certain, and Lincoln essentially told the rebellious states that if they stopped fighting they could get fairly easy terms for re-entry into the Union. If they continued to fight, the future might hold far harsher terms. Lincoln had little constitutional authority to initiate reconstruction, despite the reference to the pardon power, and he realized it. Note the several caveats at the end, especially the caution that Congress might not choose to seat representatives from these governments. But in the absence of direct constitutional or congressional guidelines, Lincoln believed that as Commander-in-Chief he could at least initiate the process. The so-called Ten Percent Plan had a number of defects, not the least of which was its return of power to the old prewar white elites and its failure to make any provision for the freedmen. In the three states where it applied, it failed to gain popular support. Lincoln saw it as an experiment, an attempt to start the process of reconciliation, rather than as a final and fixed procedure.

The plan did not work, and the following year Congress passed the Wade-Davis bill, embodying its own proposals. The bill enlarged civilian control over military components of the state reconstruction governments and called for the President to name, with Senate confirmation, a provisional governor for each conquered state, who would be responsible for civil administration until Congress recognized the reconstituted state government. The bill went on to spell out the type of republican government Congress hoped for, and by doing so, rested its claim for constitutionality on the Guarantee Clause (Article IV, Section 4).

Differences between Lincoln's plan and Wade-Davis were substantial but not irreconcilable. Lincoln's major objection was that it prematurely foreclosed options. The nation was still at war, and the bill dealt with reconstruction before all military objectives had been achieved; whatever else may be said about Lincoln, he was a president who kept all options open as long as possible. He was also a superb politician, and he recognized that something would have to be done to ease growing friction between the Executive and Congress. Instead of directly vetoing the bill, which had come to him at the very end of the congressional session, he let it die by pocket veto, and then later explained that he was unprepared to become "inflexibly committed to any single plan of restoration," even his own. As a result, it seemed that states could choose to re-enter the Union either through the presidential or the congressional plans.

Lincoln's plan, as well as his explanation of why he had rejected the congressional proposal, failed to satisfy critics, who pointed out that the presidential proposals did not pay sufficient attention to protecting the rights of the freedmen. In a statement issued in response to the President, Benjamin Wade and Henry Davis pointed out the insecurity felt by Southern blacks. But just as Lincoln had carefully avoided making his differences with Congress irreconcilable, so the congressional leaders also stopped their criticism far short of an open break. It was an election year, and the Republican Party could not afford a schism. Moreover, they recognized Lincoln's educability; they had made their point, and they assumed that, as in the past, there would be a meeting someplace between the two positions.

See W. B. Hesseltine, *Lincoln's Plan of Reconstruction* (1960); P. McCrary, *Abraham Lincoln and Reconstruction* (1978); H. Belz, *Reconstructing the Union: Theory and Policy During the Civil War* (1969); and M. L. Benedict, *A Compromise of Principle: Congressional Republicans and Reconstruction* (1974).

Ten Percent Plan (1863)

ABRAHAM LINCOLN

Whereas, in and by the Constitution of the United States, it is provided that the President "shall have power to grant reprieves and pardons for offenses against the United States, except in cases of impeachment"; and

Whereas a rebellion now exists whereby the loyal State governments of several States have for a long time been subverted, and many persons have committed, and are now guilty of, treason against the United States; and

Whereas, with reference to said rebellion and treason, laws have been enacted by Congress, declaring forfeitures and confiscation of property and liberation of slaves, all upon terms and conditions therein stated, and also declaring that the President was thereby authorized at any time thereafter, by proclamation, to extend to persons who may have participated in the existing rebellion, in any State or part thereof, pardon and amnesty, with such exceptions and at such times and on such conditions as he may deem expedient for the public welfare; and

Whereas the congressional declaration for limited and conditional pardon accords with well-established judicial exposition of the pardoning power; and

Whereas, with reference to said rebellion, the President of the United States has issued several proclamations, with provisions in regard to the liberation of slaves; and

Whereas it is now desired by some persons heretofore engaged in said rebellion to resume their allegiance to the United States, and to reinaugurate loyal State governments within and for their respective States; therefore

I, Abraham Lincoln, President of the United States, do proclaim, declare, and make known to all persons who have, directly or by implication, participated in the existing rebellion, except as hereinafter excepted, that a full pardon is hereby granted to them and each of them, with restoration of all rights of property, except as to slaves, and in property cases where rights of third parties shall have intervened, and upon the condition that every such person shall take and subscribe an oath, and thenceforward keep and maintain said oath inviolate; and which oath shall be registered for permanent preservation, and shall be of the tenor and effect following, to-wit:

I, _____, do solemnly swear, in presence of almighty God, that I will henceforth faithfully support, protect, and defend the Constitution of the United States, and the union of the States thereunder; and that I will, in like manner, abide by and faithfully support all acts of Congress passed during the existing

---

Source: Nicolay and Hay, 9 *Complete Works of Abraham Lincoln* 218 (1905).

rebellion with reference to slaves, so long and so far as not repealed, modified, or held void by Congress, or by decision of the Supreme Court; and that I will, in like manner, abide by and faithfully support all proclamations of the President made during the existing rebellion having reference to slaves, so long and so far as not modified or declared void by decision of the Supreme Court. So help me God.

The persons exempted from the benefits of the foregoing provisions are all who are, or shall have been, civil or diplomatic officers or agents of the so-called Confederate Government; all who have left judicial stations under the United States to aid the rebellion; all who are or shall have been military or naval officers of said so-called Confederate Government above the rank of colonel in the army or of lieutenant in the navy; all who left seats in the United States Congress to aid the rebellion; all who resigned commissions in the army or navy of the United States and afterward aided the rebellion; and all who have engaged in any way in treating colored persons, or white persons in charge of such, otherwise than lawfully as prisoners of war, and which persons may have been found in the United States service as soldiers, seamen, or in any other capacity.

And I do further proclaim, declare, and make known that whenever, in any of the States of Arkansas, Texas, Louisiana, Mississippi, Tennessee, Alabama, Georgia, Florida, South Carolina, and North Carolina, a number of persons, not less than one tenth in number of the votes cast in such State at the presidential election of the year of our Lord one thousand eight hundred and sixty, each having taken the oath aforesaid and not having since violated it, and being a qualified voter by the election law of the State existing immediately before the so-called act of secession, and excluding all others, shall reëstablish a State government which shall be republican, and in no wise contravening said oath, such shall be recognized as the true government of the State, and the State shall receive thereunder the benefits of the constitutional provision which declares that "the United States shall guaranty to every State in this Union a republican form of government, and shall protect each of them against invasion; and, on application of the legislature, or the executive (when the legislature cannot be convened), against domestic violence."

And I do further proclaim, declare, and make known, that any provision which may be adopted by such State government in relation to the freed people of such State, which shall recognize and declare their permanent freedom, provide for their education, and which may yet be consistent as a temporary arrangement with their present condition as a laboring, landless, and homeless class, will not be objected to by the national executive.

And it is suggested as not improper that, in constructing a loyal State government in any State, the name of the State, the boundary, the subdivisions, the constitution, and the general code of laws, as before the rebellion, be maintained, subject only to the modifications made necessary by the conditions hereinbefore stated, and such others, if any, not contravening said conditions, and which may be deemed expedient by those framing the new State government.

To avoid misunderstanding, it may be proper to say that this proclamation, so far as it relates to State governments, has no reference to States wherein loyal State governments have all the while been maintained.

And, for the same reason, it may be proper to further say, that whether members sent to Congress from any State shall be admitted to seats, constitutionally rests exclusively with the respective houses, and not to any extent with the executive. And still further, that this proclamation is intended to present the people of the States wherein the national authority has been suspended, and loyal State governments have been subverted, a mode in and by which the national authority and loyal State governments may be reëstablished within said States, or in any of them; and while the mode presented is the best the executive can suggest, with his present impressions, it must not be understood that no other possible mode would be acceptable.

107b

Wade-Davis Bill (1864)

Be it enacted, That in the states declared in rebellion against the United States, the President shall, by and with the advice and consent of the Senate, appoint for each a provisional governor, . . . who shall be charged with the civil administration of such state until a state government therein shall be recognized as hereinafter provided.

SEC. 2.   That so soon as the military resistance to the United States shall have been suppressed in any such state, and the people thereof shall have sufficiently returned to their obedience to the constitution and the laws of the United States, the provisional governor shall direct the marshal of the United States, as speedily as may be, to name a sufficient number of deputies, and to enroll all white male citizens of the United States, resident in the state in their respective counties, and to request each one to take the oath to support

Source: Richardson, ed., 6 *Messages and Papers of the Presidents* 223 (1897).

the constitution of the United States, and in his enrollment to designate those who take and those who refuse to take that oath, which rolls shall be forthwith returned to the provisional governor; and if the persons taking that oath shall amount to a majority of the persons enrolled in the state, he shall, by proclamation, invite the loyal people of the state to elect delegates to a convention charged to declare the will of the people of the state relative to the reëstablishment of a state government subject to, and in conformity with, the constitution of the United States.

SEC. 3.   That the convention shall consist of as many members as both houses of the last constitutional state legislature, apportioned by the provisional governor among the counties, parishes, or districts of the state, in proportion to the white population, returned as electors, by the marshal, in compliance with the provisions of this act. The provisional governor shall, . . . provide an adequate force to keep the peace during the election.

SEC. 4.   That the delegates shall be elected by the loyal white male citizens of the United States of the age of twenty-one years, and resident at the time in the county, parish, or district in which they shall offer to vote, and enrolled as aforesaid, or absent in the military service of the United States, and who shall take and subscribe the oath of allegiance to the United States in the form contained in the act of July 2, 1862; and all such citizens of the United States who are in the military service of the United States shall vote at the headquarters of their respective commands, under such regulations as may be prescribed by the provisional governor for the taking and return of their votes; but no person who has held or exercised any office, civil or military, state or confederate, under the rebel usurpation, or who has voluntarily borne arms against the United States, shall vote, or be eligible to be elected as delegate, at such election.

SEC. 5.   That the said commissioners, . . . shall hold the election in conformity with this act and, . . . shall proceed in the manner used in the state prior to the rebellion. The oath of allegiance shall be taken and subscribed on the poll-book by every voter in the form above prescribed, but every person known by, or proved to, the commissioners to have held or exercised any office, civil or military, state or confederate, under the rebel usurpation, or to have voluntarily borne arms against the United States, shall be excluded, though he offer to take the oath; and in case any person who shall have borne arms against the United States shall offer to vote he shall be deemed to have borne arms voluntarily unless he shall prove the contrary by the testimony of a qualified voter. . . .

SEC. 6.   That the provisional governor shall, by proclamation, convene the delegates elected as aforesaid, at the capital of the state, on a day not more than three months after the election, giving at least thirty days' notice of such day. In case the said capital shall in his judgment be unfit, he shall in his proclamation appoint another place. He shall preside over the deliberations of the convention, and administer to each delegate, before taking his seat in the convention, the oath of allegiance to the United States in the form above prescribed.

SEC. 7.   That the convention shall declare, on behalf of the people of the state, their submission to the constitution and laws of the United States, and shall adopt the following provisions, hereby prescribed by the United States in the execution of the constitutional duty to guarantee a republican form of government to every state, and incorporate them in the constitution of the state, that is to say:

First. No person who has held or exercised any office, civil or military, except offices merely ministerial, and military offices below the grade of colonel, state or confederate, under the usurping power, shall vote for or be a member of the legislature, or governor.

Second. Involuntary servitude is forever prohibited, and the freedom of all persons is guaranteed in said state.

Third. No debt, state or confederate, created by or under the sanction of the usurping power, shall be recognized or paid by the state.

SEC. 8.   That when the convention shall have adopted those provisions, it shall proceed to reëstablish a republican form of government, and ordain a constitution containing those provisions, which, when adopted, the convention shall by ordinance provide for submitting to the people of the state, entitled to vote under this law, at an election to be held in the manner prescribed by the act for the election of delegates; but at a time and place named by the convention, at which election the said electors, and none others, shall vote directly for or against such constitution and form of state government, and the returns of said election shall be made to the provisional governor, who shall canvass the same in the presence of the electors, and if a majority of the votes cast shall be for the constitution and form of government, he shall certify the same, with a copy thereof, to the President of the United States, who, after obtaining the assent of congress, shall, by proclamation, recognize the government so established, and none other, as the constitutional government of the state, and from the date of such recognition, and not before, Senators and Representatives, and electors for President and Vice-President may be elected in such state, according to the laws of the state and of the United States.

SEC. 9.   That if the convention shall refuse to reëstablish the state government on the conditions aforesaid, the provisional governor shall declare it dissolved; but it shall be the duty of the President, whenever he shall have reason to believe that a sufficient number of the people of the state entitled to vote under this act, in number not less than a majority of those enrolled, as aforesaid, are willing to reëstablish a state government on the conditions aforesaid, to direct the provisional governor to order another election of delegates to a convention for the purpose. . . .

SEC. 10.   That, until the United States shall have recognized a republican form of state government, the provisional governor in each of said states shall see that this act, and the laws of the United States, and the laws of the state in force when the state government was overthrown by the rebellion, are faithfully executed within the state; but no law or usage whereby any person was heretofore held in involuntary servitude shall be recognized or enforced by any court or officer in such state, and the laws for the trial and punishment of white persons shall extend to all persons, and jurors shall have the qualifications of voters under this law for delegates to the convention. . . .

SEC. 11.   That until the recognition of a state government as aforesaid, the provisional governor shall, under such regulations as he may prescribe, cause to be assessed, levied, and collected, for the year eighteen hundred and sixty-four, and every year thereafter, the taxes provided by the laws of such state to be levied during the fiscal year preceding the overthrow of the state government thereof, in the manner prescribed by the laws of the state, as nearly as may be; . . . The proceeds of such taxes shall be accounted for to the provisional governor, and be by him applied to the expenses of the administration of the laws in such state, subject to the direction of the President, and the surplus shall be deposited in the treasury of the United States to the credit of such state, to be paid to the state upon an appropriation therefor, to be made when a republican form of government shall be recognized therein by the United States.

SEC. 12.   That all persons held to involuntary servitude or labor in the states aforesaid are hereby emancipated and discharged therefrom, and they and their posterity shall be forever free. And if any such persons or their posterity shall be restrained of liberty, under pretence of any claim to such service or labor, the courts of the United States shall, on habeas corpus, discharge them.

SEC. 13.   That if any person declared free by this act, or any law of the United States, or any proclamation of the President, be restrained of liberty, with intent to be held in or reduced to involuntary servitude or labor, the person convicted before a court of competent jurisdiction of such act shall be punished by fine of not less than fifteen hundred dollars, and be imprisoned not less than five nor more than twenty years.

SEC. 14.   That every person who shall hereafter hold or exercise any office, civil or military, except offices merely ministerial, and military offices below the grade of colonel, in the rebel service, state or confederate, is hereby declared not to be a citizen of the United States.

107c

Proclamation Concerning Reconstruction (1864)

ABRAHAM LINCOLN

Whereas, at the late Session, Congress passed a Bill, "To guarantee to certain States, whose governments have been usurped or overthrown, a republican form of Government," a copy of which is hereunto annexed:

And whereas, the said Bill was presented to the President of the United States, for his approval, less than one hour before the *sine die* adjournment of said Session, and was not signed by him:

And whereas, the said Bill contains, among other things, a plan for restoring the States in rebellion to their proper practical relation in the Union, which plan expresses the sense of Congress upon that subject, and which plan it is now thought fit to lay before the people for their consideration:

Now, therefore, I, Abraham Lincoln, President of the United States, do proclaim, declare, and make known, that, while I am, (as I was in December last, when by proclamation I propounded a plan for restoration) unprepared, by a formal approval of this Bill, to be inflexibly committed to any single plan of restoration; and, while I am also unprepared to declare, that the free-state constitutions and governments, already adopted and installed in Arkansas and Louisiana, shall be set aside and held for nought, thereby repelling and discouraging the loyal citizens who have set up the same, as to further effort; or to declare a constitutional competency in Congress to abolish slavery in States, but am at the same time sincerely hoping and expecting that a constitutional amendment, abolishing slavery throughout the nation, may be adopted, nevertheless, I am fully satisfied with the system for restoration contained in the Bill, as one very proper plan for the loyal people of any State choosing to adopt it; and that I am, and at all times shall be, prepared to give the Executive aid and assistance to any such people, so soon as the military resistance to the United States shall have been suppressed in any such State, and the people thereof shall have sufficiently returned to their obedience to the Constitution and the laws of the United States,—in which cases, military Governors will be appointed, with directions to proceed according to the Bill.

Source: R. Basler, ed., 7 *Collected Works of Abraham Lincoln* 433 (1953).

107d

Wade-Davis Manifesto (1864)

We have read without surprise, but not without indignation, the Proclamation of the President of the 8th of July. . . .

The President, by preventing this bill from becoming a law, holds the electoral votes of the rebel States at the dictation of his personal ambition.

If those votes turn the balance in his favor, is it to be supposed that his competitor, defeated by such means, will acquiesce?

If the rebel majority assert their supremacy in those States, and send votes which elect an enemy of the Government, will we not repel his claims?

And is not that civil war for the Presidency inaugurated by the votes of rebel States?

Seriously impressed with these dangers, Congress, *"the proper constituted authority,"* formally declared that there are no State governments in the rebel States, and provided for their erection at a proper time; and both the Senate and the House of Representatives rejected the Senators and Representatives chosen under the authority of what the President calls the free constitution and government of Arkansas.

The President's proclamation *"holds for naught"* this judgment, and discards the authority of the Supreme Court, and strides headlong toward the anarchy his proclamation of the 8th of December inaugurated.

If electors for President be allowed to be chosen in either of those States, a sinister light will be cast on the motives which induced the President to "hold for naught" the will of Congress rather than his government in Louisiana and Arkansas.

That judgment of Congress which the President defies was the exercise of an authority exclusively vested in Congress by the Constitution to determine what is the established government in a State, and in its own nature and by the highest judicial authority binding on all other departments of the Government. . . .

A more studied outrage on the legislative authority of the people has never been perpetrated.

Congress passed a bill; the President refused to approve it, and then by proclamation puts as much of it in force as he sees fit, and proposes to execute those parts by officers unknown to the laws of the United States and not subject to the confirmation of the Senate!

Source: *New York Tribune,* 5 August 1864.

The bill directed the appointment of Provisional Governors by and with the advice and consent of the Senate.

The President, after defeating the law, proposes to appoint without law, and without the advice and consent of the Senate, *Military* Governors for the rebel States!

He has already exercised this dictatorial usurpation in Louisiana, and he defeated the bill to prevent its limitation. . . .

The President has greatly presumed on the forbearance which the supporters of his Administration have so long practiced, in view of the arduous conflict in which we are engaged, and the reckless ferocity of our political opponents.

But he must understand that our support is of a cause and not of a man; that the authority of Congress is paramount and must be respected; that the whole body of the Union men of Congress will not submit to be impeached by him of rash and unconstitutional legislation; and if he wishes our support, he must confine himself to his executive duties—to obey and execute, not make the laws—to suppress by arms armed rebellion, and leave political reorganization to Congress.

If the supporters of the Government fail to insist on this, they become responsible for the usurpations which they fail to rebuke, and are justly liable to the indignation of the people whose rights and security, committed to their keeping, they sacrifice.

Let them consider the remedy for these usurpations, and, having found it, fearlessly execute it.

108

Constitutionality of Draft (1863)

ABRAHAM LINCOLN

During the Civil War the United States witnessed the greatest growth in federal power since the founding of the Republic. The single largest area involved the raising of an army, first through volunteers and then

Source: R. Basler, ed., 6 *Collected Works of Abraham Lincoln* 444 (1953).

by conscription. The Constitution (Article I, Section 8) gives Congress the power to "raise and support Armies" and to call out and direct state militias. But did this allow for forced service, and did it allow the President to assign quotas to the states for their militias? The 1863 Draft Law applied to all male citizens between twenty and forty-five, as well as to immigrants who had declared their intention to become citizens. While necessary, it aroused fierce resentment, which occasionally turned into mob violence. No test case of the draft's constitutionality ever reached the Supreme Court, but New York governor Horatio Seymour urged Lincoln to suspend the draft because of its alleged unconstitutionality. Lincoln's defense of the draft, in this memorandum later found in his papers, indicates his understanding of the "adequacy-of-the-Constitution" argument.

See M. Dowd, "Lincoln, the Rule of Law and Crisis Government: A Study of His Constitutional Law Theories," 39 *U. Det. L. J.* 633 (1962); J. F. Leach, *Conscription in the United States* (1952); E. C. Murdock, *Patriotism Limited, 1862–1865: Draft and Bounty System* (1967); and A. B. Moore, *Conscription and Conflict in the Confederacy* (1924).

~~~~~~

It is at all times proper that misunderstanding between the public and the public servant should be avoided; and this is far more important now, than in times of peace and tranquility. I therefore address you without searching for a precedent upon which to do so. Some of you are sincerely devoted to the republican institutions, and territorial integrity of our country, and yet are opposed to what is called the draft, or conscription.

At the beginning of the war, and ever since, a variety of motives pressing, some in one direction and some in the other, would be presented to the mind of each man physically fit for a soldier, upon the combined effect of which motives, he would, or would not, voluntarily enter the service. Among these motives would be patriotism, political bias, ambition, personal courage, love of adventure, want of employment, and convenience, or the opposites of some of these. We already have, and have had in the service, as appears, substantially all that can be obtained upon this voluntary weighing of motives. And yet we must somehow obtain more, or relinquish the original object of the contest, together with all the blood and treasure already expended in the effort to secure it. To meet this necessity the law for the draft has been enacted. You who do not wish to be soldiers, do not like this law. This is natural; nor does it imply want of patriotism. Nothing can be so just, and necessary, as to make us like it, if it is disagreeable to us. We are prone, too, to find false arguments with which to excuse ourselves for opposing such disagreeable things. In this case those who desire the rebellion to succeed, and others who seek reward in a different way, are very active in accomodating us with this class of arguments. They tell us the law is unconstitutional. It is the first instance, I believe, in which the power of congress to do a thing has ever been questioned, in a case when the power is given by the constitution in express terms. Whether a power can be implied, when it is not expressed, has often been the subject of controversy; but this is the first case in which the degree of effrontery has been ventured upon, of denying a power which is plainly and distinctly written down in the constitution. The constitution declares that "The congress shall have power . . . To raise and support armies; but no appropriation of money to that use shall be for a longer term than two years." The whole scope of the conscription act is "to raise and support armies." There is nothing else in it. It makes no appropriation of money; and hence the money clause just quoted, is not touched by it. The case simply is the constitution provides that the congress shall have power to raise and support armies; and, by this act, the congress has exercised the power to raise and support armies. This is the whole of it. It is a law made in literal pursuance of this part of the United States Constitution; and another part of the same constitution declares that "This constitution, and the laws made in pursuance thereof . . . shall be the supreme law of the land, and the judges in every state shall be bound thereby, anything in the constitution or laws of any state to the contrary notwithstanding."

Do you admit that the power is given to raise and support armies, and yet insist that by this act congress has not exercised the power in a constitutional mode?—has not done the thing, in the right way? Who is to judge of this? The constitution gives congress the power, but it does not prescribe the mode, or expressly declare who shall prescribe it. In such case congress must prescribe the mode, or relinquish the power. There is no alternative. Congress could not exercise the power to do the thing, if it had not the power of providing a way to do it, when no way is provided by the constitution for doing it. In fact congress would not have the power to raise and support armies, if even by the constitution, it were left to the option of any other, or others, to give or withhold the only mode of doing it. If the constitution had prescribed a mode, congress could and must follow that mode; but as it is, the mode necessarily goes to congress, with the power expressly given. The power is given fully, completely, unconditionally. It is not a power to raise armies *if* State authorities consent; nor *if* the men to compose the armies are entirely willing; but it is a power to raise and support armies given to congress by the constitution, without an *if*.

It is clear that a constitutional law may not be expedient or proper. Such would be a law to raise armies when no armies were needed. But this is not such. The republican institutions, and territorial integrity of our country can not be maintained without the further raising and supporting of armies. There can be no army without men. Men can be had only voluntarily, or involuntarily. We have ceased to obtain them voluntarily; and to obtain them involuntarily, is the draft—the conscription. If you dispute the fact, and declare that men can still be had voluntarily in sufficient numbers prove the assertion by yourselves volunteering in such numbers, and I shall gladly give up the draft. Or if not a sufficient number, but any one of you will volunteer, he for his single self, will escape all the horrors of the draft; and will thereby do only what each one of at least a million of his manly brethren have already done. Their toil and blood have been given as much for you as for themselves. Shall it all be lost rather than you too, will bear your part?

I do not say that all who would avoid serving in the war, are unpatriotic; but I do think every patriot should willingly take his chance under a law made with great care in order to secure entire fairness. This law was considered, discussed, modified, and amended, by congress, at great length, and with much labor; and was finally passed, by both branches, with a near approach to unanimity. At last, it may not be exactly such as any one man out of congress, or even in congress, would have made it. It has been said, and I believe truly, that the constitution itself is not altogether such as any one of its framers would have preferred. It was the joint work of all; and certainly the better that it was so. . . .

The principle of the draft, which simply is involuntary, or enforced service, is not new. It has been practiced in all ages of the world. It was well known to the framers of our constitution as one of the modes of raising armies, at the time they placed in that instrument the provision that "the congress shall have power to raise and support armies." It has been used, just before, in establishing our independence; and it was also used under the constitution in 1812. Wherein is the peculiar hardship now? Shall we shrink from the necessary means to maintain our free government, which our grand-fathers employed to establish it, and our own fathers have already employed once to maintain it? Are we degenerate? Has the manhood of our race run out?

Again, a law may be both constitutional and expedient, and yet may be administered in an unjust and unfair way. This law belongs to a class, which class is composed of those laws whose object is to distribute burthens or benefits on the principle of equality. No one of these laws can ever be practically administered with that exactness which can be conceived of in the mind. A tax law, the principle of which is that each owner shall pay in proportion to the value of his property, will be a dead letter, if no one can be compelled to pay until it can be shown that every other one will pay in precisely the same proportion according to value; nay even, it will be a dead letter, if no one can be compelled to pay until it is certain that every other one will pay at all—even in unequal proportion. Again the United States House of representatives is constituted on the principle that each member is sent by the same number of people that each other one is sent by; and yet in practice no two of the whole number, much less the whole number, are ever sent by precisely the same number of constituents. The Districts can not be made precisely equal in population at first, and if they could, they would become unequal in a single day, and much more so in the ten years, which the Districts, once made, are to continue. They can not be re-modelled every day; nor, without too much expence and labor, even every year.

This sort of difficulty applies in full force, to the practical administration of the draft law. In fact the difficulty is greater in the case of the draft law. First, it starts with all the inequality of the congressional Districts; but these are based on entire population, while the draft is based upon those only who are fit for soldiers, and such may not bear the same proportion to the whole in one District, that they do in another. Again, the facts must be ascertained, and credit given, for the unequal numbers of soldiers which have already gone from the several Districts. In all these points errors will occur in spite of the utmost fidelity. The government is bound to administer the law with such an approach to exactness as is usual in analogous cases, and as entire good faith and fidelity will reach. If so great departures as to be inconsistent with such good faith and fidelity, or great departures occurring in any way, be pointed out, they shall be corrected; and any agent shown to have caused such departures intentionally, shall be dismissed.

With these views, and on these principles, I feel bound to tell you it is my purpose to see the draft law faithfully executed.

109

Ex parte Vallandigham (1864)

Although the decision in the *Prize Cases* (Document 105) upheld the Lincoln administration's prosecution of the war, the narrow majority as well as the cogency of Justice Nelson's dissenting opinion led opponents of the war to hope that in a different case they might get the fifth vote. That chance never came. In Roosevelt v. Meyer, 1 Wall. 512 (1863), the Court declined to take jurisdiction in a case questioning the constitutionality of the government's issue of paper currency, and in *Vallandigham* the Court again refused to interfere with the direction of the war. Clement L. Vallandigham, an antiwar Democrat, had been convicted by a military court of violating a ban against pro-Confederate

Source: 1 Wallace 243 (1864).

expressions of sympathy. Lincoln commuted his sentence to banishment to the South. Vallandigham then ran the blockade to Canada and came back into Ohio, and from there appealed his military conviction on grounds that he had been unlawfully arrested. His appeal challenged the very authority of Congress and the President to continue the war, as well as the government's power to arrest a civilian and try him before a military panel in wartime. Although a dying Roger Taney wanted to take up the challenge, a majority of the Court sidestepped the issue, believing that such questions had to await the end of the conflict (see Document 113).

See F. Klement, *Limits of Dissent: Vallandigham and the Civil War* (1970).

Justice Wayne delivered the opinion of the Court.

General Burnside acted in the matter as the general commanding the Ohio Department, in conformity with the instructions for the government of the armies of the United States, approved by the President of the United States, and published by the Assistant Adjutant-General, by order of the Secretary of War, on the 24th of April, 1863.

It is affirmed in these instructions, that military jurisdiction is of two kinds. First, that which is conferred and defined by statute; second, that which is derived from the common law of war. "Military offences, under the statute, must be tried in the manner therein directed; but military offences, which do not come within the statute, must be tried and punished under the common law of war. The character of the courts which exercise these jurisdictions depends upon the local law of each particular county."

In the armies of the United States, the first is exercised by courts-martial, while cases which do not come within the "rules and regulations of war," or the jurisdiction conferred by statute or court-martial, are tried by *military commissions.*

These jurisdictions are applicable, not only to war with foreign nations, but to a rebellion, when a part of a country wages war against its legitimate government, seeking to throw off all allegiance to it, to set up a government of its own.

Our first remark upon *the motion for a certiorari* is, that there is no analogy between the power given by the Constitution and law of the United States to the Supreme Court, and the other inferior courts of the United States, and to the judges of them, to issue such processes, and the prerogative power by which it is done in England. The purposes for which the writ is issued are alike, but there is no similitude in the origin of the power to do it. In England, the Court of King's Bench has a superintendence over all courts of an inferior criminal jurisdiction, and may, by the plenitude of its power, award a certiorari to have any indictment removed and brought before it; and where such certiorari is allowable, it is awarded at the instance of the king, because every indictment is at the suit of the king, and he has a prerogative of suing in whatever court he pleases. The courts of the United States derive authority to issue such a writ from the Constitution and the legislation of Congress. . . .

The appellate powers of the Supreme Court, as granted by the Constitution, are limited and regulated by the acts of Congress, and must be exercised subject to the exceptions and regulations made by Congress. In other words, the petition before us we think not to be within the letter or spirit of the grants of appellate jurisdiction to the Supreme Court. It is not in law or equity within the meaning of those terms as used in the 3d article of the Constitution. Nor is a military commission a court within the meaning of the 14th section of the Judiciary Act of 1789. That act is denominated to be one to establish the judicial courts of the United States, and the 14th section declares that all the "before-mentioned courts" of the United States shall have power to issue writs of *scire facias, habeas corpus,* and all other writs not specially provided for by statute, which may be necessary for the exercise of their respective jurisdictions, agreeably to the principles and usages of law. The words in the section, "the before-mentioned" courts, can only have reference to such courts as were established in the preceding part of the act, and excludes the idea that a court of military commission can be one of them.

Whatever may be the force of Vallandigham's protest, that he was not triable by a court of military commission, it is certain that his petition cannot be brought within the 14th section of the act; and further, that the court cannot, without disregarding its frequent decisions and interpretation of the Constitution in respect to its judicial power, originate a writ of certiorari to review or pronounce any opinion upon the proceedings of a military commission. . . . *The rule of construction of the Constitution being, that affirmative words in the Constitution, declaring in what cases the Supreme Court shall have original jurisdiction, must be construed negatively as to all other cases.* The nature and extent of the court's appellate jurisdiction and its want of it to issue writs of *habeas corpus ad subjiciendum* have been fully discussed by this court at different times. We do not think it necessary, however, to examine or cite many of them at this time. . . .

For the reasons given, our judgment is, that the writ of certiorari prayed for to revise and review the proceedings of the military commission, by which Clement L. Vallandigham was tried, sentenced, and imprisoned, must be denied, and so do we order accordingly.

CERTIORARI REFUSED.

110

Black Code of Alabama (1865)

Even though they no longer "owned" black slaves, many Southerners continued to view the freedmen as if emancipation had not taken place. They chose a number of devices to keep blacks in their "place," including organized terrorism through groups such as the Ku Klux Klan. But they also adopted so-called "Black Codes" to govern the movement and activities of the former bondsmen, and in many ways these differed very little in intent or design from the prewar slave codes (see Document 93). The Black Codes led directly to the 1866 Civil Rights Act (Document 111) and to the protective clauses of the Fourteenth Amendment. Here again, one must remember that the law is always an agent of social control as well as a protector of rights.

See W. Cohen, "Negro Involuntary Servitude in the South," 42 *J. So. His.* 31 (1976); R. Cruden, *The Negro in Reconstruction* (1969); J. Williamson, *After Slavery: The Negro in South Carolina During Reconstruction, 1861–1877* (1965), and T. Wilson, *The Black Codes of the South* (1965).

To protect freedmen in their rights of person and property in this State

. . . All freedmen, free negroes and mulattoes, shall have the right to sue and be sued, plead and be impleaded in all the different and various courts of this State, to the same extent that white persons now have by law. And they shall be competent to testify only in open court, and only in cases in which freedmen, free negroes and mulattoes are parties, either plaintiff or defendant, and in civil and criminal cases, for injuries in the persons and property of freedmen, free negroes and mulattoes, and in all cases, civil or criminal, in which a freedman, free negro or mulatto is a witness against a white person, or a white person against a freedman, free negro or mulatto, the parties shall be competent witnesses, and neither interest in the question or suit, nor marriage, shall disqualify any witness from testifying in open court.

Source: *Acts of the Session of 1865–6, of the General Assembly of Alabama* (1866).

To prevent persons from interfering so as to induce laborers or servants to abandon their contracts, or to employ such without the consent of their original employer before the expiration of the contract, &c.

SECTION 1.   It shall not be lawful for any person to interfere with, hire, employ or entice away or induce to leave the service of another, any laborer or servant, who shall have stipulated or contracted in writing, to serve for any given number of days, weeks or months, or for one year, so long as the said contract shall be and remain in force and binding upon the parties thereto, without the consent of the party employing or to whom said service is due and owing in writing or in the presence of some veritable white person, and any person who shall knowingly interfere with, hire, employ or entice away or induce to leave the service aforesaid, without justifiable excuse therefor, before the expiration of said term of service, so contracted and stipulated as aforesaid, shall be guilty of a misdemeanor, and on conviction thereof, must be fined in such sum not less than fifty nor more than five hundred dollars, as the jury trying the same may assess and in no case less than double the amount of the injury sustained by the party from whom such laborer or servant was induced to leave, one half to go to the party injured and the other to the county as fines and forfeitures.

SEC. 2.   *Be it further enacted,* That the party injured shall be a competent witness in all prosecutions under the act, notwithstanding his interest in the fine to be assessed.

SEC. 3.   *Be it further enacted,* That when any laborer or servant, having contracted as provided in the first section of this act, shall afterward be found, before the termination of said contract, in the service or employment of another, that fact shall be *prima facie* evidence that such person is guilty of a violation of this act—if he fail and refuse to forthwith discharge the said laborer or servant, after being notified and informed of such former contract and employment.

Concerning vagrants and vagrancy

SECTION 1.. . . The commissioners' court of any county in this State may purchase, rent, or provide such lands, buildings and other property as may be necessary for a poor-house, or house of correction for any such county, and may appoint suitable officers for the management thereof, and make all necessary by-laws, rules and regulations for the government of the inmates thereof, and cause the same to be enforced; but in no case shall the punishment inflicted exceed hard labor, either in or out of said house; the use of chain-gangs, putting in stocks, if necessary, to prevent escapes; such reasonable correction as a parent may inflict upon a stubborn, refractory child; and solitary confinement for not longer than one week, on bread and water; and may cause to be hired out such as are vagrants, to work in chain-gangs or otherwise, for the length of time for which they are sentenced; and the proceeds of such hiring must be paid into the county treasury, for the benefit of the helpless in said poor-house, or house of correction.

SEC. 2.   *Be it further enacted,* That the following persons are vagrants in addition to those already declared to be vagrants by law, or that may hereafter be so declared by law; a stubborn or refractory servant; a laborer or servant who loiters away his time, or refuses to comply with any contract for a term of service without just cause; and any such person may be sent to the house of correction in the county in which such offense is committed and for want of such house of correction, the common jail of the county may be used for that purpose.

SEC. 3.   *Be it further enacted,* That when a vagrant is found, any justice of the peace of the county must, upon complaint made upon oath, or on his own knowledge, issue his warrant to the sheriff or any constable of the county, to bring such person before him; and if, upon examination and hearing of testimony, it appears to the justice, that such person is a vagrant, he shall assess a fine of fifty dollars and costs against such vagrant; and in default of payment, he must commit such vagrant to the house of correction; or if no such house, to the common jail of the county, for a term not exceeding six months and until such fine, costs and charges are paid, or such party is otherwise discharged by law; Provided, that when committed to jail under this section, the commissioners' court may cause him to be hired out in like manner as in section one of this act.

SEC. 4.   *Be it further enacted,* That when any person shall be convicted of vagrancy, as provided for in this act, the justice of the peace, before whom such conviction is had, may, at his discretion, either commit such person to jail, to the house of correction, or hire such person to any person who will hire the same, for a period not longer than six months, for cash, giving three days' notice of the time and place of hiring; and the proceeds of such hiring, after paying all costs and charges, shall be paid into the county treasury for the benefit of the helpless in the poor-house.

SEC. 5.   *Be it further enacted,* That all fines received by any justice of the peace under the provisions of this act, shall be paid into the county treasury for the purposes as set forth in section one of this act. . . .

To define the relative duties of master and apprentice

SECTION 1.   *Be it enacted by the Senate and House of Representatives of the State of Alabama in General Assembly convened,* That it shall be the duty of all sheriffs, justices of the peace, and other civil officers of the several counties in this State, to report to the probate courts of their respective counties, at any time, all minors under the age of eighteen years, within their respective counties, beats, or districts, who are orphans without visible means of support, or whose parent or parents have not the means, or who refuse to provide for and support said minors, and thereupon it shall be the duty of said probate court to apprentice said minor to some suitable and competent person, on such terms as the court may direct, having a particular case to the interest of said minor; Provided, If the said minor be the child of a freedman the former owner of said minor shall have the preference when proof shall be made that he or she shall be a suitable person for that purpose, and provided, that the judge of probate shall make a record of all the proceedings in such case, for which he shall be entitled to a compensation of one dollar, to be paid by the master or mistress.

SEC. 2.   *Be it further enacted,* That when proof shall be fully made before such court, that the person or persons to whom said minor shall be apprenticed shall be a suitable person to have the charge and care of said minor, and fully to protect the interest of said minor, the said court shall require the said master or mistress to execute bond with security to the State of Alabama, conditioned that he or she shall furnish said minor with sufficient food and clothing, to treat said minor humanely, furnish medical attention in case of sickness, teach or cause to be taught him or her to read and write, if under fifteen years old, and will conform to any law that may be hereafter passed for the regulation of the duties and relation of the master and apprentice.

SEC. 3.   *Be it further enacted,* That in the management and control of said apprentices, said master or mistress shall have power to inflict such moderate corporeal chastisement as a father or guardian is allowed to inflict on his or her child, or ward at common law; Provided, That in no case shall cruel or inhuman punishment be inflicted.

SEC. 4.   *Be it further enacted,* That if any apprentice shall leave the employment of his or her master or mistress without his or her consent, said master or mistress may pursue and recapture said apprentice and bring him or her before any justice of the peace of the county, whose duty it shall be to remand said apprentice to the service of his or her master or mistress; and in the event of a refusal on the part of said apprentice so to return, then said justice shall commit said apprentice to the jail of said county on failure to give bond until the next term of the probate court, and it shall be the duty of said court, at the first term thereafter, to investigate said case, and if the court shall be of opinion, that said apprentice left the employment of his or her master or mistress without good cause, to order him or her to receive such punishment as may be provided by the vagrant laws which may be then in force in this State, until he or she shall agree to return to his or her master or mistress; Provided, That the court may grant continuances as in other cases; and provided, that if the court shall believe that said apprentice had good cause to quit the employment of his or her master or mistress, the court shall discharge such apprentice from said indenture, and may also enter a judgment against the master or mistress, for not more than one hundred dollars, for the use and benefit of said apprentice, to be collected on execution, as in other cases.

SEC. 5. *Be it further enacted,* That if any person entice away any apprentice from his or her master or mistress, or shall knowingly employ an apprentice, or furnish him or her food or clothing without the written consent of his or her master or mistress, or shall give or sell said apprentice ardent spirits, without such consent, such person so offending shall be deemed guilty of a misdemeanor, and shall, on conviction thereof, be fined in a sum not exceeding five hundred dollars.

111

Civil Rights Act (1866)

The ending of the war and the abolition of slavery left the status of several million freedmen in limbo. In *Dred Scott* (Document 97), the Court had held that slaves could not be citizens. Citizenship at that time was more a state than a national function, and the Southern states had little inclination to grant their former bondsmen the perquisites of citizenship. The Civil Rights Act represents Congress's first effort to deal with these problems in a comprehensive manner. It also represents a major shift in constitutional perceptions. Until then protection of individual rights had been a state responsibility; afterward people looked to the federal government for such protection. The Act attempted to establish national standards for what constituted an individual's civil rights, and then to create legal mechanisms to enforce those rights. Congress had considerable doubts about the constitutionality of the measure, since there had previously been no national standards. The subsequent veto by President Johnson (see Document 112), even

Source: 14 *Statutes at Large* 27 (1866).

though overridden, left many doubts as to congressional power in this area, and led directly to passage of the Fourteenth Amendment.

See M. L. Benedict, *A Compromise of Principle: Congressional Republicans and Reconstruction* (1974); D. Donald, *Charles Sumner and the Rights of Man* (1970); and H. L. Trefousse, *The Radical Republicans* (1969).

Be it enacted by the Senate and House of Representatives of the United States of America in Congress assembled, That all persons born in the United States and not subject to any foreign power, excluding Indians not taxed, are hereby declared to be citizens of the United States; and such citizens, of every race and color, without regard to any previous condition of slavery or involuntary servitude, except as a punishment for crime whereof the party shall have been duly convicted, shall have the same right, in every State and Territory in the United States, to make and enforce contracts, to sue, be parties, and give evidence, to inherit, purchase, lease, sell, hold, and convey real and personal property, and to full and equal benefit of all laws and proceedings for the security of person and property, as is enjoyed by white citizens, and shall be subject to like punishment, pains, and penalties, and to none other, any law, statute, ordinance, regulation, or custom, to the contrary notwithstanding.

SEC. 2.   *And be it further enacted,* That any person who, under color of any law, statute, ordinance, regulation, or custom, shall subject, or cause to be subjected, any inhabitant of any State or Territory to the deprivation of any right secured or protected by this act, or to different punishment, pains, or penalties on account of such person having at any time been held in a condition of slavery or involuntary servitude, except as a punishment for crime whereof the party shall have been duly convicted, or by reason of his color or race, than is prescribed for the punishment of white persons, shall be deemed guilty of a misdemeanor, and, on conviction, shall be punished by fine not exceeding one thousand dollars, or imprisonment not exceeding one year, or both, in the discretion of the court.

SEC. 3.   *And be it further enacted,* That the district courts of the United States, within their respective districts, shall have, exclusively of the courts of the several States, cognizance of all crimes and offences committed against the provisions of this act, and also, concurrently with the circuit courts of the United States, of all causes, civil and criminal, affecting persons who are denied or cannot enforce in the courts or judicial tribunals of the State or locality where they may be any of the rights secured to them by the first section of this act; and if any suit or prosecution, civil or criminal, has been or shall be commenced in any State court, against any such person, for any cause whatsoever, or against any officer, civil or military, or other person, for any arrest or imprisonment, trespasses, or wrongs done or committed by virtue or under color of authority derived from this act or the act establishing a Bureau for the relief of Freedmen and Refugees, and all acts amendatory thereof, or for refusing to do any act upon the ground that it would be inconsistent with this act, such defendant shall have the right to remove such cause for trial to the proper district or circuit court in the manner prescribed by the "Act relating to habeas corpus and regulating judicial proceedings in certain cases," approved March three, eighteen hundred and sixty-three, and all acts amendatory thereof. The jurisdiction in civil and criminal matters hereby conferred on the district and circuit courts of the United States shall be exercised and enforced in conformity with the laws of the United States, so far as such laws are suitable to carry the same into effect; but in all cases where such laws are not adapted to the object, or are deficient in the provisions necessary to furnish suitable remedies and punish offences against law, the common law, as modified and changed by the constitution and statutes of the State wherein the court having jurisdiction of the cause, civil or criminal, is held, so far as the same is not inconsistent with the Constitution and laws of the United States shall be extended to and govern said courts in the trial and disposition of such cause, and, if of a criminal nature, in the infliction of punishment on the party found guilty.

SEC. 4. *And be it further enacted,* That the district attorneys, marshals, and deputy marshals of the United States, the commissioners appointed by the circuit and territorial courts of the United States, with powers of arresting, imprisoning, or bailing offenders against the laws of the United States, the officers and agents of the Freedmen's Bureau, and every other officer who may be specially empowered by the President of the United States, shall be, and they are hereby, specially authorized and required, at the expense of the United States, to institute proceedings against all and every person who shall violate the provisions of this act, and cause him or them to be arrested and imprisoned, or bailed, as the case may be, for trial before such court of the United States or territorial court as by this act has cognizance of the offence. . . .

SEC. 5. *And be it further enacted,* That it shall be the duty of all marshals and deputy marshals to obey and execute all warrants and precepts issued under the provisions of this act, when to them directed; and should any marshal or deputy marshal refuse to receive such warrant or other process when tendered, or to use all proper means diligently to execute the same, he shall, on conviction thereof, be fined in the sum of one thousand dollars, to the use of the person upon whom the accused is alleged to have committed the offence. And the better to enable the said commissioners to execute their duties faithfully and efficiently, in conformity with the Constitution of the United States and the requirements of this act, they are hereby authorized and empowered, within their counties respectively, to appoint, in writing, under their hands, any one or more suitable persons, from time to time, to execute all such warrants and other process as may be issued by them in the lawful performance of their respective duties; and the persons so appointed to execute any warrant or process as aforesaid shall have authority to summon and call to their aid the bystanders or posse comitatus of the proper county, or such portion of the land or naval forces of the United States, or of the militia, as may be necessary to the performance of the duty with which they are charged, and to insure a faithful observance of the clause of the Constitution which prohibits slavery, in conformity with the provisions of this act; and said warrants shall run and be executed by said officers anywhere in the State or Territory within which they are issued.

SEC. 6. *And be it further enacted,* That any person who shall knowingly and wilfully obstruct, hinder, or prevent any officer, or other person charged with the execution of any warrant or process issued under the provisions of this act, or any person or persons lawfully assisting him or them, from arresting any person for whose apprehension such warrant or process may have been issued, or shall rescue or attempt to rescue such person from the custody of the officer, other person or persons, or those lawfully assisting as aforesaid, when so arrested pursuant to the authority herein given and declared, or shall aid, abet, or assist any person so arrested as aforesaid, directly or indirectly, to escape from the custody of the officer or other person legally authorized as aforesaid, or shall harbor or conceal any person for whose arrest a warrant or process shall have been issued as aforesaid, so as to prevent his discovery and arrest after notice or knowledge of the fact that a warrant has been issued for the apprehension of such person, shall, for either of said offences, be subject to a fine not exceeding one thousand dollars, and imprisonment not exceeding six months, by indictment and conviction before the district court of the United States for the district in which said offence may have been committed, or before the proper court of criminal jurisdiction, if committed within any one of the organized Territories of the United States. . . .

SEC. 8. *And be it further enacted,* That whenever the President of the United States shall have reason to believe that offences have been or are likely to be committed against the provisions of this act within any judicial district, it shall be lawful for him, in his discretion, to direct the judge, marshal, and district attorney of such district to attend at such place within the district, and for such time as he may designate, for the purpose of the more speedy arrest and trial of persons charged with a violation of this act; and it shall be the duty of every judge or other officer, when any such requisition shall be received by him, to attend at the place and for the time therein designated.

SEC. 9. *And be it further enacted,* That it shall be lawful for the President of the United States, or such person as he may empower for that purpose, to employ such part of the land or naval forces of the United States, or of the militia, as shall be necessary to prevent the violation and enforce the due execution of this act.

SEC. 10.   *And be it further enacted,* That upon all questions of law arising in any cause under the provisions of this act a final appeal may be taken to the Supreme Court of the United States.

112

Veto of Civil Rights Act (1866)

ANDREW JOHNSON

Andrew Johnson, for all he had been Lincoln's running mate in 1864, was never really an advocate of Republican policy, and remained a firm, indeed rigid, supporter of states' rights. Despite the enormous growth of federal power during the Civil War, Johnson clung to Jeffersonian and Jacksonian beliefs in the very limited power of the national government. His opposition to even the mildest congressional programs for the South and his gross political ineptitude were major causes of the ultimate tragedy of Reconstruction. In his veto of the 1866 Civil Rights Act, a veto promptly overridden by Congress, Johnson set out his constitutional arguments, which, in effect, denied Congress any power over the former Confederate states. Whatever Johnson's views about the "adequacy-of-the-Constitution" theory during the war, he insisted that with the end of hostilities the only constitutionally permissible policy for the national government was to acknowledge the return of the former Confederate states to their normal status within the Union, and for the national government to become, once again, a government of very limited powers, especially vis-à-vis the states. His views won few

Source: Richardson, ed., 6 *Messages and Papers of the Presidents* 405 (1897).

adherents but did raise enough questions to lead the Republicans to propose the Fourteenth Amendment.

See E. McKitrick, *Andrew Johnson and Reconstruction* (1960); J. Cox and L. Cox, *Politics, Principle, and Prejudice* (1963); A. Castel, *The Presidency of Andrew Johnson* (1979); and J. E. Sefton, *Andrew Johnson and the Uses of Constitutional Power* (1980).

To the Senate of the United States:

I regret that the bill, which has passed both Houses of Congress, entitled "An act to protect all persons in the United States in their civil rights and furnish the means of their vindication," contains provisions which I can not approve consistently with my sense of duty to the whole people and my obligations to the Constitution of the United States. I am therefore constrained to return it to the Senate, the House in which it originated, with my objections to its becoming a law.

By the first section of the bill all persons born in the United States and not subject to any foreign power, excluding Indians not taxed, are declared to be citizens of the United States. This provision comprehends the Chinese of the Pacific States, Indians subject to taxation, the people called gypsies, as well as the entire race designated as blacks, people of color, negroes, mulattoes, and persons of African blood. Every individual of these races born in the United States is by the bill made a citizen of the United States. It does not purport to declare or confer any other right of citizenship than Federal citizenship. It does not purport to give these classes of persons any status as citizens of States, except that which may result from their status as citizens of the United States. The power to confer the right of State citizenship is just as exclusively with the several States as the power to confer the right of Federal citizenship is with Congress.

The right of Federal citizenship thus to be conferred on the several excepted races before mentioned is now for the first time proposed to be given by law. If, as is claimed by many, all persons who are native born already are, by virtue of the Constitution, citizens of the United States, the passage of the pending bill can not be necessary to make them such. If, on the other hand, such persons are not citizens, as may be assumed from the proposed legislation to make them such, the grave question presents itself whether, when eleven of the thirty-six States are unrepresented in Congress at the present time, it is sound policy to make our entire colored population and all other excepted classes citizens of the United States. Four millions of them have just emerged from slavery into freedom. Can it be reasonably supposed that they possess the requisite qualifications to entitle them to all the privileges and immunities of citizens of the United States? Have the people of the several

States expressed such a conviction? It may also be asked whether it is necessary that they should be declared citizens in order that they may be secured in the enjoyment of the civil rights proposed to be conferred by the bill. . . . The policy of the Government from its origin to the present time seems to have been that persons who are strangers to and unfamiliar with our institutions and our laws should pass through a certain probation, at the end of which, before attaining the coveted prize, they must give evidence of their fitness to receive and to exercise the rights of citizens as contemplated by the Constitution of the United States. The bill in effect proposes a discrimination against large numbers of intelligent, worthy, and patriotic foreigners, and in favor of the negro, to whom, after long years of bondage, the avenues to freedom and intelligence have just now been suddenly opened. He must of necessity, from his previous unfortunate condition of servitude, be less informed as to the nature and character of our institutions than he who, coming from abroad, has, to some extent at least, familiarized himself with the principles of a Government to which he voluntarily intrusts "life, liberty, and the pursuit of happiness." Yet it is now proposed, by a single legislative enactment, to confer the rights of citizens upon all persons of African descent born within the extended limits of the United States, while persons of foreign birth who make our land their home must undergo a probation of five years, and can only then become citizens upon proof that they are "of good moral character, attached to the principles of the Constitution of the United States, and well disposed to the good order and happiness of the same."

The first section of the bill also contains an enumeration of the rights to be enjoyed by these classes so made citizens "in every State and Territory in the United States." These rights are "to make and enforce contracts; to sue, be parties, and give evidence; to inherit, purchase, lease, sell, hold, and convey real and personal property," and to have "full and equal benefit of all laws and proceedings for the security of person and property as is enjoyed by white citizens." So, too, they are made subject to the same punishment, pains, and penalties in common with white citizens, and to none other. Thus a perfect equality of the white and colored races is attempted to be fixed by Federal law in every State of the Union over the vast field of State jurisdiction covered by these enumerated rights. In no one of these can any State ever exercise any power of discrimination between the different races. In the exercise of State policy over matters exclusively affecting the people of each State it has frequently been thought expedient to discriminate between the two races. By the statutes of some of the States, Northern as well as Southern, it is enacted, for instance, that no white person shall intermarry with a negro or mulatto. . . .

I do not say that this bill repeals State laws on the subject of marriage between the two races, for as the whites are forbidden to intermarry with the blacks, the blacks can only make such contracts as the whites themselves are allowed to make, and therefore can not under this bill enter into the marriage contract with the whites. I cite this discrimination, however, as an instance of the State policy as to discrimination, and to inquire whether if Congress can abrogate all State laws of discrimination between the two races in the matter of real estate, of suits, and of contracts generally Congress may not also repeal the State laws as to the contract of marriage between the two races. Hitherto every subject embraced in the enumeration of rights contained in this bill has been considered as exclusively belonging to the States. They all relate to the internal police and economy of the respective States. They are matters which in each State concern the domestic condition of its people, varying in each according to its own peculiar circumstances and the safety and well-being of its own citizens. . . .

The object of the second section of the bill is to afford discriminating protection to colored persons in the full enjoyment of all the rights secured to them by the preceding section. . . .

This section seems to be designed to apply to some existing or future law of a State or Territory which may conflict with the provisions of the bill now under consideration. It provides for counteracting such forbidden legislation by imposing fine and imprisonment upon the legislators who may pass such conflicting laws, or upon the officers or agents who shall put or attempt to put them into execution. It means an official offense, not a common crime committed against law upon the persons or property of the black race. Such an act may deprive the black man of his property, but not of the *right* to hold property. It means a deprivation of the right itself, either by the State judiciary or the State legislature. It is therefore assumed that under this section members of State legislatures who should vote for laws conflicting with the provisions of the bill, that judges of the State courts who should render judgments in antagonism with its terms, and that marshals and sheriffs who should, as ministerial officers, execute processes sanctioned by State laws and issued by State judges in execution of their judgments could be brought before other tribunals and there subjected to fine and imprisonment for the performance of the duties which such State laws might impose. The legislation thus proposed invades the judicial power of the State. It says to every State court or judge, If you decide that this act is unconstitutional; if you refuse, under the prohibition of a State law, to allow a negro to testify; if you hold that over such a subject-matter the State law is paramount, and "under color" of a State law refuse the exercise of the right to the negro, your error of judgment, however conscientious, shall subject you to fine and imprisonment. I do not apprehend that the conflicting legislation which the bill seems to contemplate is so likely to occur as to render it necessary at this time to adopt a measure of such doubtful constitutionality.

In the next place, this provision of the bill seems to be unnecessary, as adequate judicial remedies could be adopted to secure the desired end without invading the immunities of legislators, always important to be preserved in the interest of public liberty; without assailing the independence of the judiciary, always essential to the preservation of individual rights; and without impairing the efficiency of ministerial officers, always necessary for the maintenance of public peace and order. The remedy proposed by this section seems to be in this respect not only anomalous, but unconstitutional; for the Constitution guarantees nothing with certainty if it does not insure to the several States the right of making and executing laws in regard to all matters arising within their jurisdiction, subject only to the restriction that in cases of conflict with the Constitution and constitutional laws of the United States the latter should be held to be the supreme law of the land. . . .

It is clear that in States which deny to persons whose rights are secured by the first section of the bill any one of those rights all criminal and civil cases affecting them will, by the provisions of the third section, come under the exclusive cognizance of the Federal tribunals. It follows that if, in any State which denies to a colored person any one of all those rights, that person should commit a crime against the laws of a State—murder, arson, rape, or any other crime—all protection and punishment through the courts of the State are taken away, and he can only be tried and punished in the Federal courts. How is the criminal to be tried? If the offense is provided for and punished by Federal law, that law, and not the State law, is to govern. It is only when the offense does not happen to be within the purview of Federal law that the Federal courts are to try and punish him under any other law. Then resort is to be had to "the common law, as modified and changed" by State legislation, "so far as the same is not inconsistent with the Constitution and laws of the United States." So that over this vast domain of criminal jurisprudence provided by each State for the protection of its own citizens and for the punishment of all persons who violate its criminal laws, Federal law, whenever it can be made to apply, displaces State law. The question here naturally arises, from what source Congress derives the power to transfer to Federal tribunals certain classes of cases embraced in this section. The Constitution expressly declares that the judicial power of the United States "shall extend to all cases, in law and equity, arising under this Constitution, the laws of the United States, and treaties made or which shall be made under their authority; to all cases affecting ambassadors, other public ministers, and consuls; to all cases of admiralty and maritime jurisdiction; to controversies to which the United States shall be a party; to controversies between two or more States, between a State and citizens of another State, between citizens of different States, between citizens of the same State claiming lands under grants of different States, and between a State, or the citizens thereof, and foreign states, citizens, or subjects." Here the judicial power of the United States is expressly set forth and defined; and the act of September 24, 1789, establishing the judicial courts of the United States, in conferring upon the Federal courts jurisdiction over cases originating in State tribunals, is careful to confine them to the classes enumerated in the above-recited clause of the Constitution. This section of the bill undoubtedly comprehends cases and authorizes the exercise of powers that are not, by the Constitution, within the jurisdiction of the courts of the United States. To transfer them to those courts would be an exercise of authority well calculated to excite distrust and alarm on the part of all the States, for the bill applies alike to all of them—as well to those that have as to those that have not been engaged in rebellion. . . .

The fourth section of the bill provides that officers and agents of the Freedmen's Bureau shall be empowered to make arrests, and also that other officers may be specially commissioned for that purpose by the President of the United States. It also authorizes circuit courts of the United States and the superior courts of the Territories to appoint, without limitation, commissioners, who are to be charged with the performance of *quasi* judicial duties. The fifth section empowers the commissioners so to be selected by the courts to appoint in writing, under their hands, one or more suitable persons from time to time to execute warrants and other processes described by the bill. These numerous official agents are made to constitute a sort of police, in addition to the military, and are authorized to summon a *posse comitatus,* and even to call to their aid such portion of the land and naval forces of the United States, or of the militia, "as may be necessary to the performance of the duty with which they are charged." This extraordinary power is to be conferred upon agents irresponsible to the Government and to the people, to whose number the discretion of the commissioners is the only limit, and in whose hands such authority might be made a terrible engine of wrong, oppression, and fraud. The general statutes regulating the land and naval forces of the United States, the militia, and the execution of the laws are believed to be adequate for every emergency which can occur in time of peace. If it should prove otherwise, Congress can at any time amend those laws in such manner as, while subserving the public welfare, not to jeopard the rights, interests, and liberties of the people. . . .

The ninth section authorizes the President, or such person as he may empower for that purpose, "to employ such part of the land or naval forces of the United States, or of the militia, as shall be necessary to prevent the violation and enforce the due execution of this act." This language seems to imply a permanent military force, that is to be always at hand, and whose only business is to be the enforcement of this measure over the vast region where it is intended to operate.

I do not propose to consider the policy of this bill. To me the details of the bill seem fraught with evil. The white race and the black race of the South have hitherto lived together under the relation of master and slave—capital owning labor. Now, suddenly, that relation is changed, and as to ownership capital and labor are divorced. They stand now each master of itself. In this new relation, one being necessary to the other, there will be a new adjustment, which both are deeply interested in making harmonious. Each has equal power in settling the terms, and if left to the laws that regulate capital and labor it is confidently believed that they will satisfactorily work out the problem. Capital, it is true, has more intelligence, but labor is never so ignorant as not to understand its own interests, not to know its own value, and not to see that capital must pay that value.

This bill frustrates this adjustment. It intervenes between capital and labor and attempts to settle questions of political economy through the agency of numerous officials whose interest it will be to foment discord between the two races, for as the breach widens their employment will continue, and when it is closed their occupation will terminate.

In all our history, in all our experience as a people living under Federal and State law, no such system as that contemplated by the details of this bill has ever before been proposed or adopted. They establish for the security of the colored race safeguards which go infinitely beyond any that the General Government has ever provided for the white race. In fact, the distinction of race and color is by the bill made to operate in favor of the colored and against the white race. They interfere with the municipal legislation of the States, with the relations existing exclusively between a State and its citizens, or between inhabitants of the same State—an absorption and assumption of power by the General Government which, if acquiesced in, must sap and destroy our federative system of limited powers and break down the barriers which preserve the rights of the States. It is another step, or rather stride, toward centralization and the concentration of all legislative powers in the National Government. The tendency of the bill must be to resuscitate the spirit of rebellion and to arrest the progress of those influences which are more closely drawing around the States the bonds of union and peace.

113

Ex Parte Milligan (1866)

Lambden P. Milligan had been sentenced to death by an army court in Indiana for allegedly disloyal activities. His attorney appealed for his release under the 1863 Habeas Corpus Act, and the circuit court divided over whether local federal courts had jurisdiction of appeals from military tribunals. Although only a procedural issue, the case gave the Court—now that the fighting was over—a chance to comment on the limits of governmental war powers. In what many people hail as a landmark in constitutional protection of civil rights, the Court ruled that military rule could not supersede the civil courts in areas where the

Source: 4 Wallace 2 (1866).

civil courts remained open and operational. In its own time the case primarily raised issues of congressional power to establish a reconstruction policy, and because with the exception of Japanese-Americans in World War II there have been no military internments in this country, *Milligan* has had limited value as a precedent. Nonetheless, the case belies traditional views of a supine Court during this era, and it also provided a useful limit on military power in civilian affairs. Southern sympathizers hoped, in vain, that the case meant the Court would act to limit federal authority in reconstruction.

See C. Fairman, *Reconstruction and Reunion, 1864–1888: Part One* (1971); S. I. Kutler, *Judicial Power and Reconstruction Politics* (1968); and S. Klaus, ed., *Milligan's Case* (1929).

~~~~~~

Justice Davis delivered the opinion of the Court.

On the 10th day of May, 1865, Lambden P. Milligan presented a petition to the Circuit Court of the United States for the District of Indiana, to be discharged from an alleged unlawful imprisonment. . . .

Milligan insists that said military commission had no jurisdiction to try him upon the charges preferred, or upon any charges whatever; because he was a citizen of the United States and the State of Indiana, and had not been, since the commencement of the late Rebellion, a resident of any of the States whose citizens were arrayed against the government, and that the right of trial by jury was guaranteed to him by the Constitution of the United States. . . .

The importance of the main question presented by this record cannot be overstated; for it involves the very framework of the government and the fundamental principles of American liberty.

During the late wicked Rebellion, the temper of the times did not allow that calmness in deliberation and discussion so necessary to a correct conclusion of a purely judicial question. *Then,* considerations of safety were mingled with the exercise of power; and feelings and interests prevailed which are happily terminated. *Now* that the public safety is assured, this question, as well as all others, can be discussed and decided without passion or the admixture of any element not required to form a legal judgment. We approach the investigation of this case, fully sensible of the magnitude of the inquiry and the necessity of full and cautious deliberation. . . .

The controlling question in the case is this: Upon the *facts* stated in Milligan's petition, and the exhibits filed, had the military commission mentioned in it *jurisdiction,* legally, to try and sentence him? Milligan, not a resident of one of the rebellious states, or a prisoner of war, but a citizen of Indiana for twenty years past, and never in the military or naval service, is, while at his home, arrested by the military power of the United States, imprisoned, and, on certain criminal charges preferred against him, tried, convicted, and sentenced to be hanged by a military commission, organized under the direction of the military commander of the military district of Indiana. Had this tribunal the *legal* power and authority to try and punish this man?

No graver question was ever considered by this court, nor one which more nearly concerns the rights of the whole people; for it is the birthright of every American citizen when charged with crime, to be tried and punished according to law. The power of punishment is, alone through the means which the laws have provided for that purpose, and if they are ineffectual, there is an immunity from punishment, no matter how great an offender the individual may be, or how much his crimes may have shocked the sense of justice of the country, or endangered its safety. By the protection of the law human rights are secured; withdraw that protection, and they are at the mercy of wicked rulers, or the clamor of an excited people. If there was law to justify this military trial, it is not our province to interfere; if there was not, it is our duty to declare the nullity of the whole proceedings. The decision of this question does not depend on argument or judicial precedents, numerous and highly illustrative as they are. These precedents inform us of the extent of the struggle to preserve liberty and to relieve those in civil life from military trials. The founders of our government were familiar with the history of that struggle; and secured in a written constitution every right which the people had wrested from power during a contest of ages. By that Constitution and the laws authorized by it this question must be determined. The provisions of that instrument on the administration of criminal justice are too plain and direct, to leave room for misconstruction or doubt of their true meaning. Those applicable to this case are found in that clause of the original Constitution which says, "That the trial of all crimes, except in case of impeachment, shall be by jury"; and in the fourth, fifth, and sixth articles of the amendments. . . .

Have any of the rights guaranteed by the Constitution been violated in the case of Milligan? and if so, what are they?

Every trial involves the exercise of judicial power; and from what source did the military commission that tried him derive their authority? Certainly no part of the judicial power of the country was conferred on them; because the Constitution expressly vests it "in one supreme court and such inferior courts as the Congress may from time to time ordain and establish," and it is not pretended that the commission was a court ordained and established by Congress. They cannot justify on the mandate of the President; because he is controlled by law, and has his appropriate sphere of duty, which is to execute, not to make, the laws; and there is "no unwritten criminal code to which resort can be had as a source of jurisdiction."

But it is said that the jurisdiction is complete under the "laws and usages of war."

It can serve no useful purpose to inquire what those laws and usages are, whence they originated, where found, and on whom they operate; they can never be applied to citizens in states which have upheld the authority of the government, and where the courts are open and their process unobstructed. This court has judicial knowledge that in Indiana the Federal authority was always unopposed, and its courts always open to hear criminal accusations and redress grievances; and no usage of war could sanction a military trial there for any offence whatever of a citizen in civil life, in nowise connected with the military service. Congress could grant no such power; and to the honor of our national legislature be it said, it has never been provoked by the state of the country even to attempt its exercise. One of the plainest constitutional provisions was, therefore, infringed when Milligan was tried by a court not ordained and established by Congress, and not composed of judges appointed during good behavior. . . .

It is claimed that martial law covers with its broad mantle the proceedings of this military commission. The proposition is this: that in a time of war the commander of an armed force (if in his opinion the exigencies of the country demand it, and of which he is to judge), has the power, within the lines of his military district, to suspend all civil rights and their remedies, and subject citizens as well as soldiers to the rule of *his will;* and in the exercise of his lawful authority cannot be restrained, except by his superior officer or the President of the United States.

If this position is sound to the extent claimed, then when war exists, foreign or domestic, and the country is subdivided into military departments for mere convenience, the commander of one of them can, if he chooses, within his limits, on the plea of necessity, with the approval of the Executive, substitute military force for and to the exclusion of the laws, and punish all persons, as he thinks right and proper, without fixed or certain rules.

The statement of this proposition shows its importance; for, if true, republican government is a failure, and there is an end of liberty regulated by law. Martial law, established on such a basis, destroys every guarantee of the Constitution, and effectually renders the "military independent of and superior to the civil power"—the attempt to do which by the King of Great Britain was deemed by our fathers such an offence, that they assigned it to the world as one of the causes which impelled them to declare their independence. Civil liberty and this kind of martial law cannot endure together; the antagonism is irreconcilable; and, in the conflict, one or the other must perish.

This nation, as experience has proved, cannot always remain at peace, and has no right to expect that it will always have wise and humane rulers, sincerely attached to the principles of the Constitution. Wicked men, ambitious of power, with hatred of liberty and contempt of law, may fill the place once occupied by Washington and Lincoln; and if this right is conceded, and the calamities of war again befall us, the dangers to human liberty are frightful to contemplate. If our fathers had failed to provide for just such a contingency, they would have been false to the trust reposed in them. They knew—the history of the world told them—the nation they were founding, be its existence short or long, would be involved in war; how often or how long continued, human foresight could not tell; and that unlimited power, wherever lodged at such a time, was especially hazardous to freemen. For this, and other equally weighty reasons, they secured the inheritance they had fought to maintain, by incorporating in a written constitution the safeguards which *time* had proved were essential to its preservation. Not one of these safeguards can the President, or Congress, or the Judiciary disturb, except the one concerning the writ of *habeas corpus.*

It is essential to the safety of every government that, in a great crisis, like the one we have just passed through, there should be a power somewhere of suspending the writ of *habeas corpus.* In every war, there are men of previously good character, wicked enough to counsel their fellow-citizens to resist the measures deemed necessary by a good government to sustain its just authority and overthrow its enemies; and their influence may lead to dangerous combinations. In the emergency of the times, an immediate public investigation according to law may not be possible; and yet, the peril to the country may be too imminent to suffer such persons to go at large. Unquestionably, there is then an exigency which demands that the government, if it should see fit in the exercise of a proper discretion to make arrests, should not be required to produce the persons arrested in answer to a writ of *habeas corpus.* The Constitution goes no further. It does not say after a writ of *habeas corpus* is denied a citizen, that he shall be tried otherwise than by the course of the common law; if it had intended this result, it was easy by the use of direct words to have accomplished it. The illustrious men who framed that instrument were guarding the foundations of civil liberty against the abuses of unlimited power; they were full of wisdom, and the lessons of history informed them that a trial by an established court, assisted by an impartial jury, was the only sure way of protecting the citizen against oppression and wrong. Knowing this, they limited the suspension to one great right, and left the rest to remain forever inviolable. But, it is insisted that the safety of the country in time of war demands that this broad claim for martial law shall be sustained. If this were true, it could be well said that a country, preserved at the sacrifice of all the cardinal principles of liberty, is not worth the cost of preservation. Happily, it is not so.

It will be borne in mind that this is not a question of the power to proclaim martial law, when war exists in a community and the courts and civil authorities are overthrown. Nor is it a question what rule a military commander, at the head of his army, can impose on states in rebellion to cripple their resources and quell the insurrection. The jurisdiction claimed is much more extensive. The necessities of the service, during the late Rebellion, required that the loyal states should be placed within the limits of certain military districts and commanders appointed in them; and, it is urged, that this, in a military sense, constituted them the theatre of military operations; and, as in this case, Indiana had been and was again threatened with invasion by the enemy, the occasion was furnished to establish martial law. The conclusion does not follow from the premises. If armies were collected in Indiana, they were to be employed in another locality, where the laws were obstructed and the national authority disputed. On *her* soil there was no hostile foot; if once invaded, that invasion was at an end, and with it all pretext for martial law.

Martial law cannot arise from a *threatened* invasion. The necessity must be actual and present; the invasion real, such as effectually closes the courts and deposes the civil administration.

It is difficult to see how the *safety* of the country required martial law in Indiana. If any of her citizens were plotting treason, the power of arrest could secure them, until the government was prepared for their trial, when the courts were open and ready to try them. It was as easy to protect witnesses before a civil as a military tribunal; and as there could be no wish to convict, except on sufficient legal evidence, surely an ordained and established court was better able to judge of this than a military tribunal composed of gentlemen not trained to the profession of the law.

It follows, from what has been said on this subject, that there are occasions when martial rule can be properly applied. If, in foreign invasion or civil war, the courts are actually closed, and it is impossible to administer criminal justice according to law, *then,* on the theatre of active military operations, where war really prevails, there is a necessity to furnish a substitute for the civil authority, thus overthrown, to preserve the safety of the army and society; and as no power is left but the military, it is allowed to govern by martial rule until the laws can have their free course. As necessity creates the rule, so it limits its duration; for, if this government is continued *after* the courts are reinstated, it is a gross usurpation of power. Martial rule can never exist where the courts are open, and in the proper and unobstructed exercise of their jurisdiction. It is also confined to the locality of actual war.

114

Articles of Impeachment (1867)

Republicans in Congress did not impeach Andrew Johnson because of his removal of Secretary of War Stanton, although that would appear to be the most serious of their charges. They sought to remove him

---

Source: Richardson, ed., 6 *Messages and Papers of the Presidents* 405 (1897).

because of political misfeasance in office and because he refused to work with them in an effort to develop a coherent reconstruction policy. They failed in their effort because the House managers of the Senate trial proved incompetent. The impeachment raised several constitutional questions that remain unresolved. Does the Constitution provide impeachment as a political device, or can it be invoked only for criminal offenses? What is the meaning of "high crimes and misdemeanors"? Is there a definitive original intent, or did the Framers intend impeachment as a flexible tool to be shaped according to particular circumstances? Certainly the Articles of Impeachment against Andrew Johnson do not strike the modern reader as so terrible, and they do not convey the sense of governmental stalemate that invoked them.

See R. Berger, *Impeachment: The Constitutional Problem* (1973); P. C. Hoffer and N. E. H. Hull, *Impeachment in America, 1635–1805* (1984); M. L. Benedict, *The Impeachment and Trial of Andrew Johnson* (1973); and H. L. Trefousse, *Impeachment of a President* (1975).

~~~~~~

Article I.   That said Andrew Johnson, President of the United States, on the 21st day of February, A. D. 1868, at Washington, in the District of Columbia, unmindful of the high duties of his office, of his oath of office, and of the requirement of the Constitution that he should take care that the laws be faithfully executed, did unlawfully and in violation of the Constitution and laws of the United States issue an order in writing for the removal of Edwin M. Stanton from the office of Secretary for the Department of War, said Edwin M. Stanton having been theretofore duly appointed and commissioned, by and with the advice and consent of the Senate of the United States, as such Secretary; and said Andrew Johnson, President of the United States, on the 12th day of August, A. D. 1867, and during the recess of said Senate, having suspended by his order Edwin M. Stanton from said office, and within twenty days after the first day of the next meeting of said Senate—that is to say, on the 12th day of December, in the year last aforesaid—having reported to said Senate such suspension, with the evidence and reasons for his action in the case and the name of the person designated to perform the duties of such office temporarily until the next meeting of the Senate; and said Senate thereafterwards, on the 13th day of January, A. D. 1868, having duly considered the evidence and reasons reported by said Andrew Johnson for said suspension, and having refused to concur in said suspension, whereby and by force of the provisions of an act entitled "An act regulating the tenure of certain civil offices," passed March 2, 1867, said Edwin M. Stanton did forthwith resume the functions of his office, whereof the said Andrew Johnson had then and there due notice; and said Edwin M. Stanton, by reason of the premises, on said 21st day of February, being lawfully entitled to hold said office of Secretary for the Department of War; which said order for the removal of said Edwin M. Stanton . . . was unlawfully issued with intent then and there to violate the act entitled "An act regulating the tenure of certain civil offices," passed March 2, 1867, and with the further intent, contrary to the provisions of said act, in violation thereof, and contrary to the provisions of the Constitution of the United States, and without the advice and consent of the Senate of the United States, the said Senate then and there being in session, to remove said Edwin M. Stanton from the office of Secretary for the Department of War, the said Edwin M. Stanton being then and there Secretary for the Department of War, and being then and there in the due and lawful execution and discharge of the duties of said office; whereby said Andrew Johnson, President of the United States, did then and there commit and was guilty of a high misdemeanor in office. . . .

Article III.   That said Andrew Johnson, President of the United States, on the 21st day of February, A. D. 1868, at Washington, in the District of Columbia, did commit and was guilty of a high misdemeanor in office in this, that without authority of law, while the Senate of the United States was then and there in session, he did appoint one Lorenzo Thomas to be Secretary for the Department of War *ad interim,* without the advice and consent of the Senate, and with intent to violate the Constitution of the United States, no vacancy having happened in said office of Secretary for the Department of War during the recess of the Senate, and no vacancy existing in said office at the time, and which said appointment, so made by said Andrew Johnson, of said Lorenzo Thomas. . . .

Article IV.   That said Andrew Johnson, President of the United States, unmindful of the high duties of his office and his oath of office, in violation of the Constitution and laws of the United States, on the 21st day of February, A. D. 1868, at Washington, in the District of Columbia, did unlawfully conspire with one Lorenzo Thomas, and with other persons to the House of Representatives unknown, with intent, by intimidation and threats, unlawfully to hinder and prevent Edwin M. Stanton, then and there the Secretary for the Department of War, duly appointed under the laws of the United States, from holding said office of Secretary for the Department of War, contrary to and in violation of the Constitution of the United States and of the provisions of an act entitled "An act to define and punish certain conspiracies," approved July 31, 1861; whereby said Andrew Johnson, President of the United States, did then and there commit and was guilty of a high crime in office. . . .

Article IX.   That said Andrew Johnson, President of the United States, on the 22d day of February, A. D. 1868, at Washington, in the District of Columbia, in disregard of the Constitution and the laws of the United States duly enacted, as Commander in Chief of the Army of the United States, did bring before himself then and there William H. Emory, a major-general by brevet in the Army of the United States, actually in command of the Department of Washington and the military forces thereof, and did then and there, as such Commander in Chief, declare to and instruct said Emory that part of a law of the United States, passed March 2, 1867, entitled "An act making appropriations for the support of the Army for the year ending June 30, 1868, and for other purposes," especially the second section thereof, which provides, among other things, that "all orders and instructions relating to military operations issued by the President or Secretary of War shall be issued through the General of the Army, and in case of his inability through the next in rank," was unconstitutional and in contravention of the commission of said Emory, and which said provision of law had been theretofore duly and legally promulgated by general order for the government and direction of the Army of the United States, as the said Andrew Johnson then and there well knew, with intent thereby to induce said Emory, in his official capacity as commander of the Department of Washington, to violate the provisions of said act and to take and receive, act upon, and obey such orders as he, the said Andrew Johnson, might make and give, and which should not be issued through the General of the Army of the United States, according to the provisions of said act, and with the further intent thereby to enable him, the said Andrew Johnson, to prevent the execution of the act entitled "An act regulating the tenure of certain civil offices," passed March 2, 1867, and to unlawfully prevent Edwin M. Stanton, then being Secretary for the Department of War, from holding said office and discharging the duties thereof; whereby said Andrew Johnson, President of the United States, did then and there commit and was guilty of a high misdemeanor in office.

And the House of Representatives, by protestation, saving to themselves the liberty of exhibiting at any time hereafter any further articles or other accusation or impeachment against the said Andrew Johnson, President of the United States, and also of replying to his answers which he shall make unto the articles herein preferred against him, and of offering proof to the same, and every part thereof, and to all and every other article, accusation, or impeachment which shall be exhibited by them, as the case shall require, *do demand* that the said Andrew Johnson may be put to answer the high crimes and misdemeanors in office herein charged against him and that such proceedings, examinations, trials, and judgments may be thereupon had and given as may be agreeable to law and justice. . . .

The following additional articles of impeachment were agreed to, viz:

Article X.   That said Andrew Johnson, President of the United States, unmindful of the high duties of his office and the dignity and proprieties thereof, and of the harmony and courtesies which ought to exist and be maintained between the executive and legislative branches of the Government of the United States, designing and intending to set aside the rightful

authority and powers of Congress, did attempt to bring into disgrace, ridicule, hatred, contempt, and reproach the Congress of the United States and
the several branches thereof, to impair and destroy the regard and respect
of all the good people of the United States for the Congress and legislative
power thereof (which all officers of the Government ought inviolably to
preserve and maintain), and to excite the odium and resentment of all the
good people of the United States against Congress and the laws by it duly
and constitutionally enacted; and, in pursuance of his said design and intent,
openly and publicly, and before divers assemblages of the citizens of the
United States, convened in divers parts thereof to meet and receive said
Andrew Johnson as the Chief Magistrate of the United States, did, on the
18th day of August, A. D. 1866, and on divers other days and times, as well
before as afterwards, make and deliver with a loud voice certain intemperate,
inflammatory, and scandalous harangues, and did therein utter loud threats
and bitter menaces, as well against Congress as the laws of the United States,
duly enacted thereby, amid the cries, jeers, and laughter of the multitudes
then assembled and in hearing, which are set forth in the several specifica-
tions hereinafter written in substance and effect.

115

Ex Parte McCardle
(1868)

Congressional Republicans both during the war and afterward worried
that the Supreme Court would find the expanded exercise of federal
powers unconstitutional, and they received little solace in the narrow
margins of those cases upholding the government. In order to prevent
the Court from striking down their reconstruction program, congressional leaders explored ways to limit the Court's jurisdiction and found
their answer in the so-called Exception Clause (Article III, Section 2).
McCardle, which raised issues similar to those raised in *Milligan* (Document 113), was played out against a background of Congress repealing
certain parts of the 1867 Habeas Corpus Act to deny the Court jurisdic-

Source: 6 Wallace 318 (1868).

tion in such suits. The Court delayed arguments until Congress had acted and then ruled that it had no jurisdiction. For years the case has been cited as an example of judicial impotence during Reconstruction (see, however, Document 116).

See C. Fairman, *Reconstruction and Reunion, 1864–1888: Part One* (1971); S. I. Kutler, *Judicial Power and Reconstruction Politics* (1968); R. J. Kaczorowski, *The Politics of Judicial Interpretation . . .* (1985); and W. Wiecek, "The Great Writ and Reconstruction: The Habeas Corpus Act of 1867," 36 *J.S.H.* 530 (1970).

***

Chief Justice Chase delivered the opinion of the Court

The motion to dismiss the appeal has been thoroughly argued, and we are now to dispose of it.

The ground assigned for the motion is want of jurisdiction, in this court, of appeals from the judgments of inferior courts in cases of *habeas corpus.*

Whether this objection is sound or otherwise depends upon the construction of the act of 1867.

Prior to the passage of that act this court exercised appellate jurisdiction over the action of inferior courts by *habeas corpus. . . .*

But, though the exercise of appellate jurisdiction over judgments of inferior tribunals was not unknown to the practice of this court before the act of 1867, it was attended by some inconvenience and embarrassment. It was necessary to use the writ of *certiorari* in addition to the writ of *habeas corpus,* and there was no regulated and established practice for the guidance of parties invoking the jurisdiction.

This inconvenience and embarrassment was remedied in a small class of cases arising from commitments for acts done or omitted under alleged authority of foreign governments, by the act of August 29th, 1842, which authorized a direct appeal from any judgment upon *habeas corpus* of a justice of this court or judge of a District Court to the Circuit Court of the proper district, and from the judgment of the Circuit Court to this court.

This provision for appeal was transferred, with some modification, from the act of 1842 to the act of 1867; and the first question we are to consider, upon the construction of that act, is whether this right of appeal extends to all cases of *habeas corpus,* or only to a particular class.

It was insisted on argument that appeals to this court are given by the act only from the judgments of the Circuit Court rendered upon appeals to that court from decisions of a single judge, or of a District Court.

The words of the act are these: "From the final decision of any judge, justice, or court inferior to the Circuit Court, an appeal may be taken to the Circuit Courts of the United States for the district in which said cause is heard, and from the judgment of said Circuit Court to the Supreme Court of the United States."

These words, considered without reference to the other provisions of the act, are not unsusceptible of the construction put upon them at the bar; but that construction can hardly be reconciled with other parts of the act.

The first section gives to the several courts of the United States, and the several justices and judges of such courts within their respective jurisdictions, in addition to the authority already conferred by law, power to grant writs of *habeas corpus* in all cases where any person may be restrained of liberty in violation of the Constitution, or of any treaty or law of the United States.

This legislation is of the most comprehensive character. It brings within the *habeas corpus* jurisdiction of every court and of every judge every possible case of privation of liberty contrary to the National Constitution, treaties, or laws. It is impossible to widen this jurisdiction.

And it is to this jurisdiction that the system of appeals is applied. From decisions of a judge or of a District Court appeals lie to the Circuit Court, and from the judgment of the Circuit Court to this court. But each Circuit Court, as well as each District Court, and each judge, may exercise the original jurisdiction; and no satisfactory reason can be assigned for giving appeals to this court from the judgments of the Circuit Court rendered on appeal, and not giving like appeals from judgments of Circuit Courts rendered in the exercise of original jurisdiction. If any class of cases was to be excluded from the right of appeal, the exclusion would naturally apply to cases brought into the Circuit Court by appeal rather than to cases originating there. In the former description of cases the petitioner for the writ, without appeal to this court, would have the advantage of at least two hearings, while in the latter, upon the hypothesis of no appeal, the petitioner could have but one.

These considerations seem to require the construction that the right of appeal attaches equally to all judgments of the Circuit Court, unless there be something in the clause defining the appellate jurisdiction which demands the restricted interpretation. The mere words of that clause may admit either, but the spirit and purpose of the law can only be satisfied by the former.

We entertain no doubt, therefore, that an appeal lies to this court from the judgment of the Circuit Court in the case before us.

Another objection to the jurisdiction of this court on appeal was drawn from the clause of the first section, which declares that the jurisdiction defined by it is "in addition to the authority already conferred by law."

This objection seems to be an objection to the jurisdiction of the Circuit Court over the cause rather than to the jurisdiction of this court on appeal.

The latter jurisdiction, as has just been shown, is coextensive with the former. Every question of substance which the Circuit Court could decide upon the return of the *habeas corpus,* including the question of its own jurisdiction, may be revised here on appeal from its final judgment.

But an inquiry on this motion into the jurisdiction of the Circuit Court would be premature. It would extend to the merits of the cause in that court; while the question before us upon this motion to dismiss must be necessarily limited to our jurisdiction on appeal. . . .

We are satisfied, as we have already said, that we have such jurisdiction under the act of 1867, and the motion to dismiss must therefore be

DENIED.

116

~~~~~~

Ex Parte Yerger (1869)

The Court heard the *Yerger* case two months after it ruled in *McCardle,* and once again we see the issue of the Court's jurisdiction. If *McCardle* is depicted as indicative of timidity on the part of the justices, then *Yerger* must be seen as its exact opposite, an outspoken assertion of judicial authority. Chief Justice Chase had hinted in the earlier case that the Court's appellate jurisdiction in habeas corpus did not derive from the 1867 act, but from the Judiciary Act of 1789. The only way to square the two cases is to acknowledge the political sensitivity of the justices to the tangled emotions of the time. In *McCardle,* the Court thought it best to retreat temporarily and avoid a confrontation with Congress. In *Yerger,* where the facts were somewhat different, a unanimous Court reasserted its authority, and placed limits on how far Congress could go under the Exceptions Clause.

See items listed for previous document.

~~~~~~

Chief Justice Chase delivered the opinion of the Court.

The argument, by the direction of the court, was confined to the single point of the jurisdiction of the court to issue the writ prayed for. We have carefully considered the reasonings which have been addressed to us, and I am now to state the conclusions to which we have come.

———

Source: 8 Wallace 85 (1869)

The general question of jurisdiction in this case resolves itself necessarily into two other questions:

1.   Has the court jurisdiction, in a case like the present, to inquire into the cause of detention, alleged to be unlawful, and to give relief, if the detention be found to be in fact unlawful, by the writ of *habeas corpus,* under the Judiciary Act of 1789?

2.   If, under that act, the court possessed this jurisdiction, has it been taken away by the second section of the act of March, 27, 1868, repealing so much of the act of February 5, 1867, as authorizes appeals from Circuit Courts to the Supreme Court?

Neither of these questions is new here. The first has, on several occasions, received very full consideration, and very deliberate judgment. . . .

. . . The first Congress under the Constitution, after defining, by various sections of the act of September 24, 1789, the jurisdiction of the District Courts, the Circuit Courts, and the Supreme Court in other cases, proceeded, in the 14th section, to enact, "that all the before-mentioned courts of the United States shall have power to issue writs of *scire facias, habeas corpus,* and all other writs, not specially provided by statute, which may be necessary for the exercise of their respective jurisdictions, and agreeable to the principles and usages of law." In the same section, it was further provided "that either of the Justices of the Supreme Court, as well as Judges of the District Courts, shall have power to grant writs of *habeas corpus* for the purpose of an inquiry into the cause of commitment; provided that writs of *habeas corpus* shall in no case extend to prisoners in jail, unless they are in custody, under, or by color of the authority of the United States, or are committed for trial before some court of the same, or are necessary to be brought into court to testify."

That this court is one of the courts to which the power to issue writs of *habeas corpus* is expressly given by the terms of this section has never been questioned. It would have been, indeed, a remarkable anomaly if this court, ordained by the Constitution for the exercise, in the United States, of the most important powers in civil cases of all the highest courts of England, had been denied, under a constitution which absolutely prohibits the suspension of the writ, except under extraordinary exigencies, that power in cases of alleged unlawful restraint, which the Habeas Corpus Act of Charles II expressly declares those courts to possess.

But the power vested in this court is, in an important particular, unlike that possessed by the English courts. The jurisdiction of this court is conferred by the Constitution, and is appellate; whereas, that of the English courts, though declared and defined by statutes, is derived from the common law, and is original. . . .

The doctrine of the Constitution and of the cases thus far may be summed up in these propositions:

(1.)   The original jurisdiction of this court cannot be extended by Congress to any other cases than those expressly defined by the Constitution.

(2.)   The appellate jurisdiction of this court, conferred by the Constitution, extends to all other cases within the judicial power of the United States.

(3.)   This appellate jurisdiction is subject to such exceptions, and must be exercised under such regulations as Congress, in the exercise of its discretion, has made or may see fit to make.

(4.)   Congress not only has not excepted writs of *habeas corpus* and *mandamus* from this appellate jurisdiction, but has expressly provided for the exercise of this jurisdiction by means of these writs.

We come, then, to consider the first great question made in the case now before us.

We shall assume, upon the authority of the decisions referred to, what we should hold were the question now for the first time presented to us, that in a proper case this court, under the act of 1789, and under all the subsequent acts, giving jurisdiction in cases of *habeas corpus,* may, in the exercise of its appellate power, revise the decisions of inferior courts of the United States, and relieve from unlawful imprisonment authorized by them, except in cases within some limitations of the jurisdiction by Congress.

It remains to inquire whether the case before us is a proper one for such interposition. Is it within any such limitation? In other words, can this court inquire into the lawfulness of detention, and relieve from it if found unlawful, when the detention complained of is not by civil authority under a commitment made by an inferior court, but by military officers, for trial before a military tribunal, after an examination into the cause of detention by the inferior court, resulting in an order remanding the prisoner to custody?

It was insisted in argument that, "to bring a case within the appellate jurisdiction of this court in the sense requisite to enable it to award the writ of *habeas corpus* under the Judiciary Act, it is necessary that the commitment should appear to have been by a tribunal whose decisions are subject to revision by this court." . . .

But it is unnecessary to enter upon this inquiry here. The action which we are asked to revise was that of a tribunal whose decisions are subject to revision by this court in ordinary modes.

We need consider, therefore, only the second branch of the proposition, namely, that the action of the inferior court must have resulted in a commitment for trial in a civil court; and the inference drawn from it, that no relief can be had here, by *habeas corpus,* from imprisonment under military authority, to which the petitioner may have been remanded by such a court.

This proposition certainly is not supported by authority. . . .

The great and leading intent of the Constitution and the law must be kept constantly in view upon the examination of every question of construction.

That intent, in respect to the writ of *habeas corpus,* is manifest. It is that every citizen may be protected by judicial action from unlawful imprisonment. To this end the act of 1789 provided that every court of the United States should have power to issue the writ. The jurisdiction thus given in law to the Circuit and District Courts is original; that given by the Constitution and the law to this court is appellate. Given in general terms, it must necessarily extend to all cases to which the judicial power of the United States extends, other than those expressly excepted from it.

As limited by the act of 1789, it did not extend to cases of imprisonment after conviction, under sentences of competent tribunals; nor to prisoners in jail, unless in custody under or by color of the authority of the United States; or committed for trial before some court of the United States, or required to be brought into court to testify. But this limitation has been gradually narrowed, and the benefits of the writ have been extended, first in 1833, to prisoners confined under any authority, whether State or National, for any act done or omitted in pursuance of a law of the United States, or of any order, process, or decree of any judge or court of the United States; then in 1842 to prisoners being subjects or citizens of foreign States, in custody under National or State authority for acts done or omitted by or under color of foreign authority, and alleged to be valid under the law of nations; and finally, in 1867, to all cases where any person may be restrained of liberty in violation of the Constitution, or of any treaty or law of the United States.

This brief statement shows how the general spirit and genius of our institutions has tended to the widening and enlarging of the *habeas corpus* jurisdiction of the courts and judges of the United States; and this tendency, except in one recent instance, has been constant and uniform; and it is in the light of it that we must determine the true meaning of the Constitution and the law in respect to the appellate jurisdiction of this court. We are not at liberty to except from it any cases not plainly excepted by law; and we think it sufficiently appears from what has been said that no exception to this jurisdiction embraces such a case as that now before the court. On the contrary, the case is one of those expressly declared not to be excepted from the general grant of jurisdiction. For it is a case of imprisonment alleged to be unlawful, and to be under color of authority of the United States. . . .

We are obliged to hold, therefore, that in all cases where a Circuit Court of the United States has, in the exercise of its original jurisdiction, caused a prisoner to be brought before it, and has, after inquiring into the cause of detention, remanded him to the custody from which he was taken, this court, in the exercise of its appellate jurisdiction, may, by the writ of *habeas corpus,* aided by the writ of *certiorari,* revise the decision of the Circuit Court, and if it be found unwarranted by law, relieve the prisoner from the unlawful restraint to which he has been remanded.

This conclusion brings us to the inquiry whether the 2d section of the act of March 27th, 1868, takes away or affects the appellate jurisdiction of this court under the Constitution and the acts of Congress prior to 1867.

In *McCardle's case,* we expressed the opinion that it does not, and we have now re-examined the grounds of that opinion.

The circumstances under which the act of 1868 was passed were peculiar. . . .

It is quite clear that the words of the act reach, not only all appeals pending, but all future appeals to this court under the act of 1867; but they appear to be limited to appeals taken under that act.

The words of the repealing section are, "that *so much* of the act approved

February 5th, 1867, as *authorizes* an appeal from the judgment of the Circuit Court to the Supreme Court of the United States, or the exercise of any such jurisdiction by said Supreme Court on appeals which have been, or may be hereafter taken, be, and the same is hereby repealed."

These words are not of doubtful interpretation. They repeal only so much of the act of 1867 as authorized appeals, or the exercise of appellate jurisdiction by this court. They affected only appeals and appellate jurisdiction authorized by that act. They do not purport to touch the appellate jurisdiction conferred by the Constitution, or to except from it any cases not excepted by the act of 1789. They reach no act except the act of 1867.

It has been suggested, however, that the act of 1789, so far as it provided for the issuing of writs of *habeas corpus* by this court, was already repealed by the act of 1867. We have already observed that there are no repealing words in the act of 1867. If it repealed the act of 1789, it did so by implication, and any implication which would give to it this effect upon the act of 1789, would give it the same effect upon the acts of 1833 and 1842. If one was repealed, all were repealed.

Repeals by implication are not favored. They are seldom admitted except on the ground of repugnancy; and never, we think, when the former act can stand together with the new act. It is true that exercise of appellate jurisdiction, under the act of 1789, was less convenient than under the act of 1867, but the provision of a new and more convenient mode of its exercise does not necessarily take away the old; and that this effect was not intended is indicated by the fact that the authority conferred by the new act is expressly declared to be "in addition" to the authority conferred by the former acts. Addition is not substitution. . . .

Our conclusion is, that none of the acts prior to 1867, authorizing this court to exercise appellate jurisdiction by means of the writ of *habeas corpus,* were repealed by the act of that year, and that the repealing section of the act of 1868 is limited in terms, and must be limited in effect to the appellate jurisdiction authorized by the act of 1867.

We could come to no other conclusion without holding that the whole appellate jurisdiction of this court, in cases of *habeas corpus,* conferred by the Constitution, recognized by law, and exercised from the foundation of the government hitherto, has been taken away, without the expression of such intent, and by mere implication, through the operation of the acts of 1867 and 1868.

The suggestion made at the bar, that the provision of the act of 1789, relating to the jurisdiction of this court by *habeas corpus,* if repealed by the effect of the act of 1867, was revived by the repeal of the repealing act, has not escaped our consideration. We are inclined to think that such would be the effect of the act of 1868, but having come to the conclusion that the act of 1789 was not repealed by the act of 1867, it is not necessary to express an opinion on that point.

The argument having been confined, by direction of the court, to the question of jurisdiction, this opinion is limited to that question. The jurisdiction of the court to issue the writ prayed for is affirmed.

117

Texas v. *White (1869)*

In this case the Court again addressed reconstruction issues, but again indirectly. During the war the Confederate government of Texas had sold prewar Union bonds held in the state treasury to defray the cost of the war. The new Reconstruction government now sued the subsequent bondholders to recover the bonds, claiming that the original sale had been void. Chase devoted three-fourths of his opinion to the jurisdictional issue—whether such a question could come before a federal court—and in doing so he gave the Court's only extended disquisition on the nature of statehood and what had happened to the states constitutionally during the war. In a memorable phrase, he declared that "The Constitution, in all its provisions, looks to an indestructible Union, composed of indestructible States," but he then explored how the states had left their proper orbit during the rebellion.

See W. W. Pierson, Jr., "Texas *versus* White," 18 *S.W. His. Q.* 341, 19 *idem* 1, 142 (1915); J. J. Templin, "Texas *v.* White . . ." 6 *Sw.L.J.* 467 (1952).

Chief Justice Chase delivered the opinion of the Court.

This is an original suit in this court, in which the State of Texas, claiming certain bonds of the United States as her property, asks an injunction to restrain the defendants from receiving payment from the National government, and to compel the surrender of the bonds to the State. . . .

Source: 7 Wallace 700 (1869).

The first inquiries to which our attention was directed by counsel, arose upon the allegations of the answer of Chiles (1), that no sufficient authority is shown for the prosecution of the suit in the name and on the behalf of the State of Texas; and (2) that the State, having severed her relations with a majority of the States of the Union, and having by her ordinance of secession attempted to throw off her allegiance to the Constitution and government of the United States, has so far changed her status as to be disabled from prosecuting suits in the National courts.

The first of these allegations is disproved by the evidence. . . .

The other allegation presents a question of jurisdiction. It is not to be questioned that this court has original jurisdiction of suits by States against citizens of other States, or that the States entitled to invoke this jurisdiction must be States of the Union. But, it is equally clear that no such jurisdiction has been conferred upon this court of suits by any other political communities than such States.

If, therefore, it is true that the State of Texas was not at the time of filing this bill, or is not now, one of the United States, we have no jurisdiction of this suit, and it is our duty to dismiss it.

We are very sensible of the magnitude and importance of this question, of the interest it excites, and of the difficulty, not to say impossibility, of so disposing of it as to satisfy the conflicting judgments of men equally enlightened, equally upright, and equally patriotic. But we meet it in the case, and we must determine it in the exercise of our best judgment, under the guidance of the Constitution alone.

Some not unimportant aid, however, in ascertaining the true sense of the Constitution, may be derived from considering what is the correct idea of a State, apart from any union or confederation with other States. The poverty of language often compels the employment of terms in quite different significations; and of this hardly any example more signal is to be found than in the use of the word we are now considering. It would serve no useful purpose to attempt an enumeration of all the various senses in which it is used. A few only need be noticed.

It describes sometimes a people or community of individuals united more or less closely in political relations, inhabiting temporarily or permanently the same country; often it denotes only the country or territorial region, inhabited by such a community; not unfrequently it is applied to the government under which the people live; at other times it represents the combined idea of people, territory, and government.

It is not difficult to see that in all these senses the primary conception is that of a people or community. The people, in whatever territory dwelling, either temporarily or permanently, and whether organized under a regular government, or united by looser and less definite relations, constitute the state. . . .

In the Constitution the term state most frequently expresses the combined idea just noticed, of people, territory, and government. A state, in the ordinary sense of the Constitution, is a political community of free citizens, occupying a territory of defined boundaries, and organized under a government sanctioned and limited by a written constitution, and established by the consent of the governed. It is the union of such states, under a common constitution, which forms the distinct and greater political unit, which that Constitution designates as the United States, and makes of the people and states which compose it one people and one country. . . .

It is needless to discuss, at length, the question whether the right of a State to withdraw from the Union for any cause, regarded by herself as sufficient, is consistent with the Constitution of the United States.

The Union of the States never was a purely artificial and arbitrary relation. It began among the Colonies, and grew out of common origin, mutual sympathies, kindred principles, similar interests, and geographical relations. It was confirmed and strengthened by the necessities of war, and received definite form, and character, and sanction from the Articles of Confederation. By these the Union was solemnly declared to "be perpetual." And when these Articles were found to be inadequate to the exigencies of the country, the Constitution was ordained "to form a more perfect Union." It is difficult to convey the idea of indissoluble unity more clearly than by these words. What can be indissoluble if a perpetual Union, made more perfect, is not? . . .

. . . Not only, therefore, can there be no loss of separate and independent autonomy to the States, through their union under the Constitution, but it may be not unreasonably said that the preservation of the States, and the maintenance of their governments, are as much within the design and care of the Constitution as the preservation of the Union and the maintenance of the National government. The Constitution, in all its provisions, looks to an indestructible Union, composed of indestructible States.

When, therefore, Texas became one of the United States, she entered into an indissoluble relation. All the obligations of perpetual union, and all the guaranties of republican government in the Union, attached at once to the State. The act which consummated her admission into the Union was something more than a compact; it was the incorporation of a new member into the political body. And it was final. The union between Texas and the other States was as complete, as perpetual, and as indissoluble as the union between the original States. There was no place for reconsideration, or revocation, except through revolution, or through consent of the States.

Considered therefore as transactions under the Constitution, the ordinance of secession, adopted by the convention and ratified by a majority of the citizens of Texas, and all the acts of her legislature intended to give effect to that ordinance, were absolutely null. They were utterly without operation in law. The obligations of the State, as a member of the Union, and of every citizen of the State, as a citizen of the United States, remained perfect and unimpaired. It certainly follows that the State did not cease to be a State, nor her citizens to be citizens of the Union. If this were otherwise, the State must have become foreign, and her citizens foreigners. The war must have ceased to be a war for the suppression of rebellion, and must have become a war for conquest and subjugation.

Our conclusion therefore is, that Texas continued to be a State, and a State of the Union, notwithstanding the transactions to which we have referred. And this conclusion, in our judgment, is not in conflict with any act or declaration of any department of the National government, but entirely in accordance with the whole series of such acts and declarations since the first outbreak of the rebellion.

But in order to the exercise, by a State, of the right to sue in this court, there needs to be a State government, competent to represent the State in its relations with the National government, so far at least as the institution and prosecution of a suit is concerned.

And it is by no means a logical conclusion, from the premises which we have endeavored to establish, that the governmental relations of Texas to the Union remained unaltered. Obligations often remain unimpaired, while relations are greatly changed. The obligations of allegiance to the State, and of obedience to her laws, subject to the Constitution of the United States, are binding upon all citizens, whether faithful or unfaithful to them; but the relations which subsist while these obligations are performed, are essentially different from those which arise when they are disregarded and set at nought. And the same must necessarily be true of the obligations and relations of States and citizens to the Union. No one has been bold enough to contend that, while Texas was controlled by a government hostile to the United States, and in affiliation with a hostile confederation, waging war upon the United States, senators chosen by her legislature, or representatives elected by her citizens, were entitled to seats in Congress; or that any suit, instituted in her name, could be entertained in this court. All admit that, during this condition of civil war, the rights of the State as a member, and of her people as citizens of the Union, were suspended. The government and the citizens of the State, refusing to recognize their constitutional obligations, assumed the character of enemies, and incurred the consequences of rebellion. . . .

There being then no government in Texas in constitutional relations with the Union, it became the duty of the United States to provide for the restoration of such a government. But the restoration of the government which existed before the rebellion, without a new election of officers, was obviously impossible; and before any such election could be properly held, it was necessary that the old constitution should receive such amendments as would conform its provisions to the new conditions created by emancipation, and afford adequate security to the people of the State.

In the exercise of the power conferred by the guaranty clause, as in the exercise of every other constitutional power, a discretion in the choice of means is necessarily allowed. It is essential only that the means must be necessary and proper for carrying into execution the power conferred, through the restoration of the State to its constitutional relations, under a republican form of government, and that no acts be done, and no authority exerted, which is either prohibited or unsanctioned by the Constitution. . . .

. . . A provisional governor of the State was appointed by the President in 1865; in 1866 a governor was elected by the people under the constitution of that year; at a subsequent date a governor was appointed by the commander of the district. Each of the three exercised executive functions and actually represented the State in the executive department.

In the case before us each has given his sanction to the prosecution of the suit, and we find no difficulty, without investigating the legal title of either to the executive office, in holding that the sanction thus given sufficiently warranted the action of the solicitor and counsel in behalf of the State. The necessary conclusion is that the suit was instituted and is prosecuted by competent authority.

The question of jurisdiction being thus disposed of, we proceed to the consideration of the merits as presented by the pleadings and the evidence.

And the first question to be answered is, whether or not the title of the State to the bonds in controversy was divested by the contract of the military board with White and Chiles?

That the bonds were the property of the State of Texas on the 11th of January, 1862, when the act prohibiting alienation without the endorsement of the governor, was repealed, admits of no question, and is not denied. They came into her possession and ownership through public acts of the general government and of the State, which gave notice to all the world of the transaction consummated by them. And, we think it clear that, if a State, by a public act of her legislature, imposes restrictions upon the alienation of her property, that every person who takes a transfer of such property must be held affected by notice of them. Alienation, in disregard of such restrictions, can convey no title to the alienee.

In this case, however, it is said that the restriction imposed by the act of 1851 was repealed by the act of 1862. And this is true if the act of 1862 can be regarded as valid. But, was it valid?

The legislature of Texas, at the time of the repeal, constituted one of the departments of a State government, established in hostility to the Constitution of the United States. It cannot be regarded, therefore, in the courts of the United States, as a lawful legislature, or its acts as lawful acts. And, yet, it is an historical fact that the government of Texas, then in full control of the State, was its only actual government; and certainly if Texas had been a separate State, and not one of the United States, the new government, having displaced the regular authority, and having established itself in the customary seats of power, and in the exercise of the ordinary functions of administration, would have constituted, in the strictest sense of the words, a *de facto* government, and its acts, during the period of its existence as such, would be effectual, and, in almost all respects, valid. And, to some extent, this is true of the actual government of Texas, though unlawful and revolutionary, as to the United States.

It is not necessary to attempt any exact definitions, within which the acts of such a State government must be treated as valid, or invalid. It may be said, perhaps with sufficient accuracy, that acts necessary to peace and good order among citizens, such for example, as acts sanctioning and protecting marriage and the domestic relations, governing the course of descents, regulating the conveyance and transfer of property, real and personal, and providing remedies for injuries to person and estate, and other similar acts, which would be valid if emanating from a lawful government, must be regarded in general as valid when proceeding from an actual, though unlawful government; and that acts in furtherance or support of rebellion against the United States, or intended to defeat the just rights of citizens, and other acts of like nature, must, in general, be regarded as invalid and void. . . .

. . . We are obliged to say that the enlarged powers of the board appear to us to have been conferred in furtherance of its main purpose, of war against the United States, and that the contract, under consideration, even if made in the execution of these enlarged powers, was still a contract in aid of the rebellion, and, therefore, void. And we cannot shut our eyes to the evidence which proves that the act of repeal was intended to aid rebellion by facilitating the transfer of these bonds. It was supposed, doubtless, that negotiation of them would be less difficult if they bore upon their face no direct evidence of having come from the possession of any insurgent State government. We can give no effect, therefore, to this repealing act.

It follows that the title of the State was not divested by the act of the insurgent government in entering into this contract. . . .

On the whole case, therefore, our conclusion is that the State of Texas is entitled to the relief sought by her bill, and a decree must be made accordingly.

Justice Grier, dissenting.

I regret that I am compelled to dissent from the opinion of the majority of the court on all the points raised and decided in this case.

The first question in order is the jurisdiction of the court to entertain this bill in behalf of the State of Texas.

The original jurisdiction of this court can be invoked only by one of the United States. The Territories have no such right conferred on them by the

Constitution, nor have the Indian tribes who are under the protection of the military authorities of the government.

Is Texas one of these United States? Or was she such at the time this bill was filed, or since?

This is to be decided as *a political fact,* not as a *legal fiction.* This court is bound to know and notice the public history of the nation.

If I regard the truth of history for the last eight years, I cannot discover the State of Texas as one of these United States. . . .

Is Texas a State, now represented by members chosen by the people of that State and received on the floor of Congress? Has she two senators to represent her as a State in the Senate of the United States? Has her voice been heard in the late election of President? Is she not now held and governed as a conquered province by military force? The act of Congress of March 2d, 1867, declares Texas to be a "rebel State," and provides for its government until a legal and republican State government could be legally established. It constituted Louisiana and Texas the fifth military district, and made it subject, not to the civil authority, but to the "military authorities of the United States."

It is true that no organized rebellion now exists there, and the courts of the United States now exercise jurisdiction over the people of that province. But this is no test of the State's being in the Union; Dacotah is no State, and yet the courts of the United States administer justice there as they do in Texas. The Indian tribes, who are governed by military force, cannot claim to be States of the Union. Wherein does the condition of Texas differ from theirs?

Now, by assuming or admitting *as a fact* the present *status* of Texas as a State not in the Union *politically,* I beg leave to protest against any charge of inconsistency as to judicial opinions heretofore expressed as a member of this court, or silently assented to. I do not consider myself bound to express any opinion judicially as to the constitutional right of Texas to exercise the rights and privileges of a State of this Union, or the power of Congress to govern her as a conquered province, to subject her to military domination, and keep her in pupilage. I can only submit to *the fact* as decided by the political position of the government; and I am not disposed to join in any essay to prove Texas to be a State of the Union, when Congress have decided that she is not. It is a question of fact, I repeat, and of fact only. *Politically,* Texas is not *a State in this Union.* Whether rightfully out of it or not is a question not before the court.

But conceding now the fact to be as judicially assumed by my brethren, the next question is, whether she has a right to repudiate her contracts? Before proceeding to answer this question, we must notice a fact in this case that was forgotten in the argument. I mean that the United States are no party to this suit, and refusing to pay the bonds because the money paid would be used to advance the interests of the rebellion. It is a matter of utter insignificance to the government of the United States to whom she makes the payment of these bonds. They are payable to the bearer. The government is not bound to inquire into the *bonâ fides* of the holder, nor whether the State of Taxes has parted with the bonds wisely or foolishly. And although by the Reconstruction Acts she is required to repudiate all debts contracted for the purposes of the rebellion, this does not annul all acts of the State government during the rebellion, or contracts for other purposes, nor authorize the State to repudiate them.

Now, whether we assume the State of Texas to be judicially in the Union (though actually out of it) or not, it will not alter the case. The contest now is between the State of Texas and her own citizens. She seeks to annul a contract with the respondents, based on the allegation that there was no authority in Texas competent to enter into an agreement during the rebellion. Having relied upon one fiction, namely, that she *is* a State in the Union, she now relies upon a second one, which she wishes this court to adopt, that she was not a State at all during the five years that she was in rebellion. She now sets up the plea of *insanity,* and asks the court to treat all her acts made during the disease as void. . . .

. . . Hardenberg . . . purchased the bonds in open market, *bonâ fide,* and for a full consideration. Now, it is to be observed that these bonds are payable to bearer, and that this court is appealed to as a court of equity. The argument to justify a decree in favor of the commonwealth of Texas as against Hardenberg, is simply this: these bonds, though payable to bearer, are redeemable fourteen years from date. The government has exercised her privilege of paying the interest for a term without redeeming the principal, which gives an additional value to the bonds. *Ergo,* the bonds are dishonored. *Ergo,* the former owner has a right to resume the possession of them, and reclaim them from a *bonâ fide* owner by a decree of a court of equity.

This is the legal argument, when put in the form of a logical sorites, by which Texas invokes our aid to assist her in the perpetration of this great wrong.

A court of chancery is said to be a court of conscience; and however astute may be the argument introduced to *defend* this decree, I can only say that neither my reason nor my conscience can give assent to it.

Justice Swayne

I concur with my brother Grier as to the incapacity of the State of Texas, in her present condition, to maintain an original suit in this court. The question, in my judgment, is one in relation to which this court is bound by the action of the legislative department of the government.

Upon the merits of the case, I agree with the majority of my brethren.

I am authorized to say that my brother Miller unites with me in these views.

Legal Tender Cases
(1871)

To finance the war, the Union had issued enormous amounts of paper money backed only by the credit of the United States. Salmon Chase, Secretary of the Treasury at the time, like most Republicans opposed paper money in principle but had accepted it in practice as a necessity of war. During the fighting the Court had evaded a challenge to the paper money in Roosevelt v. Meyer, 1 Wallace 512 (1863). In February 1870, however, Chase led a four-man majority in striking the paper money down in Hepburn v. Griswold, 8 Wallace 603, a decision widely attacked then and now by legal scholars. President Grant then made two appointments to the Court, and the new justices, William Strong and Joseph Bradley, joined with the dissenters in *Hepburn* in the rehearing of the issue to uphold the government's constitutional power to determine what would pass as legal tender. The following excerpts are, therefore, from the second decision of the Court on the wartime paper money. There have been charges that Grant "packed" the Court to secure this reversal, since the government would have been financially embarrassed had the earlier decision stood. But the sequence of events makes it fairly clear that Grant had determined upon the two men before either he or Congress received word of the *Hepburn* decision.

See G. T. Dunne, "President Grant and Chief Justice Chase: A Footnote to the Legal Tender Cases," 5 *St. Louis Univ. L. J.* 539 (1959); C. Fairman, "Mr. Justice Bradley's Appointment . . . and the Legal Tender Cases," 54 *Harv. L. R.* 977, 1128 (1941); and J. M. Cormack, "The Legal Tender Cases," 16 *Va. L.R.* 132 (1929).

Justice Strong delivered the opinion of the Court

The controlling questions in these cases are the following: Are the acts of Congress, known as the legal tender acts, constitutional when applied to contracts made before their passage; and, secondly, are they valid as applicable to debts contracted since their enactment? These questions have been elaborately argued, and they have received from the court that considera-

---

Source: 12 Wallace 457 (1871).

tion which their great importance demands. It would be difficult to overestimate the consequences which must follow our decision. They will affect the entire business of the country, and take hold of the possible continued existence of the government. If it be held by this court that Congress has no constitutional power, under any circumstances, or in any emergency, to make treasury notes a legal tender for the payment of all debts (a power confessedly possessed by every independent sovereignty other than the United States), the government is without those means of self-preservation which, all must admit, may, in certain contingencies, become indispensable, even if they were not when the acts of Congress now called in question were enacted. It is also clear that if we hold the acts invalid as applicable to debts incurred, or transactions which have taken place since their enactment, our decision must cause, throughout the country, great business derangement, widespread distress, and the rankest injustice. . . . These consequences are too obvious to admit of question. And there is no well-founded distinction to be made between the constitutional validity of an act of Congress declaring treasury notes a legal tender for the payment of debts contracted after its passage and that of an act making them a legal tender for the discharge of all debts, as well those incurred before as those made after its enactment. There may be a difference in the effects produced by the acts, and in the hardship of their operation, but in both cases the fundamental question, that which tests the validity of the legislation, is, can Congress constitutionally give to treasury notes the character and qualities of money? Can such notes be constituted a legitimate circulating medium, having a defined legal value? . . .

The consequences of which we have spoken, serious as they are, must be accepted, if there is a clear incompatibility between the Constitution and the legal tender acts. But we are unwilling to precipitate them upon the country unless such an incompatibility plainly appears. A decent respect for a coordinate branch of the government demands that the judiciary should presume, until the contrary is clearly shown; that there has been no transgression of power by Congress—all the members of which act under the obligation of an oath of fidelity to the Constitution. Such has always been the rule. . . .

Nor can it be questioned that, when investigating the nature and extent of the powers conferred by the Constitution upon Congress, it is indispensable to keep in view the objects for which those powers were granted. This is a universal rule of construction applied alike to statutes, wills, contracts, and constitutions. If the general purpose of the instrument is ascertained, the language of its provisions must be construed with reference to that purpose and so as to subserve it. In no other way can the intent of the framers of the instrument be discovered. . . . The powers conferred upon Congress must be regarded as related to each other, and all means for a common end. Each is but part of a system, a constituent of one whole. No single power is the ultimate end for which the Constitution was adopted. It may, in a very proper sense, be treated as a means for the accomplishment of a subordinate object, but that object is itself a means designed for an ulterior purpose. Thus the power to levy and collect taxes, to coin money and regulate its value, to raise and support armies, or to provide for and maintain a navy, are instruments for the paramount object, which was to establish a government, sovereign within its sphere, with capability of self-preservation, thereby forming a union more perfect than that which existed under the old Confederacy.

The same may be asserted also of all the non-enumerated powers included in the authority expressly given "to make all laws which shall be necessary and proper for carrying into execution the specified powers vested in Congress, and all other powers vested by the Constitution in the government of the United States, or in any department or officer thereof." It is impossible to know what those non-enumerated powers are, and what is their nature and extent, without considering the purposes they were intended to subserve. Those purposes, it must be noted, reach beyond the mere execution of all powers definitely entrusted to Congress and mentioned in detail. They embrace the execution of all other powers vested by the Constitution in the government of the United States, or in any department or officer thereof. . . .

And it is of importance to observe that Congress has often exercised, without question, powers that are not expressly given nor ancillary to any single enumerated power. Powers thus exercised are what are called by Judge Story in his Commentaries on the Constitution, resulting powers, arising from the aggregate powers of the government. . . .

Indeed the whole history of the government and of congressional legislation has exhibited the use of a very wide discretion, even in times of peace and in the absence of any trying emergency, in the selection of the necessary and proper means to carry into effect the great objects for which the government was framed, and this discretion has generally been unquestioned, or, if questioned, sanctioned by this court. This is true not only when an attempt has been made to execute a single power specifically given, but equally true when the means adopted have been appropriate to the execution, not of a single authority, but of all the powers created by the Constitution. . . . Before we can hold the legal tender acts unconstitutional, we must be convinced they were not appropriate means, or means conducive to the execution of any or all of the powers of Congress, or of the government, not appropriate in any degree (for we are not judges of the degree of appropriateness), or we must hold that they were prohibited. This brings us to the inquiry whether they were, when enacted, appropriate instrumentalities for carrying into effect, or executing any of the known powers of Congress, or of any department of the government. Plainly to this inquiry, a consideration of the time when they were enacted, and of the circumstances in which the government then stood, is important. It is not to be denied that acts may be adapted to the exercise of lawful power, and appropriate to it, in seasons of exigency, which would be inappropriate at other times.

We do not propose to dilate at length upon the circumstances in which the country was placed, when Congress attempted to make treasury notes a legal tender. They are of too recent occurrence to justify enlarged description. Suffice it to say that a civil war was then raging which seriously threatened the overthrow of the government and the destruction of the Constitution itself. It demanded the equipment and support of large armies and navies, and the employment of money to an extent beyond the capacity of all ordinary sources of supply. Meanwhile the public treasury was nearly empty, and the credit of the government, if not stretched to its utmost tension, had become nearly exhausted. Moneyed institutions had advanced largely of their means, and more could not be expected of them. They had been compelled to suspend specie payments. Taxation was inadequate to pay even the interest on the debt already incurred, and it was impossible to await the income of additional taxes. The necessity was immediate and pressing. . . .

It was at such a time and in such circumstances that Congress was called upon to devise means for maintaining the army and navy, for securing the large supplies of money needed, and, indeed, for the preservation of the government created by the Constitution. It was at such a time and in such an emergency that the legal tender acts were passed. Now, if it were certain that nothing else would have supplied the absolute necessities of the treasury, that nothing else would have enabled the government to maintain its armies and navy, that nothing else would have saved the government and the Constitution from destruction, while the legal tender acts would, could any one be bold enough to assert that Congress transgressed its powers? Or if these enactments did work these results, can it be maintained now that they were not for a legitimate end, or "appropriate and adapted to that end," in the language of Chief Justice Marshall? That they did work such results is not to be doubted. Something revived the drooping faith of the people; something brought immediately to the government's aid the resources of the nation, and something enabled the successful prosecution of the war, and the preservation of the national life. What was it, if not the legal tender enactments? . . .

Concluding, then, that the provision which made treasury notes a legal tender for the payment of all debts other than those expressly excepted, was not an inappropriate means for carrying into execution the legitimate powers of the government, we proceed to inquire whether it was forbidden by the letter or spirit of the Constitution. It is not claimed that any express prohibition exists, but it is insisted that the spirit of the Constitution was violated by the enactment. Here those who assert the unconstitutionality of the acts mainly rest their argument. They claim that the clause which conferred upon Congress power "to coin money, regulate the value thereof, and of foreign coin," contains an implication that nothing but that which is the subject of coinage, nothing but the precious metals can ever be declared by law to be money, or to have the uses of money. . . . To assert, then, that the clause enabling Congress to coin money and regulate its value tacitly implies a denial of all other power over the currency of the nation, is an attempt to introduce a new rule of construction against the solemn decisions of this court. So far from its containing a lurking prohibition, many have thought it was intended to confer upon Congress that general power over the currency which has always been an acknowledged attribute of sovereignty in every other civilized nation than our own, especially when considered in connection with the other clause which denies to the States the power to coin money, emit bills of credit, or make anything but gold and silver coin a tender in payment of debts. We do not assert this now, but there are some considerations touching these clauses which tend to show that if any implications are to be deduced from them, they are of an enlarging rather than a restraining character. . . .

We come next to the argument much used, and, indeed, the main reliance of those who assert the unconstitutionality of the legal tender acts. It is that they are prohibited by the spirit of the Constitution because they indirectly impair the obligation of contracts. . . .

If, then, the legal tender acts were justly chargeable with impairing contract obligations, they would not, for that reason, be forbidden, unless a different rule is to be applied to them from that which has hitherto prevailed in the construction of other powers granted by the fundamental law. But, as already intimated, the objection misapprehends the nature and extent of the contract obligation spoken of in the Constitution. As in a state of civil society property of a citizen or subject is ownership, subject to the lawful demands of the sovereign, so contracts must be understood as made in reference to the possible exercise of the rightful authority of the government, and no obligation of a contract can extend to the defeat of legitimate government authority. . . .

We are not aware of anything else which has been advanced in support of the proposition that the legal tender acts were forbidden by either the letter or the spirit of the Constitution. If, therefore, they were, what we have endeavored to show, appropriate means for legitimate ends, they were not transgressive of the authority vested in Congress.

[The Chief Justice, and Justices Clifford, Field, and Nelson, dissented.]

119

Slaughterhouse Cases (1873)

An 1869 Louisiana statute chartered the Crescent City Live-Stock Landing and Slaughter-House Company, gave it a twenty-five-year monopoly over three parishes having a population of two hundred thousand and including the city of New Orleans, and set rates that could be charged at the company's facilities. Butchers not included in the monopoly argued that they had been deprived of an important "right," the right to exercise their trade, and they challenged the statute under the Thirteenth and Fourteenth Amendments. The plaintiffs were, in fact, not completely deprived of their livelihood, only inconvenienced, since they could continue to butcher animals but only at the facilities of the monopoly company.

Their suit did, however, raise the issue of substantive due process, that is, whether there were certain rights behind and more fundamental than the bundle of procedural safeguards normally associated with the phrase "due process of law." There had been a few prewar references to the notion that due process also included certain rights in property, but the justices here rejected that notion. By a five-to-four majority, the Court ruled that the Civil War amendments had no purpose other than protecting the rights of slaves. The issue would not go away, however, and in 1897 the Court finally accepted the idea that the fourteenth Amendment's Due Process Clause protected substantive rights as well as procedural safeguards in Allgeyer v. Louisiana, 165 U.S. 578 (1897).

See E. S. Corwin, "The Supreme Court and the Fourteenth Amendment," 7 *Mich. L. R.* 643 (1909); L. Beth, "The Slaughterhouse Cases," 23 *La. L. R.* (1963); J. TenBroek, *Antislavery Origins of the Fourteenth Amendment* (1951); and the chapters on law in R. G. McCloskey, *American Conservatism in the Age of Enterprise* (1964).

Justice Miller delivered the opinion of the Court.

The regulation of the place and manner of conducting the slaughtering of animals is among the most necessary and frequent exercises of the police power. The 1869 law is aptly framed to remove from the more densely

---

Source: 16 Wallace 36 (1873).

populated part of the city, the noxious slaughter-houses, and large and offensive collections of animals necessarily incident to them, and to locate them where the convenience, health, and comfort of the people require they shall be located. And it must be conceded that the means adopted by the act for this purpose are appropriate, are stringent, and effectual. But it is said that in creating a corporation for this purpose, and conferring upon it exclusive privileges—privileges which it is said constitute a monopoly—the legislature has exceeded its power. . . .

The most cursory glance at [the three post-Civil War Amendments] discloses a unity of purpose, when taken in connection with the history of the times, which cannot fail to have an important bearing on any question of doubt concerning their true meaning. . . . Fortunately that history is fresh within the memory of us all, and its leading features, as they bear upon the matter before us, free from doubt.

. . . The overshadowing and efficient cause [of the war] was African slavery. In that struggle slavery, as a legalized social relation, perished. It perished as a necessity of the bitterness and force of the conflict. . . . But the war being over, those who had succeeded in re-establishing the authority of the Federal government were not content to permit this great act of emancipation to rest on the actual results of the contest or the proclamation of the Executive, both of which might have been questioned in after times, and they determined to place this main and most valuable result in the Constitution of the restored Union as one of its fundamental articles. Hence the [13th Amendment].

To withdraw the mind from the contemplation of this grand yet simple declaration of the personal freedom of all the human race within the jurisdiction of this government—a declaration designed to establish the freedom of four millions of slaves—and with a microscopic search endeavor to find in it a reference to servitudes, which may have been attached to property in certain localities, requires an effort, to say the least of it. That a personal servitude was meant is proved by the use of the word "involuntary," which can only apply to human beings. [The] word servitude is of larger meaning than slavery, as the latter is popularly understood in this country, and the obvious purpose was to forbid all shades and conditions of African slavery. . . .

. . . Notwithstanding the formal recognition by those [southern] States of the abolition of slavery, the condition of the slave race would, without further protection of the Federal government, be almost as bad as it was before. Among the first acts of legislation adopted by several of the States were laws which imposed upon the colored race onerous disabilities and burdens, and curtailed their rights in the pursuit of life, liberty, and property to such an extent that their freedom was of little value, while they had lost the protection which they had received from their former owners from motives both of interest and humanity. They were in some States forbidden to appear in the towns in any other character than menial servants. They were required to reside on and cultivate the soil without the right to purchase or own it.

They were excluded from many occupations of gain, and were not permitted to give testimony in the courts in any case where a white man was a party. It was said that their lives were at the mercy of bad men, either because the laws for their protection were insufficient or were not enforced.

These circumstances, whatever of falsehood or misconception may have been mingled with their presentation, forced upon the statesmen who had conducted the Federal government in safety through the crisis of the rebellion, and who supposed that by the thirteenth article of amendment they had secured the result of their labors, the conviction that something more was necessary in the way of constitutional protection to the unfortunate race who had suffered so much. They accordingly [proposed the 14th Amendment].

A few years' experience satisfied the thoughtful men who had been the authors of the other two amendments that, notwithstanding the restraints of those articles on the States, and the laws passed under the additional powers granted to Congress, these were inadequate for the protection of life, liberty, and property, without which freedom to the slave was no boon. They were in all those States denied the right of suffrage. The laws were administered by the white man alone. It was urged that a race of men distinctively marked as was the negro, living in the midst of another and dominant race, could never be fully secured in their person and the property without the right of suffrage. Hence [the 15th Amendment].

We repeat, then, in the light of this recapitulation of events, almost too recent to be called history, but which are familiar to us all; and on the most casual examination of the language of these amendments, no one can fail to be impressed with the one pervading purpose found in them all, lying at the foundation of each, and without which none of them would have been even suggested; we mean the freedom of the slave race, the security and firm establishment of that freedom, and the protection of the newly-made freeman and citizen from the oppressions of those who had formerly exercised unlimited dominion over him. . . .

We do not say that no one else but the negro can share in this protection. Both the language and spirit of these articles are to have their fair and just weight in any question of construction. Undoubtedly while negro slavery alone was in the mind of the Congress which proposed the thirteenth article, it forbids any other kind of slavery, now or hereafter. . . .

Up to the adoption of the recent amendments, no claim or pretence was set up that those rights depended on the Federal government for their existence or protection, beyond the very few express limitations which the Federal Constitution imposed upon the States—such, for instance, as the prohibition against ex post facto laws, bills of attainder, and laws impairing the obligation of contracts. But with the exception of these and a few other restrictions, the entire domain of the privileges and immunities of citizens of the States, as above defined, lay within the constitutional and legislative power of the States, and without that of the Federal government. Was it the purpose of the fourteenth amendment, by the simple declaration that no State should make or enforce any law which shall abridge the privileges and immunities of *citizens of the United States,* to transfer the security and protection of all the civil rights which we have mentioned, from the States to the Federal government? And where it is declared that Congress shall have the power to enforce that article, was it intended to bring within the power of Congress the entire domain of civil rights heretofore belonging exclusively to the States?

All this and more must follow, if the proposition of the plaintiffs in error be sound. For not only are these rights subject to the control of Congress whenever in its discretion any of them are supposed to be abridged by State legislation, but that body may also pass laws in advance, limiting and restricting the exercise of legislative power by the States, in their most ordinary and usual functions, as in its judgment it may think proper on all such subjects. And still further, such a construction followed by a reversal of the judgments of the Supreme Court of Louisiana in these cases, would constitute this court a perpetual censor upon all legislation of the States, on the civil rights of their own citizens, with authority to nullify such as it did not approve as consistent with those rights, as they existed at the time of the adoption of this amendment. The argument we admit is not always the most conclusive which is drawn from the consequences urged against the adoption of a particular construction of an instrument. But when, as in the case before us, these consequences are so serious, so far-reaching and pervading, so great a departure from the structure and spirit of our institutions; when the effect is to fetter and degrade the State governments by subjecting them to the control of Congress, in the exercise of powers heretofore universally conceded to them of the most ordinary and fundamental character; when in fact it radically changes the whole theory of the relations of the State and Federal governments to each other and of both these governments to the people; the argument has a force that is irresistible, in the absence of language which expresses such a purpose too clearly to admit of doubt. We are convinced that no such results were intended by the Congress which proposed these amendments, nor by the legislatures of the States which ratified them. . . .

Unquestionably [the civil war] added largely to the number of those who believe in the necessity of a strong National government. But, however pervading this sentiment, and however it may have contributed to the adoption of the amendments we have been considering, we do not see in those amendments any purpose to destroy the main features of the general system. Under the pressure of all the excited feeling growing out of the war, our statesmen have still believed that the existence of the States with powers for domestic and local government, including the regulation of civil rights—the rights of person and of property—was essential to the perfect working of our complex form of government, though they have thought proper to impose additional limitations on the States, and to confer additional power on that of the Nation.

But whatever fluctuations may be seen in the history of public opinion on this subject during the period of our national existence, we think it will be found that this court, so far as its functions required, has always held with a steady and an even hand the balance between State and Federal power, and we trust that such may continue to be the history of its relation to that subject.

Affirmed.

Justice Field, joined by Chief Justice Chase and Justices Swayne and Bradley, dissented.

Upon the theory on which the exclusive privileges granted by the act in question are sustained, there is no monopoly, in the most odious form, which may not be upheld. The question presented is, therefore, one of the gravest importance, not merely to the parties here, but to the whole country. It is nothing less than the question whether the recent amendments to the Federal Constitution protect the citizens of the United States against the deprivation of their common rights by State legislation. In my judgment the fourteenth amendment does afford such protection. . . .

The amendment does not attempt to confer any new privileges or immunities upon citizens, or to enumerate or define those already existing. It assumes that there are such privileges and immunities which belong of right to citizens as such, and ordains that they shall not be abridged by State legislation. If this inhibition has no reference to privileges and immunities of this character, but only refers, as held by [the majority], to such privileges and immunities as were before its adoption specifically designated in the Constitution or necessarily implied as belonging to citizens of the United States, it was a vain and idle enactment, which accomplished nothing, and most unnecessarily excited Congress and the people on its passage. With privileges and immunities thus designated or implied no State could ever have interfered by its laws, and no new constitutional provision was required to inhibit such interference. The supremacy of the Constitution and the laws of the United States always controlled any State legislation of that character. But if the amendment refers to the natural and inalienable rights which belong to all citizens, the inhibition has a profound significance. . . .

The terms, privileges and immunities, are not new in the amendment; they were in the Constitution before the amendment was adopted. . . . The privileges and immunities designated are those *which of right belong to the citizens of all free governments.* Clearly among these must be placed the right to pursue a lawful employment in a lawful manner, without other restraint than such as equally affects all persons. . . .

What [Art. IV, § 2] did for the protection of the citizens of one State against hostile and discriminating legislation of other States, the fourteenth amendment does for the protection of every citizen of the United States against hostile and discriminating legislation against him in favor of others, whether they reside in the same or in different States. If under the fourth article of the Constitution equality of privileges and immunities is secured between citizens of different States, under the fourteenth amendment the same equality is secured between citizens of the United States. . . .

This equality of rights, with exemption from all disparaging and partial enactments, in the lawful pursuits of life, throughout the whole country, is the distinguishing privilege of citizens of the United States. To them, everywhere, all pursuits, all professions, all avocations are open without other restrictions than such as are imposed equally upon all others of the same age, sex, and condition. The State may prescribe such regulations for every pursuit and calling of life as will promote the public health, secure the good order and advance the general prosperity of society, but when once prescribed, the pursuit or calling must be free to be followed by every citizen who is within the conditions designated, and will conform to the regulations. This is the fundamental idea upon which our institutions rest, and unless adhered to in the legislation of the country our government will be a republic only in name. The fourteenth amendment, in my judgment, makes it essential to the validity of the legislation of every State that this equality of right should be respected. It is to me a matter of profound regret that the validity [of the Louisiana law] is recognized by a majority of this court, for by it the right of free labor, one of the most sacred and imprescriptible rights of man, is violated. Grants of exclusive privileges are opposed to the whole theory of free government, and it requires no aid from any bill of rights to render them void. That only is a free government, in the American sense of the term, under which the inalienable right of every citizen to pursue his happiness is unrestrained, except by just, equal, and impartial laws.

Appendix I
Justices of the United States Supreme Court

Name*	Term	Appointed By
John Jay	1789–1795	Washington
John Rutledge	1789–1791	Washington
William Cushing	1789–1810	Washington
James Wilson	1789–1798	Washington
John Blair	1789–1796	Washington
James Iredell	1790–1799	Washington
Thomas Johnson	1791–1793	Washington
William Paterson	1793–1806	Washington
John Rutledge	1795	Washington
Samuel Chase	1796–1811	Washington
Oliver Ellsworth	1796–1800	Washington
Bushrod Washington	1798–1829	John Adams
Alfred Moore	1799–1804	John Adams
John Marshall	1801–1835	John Adams
William Johnson	1804–1834	Jefferson
H. Brockholst Livingston	1806–1823	Jefferson
Thomas Todd	1807–1826	Jefferson
Gabriel Duval	1811–1835	Madison
Joseph Story	1811–1845	Madison
Smith Thompson	1823–1843	Monroe
Robert Trimble	1826–1828	John Quincy Adams
John McLean	1829–1861	Jackson
Henry Baldwin	1830–1844	Jackson
James M. Wayne	1835–1867	Jackson
Roger B. Taney	1836–1864	Jackson
Philip P. Barbour	1836–1841	Jackson
John Catron	1837–1865	Van Buren
John McKinley	1837–1852	Van Buren
Peter V. Daniel	1841–1860	Van Buren
Samuel Nelson	1845–1872	Tyler
Levi Woodbury	1845–1851	Polk
Robert C. Grier	1846–1870	Polk

*Chief Justices in italics.

Name	*Term*	*Appointed by*
Benjamin R. Curtis	1851–1857	Fillmore
John A. Campbell	1853–1861	Pierce
Nathan Clifford	1858–1881	Buchanan
Noah H. Swayne	1862–1881	Lincoln
Samuel F. Miller	1862–1890	Lincoln
David Davis	1862–1877	Lincoln
Stephen J. Field	1863–1897	Lincoln
Salmon P. Chase	1864–1873	Lincoln
William Strong	1870–1880	Grant
Joseph P. Bradley	1870–1892	Grant
Ward Hunt	1872–1882	Grant
Morrison R. Waite	1874–1888	Grant
John Marshall Harlan	1877–1911	Hayes
William B. Woods	1880–1887	Hayes
Stanley Matthews	1881–1889	Garfield
Horace Gray	1881–1902	Arthur
Samuel Blatchford	1882–1893	Arthur
Lucius Q. C. Lamar	1888–1893	Cleveland
Melville W. Fuller	1888–1910	Cleveland
David J. Brewer	1889–1910	Benjamin Harrison
Henry B. Brown	1890–1906	Benjamin Harrison
George Shiras	1892–1903	Benjamin Harrison
Howell E. Jackson	1893–1895	Benjamin Harrison
Edward D. White	1894–1910	Cleveland
Rufus W. Peckham	1895–1909	Cleveland
Joseph McKenna	1898–1925	McKinley
Oliver Wendell Holmes	1902–1932	Theodore Roosevelt
William R. Day	1903–1922	Theodore Roosevelt
William H. Moody	1906–1910	Theodore Roosevelt
Horace H. Lurton	1909–1914	Taft
Charles E. Hughes	1910–1916	Taft
Edward D. White	1910–1921	Taft
Willis Van Devanter	1910–1937	Taft
Joseph R. Lamar	1910–1916	Taft
Mahlon Pitney	1912–1922	Taft
James C. McReynolds	1914–1941	Wilson
Louis D. Brandeis	1916–1939	Wilson
John H. Clarke	1916–1922	Wilson
William H. Taft	1921–1930	Harding
George Sutherland	1922–1938	Harding
Pierce Butler	1922–1939	Harding
Edward T. Sanford	1923–1930	Harding
Harlan F. Stone	1925–1941	Coolidge
Charles E. Hughes	1930–1941	Hoover
Owen J. Roberts	1930–1945	Hoover
Benjamin N. Cardozo	1932–1938	Hoover
Hugo L. Black	1937–1971	Franklin D. Roosevelt

Name	Term	Appointed by
Stanley F. Reed	1938–1957	Franklin D. Roosevelt
Felix Frankfurter	1939–1962	Franklin D. Roosevelt
William O. Douglas	1939–1975	Franklin D. Roosevelt
Frank Murphy	1940–1949	Franklin D. Roosevelt
James F. Byrnes	1941–1942	Franklin D. Roosevelt
Harlan F. Stone	1941–1946	Franklin D. Roosevelt
Robert H. Jackson	1941–1954	Franklin D. Roosevelt
Wiley B. Rutledge	1943–1949	Franklin D. Roosevelt
Harold H. Burton	1945–1958	Truman
Fred M. Vinson	1946–1953	Truman
Tom C. Clark	1949–1967	Truman
Sherman Minton	1949–1956	Truman
Earl Warren	1953–1969	Eisenhower
John Marshall Harlan	1955–1971	Eisenhower
William J. Brennan, Jr.	1956–	Eisenhower
Charles E. Whittaker	1957–1962	Eisenhower
Potter Stewart	1958–1981	Eisenhower
Arthur J. Goldberg	1962–1965	Kennedy
Byron R. White	1962–	Kennedy
Abe Fortas	1965–1969	Lyndon B. Johnson
Thurgood Marshall	1967–	Lyndon B. Johnson
Warren E. Burger	1969–1986	Nixon
Harry A. Blackmun	1970–	Nixon
Lewis F. Powell, Jr.	1972–1987	Nixon
William H. Rehnquist	1972–	Nixon
John Paul Stevens	1975–	Ford
Sandra Day O'Connor	1981–	Reagan
Antonin Scalia	1986–	Reagan
Anthony Kennedy	1988–	Reagan

Appendix II
Cross References to
Main Textbooks

Document	Urofsky *A March of Liberty*	Kelly, Harbison, and Belz *The American Constitution* 6th ed.
Part I		
1 Magna Carta	2–5	—
2 Letters Patent	7	—
3 Virginia Rules	—	—
4 Mayflower Compact	12	9
5 Fundamental Orders	12	10–11
6 Williams, "Bloudy Tenent"	—	—
7 Penn, "Frame of Government"	—	18
8 Zenger's Case	172	—
9 Indian, White Views on Property	18–20	—
Part II		
10 Writs of Assistance	40–41	65–66
11 Blackstone, "Parliament"	—	—
12 Virginia Stamp Act Resolution	48	48
13 Stamp Act Congress	48	48
14 Declaratory Act	49	52
15 Dickinson, Letter from a Farmer	50–51	49–50
16 Paine, "Common Sense"	56	61
17 Adams, "Thoughts on Government"	66	—
18 Declaration of Independence	57–58	62–64, 70–72
19 Pennsylvania Bill of Rights	—	—
Part III		
20 Articles of Confederation	63–65	79–85
21 Vermont Reception Statute	74–75	—

542

		Urofsky	*K. H. B.*
22	Land Ordinance (1785)	84	—
23	Honestus, "Observations on Lawyers"	30, 165	—
24	Statute for Religious Freedom	72	—
25	Northwest Ordinance (1787)	84	98
26a	Virginia Plan	91	91–95
b	New Jersey Plan	91	95–96
c	Hamilton's Plan	106	95, 100
27	Constitution of United States	passim	passim
28	Mason, "Objections to Constitution"	98	107–10
29	The Federalist	96–97	111–112

Part IV

		Urofsky	*K. H. B.*
30	Judiciary Act (1789)	131–133	162–165
31	Jefferson on National Bank	117–118	130–131
32	Hamilton on National Bank	118–119	131–132
33	Jay's Reply to Washington	138–139	165
34	Hamilton, Pacificus	124–125	—
35	Madison, Helvidius	125	—
36	Chisholm *v.* Georgia (1793)	142–144	166
37	Hilton *v.* United States (1796)	146–148	178
38	Virginia & Kentucky Resolutions	173–174	136–139
39	Georgia Judiciary Act (1799)	163–165	—
40	Virginia Assembly on Common Law	155	170

Part V

		Urofsky	*K. H. B.*
41	Jefferson, First Inaugural (1801)	176	143
42	Marbury *v.* Madison (1803)	182–186 and passim	176–182 and passim
43	Eakin *v.* Raub (1825)	185	—
44	Gallatin, Memo on Louisiana Purchase (1803)	186–187	147–150, 155, 157
45	Am. Ins. Co. *v.* Canter (1828)	187, 368, 484	264
46	Chase, Grand Jury Charge (1803)	189–191	174–176
47	Ex parte Bollman (1807)	193–195	183
48	United States *v.* Peters (1809)	203–204	186
49	Fletcher *v.* Peck (1810)	226–229, 285	186, 195
50	U.S. *v.* Hudson & Goodwin (1812)	155, 323	171, 242
51	Martin *v.* Hunter's Lessee (1816)	206–209	187
52	Dartmouth College Case (1819)	236–239, 285, 288, 290, 321	198–99, 231, 233
53	Sturges *v.* Crowinshield (1819)	240–241, 307	199–200, 236
54	McCulloch *v.* Maryland (1819)	211–215 and passim	190–92 and passim

		Urofsky	*K. H. B.*
55	Jackson, Bank Bill Veto (1832)	281–283	212–214
56	Cohens *v.* Virginia (1821)	215–216	188–189
57	Gibbons *v.* Ogden (1824)	216–219, 224, 285	202–204, 238
58	Worcester *v.* Georgia (1832)	271–272	211
59	Barron *v.* Baltimore (1833)	378, 640	205, 229, 286, 526
60	Story, *Commentaries* (1833)	—	—

Part VI

		Urofsky	*K. H. B.*
61	Palmer *v.* Mulligan (1805)	250	—
62	Commonwealth *v.* Pullis (1806)	305–306	—
63	Sands *v.* Taylor (1810)	162, 264	—
64	Kent, Against Suffrage (1821)	294	224
65	Tyler *v.* Wilkinson (1827)	160, 250	—
66	Lansing *v.* Smith (1828)	253	—
67	Jackson, Maysville Road Veto (1830)	280	209
68	New York *v.* Miln (1837)	321	238–239
69	Charles River Bridges Case (1937)	289–291 and passim	231–234
70	Nickerson's Case (1837)	304	—
71	Parker *v.* Foote (1838)	160	—
72	Mercein *v.* People (1840)	304	—
73	Swift *v.* Tyson (1842)	323–324, 696–699 & passim	243–244, 520–521
74	Farwell *v.* B&W RR (1842)	257	—
75	Commonwealth *v.* Hunt (1842)	306–307, 562	409
76	Field, Code Reform (1847)	313, 314, 321	—
77	Seneca Falls Declaration (1848)	302, 603	—
78	Commonwealth *v.* Alger (1851)	325	—
79	Cooley *v.* Bd. of Wardens (1851)	328, 330, 699	241, 244, 606
80	Ohio Constitution (1851)	295–297	224–226
81	Hentz *v.* LIRR (1852)	253–254	—

Part VII

		Urofsky	*K. H. B.*
82	Maryland Slave Law (1664)	25–26	—
83	Somerset *v.* Stewart (1772)	355, 356, 358, 364	252
84	Taylor, States' Rights (1820)	350	—
85	South Carolina Exposition (1828)	273–274	214–216
86	S.C. Nullification (1832)	277–279	216–219
87	Anti-Slavery Declaration (1833)	353	—
88	Commonwealth *v.* Aves (1836)	355–356	253–254
89	Prigg *v.* Pennsylvania (1842)	358–359	255–256

		Urofsky	*K. H. B.*
90	Jones *v.* Van Zandt (1847)	340, 359–360, 378	—
91	Luther *v.* Borden (1849)	333–334, 409, 466, 469	227, 245, 639–640
92	State *v.* Caesar (1849)	345	—
93	Virginia Slave Code (1860)	341	—
94	Roberts *v.* Boston (1849)	355	—
95	Fugitive Slave Act (1850)	375, 377–379	245, 256–257, 287, 292
96	Mass. Personal Liberty Law (1855)	381	256, 287
97	Dred Scott *v.* Sandford (1857)	384–390 & passim	276–283 and passim
98	Lincoln-Douglas Debates (1858)	389–390, 394	283–287
99	Ableman *v.* Booth (1859)	379–380, 381, 408	245, 287–288
100	Black, Limits of Fed. Power (1860)	397	—
101	S.C. Secession Ordinance (1861)	395–396	291

Part VIII

102	Confederate Constitution (1861)	399–404	293–294
103	Ex parte Merryman (1861)	408–409, 414	312
104	Emancipation Proclamation (1863)	418	325–326
105	Prize Cases (1863)	414	304–305, 308
106	Whiting, Adequacy of Const. (1863)	412–413, 426	—
107a	Lincoln, Ten Percent Plan (1863)	428, 429	330
b	Wade-Davis Bill (1864)	430–431	330–331
c	Lincoln Proclamation (1864)	431	331
d	Wade-Davis Manifesto (1864)	431	331
108	Lincoln, Const. of Draft (1863)	417–418	320–321
109	Ex parte Vallandigham (1864)	415	315
110	Alabama Black Code (1865)	436–437	335, 337–338, 340
111	Civil Rights Act (1866)	438–440, 797, 843	339–341, 365, 369, 618, 623, 627
112	Johnson, Veto of Rights Act (1866)	440	341
113	Ex parte Milligan (1866)	463–464, 470, 727	315, 346, 362, 525, 566
114	Articles of Impeachment (1867)	456–462	350–356
115	Ex parte McCardle (1868)	467–468	363–364
116	Ex parte Yerger (1869)	468, 470	364
117	Texas *v.* White (1869)	94, 469–470	327, 348, 364
118	Legal Tender Cases (1871)	471–472	370
119	Slaughterhouse Cases (1873)	441, 497, 699	365, 399–400

Index of Documents